# North American Exploration

# North American Exploration

## VOLUME 3

## A CONTINENT COMPREHENDED

JOHN LOGAN ALLEN, EDITOR

UNIVERSITY OF NEBRASKA PRESS   LINCOLN AND LONDON

© 1997 by the University of Nebraska Press
All rights reserved
Manufactured in the United States of America
⊖ The paper in this book meets the minimum
requirements of American National Standard
for Information Sciences—Permanence of
Paper for Printed Library Materials,
ANSI Z39.48-1984.
Library of Congress Cataloging-in-
Publication Data
North American exploration / John Logan
Allen, editor.
p.   cm.
Includes bibliographical references and index.
Contents: v. 1. A new world disclosed—
v. 2. A continent defined—v. 3. A continent
comprehended.
ISBN 0-8032-1015-9 (cloth : alk. paper).—ISBN
0-8032-1023-x (cloth : alk. paper).—ISBN
0-8032-1043-4 (cloth : alk. paper)
1. North America—Discovery and
exploration.   I. Allen, John Logan, 1941–
E45.N67   1997   917.04—dc20   96-33025   CIP

# Contents

# Illustrations

# Maps

# A Continent Comprehended

# Introduction to Volume 3
# A Continent Comprehended

JOHN L. ALLEN

During the nineteenth century a dramatic shift in the purpose, priorities, and results of the exploration of North America occurred. As the century opened, much of the exploratory activity of British, Russian, Spanish, and American explorers was still linked with the game of empire. By the 1830s, commercial interests—primarily of the fur trade—had become the primary exploratory incentive, although imperial clashes between the British and the Americans were still very much a factor in exploration. But by midcentury, with the resolution of most international political issues involving North America and with the decline in the economic benefits of the fur trade, exploration of the continent began to take on a different flavor—that of scientific inquiry. This new spirit of science was not necessarily science conducted for science's sake. Some was motivated by the search for new resources or new transportation routes and some by military purposes. But a clear transition took place as the spirit of the Enlightenment gave way to economic imperatives and then to the "new" science of the post-Darwinian world. If the earlier centuries of exploration had resulted in the discovery of the continent and in its geographical definition, exploration in the nineteenth century led to the comprehension of the continent, including a fuller understanding of its native peoples. Fur trade exploration, in particular, relied on geographical lore and data from Native Americans, as did, to a lesser degree, military and scientific exploration.

In the opening chapter, James P. Ronda, H. G. Barnard Professor of History at the University of Tulsa, articulates the beginning stage of nineteenth-century exploration. Ronda notes, "Between the 1790s and the 1820s, the American West was both battleground and prize in an epic clash involving Russians, Spaniards, Americans, Canadians, and native peoples." Men like Meriwether Lewis, William Clark, and Zebulon Montgomery Pike were, in William Goetzmann's phrasing, "diplomats in buckskin."

Ronda adds: "Explorers were part of a swirl of nations, the great rage for imperial sway that had dominated America since the Age of Columbus."

In the next two chapters, I recount the explorations undertaken by the Canadian and the American fur trade during the first half of the nineteenth century. I note three primary motivations for the fur trade explorers' persistent campaigns toward the Pacific and the Arctic. The first was geopolitical. Just as the American government viewed the fur trade as a tool of imperial ambition, so the English used the Canadian fur trade as an instrument in the clash of rivals for the domination of western North America. British, Spanish, Russians, and Americans all saw western North America as the key to ultimate control over the entire continent. A second factor was simple economic competition as Canadian and American trappers and traders vied with one another for access to both territory and Native American loyalty. This competition was related to the nature of the extractive industry of the fur trade: new territory with unexploited resources and native populations unaffiliated with other fur companies was a requirement for the continued economic success of the fur trade enterprise. Third, fur trade exploration needed geographical information, sometimes of a practical, localized nature and other times with a more continental focus, related to the longer-range ambitions of commercial enterprises based in eastern North America for good transportation routes to western North America, the Pacific, and the Orient. Together, these three motives display the transitional nature of nineteenth-century exploratory objectives.

The transition from imperial ambition to commercial incentive to scientific curiosity is detailed in the remaining chapters. Suzanne Zeller, associate professor of history at Wilfred Laurier University, notes that the territories of British North America had piqued curiosity during the Napoleonic Wars because of their needed natural resources. According to Zeller, the nature and extent of these resources could be made known quickly and efficiently only through "statistical," rational surveys borrowed from the German tradition of the late 1700s. This utilitarian exploratory impulse was reinforced in the post-Napoleonic period with a surplus of scientifically trained British military officers who combined practical and theoretical sciences to convert geographical investigation from aesthetic description to the systematic collection and classification of standardized forms of information. Zeller compares the scientific explorers of Canada to the two main protagonists of classic travel literature: Gulliver and Crusoe. Like Gulliver, some explorers arrived in Canada eager to "see the country and make what discoveries [they] could," reporting their observations in terms relative to the familiar standards of home. Many of these "Gullivers" were ex-officers who justified their retention in the service and even carved out new careers by providing the personnel and expertise for major scientific expeditions. In contrast, immigrants and native British North Americans also used science to explore, yet not as visitors but as inhabitants. Although they were part of the larger scientific tradition of Europe, they also strived, like Crusoe, to duplicate British life in their new environment. Thus, their tools of exploration included ideas borrowed from Europe and reapplied to their new North American situation.

W. Gillies Ross, professor of geography at Bishop's University, articulates a similar process that operated throughout the Arctic regions for most of the century. For Europeans, the Arctic was "a part of the globe which had no care for human life, which was not built to man's scale, a remnant of the Ice Age which long ago had withered the world." Ross notes: "It had no prospects for settlement other than posts and missions; without the incentives of gold and silver, tall trees and fertile fields, or water power and coal, it held little attraction for Europeans except where it provided access to the fur resources of subarctic forests or where its offshore waters yielded bountiful supplies of sea mammal oil, baleen, and ivory." But Ross adds that exploration was driven as much by curiosity as by economic incentives and that much of the Arctic became known to Europeans as the result of the quest for scientific knowledge in an exotic environment. For example, European explorers persisted in the search for a Northwest Passage, "not because they still dreamed that a practical shipping route existed within the icy seas north of 65° or 70° north but because the question of what lay beyond the known world had to be answered." Exploration of this vast region was a slow process, but by the end of the century, scientific curiosity and economic incentive had together provided a map of the Arctic.

In another remote region, albeit not one as hostile as the Arctic, a similar mixture of scientific curiosity, adventure, and economic imperative was driving exploration. Vincent Ponko Jr., former Distinguished Professor of History at Dominican College, describes the exploration of the U.S. military—particularly the U.S. Army Corps of Topographical Engineers—in the western United States as a process that also depended on a blend of objectives. Ponko notes that before the 1840s, American exploring activities in the name of "practical science" had been largely a means whereby private citizens could utilize the rich resource base of the continent. With the exception of Jeffersonian government-sponsored exploration, most investigations had been dominated by the commercial interests of the fur trade.

By the end of the 1840s, however, "official" objectives of the nation began to prevail over more private and commercial goals. Among the newer national objectives was the desire "to increase the international scientific and philosophical significance" of the United States "through the application of Humboldtean rather than Enlightenment principles of scientific exploration." Of equal importance was the wish "to expand American political and economic influence and control over the entire continent as far as the Pacific." Finally, there was the incentive to learn about the continental resource base "for the longer-range objectives of an expanding agricultural and industrial civilization." The beginnings of military exploration by the U.S. government between the end of the fur trade era and the beginning of the Civil War were firmly grounded in the first desire: to "show the flag" both of the U.S. political entity and of American science. Soon, however, military exploration became directed primarily to the latter two objectives: to expand political and economic influence and to acquire practical knowledge of the continental resource base. Even in the short time period of two decades, military exploration underwent a significant transition in goals, mirroring the general process of U.S. exploration.

The last two chapters deal with the "end game," the final process in the transition of exploration into an activity that, though not purely science conducted for the sake of science, was more attuned to intellectual inquiry than to commercial or political gain. This is not to say that the government explorers in Canada and the United States in the latter third of the nineteenth century did not have economic or political objectives in mind; they certainly did, and explorers such as John Wesley Powell produced reports that were both groundbreaking scientific studies of the western regions and economic treatises on the utility of lands and environments unfamiliar to the general public.

William A. Waiser, professor of history at the University of Saskatchewan, carries the story of scientific exploration in Canada beyond the time frame covered in Zeller's chapter. Waiser begins by quoting the scientist George Dawson in 1890: "It is very commonly supposed, even in Canada, but to a greater extent elsewhere, that all parts of the Dominion are now so well known that exploration, in the true sense of the term, may be considered as a thing of the past." In spite of this prevalent opinion, some scientists continued to appeal publicly for the continuation of the kind of government-sponsored exploratory surveys that had been performed since midcentury. Dawson, speaking before the Ottawa Field-Naturalists' Club, identified sixteen areas of mainland Canada that remained "almost or altogether unmapped." He also reported that "the whole topographical fabric of large parts" of existing maps of the country rested on "information of the vaguest kind." Waiser comments: "Far from believing that Canada's main features had been delineated, Dawson advised his audience that about one million square miles were 'for all practical purposes entirely unknown.'" On the strength of such opinion the new Canadian government, believing that Canada faced stagnation and an uncertain future unless it expanded westward, began a program of scientific exploration designed to acquaint Canadians with the massive areas added to the country within three years of Confederation. Now covering half a continent, Canada embarked on a program of scientific exploration designed not only to enlarge the boundaries of scientific knowledge but also to evaluate the new western regions for occupation and utilization. At the time of the 1870 land transfer, large areas required the most basic exploration. Two decades later, the Canadian-American boundary had been established along the forty-ninth parallel, much of the western interior had been divided into homesteads, the telegraph and the railway to the Pacific were in place, and the Canadian Shield had been traversed by geological and topographical parties. Moreover, a substantial amount of scientific information had been gathered. But Waiser notes: "Much remained to be learned about the country's basic features. Wide-ranging reconnaissance surveys, with their associated mapping and resource assessment, therefore continued under federal sponsorship until the outbreak of World War I."

At the same time that Canada was opening its western territories through scientific exploration, the U.S. government was engaged in similar activity. Collectively known as the "Great Surveys," American scientific exploration from 1865 to 1900 is the subject of the chapter written by Richard A. Bartlett, professor emeritus of history at Florida State University. Bartlett states: "As the scientists looked to the American West, which was their primary though not exclusive geographical area of interest, they perceived a region becoming well-known but still full of challenging mysteries in all the earth and physical sciences. The West they looked to was changing with great rapidity, so much so that scientific reconnaissance—the wide-ranging survey—would soon give way to more-precise fieldwork and scientific investigation of regions already 'explored' in the conventional sense." Given what was already known of the region by the end of the Civil War, the burst of exploratory activity that continued until the end of the nineteenth century was both unexpected and unexpectedly productive.

Following the Civil War, a major paradigm shift occurred in American science, form the Humboldtean exercise of demonstrating the unity and purpose of God's plan for the cosmos to a Darwinian investigation of change and progression. Nowhere was this paradigm shift more clearly expressed than in exploration in the American West, where the "Great Reconnaissance" view of the West as a magnificent testimony to the creator gave way to the Great Surveys—more compartmentalized, more detailed, more thorough investigations with considerably higher standards of performance than those of the pre–Civil War explorations. At the same time that the Great Surveys were more "scientific," as we understand the word today, they were pragmatic in that the explorers of the West recognized that their exploratory efforts could not be separated from the needs of the nation's miners, farmers, ranchers, lumbermen, and railroad barons.

Out of these Great Surveys came knowledge that is still a part of our basic scientific paradigms and government policies that continue to govern the management of the public lands of the American and Canadian West. The last stage of North American exploration, like the very beginnings, had consequences far beyond those expected by the participants in the adventure.

By 1900, then, the story of North American exploration was complete and the continent had been comprehended. Knowledge had increased dramatically since the first tentative Norse landing on North American shores nearly a millennium earlier. And in the four centuries since Columbus set in motion the events that have provided the essence of our work in these three volumes, more expansion of geographical knowledge was accomplished than ever before in human history.

We will never again see such a period, incorporating, as William Goetzmann notes in the concluding chapter of this volume, the three Great Ages of Discovery that were stimulated by (and in turn stimulated) revolutions in knowledge and scientific thought. During the First Age of Discovery, figures like Columbus were attuned to the rediscovery of ancient and classical knowledge, and their explorations reflected the growth of imperialism and international competition. The Second Great Age began with the birth of modern scientific thought and was typified by explorers such as Lewis and Clark, who sought nothing less than redefinition of their world. The Third Great Age began in the turmoil of the Darwinian revolution and the corresponding drive of explorers to frame their discoveries in the context of biological and geological change through time. The explorers with whom this volume concludes are the epitome of the explorers of Goetzmann's Third Great Age.

The three Great Ages of Discovery are characteristic of exploration not just in North America but throughout the world. Yet North America, as Goetzmann points out, is perhaps the clearest and most accessible case study; it certainly should be the best known. North American exploration should also be most clearly portrayed, throughout this volume and its predecessors, as imbued with what Goetzmann, following F. Scott Fitzgerald, has called the human "capacity for wonder" and what John K. Wright and Bernard DeVoto expressed as the power of the imagination or the sirens' songs of knowledge. Thus the story of North American exploration began in the pre-Columbian yearnings for the terrestrial paradise to the west (or east), was seasoned by the Scottish Enlightenment explorations of Alexander Mackenzie and David Thompson, and culminated in the Canadian and American scientific surveys of the latter nineteenth century. It is not just a continental epic but a global one. It should therefore be understood and appreciated for what it was: a crowning achievement and a validation of that which makes us human.

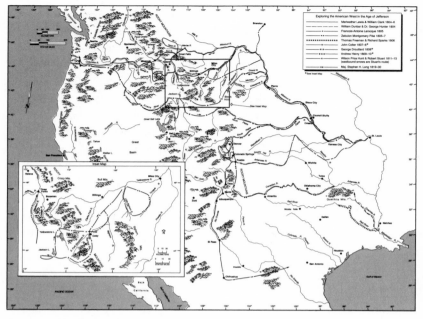

*Map 15.1 Exploring the American West in the Age of Jefferson.*

# 15 / Exploring the American West in the Age of Jefferson

JAMES P. RONDA

Early in 1793 the American Philosophical Society engaged French naturalist Andre Michaux to undertake a journey "Westwardly to the Pacific."[1] Later that same year Thomas Jefferson drafted instructions for the prospective explorer—instructions that portrayed a West both mysterious and remote. The future president imagined a land where mammoths still thundered and herds of llamas roamed free. Jefferson's West was laced with interlocking rivers and low mountains easily portaged. A few years later he conjured up a landscape dotted by volcanoes and by mountains of salt. Thirty years later, much of the mystery and a good deal of the fantasy had vanished—or so it seemed to readers scanning *Niles' Weekly Register* for 23 November 1822. Reprinting press clippings from St. Louis, *Niles' Weekly* informed its subscribers: "It is very possible that the citizens of St. Louis on the Mississippi may eat fresh salmon from the waters of the Columbia! for distance seems annihilated by science and the spirit of adventure."[2]

Although that claim carried more than its share of brash nationalism, it also touched a profound truth. Between the 1790s and the 1820s, the American West was both battleground and prize in an epic clash involving Russians, Spaniards, Americans, Canadians, and native peoples. The results of that confrontation were often sealed in treaties and agreements negotiated by diplomats far from any western region. But behind every polite proposal or negotiating ploy were the journeys and struggles of explorers. Men like Alexander Mackenzie, Meriwether Lewis, William Clark, and Zebulon Montgomery Pike were, in William Goetzmann's felicitous phrase, "diplomats in buckskin."[3] Explorers were part of a swirl of nations, the great rage for imperial sway that had dominated America since the Age of Columbus.

Historians have long used the intellectual shorthand "the Age of ———" to set off one era from another. This chapter uses the tag line "Age of Jefferson" to encompass the first two decades of the nineteenth century. Jefferson and his successors were not the only American voices in the period, but they did set the tone and pace for much of the early republic's national business. By making exploration of the West an official concern, Jefferson stamped those ventures with his unmistakable imprint.

From the late 1400s, North American history was increasingly shaped by imperial contests. The emerging European nations all launched voyages of discovery aimed at building colonial empires. That rush for empire had more than a political dimension. A war of cultures pitted Europeans against native Americans. By the mid-1700s these struggles had reached an unprecedented intensity. In every European capital, bureaucrats, businessmen, philosophers, and scientists looked to America as a source of national power, personal wealth, cultural rejuvenation, and scientific knowledge. Explorers like James Cook, Jean François de La Pérouse, Peter Pond, and James Mackay searched for more than high adventure. They were part of an imperial encounter that would shape the destiny of the American West.

Histories of exploration have often been lumped together with volumes about travel and adventure. The word *explorer* conjures up visions of hazardous treks through uncharted lands. Such an image does little to help us understand the explorers and their journeys. Standing back from the voyages of the late eighteenth and early nineteenth centuries, we can discern three distinct motives that sparked exploration. The first of those was empire. In the sixteenth and seventeenth centuries much of the exploration of the Americas had been undertaken by Christian missionaries. Wide-ranging travelers like Paul LeJeune and Jacques Marquette sought to save souls. Yet the missionary explorer's place was increasingly taken by agents of empire. If missionary zeal had powered exploration in the Age of the Fathers, the drive for national sovereignty beyond the seas fired discovery in later years. Ship captains like Cook, army officers like Pike, and fur traders like the Astorians represented a brand of exploration stamped with the marks of Great Power rivalry. Each nation, whether European or American, sent its explorers into the West hoping to capture what diplomats termed "the right of discovery." In an Atlantic civilization that measured national status in terms of land and commerce, the stakes for empire in the West were high indeed.

The drive for empire was not an undifferentiated motive for either explorers or expedition planners. The British vision of empire in the American West was quite different from the perspective of Thomas Jefferson and James Madison. Promoters and explorers from Montreal and London saw exploration as a means to expand a mercantilist state. New territories promised profit for state-chartered monopoly companies. Thus, Alexander Mackenzie viewed the West as an integral part of a highly structured international economy, an economy that would enhance the wealth and prestige of Britain at the expense of other imperial rivals. This model of exploration for development neatly fit British market-oriented views.

Political thinkers schooled in the republican tradition also pondered the relationship between exploration and empire. The American dilemma centered on the issue of republics and expansion. Eighteenth-century political theory maintained that republics were by definition geographically small, socially homogeneous states. An expanding republic seemed a contradiction in terms. American republicans challenged that wisdom, arguing that expansion would preserve the agricultural nature of the American economy. Since American republicans insisted that farming best preserved public and private virtue, expansion could be the salvation of the republic. The hidden danger was potential conflict with other imperial powers. How could an empire dedicated to liberty and virtue survive alongside one based solely on capitalist expansion and mercantilist national security? Perhaps the only answer was for the United States to dominate the West.[4]

Fashioning empires, whether for national prestige or for republican virtue, was a prominent motive for exploration. But private profit was an equally important reason to head west. By the mid-1700s the image of the entrepreneur had undergone a remarkable shift in meaning. The European world had long looked askance at the acquisition of substantial private wealth. Merchant capitalists, those not involved in gaining wealth from land, were seen as somehow working outside the realm of the social good. Concepts like "just price" and "the good of the community" acted to slow the growth of capitalism. Adventurers like Sir Walter Raleigh and Sir Francis Drake captured the imagination but had few successors. By the time John Astor began to advance his schemes for western exploration, some of those cultural barriers to capitalism were beginning to fall. The accumulation of personal gain beyond one's own physical labor was increasingly seen as a sign of diligence and industry—sound republican virtues. The West might yield honest empires of wealth. Jefferson admitted as much when he openly wished that men of private means would continue the explorations begun by Lewis and Clark. The capitalist was no longer a social outlaw.

No other part of the emerging capitalist world was more closely linked to western exploration than the fur trade. Through the Hudson's Bay Company, the North West Company, and John Astor's various enterprises, the fur business became highly structured and carefully rationalized. The constant search for new supplies of fur led the most aggressive companies to mount expeditions such as those by undertaken by David Thompson, Simon Fraser, and the Astorians. The North West Company, the most westward-thinking of the Canadian concerns, put the connection between fur and exploration in sharp focus: "It is the peculiar nature of the Fur Trade to require a continual extension of its limits, into new countries."[5]

Scientific inquiry stood alongside empire and wealth as a fundamental exploration motive. Veteran fur trader Alexander Ross best summed up the interrelationship of all three: "The progress of discovery contributes not a little to the enlightenment of mankind; for mercantile interest stimulates curiosity and adventure, and combines with them to enlarge the circle of knowledge. To the spirit of enterprise developed in the service of commercial speculation, civilized nations owe not only wealth and territorial acquisitions, but also their acquaintance with the earth and its productions."[6] Voyages of discovery in the Age of Jefferson were part of an Enlightenment tradition that emphasized global scientific inquiry. Jefferson described such ventures as part of a republic of science, "a great fraternity spreading over the whole earth."[7]

## The Legacy of European and Colonial Exploration

The intimate connection between science and exploration became part of British national policy in a series of voyages launched during the last half of the eighteenth century. Those Pacific journeys united the talents of two extraordinary men—Captain James Cook and Sir Joseph Banks. Cook was the consummate maritime explorer, an exceptionally skilled sailor whose knowledge went well beyond knowing the winds and following the currents. But it was Banks who best represented the joining of scientific investigation and geographical discovery. As president of the Royal Society and an influential government adviser, Banks had both power and opportunity to advance exploration. One enthusiastic admirer described him as "the common Center of we discoverers."[8] Banks made the three Cook voyages into models of Enlightenment science.

No other expedition in the Age of Jefferson could boast the variety of professional scientists that sailed with Cook. Enlightenment science had to be tailored to the needs, skills, and resources of travelers not professionally trained in the sciences. Science for Jefferson's explorers meant natural history, long the province of gifted amateurs. The methods of natural history fit the quick minds of men like Lewis, John Bradbury, Robert Stuart, and Peter Custis. These explorers observed the natural world, collected specimens, and described and categorized each sample for future study. As a descriptive science, natural history embraced botany, zoology, geology, geography, and ethnography. Writing about differing classification systems, Jefferson noted, "It would certainly be better to adopt as much as possible such exterior and visible characteristics as every traveler is competant to observe, to ascertain and to relate."[9] But natural history had weaknesses as well. Jefferson's phrase "exterior and visible characteristics" betrays the trouble: expedition science described but rarely analyzed. Surface features, often misleading, seemed more important than internal structures. Enlightenment explorers were not "scientists" as we now understand the term, since the meaning of their samples and observations would have to wait for a more analytical age.

Before Europeans and Americans traveled the West, they filled the space with imaginary empires. Quivira, unicorns, volcanoes, Welsh Indians—all were in the West, a storehouse of treasures. Looking west, Europeans fashioned kingdoms crowded with exotic peoples living in fantastic landscapes. The Age of Columbus had fancied an America populated by one-legged men and Amazonian women, cities of gold and rivers that ran straight to China. Imagination in the Age of Jefferson, supposedly rational and enlightened, was likewise unfettered. The West might hold wonders beyond anything seen in Charles Wilson Peale's American Museum.

Those imaginary western landscapes can be found in contemporary maps. By the late 1700s, the interested student could consult over a dozen maps, atlases, and geographies—all exercises in conjectural geography. These sources took bits of geographical lore and blended that information with notions about supposedly universal characteristics of landscape, climate, and non-European peoples. The result was a series of images of the West, images that were important not only because they reflected a geographical state of mind but also because they shaped exploring strategies. A cartographic vision of the West in 1800 reveals not only the region imagined but also the West expected.[10]

No map stands without ancestry. Printed maps of the West available at the beginning of the Age of Jefferson drew on an impressive cartographic heritage that included maps from the journeys of French explorers such as Marquette, Joliet, and La Salle and from the books of gentleman travelers

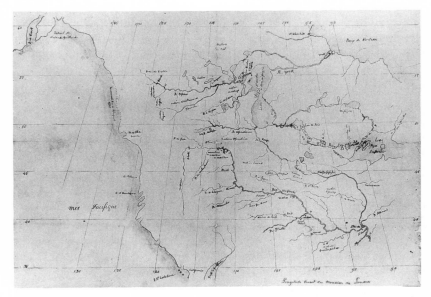

*15.1 Anonymous map from Spanish Louisiana (Antoine Soulard [?], c. 1798). This map, probably by Antoine Soulard of Saint Louis, illustrates the latest conception of the territory of Louisiana before the purchase of the region by the United States in 1803. The map played an important role in the planning of the Lewis and Clark expedition. Courtesy of the Library of Congress.*

such as the Baron Lahontan and Antoine Simon le Page du Pratz. That French legacy emphasized the role of the Missouri River as the principal water passage from Atlantic to Pacific. Virtually every French commentary on the West, whether written or graphic, carried the same message. French Jesuit Pierre F. X. Charlevoix stated, "I have good reason to think that after sailing up the Missouri as far as it is navigable you come to a great river which runs westward and discharges into the sea."[11]

The French legacy was unquestionably important, but maps at this time probably drew inspiration from more immediate sources. For example, in the 1760s Robert Rogers, associated with guerrilla warfare against the Indians of northern New England, began to promote western exploration. Perhaps influenced by French sources, he was convinced that a river called the "Oregan" or the "River of the West" flowed from somewhere near the headwaters of the Mississippi directly to the Pacific. Here was the passage to India uninterrupted by any troublesome mountains. Rogers also imagined a West cut through by a high range of steep mountains, what geographers now call a pyramidal height of land, from which rivers flowed east and west.[12]

Rogers did more than simply petition the Board of Trade in London, begging for financial support for his western enterprise. In 1766 he hired Jonathan Carver and James Tute to lead a search for the river Oregan. Although the Carver-Tute journey (1767) into present-day Minnesota failed to locate the elusive Oregan, the trek did produce maps and a narrative. Carver's *Travels through the Interior Parts of North America*, first published in 1778, offered a vision of remarkable durability and appeal. Carver advanced Rogers's pyramidal height-of-land notion, arguing that the four major rivers in North America—the Saint Lawrence, the Nelson, the Mississippi, and the Oregan—all had "their sources in the same neighbourhood."[13] And the Missouri, Carver insisted, found its headwaters in the same region. The message was plain: a journey up the Missouri could take travelers to the source of the Oregan; from there, the passage to Pacific waters was clear.[14] Few students of the West in 1800 knew about Rogers, but nearly all had read Carver's book. His words and maps presented an optimistic picture, one sure to appeal to Jefferson.

Carver's impact was out of proportion to his westering experience. By contrast, Peter Pond was a much-traveled trader and explorer. He also proved to be the premier fur trade geopolitician of the era. During the 1770s Pond was one of those intrepid "pedlars from Quebec" who drove their way into the heart of western Canada. By the spring of 1778 Pond and his men were in the fur-rich Athabasca country, trading the clothes off their backs in exchange for the "brown gold" of beaver pelts. At his Athabasca River post the inquisitive Pond gathered geographical information from Indians as well as from fellow traders like Alexander Henry the elder. As he listened, Pond began to fashion images of vast lakes and swift rivers that dominated the landscape. Might these somehow be a path to the Pacific?

That question found something of an answer when Pond learned about the last Cook voyage. In 1778, the same year that Pond crossed Methye Portage into Athabasca, Cook and his ships *Resolution* and *Discovery* were probing the Alaska coast, searching for the Northwest Passage. Late in May, Cook found an opening north of the Kenai Peninsula. The shape of the bay and the presumed river beyond seemed to fit prevailing notions about the passage. After several days of exploring, Captain Charles Clerke of the *Discovery* characterized the waterway as "a fine spacious river . . . but a cursed unfortunate one for us." Cook agreed that the river (a river they had not really seen) was probably not *the* passage, but like Clerke, he thought it stretched deep into the interior and would someday serve as "a very extensive inland communication."[15] Not until 1794, fifteen years after Cook's death, did Captain George Vancouver find that Cook's River was a dead end, now properly known as Cook's Inlet. But throughout the 1780s, published accounts of the final Cook voyage kept the illusion alive. Speculation about the river intensified with the rapid growth of the fur trade between the Northwest coast and China. Cook's mysterious river and the immense profits to be made selling sea otter pelts at Canton tantalized Pond and his entire generation.

Wintering at Athabasca in 1784, Pond was now convinced that one of the great rivers of the Athabasca country was in fact Cook's River. He drew an early sketch, now lost, but the four surviving Pond maps all express the same optimistic vision. Lake Athabasca and the Great Slave Lake form a giant water hub for the entire Northwest. Pond imagined several rivers reaching out like spokes in a wheel toward the north and west. He was partly right. The Mackenzie, Peace, and Athabasca Rivers do indeed point north and west from the lakes, but none is Pond's navigable highway. His optimism about rivers extended to mountains. Pond's 1785 map, presented to the American Congress, and his 1790 *Gentleman's Magazine* map show the Rockies as a single ridge with many breaks for convenient portaging.[16]

Pond's maps advanced a powerful imperial message. In the late 1780s he began to preach an expansionist gospel. Through maps and petitions directed to both American and Canadian officials, the trader argued that armed posts throughout the West could hold a vast empire. Acknowledging the growing rivalries between American, Canadian, and Russian interests, he argued that his chain of trading houses promised wealth and power to whatever nation proved audacious enough to pursue his strategy. Pond's apt pupil in all this was Alexander Mackenzie. In the 1790s Mackenzie based his explorations on Pond's ideas, but more important, Mackenzie's proposals for British commercial occupation of the West—ideas presented at the end of his *Voyages from Montreal*—were vintage Pond. After reading the work, Thomas Jefferson took actions leading directly to the Lewis and Clark expedition.[17]

Two major geographical works, both of which codified and advanced earlier speculations, appeared in 1797. Jedediah Morse's *American Gazetteer* drew on Carver and Pond for its image of the West. Morse's "A New Map of North America" claimed to be based on "all the New Discoveries." From Carver, Morse took the "River of the West"—running due east out of present-day Puget Sound. The Missouri reached out almost to touch the wild

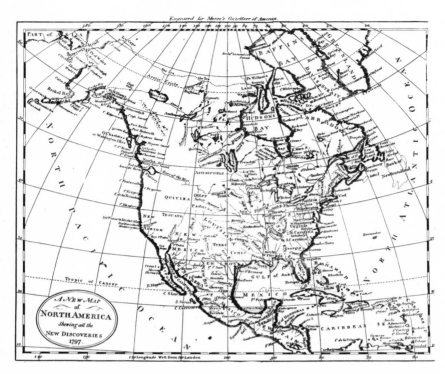

15.2 "A New Map of North America Shewing all the New Discoveries 1797" (Jedediah Morse, 1801), published in Morse, New American Universal Geography. *Morse's geographies were the most commonly used in American schools of the late eighteenth and early nineteenth centuries. This map is based primarily on British cartography, particularly that of Aaron Arrowsmith, but also shows the influence of Spanish and French mapping in the Territory of Louisiana. Collection of John L. Allen.*

Oregan. Taken directly from Pond's 1790 map was a river connection between the Great Slave Lake and the Pacific. Neither Carver nor Pond emphasized the Rockies, and Morse erased the mountains completely. Only empty space, aptly labeled Quivira, stood between the new American nation and the Pacific coast.[18]

The other 1797 work was *A Topographical Description of the Western Territory*, by Gilbert Imlay, Kentucky land promoter. Like Morse, Imlay drew heavily on Carver for details about land, rivers, and mountains. The Rockies were simply "a ridge of hills" stretching from the Canadian Northwest to Mexico. Major rivers like the Oregan and the Missouri had sources within a pyramidal height of land. According to Imlay, the imperial message was embedded in the land itself. "Thus in the centre of the earth," boasted Imlay, "governing by the laws of reason and humanity, we seem calculated to become at once the emporium and protectors of the world."[19]

At the end of the eighteenth century the name Arrowsmith symbolized cartographic accuracy. Aaron Arrowsmith's 1795 and 1802 maps of North America relied on the fur trade explorations done by Pond, Mackenzie, David Thompson, and Peter Fidler. The maps portray the Rockies as a narrow, almost unbroken ridge. Leaning on Mackenzie and Thompson, Arrowsmith emphasized low-elevation passes through the Stony Mountains and the possibility of short portages to the Pacific side. Whereas the 1795 map showed only an isolated fragment of the Missouri, the 1802 chart, consulted by Jefferson's geographical adviser Albert Gallatin, had dotted lines for the course of the river directly to the base of the Rockies. Passing over a trifling divide, travelers would find streams leading straight to the Oregan. And on the 1802 map, the "River of the West" was now properly the Columbia. As John L. Allen has written, "Arrowsmith's map added fuel to the theoretical fire of belief about the possible connections between the waters that ran east and those that ran west."[20]

Arrowsmith eschewed fantasy and readily labeled the conjectural. The white spaces on his maps showed a willingness to acknowledge uncertainty. Yet even though his maps appealed to Jefferson, they may not have reflected what most educated Americans believed about the West. This popular conception was instead portrayed in Samuel Lewis's map of Louisiana, published as part of *A New and Elegant General Atlas* in 1804. In this foreshortened vision of the West, the Rockies were a low range broken by several water gaps. Rivers like the Platte and the Missouri reached straight to the dividing ridge, and a branch of the Missouri stopped right at a broad gap in the mountains. Here, in cartographic expression, was the optimism that fueled American imperialism.[21]

Early-nineteenth-century maps of the West differed in some details, but nearly all agreed on the essentials. Western rivers, their navigability unquestioned, flowed east and west from sources in close proximity. Water routes through the continent did exist, an article of geographical faith that was directly linked to what Allen has termed "the fundamental core of misconception about western geography on the eve of the Lewis and Clark expedition."[22] Most maps showed the Rockies as an easily portaged range. Other commentators suggested a broad, gently sloped height of land rather than a mountain ridge. No one fully comprehended the awesome complexity of the Rockies. Their sheer ascent and precise location eluded even the most diligent geographers. Thinking in terms of eastern mountains and conditioned by concepts of symmetrical geography, Jefferson and his contemporaries simply imagined the Rockies as a distant version of the familiar Blue Ridge.[23]

## The Lewis and Clark Expedition, 1804–1806

Throughout the 1780s and 1790s Thomas Jefferson had noted the steady progress of British and French explorers and their search for routes to the Pacific. Preoccupied with personal and political duties, Jefferson worried about growing British power but did little else. Rumors of Anglo-Canadian expeditions to the Pacific prompted Jefferson's letter in 1783 to George Rogers Clark, asking if the now retired conqueror of the Illinois country might lead an American party westward to the coast. In addition, concern about the La Pérouse expedition and about French influence on the Northwest Coast was behind at least some of the attention Jefferson paid to the eccentric adventurer John Ledyard. And renewed efforts by the Canadians to create a fur trade empire in the West were a major factor in the abortive Michaux expedition. In each case, however, Jefferson's response proved either too little or too late. Then suddenly, in the summer of 1802, Jefferson ordered a copy of Mackenzie's recently published *Voyages from Montreal*. At the same time the president asked his New York bookseller for a copy of Arrowsmith's new map of North America.

Mackenzie's commentary at the end of his book captured Jefferson's attention. Repeating ideas gained largely from Pond, Mackenzie sketched out his strategy for British domination of the West. "By opening this intercourse between the Atlantic and Pacific Oceans, and forming regular establishments through the interior, and at both extremes, as well as along the coasts and islands, the entire command of the fur trade of North America might be obtained."[24] In addition Mackenzie suggested that the lands along the Columbia, increasingly thought of as the River of the West, were ideal for colonization. Thus British colonial and commercial power would be planted in the very region that Jefferson hoped would provide renewal, through expansion, for the American republic.

By the fall of 1802 Jefferson intended to send a modest expedition, perhaps one or two officers and a handful of soldiers, to the Pacific. Its aims were imperial, and its support had to be national. Although scientific and geographical discovery were important goals even at this early date, the expedition was essentially an expression of American expansionism, an imperial reconnaissance through territories still claimed by France and Spain. Jefferson's proposal came at a time when relations between the United States, Britain, and the European powers were unsettled at best and potentially violent at worst. American transit rights on the Mississippi, the revival of French power in Louisiana, and rumors about negotiations in Paris over the future of the western country all disturbed an already volatile diplomatic climate. Political controversies in the newly convened Seventh Congress enveloped Federalists and Jeffersonians as many in both parties predicted a storm in the West.[25] Not surprisingly, Jefferson's next moves were shrouded in secrecy.

Although the precise sequence of events is now unclear, in the first months of 1803 the president was pressing ahead with his western expedition. Money and a reliable leader were much on his mind. An early draft of his annual message to Congress (December 1802) contained a request for expedition funds, but the politically astute Secretary of the Treasury Albert Gallatin persuaded Jefferson to delete the item. Gallatin and other Republican politicians feared that any hint of a federally sponsored journey "out of our territory" would spark even more congressional trouble.[26] The alternative was to send Congress a confidential appropriation bill. Dated 18 January 1803, the request was a masterpiece of slippery language and sleight of hand. Purporting to be the president's thoughts on Indian policy and the long-standing use of federal trading houses, the bill mentioned, in its last paragraph, a modest, inexpensive tour to the Pacific. Jefferson even went so far as to claim that Spain "would not be disposed to view it [the expedition] with jealousy."[27] The subterfuge evidently worked, and on 28 February the confidential message became law.

Jefferson had meanwhile been looking for an expedition commander. He did not want a professional naturalist: "These expeditions are so laborious and hazardous, that men of science, used to the temperature and inactivity of their closet, cannot be induced to undertake them."[28] English, French, and Spanish expeditions were, with some exceptions, led by military officers, and Jefferson followed that pattern. He turned to his young private secretary, Meriwether Lewis. Captain Lewis, former paymaster for the First Infantry Regiment, had joined the president's official family in the spring of 1801 partly because of his "knolege of the Western country."[29] However, that knowledge, gained while serving in the Ohio Indian wars, did not reach beyond the Mississippi. No compelling evidence supports the often-made claim that Jefferson was already planning an expedition when he appointed Lewis as his secretary. As historian Donald Jackson has shown, Jefferson had thought Lewis's western experience would be helpful in trimming the army's officer corps—a reduction in force that was done with clearly political motives. But Lewis did have some of the qualifications necessary for the kind of initial western probe that Jefferson envisioned. He was a good woodsman and possessed a keen naturalist's eye.

By the spring of 1803 Lewis had already drafted a preliminary estimate of expedition expenses and was now ready to begin preparations in earnest. He next went to Harpers Ferry federal arsenal with a long list of items needed for frontier travel. Guns, knives, tomahawks, and even an ingenious but ill-fated iron-framed boat were issued from the arsenal's workshops and storerooms. While Lewis attended to the material foundations of the expedition, Jefferson hurried to extend its intellectual roof. Letters to Andrew Ellicott, Robert Patterson, Caspar Wistar, Benjamin Rush, and Benjamin Smith Barton put the expedition in touch with some of the best scientific minds in the new republic. Notes to cabinet members Levi Lincoln, Albert Gallatin, and James Madison solicited their political advice. From Harpers Ferry Lewis traveled to Lancaster, Pennsylvania, to study with the noted surveyor and astronomer Andrew Ellicott. Two weeks with Ellicott hardly made for an impressive apprenticeship, but by early May the prospective explorer was in Philadelphia, home to the American Philosophical Society and the republic's intellectual center. Lewis's short stay in Philadelphia has sometimes been described as his scientific education. Yet in the middle of considerable socializing and buying supplies, he had little time to spend with the likes of Rush, Patterson, and Barton. There is no sure evidence that Lewis ever used Jefferson's vast library—a library, it must be remembered, that was at Monticello, not Washington—and his contacts with Philadelphia savants were almost perfunctory.[30]

Dr. Samuel Johnson, the eighteenth century's famous "Dictionary Johnson," was known to say that "a man must carry knowledge with him, if he would bring home knowledge."[31] Explorers of the Americas were always armed with instructions, both to condition their understanding of the landscape and to guide their paths through it. During the early months of 1803 Jefferson circulated a preliminary instruction draft to several cabinet members. Secretary of State Madison offered little in the way of advice. Gallatin, on the other hand, had a lively interest in geography, ethnography, and linguistics. His letter was filled with valuable scientific advice.

Like Jefferson, the secretary of the treasury was committed to expansion. "The great object to ascertain," he argued, "is whether from its extent and fertility that country is susceptible of a large population."[32]

In his reply, Attorney General Levi Lincoln, one of Jefferson's closest political advisers, blasted the Federalists as "the perverse, hostile, and malignant opposition." He feared that a failed expedition would call down even more partisan fury on the administration. The initial instruction draft contained little about scientific study, and Lincoln urged Jefferson to expand the expedition's agenda to include the investigation of all aspects of Indian life. That way, should the party fall short of its Pacific goal, it could still claim scientific laurels. In addition Lincoln had some sharp things to say about Lewis, who could be both moody and impetuous. Lincoln worried that an overzealous Lewis might be inclined, "in case of difficulty, to push too far, [rather] than to recede too soon." The cabinet officer suggested that the instructions be modified to more fully restrain Lewis.[33]

Two key concerns dominated Jefferson's final instructions, dated 20 June 1803. First was the matter of the expedition's ultimate purpose. Jefferson was very plain on this point: "The object of your mission is to explore the Missouri river, and such principal stream of it, as, by it's course and communication with the waters of the Pacific ocean, whether the Columbia, Oregan, Colorado or any other river may offer the most direct and practicable water communication across this continent for the purposes of commerce."[34] These lines represent Jefferson's testimony of geographical faith. Having examined the best maps and the most enlightened commentaries of the day, he had no doubt that a water passage through the American garden did exist. There is also the matter of that intriguing word "commerce." On one level it meant the fur trade and Jefferson's hope that a Missouri-based trade system could stop British commercial penetration of the West. But commerce meant something more, something not readily apparent to the modern reader. Jefferson once wrote, "All the world is becoming commercial." Americans had "too full a taste of the comforts furnished by the Arts and manufactures to be debarred the use of them."[35] Jefferson understood that the image of the self-sufficient, noncommercial yeoman farmer was a drawing-room theory, one that no pragmatic American politician could afford to embrace. Jeffersonians hoped to tame commerce and enjoy its benefits by binding it to agriculture. Just as farmers needed an expanding land base, so they required foreign markets for their produce. Without a commercial system—and that meant banks, transportation, and treaties with foreign powers—American agriculture would col-

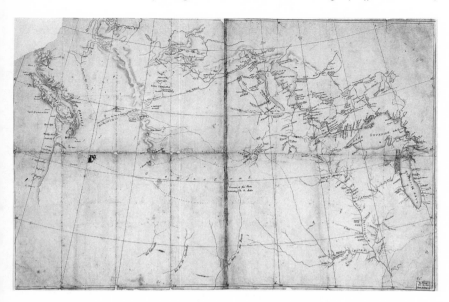

*15.3 Untitled map of the American West (Nicholas King, 1803). King's map, carried on the Lewis and Clark expedition, was long classified as "anonymous" by the Library of Congress but was discovered in the early 1970s to be the map discussed by Lewis, Jefferson, and Gallatin in correspondence in 1803. It represents what was probably the most precise American image of the western interior before Lewis and Clark. Courtesy of the Library of Congress.*

lapse. When Jefferson talked about commerce in this positive sense, he meant a diversified economy, one that might be commercial without fostering avarice and luxury. Land and commerce were to join forces in the West to ensure the republic's future.

Jefferson's second key concern was the native people. Support from and information about the Indians were essential. Jefferson saw western Indians both as objects of scientific study and as potential allies in the struggle for empire. The largest topical section in Lewis's instructions was devoted to Indian matters, particularly the daily relations between native people and explorers. Sending army officers and frontiersmen—men quick to take offense and to defend against imagined slights to national and personal honor—was a real gamble. Sensing the danger, Jefferson ordered his explorers to treat Indians "in the most friendly and conciliatory manner which their own conduct will permit."[36] Peaceful relations with the native people would enable the success of the expedition's diplomatic, commercial, and scientific missions. With the completion of the Louisiana Purchase negotiations, the expedition was charged with announcing the arrival of a new "great father" along the river. Jefferson expected his explorers to hold frequent conferences with tribal leaders, to organize delegations to visit the new federal city, and to establish commercial ties between native groups and white merchants, as well as sites for future trading houses. In addition, Jefferson drafted a series of questions aimed at studying seventeen areas of Indian life and culture, ranging from language and law to trade and technology. The explorers were to record what Indians ate, what they wore, how they made a living, and what they believed. In short, Jefferson told Lewis, "You will therefore endeavor to make yourself acquainted as far as a diligent pursuit of your journey shall admit, with the names of the nations and their numbers."[37]

Throughout the summer of 1803, Lewis's expedition grew in both numbers and sense of mission. What had begun as a modest-sized party on a western "tour" was now the Corps of Northwestern Discovery, the Lewis and Clark expedition. The addition of William Clark acknowledged the expedition's importance and complexity. A frontiersman with far greater experience than Lewis, Clark brought to the venture not only his wilderness and military skills but also his considerable ability as a cartographer. He also had an empathic way in talks with native people. Balancing Lewis's sometimes mercurial and overly sensitive ways, Clark brought steadiness and good sense.

The voyage of western discovery began "under a jentle brease" from St. Louis on 14 May 1804. The party was now a substantial military expedition of forty-two men, recruits representing a virtual cross-section of frontier life. Soldiers and civilian hunters found their places alongside French-Canadian boatmen and Clark's slave York. Equipment of all sorts, from camp gear to Indian trade goods, was stowed in two flat-bottomed pirogues and a large Pittsburgh-built keelboat. Not all these men or all these boxes and bales were bound for the Pacific. At the end of the Fort Mandan winter, Corporal Richard Warfington's detachment took the keelboat and its valuable cargo of scientific specimens back to St. Louis. The thirty-three members of the permanent party, including the captains, Sacagawea, and her infant son, Jean Baptiste, left Mandan on 7 April 1805 to find their way west.

In many ways, the Missouri River route from St. Louis to the Mandan villages was a journey through the known. The twists of the muddy river, its falling banks and sudden shallows, were all familiar to men such as Pierre Cruzatte and Francois Labiche. From mid-May until the end of October, the expedition followed the river highway, a route that took them through present-day Missouri, Kansas, Iowa, Nebraska, and the two Dakotas. But those modern political boundaries are less important to students of the expedition than the explorers' perceptions of the changing terrain, weather, plants, and animals. By the time the expedition reached the Platte River, the world of eastern forests had given way to a plains environment.

When the expedition members left Fort Mandan in early April 1805, all were filled with a sense of excitement. Lewis caught the moment when he wrote that he and his companions were about to embark on a grand enterprise like that of Columbus or Cook. In the following weeks, an upper Missouri world unfolded before them, a world increasingly alien to eyes accustomed to green landscapes and rounded eastern hills. As the river twisted through present-day northeastern Montana, the expedition saw the fantastic shapes of the White Cliffs. In one memorable phrase, Lewis described the view as "seens of visionary inchantment."

By mid-June the explorers were at the Great Falls of the Missouri, where they confronted their first serious physical barrier. A month of demanding work tested the Corps of Discovery's courage and endurance. Once past the Great Falls, they followed the Missouri south through present-day west-central Montana. Passing through the soaring cliffs of the Gates of the Mountains, the expedition pushed and paddled toward the Three Forks of the Missouri. Spending several days (25–30 July) at what Lewis called "an essential point in the geography of this western part of the Continent," the explorers named the three streams that were the headwaters of the Missouri: the Madison, the Jefferson, and the Gallatin.

It was the lack of progress, however, that increasingly worried Lewis and Clark. Lost time at the Great Falls portage put the expedition off schedule. But lost time was just that—lost time. What now obsessed the captains was the search for horses to take them over the continental divide and on to Pacific waters. From the Great Falls on, they had seen signs of Indians, but native people and their horses proved elusive. At Three Forks, Sacagawea once again assured the captains that her Shoshoni kin were nearby. Throughout August, Lewis, George Drouillard, John Shields, and Hugh McNeil worked their way through Shoshoni Cove toward Lemhi Pass. Gradually they realized that the vision of an easy mountain portage was a geographical pipe dream. Standing at Lemhi Pass (on the border of present-day Montana and Idaho), the captains saw the seemingly endless, snow-clad expanse of the Bitterroot Mountains.

At the divide, the expedition recorded scientific and ethnographic observations. After a surprise meeting with Cameahwait's band of Lemhi Shoshonis, the men acquired horses, a Shoshoni guide, and some sketchy information about the Lolo Trail. The expedition left the Lemhi River camps near the end of August. Clark's reconnaissance of the Salmon River revealed that this was not the water highway the expedition sought. Instead, the Corps of Discovery took trails north through broken, densely forested country. Struggling in cold rain and snow, the explorers crossed Lost Trail Pass and came into a narrow, beautiful intermountain cove known today as Ross's Hole. Near present-day Sula, Montana, the cove was a home camp for the Flathead (Interior Salish) Indians. Horse trading and good times filled the short September days. Leaving the Flatheads on 6 September, the explorers pressed north to what they believed was a quick mountain passage to western waters.

The Great Falls of the Missouri had been a formidable barrier for the expedition. But the memory of that month laboring under a blazing sun must have dimmed in the days of cold and hunger on the Lolo Trail. The expedition spent from 12 to 20 September in bitter snows, marching through northern Idaho's most demanding terrain. Numbed by cold and dizzy in the thin air, the explorers braved the Lolo passage. Clark, never one to complain in the face of adversity, admitted that he had never in his life been so cold and wet. Finally Clark led a small advance to the end of the trail at Weippe Prairie near present-day Orofino, Idaho, where Clark met Nez Percé Indians who were digging camas roots and fishing along the nearby Clearwater River. Welcomed by the Nez Percé people, the expedition took time to rest and refit before making a final dash for the Pacific.

Much prejourney planning was based on the assumption that the explorers would exchange horses for canoes soon after crossing the continental divide. But the harsh western geography derailed that scheme. The party did not leave Canal Camp on the Clearwater River until early October. In the next two months the explorers left the mountains and ponderosa pines of the plateau and sailed through the awesome and seemingly desolate Columbia Plain. Navigating hazardous rivers, the Corps of Discovery paddled the Clearwater to the Snake and on at last to the Columbia. The expedition's Columbia days were marked by high winds, terrifying storms, and often tense confrontations with river Indians. By early December the explorers finally reached the Pacific—and faced the task of building a winter post, Fort Clatsop, and readying for the return to St. Louis.

When the captains eventually left Fort Clatsop in late March 1806, they had an exploring agenda every bit as complex as the one that had guided their trek west. During the winter, Lewis and Clark had heard from natives about a river that struck south from the Columbia to the "gulph of California." That river, known to both Indians and explorers as the Multnomah, raised expedition hopes for a trade connection to the Southwest. Equally important were charting the northern course of the Marias River and exploring the Yellowstone. Finally, Lewis and Clark needed to verify Indian information concerning a shorter route between Travelers' Rest at the eastern end of the Lolo Trail and the Great Falls of the Missouri. All this exploring demanded skill and coordination in field operations beyond anything yet attempted by the expedition.

Eager to leave the Northwest and get on the road home, the expedition left Fort Clatsop far too soon, as it turned out, to make a passage through the heavy snows still on the Lolo Trail. By the time the explorers got to the Nez Percé villages along the Clearwater River, their mistake was obvious. Building a makeshift base—Camp Chopunnish—near present-day Kamiah, Idaho, the party spent a month (14 May–15 June 1806) in Nez Percé country. Here the days were filled with hunting, visiting, doctoring, and diplomacy. Yet even while Lewis and Clark enjoyed native hospitality, they chafed at the restraints imposed by time and weather. Determined to be on their way, even if that meant bulling through the snows of the Lolo Trail, the expedition left Camp Chopunnish on 15 June.

That decision was nearly fatal. By 17 June the party was again deep in the Lolo snows. Struggling through drifts sometimes twelve to fifteen feet deep, the explorers must have recalled those terrible days of September 1805, when it had seemed as if the Lolo would be a cold grave. Exhausted and dispirited, the expedition members turned around and did what Lewis blandly described as a "retrograde march." By any name, this was still a retreat, the first in the expedition's history. But fortunes soon changed, and once they were off the trail the explorers engaged three Nez Percé guides. Once again native skill and knowledge saved the expedition and guaranteed success. By the first of July the explorers were over the trail and recuperating at Travelers' Rest.

At Travelers' Rest the captains put the finishing touches on an intricate exploratory plan that promised to fulfill many of their return-trip objectives. The complex strategy would also test field skills to a degree not yet tried. Lewis would take a small party overland to the Great Falls of the Missouri. Three privates would remain at the falls to retrieve and refurbish goods cached there in 1805. In the meantime, Lewis would take a handful of volunteers up the Marias River to chart its northern course, explore the country, and contact the Blackfeet and Atsina Indians. Clark's assignment was every bit as important, if not as dramatic. He was to proceed south from Travelers' Rest through the Bitterroot Valley and eventually cross the divide to Three Forks to Great Falls and link up with the men left behind by Lewis. Eventually the whole Corps of Discovery would reassemble at the Yellowstone-Missouri confluence.

Good fortune, skill, and fortitude were required for such a complex plan. Except for Lewis's angry confrontation with Piegan Blackfeet, a dispute that left two Indians dead, the strategy proved remarkably successful. By the time of the grand reunion on 12 August, much had been accomplished. Clark's exploration of the Yellowstone added to the knowledge of the region. Lewis's northern probe yielded more ambiguous results, both for geographical information and for future Indian-white relations. What remained now was some last-minute Missouri River Indian diplomacy, followed by a quick homebound run down the river. By late September 1806 the voyage was over, and the struggle for meaning and understanding was about to begin.

Our effort to analyze the significance of the expedition might best focus on one key aspect of the journey. Toward the end of the long, dreary Fort Clatsop winter, Lewis set down his thoughts on relations between Indians and the Corps of Discovery. Honesty forced him to admit that the moments of tension and hostility had been far outweighed by months of generosity and goodwill. Nevertheless, in a torrent of angry words harkening back to blood-drenched eastern frontiers, Lewis lashed out at what he insisted was the fundamentally treacherous nature of all native peoples. The explorer maintained that kindness from whites was always repaid with brutality from Indians. "The too great confidence of our countrymen in their sincerity and friendship has caused the destruction of many hundreds of us." Turning his attention to the expedition, Lewis admitted that long months of good relations with Indians made it difficult to believe the party would be attacked. Against that general good feeling, however, Lewis charged that Indians did not deserve the expedition's confidence, no matter how helpful they had been. And Lewis was determined to do everything in his power to undermine any favorable impression his men had of Indians. The Corps of Discovery had to be taught to hate. Lewis repeated his conviction "that our preservation depends on never loosing sight of this trait [treachery] in their character, and being always prepared to meet it in whatever shape it may present itself."[38] That verbal abuse heaped on native people reveals more about Lewis than about the state of expedition-Indian affairs. As much as Jefferson's captains wanted to believe they were masters of a new American domain, Indians usually determined expedition successes or failures. This republican march had its pace set not by Washington or Monticello but by those who had come first to the land.

No situation reveals this more clearly than the expedition's confrontation with the Teton Sioux in September 1804. At the confluence of the Bad and Missouri Rivers, near present-day Pierre, South Dakota, Lewis and Clark had their first lesson in native politics. Long before those tense September days, they had worried about a Sioux encounter. Jefferson had hoped his explorers would pay close attention to the Sioux. "On that nation," wrote the president, "we wish most particularly to make a friendly impression, because of their immense power, and because we learn they are very desirous of being on the most friendly terms with us."[39] Yet Jefferson engaged in wishful thinking when he thought that the Sioux were looking for American friends; he was closer to the mark in noting "their immense power." Lewis and Clark would have to confront that economic and military power, convince the Indians that St. Louis merchants did not endanger the Sioux role in upper Missouri trade, and persuade the Tetons to bring their business to American posts. The captains would have to deal with Indian leaders who clearly understood tribal needs and had both the diplomatic skill and the military force to command attention. A tangled web of economic, personal, and imperial considerations, the Teton Sioux negotiation was perhaps the most demanding piece of Indian diplomacy assigned to the expedition.

Dealing with the well-armed bearded strangers was just as challenging for men such as Black Buffalo, Tortohongar, and Buffalo Medicine. For the Brulé bands of the Tetons and their leaders, the stakes were very high. In the intricate trade network of the upper Missouri, the Teton Sioux played a dangerous and precarious game. Each year the Brulé, Oglala, and Miniconjou bands of Tetons traveled to a trade fair known as the Dakota Rendezvous, held on the James River in present-day east-central South Dakota. There these bands met Sisseton and Yankton Sioux who had obtained trade goods from North West Company posts on the Des Moines and St. Peters Rivers. The Teton bands used those items and buffalo robes in their agricultural trade with the Arikara farmers. With the growing

Teton population, a secure food supply was essential. So long as the Tetons could control the flow of European goods to the villagers, their position would be reasonably strong. But if the villagers gained easy, direct access to St. Louis traders, the role of the Tetons as brokers and middlemen
would be lost. These commercial realities required the Tetons to at most
blockade the Missouri or, at least, exact considerable tribute from traders
coming upriver. The American expedition, representing St. Louis interests
and determined to make direct contact with Arikara, Mandan, and Hidatsa
villages, was a threat that could not be ignored.

But there was more than economic survival at stake for the Brulé leaders. As Lewis and Clark soon discovered, they were caught in the toils of
factional politics. In Brulé politics the leading players were Black Buffalo,
Buffalo Medicine, and Tortohongar. Black Buffalo, headman of the largest
Brulé band, was described by one experienced Missouri trader as a man "of
good character, although angry and fierce in his fits of passion." His authority and prestige had long been questioned by Tortohongar (known to
the whites as the Partisan), headman of the second-ranked band. Pierre-
Antoine Tabeau, whose trade goods had been ransacked by the Partisan
and some of his men, described this Indian as "a true Proteus, who is seen
in the selfsame day faint-hearted and bold, audacious and fearful, proud
and servile, conciliator and firebrand."[40] Buffalo Medicine's role remains
unclear; he was called "the third chief" by Lewis and Clark in what was
perhaps a statement about his place in the larger power struggle. As negotiations with Lewis and Clark were about to begin, both Black Buffalo and
the Partisan looked to use the talks to increase personal standing. Playing
to the Indian galleries, each man tried to outdo the other in spirited defense
of Sioux privilege.

Despite the high stakes for all involved, the explorers and their Teton
hosts enjoyed many hours of genuine hospitality, of good food and spirited dancing. And the captains received a gift that did not translate well
across the cultural divide—bedmates, a mark of respect accorded to distinguished guests. But these good times could not cover harsh words and
provocative gestures. The swirl of talk, poorly interpreted by expedition
member Pierre Cruzatte, was punctuated by moments of violence and confusion. The Partisan and his retinue proved the most aggressive, at one
point causing the usually unflappable Clark to draw his sword. Clark later
recalled that he "felt My Self warm and Spoke in verry positive terms."
Such incidents continued throughout the week. Failing to make any trade
agreement with the Tetons, Lewis and Clark eventually decided to press

upriver. At that moment some of the Partisan's warriors seized the keelboat's bow cable. As Indian women and children hurried away, Clark engaged in a shouting match with Black Buffalo and the Partisan. On the brink of bloodshed, Black Buffalo calmed the nasty scene. After Lewis agreed to a symbolic gift of tobacco, Black Buffalo jerked the cable from the warriors' hands, ending the confrontation.[41]

Lewis and Clark got past the Teton Indians in one piece, but they failed the diplomatic test. The Tetons were still masters of the river, a painful fact that prompted Clark to denounce them as "the pirates of the Missouri."[42] Rebuffed by the Tetons, Lewis and Clark attempted to forge an alliance of Arikara, Mandan, and Hidatsa villages against the Sioux. That strategy, running counter to the economic ties that bound nomads and villagers together, was doomed to failure. The days at Bad River symbolize the two sides of expedition-Indian relations. Native peoples up the Missouri and across the mountains offered information and support vital for the expedition's survival. But when Lewis and Clark tried to shape Indians to a federal course, they met resistance and rejection. The captains could proclaim the arrival of a new republican father, but native people continued to keep their own counsel.

Lewis and Clark never called themselves explorers. But if *exploration* means a carefully planned journey that constantly measures expectation against reality, then Jefferson's soldiers were explorers indeed. That juxtaposition of image and reality can be seen in the first days of June 1805. During the previous winter at Fort Mandan, the Indians had told the explorers that once they passed the Milk River (the "River That Scolds at All Others," as the Hidatsas termed it), they would see no other major streams until past the Great Falls. Now, on 2 June as the expedition made camp in a clump of cottonwoods, they could see "a very considerable river" entering the Missouri from the north. That stream nearly matched the size of the Missouri. Lewis and Clark had to make a crucial choice, one that geographer John L. Allen has termed "decision at the Marias."[43]

The next morning, as the Corps of Discovery got a good look at both rivers, the magnitude of the problem became evident. According to both formal cartographic knowledge and geographical lore, the Missouri trended south to a headwaters near a tributary of the Columbia. The party was at a crossroads. Which stream, north or south, was the true Missouri? Making the wrong choice might fatally delay the expedition. Since the captains were still thinking they could return to Fort Mandan without wintering on the Pacific coast, the decision was vital. For the next week Lewis and Clark attempted to gather accurate information and reach a rational conclusion. As Allen has written, "The captains had come across the first major disjunction between the geography of reality and the image shaped by the previous winter."[44] The test here would be as severe as at any Indian confrontation or council.

Jefferson wanted the explorers to make "very exact descriptions" of what they saw.[45] Direct observation, not tradition or received wisdom, was an Enlightenment fundamental, one that Lewis and Clark followed at the junction of the Missouri and the Marias. Looking at the soon-to-be-named Marias River, Lewis surmised that it was not the true Missouri. Nevertheless, most members of the expedition, including some very experienced frontiersmen, were convinced that the northern stream was the route to follow. On 4 June Lewis and Clark took separate parties to scout each waterway, Lewis along the Marias and Clark along the Missouri. By the time the captains were back in camp on 8 June, both were convinced that the Marias was merely a tributary—important but not the true route to the Pacific.

Lewis and Clark may have been convinced that they knew the right course, but their men were not. Pierre Cruzatte, the Corps' most accomplished waterman, spoke for all when he declared, "The N. fork [the Marias] was the true genuine Missouri and could be no other."[46] The captains could have ignored such opinions and ordered the expedition to follow the southern route. But the party had become what Lewis would later call "the best of families." Respect for other views and a strong sense of company unity made Lewis and Clark conduct a second reconnaissance. On 11 June Lewis took the southern path and two days later came to the Great Falls, incontrovertible evidence of the Missouri. The route to the Pacific ran past the falls toward the Rockies. All the measuring, testing, and judging had paid off at a crucial place.

In two and a half years of western travel, the explorers' days were generally filled with hours of hard work and numbing boredom. Moments of exhilaration and delight were few. From all of this, Jefferson wanted results. Whereas modern followers of the Lewis and Clark epic are fascinated by the journey, Jefferson cared only for facts that could be listed, compared, and used. No sooner had the expedition returned to St. Louis in September 1806 than the president proclaimed his venture a great success. Long on praise and short on specifics, he told Congress that the explorers "had all the success which could have been expected."[47]

Did the journey actually fulfill Jefferson's dreams? The president's

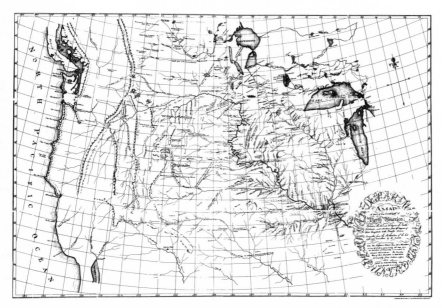

*15.4 "A Map of part of the Continent of North America" (William Clark, 1805). Drawn during the winter of 1804–5 and sent back to Jefferson with other materials in the spring of 1805, this map illustrates the information gathered during the first summer of exploration, as well as data obtained during the winter at Fort Mandan. It was copied by Nicholas King. Collection of John L. Allen.*

greatest hope was that the expedition would find what he called a "channel of communication" across the continent. In instructions for the expedition, he emphasized the primacy of locating that passage. Safely back in St. Louis, the president's men had to face the uncomfortable fact that they had failed to find the fabled passage. When Lewis wrote Jefferson one day after ending the journey, he smoothly assured the president that the party had "penitrated the Continent of North America to the Pacific Ocean, and sufficiently explored the interior of the country to affirm with confidence that we have discovered the most practicable rout which does exist across the continent." But Lewis admitted that the passage was not Jefferson's highway to the Pacific. No direct "channel of communication" reached across the West. As Lewis gingerly put it, the overland route was useful only for goods "not bulky brittle nor of a very perishable nature."[48]

Jefferson's cherished image of the West was a mirage. Lewis and Clark struggled to escape the thrall of that old image by replacing conjecture and fantasy with observation and reality. Nowhere can this be seen more clearly than in Clark's 1810 manuscript map of western North America. Sometimes called Clark's master map, this incorporated not only expedition discoveries but also information from fur traders and other government-sponsored journeys. Even at first glance the map is complex—a tangle of rivers and a maze of mountains. Gone are the comforting simplicities of a single range of mountains, easy portages, and interlocking river systems. In place of deceptive simplicity Clark aimed for geographical accuracy. He correctly positioned the east-west extent of the Rockies and at the same time drafted a reasonably precise depiction of the continental divide. Using his remarkable ability to stand back from the welter of terrain features and visualize very large geographical systems, Clark drew, with unerring skill, two distinct mountain ranges—the Rockies and the Cascades. He also accurately placed the headwaters and tributaries of the Missouri and the Columbia, revealing the illusion of Jefferson's dream of a water highway. But illusions die hard, and Clark did succumb to at least one major geographical deception. The map shows a river called the Multnomah running into the Columbia from far to the south, in present-day Nevada, and rising from the western slope of the Rockies, just opposite the Rio del Norte. The latter river was a phantom as well, and these two illusions were Clark's last tilt at the windmill of Northwest Passage fantasy.[49]

Levi Lincoln's gloomy prediction had come true. The expedition had failed to accomplish its core mission. But Lincoln's suggestions had planted the seeds for the venture's salvation. Science saved the expedition's reputation and kept congressional critics at bay. By the summer of 1808 Jefferson was busy transforming the meaning of the journey. In letters to the scientists Charles Wilson Peale and Bernard McMahon, he emphasized the expedition's intellectual accomplishments. Lewis plainly agreed, and his initial plans for the expedition's three-volume published report promised two volumes filled with botany, zoology, ethnography, and "other natural phenomena."[50] This bright promise was shattered by Lewis's death in 1809. What finally appeared in 1814 was Lewis's proposed volume one—a narrative of the expedition. As Jefferson lamented to Alexander von Humboldt, "The botanical and zoological discoveries of Lewis will probably experience greater delay, and become known to the world thro other channels."[51]

What were those discoveries, and how did they become known to science? As the expedition's principal naturalist, Lewis had spent much time collecting plant and animal specimens and writing detailed observations. His forte was botany, and here the explorer made important scientific contributions. The Academy of Natural Sciences in Philadelphia today contains 216 herbarium sheets with Lewis and Clark samples. Paul Cutright, a leading student of the expedition's scientific endeavors, estimated that perhaps 70 to 75 of those samples were new to science when they were collected. Zoological specimens fared less well, due to rough handling, insect damage, and the eventual dispersal of Peale's American Museum, where they had been deposited after the expedition. Nonetheless, scientists such as Frederick Pursh, Alexander Wilson, and Thomas Say did make good use of what the explorers had so diligently collected and described.[52]

Sometime in the summer of 1806, during a reconnaissance of the Yellowstone River, Clark had paused to write a speech to Indians he would never meet. Two sentences in that talk signify the expedition's relations with native people: "We have been to the great lake of the west and are now on our return to our country. I have seen all my read [red] children quite to that great lake and talked with them, and taken them by the hand in the name of their great father the Great Chief of all the white people."[53] Clark and his companions had indeed seen many Indians, and the daily dealings between explorers and native people had indeed been mostly cordial. But when the captains plunged into the world of diplomacy, whether with plains, plateau, or coastal peoples, and began to treat Indians as children, they met either studied indifference or open hostility. Native diplomats had their own strategies and goals. Accepting the direction of a distant and untried great father seemed a witless course. So long as native sovereignty remained intact, the schemes of a young republic would count for little.

What counted more was the ethnographic knowledge brought back by the expedition. Guided by Jefferson's precise instructions and their own curiosity, the explorers gathered a virtual library of journal entries, vocabularies, drawings, maps, artifacts, and population estimates, all containing priceless information about Indian ways. In their writing, drawing, and collecting, Lewis and Clark captured an essential part of American life on the edge of profound change.

## Dunbar, Freeman, and Custis in Louisiana and the Southwest

Jefferson never intended the Lewis and Clark expedition to be the only American probe of the West. Like his contemporary Sir Joseph Banks in England, Jefferson envisioned exploration as a coordinated enterprise involving many travelers and scientists. After the United States acquired the Louisiana lands, he had even more reason to launch additional expeditions—to address Indian relations, boundary surveys, and scientific concerns.

In March 1804, while Lewis and Clark were still camped outside St. Louis, Jefferson wrote William Dunbar, a Natchez planter and accomplished naturalist who had been a Jefferson correspondent for several years. The president wanted Dunbar to explore the Mississippi's major tributaries, which defined large portions of the Louisiana Purchase, lands bordering on Spain's Internal Provinces. Jefferson's broad vision of the purchase also included the region drained by the Red River, that is, substantial parts of present-day eastern Texas. For Spanish officials, talk about exploring these rivers constituted armed invasion. Jefferson wrote Dunbar, "These surveys will enable us to prepare a map of Louisiana which in its contours and main waters will be perfectly accurate."[54] Spanish fears were surely increased.

During the spring of 1804 Dunbar received authorization from Secretary of War Henry Dearborn to begin selecting personnel for the journey to the Red and Arkansas Rivers. Considering the implications of the expedition, Dunbar saw two problems, both equally dangerous. First was the possible Spanish response. Dunbar knew how committed the Spanish were to the defense of the Internal Provinces. According to geographical lore, the Red River rose near Santa Fe, yet another reason for the Spanish to keep the restless Americans from pushing up the Red. Had Dunbar known of Spanish actions taken against Lewis and Clark, he would have been even more concerned. Second was a genuine worry about the possible Osage reaction. The Arkansas Osages, led by Great Track (Cashesegra), were sure to hinder the expedition's progress.[55]

While Dunbar counted the dangers, Jefferson retired to Monticello to draft instructions for the party. By now the president had abundant experience for such an undertaking. Drawing on the directions prepared for Lewis and Clark, Jefferson drafted guidelines for a journey that would be both scientific and imperial. Jefferson knew that the potential for Spanish-American conflict was great. He told his explorers to announce to the Indians that the Spanish had freely withdrawn their troops from the Mississippi, the Missouri, and all their tributaries. The American president was now the great father to all native people. Such an astounding declaration reflected Jefferson's wish but hardly frontier realities.[56]

No sooner had these initial steps been taken than plans began to unravel. In early July 1804 an Osage delegation led by White Hair I arrived in

Washington. That delegation, organized by Meriwether Lewis, was the first in a series of Indian visitations to result from Lewis and Clark's Indian diplomacy. White Hair I urged Jefferson to abandon the planned venture, saying it would upset both the Spanish and his own people. The president agreed, deciding to delay any Red-Arkansas journey until the spring of 1805. But he was not about to quit all exploration. Dunbar had expressed interest in a short reconnaissance of the Ouachita River through northern Louisiana, past the Sabine River, and into present-day Arkansas. Such a venture might be a good test for the larger enterprise and would also give Pierre Chouteau, the government Indian agent, time to conciliate the disaffected Arkansas Osages. And of course Jefferson would now have a chance to deal with what Dunbar blandly called the "Spanish impediments."[57]

Before abandoning a Red-Arkansas expedition for 1804, Jefferson had selected a naturalist for the undertaking: Dr. George Hunter, a Philadelphia chemist. Jefferson always ranked chemistry a bit lower than botany and zoology, but Hunter was not a bad choice. In the fall of 1804, with Hunter already in Natchez, preparations were under way for the Ouachita journey. When the expedition left Natchez on 16 October, however, its prospects seemed dim. The Dunbar-Hunter expedition was hardly an impressive-looking affair. Hunter's experimental boat, something he called "a Chinese scow," would prove to be a miserable failure. Daily expedition duties were performed by twelve privates commanded not by a commissioned officer but by a sergeant. An unruly crew and scientists unfamiliar with wilderness travel made for difficult days. By early November the party reached what is today Monroe, Louisiana, and soon the travelers entered present-day Arkansas. After reaching the head of navigation on the Ouachita, the expedition portaged to present-day Hot Springs. A month's stay at the springs probably soothed aching muscles and angry tempers, and by the end of January 1805 the travelers were back in Natchez.[58]

The Dunbar-Hunter expedition was hardly a significant exploring adventure, but it did yield valuable information. Cartographer Nicholas King was able to draft the first accurate map of the Ouachita River. Dunbar and Hunter's scientific observations, though not of the highest quality, were greeted with considerable enthusiasm. More important, the Ouachita trip suggested three important lessons for future journeys. First, river craft better suited for exploring southwestern rivers was needed. Second, the Red-Arkansas expedition needed to have a commissioned army officer in the party for discipline and effective leadership. Finally, the Ouachita trip suggested that Dunbar's plan for the later expedition—to go up one river, perhaps the Red, and then portage to the Arkansas—was both unwise and impractical.[59]

The Ouachita jaunt should have made planning the more important Red-Arkansas expedition much easier. In fact, Jefferson had more troubles than he could count. The confusion began with personnel. Neither Dunbar nor Hunter wanted any direct part in the longer voyage. When Jefferson wrote Dunbar about a man named Colonel Freeman as a possible leader of the expedition, Dunbar assumed the president meant Lieutenant Colonel Constant Freeman, currently military commander at New Orleans. But when Dunbar talked with the soldier he soon discovered that this Freeman knew nothing about the proposed journey. Baffled, Dunbar slowed expedition planning until he found out that the man Jefferson had in mind was Thomas Freeman, an accomplished surveyor. This Freeman had been part of Andrew Ellicott's Spanish-American southern boundary survey. Dunbar knew Thomas Freeman and was not especially impressed. These time-consuming misunderstandings were compounded by a frustrating search for an expedition naturalist. Two prime candidates, Constantine Rafinesque and Alexander Wilson, missed expedition berths due to letters poorly timed or gone astray. A desperate Jefferson finally turned to Benjamin Smith Barton, who in turn recommended Peter Custis, a young medical student just finishing his education in Philadelphia under Barton's direction. Custis had some botanical and zoological experience but shared his mentor's scientific conservatism in naming and classification. He had no wilderness travel experience, and his days on the Red River were hard indeed.[60]

Neither Dunbar nor Jefferson could decide which river to explore first. Jefferson voted for the Red, whereas Dunbar advanced a more deceptive strategy, suggesting that the Spanish be told the target was the Red while the group really headed for the Arkansas. The president finally told Dunbar to make his own choice. Far more worrisome was the growing fear that Spanish military forces might actively oppose any move up the Red. Although the Marques de Casa Calvo, the Spanish boundary commissioner, had given grudging assent to the expedition, other royal officers were less willing to allow an American intrusion. No one was more determined to stop all American expansion than Nemesio Salcedo, military commander of the Internal Provinces. He saw this expedition, along with the Lewis and Clark party, as part of a coordinated plan to extend American power at the expense of Spanish influence.[61] The Freeman-Custis expedition could not have come at a more unsettled time in Spanish-American relations.

By 19 April 1806 the explorers were ready to make their way from Fort

Adams, just south of Natchez, up the Mississippi to the Red. The expedition now boasted two flat-bottomed barges and a pirogue. On the roster were twenty-four men, including Freeman, Custis, and two army officers, Captain Richard Sparks and Lieutenant Enoch Humphreys. Later the party comprised seven boats and some forty adventurers. The plan was to sail up the Red to its head of navigation, where the explorers would abandon their boats, buy horses from the Pawnees, and locate the headwaters of the Red. The Pawnee negotiation would be especially important because those Indians had long been of intense interest to the Spanish. Since Salcedo believed they were faithful Spanish allies, the prospect of Americans luring them out of the royal fold was yet another reason to stop Freeman's company.

The expedition reached Campti, the last American outpost on the Red, some forty-five miles above Natchitoches, on 7 June 1806. Lucas Talapoon, a guide hired at Natchitoches, arrived the next day with news that Spanish troops were on the way from Nacogdoches to intercept the expedition. After some discussion, the explorers decided to go as far up the Red as the Coashatta Indian village and wait for federal agent Dr. John Sibley.[62] But to reach that village, the expedition had to face the most formidable barrier on the Red: the Great Raft, a twisted mass of jammed timber and brush some one hundred miles long. From 11 to 24 June, the explorers struggled, hauled, and cursed their way through this morass. As Freeman put it, "After fourteen days of incessant fatigue, toil and danger, doubt and uncertainty, we at length gained the river above the Great Raft, contrary to the decided opinion of every person who had any knowledge of the difficulties we had to encounter."[63]

What lay ahead was a far greater challenge. From 26 June to 11 July the explorers enjoyed the hospitality at the Caddo Coashatta village. Diplomacy, botanizing, and socializing filled the days. On 11 July the expedition, guided by several Caddo Indians, resumed travel up the Red. After two weeks, Indian runners brought the inevitable news that Spanish forces were nearby. With navigation becoming more difficult and the supply of Indian gifts dwindling, this information was one more blow to an already faltering expedition. Like Lewis and Clark, Freeman had been instructed not to challenge any superior military force, whether Indian or European.

Early on the morning of 28 July the expedition, in present-day Bowie County, Texas, sighted a Spanish patrol. The next day Americans and Spaniards met face to face. Francisco Viana, an experienced soldier and a supporter of the Salcedo hard line toward American expansion, had skillfully deployed his troops on a bluff along the southern bank of the Red. Viana made it plain that "his orders were not to suffer any body of armed troops to march through the territory of the Spanish Government; to stop the exploring party by force, and to fire on them if they persisted in ascending the river, before the limits of the territory were defined."[64] Freeman's objections were hastily brushed aside. Having little choice, Freeman agreed to begin a retreat the next day.[65]

What happened at Spanish Bluff was not unexpected, nor was it the untimely end to an expedition bound for success. Freeman admitted as much when he acknowledged that shallow water had already made "further progress impracticable."[66] The Spanish military presence simply hurried the end of an expedition already in deep trouble. But the Freeman-Custis expedition was not a complete failure. As the recent publication of Custis's natural history catalog shows, the explorers made many important ethnographic and environmental observations. Their geographical labors were reflected in maps by Nicholas King (1806), Anthony Nau (1807), and William Clark (1810). As historian Dan Flores has written, "In the present day, their Accounts have become the most valuable primary source for researchers attempting to reconstruct the wilderness frontier and original environmental setting of the lower half of the Red River valley."[67]

In the fall of 1806 Jefferson most likely knew that the Freeman-Custis expedition had been stopped at Spanish Bluff. Nevertheless, he pressed ahead with surveys of important southwestern rivers. On 14 February 1807 Jefferson wrote Secretary of War Dearborn on the subject of future explorations under Freeman's command. Freeman and Lieutenant James B. Wilkinson, the son of General James Wilkinson, were to undertake a thorough study of the Arkansas River. But once again everything went awry. Dunbar could not find a suitable naturalist, and Congress failed to appropriate funds for the journey. Mired in troubles both domestic and foreign, Jefferson found it hard to concentrate on the West and Southwest. Whatever opportunities had beckoned, they were now lost through inaction. For a president once so committed to a comprehensive program of exploration, this was a feeble ending to an impressive beginning.[68]

## The Explorations of Zebulon Montgomery Pike

Zebulon Montgomery Pike was a young army officer cursed by galloping ambition, an inadequate education, and a misplaced loyalty to his commanding officer, General James Wilkinson, the sometime Spanish secret agent. Born in Maryland in 1757, Wilkinson seemed headed toward a medical and scientific career when he attended the University of Pennsylvania. As correspondents such as Jefferson were to discover, Wilkinson had a genuine interest in natural history. But a seat in the republic of science was not what the ambitious young man sought. Marriage to Ann Biddle moved Wilkinson into the world of wealth and privilege, things he would covet for the rest of his life. When the American Revolution burst in the spring of 1775, Wilkinson joined the Continental Army. His war service was not especially distinguished. As clothier-general, the "querulous, litigious, and conniving" Wilkinson managed to antagonize everyone, including George Washington.[69]

In 1784 Wilkinson set out for Kentucky and soon joined in conspiracies to separate that territory from the Union. Here he became a Spanish agent, a connection he would maintain for profit for years to come. In 1791 he returned to military service as an officer in General Anthony Wayne's Ohio army. Wilkinson spent most of his time criticizing Wayne, sniping that made him the darling of junior officers, including the young William Clark. Wayne's untimely death in mid-December 1796 opened the way for Wilkinson, who soon became commanding general of the U.S. Army. Known to the Spanish as "agent thirteen," Wilkinson became governor of Upper Louisiana in 1805. He had already urged his Spanish employers to act against Lewis and Clark. Now his private ambitions led him to launch a troubled journey of discovery.[70]

In early February 1805 Secretary of War Dearborn, influenced by Wilkinson's numerous anti-Spanish reports, suggested a secret reconnaissance into Texas.[71] In the summer of 1805 Wilkinson, now both general and governor of the new Louisiana Territory, visited Fort Massac and selected Pike, district paymaster for the First Infantry Regiment, to lead a journey up the Mississippi River. What brought the inexperienced lieutenant to Wilkinson's attention is unclear. The general did know Pike's father, Colonel Zebulon Pike, and Pike's wife, Clarissa, was the daughter of a Kentucky friend. Armies have a way of taking care of their own; perhaps Wilkinson was looking to add another member to his unofficial family. In any case Pike, always eager for distinction, now suddenly had what seemed his great opportunity.

Orders drawn for Pike on 30 July 1805 spelled out the dimensions of his first "tour of discovery." The expedition was to chart the Mississippi, observe its natural resources, note suitable places for military and commercial establishments, and arrange for Indian delegations to visit St. Louis. Pike expanded the orders, at least in his own mind, to include a search for the source of the Mississippi and a diplomatic thrust against North West Company traders dealing in present-day Minnesota. On 9 August 1805 Pike took twenty men and a keelboat up the Mississippi. By the time winter closed in, the explorers were somewhere near Little Falls, Minnesota. While most of his men spent the winter in a stockaded fort, Pike and a small party sledded into northern Minnesota looking for the headwaters of the Mississippi. They got close, but the prize would go years later to Henry R. Schoolcraft. By 30 April 1806 Pike was back in St. Louis, proud of his maps and scientific observations. Wilkinson's only remark was that Pike had "stretched his orders."[72]

Pike may have imagined that his exploits up the Mississippi shaped his future, but in fact the lieutenant's destiny was increasingly in the hands of others, particularly former vice-president Aaron Burr and his political associate Wilkinson. Burr and Wilkinson had set their sights on the West. Just what they hoped to gain remains a source of lively scholarly debate. Whatever their plans—invading Mexico or establishing a new republic in the West—the result was increased pressure to probe into Spanish territories.[73]

Thus, less than a month and a half after Pike's return from the Mississippi, the young explorer learned he was to have a new assignment. He described his forthcoming journey as "long and Ardious" but gave no details.[74] Those details came a week later in formal instructions from Wilkinson. Pike's first objective, and certainly the least demanding, was to return fifty-one Osage captives to their homes. Those Indians, held prisoner by the Potawatomis, had been ransomed and were now being escorted west as a sign of American good faith. Wilkinson insisted that this duty was the "primary object" of the journey, but neither the general nor the lieutenant believed those words. Second, Pike was to negotiate a peace between Kansas and Osage bands. Third, Pike was ordered to find the Comanches— or the Ietans, as Europeans called them—and negotiate an anti-Spanish alliance.[75]

Both Wilkinson and Pike recognized that the search for the Comanches could have grave international consequences. The general admitted that Pike's route would take him "approximate to the settlements of New Mexico." Acknowledging that Pike was going to travel through Spanish territory, Wilkinson ordered him to "move with great circumspection."[76] Such polite phrasing barely hid the obvious: Pike was headed toward the Internal Provinces on a spying mission. The extent of that spying and its beneficiaries remain unclear. The secretary of war had authorized such clandestine probes early in 1805, when tensions between Spain and the United States were at fever pitch. By the end of the year, tensions had somewhat subsided. Perhaps the spying was planned to benefit Wilkinson's own commercial Santa Fe schemes. The general may have hoped that Pike's capture (something Wilkinson probably felt was inevitable) might spark an ugly incident with Spain. How much of this Pike knew is difficult to judge. In a letter to Wilkinson written just days after the expedition left St. Louis, Pike insisted that a journey to Santa Fe under Spanish guard "would gratify our most sanguine expectations."[77] Pike had always supported an American invasion of the Southwest as a means to spread republican light and liberty. Perhaps he saw his mission in such imperialist terms.

Pike's mission, however defined, hung on a persistent geographical delusion. Wilkinson, Pike, and virtually everyone else on the frontier who gave systematic thought to western geography believed that the sources of the Red and the Arkansas Rivers were close together. According to geographical lore, the Red rose just east of Taos. All this seemed confirmed by Alexander von Humboldt's "General Map of the Kingdom of New Spain." As Donald Jackson has shown, Humboldt drew on the work of Bernardo Miera y Pacheco, cartographer for the Dominguez-Escalante expedition. With a conceptual geography so at odds with reality, it was little wonder that Pike soon became disoriented and lost.

Pike traveled through present-day Missouri, Kansas, and Nebraska in the summer and fall of 1806. By mid-October the expedition was on the Great Bend of the Arkansas River. There the party divided, with Wilkinson's son James leading a small group back downriver. Pike imagined that he could track the Arkansas to its source and then easily reconnoiter the Red. On 5 December 1806 the explorers were just below present-day Canon City, Colorado, where the Arkansas comes through the cavernous Royal Gorge. A quick scouting of the terrain revealed two creeks, the Grape and the Oil. Pike now faced a decision much like the one Lewis and Clark had been forced to make at the Marias. Whereas those captains made the right choice, Pike chose the wrong course. Thinking he had found the headwaters of the Arkansas and believing that the Red River was nearby, Pike decided (on 9 December) to follow what he thought was a fresh Spanish trail north. He then intended to swing south to Santa Fe and the waters of the Red. Given his conceptual geography, this was not a wholly illogical strategy.

Pike's expedition traveled north to the waters of the South Platte. He then turned west to intercept the main stem of the Arkansas, which he was sure was the Red. By 14 December 1806 the Pike expedition was in deep trouble. Dressed in summer uniforms, they faced a Rockies winter. Pike had begun to realize that his geographical image and the landscape reality did not match. "The geography of the country," he confessed in his journal, "had turned out to be so different from our expectation; we were somewhat at a loss which course to pursue."[78] The explorers may have been bewildered, but Pike evidently did not doubt that the river he was on—the Arkansas—was the Red. Only on 5 January 1807, after an exhausting struggle through Royal Gorge, did he recognize the Arkansas for what it was.

In self-admitted despair, Pike faced a second crucial decision, complicated by short supplies, inadequate clothing, no horses, and geographical confusion. "I now felt at considerable loss how to proceed."[79] If he turned down the Arkansas and then tracked south, he would strike the north fork of the Canadian River. On the other hand, if the explorers marched southwest and crossed the awesome Sangre de Cristo Range, they would meet the Rio Grande. In either case, Pike would no doubt think that he had found the Red. On 9 January he made his choice. For eighteen days (14–31 January) Pike and his men labored over the snow-choked mountains in a state of hunger, exhaustion, and terrible suffering. Two soldiers, John Sparks and Thomas Dougherty, were so badly frostbitten that they had to be left in the snows with scant provisions and promises that the party would return for them. By the end of January the expedition was in the San Luis Valley. There, some five miles up the Conejos River and twelve miles south of present-day Alamosa, Colorado, Pike's men built a log stockade. Their commanding officer was sure he was on the Red River and plainly within the territorial limits of the United States.[80]

Pike's fort was destined for a short life under American colors. In early February Dr. John H. Robinson suddenly announced that he would be leaving the fort to reach Santa Fe on his own. Robinson had joined the expedition just days before it had left St. Louis, and his presence has always been a mystery. The doctor plainly had some sort of ties to Wilkinson. He may have begun the journey partly to look after the younger Wilkinson, but that explanation hardly fits Robinson's later career as an ardent Mexican revolutionary. Yet there is no evidence that he carried any secret letters from Wilkinson to Salcedo. Giving the excuse that he had promised a Kas-

kaskia merchant he would collect a long-overdue debt, Robinson struck off toward Santa Fe.[81]

Next, on the morning of 26 February, a sentry suddenly broke daily drill to report the presence of two scouts. Those men were the advance party for a large Spanish detachment under the command of Lieutenants Ignatio Saltelo and Bartholomew Fernandez. When the officers confronted Pike with the fact that he was on the Rio Grande and in Spanish territory, he exclaimed, "What . . . is not this the Red river [?]" After being assured that the Red was many miles distant, Pike hauled down the U.S. flag and prepared to go under escort to Santa Fe. Pike's assertion that he was lost and had blundered into the Spanish domain has sometimes been doubted as a transparent ruse. Those who believe that Pike purposely entered New Mexico and openly courted capture cite the Dearborn-Wilkinson plans for secret probes into the Southwest and point to a letter that Pike wrote to Wilkinson a few days into the journey. Pike recognized that his pursuit of the Comanches might lead him into Spanish territory, and he suggested that if this should happen, he might claim he was lost. By the time Spanish troopers found him on the Conejos, he was lost and had been for some time; his assertion was more accurate than he knew. As Donald Jackson observed, Pike was not only a spy but a hopelessly lost one.[82]

Pike and his men spent the next four months traveling under Spanish guard. The route took the Americans south through Santa Fe and into present-day Mexico. After a stay at Chihuahua, the party proceeded northeast across the Sierra Madre Oriental mountains and into present-day Texas. A brief visit to San Antonio was all Pike saw of a place of considerable military importance. On the evening of 30 June the explorers were back on American soil at Natchitoches.

The Pike expedition never captured the American imagination in the way that the journeys of Lewis and Clark or even John C. Frémont did. Pike's Peak remains the single recognizable remnant of his adventure. Pike certainly thought he and his men deserved better. But as Donald Jackson has written, "Nothing that Pike ever tried to do was easy, and most of his luck was bad."[83] A faulty sense of geography, poor expedition planning, devotion to an unworthy commanding officer, and an inadequate scientific education made the journey both rough and unproductive. The Spanish seizure of his papers damaged whatever Pike had to say. The explorer struggled to get his report into print and failed to gain suitable rewards for his men. Pike's maps and observations were derivative and unenlightening. Zebulon Montgomery Pike proved no southwestern Homer.

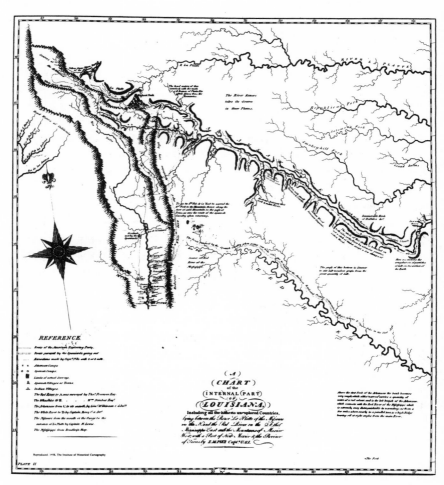

15.5 *"A Chart of the Internal Part of Louisiana"* (Zebulon Montgomery Pike, 1810). *This map accompanied the publication of Pike's* Account of Expeditions to the Sources of the Mississippi, and through the Western Parts of Louisiana. *Pike's map reinforced several key geographic concepts advanced by Clark's cartography, including the concept of a common source area for major western rivers. Reproduced from the original by the Institute of Historical Cartography, San Francisco, California.*

# Early Fur Trade Exploration

Official government expeditions probing the West were a hallmark of the Jefferson era. But military men were not the only explorers who paddled up rivers and marched across mountains. Some of the most important exploring in the early 1800s was undertaken by traders working for rival fur companies. Men such as David Thompson, Alexander Mackenzie, Simon Fraser, and Robert Stuart made their mark with published journals and printed maps. Others, less literate or less fortunate, have slipped through the grasp of recorded history.

Well before Lewis and Clark headed up the the Missouri in the summer of 1804, the fur trade was a going concern. Thanks to both St. Louis and Canadian entrepreneurs, the Missouri River and the northern plains had become part of a global business system. On one day alone Lewis and Clark met seven canoes taking pelts down to St. Louis: four from the Osage villages, two from the Omahas, and one from the Pawnees on the Platte.[84] Other days brought encounters with traders doing business with the Sioux far up the Missouri. At Fort Mandan, Lewis and Clark met the merchants Hugh Heney, Francois-Antoine Larocque, and Rene Jusseaume. Larocque was an important explorer in his own right, making the first major European reconnaissance of the Yellowstone River a full year before Clark's 1806 journey.

But the merchants' business system had geographical limits in the West. When Lewis and Clark returned to St. Louis in late September 1806, carrying notebooks crammed with information on virtually every aspect of the West and the Pacific Northwest, it was the economic news that captured the imaginations of many St. Louis entrepreneurs. The captains and their men spoke of seemingly endless supplies of beaver, and of Indians eager to become partners in the trade. Listening attentively was Manuel Lisa, a Spanish trader who had come to St. Louis in the late 1790s and soon challenged the powerful Chouteaus for a place in the fur business. By the summer of 1806 Lisa and his partners were organizing a trading journey to Santa Fe. The planned adventure angered Wilkinson, who evidently did all he could to block Lisa's plans. Wilkinson was a dangerous enemy, and Lisa wisely gave up his Santa Fe plan. No sooner had that decision been made than Lewis and Clark pulled into town.[85]

Lisa never lacked energy. What he needed was knowledge and experience. Lisa quickly recognized those commodities in George Drouillard, perhaps the ablest of Lewis and Clark's men. Lewis described Drouillard as "a man of much merit" with "uncommon skill as a hunter and woodsman."[86] By the spring of 1807 Drouillard was busy hiring other expedition veterans for a major trapping venture that soon journeyed up the Missouri and into the Yellowstone and Bighorn country. From a post (Fort Raymond) just above the confluence of the Yellowstone and the Bighorn, the Lisa party could survey a vast trading range. Needing to bring Indians to Fort Raymond, Lisa sent John Colter on a reconnaissance of present-day northwestern Wyoming. Colter, one of the young Kentucky hunters recruited for the Lewis and Clark expedition, had become a skilled frontiersman.

Sometime during the late fall or early winter of 1807 Colter set out alone, packing no more than his gun and what supplies he could carry. Although his exact route has been debated for years, he apparently followed a rough figure-eight-shaped track that took him over the Pryor Mountains, along Clark's Fork of the Yellowstone, and into today's Sunlight Basin. Confronted by the Absaroka Mountains, Colter angled southeast past Heart Mountain to the Shoshone River near present-day Cody, Wyoming. There he found thermal springs and tar pits, resulting in the name "Colter's Hell." Skirting the Absarokas, Colter finally reached the Wind River valley. As he traveled west through the valley Colter may have been surprised to find no Spanish settlements; according to geographical lore, such establishments were in the region. Colter's western route took him over Togwotee Pass and into Jackson's Hole and the Grand Tetons. His reconnaissance of what is today Yellowstone National Park did not include geyser country, but he did discover Yellowstone Lake and Mammoth Springs. At the springs he found the well-traveled Bannock Indian trail and the way back to Fort Raymond.[87]

Colter's extraordinary journey puts him in the front rank of fur trade explorers. But he may not have been the only American explorer in the mountains during 1807. Another expedition, one backed directly by Wilkinson, may also have been scouting the western landscape. On 17 September 1806, as the Lewis and Clark expedition was hurrying down the Missouri toward St. Louis, the explorers came upon John McClellan and a modest trading party just above the mouth of the Grand River. Lewis quickly recognized McClellan, a recently resigned army captain. McClellan volunteered that "he was on reather a speculative expedition to the confines of New Spain, with a view to introduce a trade with those people." McClellan expected to build a post at the mouth of the Platte, make business arrangements with the Pawnees and Otoes, and then head for Santa Fe. There he planned to "appear in a stile calculated to atract the

Spanish government in that quarter and through the influence of a handsome present he expects to be promited to exchange his merchandize for Silver and gold of which those people abound."[88]

This ambitious scheme was hardly the product of one ex-artillery officer's discontent with army life. McClellan himself gave an important clue to the origin of his enterprise when he displayed "a kind of introductory Speach from Gov. Wilkinson to the Panias and Ottoes."[89] Wilkinson had already sent Pike on one southwestern mission, and now McClellan was also pointed toward Santa Fe. As early as September 1805 the scheming general reported that he had "engaged a bold adventurer, who served under me during the late Indian War, and is now a Pensioner of the U.S.—(McClellan) to look at Saint Afee in person pending the winter."[90] But after Wilkinson's "bold adventurer" heard Lewis and Clark extol the riches of Rocky Mountain beaver streams, the destination changed. McClellan evidently abandoned thoughts of Spanish silver and now dreamed of "brown gold."

McClellan and his traders probably wintered at the old post built by Regis Loisel on the Great Bend of the Missouri in present-day southern South Dakota. During the winter McClellan's expedition grew in both size and knowledge. From the time Lewis and Clark met the party in September 1806 to the summer of 1807, the group increased from eighteen to forty-two members. A substantial number of experienced traders wintered over on the northern plains in 1806–7, and McClellan probably recruited from their ranks. But there was an additional source for valuable employees. When Kutenai Indians reported McClellan's presence in Montana in the summer of 1807, they told David Thompson that the party included Lewis and Clark veterans. One historian has argued that those men were probably Joseph Field and John B. Thompson. These two would have made especially good candidates for McClellan's expedition, since they were part of Lewis's reconnaissance in 1806.[91]

The expedition probably left Loisel's fort in March 1807 and followed the route blazed by Lewis and his men into present-day Montana. A reasonable route and pace of march would have put McClellan in Flathead country (northwestern Montana) by midsummer. Far to the north, at Kootenay House just above Lake Windermere in present-day British Columbia, David Thompson and his North West Company men were exploring the upper Columbia River. In mid-August 1807 two Kutenai Indians brought Thompson a remarkable letter. Written by one "Captain Zachary Perch" from Fort Lewis on Yellow River, the note carried the date 10 July 1807. In the form of a list of trade regulations, the letter announced a broad American claim to western lands and warned off any Canadian traders. From the Kutenais, Thompson learned that the American party had a fortified post on the lower Flathead River near what is today Dixon, Montana. The presence of a large American expedition and its open commercial and political challenge worried Thompson. "This establishment of the Americans," wrote the Nor'wester, "will give a new Turn to our so long delayed settling of this Country, in which we have entered it seems too late."[92]

Thompson had not heard the last of those elusive Americans. On 24 December 1807 Kutenais brought a second letter, signed this time by "Lieutenant Jeremy Pinch." That note, dated 29 September 1807 at Poltito palton Lake (Flathead Lake), was far more abrasive than the first message. Thompson was warned that his supposed violations of American trade regulations would not go unpunished. The letter writer was evidently convinced that Thompson was arming Piegans and Atsinas for raids against Flathead villages. "We expect Sir," blustered the American, "you will no longer supply these Marauders with Arms and Ammunition." Thompson's bland reply reminded his officious correspondent of previous British claims of discovery and promised only to place all customs questions before North West Company partners.[93]

In the summer or fall of 1807 a large party of Americans was obviously in northwestern Montana. But who they were, the nature of their mission, and the identity of Perch/Pinch have long remained a puzzle. Harry M. Majors, the most recent scholar to examine the fragmentary evidence, argues that Perch/Pinch was John McClellan. Drawing on substantial geographical and ethnographic research, Majors places McClellan and his men first at a post on the lower Flathead River and later at Flathead Lake. The pseudonymous letters to Thompson were a clever, perhaps desperate ploy to frighten rival traders out of a rich beaver country. After 1807 McClelland and his expedition drop from sight for good. Majors believes that Wilkinson's "bold adventurer" was killed by Piegans who assaulted American traders throughout the upper Missouri country in the fall of 1810.[94]

Colter's grand tour of the Yellowstone and McClellan's probable Flathead adventure point to a quickening of western fur trade exploration. The driving force behind St. Louis ventures was Manuel Lisa. In a revealing letter to William Clark, Lisa summed up his own drive to succeed: "I put into my operation great activity; I go a great distance while some are considering whether they will start today or tomorrow."[95] During the winter of 1808–9 Lisa and others formed the Saint Louis Missouri Fur Company, known locally as the Missouri Fur Company. The firm attracted some of the city's most influential merchants and politicians, including Pierre Chouteau, Reuben Lewis (Meriwether's brother), and William Clark. George Drouillard, soon to die at Three Forks in company service, was not a partner. Andrew Henry, the company's able field captain, became a partner later. As Lisa saw it, his company bid fair to engross the fur trade not only of the Missouri but also of those lands up to the Rockies. Indeed, Lisa may also have also imagined his traders spreading south to New Spain and west over the Great Divide to the Columbia.[96]

Headed up the Missouri in the spring of 1809 were two distinct parties. A substantial contingent of militiamen, under the command of Pierre Chouteau, escorted the Mandan headman Sheheke back to his village. That military force left St. Louis in mid-May 1809. A month later Lisa's trappers, nearly 190, started upriver. Lisa's plan was to use Fort Manuel on the Yellowstone as a staging base for trapping in and around the Three Forks of the Missouri. But massive desertions among the inexperienced American employees undermined Lisa's scheme. Nonetheless an impressive trapping expedition led by Pierre Menard and Andrew Henry and guided by John Colter did cross Bozeman Pass and reach Three Forks in early April 1810. Thomas James's *Three Years among the Indians and Mexicans*, first published in 1846, vividly recounted this expedition, from the Montana landscape to the trappers' running battles with the Blackfeet. More recently an account and a map based on the experiences of John Dougherty, another expedition member, have come to light.

Using these two sources, we can reconstruct the travels of the various Missouri Fur Company parties. One trapping group took beaver from Three Forks to the Great Falls of the Missouri. The Blackfeet killed the members of a second party, including two Lewis and Clark veterans, John Potts and the redoubtable George Drouillard. A third contingent, led by Andrew Henry, made the most important journey. Taking the Bannock Indian Trail (the same route perhaps used by the McClellan expedition), Henry and his men crossed the continental divide and came to a tributary of the Snake River. With winter closing in, the trappers built Henry's Fort on the river now called Henry's Fork. If the McClellan expedition is discounted because of lack of evidence, Henry and his companions were the first American trappers to build a permanent post west of the divide. The geography of the northern plains and the Rockies was slowly becoming better understood by those looking west from St. Louis.[97]

The business of collecting trader lore and reducing it to cartographic scale fell to William Clark. The explorer had proven to be an intuitive car-

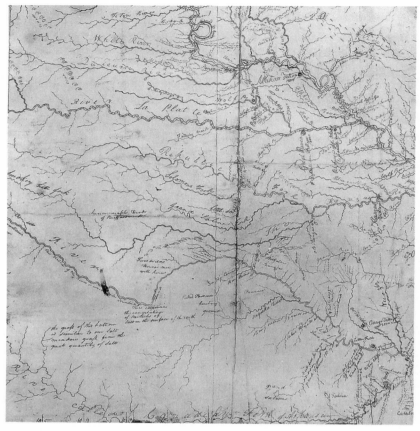

15.6 "A Map of part of the Continent of North America" (William Clark, c. 1810). Clark's "master map" of the American West contained not only the results of the Lewis and Clark journey but also information obtained by early fur traders in the West, including the Astorians. This map formed the basis for the published map

tographer, and now, as Superintendent of Western Indian Affairs in St. Louis, he began a large "master map" of the American West. Seeking reliable information, Clark questioned men such as Drouillard and Colter about their travels. When Drouillard returned to St. Louis in August 1808 he made a rough map of his travels in the Bighorn River country. Clark copied that map and incorporated its views into his own work. The result, as described by one historian, was "a remarkable exercise in fictional geography."[98] Clark believed that the upper reaches of the Yellowstone and the

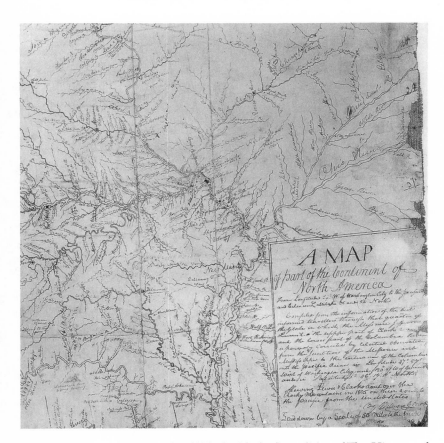

*produced by Samuel Lewis and published with the first edition of* The History of
the Expedition *(ed. Nicholas Biddle). Yale Collection of Western Americana, Beinecke Rare Book and Manuscript Library.*

Bighorn were close to rivers leading to Spanish territories. Drouillard's map
seemed to confirm that misconception. And fresh evidence for the illusion
came from Andrew Henry, who returned to St. Louis in the fall of 1811. The
*Louisiana Gazette* offered this optimistic version of Henry's geography:

> Mr. Henry, a member of the Missouri Fur Company, and his hunters,
> have discovered several passes, not only very practicable, but even
> in their present state, less difficult than those of the Allegany Moun-
> tains. These are considerably south of the source of the Jefferson
> River. It is the opinion of the gentleman last mentioned, that loaded

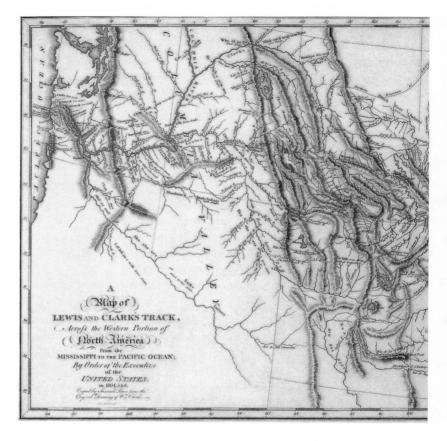

15.7 "A Map of Lewis and Clark's Track across the western portion of North America" (drawn and engraved by Samuel Lewis, 1814, from William Clark's 1810 manuscript map). This map, which illustrated the Nicholas Biddle edition of The History

horses, or even wagons, might in its present state, go in the course of 6 or 8 days from a navigable point on the Columbia, to one on the waters of the Missouri—Thus, rendering an intercourse with settlements which may be formed on the Columbia, more easy than between those on the heads of the Ohio, and the Atlantic states.[99]

Imagining a "river Collarado" or a "Rio del Norte," Clark now fashioned another version of the pyramidal height of land and a water route across the continent.

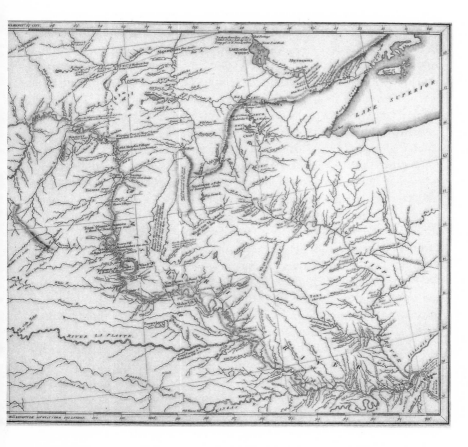

of the Expedition, *was the primary source of geographical information on the far-ther West until the 1840s. American Philosophical Society.*

The Lewis and Clark, Pike, and fur trade explorations were fully expressed in the map Clark sent Nicholas Biddle in December 1810. That map became the basis for the engraved "Map of Lewis and Clark's Track Across the Western Portion of North America" published in Biddle's 1814 *History of the Expedition under the Command of Captains Lewis and Clark*.[100] Clark's "master map" (as well as, to a lesser degree, the published version) demonstrates the subtle interaction of persistence and change in western cartography. Even the most casual comparison of Clark's 1805 map of the West made during the Fort Mandan winter and his effort five years later reveals the leap forward in both geographical knowledge and cartographic imagination. John L. Allen has pointed to two places where change is most evident. Like its predecessors, Clark's 1805 map portrayed the Rockies as narrow, disconnected ridges. But direct field experience forever transformed that image. Clark now knew about the multiple, complex ranges of the Rockies. His 1810 map almost overwhelms the viewer with a tangle of mountain terrain. In that detail, sometimes blurred by the soft end of Clark's pen, a powerful myth finally died. Earlier sources had claimed that a traveler could catch a glimpse of the Pacific from the crest of the Rockies. Clark's depiction of the Cascades country virtually ended such optimistic speculation.

An equally dramatic change is the expression of western rivers. Earlier maps had ghost rivers, phantom lakes, and the powerful concept of headwaters near one another. Clark's "master map" erased most of these features, instead offering a reasonably clear portrayal of the Missouri and Columbia. Thanks to his field experience, Clark now understood that the Columbia and the Missouri headwaters were narrow mountain streams, not broad navigable water highways. But for all this accuracy, the 1810 map did hold one grand river illusion. Clark not only accepted the notion of an easy journey from the upper Bighorn to the "Spanish river" but also fashioned a new north-south waterway. During their explorations of the Columbia, Lewis and Clark had heard about the river known today as the Willamette. Drawing on Indian information garbled in translation and on their own geographical notions, the captains created the Multnomah—a river that would haunt explorers for the next thirty years. Clark sketched the Multnomah from its Columbia junction to headwaters in a region that also gave birth to the Yellowstone, Snake, Platte, Bighorn, Arkansas, Colorado, and Rio Grande Rivers. One passage to India—the easy portage from the Missouri to the Columbia—had died, only to be reborn farther south.[101]

## The Astorians' Vision of Empire

Thomas Jefferson often used quiet dinners to test the political waters or advance a new idea. At one such gathering in late November 1806 the president offered his thoughts on the next steps in the American exploration of the West and Pacific Northwest. He had just finished reading a long letter from Lewis detailing the explorer's journeys and the imperial future of the Columbia country. As Senator William Plumer later recalled, the president hoped "some enterprizing mercantile Americans" would travel "to the river Columbia and near the Pacific ocean, and settle the land there." The president insisted that no other nation had legitimate claims to the region, an assertion sure to raise hackles in European capitals. Would the U.S. government organize, fund, and support such ventures? Private investors might follow in the tracks of official explorers, but the traders and settlers were largely on their own. As Plumer recollected, the president "doubted whether it would be prudent for the government of the United States to attempt such a project."[102] Jefferson hoped and expected that Americans would follow in the footsteps of his Corps of Discovery but felt that the personnel and funding would have to come from outside official Washington.

One American "enterprizing mercantile" was eager to take up the challenge. John Jacob Astor was already a prosperous New York fur merchant. With good connections in the Montreal fur market and a remarkable attention to detail, Astor had both the energy and the intellect for a struggle of imperial dimensions. In the last months of 1807 Astor first mentioned his western ideas to De Witt Clinton. Mayor of New York and sometime lieutenant governor of the state, Clinton was the ideal sounding board. He had influential political friends and considerable business savvy, and Clinton's uncle George was Jefferson's vice-president. No direct record of those earliest talks between Astor and Clinton survives, but clearly the mayor urged the merchant to pursue a Pacific enterprise, about which Astor had been thinking for some time.[103]

Writing to Clinton on 25 January 1808, Astor precisely spelled out his "plans on the Subject of a company for carrying on the furr trade in the United States even more extensive than it is done by the companys in Canada." Astor proposed an ambitious design to control the entire Great Lakes and upper Missouri fur trade and then to extend that control to the Pacific coast. He envisioned a series of trading posts from the Missouri to the Pacific, dotting the route followed by Lewis and Clark. Because Astor lacked reliable connections in St. Louis, he initially selected New Orleans as his midcontinent base.[104] Later he came to see the value of St. Louis, as well as the need to build a large entrepôt at the mouth of the Columbia. Although Astor did not mention China and the booming sea otter trade, Clinton surely knew that Astor was interested in more than the domestic fur business. Here, in outline, was an attractive plan for expanding the republic. As Astor wrote years later, his effort was aimed to "extend it [the United States] dominion over a most interesting part of the opposite coast of the North American continent, and perhaps open communications of no small moment with Japan and the East Coast of Asia."[105]

Astor's imperial vision was inspired neither by Jefferson's concept of an expanding republic nor by Lewis and Clark's example. Rather, he took his direction from Canadian sources. Beginning in 1787, Astor made annual trips each fall to the Montreal fur market. Astor, who sometimes brought his family on these journeys, enjoyed invitations to dine with prominent members of the North West Company. At a time when Montreal and its merchants were filled with talk about the Rockies, western rivers, and the Pacific trade to China, Astor heard it all, and what he heard went by the name of the North West Company's Columbian Enterprise. That plan, born from the explorations and geographical ruminations of Peter Pond, Alexander Henry the elder, and Alexander Mackenzie, sought to seize the West for Britain by means of a vast fur trade system. The Pond-Henry-Mackenzie plans had challenged Jefferson; now they would inspire Astor as well.

From the beginning, Astor understood that his plans required the creation of a company both to launch the enterprise and to protect him in case of failure. That firm, Pacific Fur Company, was organized along North West Company lines with partners, clerks, and laborers. Corporate strategy was firmly within the Pond-Henry-Mackenzie tradition: overland expeditions carrying pelts, employees, and information from St. Louis to the Columbia and back. Ships bound out of New York for the Northwest coast would transport heavier goods not suitable for overland transit.[106]

In the midst of preparations for such journeys, Astor suddenly had the opportunity to extend the reach of his company far to the north. The Russian fur trade, represented by the Russian-American Company, was faltering. Competition from shrewd Americans, weapons in the hands of unfriendly local people, and the grim prospect of short rations all haunted the company and its poorly paid employees. In addition, although the domestic fur market in Russia was substantial, it could never yield the kind of bumper profits realized in China. Yet Canton, the only Chinese port open to foreigners, was shut to the Russians. Their only access to the Chinese market was the remote frontier post at Kyakhta on the border between Siberia and present-day Mongolia. Furs sold there fetched a much lower price than at Canton, and even those profits were diminished by high transportation costs. Plainly the Russian-American Company needed to gain access to Canton.[107] To help it do this, the company decided to find a private American merchant. By late fall 1809 the Russian-American Company and Astor's Pacific Fur Company were discussing ways that the two might cooperate on the Northwest coast. An agreement was finally reached in May 1812, giving Astoria a northern prospect.[108]

When Astor had begun planning his overland enterprise in 1808, he had assumed that his traders, led by Wilson Price Hunt, would follow the Lewis and Clark track up the Missouri, across the mountains, and on to the Columbia.[109] At the time Hunt and his party got to St. Louis in September 1810, there seemed no reason to doubt that the Lewis and Clark trail was the best highway across the continent. Hunt had heard about this route since his days in St. Louis as a young merchant. He clearly knew about the course of the Missouri, the nature of the Great Falls on that river, and the mountain passage to the Pacific. Yet his image of that passage was a curious mix of preexpedition notions and more accurate information brought back by Lewis and Clark. Like most geographers before Lewis and Clark, Hunt believed that only a short distance separated the heads of rivers flowing east and west. But after hearing about expedition experiences, he recognized that "the dividing is a mountain on which there is snow all year."[110]

That the Astorians were headed west by the northern Rockies route soon became common knowledge in St. Louis. William Clark noted that Hunt's party was "preparing to proceed up the Missouri, and prosue my trail to the Columbia."[111] Yet Clark and Lewis, even before returning to St. Louis, knew that there were quicker and safer routes to the Pacific. By 1810 knowledge of those routes had been enhanced by the fur trade explorations of men such as John Colter and George Drouillard. In St. Louis, Hunt could not have escaped hearing about such new ways west. And he certainly could not have escaped Clark, who always sought out anyone either coming or going west. Indeed, part of Hunt's 1811 overland route found its place on Clark's "master map." And Hunt's alterations of his plans while in St. Louis may have resulted from conversations with Clark. Clark's exploration of the Yellowstone in the late summer of 1806 convinced him that the river was an important western trail. Writing that year, he characterized the Yellowstone as "a large and navagable river with but fiew obstructions quite to the rocky Mountains."[112] Both Lewis and Clark believed that the Yellowstone could take a traveler to the eastern slopes of the Rockies more quickly than any other southern route. And southern routes were increasingly important. Conflict between the Blackfeet and American trappers, coupled with constant threats from both the Teton Sioux and the Arikaras, made northern trails chancy. Clark may have told Hunt about these hazards and the possibility of an attractive Yellowstone detour.

But federal officials like Clark were not the only people in the city with valuable information. St. Louis was the great clearinghouse for both pelts and western lore. Geography—the courses of rivers and the shape of the land—was a topic eagerly discussed at William Christy's city tavern and every other watering hole. Trapper lore was in the air, and the Astorians could not have avoided hearing it. Of all the traders now living around St. Louis, none had seen more of the West than John Colter. First hired by Lewis and Clark and later employed by the Missouri Fur Company, Colter had trapped and explored from the Three Forks of the Missouri to the farthest reaches of the Yellowstone country. Colter returned to the St. Louis vicinity in 1810, married, and settled down along the Missouri above La-Charette. Here Hunt met him in March 1811. Colter's ideas about western geography were well-known, and the Astorians were probably acquainted with them some months before that meeting. Like Clark, Colter was convinced that a southern course was the surest way to the Pacific. In an interview published in the *Louisiana Gazette*, Colter insisted, "At the head of Gallatin fork, and of the Grosse Corne [Bighorn River] of the Yellowstone it is found less difficult to cross [the Rocky Mountains] than the Alleghany Mountains." Colter thought that both the Bighorn and the Gallatin would provide access to passes such as Union and Teton, over which, he claimed, "a loaded wagon would find no obstruction in passing."[113]

Information from Clark and Colter influenced Hunt. Sometime before making the final push up the Missouri in March 1811 he changed his plans. The notion of simply following Lewis and Clark's northern route was abandoned. Instead Hunt selected a Yellowstone path to one of Colter's "southern passes." This Yellowstone strategy dominated Hunt's decisions as his large expedition moved up the Missouri during the early spring of 1811. But by the end of May, with the party ready to leave the Ponca Indians in present-day northeastern Nebraska, he suddenly changed his plans again. On 26 May three grizzled mountain men—Edward Robinson, John Hoback, and Jacob Reznor—appeared in camp. As members of Andrew Henry's 1809 western expedition, these men had traveled from Three Forks and the upper Yellowstone to the Snake River country over Bannock Pass. After leaving Henry, the trappers had crossed the Teton Range into Jackson Hole. Departing the valley by way of Togwotee Pass, the men had headed southwest along the Wind River. By the time they reached Hunt, they had seen much of the mountain West virtually unknown to the best-informed trader or explorer.

Hunt initially hired the three men to beef up company firepower in the face of potential Indian confrontations. But he soon realized that these mountain men had more to offer than quick eyes and ready guns. Learning that Hunt's party was preparing to follow a Yellowstone trail, the trappers offered an even more southerly passage. They argued that both the original Lewis and Clark route and a Yellowstone march would expose the Astorians to unnecessary Indian dangers, and they suggested what seemed a more direct and less hazardous highway across the mountains. The trappers advised Hunt that his party should go no farther up the Missouri than the Grand River Arikara villages. Once there, Hunt could purchase horses for the overland trek. The trappers proposed a journey that would run southwest through present-day South Dakota and Wyoming to meet the Wind River near today's Shoshoni, Wyoming. From that point the traders were sure that "by following up Wind River, and crossing a single mountain ridge, he [Hunt] would come upon the headwaters of the Columbia."[114]

Hunt's new recruits had an accurate picture of much of the route they advocated. They certainly understood the role of the Wind River valley, although they may have confused Togwotee and Union Passes. What the trappers did not fully grasp was the demanding nature of the Snake River and the country around it. They had seen the Snake around Henry's Fort, where it was a broad, easy river. They had no hint of the white-water hell in places like Caldron Linn.

The trappers' information became what naturalist John Bradbury called "a subject of anxious inquiry." To Hunt's mind, however, the traders made a persuasive case. He now committed the Astorians to an overland voyage on trails unmarked and perhaps not fully comprehended.[115] Throughout the summer and early fall of 1811, Hunt and his overlanders tracked west. Late August found them in the grass ocean of Wyoming's Thunder Basin. Difficult passages through the Big Horns and over Teton Pass tested both mind and body. By early October the Astorians were at Henry's Fort. At the abandoned post, Hunt began to plot his next moves. With a mental geography still bound by the notion of an easy water passage to the Pacific, Hunt looked at Henry's Fork—the north fork of the Snake—and was sure this was the way west. He did not know that the stream he called Canoe River was still the dreaded Snake. Hunt now decided to leave his horses in Shoshoni hands and set his men to building canoes. That decision, which eventually cost several lives, has since been criticized, but Hunt's choice needs to be understood in the context of his geographical notions about the West.

From the beginning of the journey, Hunt believed that practical water routes west of the divide could provide quick and safe access to the Columbia. From his earliest conversations with Lewis in 1806 to his later contacts with Clark and Colter, Hunt thought all evidence pointed to the existence of such navigable rivers. Trapper lore only reenforced what he already trusted as geographical gospel. Hunt knew that his Canoe River was unexplored by any European. But in his foreshortened view of the West, that river simply had to flow into the Columbia. Even more important, it had to be a navigable waterway. Using the best available information, Hunt took his chances. Had he known that the Mad and the Canoe were one and the same river—the Snake—he might have been more wary. But in the end, commerce and empire required water routes, and Hunt was bent on finding such a path to the Pacific.[116]

That determination nearly destroyed the Hunt expedition. Shattered by the white-water fury of the Snake River and stymied by the river's awesome canyon, the expedition split into several small parties. As temperatures fell and rations ran low, each group struggled to survive the treacherous conditions and to escape the Snake's deadly embrace. Hunt's party finally reached Astoria in February 1812.

At Astoria, Hunt and his exhausted overlanders found a thriving fur trade community. But Astoria's days as an outpost of American empire were numbered. The War of 1812 renewed the North West Company's hopes of Crown support for a strike against Astoria. After difficult negotiations, the British admiralty agreed to send a warship to the Columbia. News of that decision reached Astoria on 16 January 1813 and set off the events that finally culminated in the sale of Astoria to the North West Company on 16 October 1813.[117]

The collapse of the Astor venture did not spell the end of Astoria. The imperial idea and the experiences that had created the community left a continuing legacy. After the Treaty of Ghent (1814) that ended the War of 1812, Astor and American diplomats asserted that the post had been captured, not sold. Under provisions of the Treaty of Ghent, this would have meant that Astoria would be returned to American ownership. After numerous, often acrimonious exchanges between the American Department of State and the British Foreign Office, in 1817 the Monroe administration and its expansionist Secretary of State John Quincy Adams decided to assert American claims by sending a warship to the Columbia to reoccupy Astoria. In the fall of 1818 the USS Ontario sailed from New York for the Northwest coast. Finding Astoria, now called Fort George, firmly and legally in Nor'wester hands, the Ontario captain simply announced American sovereignty and sailed away. When American Commissioner John G.

Prevost went to Astoria in October 1818, he gave official permission for the Canadian company to control the post.

These confusing events and the growing tensions between the United States and Great Britain over Pacific claims made Astoria an increasingly important diplomatic issue. Writing to geographer John Melish, Jefferson asserted, "If we claim that country at all, it must be on Astor's settlement near the mouth of the Columbia."[118] Jefferson's statement became gospel for his successors. Missouri senator Thomas Hart Benton, leader of a loosely organized expansionist movement, seized on Astoria and, in the years after 1820, made the post a symbol for American imperialism. Benton and his allies urged the federal government to reoccupy the Columbia, contributing to the superheated rhetoric that elevated Astoria to symbol and imperial icon.

When Irving published his *Astoria* in 1836, he contended that Pacific Fur Company records were "kept by men of business little versed in science, or curious about matters not immediately bearing upon their interests."[119] Alexander Ross and other inquisitive Astorians would have lodged a stiff protest against such a cavalier judgment. As Ross wrote in the preface to his own memoir of the Astoria years, "The progress of discovery contributes not a little to the enlightenment of mankind."[120] Although company men did not actively seek scientific discoveries as a principal duty, men such as Robert Stuart, Gabriel Franchere, Ross Cox, and Alexander Ross himself did make important observations. Natural history and ethnography benefited from the published work of several Astorians. And the Astoria journey up the Missouri attracted professional naturalists like John Bradbury and Thomas Nuttall. Taken together, the Astorians' works formed an enviable record of scientific achievement.

Geographical discovery was an essential part of Astoria's scientific world. Patrons of exploration, men such as Thomas Jefferson and Sir Joseph Banks, expected their explorers to find new mountain ranges, passes, and rivers. The overland Astorians surely qualify as important explorers of the American West. Hunt's expedition, the second U.S. transcontinental crossing, traveled through parts of Wyoming, Idaho, and Oregon yet unpathed by Europeans. The Astorians' most notable geographical accomplishment came in 1812 when Robert Stuart and his eastbound party found South Pass in Wyoming's Wind River Range. South Pass eventually became an essential part of the Oregon Trail migration after the pass was rediscovered in the 1820s by Jedediah Smith. The Astorians deserve credit as the initial discoverers.[121]

## The Explorations of Stephen Long

The War of 1812 had a profound effect on American exploration of the West. Astoria and the fur trade of the Northwest ended up in Canadian hands. Travel and business on the upper Missouri and Mississippi came to a halt. From his headquarters in St. Louis, General William Clark saw a powerful alliance of Indians and Canadian traders effectively closing the West to any American advance. If nothing else, the war was a painful reminder of federal weakness in the West. Republican ideology might call for expansion, but words alone could not forge liberty's empire.

After the Treaty of Ghent, a War Department review of western defenses resulted in the eventual construction of military posts from Fort Smith on the Arkansas River to Fort Snelling on the upper Mississippi. More aggressive steps were taken when John C. Calhoun became secretary of war in 1817. Both Calhoun and Secretary of State John Quincy Adams, influential members of President James Monroe's cabinet, preached an expansionist, anti-British gospel that found the president an eager convert. Calhoun was especially concerned about Canadian influence in the region between the Mississippi and the Rockies, particularly Lord Selkirk's Red River colony. From that post Canadian traders could easily dominate the northern plains and stop American expansion. To curb such power, Calhoun proposed what came to be known as the Yellowstone Expedition, a plan to send substantial numbers of troops up the Missouri and Mississippi Rivers to establish fortified posts. Calhoun's scheme involved three coordinated ventures: the Mississippi Expedition, during which Colonel Henry Leavenworth ascended the river and built Fort Snelling on the site of present-day Minneapolis–St. Paul; the Missouri Expedition; and the Scientific Expedition. As the secretary explained to the Committee on Military Affairs, the expeditions were "part of a system of measures, which has for its objects, the protection of our northwestern frontier, and the greater extension of our fur trade."[122]

The Missouri Expedition was a large-scale troop movement commanded by Colonel Henry Atkinson. After assembling the Rifle Regiment and the Sixth Infantry Regiment near present-day Leavenworth, Kansas, Atkinson prepared for the trip upriver in six steamboats, the latest in exploration technology. Atkinson's objective was the confluence of the Missouri and the Yellowstone. Poor planning, slow progress, and insufficient federal funding hobbled the venture, and by early October 1819 the soldiers began to build Cantonment Missouri at present-day Fort Calhoun, Nebraska. During the winter of 1819–20, disease and malnutrition debilitated the detachment. On one day alone Surgeon Thomas Gale noted that there were "two hundred and eighty sick principally with the scurvy." Two weeks later, in early March 1820, Gale listed seven burials and 360 soldiers on sick report.[123] Busy counting its dead, the Missouri Expedition would count no more miles up the muddy river.

While the Missouri Expedition floundered in a sea of mud, sickness, and bureaucratic squabbling, hopes were still high for the Scientific Expedition. The expedition was led by Major Stephen H. Long, an experienced officer in the army's Topographic Bureau. Educated at Dartmouth and interested in mathematics and civil engineering, Long was eager to recruit the best scientists available for the venture. Thomas Say, Long's zoologist, was a charter member of the Academy of Natural Sciences in Philadelphia and the author of important works in entomology and conchology. The expedition's first botanist, Dr. William Baldwin, had already done fieldwork in Georgia, Florida, and South America. In poor health, Baldwin hoped a western journey might prove a tonic. Although not a professional geologist, Philadelphia merchant Augustus Jessup had read widely in the field and was also a member of the Academy of Natural Sciences.

Long was acutely aware of the need to provide graphic documentation for his discoveries. Two skilled artists came from the Philadelphia circle. Samuel Seymour, recently arrived from England, was an able landscape painter. Little is known about Seymour's life either before or after the journey, but his work provided the earliest published views of the western lands. Titian Ramsay Peale, the youngest son of the famous artist Charles Wilson Peale, was a talented naturalist-illustrator. Like his contemporary Karl Bodmer, the young Peale could capture both the detail and the essence of a plant or animal. To round out the party, Long enlisted Major Thomas Biddle as journalist and Lieutenant James D. Graham and Cadet William Swift as personal aides.[124]

Leaving Pittsburgh in early May 1819, Long's intrepid scientists chugged along the Ohio on board a remarkable steamboat appropriately named the *Western Engineer*. This was no ordinary river steamer. Paddle wheels rode astern, one wheel carrying the name "Monroe" and the other bearing the name "Calhoun." Peale joked that this arrangement was fitting because the two politicians were "the two propelling powers of the expedition."[125] The ship's most noteworthy feature was an elaborately carved dragon that served as both figurehead and steam exhaust. An observer wrote, "The bow of this vessel exhibits the form of a huge serpent, black and scaly, rising out of the water from under the boat, his head as high as the deck, darting forward, his mouth open, vomiting smoke, and apparently carrying the boat on his back."[126] The *Western Engineer* may have been a grand tourist attraction, but it had an unreliable engine and a leaky cabin. The expedition did not reach St. Louis until early June.

After a two-week stay, Long pointed his puffing dragon into the Missouri current. His immediate objective was to establish a base camp at Council Bluffs, on the western bank of the river twenty miles above present-day Omaha, Nebraska. But the *Western Engineer* was seriously underpowered and had a hard time bucking the river's spring current. Hidden logs ("sawyers") and shifting sandbars made each day a dangerous, tedious struggle. And there were personnel difficulties as well. Long and Biddle had been at odds for some time, and now the temperamental Biddle challenged Long to a duel. But the prospect of pistols at twenty paces was the least of Long's worries. Dr. Baldwin's health had steadily declined throughout the trip, and on 13 July the botanist resigned from the expedition, a decision made perhaps too late, since he died a month later. Compounding the personnel problems, Jessup was unwilling to stay with the expedition for a second season of exploring. Despite all these difficulties and an abortive land journey made by some of the explorers, the expedition finally reached its destination in late September.

Long dubbed his wintering post Engineer Cantonment, a rather grand title for what was probably a scattering of modest cabins. From that camp the expedition's scholars—Say, Seymour, Peale, Jessup, and guide-interpreter John Dougherty—made short trips to gather ethnographic and natural history materials. The harvest of Indian information was especially valuable, as were the drawings and sketches made by the two artists. While science moved ahead, Long prepared to return to Washington. His expedition needed not only new personnel but also additional funding.

When Long reached the federal city in the early days of 1820, he found that much had changed. Congressional critics of the military expedition had cut funds for that effort; clearly, Atkinson's soldiers were not going to advance beyond Cantonment Missouri. Long enjoyed good connections in the military establishment, and now he used those ties to save his part of the larger scheme. Calhoun was evidently convinced by Long's well-planned campaign, and the journey got additional funds and personnel as well as new marching orders. Those directions reflected recent diplomatic developments between the United States and Spain. The Adams-Onis Treaty (1819) attempted to mark out the border between Louisiana and

Spanish territory by using the Arkansas and the Red, rivers that had proved elusive for many explorers. Calhoun ordered the Scientific Expedition to trace the Platte to its source and then turn south to probe the Red and Arkansas. The expedition was to terminate at Fort Smith, Arkansas, then called Belle Pointe. The secretary believed that such an overland journey would serve both diplomacy and science.

By early spring 1820 Long was ready to return west. Joining him were two new members of the party. Biddle's replacement as journalist was Captain John R. Bell, a no-nonsense regular eager to escape boring garrison life. Long's most important acquisition was Dr. Edwin James. A New Englander like Long, James had studied at Middlebury College in Vermont before joining his two brothers in their Albany, New York, medical practice. James had studied widely in a number of fields, cultivating broad interests that served him well in his new duties as a western explorer. By late May, Long and his companions were back at Engineer Cantonment and began preparing for the trip west.

For all Long's determination to be a serious explorer, his enterprise was poorly planned and woefully undersupplied. The expedition had just six extra horses and a food supply good for only one month's travel. The supply of Indian trade goods was also slim. Equally worrisome, the scientific equipment was wholly inadequate for the task. The expedition even lacked a sufficient number of boxes to store scientific samples. Nevertheless, on 6 June the Long expedition—scientists and thirteen helpers—headed west. Some two weeks later, after a brief stay at the Grand Pawnee village, the expedition struck the Platte River. On 22 June the party reached the junction of the North and the South Platte at present-day North Platte, Nebraska. There they forded the north branch and crossed to the southern side of the South Platte. While Long looked for the river's source, others in the expedition noted the land, its climate, and the many plants and animals of the Great Plains. Expedition records soon became filled with words like "arid," "barren," and "sterile." For New Englanders like Long and James, plains landscapes were both foreign and strangely unsettling. As James wrote later, "The monotony of a vast unbroken plain, like that in which we had now travelled, nearly one hundred and fifty miles, is little less tiresome to the eye, and fatiguing to the spirit, than the dreary solitude of the ocean."[127] Dwindling supplies and long days under the blistering sun sapped the party's morale, but the sight (on 30 June) of the distant Rockies cheered the explorers. By 5 July the expedition was at the site of present-day Denver. Some days later a small contingent undertook an ascent of Pikes Peak. The climb showed the Platte headwaters running from the mountains. Long could now claim he had achieved an important expedition goal without actually tracing the river to its source.

With the Platte question settled to his satisfaction, Long pointed his party south to find the Arkansas. On 17 July, James, Bell, and two others carried out a brief reconnaissance around the Royal Gorge of the Arkansas. The secretary of war hoped for a western probe along the Arkansas, but instead Long began to lay plans for a homeward journey. His strategy for that trip was to divide the expedition into two parties. Captain Bell was ordered to take one group down the Arkansas to Belle Pointe. In the meantime Long's contingent would head south to intercept the Red and then proceed on to Belle Pointe. Bell's passage proved a rough one. Three of his men deserted, taking with them not only horses and equipment but also valuable field notes compiled by Say and Swift. But Long and his men suffered far greater disappointment. Finding a river they assumed to be the Red, they followed it southeast. As had happened so often before, the Red proved an elusive quarry. The river they were on was the Canadian, a discovery that "defeated one principal aspect of our summer's labor."[128] The two divisions finally reunited at Belle Pointe in mid-September 1820.

If Long had hoped to lead a grand scientific reconnaissance of the West, he must have been bitterly disappointed. The explorers suffered from poor planning and insufficient funding. Long proved an often indecisive field commander. He did not track the Platte, he retreated from a probe of the Arkansas, and he mistook the Canadian for the Red. More than anything else, Long's expedition has been faulted for its role in the myth of the Great American Desert. Long was charged with advancing the "misconception" of the West as largely an arid wasteland when he put the term "Great American Desert" on his important 1823 map. But as historical geographer Martyn J. Bowden has shown, the desert image had only limited currency. The West as garden was a far more popular and pervasive nineteenth-century image.[129] Yet Long certainly gave the desert notion a powerful boost. His official report to Calhoun declared that the northern plains were "almost wholly unfit for cultivation, and of course uninhabitable by a people depending on agriculture for their subsistence."[130] Arguing along the lines of those who worried about the danger of expansion, Long thought that the desert West might serve as an effective "barrier to prevent too great an extension of our population westward, and secure us against the machinations or incursions of an enemy, that might otherwise be disposed to annoy us in that quarter."[131]

Given Long's own cultural background, his image of the West was hardly a surprise. Nor was it wholly wide of the mark. As settlers in the West soon learned, the soil, rainfall, and temperature dictated a farming life quite unlike that in Ohio, Illinois, or even eastern Nebraska. Well before John Wesley Powell wrote his seminal *Report on the Lands of the Arid Regions* (1878), Long had important things to say about water and the world beyond the one hundredth meridian. The dusty times of the 1930s suggest how well Long and Powell understood the limits of eastern agriculture in the West.

Too much emphasis on Long and the Great American Desert has caused some students of the expedition to overlook the substantial contributions made by the explorers. Paintings and sketches by Seymour and Peale gave visual definition to a West heretofore fixed only in words. Edwin James, the author of the expedition's published account (1823), was an astute observer of western geology and climate. As Maxine Benson, James's biographer, has found, the expedition's scientific contributions must also be sought beyond the pages of James's *Account*. James, Long, Peale, Say, and Jessup all published important findings in a number of scientific journals. The expedition also enriched the world of literature. When James Fenimore Cooper wrote his popular book *The Prairie* in 1827, he used James's *Account* as a research tool. Art, science, literature—all found value in what at first glance appeared a failed venture.

The Long expedition marks a transition in the history of western exploration. Jefferson's Corps of Discovery was taking on a new shape in the 1820s and 1830s. In the first two decades of the century, exploration had been conducted by relatively small parties. By the 1830s, expeditions had grown in size and complexity. Expedition personnel was changing as well. Long knew that he had to recruit professional scientists in order to make any real contribution to the knowledge of the West. Gone were the days when an amateur naturalist like Lewis or a part-time ethnographer like Ross could provide the necessary scientific skill. As American science matured, exploration drew on the resources of the growing professionalism. With the Long expedition one can also see the beginnings of important changes in exploration goals. Government explorers and fur traders had set their sights on the Pacific. For those travelers and their patrons, the Northwest was both imperial battleground and commercial prize. By the time Calhoun's War Department sent Long into the West, Joint-Occupation Treaties between Britain and the United States seemed to have fixed the destiny of the Northwest. Perhaps the lands between the Mississippi

15.8 "*Country drained by the Mississippi, western section*" *(Stephen Long, 1823).* Published with Long's Account of an Expedition from Pittsburg to the Rocky Mountains, *this map was the first to carry the words "Great American Desert" across a portion of the Great Plains. Courtesy of the Special Collections Division, Babbidge Library, University of Connecticut.*

and the Rockies, territories that Jefferson's captains had hurried over, deserved more attention.

Throughout the fall of 1818 the American ambassador Richard Rush held meetings with George Canning, president of Great Britain's powerful Board of Control. Canning, who would soon become foreign minister, had kept a watchful eye on the rapid growth of the American republic. In Rush's words, the English statesman seemed "very much awake to our present and growing power." Rush too was astounded by the national expansion. "Indeed," he wrote, "we have sprung, as it were by a leap, into the rank of one of the great nations of the world."[132] There seemed much to celebrate. The Jeffersonian Corps of Discovery had laid the foundation for the United States to become a continental power. That new place in the world of nations had certainly increased the power of the federal government, especially in western matters, and meant new sources of wealth and influence for eastern entrepreneurs. Exploration advanced the worlds of science and art. Neatly capturing the ways that discovery stimulated artistic and scientific creativity, Ross wrote that exploration "enlarged the circle of knowledge."[133]

Nowhere was that circle drawn wider than in the cartographic image of the West. One need only compare Samuel Lewis's map of Louisiana (1804) or Jedediah Morse's map of North America (1797) with maps by John Melish (1816), William Rector and Isaac Roberdeau (1818), and Stephen H. Long (1821, 1823) to see what two decades of exploring had wrought. Melish's "Map of the United States with the Contiguous British and Spanish Possessions" not only was the first American-produced wall map giving a coast-to-coast view but also marked a break with the simple copying of Arrowsmith maps. Melish drew heavily on the published maps of Lewis and Clark and Pike to offer reasonably accurate depictions of the Rockies, the Cascades, and the Yellowstone country. Nonetheless, his map still showed ghost rivers like the San Buenaventura and the Multnomah. The Southwest remained a tangle while the Great Basin stood blank and unnamed.[134]

When the War Department ordered Topographical Corps officers William Rector and Isaac Roberdeau to prepare a western map based on the most current sources, the result was a competent but unimaginative compilation. The Rector-Roberdeau "Sketch of the Western Part of the Continent of North America" had its blank spaces, mysterious rivers, and geographical distortions. But like the Melish map of two years before, this military production was a testimony to how much had been seen and understood in so short a time.[135] Finally, despite the criticism leveled against Long's western expedition, the journey produced two maps of exceptional importance. Long's 1821 and 1823 maps represent the best understanding of the West at the end of the Jeffersonian period. Long's 1821 map, drawn soon after he returned from his journey, contained the explorer's vision of the central and southern plains. John Allen has written that the 1823 map "may have been one of the most important of all maps of the plains produced before the Civil War."[136] Both maps had considerable influence on commercial maps made during the period. Long's descriptive label "Great American Desert" became standard on many western maps. But to overemphasize the desert image is to miss the substantial advances made by Long's maps. His 1823 map displayed a remarkably clear expression of the plains from the Yellowstone River south to Santa Fe. And with an eye to the future, Long noted the presence of "the Great Spanish Road," soon to be the Santa Fe Trail.[137] Such maps represented not only significant cartographic advances but also the promise of an expanding American empire. Each map grew out of and contributed to a powerful expansionist ideology.

Long's exploration represented the penultimate stage of Jeffersonian exploration: there remained the inventory work undertaken by the federal land surveyors operating east of the Mississippi River. Although much of this activity was actually the delineation of lands already well-known and understood (and, in many cases, occupied by a farming population), one important geographical question remained to be answered by the final stages of Jefferson-era exploration: where was the source of the Mississippi River? An expedition led by Michigan Governor Lewis Cass, accompanied by scientist Henry Rowe Schoolcraft, was mounted in 1820 to locate "the sources of the Mississippi river, which have continued to be the subject of dispute between geographical writers."[138] Traveling from Detroit to Michilimackinac, thence to the Sault Sainte Marie and up the Mississippi to Upper Red Cedar or "Cassina" Lake, the expedition extensively inventoried the region, following the Jeffersonian principles of exploration as conducted by Lewis and Clark and others. Schoolcraft judged that they had located "the true source of the Mississippi River" in Cassina Lake, although he noted that a greater volume of water flowed from another branch.[139] The final solution to the riddle was not found until 1832, when another expedition led by Schoolcraft, by then Indian agent at Michilimackinac, determined the source of the river to be in a lake that Schoolcraft named "Itasca, a name compounded from the last two syllables of *veritas* and the first syllable of *caput*."[140] On the accompanying map drawn by Lieutenant James Allen, just west of Itasca Lake was shown the "Hauteurs des Terres Mountains," the dividing ridge between the drainage of the Mississippi and that of the Red River of the North. It was this drainage divide that would become the focal point of Joseph Nicollet in 1838 in an expedition sponsored by the U.S. Army Corps of Engineers—the successor and heir to the principles of Jeffersonian exploration.

Explorers and their patrons laid the foundations of empire. But that handiwork did not promise all North Americans an equally bright future. In his penetrating novel *Heart of Darkness*, Joseph Conrad probed the grimmer consequences of exploration: "The conquest of the earth, which mostly means the taking of it away from those who have a different complexion or slightly flatter noses than ourselves, is not a pretty thing when you look at it too much."[141] A close look at the consequences of exploration in the first two decades of the nineteenth century reveals not the steady progress of a westering republic but scenes of uncertainty, confusion, and invasion. Canning had every reason to be worried about American ventures to the West. Such journeys expanded and intensified international rivalries. Concerned Spanish officials knew that in the wake of Jefferson's explorers there would be an "eruption of ferocious men who know neither law nor subjection."[142] Pike's filibustering thoughts on the conquest of Mexico pointed to eventual war with that nation. The dreams and schemes of Astor and Benton set them at odds with their Anglo-Canadian rivals and made the Oregon Question a lingering source of British-American controversy until 1846.

If exploration heightened international tensions, it also raised troubling domestic questions. Explorers, whether army officers or private traders, brought the claims of federal sovereignty to native people. Although expediency and good judgment made most relations between early explorers and Indians reasonably peaceful, what followed was anything but that. In the new American empire, Indians were expected either to conveniently vanish or to meekly surrender land and power. In a now-famous letter written to Senator John Breckinridge soon after the announcement of the Louisiana Purchase, Jefferson envisioned a process of national expansion: "We may lay off a range of States on the Western bank [of the Mississippi], from the head to the mouth, and so, range after range, advancing compactly as we multiply."[143] Such political imperialism promised just the sort of conflict and conquest that Jefferson abhorred in the British Empire. It also raised what was rapidly becoming the central question in American life: would slavery be allowed to extend into the new western territories? These were the very lands the explorers had made part of the republic. More important, they were the lands Jefferson hoped would secure republicanism for future generations. Now they seemed to breed only discord. Writing in 1820, a plainly fearful Jefferson likened the Slave Question to holding a wolf by the ears. Whether held or set free, the wolf was bound to bite.[144] Jefferson's explorers brought back many wonderful things, but they also helped put the wolf in the nation's hands.

Finally, something else was in the air, something hard to fix precisely. Explorers in the early 1800s saw themselves as faithful agents. They went on journeys at the bidding of a nation-state or a powerful trading enterprise. Any glory properly belonged to the cause or the company. Meriwether Lewis and Robert Stuart were not immune from the lure of fame and the spur of ambition, but at heart they and their companions were self-effacing men doing dangerous work as ordered. They understood themselves to be ordinary men who faced sometimes extraordinary challenges. Such a style, well suited to republican simplicity, could not last in the tumult of the new nation. Public men now courted public audiences for national reputation. A hint of that came when Long used carefully placed newspaper interviews to lobby Calhoun and the War Department. The explorer as private agent was giving way to the adventurer as public hero. In a romantic age, the western journey was now a celebrity circuit. The cultural distance traveled can be roughly measured by looking from William Clark, the dutiful soldier of empire, to John C. Frémont, the self-proclaimed pathfinder. Lewis and Clark had modestly described their journey as a "tour." Their successors would use language far grander and perhaps more self-indulgent.

Exploration gave the American republic room to grow, no matter the consequences of that growth. Secretary of State John Quincy Adams minced no words when he explained the meaning of such growth: "The world shall be familiarized with the idea of considering our proper dominion to be the continent of North America."[145] Not surprisingly, such sentiments and the actions that grew out of them angered some neighbors, dispossessed others, and seemed destined to spark violence of almost unimagined ferocity. The *Niles' Weekly Register* for 23 November 1822 was almost prophetic. Two decades of intense western exploration had indeed "annihilated" distance. Saint Louis diners might soon taste Columbia River salmon. Here, in a commonplace language, was the Jeffersonian image of an expanding republic. But the price paid for that salmon proved high indeed.

# 16 / The Canadian Fur Trade and the Exploration of Western North America, 1797–1851

JOHN L. ALLEN

Westward and northward exploration in what is now Canada was inextricably linked with the twin desiderata of a profitable fur trade and an easy passage through North America to the Pacific and thus to the rich trade of the Orient. Voyaging into the Hudson Bay region, British explorers failed to locate the easy passage to the South Sea but did discover an abundant fur resource. Similarly, the French, from their colonial base of New France in the St. Lawrence Valley, searched westward for a passage to China and discovered instead a potential fur trade that would dominate the economy of their North American colony.

Just before the establishment of the Hudson's Bay Company by the British in 1670, the geographical information obtained by explorers searching for the Pacific was joined with economic data on the fur trade. "Two Frenchmen [Pierre Radisson and Sieur de Groseilliers] who have lived long in Canada & have been up in ye great lakes that lye in the midst of that part of America" informed English merchants that they had discovered a plentiful fur resource in the Great Lakes region; they added, "There is great hope of finding some passage through those Lakes into the South Sea."[1] On the strength of this information, the "Governor and Company of Adventurers of England trading into Hudson's Bay" was founded; for more than a century "the Company" dominated exploration and economic utilization of the drainage basin of Hudson Bay.[2] At the same time that the company was expanding west and northwest from posts at the mouths of the major rivers flowing into Hudson Bay, the French in the St. Lawrence Valley explored westward from Montreal through the Great Lakes to Lake Winnipeg and the upper Missouri and beyond. Although France lost its colonial possessions in North America in 1763 after the French and Indian Wars, this Montreal-based fur trade continued. Thus two commercial en-

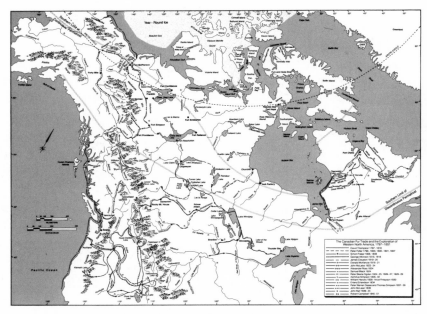

*Map 16.1 The Canadian Fur Trade and the Exploration of Western North America, 1797–1851.*

terprises devoted to the fur trade and to the continuing search for a route to the Pacific existed in the late 1700s: the Hudson's Bay Company, English in origin and dominated by Englishmen and Scots; and the North West Company of Montreal, originally French but now controlled by English merchants (although still employing many French-Canadians).[3] As rivals for the fur trade of the western interior, these two companies were responsible for nearly all major explorations in interior and western Canada in the late 1700s and early 1800s, carrying the fur trade economy as far as the Pacific shores of British Columbia and the interior of the American Pacific Northwest.

In 1821 the North West Company and the Hudson's Bay Company merged; the new company (still called "the Hudson's Bay Company") maintained oligopolistic control over the fur trade of Canada and also held a monopoly on most of the exploration that took place into the Canadian West and North until the emergence of the scientific explorers of the interior in the 1850s. With the possible exception of the explorations of David Thompson, no nineteenth-century Canadian fur trade explorations could rival the eighteenth-century fur-trade explorations of Alexander Mackenzie or the American fur-trade explorations of Jedediah Smith in the 1820s. But several significant explorations conducted by Canadian fur trappers in the 1800s not only helped to fill the map of western and northern Canada with geographical data but also provided the information on which the Canadian settlement of the interior and farther West would be based.

During the first half of the nineteenth century, three primary motivations propelled fur trade explorers toward the Pacific and the Arctic.[4] The first was geopolitical. Just as the U.S. government viewed the American fur trade of the upper Missouri and the Rocky Mountain regions as a tool of imperial ambition, so the English used the Canadian fur trade (whether by the North West Company, the Hudson's Bay Company, or the merged concerns after 1821) as an instrument in the clash of rivals for domination of western North America. British, Spanish, Russians, and Americans all cast covetous glances at western North America as the key to ultimate control over both the economic and the political destiny of the entire continent. The continued expansion of the fur trade, as well as the acquisition of knowledge through fur trade exploration, was essential to imperial ambition.[5]

The second motivation for fur trade exploration was simple economic competition. In the years before the merger of 1821, the North West Company and the Hudson's Bay Company competed with one another for access to both territory and tribal loyalty among the various native American populations on which they relied for much of their fur supply. Both companies competed with the St. Louis–based fur trade of the upper Missouri; after the merger, the Hudson's Bay Company continued to seek geographical information through exploration that would allow it to outflank its new rivals, the American Fur Company and the Rocky Mountain Fur Company based in St. Louis, for both the upper Missouri and the Rocky Mountain trade regions. Also before the merger, the North West Company competed with John Jacob Astor's short-lived enterprise at the mouth of the Columbia and, after the War of 1812 and the purchase of Astor's establishment by the North West Company, with the continuing encroachment of other American companies working their way into the Rocky Mountains via the Platte Valley. After the merger, the Hudson's Bay Company planned to expand its domination of the fur trade of the western slope of the Rockies and even engaged in a "scorched earth" policy in the Columbian Basin and Snake River country to forestall American trade.[6] Similarly, along the Pacific coast, the company engaged in exploration designed to intercept furs that might otherwise have been traded by Native Americans to Russian and American enterprises. Part of this competitive incentive was tied to Great Britain's imperial ambitions for western North America, but an equal part was related to the extractive nature of the industry itself. New territory with unexploited resources and with native populations unaffiliated with other fur companies was a basic requirement for the continued economic growth and success of the fur trade enterprise.

Finally, a third motivation for fur trade exploration was the need for geographical information. Often this information was practically oriented and was used in the annual operation of the fur trade. Other times it had a more continental focus and was related to longer-range ambitions for good transportation routes to western North America, the Pacific, and the Orient. Certainly, the fur trade explorations of the late eighteenth century were motivated by the search for routes to the western sea. Although the belief in a "Great River of the West" or in an easy all-water commercial route across the continent was less pervasive after Mackenzie and the Lewis and Clark expedition, the members of the fur trade still sought to locate the lowest and easiest mountain passes that could give their companies an advantage over rivals. Thus, the explorations of the Canadian fur trade in the first half of the nineteenth century were a blend of imperial ambition, economic motivation, and geographical curiosity.

As the explorer-traders of the Hudson's Bay and North West Companies moved into the West and North in the early 1800s, they encountered regions that were poorly known and even less understood. The Hudson Bay trade and the Montreal trade had made extensive contacts with Indians who provided data on the western and northern interior regions (much more so than had their American counterparts to the south). The traders themselves, on their journeys toward the interior, had gathered much data on the forest and grassland regions east of the Rockies, adding to the mental maps of Canada before the early 1800s. And the travels of Mackenzie between 1789 and 1793 had added the Mackenzie River basin and the upper Peace River–upper Fraser River region of the Canadian Rockies to the fund of available geographical lore by 1800.

In the basic geographical image of western Canada in the early 1800s,[7] four major regions lay west of Hudson Bay and north of the Great Lakes: (1) the narrow taiga-clad coastal plain region of "New South Wales" in the southeastern corner of Hudson Bay, where the primary Hudson's Bay Company posts of Churchill Factory, York Factory, and Severn Factory were located; (2) the lake-dotted Canadian Shield region or "Stoney Region," stretching northwestward from the Great Lakes to the Arctic shores, with the northeastern section from Churchill Factory to the Coppermine River being defined as the "Barren Grounds" of the tundra ecosystem, the region to the west of the barrens and north of Lakes Athabasca and Great Slave as the "Land of Little Sticks" or taiga ecosystem, and the remainder as the "Great Western Forest"; (3) the "Great Plains," forest north of the North Saskatchewan River and grassland to the south with an aspen and park-grove (the "Íclets de bois") transitional zone between forest and grassland, separated from the "Stoney Region" by a line running northwest from Lake of the Woods to Lake Winnipeg and thence to near the Hudson's Bay Company's Cumberland House on the lower Saskatchewan and continuing northwestward just east of the Athabasca and Mackenzie Rivers; and (4) the virtually unknown (except for Mackenzie's narrow traverse to the Pacific) forested and rugged region of the Rocky Mountains or "Stoney Mountains" extending from the western margin of the plains all the way to the Pacific, with the Pacific slope portions of the mountains being known as "New Caledonia." In addition to these four major geographical provinces was a fifth transitional region: the "Valley of the Lakes" extending from the Great Lakes to the Beaufort Sea, roughly approximating the boundary zone between the Canadian Shield and the Great Plains and containing the major lakes Winnipeg and Winnipegosis, Reindeer, Athabasca, Great Slave, and Great Bear.

Although it was not viewed as a major geographical province, this fifth region was of crucial importance and was probably the best understood of the regions of the interior, partly because of the traders' long reliance on water travel. Both the Hudson's Bay Company and the North West Company based their administrative divisions on drainage basins or river-lake regions. The Northern Department of the Hudson's Bay Company consisted of Canada west of the Severn River and included Churchill Factory of the Churchill River basin, York Factory of the Nelson and Hayes basins, Winnipeg Factory of the Lake Winnipeg region, and Saskatchewan Factory of the Saskatchewan River west of Cumberland House, which lay northwest of Lake Winnipegosis. The North West Company's administrative departments often overlapped those of the Hudson's Bay Company. North and west of Lake Superior were the Nipigon Lake district, the Lac de la Pluie (Lake of the Woods) district, and the Lake Winnipeg district; more or less coterminous with the latter were the Red River and Assiniboine district southwest of Lake Winnipeg and the Fort Dauphin district west of Lake Winnipeg. Northwest of Winnipeg were the overlapping English River and Saskatchewan districts between the Churchill River and the

North Saskatchewan; still farther northwest was the huge Athabasca district, which extended from the North Saskatchewan to Great Bear Lake.

Through these administrative regions ran the three major transportation routes on which the Canadian fur trade depended: a southern route, primarily used by the North West Company men (the "Nor'Westers"), from Lake Superior following various river systems into the Lake Winnipeg region and then up the north branch of the Saskatchewan to the mountains; a central Hudson's Bay Company route from Churchill and York Factories west into the interior, where Hudson's Bay Company traders used the same river systems as did the Nor'Westers to penetrate southward to the upper Missouri and westward to the Rockies; and a northern route pioneered by North West Company explorer Mackenzie and including the routes of the Athabasca and Peace Rivers west to the mountains and the Mackenzie River route north to the Arctic.

The cartographic records of the major fur-trading concerns seem to indicate that the western and northern interior of Canada was much better known in the early 1800s than was the western interior of the United States to the south. To a certain degree this is true. The Canadian fur trade, after all, had been active over a longer period of time than the St. Louis fur trade and had, until the 1830s, many more men in the field than the American fur trade ever did. But even though much was known about the country bounded by Hudson Bay on the east, the Great Lakes on the south, the Rockies on the west, and the Arctic on the north, major portions of the interior were still virtual terrae incognitae, and much basic geographical information was either inaccurate or missing altogether. Even less known were the regions of the Rockies, the Columbian Plateau, and the "New Caledonia" Pacific slope.

## The North West Company in the Far West, 1797–1821

The explorers of the North West Company were the first to make significant contributions to the geographical knowledge of the western interior during the nineteenth century, building on the first transcontinental crossing, by the North West Company's Alexander Mackenzie in 1793. Most of the important early contributions came from Welshman David Thompson, who ranks with William Clark, Peter Skene Ogden, and Jedediah Smith among the greatest explorer-geographers of the 1800s.[8] In the spring of 1797, the twenty-seven-year-old Thompson, who had been a Hudson's Bay

Company employee since he was fourteen, departed his post at Reindeer Lake in the Churchill district and joined the "Company of the Merchants from Canada," or the North West Company. By this time Thompson had already traveled nearly nine thousand miles along the inland waterways of the interior; as a trained mathematician and astronomer who made careful geographical surveys and recordings of climatic and other natural phenomena, he had added important information to the geographical lore being assembled by the Hudson's Bay Company in its London archives.[9]

Partly because of the continental outlook of the North West Company typified by Mackenzie's explorations, and partly because of the Nor'Westers' geographical position abutting the new United States, Thompson's new employers (quite unlike his old) were more interested in his skills with surveying, mapping, and other traditional exploration methodologies than they were in his abilities as a fur trader. Accordingly, almost immediately on his attachment to the North West Company, he was dispatched on an extensive reconnaissance of the region between British territory and American territory west of Lake Superior. The breadth of his instructions reveals the Nor'Westers' deep interest in geographical information. He was instructed to "learn the true positions of their [North West Company] Trading Houses, in respect to each other," and to determine how the company's trading posts were located with respect to "the forty-ninth parallel of Latitude North, as since the year 1792 . . . had become the boundary line between the British Dominions and the Territories of the United States." He was further instructed to travel overland to the upper Missouri River to "visit the villages of the ancient agricultural Natives who dwelt there [the Mandans]" and to "enquire for fossil bones of large animals, and any monuments, if any, that might throw light on the ancient state of the unknown countries [he] had to travel over and examine."[10] How very different, noted Thompson, was the "liberal and public spirit" of the North West Company from the "mean selfish policy" of the Hudson's Bay Company; Thompson was being asked to do what he did best—explore and map. If the Hudson's Bay Company had given him freedom to do this, it could have had, in Thompson's opinion, "at little expense . . . the northern part of this Continent surveyed to the Pacific Ocean, and greatly extended their Trading Posts."[11] This entry from Thompson's journal may reveal his motives for defecting from the Hudson's Bay Company to join its greatest rival.

Thompson's first journey of exploration for his new employers took place in 1797–98, during which he completed a great circle of four thousand miles by foot, snowshoe, horseback, and canoe from the North West port at Grand Portage on the northwestern shore of Lake Superior and back again. This trek took him first to Lake Winnipeg, via the Rainy Lake and Lake of the Woods route, through a country that he noted was "at present, of no value to the farmer, [although] time may do something for it as a grazing country, from it's many Brooks and small Lakes of clear water."[12] From the "rude Paraelelogram" of Lake Winnipeg, Thompson traveled south into the valleys of the Red and Assiniboine Rivers, surveying and mapping the sites of North West posts. From the Assiniboine, he struck out southward over the prairie country to the Missouri River (labeled as the "Missisourie" on his maps), which he reached near the villages of the Mandan and Hidatsa nations. These villages, where Lewis and Clark would winter in 1805–6, were the nerve center of the upper Missouri fur trade, attracting both the Montreal trade and the St. Louis trade. Thompson described the culture of the Mandans thoroughly, obviously fascinated by the differences between the Mandans and other northern plains tribes. Typical of his careful and scientific reporting, he omitted any commentary on the long-supposed lineage of the Mandans as the descendants of Madoc ap Gwynedd, Prince of Wales, who, according to European legend, had settled in lands in the western Atlantic in the thirteenth century.[13] Other Welsh travelers who visited the Mandans at the same time were far less restrained.

From the Mandan villages, Thompson worked his way eastward to the source region of the Mississippi River and from there along the southern shore of Lake Superior to Sault Sainte Marie and, completely circling Lake Superior, back to Grand Portage in the summer of 1798. His first exploration under North West direction was a considerable success. Thompson not only had accurately located and mapped all North West Company trading houses in the region but also had opened the upper Missouri River region for the Nor'Westers. Perhaps most important, he provided geographical science with one of its first and, for the time, most accurate views of the Great Plains. Almost alone among his contemporaries, Thompson provided both a physiographic and a vegetative description of the plains.[14] This vast level region, he wrote, reached from the Gulf of Mexico to the fifty-fourth parallel of latitude and from the Mississippi to the Rockies. The level character of this region was broken only by the rivers that, fed by "the perpetual snows and Glaciers" of the Rocky Mountains, flowed eastward across the plains and cut deep valleys through the thick soil rather than forming lakes as did rivers in the "Stoney Region" of the Shield to the east. The chief vegetative difference between the plains and surrounding re-

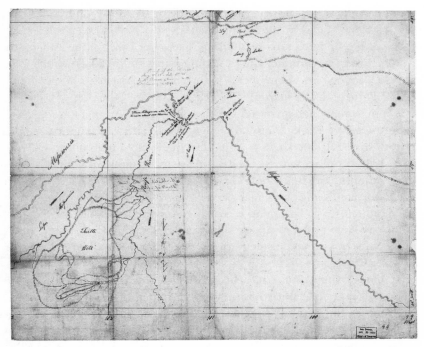

*16.1 Map of the northern bend of the Missouri River and the Mandan villages (David Thompson, 1798). This first detailed map of the trade center of the upper Missouri was one of the maps used by Jefferson and Lewis in assessing the state of geographical knowledge of the West before the Lewis and Clark expedition. Courtesy of the Library of Congress.*

gions was the grassland cover of the plains. Thompson accurately described this cover as ranging from tall-grass prairies in the east to short-grass steppes in the west; this portrayal of the vegetative transition between the Mississippi and the high plains was remarkable when compared with others of the time. The plains north of the forty-fourth parallel would, he believed, support an agricultural civilization adapted to the grazing of cattle and sheep and would be limited only by the distance to market. A modern geographer reading Thompson's description of the Great Plains will find little to criticize in the explorer-geographer's portrait of this region.

Less dramatic—if, perhaps, equally valuable for the North West Company—were Thompson's explorations in 1799. Given permission by the company to engage in both exploration and fur trading, he traveled into the Athabasca country, surveying the route between the Churchill River and Athabasca Lake, including the crucial Methy Portage between Lac La Loche of the upper Churchill and the Clearwater River of the Athabasca system during the summer and providing astronomical observations for a precise locating of company posts in the Athabasca district. Returning to Grand Portage in the fall (after having acquired a Scot-Chippewa wife, to whom he remained married for nearly fifty years), Thompson prepared to head west for Rocky Mountain House, the North West Company post on the North Saskatchewan—in sight of the Rocky Mountains—early in 1800. Well supplied with surveying and astronomical equipment, high-quality drafting instruments, and mapmaking supplies, he was instructed to attempt a crossing of the mountains. By this time, an easy route across the mountains was becoming increasingly important to the North West Company. Two of the company's principals, Simon McTavish and Alexander Mackenzie, had engaged in a long dispute that resulted in Mackenzie's departure from the North West Company to join a new fur trade concern, the XY Company, which became popularly known as "Alexander Mackenzie and Co."[15] With this new player competing for the furs of southern Canada, the North West Company was determined to be the first to find a commercially usable route across the Rockies to the Pacific.

For the next two years, Thompson spent most of his time east of the Rockies surveying the region between Rocky Mountain House and the mountains and from the Bow River north to the Saskatchewan. At least some of his efforts during this time seem to have been directed at providing support for his superior, Duncan McGillivray, who had joined him at Rocky Mountain House late in 1800 and was, in Thompson's words, "prepared to cross the mountains."[16] During the fall of 1800 and throughout most of 1801 Thompson and McGillivray probed the river systems issuing from the Rockies in search of possible passes, McGillivray exploring the region between the North Saskatchewan and the Athabasca Rivers and Thompson exploring the area between the Clearwater tributary of the North Saskatchewan and the Bow River tributary of the South Saskatchewan. Sometime during the summer of 1801, McGillivray may actually have reached the upper waters of the North Saskatchewan and crossed the continental divide to the Kootenay River, a tributary of the Columbia; in his journals, Thompson indicates that belief and gives McGillivray credit for the discovery and naming of "McGillivray's River" (the Kootenay).[17] If so, then McGillivray was only the second white to cross the continental divide north of Mexico and to discover Howse Pass, by which Thompson would make a well-documented crossing of the Rockies in 1807. If McGillivray did discover a pass across the Rockies to the Columbia system in 1801, however, there was no follow-up. McGillivray became ill and was forced to leave Rocky Mountain House; Thompson made a trip into the mountains in 1802, but since his journals for that year are missing, we do not know whether he was even attempting a mountain crossing.[18]

Between 1802 and 1806, the North West Company conducted little active exploration in the farther West. The company's most talented explorer, Thompson, was occupied with business matters during most of this time, although he did survey and map much of the country east of Cumberland House between the Saskatchewan and Churchill Rivers. One of the company's other capable explorers, Simon Fraser, a Vermont-born fur trader who became a partner in the company in 1801, traveled in the upper Peace River and upper Fraser River regions in 1805, but he did not explore any territory that had not already been crossed and mapped by Mackenzie. Alexander Henry the younger reexplored the Red and Assiniboine regions, adding to Thompson's geographical descriptions of the region between the Missouri Valley and Lake Winnipeg. And Daniel Harmon explored the region between the Red and Swan Rivers, also covering country that had already been mapped, at least in part, by Thompson.[19] Other events occupied the attention of the company during this period. In 1803 the Nor'-Westers had to move their headquarters from Grand Portage (which had become American territory) to Fort William, a bit farther north on Lake Superior's northwestern shore. Also in 1803, the United States purchased the Territory of Louisiana from France, diverting company attention southward; the company was even more attentive in 1804–6 when Meriwether Lewis and William Clark crossed from the upper Missouri to the Columbia system, making the first documented crossing of the divide since Mackenzie and staking an American claim to control over the lower Columbia River and its mouth. In 1804 McTavish, a principal member of the company, died; also in that year, following a period of conflict that verged on open warfare, the North West and XY Companies merged, and for the next two years the company attempted to consolidate its business activities east of the mountains.

By 1805 the Nor'Westers were again prepared to attempt a Rocky Mountain crossing and to search for a route to the Pacific—more specifically, a route to the Columbia River, which was viewed as the key to the development of a continent-spanning trading empire that would stretch from the St. Lawrence to the mouth of the Great River of the West. The obvious choices for men to lead this endeavor were Thompson (by now a partner in the North West Company) and Fraser. In 1806 the company planned a two-pronged assault on the mountain crossing: Fraser, working out of the Peace River country, was to attempt a crossing to the river discovered by Mackenzie, a river that everyone still believed to be the Columbia (actually the Fraser River); Thompson, working out of Rocky Mountain House, was to follow the leads uncovered by himself and McGillivray in 1801–2 and explore the upper North Saskatchewan drainage in an attempt to locate (or relocate) a pass across the mountains to the Columbia. Both of these efforts to reach Pacific slope waters proved successful; only one, however, was successful in the ultimate objective of reaching the Columbia River.

In late 1805 Fraser was on the upper Peace River. During the next two years, in preparation for an exploration westward to the Pacific, he worked to set up the fur trade of the area. A post was built at Rocky Mountain Portage (the site of Mackenzie's crossing of the divide between the upper Peace and upper Fraser Rivers in 1793); posts were also constructed west of the divide in what is now British Columbia at Fort McLeod near the upper Finlay River, at Fort Saint James at the southern end of Stuart Lake, and at Fort George on the Fraser. These posts were to form the nucleus of the North West Company's New Caledonia district. Fraser's activities during these two years are an excellent example of the merchant companies' tendency to prioritize economic endeavors over exploratory objectives—even when the latter could be viewed, in the long run, as beneficial to the struggle for economic and imperial control over territory.

By May 1808 Fraser, accompanied by company surveyor John Stuart and a small party, was ready to embark from Fort George on the upper Fraser River and search for a route to the Pacific. His plans were to follow this river (mistakenly identified as the Columbia) downstream to its mouth. The first part of the journey was deceptively easy; the Fraser River near Fort George is a placid and wide stream, flowing along an easy and level course to the south. Before long Fraser's hopes of an easy route to the Pacific were dashed, and he learned why Mackenzie had left the Fraser's waters. As the river entered the long and deep gorge that it has carved through the mountains on its southward path to the Straits of Georgia, it became turbulent and treacherous. Natives of the region told Fraser of "whirlpools that would swallow up canoes." Their assessment, the Vermonter learned, was not far off: "It is so wild that I cannot find words to describe our situation at times. We have to pass where no human being should venture."[20] Once in the Fraser's gorge, the explorers could only continue downstream; the canoes could not be carried on land because of the steepness of the canyon walls, and Fraser and his men were forced to plunge through boiling rapids, from which they escaped only to encounter other rapids further downstream. By late June, Fraser began to notice signs that the ocean was near, and on 2 July 1808 he recorded his glimpse of the Pacific—which, like Mackenzie before him, he would not be able to attain. "We came in sight of a gulf or bay of the sea . . . seeing nothing but dangers and difficulties in our way, we therefore relinquished our designs and turned our thoughts toward home. . . . Here I must again acknowledge my great disappointment in not seeing the *main* Ocean, having gone so near it as to be almost within view. . . . The latitude is 49° nearly, while that of the entrance of the Columbia is 46°20'. This river therefore is not the Columbia!"[21]

A second North West company explorer had crossed the mountains to the Pacific; unlike his predecessor, Fraser had accomplished his crossing mostly by water. But the water crossing did him no good. The river that he and Mackenzie had assumed to be the Columbia was not—nor was it navigable for canoes laden with furs. The Columbia River route to the sea was still firmly in the hands of the Americans.

Even before Fraser began struggling down the river that now bears his name, the other North West Company explorer was engaged in his own mountain crossing. Thompson left Rocky Mountain House in the spring of 1807, bound for the Rockies pass that he believed had been discovered by McGillivray in 1801. The Piegan division of the Blackfeet nation had prevented white traders from entering the mountains in this area for several years, but now, with the Piegans drawn southward to avenge themselves against the Americans for the loss of two warriors in a battle with Meriwether Lewis on the Marias River in 1806, the way to the mountains was open to Thompson. Traveling with his family, Thompson passed through the Kootenay Plain of the upper North Saskatchewan and successfully negotiated a mountain crossing via "the defiles of the Saskatchewan River, which led to the head water of the Columbia River."[22] His crossing was probably via Howse Pass, named for the Hudson's Bay Company man who would cross it several years later, and it took him into the long northward stretch of the Columbia River east of the Selkirk Range before the river bends to the south and then the west and the Pacific. After a conflict with the Kootenai Indians, Thompson and his party canoed south up the Columbia to its virtual source in Lake Windemere, where he built the log houses that formed Kootenay House, the first trading post on the waters of the Columbia. Here, over the next four years, Thompson would complete his surveys of the Columbia River.

Curiously, Thompson made no attempt to follow the Columbia to the sea in 1807 but instead explored southward into the valley of the Kootenay River, surveying and building trading posts in the Flathead and Pend d'Oreille country of Idaho. After wintering at Fort Kootenay in 1807–8, he packed up his winter's accumulation of furs and, with his family, traveled back across the mountains to the North Saskatchewan. Leaving his pregnant wife at the small post of Boggy Hall, Thompson traveled all the way east to Rainy Lake Post, where he delivered his furs and rested for two days before returning to the mountains, arriving back on the Columbia at the end of October, having traveled five thousand miles. He followed a similar route in 1809, although he traveled with his winter furs only as far as Fort Augustus on the Saskatchewan before returning to the Pacific slope. During the remainder of 1809 he and his North West Company men continued to search unsuccessfully for a practical trade route across the mountains east of Lake Pend d'Oreille and to develop successfully the fur trade toward the south, building "Kullyspell" (Kalispell) House on Lake Pend d'Oreille in Idaho, "Saleesh" (Salish) House near the mouth of Ashley Creek (part of the Kootenay system) in Montana, and Spokane House on the Spokane River south of the Columbia in Washington.[23] In 1810 Thompson again returned east across the mountains and plains all the way to Rainy Lake Post, following the by-now familiar route along the upper Columbia and through Howse Pass. On his return to the Columbia late in 1810, forced by the warlike Piegans to detour north of his regular Howse Pass route, he crossed the divide via Athabasca Pass in January 1811, his second discovery of a major route across the mountains.

During all these travels Thompson had made astronomical observations and had carefully recorded the latitude and longitude of numerous geographical features, both natural and man-made, for the purpose of completing his large map of British possessions in North America. The one major geographical feature still missing from his observations and logs was the Columbia River's lower course, and in 1811 he was ready to complete his surveys by exploring the Columbia from near Kettle Falls, Washington, to its mouth. As a geographer, Thompson needed to complete his work on the Columbia system; as a fur trader, he had more economic motives: "We set off on a voyage down the Columbia River to explore this river in order to open out a passage for the interior trade with the Pacific Ocean."[24] Only twelve days were required to journey from Kettle Falls down the Columbia to the Pacific: through the Grand Coulee, past the mouth of the Snake River (where Thompson posted a sign claiming the area for Great Britain, never mind that Lewis and Clark had traversed this area six years before), and through the Dalles and the Gorge of the Columbia to Tongue Point, where he had "a full view of the Pacific Ocean." The arrival at the Pacific was the zenith of Thompson's career as a geographer-explorer; it may have been the nadir of his career as a fur trader. He had arrived at the Columbia only to find "the fur trading post of Mr. J.J. Astor of the City of New York; which was four low log huts, the far famed Fort Astoria of the United States."[25] After spending a short time at Astoria, Thompson headed back up the Columbia for his post at Kootenay House; in 1812 he left the mountains and the West for good.

During the years 1813 and 1814 Thompson worked on the large (more than ten feet by six feet) map that was to culminate his life's work as an explorer. During his service with the North West Company, he had traveled more than fifty thousand miles in the West and had made accurate trigonometrical and astronomical observations for most of his journeys. His map was a magnificent contribution to geographical knowledge, not just because it was so accurate but also because it reflected Thompson's interest in the character of the country: "The lengths of the rivers, the heights of the mountains, the extent of the plains, were all alike investigated, and the results were recorded by him."[26] Unlike other explorers who were content to merely map lines on the ground, Thompson attempted to give a picture of terrain and climate, of vegetation and animal populations other than simply beaver, of native American life and customs. In his geographical approach to his profession, he was exceeded only by a handful of western explorers—and none of them were engaged in the business of developing and maintaining a far-flung fur-trading enterprise at the same time that they were busy exploring. The title of Thompson's map reflects his achievements:

> Map of the North West Territory of the Province of Canada from actual survey during the years 1792 to 1812. This Map was made for the North West Company in 1813 and 1814 and delivered to the Honorable William McGillivray, their agent. Embraces the region lying between 45 and 60 Degrees North Latitude and 84 and 124 degree West Longitude comprising the Discovery and Survey of the Oregon Territory, to the Pacific Ocean, the Survey of the Athabasca Lake, Slave River and Lake, from which flow Mackenzie's River to the Arctic Sea

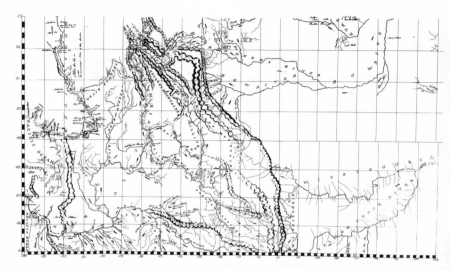

*16.2 Map of the northwestern part of North America (David Thompson, 1812). Thompson may have been the most skilled of all the British explorers in putting the results of his journeys into cartographic form. This map is a classic example of his mapping abilities. Collection of John L. Allen.*

by Mr. Philip Turner, the Route of Sir Alexander Mackenzie in 1792 [1793] down part of Fraser's River together with the Survey of this River to the Pacific Ocean by the late John Stuart of the North West Company, by David Thompson, Astronomer & Surveyor.[27]

When Thompson left the west in 1812, Britain and the United States were on the brink of war. When he arrived at North West Company headquarters at Fort William, the United States had declared war on the United Kingdom. Over the next few years, the company's western activities would be conditioned by the War of 1812 as economic competition between the Nor'Westers and Astor's Pacific Fur Company evolved into a military struggle for imperial territorial control. It was to the North West Company, not the Royal Navy, that Fort Astoria surrendered in 1813, and the Western Department of the North West Company took over Astor's empire at the mouth of the Columbia, renaming Astoria "Fort George" in honor of the king.[28] The fortunes of war had given to the Nor'Westers territorial and economic control over the entire Pacific coastal region of North America between San Francisco and Alaska. The period of glory was brief, however: the North West Company and its rival, the Hudson's Bay Company, merged in 1821. But during that short interlude, North West Company employees carried out significant explorations in this vast region.

Following the transfer of Astoria to British control, many of Astor's employees decided to remain on the Columbia and join the ranks of the Nor'Westers. Two of these men, Ross Cox and Alexander Ross, recorded important observations of regional geography and native life. These works, along with Washington Irving's *Astoria* (1836), provided British, Canadians, and Americans with their first look at life in the Northwest.[29] Cox, in his *Adventures on the Columbia River* (1831), enthusiastically noted the size of the trees, the climate and soil, and the wildlife of the lower Columbia and Willamette Valleys; the Columbia itself he called "a noble river." About the interior east of the Columbia Gorge, he harshly commented: "The country assumes a new aspect: it is free from any rising grounds, or timber, and on each side nothing is to be seen but immense plains stretching a great distance to the north and south: the soil is dry and sandy, and covered with a loose parched grass, growing in tufts." He also noted that an enormous number of rattlesnakes inhabited the Columbian plain and that the plains were covered with "immense quantities of prickly pear, which was a source of great annoyance."[30] Ross, in his *Adventures of the First Settlers on the Oregon or Columbia River* (1849), offered a narrative of the Astoria adventure and its aftermath; this valuable historical document discusses the Astoria settlement from the perspective of a participant. The daily life of the "settlers," the customs of the local natives, the nature of the fur-trading operations, and the character of the environment are all treated in Ross's narrative. About the country near the mouth of the Columbia where Fort George stood, Ross noted: "The country is low, and the impervious forests give to the surrounding coast a wild and gloomy aspect . . . while toward the south, the impervious and magnificent forest darkened the landscape as far as the eye could reach. The place thus selected for the emporium of the west, might challenge the whole continent to produce a spot of equal extent presenting more difficulties to the settler." He commented that the "people suffered greatly from the humidity of the climate" on the coast while the climate of the interior valleys, particularly the Willamette, "was salubrious and dry, differing materially from that of the sea-coast; and the heat is sufficiently intense to ripen every kind of grain in a short time . . . but, however inviting may be the soil, the remote distance and savage aspect of the boundless wilderness along the Pacific seem to defer the colonization of such a region to a period far beyond the present generation; and yet, if we consider the rapid progress of civilization in other new and equally remote countries, we might still indulge the hope of seeing this, at no distant time, one of the most flourishing countries on the globe." Finally, Ross shared Cox's harsh view of the interior east of the Cascades: "The face of the country is one wide and boundless plain, with here and here some trifling inequalities, but not a tree nor bush to be seen. . . . One boundless rough and barren plain . . . the whole contry . . . studded with towering heights and rocks, giving the whole face of the country, in that direction, a bleak, broken, and mountainous appearance."[31]

Among the North West Company employees who acted as explorers, as well as landscape observers, during the 1813–21 period, only one man distinguished himself. In 1816 Donald McKenzie, a former Astor man who had chosen to stay in the Northwest after the surrender of Fort Astoria, was appointed leader of the new "Columbia Department" of the North West Company in the Pacific Northwest.[32] Between 1816 and 1819, McKenzie and his men explored "the inland empire," or the intermountain West— the area between the western slopes of the Rocky Mountains and the eastern slopes of the Cascade Range. Lewis and Clark, of course, had already explored the connections between the Missouri River and the Clearwater River in Idaho and then had traveled down the Snake and Columbia to the Pacific. Fur company employees of Manuel Lisa of the Missouri Fur Company of St. Louis and of Astor's Pacific Fur Company had traveled into the inland empire by way of Teton Pass and knew something of the Snake River's tortuous route across Idaho to its junction with the Columbia. McKenzie and his men added to all this knowledge by traveling throughout the areas west of the continental divide, areas explored by Lewis and Clark, Andrew Henry, Wilson Price Hunt, and Robert Stuart.

Through their travels, the North West Company men changed the way that the fur trade would operate in western North America. Ever since the French had begun exploiting the fur resource of the St. Lawrence Valley in the sixteenth century, the usual practice was to go into fur country, build a trading post, and wait there for Indians to bring furs to be traded for items of European manufacture. McKenzie, however, concluded that the fur trade could be made more profitable by eliminating the middlemen, that is, the Indians. Instead of building posts for trading purposes, the North West Company decided to trap rather than trade. Trappers would go into the Northwest and gather the beaver furs rather than depending on the Indians. These trappers would then return their furs to the post, where they would be paid wages, much of which would be spent to purchase supplies and equipment for use in the next season's trapping. This change, immensely profitable for the fur merchants, also almost guaranteed that instead of a few solitary fur trade explorers seeking Indians with whom to trade, large numbers of white trappers would invade the beaver country. These trappers became explorers, searching for beaver and for the best routes over which to carry their catch to the fur-trading posts. As a result, the rate at which fur trade exploration uncovered new geographical information greatly increased.[33]

McKenzie's efforts in the inland empire formed the first test of this innovative commercial enterprise. In 1816 McKenzie and his men traveled into the interior of the Columbian Basin region as far as Thompson's Spokane House, near the present location of Spokane, Washington. Two years later they built a trading post near the junction of the Columbia and Snake Rivers at Walla Walla, and from here they began to explore eastward to the Boise River in Idaho and southeastward to the barren sagebrush flats between the Snake and Green Rivers, finding a vast region unknown to the white man. In the Snake River plain the valleys of the rivers were found to be deep, tortuous, and inaccessible; they were also found to be teeming with beaver. In 1819 McKenzie's men trapped as far south as the Bear Lake region of northern Utah, although they did not discover the Great Salt Lake, only a short distance to the south. In reaching this region, however, McKenzie's trapper-explorers closed the gap that had existed since the eighteenth century between the Spanish penetrations northward from Mexico into the Great Basin and the British and American explorations of the northern Rockies. The trappers also thrust north, and McKenzie, in an innovation typical of North West Company operations, established the first link between the company's Columbia and New Caledonia Departments by exploring and developing a combined packhorse-canoe route between Fort Okanagan on the Columbia River and Fort McLeod on the Peace River. Yet McKenzie's travels represent the end of fur trade exploration under the aegis of the North West Company: in 1821 the company merged with its ancient rival, the Hudson's Bay Company.[34]

## Hudson's Bay Company Explorations, 1800–1821

While the North West Company was opening up the farther West and developing the rich fur trade of the Saskatchewan basin, the Pacific coastal region, and "Oregon Country," the Hudson's Bay Company (HBC) was largely quiescent in exploration. Only one Hudson's Bay Company employee penetrated the Rocky Mountains during the years when Thompson and Fraser and other Nor'Westers were developing a thriving trade between the Saskatchewan region and the Columbia and New Caledonia region. This HBC man, Joseph Howse, a writer and surveyor, had been on both the northern and the southern branches of the Saskatchewan between 1805 and 1808. In 1809, in response to the HBC decision to compete with the Nor'Westers in the Rockies and beyond, Howse traveled up the North Saskatchewan in search of a suitable pass across the mountains. He may have crossed the mountains by way of Howse Pass, used two years earlier by Thompson, but no journals or maps of Howse's first expedition have survived.[35] In 1810 Howse crossed the divide again, presumably via the same route, and traveled into the upper Columbia country and as far south as Flathead Lake, Montana, where he erected a small cabin and spent the winter before returning by way of the Saskatchewan in the summer of 1811. His map of this journey is now lost, though it apparently showed the headwaters regions of the Athabasca, Saskatchewan, and Missouri Rivers east of the divide and the Columbia, Kootenay, and Flathead Rivers to the west. This map may have passed from Hudson's Bay Company hands to Aaron Arrowsmith's cartographic firm; if so, it—along with Thompson's map—provided crucial geographical data for subsequent Arrowsmith maps of North America. Howse returned to the Saskatchewan in 1811 with thirty-six bundles of prime furs, ample evidence of the richness of the fur resource of the Pacific slope. Yet these furs were not enough to push other HBC men into territory controlled by the Nor'Westers, and Howse's penetration was the first and only expedition by the Hudson's Bay Company west of the Rockies until after the merger.

The only other significant HBC explorations before 1821 were east of the mountains and were largely attempts to obtain new information on the farther West from Indians rather than through white exploration, to consolidate knowledge of the Saskatchewan and Athabasca countries, and to fill in the remaining holes in the maps of the Hudson's Bay Company region to the east. The leading figure in HBC exploration during this period was Peter Fidler, who had long been a prime player in the development of geographical knowledge of the Canadian interior and who had spent most of his time obtaining and attempting to translate geographical lore from native Americans. In 1800 Fidler, who had been in the Athabasca country before the turn of the century, traveled to Cumberland House, the HBC post on the Sas-

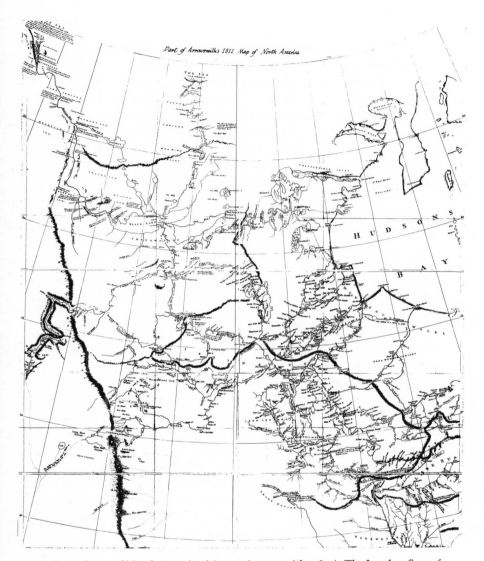

16.3 *Part of map of North America (Aaron Arrowsmith, 1811). The London firm of Arrowsmith had ready access to sketch maps and other materials from the fur trade, particularly the Hudson's Bay Company. This map presents the best-available British information on the West at the end of the first decade of the nineteenth century. Collection of John L. Allen.*

katchewan River. Receiving instructions to construct the first HBC house in the grassland region of the South Saskatchewan, he traveled west to the site where Chesterfield House was to be erected, just below the confluence of the Red Deer River with the South Saskatchewan. The idea seemed to be to attract the Blackfeet and Piegan Indians eastward from the mountains and to attract the Missouri River tribes northward.[36] Fidler spent the next two years at this location, far out on the Great Plains; he seldom traveled far from Chesterfield House, remaining at the post to gather furs and, more important, geographical data from the Indians. Fidler was extraordinarily skilled in asking the right questions of his native informants and in translating their responses into a geographical context that had meaning for the European worldview. The maps he fashioned from Indian lore were easily transferred to maps such as those of Arrowsmith.[37] During his stay at Chesterfield House, Fidler—even though he traveled only a few miles west—was able to develop a reasonably accurate picture of the high plains from the North Saskatchewan to the Missouri and of the eastern front of the Rocky Mountain cordillera.

Fidler left the South Saskatchewan in 1802 and for the next four years was in the Athabasca region, where he obtained additional information for his maps of the west while trying to maintain HBC trade in the face of increasing competition from the Nor'Westers. Here, Fidler's most important data came from other travelers rather than from his own observations; nevertheless, he completed the first HBC map of the transmontane region, delineating the territory from the northern bend of the Columbia River south to Flathead Lake. In 1807 Fidler explored and surveyed the trade route from Reindeer Lake to Lake Athabasca via Methy Portage, a well-known and long-used route but one for which no accurate maps existed. In the same year he surveyed the route from Reindeer Lake to the Churchill River and down that river to Churchill Factory on Hudson Bay.[38] The following year Fidler surveyed trading routes in the Lake Winnipeg–Assiniboine River–Red River region. His first two explorations took him through the Canadian Shield, or the "Stoney Region," in the transition zone between the taiga and forest zones; a third placed him in the aspen grove and parkland country of the forest-grassland margins. His perceptive geographical comments on these regions—along with his accurate surveys—provided the HBC with its first true picture of an area that had been in use by the fur trade for a half-century.

During the final phase of Fidler's career with the Hudson's Bay Company, from 1811 to 1819, he transcribed data from Indians and fellow traders and from western and northern maps collected during two decades of fieldwork. There were hardly any areas of the Northwest—from the Missouri to the Arctic and from Hudson Bay to the Rocky Mountains—for which he did not have at least some geographical information. His days as a primary explorer were over by 1810, but his intellectual exploration continued as he analyzed his maps and sketches and drafted fairly large-scale maps of small regions. Fidler produced a number of precise maps—one showing the village locations, farm fields, and cart trails of Lord Selkirk's agricultural colony in the Red River district is perhaps the best example—but unlike Thompson, he never consolidated his considerable knowledge of the western interior into one large, small-scale map. Thus one of the more prolific mapmakers and explorers of the early nineteenth century is not as well-known as many travelers who covered less ground with less precision.

During the last years before the 1821 merger, the exploratory activities of the Hudson's Bay Company in the western interior virtually stopped. The internecine conflict that had characterized the years immediately before the XY and the North West Companies had combined spilled over to relations between employees of the North West and the Hudson's Bay Companies, leaving little time or energy for pushing the frontiers of geographical knowledge farther north and west. The one area where some significant HBC exploration did take place was in the region of the Eastmain, the vast and still unknown territory east of Hudson Bay.

That the Eastmain should have remained generally terra incognita while lands clear to the Pacific shores were being explored is curious. In part, the environment—rocky shield areas with little vegetative cover and few rich fur areas, a harsh climate, and natives resentful of European intrusion into their trading areas—may have prevented the company from attempting to learn about the Eastmain while more profitable and accessible lands lay on the other side of the bay. Nevertheless, by 1817 the company had determined to try to use some of the rivers entering the bay north of the Eastmain River (flowing into James Bay north of the company post at Rupert House) to cross eastward into Labrador. James Clouston, a former schoolteacher, had in fact already traveled and mapped portions of this territory between 1812 and 1816; he had explored the lower ends of the Rupert and Slude (Eastmain) Rivers (1812) and the basins of the upper Rupert, Broadback, and Nottaway Rivers into the Lake Mistassini region (1813–16). And HBC trader George Atkinson had ascended the Great Whale River at least as far as Lac Bienville in 1816. On the strength of information provided by Clouston's and Atkinson's preliminary investigations, the company leaders decided to explore the region so as to have "a distinct idea of all the interior of Eastmain as far as the [Hudson?] streights."[39] Although not indicated by company records, a probable goal of this proposed exploration was a rumored river, north and east of the Eastmain River, that flowed to Labrador and the Atlantic. Such a stream, if it could be located, might offer the company a trading route directly from the Atlantic to James Bay in latitudes low enough to allow the transportation of trade goods from England to Hudson and James Bays throughout more of the year than was possible via the Hudson Strait route then in use.

In the summer of 1817 the HBC built Nitchequon House on Nichicun Lake in the headwaters region of the Big River; Clouston surveyed the route between this new establishment in the interior and Neoskweskau on the coast of James Bay and prepared to search for an eastward-flowing stream that would lead to the Atlantic. He was delayed for three years by business matters at the new establishment at Nichicun Lake, and while he tarried, Atkinson followed the coast of the bay north from the mouth of the Great Whale River to Richmond Gulf and thence inland to Lac des Loups Marins, south and west to the Little Whale River, and back downstream to the bay. Atkinson found no trace of any river flowing eastward, nor could he locate a height of land that might separate Atlantic from Hudson Bay drainage; thus Clouston's ambitions for the discovery of an eastward water route from the bay were still safe. Finally, in 1820 Clouston and a small party traveled northeast searching for a lake called Caniapiscau, which Indian information had led him to believe was "over the height of country Towards the Labrador Coast."[40] Clouston reached the Koksoak River, which flows north to Ungava Bay, and actually sighted the estuary of the river before deciding that it led to Ungava Bay rather than the Atlantic. In defeat, he turned west from the Koksoak and traveled overland to Richmond Gulf and then south along the coast to Rupert House. In his map and journal of this exploration, he concluded that a line of mountains might well parallel the Labrador coast, providing a height of land between Atlantic and Hudson drainages. But considering the difficulties of travel in the interior, he also recommended that HBC activities be focused on the area south of established houses. Given the alterations in the organization and structure of the Hudson's Bay Company after the merger with the North West Company, it is not unusual that his recommendations were followed and that the interior of Eastmain remained a geographical mystery for many years.

# The Hudson's Bay Company in Oregon Country and California, 1822–1842

The merger of the North West Company and the Hudson's Bay Company in 1821 precipitated a renewal in exploratory endeavors, a revitalization based largely on the major operational shift that Nor'Wester Donald McKenzie had pioneered in the Snake River country in 1816–19. Following McKenzie's example, the Hudson's Bay Company formed "the Snake River Brigade" in 1822 as a group of free trappers and gave the Brigade the responsibility of exploring and trapping the Snake River country. Its purpose was twofold: to exploit the rich fur resource of that region and to prevent the entry of the St. Louis–based American fur trade into the Snake River region west of the Rockies. Once again, the Hudson's Bay Company was functioning both as an economic entity interested in the profits to be made from the fur trade and as an imperial agent engaging in what amounted to a foreign policy on behalf of the British government. The 1818 Joint Occupation convention between Britain and the United States had stipulated, "It is agreed that any country that may be claimed by either party on the northwest coast of America westward of the Stoney Mountains shall, together with all its harbors, bays and creeks, and the navigation of all rivers within the same, be free and open, for the term of 10 years from the date of the signature of this convention to the vessels, citizens and subjects of the two powers."[41] Treaty or no, the Hudson's Bay Company was determined that "free and open" would not extend to the members of the St. Louis–based fur trade.

Between 1822 and 1824, under the command of former Astorian and Nor'Wester Alexander Ross, the company's Snake River Brigade trapped as far south as the Bear Lake region of northern Utah and as far east as the Blackfoot River in southeastern Idaho. It probably also worked into the upper portions of the Green River valley in western Wyoming and even into the area east of the Rockies around the Great Falls of the Missouri River in Montana. Ross, who had kept an extensive journal during his days with the North West Company, did not leave much record of this period, and little is known about the extent of the trapper activity until the next phase of HBC exploration of the inland empire in 1824. In that year a new governor of the company was named; although not an explorer himself, Governor George Simpson made significant contributions to the expansion of geographical knowledge of the area west of the Rockies. He consolidated the coastal trade in sea otter pelts near the mouth of the Columbia; he built Fort Vancouver at the junction of the Willamette River and the Columbia, a post that would serve as the nerve center of fur trade and other activities in the Pacific Northwest until the 1840s; he appointed former Nor'Wester Dr. John McLoughlin as chief factor of the Columbia Department (a post McLoughlin held until 1846, when Oregon Country became American territory); and he appointed Peter Skene Ogden as commander of the Snake River Brigade and charged him with expanding company activities far to the south and with taking as many beaver from the inland empire as possible.[42] Simpson's idea was simple: by taking all the available beaver from the waters of the Snake River country, American fur merchants would have no interest in that region, and the inland empire would remain in British hands. It was a clever strategy, even if it did not achieve Simpson's ultimate goal. But his appointment of Ogden did bear fruit—in the form of additional geographical knowledge.

Between 1824 and 1830, in six separate expeditions, Ogden's explorations covered the following areas: (1) nearly all the region drained by the Snake River between the Rockies and the Columbia; (2) much of what is now the state of Oregon, on both sides of the Cascade Range; (3) the Bear Lake–Bear River–Great Salt Lake region of southern Idaho and northern Utah; (4) the northern parts of the Great Basin and the valley of the Humboldt River, including much of northern Utah and Nevada; (5) most of California north of San Francisco Bay, including the Klamath Lake and Mount Shasta region; (6) the western side of the Great Basin, from Humboldt Sinks near present-day Reno, Nevada, all the way south to the Gulf of California; and (7) the southern end of the Sierra Nevada Range and northward through the Great Valley of California to Klamath Lake in southern Oregon.[43]

At the beginning of Ogden's explorations in 1824, he clearly believed in the geographical fiction of a common source area for all western rivers below the fiftieth parallel of latitude, a fiction firmly embedded in geographical thought by the journals and maps of Lewis and Clark. In particular, Ogden accepted the concepts of the Multnomah of Lewis and Clark and the Rio San Buenaventura of the Spanish and American fur trappers operating out of Taos, New Mexico. The first of these imaginary rivers had some basis in fact, being a greatly lengthened version of the Willamette River, but was viewed as draining the country south of the Snake River and having a source in the Rockies near the headwaters of other major rivers such as the Yellowstone, Missouri, Rio Grande, Arkansas, and Colorado. The second imaginary river was pure myth, derived from Spanish geo-

graphical lore of the late eighteenth century; in the absence of any awareness of the vast region of interior drainage represented by the Great Basin
between the Rockies and the Sierras, theorists believed that some large
stream drain was necessary in that region. Ogden wrote that he agreed
"there must be large Rivers" draining the country between the Rockies and
the Pacific.[44] He would be the first explorer to prove that this was not the
case.

Ogden's travels in 1824–25 took him from Flathead Lake, Montana,
eastward into the Bitterroot Valley near Missoula and thence south to near
present Grace, Idaho, and the Bear River, which, Ogden believed, "takes
its rise due east & was supposed to be the Rio Colorado & even now said to
be a Fork of the same."[45] During part of this trek, Ogden was accompanied
by Jedediah Smith and a group of American trappers—exactly the people
he was trying to keep out of the region. Smith and his men left Ogden near
the Bear River, however, and the HBC men moved south into the Cache
Valley of Idaho. At some point during this southward thrust, one of Ogden's men climbed a peak from which he obtained a view of the Bear River
flowing into a lake as big (according to the trapper) as Lake Winnipeg.
From this information, Ogden understood that the Bear River had "nothing to do with the Spanish River";[46] in other words, it was not the Colorado. He also learned that the large lake—the Great Salt Lake of Utah—had
a river flowing out of it toward the west; he assumed this river was the
Umpqua River of Oregon, a belief confirmed by one of his men, Thomas
McKay, who had earlier learned from Indians on the Umpqua that the river
headed in a lake east of the Cascades (a probable reference to Crater Lake,
which is just east of the crest of the Cascades and east of the Umpqua's
source region).[47] In a final bit of imaginary geography, he learned that from
his camp at Cache Valley, he was only "15 days march from the Spanish Village [Taos]."[48]

Had Ogden's career as an explorer been based on this first journey, he
would have been judged a miserable failure. Not only was his geography
confused beyond hope, but in May 1825, while camped at Mountain
Green, Utah, just east of the Great Salt Lake, most of his men deserted him
(taking the winter's catch of furs with them) for an American trapping
party. Ogden returned to the company post, Fort Nez Percé near Walla,
Washington, with little to show for a year in the field but with a belief that
he had come close to the core drainage region and had possibly located the
lake out of which a great river—the San Buenaventura?—flowed west to
the Pacific.

The hope of discovering such a river was strengthened late in 1825 when, before departing on his second trek, Ogden learned that there was "a River three days South of the Umpqua said to Extend a great way into the Interior."[49] He had also heard rumors of a large lake south of the Columbia—probably Klamath Lake—from which a river flowed, although it was not clear in which direction. In Ogden's mind, a lake and river system was the key to finding a water route from the Rockies to the Pacific, but this was not really his goal when he departed Fort Nez Percé on the winter and spring hunt and exploration of 1825–26. Needing to recoup the losses caused by the desertion of the preceding spring, the second expedition was primarily a trapping one. His route took him up the Snake River through its lava-bed plains—a "wretched place" and "a cursed country" in Ogden's view[50]—all the way to the Portneuf River of eastern Idaho near the Wyoming border. The hunt was a success; laden with furs, Ogden returned to the Columbia, where he immediately began planning a third expedition to test the hypothetical geography he had worked out in 1825 and to determine whether a great river did flow westward to the Pacific through the vast country south of the Columbia and Snake.

Late in 1826, while still at his post at Walla, Ogden spoke with some Snake Indians who had been on the Klamath Lake and who also had a considerable amount of "Spanish goods." This fixed in his mind the idea that the large lake he had heard about south of the Columbia (Klamath Lake) and the Great Salt Lake were one and the same; it also provided the goal for his travels of 1826–27: "There was no other alternative left from this information I obtained but to proceed to the South branch of the Columbia and endeavor to reach the lake on which so much *Stress* had been laid, and which I have since ascertained beyond a doubt both from the Americans as well as from many Indians who are in the habit of resorting to the Clammit country is the same Lake I saw last year on the Spanish waters and within 6 days march of the Spanish Settlement (called Taos)."[51]

To test this assumption, in 1826–27 Ogden journeyed south from Fort Vancouver (to which he had moved his headquarters) into the headwaters region of the Des Chutes tributary of the Columbia and across the Malheur Lake desert country of southeastern Oregon east of the Cascades, back west to Klamath Lake and—although his route is far from clear—probably as far as the Rogue River and possibly even as far as the Stanislaus River (tributary of the Sacramento) in northern California. He discovered that the "great river" of the Klamath country did flow to the Pacific but that it headed in Klamath Lake (which, as it turned out, was far from the Great

Salt Lake); this could not, therefore, be the Buenaventura he was searching for, which he decided must lie still farther south. He wanted to continue southward until he either struck the Buenaventura or was forced to turn eastward to the Snake, but difficult travel conditions and other matters interfered.[52] Ogden instead returned to Fort Vancouver, leaving further explorations toward the Buenaventura for the his fourth expedition, in 1827–28.

On this next trip, Ogden's original intention of searching for the Buenaventura to the south had to give way to expediency. His superiors told him that he needed to obtain enough value in furs to warrant HBC activities in the Snake country if he wanted to continue his explorations. Accordingly, this expedition concentrated on the rich fur country of the Snake Basin, roughly between the Idaho-Wyoming border on the east and the Idaho-Oregon border on the west, much of it country over which Ogden had already traveled. His familiarity with the country is evidenced by his journal entries for 1827–28; whereas previous journals had contained substantial information on actual and speculative geography, these daily entries were place-specific and matter-of-fact, often ending with the tally of the day's take in beaver pelts.[53]

By contrast, Ogden's next expedition, in 1828–29, journeyed from Fort Nez Percé southward in search of the Buenaventura, moving deep into new territory—into that vast unexplored region south of Malheur Lake, east of the Sierras, and west of the Great Salt Lake—making the first major penetration of the Great Basin. Ogden discovered the Humboldt River, which he explored from its source in the Ruby Mountains near the Utah-Nevada border to its sink in the western reaches of the Basin. Shortly after reaching the Humboldt, Ogden learned from Indians that "the distance was great to its sources, not less than ten days march—there we shall find five forks, on three of these beaver, that the river discharges in a large lake, and that salmon does not ascend this stream and consequently has no communication with the waters of the ocean."[54] The Buenaventura, therefore, still had to lie toward the south; after trapping eastward toward the Rockies, mostly along the Humboldt and its tributaries, Ogden came once again to the Great Salt Lake. His journal entry for 28 December 1828 notes: "Here we now are at the end of Great Salt Lake having this season explored one half of the north side of it and can safely assert as the Americans have of the south side that it is truly a barren country, almost destitute of everything."[55] Yet Ogden's description of the Great Salt Lake held out promise: "On both sides of Salt Lake is very high land and as far as the eye [can see] it appears surrounded by mountains, but beyond these mountains at the west end although the lake has no discharge I am of the opinion there must be large rivers and probably an object worthy of exploring at a future day."[56]

Not until the explorations of U.S. Army Topographical Engineer John Charles Frémont in the 1840s was the true nature of the Great Basin fully understood as a region without the large rivers that Ogden believed must be there. In the meantime, Ogden's exploration of 1828–29 had contributed much geographical knowledge on the intermountain West: he had discovered the Humboldt and had learned that it did not lead to the ocean; he had also learned that the Bear River drained not into the Columbia but south into the Great Salt Lake, which lacked an outlet to the Pacific. In all his wanderings, Ogden had found no river that headed in the supposed common-source region and that flowed directly to the Pacific.

Before the end of his reign as the Hudson's Bay Company's leading explorer, Ogden had one more journey to make. Little is known about this expedition, perhaps his most significant geographically. Ogden's journals for his travels of 1829–30 were destroyed in a boat accident in a whirlpool of the Columbia, just before he reached Fort Vancouver on his return journey; the record of this last trek is found only in a letter he wrote to Simpson.[57] Apparently, Ogden was attempting finally to resolve the issue of the Buenaventura. From a variety of sources, we can trace the 1829–30 route as follows: from Fort Vancouver up the Deschutes River to near its head and then southward to Malheur Lake; from Malheur Lake south to the Humboldt River and up the Humboldt to the Sinks and then south to Walker Lake in western Nevada; from Walker Lake up into the Sierras and southward through the mountains until turning east to strike the Colorado River below its junction with the Virgin River (probably somewhere near Needles, California); southward along the Colorado to the Gulf of California, then back up the river for one hundred miles or so; from the Colorado River westward into California, across Cajon Pass to the San Bernadino area and then north through Walker's or Tehachapi Pass into the San Joaquin Valley; northward through the San Joaquin Valley (where he traveled, for a time, with an American party headed by Ewing Young) and the Sacramento Valley to the Pit River of northern California. By now he was approaching familiar ground, and he traveled from the Pit River northeast to Klamath Lake, the Deschutes, the Columbia, and Fort Vancouver.[58]

This last journey alone would place Ogden in the first rank of fur trade explorers; when all his expeditions are combined, his accomplishments are staggering, exceeded only by one or two other individuals in the annals of western North America. Unlike American fur trade explorations, Ogden's had direct consequences for the development of geographical knowledge. The journals and maps that resulted from his travels were deposited in the archives of the Hudson's Bay Company in London, where they became available to the British cartographic firm of Aaron Arrowsmith; after 1830, the geographical knowledge obtained from Ogden's travels appeared on British maps.[59] In Ogden's final reports and maps, the common source area for western rivers, as envisaged by Clark and others of the early nineteenth century, was shown as a core drainage region containing the upper waters of the Missouri, Columbia, Colorado, Rio Grande, and Arkansas. But the Buenaventura and the Multnomah were absent from his maps; as a result, British cartography no longer included these mythical streams as part of the geography of western North America. This was Ogden's major contribution to geographical knowledge.

HBC exploration in Oregon and California after 1830 was anticlimactic, although eleven expeditions were sent out. John Work's California expedition of 1832–33 (preceded by Michael Laframboise's entry into California from Oregon via the coastal route) was probably the most important of this latter stage of HBC activity in what became the American West. Leaving Fort Vancouver in the spring of 1832, Work's brigade traveled up the Columbia to Fort Nez Percé (Walla Walla) and from there south to Malheur Lake. Near Malheur Lake, Work noted that he had originally intended to travel southeast "to Ogdens river [the Humboldt] and searched to the Southward of it for a river which the Indians give some vague account of" but that the season was too far advanced;[60] this is Work's only reference to any purpose for his trip other than fur trapping. From the Malheur Lake region the party went west to Alkali Lake, Lake Abert, and Abert Rim in the central Oregon desert country, then southwest to Goose Lake and to the Pit River of southern Oregon, then down the Pit River and west across the Cascades into the Sacramento River headwaters region. The Sacramento was known to the HBC as "the Bonaventura," but Work's journal, which gave the river limits and course, clearly indicates that the name had nothing to do with the Buenaventura that Ogden had sought fruitlessly.[61] From the Sacramento River, Work's party journeyed south to Sutter Buttes—with a side trip to the American River—and then in the spring of 1833 headed west across the coastal hills and then south to San Francisco Bay. From here they traveled north along the coast and then inland to the Great Valley (Sacramento Valley) once again, which they followed north as far as the Stanislaus River; from the Stanislaus they returned to Fort Vancouver by way of the Mount Shasta and Klamath River–Klamath Lake regions.

Some minor expeditions followed: in 1834 Michael Laframboise led a brigade into Sacramento Valley; in 1836 Tom McKay (who had traveled with Odgen) and Stephen Meek trapped on the Pit River; in 1836–37 Laframboise again led brigades into northern California; and in 1841–42 Francis Ermatinger and Laframboise "made out poorly" trapping in California. In twenty years, the Hudson's Bay Company had converted much of the Pacific slope south of the Columbia into a fur wasteland. When the furs were gone, the company had little reason to continue activities in Oregon and California, and it abandoned most of its facilities in this region even before the area became American territory in 1846. That the area became American territory at all was at least partly the result of Hudson's Bay Company operations and pointed up the dangers of using the fur trade as an agent of foreign policy. Unlike the American fur trappers in the Rockies and farther west—who were the advance guard for an American agricultural settlement—the traders and trappers of the Hudson's Bay Company were the employees of a "gigantic and semifeudal governing monopoly" that embodied the values of British mercantilism: primarily interested in profit and, therefore, much less interested in agricultural use of the lands from which it was taking furs. Each HBC brigade leader in the Columbia Department (and elsewhere) was controlled by commerce.[62]

## Exploration in the Eastmain and Southern Interior, 1821–1841

The 1821 decision by the Hudson's Bay Company to ignore the Eastmain region in favor of more established sites lasted only until 1824 and Simpson's appointment as governor of the company. Early in his tenure as governor, Simpson recognized that existing areas of fur trapping were overexploited and that the resource, particularly beaver, was imperiled. Thus, he promoted the expansion of the company's trading activities from the bay southeast toward the St. Lawrence and into the unexplored territory south of Ungava Bay between the Koksoak and Caniapiscau (South) Rivers and the coast of Labrador.[63] Of these areas, only the Koksoak region had been investigated at all (by Clouston in 1820), and Simpson planned to expand both geographical knowledge and the fur trade of this area by building a trading post near where Clouston had viewed Ungava Bay. In conjunction with this decision, William Hendry and George Atkinson were instructed to explore and survey the region first visited by Clouston. In 1828 they traveled overland to the mouth of the Caniapiscau River (a tributary of the Koksoak), followed the Koksoak down to Ungava Bay, and then explored the shores of the bay on both sides of the mouth of the Koksoak. Although Henry and Atkinson surveyed the region carefully, no site for a trading house was established.

Two years later, a party led by Nicol Finlayson and Erland Erlandson traveled into the region of the lower Koksoak and erected a house some twenty-seven miles up the Koksoak River. From this establishment, named Fort Chimo, exploring parties were sent out along the coast and into the interior between 1830 and 1834. Two parties in 1830 explored the coast of Ungava Bay to the northwest and the northeast; the trek to the northeast penetrated as far as the mouth of the George River, but the northwestern thrust was turned back by ice a short distance from the mouth of the Koksoak. In the following year a small party traveled up the Caniapiscau River as far as the first major waterfall; in 1832 a party under Erlandson built a trading post on the Caniapiscau River near its mouth. By this time the hostile nature of the environment and the paucity of furs had convinced the traders—particularly Finlayson and Erlandson—that any further interior exploration and development should be to the south rather than the north. Additional trading houses in the interior of Eastmain would, in their opinion, be of little value unless located close to a height of land from which water travel south to the St. Lawrence was possible.[64]

Following instructions from Simpson to locate a route south to the St. Lawrence, Finlayson and Erlandson recruited Indian guides to lead Erlandson south from Fort Chimo to the St. Lawrence. They succeeded in locating Indians who claimed to know the way, but they failed to reach their goal of the Mingan post on the northern shore of the St. Lawrence. In 1834 Erlandson, with a party of Indian guides, headed southeast from Fort Chimo up the Caniapiscau River and then through a complex and interlocking set of waterways (typical of the Canadian Shield environment) as far as Lake Petitsikapau in western Labrador near the Quebec border. The Indians refused to go any farther south and steered Erlandson east to Lake Melville and Hamilton Inlet on the Labrador coast.[65] The desired route to the St. Lawrence had not been found. But a major portion of the interior of the northeastern portion of the Eastmain peninsula had been explored.

The Fort Chimo–Hamilton Inlet route discovered by Erlandson (with Indian directions) would become a regularly used trade connection between the Atlantic coast and Ungava Bay—but only after further exploration. Erlandson's potential route discovered on his 1834 journey was arduous, and he and his Indian party had achieved the crossing to the Atlantic only with great difficulty. If the route was to be effective in supplying the remote Fort Chino from the Atlantic, it would have to be mapped and surveyed more completely. Between 1837 and 1841 John McLean (the new factor at Fort Chimo) undertook a series of journeys, possibly four total, through the northeastern Eastmain to determine the most feasible commercial supply route between the company's North West River House (Fort Smith) on Lake Melville (the inland extension of Hamilton Inlet) to his own post at Chimo and, thus, to Ungava Bay.[66] He succeeded in establishing this route, using the Naskaupi River, which flows to Lake Melville, and the George River, which flows to Ungava Bay, as the primary path. Although this route placed travelers some distance east up the Ungava shoreline from Fort Chimo, it was certainly a feasible solution to a problem that had been plaguing the company for years.

Development of the Ungava Bay–Hamilton Inlet route not only solved an economic problem but also stimulated continuing exploration in the northern portions of Eastmain between the two termini of the trade route. Little is known of these explorations, but maps drawn by company personnel between 1837 and 1840 suggest active exploration, particularly in the Labrador coastal region adjacent to Fort Smith.[67] The master trader at Fort Smith, W. H. A. Davis, seems to have made a number of journeys up and down the Labrador coast from Hamilton Inlet during this period. Of particular interest was Kaipokok Bay, the next inlet of the ocean north of Hamilton; Davis apparently not only traveled up the coast from Hamilton to Kaipokok but also—probably in 1840—journeyed overland from Melville Lake to Kaipokok Bay in an attempt to locate a more direct trade route and avoid the long and circuitous route following the ocean's edge. His sketchy reports of this 1840 journey provide some of the earliest firsthand accounts of the interior: a country of "abrupt hills" and "numerous swale[s] & shallow lakes"; a region that, recently ravaged by fires, had a "naked & desolate appearance."[68] In addition to Davis's efforts, George Duberger, a company trader operating out of Fort Smith at this time under Davis's orders, explored toward the west and south in an attempt to establish a trade connection between Fort Smith and the St. Lawrence. The advantages of such a connection were obvious: the company would have north-south access from Ungava Bay through the interior to Montreal, access it had long sought, even if a detour eastward to Lake Melville and Hamilton Inlet had to be thrown into the bargain. This attempt to secure a route to the St. Lawrence failed; the country west and south of Fort Smith was too boggy and the lakes too shallow to support the large canoes favored by the company in hauling trade goods to the interior and shipping furs back out.

Duberger's failure to locate a route between Labrador and northern Quebec and the St. Lawrence did not deter the company from making other explorations in the southern portions of the Eastmain in the late 1830s and early 1840s. Independent traders working northward from the St. Lawrence had severely cut into the company's supposed monopoly over the fur trade in the southern Eastmain and Quebec. To counter these independents, the company increased its activities in the area south of the Rupert River and Lake Mistassini in the center of the peninsula almost halfway between Ungava Bay and the Gulf of St. Lawrence. Operating out of the company post at Nitchequon, north of Lake Mistassini, John Spencer and Thomas Beads mapped the area from Mistassini south and east to the St. Lawrence, apparently between 1837 and 1841; no records exist, but an 1841 map produced by Beads and Spencer indicates the expansion of geographical knowledge of the southern portions of interior Quebec.[69] The mountainous height of land north of the St. Lawrence River is shown on the map, as is the dense river and lake network through which the fur traders moved. The map was far from perfect—the company did not have cartographers the equivalent of David Thompson or Peter Fidler working in this area. But until the scientific surveys of the 1860s and 1870s, this map was probably the most accurate picture of one of the most difficult regions of the North American continent to understand geographically. With this last effort, exploration east and south of Hudson Bay by the company (and the fur trade) was virtually over.

## Exploration in the Canadian Pacific West, 1821–1846

Even before Ogden's far-reaching explorations in the Snake River country in the 1820s, the Hudson's Bay Company had made a crucial decision about the future of its western fiefdom and had divided the region west of the continental divide into two administrative districts: the Columbia Department, consisting of the bulk of the drainage basin of the Columbia River; and the New Caledonia Department, including the region north of the Columbia basin and up the coast to Alaska—the Canadian Pacific West.

Whereas the Snake and Columbia Rivers were the determining paths of exploration in the Columbia Department, enticing Ogden and others to seek to reveal the outlines of that area even before American entry into the intermountain West, the focal point of exploration in New Caledonia was the Fraser River. Governor Simpson described this mighty stream as having been "formed by Nature" to provide a communication from the interior to the coast; since, in Simpson's opinion, the Americans were probably destined to take over most of the Columbia district, the Fraser and other Pacific slope streams constituted the probable entries for the Hudson's Bay Company into the interior from the coast—entries that would assume even more importance if the Americans did indeed gain control of the Columbia and Fort Vancouver.[70] The interests of HBC men in New Caledonia, therefore, were the Fraser and other great rivers of the Pacific slope and the possible interconnections with eastward-flowing streams, particularly the Finlay River, the northern branch of the Peace River, reached by North West Company explorer John Finlay in 1797 but still essentially unknown.

Also of concern was the Russian presence, more to be feared in the coastal region in the 1820s than the as-yet only speculative competition from the Americans inland. Governor Simpson was convinced, on the basis of his interpretations of the journals of Captain James Cook and the travel accounts of Alexander Mackenzie, that some other great river (in addition to the Fraser and the Columbia) drained the reach of country between the mouth of the Fraser and Cook's Inlet.[71] In response to both the need to know more about the Fraser and other rivers of the Pacific slope and their potential use as avenues to Hudson Bay's drainage and the desire to learn how far inland the Russian influence extended, Simpson dispatched Peter Warren Dease to the Finlay River. Dease was instructed to follow the Finlay upstream to a point at which its waters intersected either with those of a great western stream (the "Great River of the West" was still a part of the company's image of the West in spite of the known Fraser and Columbia) or with the headwaters of the Liard River, a southern branch of the Mackenzie. Perhaps because of these rather confusing instructions to locate a connection either between the Finlay and the Pacific or between the Finlay and the Arctic, Dease vacillated, causing Simpson to note that he had been trying to get the western country explored but "could not succeed in procuring anyone to undertake it."[72] Finally, in 1824, Simpson's search for an explorer ended in his selection of Samuel Black.

Black had more field experience than most other North American explorers. A loyal member of the North West Company since 1804, he had traveled widely between Montreal and the Lake Athabasca region and beyond. More important, perhaps, he was widely read in the literature of North American exploration and had, according to his own accounts, long desired to make some significant contribution to geographical knowledge. The expedition to explore the connections between the Finlay River and the still-conjectural rivers of Pacific drainage must have seemed a great opportunity for him; putting aside his long-standing resentment toward the Hudson's Bay Company, he accepted Simpson's invitation. In preparation for his journey, he spent the winter of 1823–24 on the Peace River, from where he would have easy access to the Finlay when the ice melted in the spring. Here he made logistical preparations and obtained as much information as he could from native peoples about the lands west of the mountains. This was a style of exploration groundwork much like that practiced by other noted explorers such as David Thompson and Jedediah Smith.

Also like Thompson, Black was given instructions to search for what amounted to a will-o'-the-wisp: the Great River of the Northwest. In spite of the discoveries of the Fraser and the Columbia (the latter being the manifestation of the hypothetical Great River of the West), British geographical thought still was locked into the eighteenth-century image of numerous cardinal rivers rising in the western interior and flowing to both the Pacific and the Arctic. A northern or western mirror image of the St. Lawrence had not been found in the Fraser, the Columbia, or the Mackenzie, and Governor Simpson, among others, persisted in the belief that such a river or rivers existed. Simpson instructed Black to search the upper Finlay until he discovered a river that paralleled the Mackenzie; he was then to turn east across the divide between this river and the Mackenzie system to the Liard River to ascertain the ease of crossing the divide; after wintering on the Liard or Mackenzie, he was to retrace his steps back across the divide to the great transmountain river (which existed only in geographers' imaginations) and follow it to its mouth in the Arctic Ocean. This would give the Hudson's Bay Company an Arctic access route considerably farther west than Mackenzie's river and would, thereby, satisfy the commercial demands of the Northwest Passage, demands that had driven much North American exploration for three centuries. As a seasoned northwestern traveler, Black presumably had a different objective in mind—a Pacific coast stream that would enter the ocean north of the Fraser but without the tortured canyons and gorges through which that river flowed and that made it unsuitable for commercial travel. He had learned of such a river by questioning Iroquois trappers, many of whom had penetrated beyond the

Rocky Mountains into the region between the Rockies and the coastal ranges.[73] The search for this river linking the interior with the Pacific occupied Black's geographical imagination during his expedition in the summer of 1824.

Black and a small party of Iroquois voyageurs (many of them probably mixed-bloods), a métis interpreter and his wife, and a company clerk left Rocky Mountain Portage on the Peace River, heading up the Finlay and, hopefully, to the Pacific. On the eastern flank of the Rockies, after passing through a tortured canyon cut through the pale sandstone, two of the voyageurs deserted. Warning the remainder of his company of his determination to continue, alone if need be, Black led his command around the canyon still known as "Deserters' Canyon." Above the canyon and out of the Rockies proper, Black could see mountains to both the east and the west. He had entered the region of the Rocky Mountain Trench, a nine-hundred-mile depression separating the Rockies from the Coastal Ranges and stretching from northern Montana to the Liard River in northernmost British Columbia. Pressing up the Finlay, Black reached an area where the river's course veered sharply, with the stream emerging from the deep canyons of the western cordillera toward the Pacific. This was, indeed, the direction in which he desired to travel, hoping to find the connections between the upper Finlay and some great river of the Pacific. Yet the rapids and small waterfalls characteristic of mountain rivers required two full weeks of laborious travel before Black and his party emerged in the meadow and lake country some fifty miles from the Finlay's source. The region was disappointingly devoid of a fur resource—Black noted that it could "by no means come under the denomination of a Beaver Country"[74]—and little information could be gained from the local native peoples (the Sekanis) regarding the connections with western streams. Black continued to follow his orders to pursue the Finlay to its source, however, and after passing still more treacherous rapids and a major waterfall and avoiding a near-mutiny by one of his Iroquois voyageurs, Black reached the ultimate source of the Finlay River in Thutade Lake (indeed, the ultimate source of the Mackenzie system, nearly twenty-four hundred miles from the Arctic Ocean) in late June 1824.

Here Black had a difficult choice to make: either he could pursue his geographically confusing orders from Simpson to search overland for the source of the Liard River and some nebulous stream supposedly flowing into the Arctic west of the mouth of the Mackenzie or he could follow his own inclinations and head westward from Thutade Lake in search of a large Pacific stream. Perhaps because two months of the travel season had already passed or perhaps because Black was a loyal company servant, he chose the first alternative. Steered northward by Sekani guides, he set out toward the Liard River and Simpson's hoped-for northwestern stream that would replace the Mackenzie as a route to the Arctic. By mid-August, Black had crossed the divide between Pacific and Arctic streams, having traversed a country with scattered and poor native peoples and with even poorer prospects as good fur country. But he had also crossed the Stikine plateau, had encountered the Nahanni Indians, who were then actively engaged in trading with the Russians along the coast, and had forded many small westward-flowing streams that, had he followed them, could have led him to the Stikine River, the key to the fur trade route from the interior to the Pacific, a key that could have opened for the British the entire area of British Columbia between the Fraser and the Russian fur post at Sitka. But he did not follow these rivers, and when Black and his party came out of the plateau onto a large eastward-flowing stream that he recognized as a probable tributary of the Liard and, thence, the Mackenzie, he was forced to admit that either Simpson's hoped-for stream did not exist or, if it did, it was much too far north to be practicable as an access route to the interior and would therefore offer little competitive advantage over the Russians ensconced in their coastal fur-trading posts. From the Kechicka branch of the Liard, Black and his command retraced their route, reaching the company's post on the Peace River in late September 1824. Black's expedition had been a failure, largely because of Governor Simpson's failure to recognize the Stikine plateau and its westward-flowing streams for what they were: the route to the interior already being used to advantage by Russian traders. But the "Finlay River Expedition" did add significantly to the fund of accurate geographical knowledge on the northwestern regions of North America by clarifying one of the most puzzling topographic conundrums of western Canada: the Rocky Mountain Trench.

Black's expedition, as "an exercise in negative discovery" typified the exploratory efforts of the Hudson's Bay Company in the New Caledonia district.[75] Little more came of company exploration in the western mountains and coastal region of what is now British Columbia. Simpson did attempt to develop a coastal trade and to complete surveys along the coast, particularly after the Anglo-Russian Convention of 1825, which allowed both English and Americans access to the coastal and interior trade south of 54°40' north latitude.[76] And the company had engaged in some preliminary coastal surveying in 1824: ships under the command of Henry Hanwell were dispatched to survey good harbors along the coast and to ascertain the prospects for trade with native peoples, and James McMillan was directed to survey the lower course of the Fraser River and any connections that might exist between the Fraser and the Columbia.[77] Hanwell's coastal investigations were unsuccessful, and McMillan's mapping was seriously flawed because of reliance on faulty native lore. By the time of the 1825 agreement with Russia, the company knew little more about the coast than it had at the opening of the century, and it had few charts to equal those prepared by Captains Cook and Vancouver.

This changed somewhat with the 1826 appointment of a former Royal Navy officer, Aemilius Simpson (a relative of Governor Simpson's), as superintendent of the company's maritime operations. With instructions to survey the coast for the most appropriate sites for posts from which the company could trade with native peoples of the interior, Simpson quickly learned the entire region between Monterey and the mouth of the Stikine River, near the proscribed parallel beyond which British interests were prohibited. Simpson, after several surveys of the lower Fraser River, condemned that stream as one that "could no longer be thought of as a practicable communication with the interior," and he turned the company's attention to the Nass River.[78] Here Fort Simpson was built in 1832—interestingly enough, by Ogden, whose explorations of the Snake River country far to the south had opened that region to exploitation first by the company and, quickly thereafter, by the American fur trade of the Rockies. Between Ogden's construction of Fort Simpson in 1832 and the Oregon Treaty of 1846, relatively little significant exploration was conducted in the New Caledonia district. The company, having decided to develop Vancouver Island for farming in order to supply the Russians up the coast with agricultural goods, ordered several Hudson's Bay Company explorers to map the agricultural lands of the island, work that would be continued under Joseph Pemberton after 1845, but that was hardly worthy of being termed "exploration."[79]

Similarly, between 1826 and 1849, company surveyors and cartographers mapped the various horse brigade trails that company explorers— beginning with Thompson—had carved between the interior and the Pacific. Among these mappers was Archibald McDonald, who, between 1826 and 1827, improved on Thompson's early maps of the region between the junction of the Thompson and Fraser Rivers, providing the first truly accurate cartographic representation of the middle Fraser basin and overland connections between that rich fur area and the company posts on the coast and, inland, at Fort Okanagan. During the next decade, Simon McGillivray mapped out what he (and his superiors) assumed was a practicable horse route across the Babine Range to the Simpson (the Bulkley on modern maps) and the Skeena Rivers and thence to the coast, even though he had not covered the entire distance. Finally, during the years immediately following the 1846 Oregon Treaty, which ceded to the Americans rights over what had been the Columbia Department of the company, surveyors and mappers such as Alexander Anderson, James Yale, and Henry Peers reconnoitered the territory between the Fraser River's southward course and the Pacific, laying out horse brigade trails that were variously useful.[80]

Although these later surveys were immensely useful in filling in the gaps in geographical information and providing reasonably accurate maps of regions only glimpsed and charted crudely by the earliest explorers, none of them located anything resembling what Governor Simpson had sought in the 1820s: a Pacific or Arctic river route north of the Columbia and west of the Mackenzie. The Pacific rivers such as the Bella Coola and the Stikine—useful as they were for relatively small areas—gave the company no major access to either the interior or the ocean, access on which could be developed a profitable fur trade and, thus, further imperial British consolidation of control over an area still contested by British and Russian fur trade interests. The convoluted river courses and rugged terrain of the Canadian Rockies and the coastal cordillera between the Rocky Mountain Trench and the Pacific had prevented the company from finding a western counterpart to the St. Lawrence. Accordingly, even while the early stages of this final mapping of New Caledonia were under way, the company's official attention turned to the Liard River and, ultimately, to the rich fur-trading region of the Yukon and Alaska far to the northwest.

## Exploration in the Far Northwest, 1821–1851

Even before Governor Simpson had presented Black with instructions for his Finlay River Expedition of 1824, the Hudson's Bay Company had begun a tentative push toward the northwest in the hope of finding Simpson's hypothetical great river. Simpson wrote Alexander McLeod, of the Mackenzie district, about the Smith-Dease expedition to "the country laying to the West of the Mountains, through which by Indian reports there is a water communication running parallel with the Mackenzie River [that] is quite unknown to us, altho supposed to be rich in Fur bearing animals."[81]

McLeod could contribute to these westward probings, wrote Simpson, by sending parties from the Mackenzie toward the western mountains to link up with the Nahanni Indians, supposedly inhabiting mountain fastnesses rich in beaver. Apparently, McLeod led an expedition into the Mackenzie Mountains west of the Mackenzie in the winter of 1822–23, although no journal of his travels has survived. McLeod did write Simpson in the spring of 1823 and indicated that he had failed to contact the Nahannis or any other beaver-rich western tribes but that he had appointed a John McLeod (no relation to himself) to lead "a voyage of discovery to the westward."[82] The official objective of McLeod's 1823 journey was to ascend the Liard River to the South Nahanni branch and open trading relationships with the Indians (presumably the rumored Nahannis) living along its banks; if he could obtain word of the great western stream across the mountains from the Mackenzie basin, so much the better.

Although McLeod's 1823 expedition was partially successful (he did succeed in contacting a small band of Nahanni Indians), he was unable to learn anything of importance regarding rivers farther west, and in the summer of 1824 he was sent forth again, this time to reestablish contact with the native peoples he had met the preceding summer and to obtain better geographical data on Simpson's theoretical river west of the Mackenzie. He was marginally successful, since he did induce a number of the natives he had met in 1823 to return with him to Fort Simpson, at the junction of the Liard and Mackenzie Rivers in the Mackenzie district. The Nahannis were now within the company's trading range (although they had to be taught how to dress and preserve the skins of any beaver they captured); more important, they provided rumors that interested the company. Although they themselves knew of no great rivers west of the mountains, they were acquainted with tribes who dwelled on the western side of the mountains and who were supposed to have trading contacts with the Pacific.[83]

Such information bore no immediate fruit, although it must have stimulated Simpson's imagination and conditioned, at least in part, the confusing instructions he presented to Black the next year. The cusp of Simpson's (and nearly everyone else's) geographical confusion was the puzzling configuration of mountains and rivers in the region west of the Mackenzie. The drainage patterns here and north of its tributary, the Liard, actually formed valleys draining to three seas, unlike the situation far to the south, where the continental divide separated waters flowing to the Atlantic from those flowing to the Pacific, and unlike the geographical anomaly of the

Rocky Mountain Trench, where the eastern mountains (the Rockies) separated streams of Hudson Bay's drainage and which itself contained rivers that flowed ultimately to the Pacific but that were divided from other Pacific streams by the coastal cordillera west of the Trench. In the confusing northern drainage, the rivers east of the Mackenzie Mountains flowed to the river of the same name and thence to the Beaufort Sea of the Arctic. West of the Mackenzie Mountains, however, some streams found their way southward to the Liard and thence to the Mackenzie and the Beaufort Sea; others, such as the Stikine River, worked through the cordillera to the Pacific; still others fell into the upper reaches of the Pelly or Porcupine Rivers, both branches of the Yukon River, with an ultimate destination in the great Yukon delta on the Bering Sea.

Nor would this early series of explorations come close to clearing up the geographical confusion. For example, at the same time that McLeod was investigating the South Nahanni River and its hoped-for but impossible connections with Pacific or Arctic streams, another company party, led by Murdock McPherson, was heading into the Beaver River country. Like the South Nahanni, the Beaver flows southwest from the Mackenzie Mountains into the Liard River; also like the South Nahanni, it has no possible connections with the sources of streams flowing to the Pacific (although its source regions border those of the upper Pelly River branch of the Yukon). McPherson was no more successful than McLeod in establishing any kind of transmountain connections. Although he discovered a rich beaver country in the lower reaches of the Beaver River, he located no native peoples to entice into Fort Simpson for trade, and in that sense, his expedition was more of a failure than McLeod's. But although both expeditions had failed in their basic objective (the discovery of Simpson's theoretical western river), they had pushed the boundaries of the Mackenzie River district of the company westward and, by exploring the Liard Valley, pointed the direction for later explorers and traders.

For more than half a decade following McLeod's and McPherson's entry into the Liard River region, the Hudson's Bay Company primarily attempted to consolidate what it believed would be a rich trade with native peoples throughout the lower Liard Valley. But remaining among the company hierarchy were men like Simpson who believed in the Liard as a route to an as-yet-undiscovered great river to the west and, ultimately, as a route to the coast, where British and Russians and Americans were all competing for supremacy in the rich trade. A British advantage could be gained if the Hudson's Bay Company could develop a route into the coastal region from one of its major bases on the Mackenzie, Fort Simpson. Accordingly, McLeod was again ordered to explore the upper drainage basin of the Liard River by following the Liard directly into the mountains and traversing its treacherous rapids and canyons.

McLeod departed Fort Simpson in June 1831 and, with a small party, advanced by canoe up the Liard, alternately towing and paddling. By the middle of July, the party had reached that point in the Liard's course where the river veers sharply from a west-to-east direction to a north-to-south one, and here they began to encounter difficult navigation points: Hell Gate, Rapids of the Drowned, Devil's Rapids.[84] A month of extremely difficult travel took McLeod through the Liard's Grand Canyon and into the northernmost ranges of the Rockies proper. From here on, the mountains would be indistinguishable as separate ranges. If there was any cause for optimism at any point in this stretch of McLeod's journey, it was that he and his party had encountered groups of Indians who had, it seemed, contact both with Hudson's Bay Company posts farther down the Liard and with Russian or British trading establishments on the Pacific. This possibility fit Simpson's imaginary geography, on which McLeod's journey was based; it also fit the ultimate commercial aims of the company.

By early August, when the worst of the rapids had been passed and a loop of exploration had been closed, the McLeod party found, nailed to a tree, a written inscription indicating that this was the farthest interior penetration made by Black in 1824.[85] McLeod's journal does not indicate whether he attached any geographical significance to the fact that both he and Black had arrived at the same point on the upper Liard—after approaching it from different directions—without having discovered Governor Simpson's great river. McLeod did note that from this point on, the country was superb for hunting and trapping; his party was in the great valley of the upper Liard, where high and rugged mountain country gives way to more gently rounded terrain.[86] He also recorded the discovery of the Liard's most important western tributary, a stream that he named Dease River after Peter Warren Dease, who could have named it after himself if he had followed Simpson's directives for western exploration nearly a decade earlier. McLeod apparently attached relatively little significance to the direction from which the Dease River entered the Liard, noting only that it offered a promising route to the "interior." What it actually offered was a route to the Stikine River and thus the Pacific. Continuing upstream beyond the mouth of the Dease, McLeod came to the last major tributary of the Liard, the Frances River, and followed it, believing this to be the main stream (as, indeed, it is except in its geographical nomenclature). Some thirty-five miles up the Frances, McLeod decided he had gone far enough and turned to retrace his route to Fort Simpson. Governor Simpson's great western stream had not been discovered, but McLeod's journey had opened up the Liard River and its major western tributaries, the Dease and the Frances, to the Hudson's Bay Company.

A clash between Russians and HBC men near the mouth of the Stikine River on the Pacific coast in 1833 made it imperative that the interior-based company reach the Stikine from the eastern side of the mountains,[87] and in 1834 McLeod was again sent up the Liard, to complete what he had begun in 1831. McLeod's official instructions for the 1834 journey were to explore "the countries situated on the west side of the Rocky Mountains from the sources of the East Branch of the Liard."[88] Technically, this meant that he was supposed to attempt to reach the Pacific from the Fort Nelson River; since this stream flowed north into the Liard well below the confluence of the Liard and Dease, he knew these instructions were geographically absurd; his goal, when he left the company's new post of Fort Halkett on the upper Liard in the spring of 1834, was the Dease River. By early July he had reached the mouth of the Dease and turned up it to the west, encountering rapids and canyons as difficult as those on the Liard below the mouth of the Dease. But these rapids were less extensive; within a week the course of the river had smoothed out, and McLeod and his small party of five voyageurs and two natives traveled with relative ease through a country rich in game. Although falls and rapids occasionally obstructed travel, McLeod continued upstream and began searching for signs of the native peoples whom Black had contacted in 1824, peoples known to trade with Europeans by way of westward-flowing streams.

In late July, evidence of native peoples became more abundant, but the fact that no Indians had appeared suggested that they were fleeing ahead of McLeod and his party. Determining to proceed by land with an interpreter, McLeod left the river and headed over treeless hills south of the Dease, following an Indian trail. He gave up this pursuit after two days, but in the interval, he had discovered something of nearly equal importance: the source of the Dease River. From a high hill overlooking the valley of the Dease, McLeod viewed a large body of water—Dease Lake—the ultimate source of the Dease and the closest approach of the Liard River system to the waters of the Stikine River of the Pacific slope. Here he made a decision typical of explorers in western Canada since Mackenzie: "A complete stop being now put to our further advance by water, my intention is to secure our canoe and baggage at this place, and proceed for some days in the same direction [west] overland, and as no Mountains of any great Magnitude approach before us, I have every expectation some of the streams flowing to the Pacific can be no great distance, and before long anticipate the hope of drinking their waters."[89]

McLeod knew precisely what he was looking for, a fact that illustrates a crucial advantage the Hudson's Bay Company explorers had over their counterparts in the American Rockies: the former had open access to the journals, maps, and records of predecessors. Black, a decade earlier, had described in his journal a tribe of Indians whom he called the "trading Nahannies" and who dwelled on the banks of "the large River west of the Mountains"; he had also noted that these people followed a trail from their homeland to a large lake to the east. For McLeod, the geographical descriptions were clear: after crossing the slight divide west of Dease Lake, he would fall onto Pacific waters and, quite probably, locate the very people known to trade with Europeans at or near the Pacific coast.

A short overland journey west of Dease Lake brought McLeod and his party to Pacific waters, possibly the Tanzilla River tributary of the Stikine. A few more days of westward travel found them on "a considerable River, equal in magnitude to the rocky parts of the West Branch Liard River."[90] This was the Stikine River, whose headwaters were discovered by Black ten years before. If the mark of a competent explorer is recognizing the significance of his discoveries, then McLeod was more than competent; this was the stream, he wrote, "so much and so long spoken of by which the Coast Indians annually come up in boats of trading excursions with the Nahany and other Indians of the interior."[91] McLeod had found the key that unlocked the door to the trading route from the Mackenzie Valley (and ultimately, from Montreal) to the Pacific coast north of the Fraser River. He went no farther but returned to Dease Lake and, eventually, to the Liard River and the company posts in the Mackenzie district. He had failed to find Governor Simpson's western analogue to the Mackenzie, but he had found something that was, for the moment, more important.

McLeod was promoted and transferred to a softer land on the Columbia River. Governor Simpson—ever a man to pursue an unexpected advantage—quickly appointed a successor, another Scot: Robert Campbell. At Fort Simpson in 1835, Campbell met with McLeod and learned of the journey of the previous summer. He also learned that the governors of the company had planned to develop a trading post at Dease Lake as a stepping-stone to another post west of the divide between Arctic and Pacific waters. The company man who had originally been selected to develop these posts had failed, and in the spring of 1837 Campbell was instructed to develop a chain of fur trade posts west of Dease Lake.[92] He was beset by difficulties, including apocryphal tales of rampaging Nahanni Indians in the interior, and he did not proceed toward Dease Lake until the spring of 1838.

Reaching the head of the Dease without incident, Campbell and a small party crossed over the slight divide between the Dease and the Stikine drainages and soon found incontrovertible evidence of the coastal trade: a recently abandoned native dwelling containing three metal pots of probable Russian manufacture. The day after that discovery, Campbell encountered the Nahanni Indians, who informed him that they were traveling to a trade rendezvous on the Stikine River. In spite of the Indians' protestations that they could not protect the company men against the dominant Tlingit nation, who functioned as middlemen between the Russians and Americans on the coast and the interior tribes, Campbell decided to accompany the Nahannis to the "trade fair." Here, Campbell noted, natives "were gathered from all parts of the Western slope of the Rockies & from along the Pacific coast."[93] Also gathered, to Campbell's surprise, were four officers from the Russian-American Company, his potential adversary for the trading area from Dease Lake to the coast. Since the Russians were accompanied by the Tlingits, Campbell's Nahanni companions feared for the safety of their guest, and after a short visit, Campbell departed the rendezvous—but not before he hoisted "the H.B.C. flag & cut H.B.C. & date on a tree, thus taking possession of the country for the Company."[94]

Campbell returned to Dease Lake, where the men he had left behind were in the beginning stages of completing a trading post. Supplies were short, however, and Campbell returned to Fort Simpson in August to report that the river that McLeod had discovered four years earlier was, in fact, the Stikine, and that he had at least initiated trading contacts with western slope peoples. Impressed with his explorations, the company factor at Fort Simpson was less hopeful of trade in the face of Russian competition and would not even provide Campbell with additional trade goods to take back to Dease Lake; apparently, the company had never really intended to develop the interior trade region but only to interfere with the Russian competition.

Campbell returned to Dease Lake virtually empty-handed, arriving in the fall of 1838 after having traveled more than two thousand miles since spring. Over the winter at the new Dease Lake post, a shortage of food brought about near-starvation; in addition, the small company of traders was continually beset by the Nahannis, encouraged by the Tlingits to harass the Hudson's Bay Company force. The Dease Lake fort was finally abandoned in the spring of 1839, and Campbell returned to the Liard River to learn that Governor Simpson had worked out a trading agreement with the Russians for the coastal region. This agreement, the "Contract of 1839," gave the British control over the trade of the coastal region south of Russian America (Alaska), excluded the Americans from the trade north of the Columbian drainage, and guaranteed the Russians an annual "rent" or "lease" of two thousand beaver pelts.[95] This made the company's drive to the Stikine from the interior unnecessary and negated, in a commercial sense, the valiant exploratory efforts of Black, McLeod, and Campbell.[96] Those efforts were, however, of considerable significance to the company mapmakers, who could now sort out the complex set of relationships between the upper Liard drainage basin and the Stikine system of the Pacific slope. Another piece of the puzzle of western North America was set into place through fur trade exploration.

With the satisfactory resolution of the coastal trade competition between Russian and British interests, the Hudson's Bay Company explorers directed their attentions northwestward rather than westward and resurrected the still-viable dream of Governor Simpson: the discovery of a western counterpart of the Mackenzie River. The new foci of fur trade exploration would be the Peel River tributary of the Mackenzie, the Colville River draining into the Beaufort Sea of the Arctic Ocean, and the Yukon. Discovered during Captain John Franklin's 1825–27 Royal Navy surveys of the Arctic coast, the Peel River, a western tributary of the Mackenzie, enters the delta region of the main stream within a hundred miles of the Arctic Ocean.[97] Although it offered, in the company's opinion, a potential route to the supposed drainage divide between the Mackenzie and Simpson's hypothetical great western river, it was not explored further until 1839–40. The mouth of the Colville River had been discovered in 1837 by Thomas Simpson (a cousin of the governor's) and Peter Warren Dease as they sought to map the Arctic coastline west of the Mackenzie delta.[98] Although the largest river of Alaska's North Slope, the Colville is a short and relatively unimportant stream, one of many that drain the North Slope region and are separated from most of Alaska (and, thus, the drainage basin of the Yukon River) by the east-west Brooks Range. However, Simpson and Dease, believing they had found Governor Simpson's great western river, encouraged the company to open up the farther Northwest for exploration and elevated the potential importance of the discovered but unexplored Peel River as an access route west to the headwaters of the Colville, assumed to drain a much larger area than it actually does. Finally, the Yukon—still in the realm of the geographical unknown as the 1830s ended—was the great river of the North, the real-world version of Governor Simpson's imaginary northwestern stream.

The first steps in the attempt to link the Mackenzie River basin with that of the Colville via the Peel River came in 1839 when John Bell, the company's commander at Fort Good Hope (located approximately four hundred miles upstream from the Mackenzie delta), was directed to take a small party and ascend the Peel River to its source to ascertain "whether a practicable communication exists between the Peel and Colville Rivers."[99] Leaving Fort Good Hope in late June 1839, Bell and a party of about a half-dozen men (including a native guide) moved up the Peel River, encountering only minor rapids until they reached the Mackenzie Mountains. Movement through this range was difficult, since the river was now full of rapids and deep canyons; the countryside abounded in beaver, however, and Bell noted the advantages of a trading post farther downstream toward the Peel's confluence with the Mackenzie. After moving nearly two hundred miles upstream, Bell had followed the Peel as close to its source as he thought "practicable" and had learned that this source was "lost in the innumerable streams and rivulets which descend from the [Mackenzie] mountains and that late in the season it becomes dry."[100] The upper Peel, in his opinion, did not provide a viable route to the Colville; he was, of course, absolutely correct, but for all the wrong reasons, since the sources of the Peel and the Colville are separated by a vast region. And the Peel does not provide an easy access to the upper Yukon, but neither Bell nor any other company men had the foggiest notions of the existence of the Northwest's major stream.

Returning to the lower Peel, Bell began to scout for another route that would lead west from the Peel drainage to what he and virtually everyone else who had any geographical knowledge of the area believed would be the valley of the upper Colville. Natives living near the mouth of the Peel had told him that a small tributary, the Rat River, which entered the Peel almost at the same point as the major stream's debouchment into the Mackenzie, could be followed to a height of land and a portage to the west; Bell decided to proceed by canoe up the Rat. After a difficult four-day journey, the source of the Rat River was reached in a broad meadow that, his native guides informed him, was the head of the portage to the great river beyond the mountains. Curiously, Bell did not follow up on this information; if he had, he would have crossed McDougall Pass at an elevation of slightly more than one thousand feet and dropped into the upper waters of a river later to bear his name, a river that could be followed downstream to the Porcupine River and thence down to the Yukon. So close to the unveiling of a low crossing of the continental divide and to the discovery of the Yukon Basin, Bell retreated downstream to begin construction of a post (known today as Fort McPherson) near the mouth of the Peel River.

Two years later, in 1841, Bell's assistant at the new Peel River post, Alexander Isbister, completed what Bell had left unfinished. Traveling up the Rat River in the early spring of the year in search of food to supply the trading post until the summer hunting season could begin, Isbister reached the Rat's source in the McDougall Pass area. About a mile from the farthest source of the Rat, Isbister found another small stream known today as the Bell River, one of the easternmost feeder streams of the Yukon Basin. During the spring melt, the source waters of the Rat and the Bell mingle and the traveler can pass from the Mackenzie Basin to the Yukon Basin by canoe without a portage. This was a real-world counterpart of the fabled "interlocking" drainage that had been a foundation of exploration of the North American western interior almost from the beginning; it was this feature that Mackenzie had sought on his famous mountain crossing between the Peace and the Fraser and that Lewis and Clark had searched for between the upper Missouri and the Columbia. If not the best route from the Mackenzie to the Yukon, this surely was one of the best, but Isbister did not recognize it as such and returned to the Peel River post with provisions acquired through trade with the Indians. It would be years before the significance of his discovery was realized.[101]

Farther south, as Bell and Isbister were traversing the Peel River country, Robert Campbell was continuing his pursuit of a route between the Mackenzie and a great western stream (now assumed to be the Colville) by way of the upper Liard River. Ordering him to locate a lake supposed to drain into the northern branches of the Liard and to then "be alert" for any rivers draining to the north or northwest, Campbell's company superiors perhaps hoped he would solve the same kind of geographical puzzle that he had pieced together by establishing the overland route between the western branch of the Liard and the Stikine River. In the spring of 1840 Campbell and a party of seven traveled up the Liard to its northern fork, the Frances River, and thence up that stream and through its seemingly innumerable canyons hemmed in between the Campbell Range of the Pelly Mountains to the west and Logan Mountain to east. In mid-July they reached Frances Lake, the source of the Frances River, and proceeded up the lake's western arm searching the mountains to the west for a break that might provide access to the great river (the Colville) supposed to lie in that direction.[102]

Some twenty-five miles up the lake's western arm, Campbell decided to strike out overland, following a small unnavigable stream toward the mountains on the west. This stream, Finlayson Creek, led to Finlayson Lake and, just beyond, to a series of small streams that ran toward the west. Campbell, with the uncanny geographical instinct that had served him well during his previous explorations, knew that he had crossed an important divide; this was confirmed a few days later when, from the top of a high ridge, he viewed "a large river in the distance flowing Northwest."[103] This was the Pelly River, one of the Yukon's major tributaries; Campbell, locked into the geographical conceptualizations of his time (and of his commander Governor Simpson), noted that he had "no doubt it is identical with the Colvile."[104] Believing that he had achieved his goal, Campbell returned to Fort Halkett, the company post on the Liard, where he would begin planning for the expansion of the Hudson's Bay Company empire into the northwestern valley that Simpson had convinced nearly all company men was geographically synonymous with the Colville River.

Campbell did not explore further into the Yukon region for another three years. Meanwhile, as early as 1841 Governor Simpson had written Campbell a letter in which he conjectured that Campbell's western river was not the Colville at all but was a stream of the Pacific. Campbell was nevertheless instructed to build and begin operating a trading establishment on Frances Lake, an activity that occupied his time until 1843. During these years, Campbell's own thinking (perhaps influenced by his superiors) began to change; the Pelly River, in his conjectural geography of early 1843, was either the Copper River or the apocryphal Cook's River that had haunted maps and minds since Captain James Cook's coastal explorations more than a half-century earlier. In either case, the Pelly was now viewed as a stream that flowed into country that was, by international agreement, part of Russian America and thence closed to the British. But it drained what appeared to be a rich fur resource; always more interested in commercial gain than the advance of pure geographical knowledge, the company determined to pursue at least its commercial operations toward the Pelly

River, and to that end, in the spring of 1843, Campbell and a small party of six men departed the new Frances Lake post he had established and headed for the great river he had discovered three years earlier.[105]

Campbell reached the Pelly River in only three days' travel from Frances Lake and proceeded downstream for about a week until he reached the confluence of the Pelly and Lewes Rivers, near which he met natives who had never before seen whites. One of the company's chief objectives—the opening of new country to trade—was already achieved. But for the timidity of his men, who refused to proceed farther, another goal might have been reached as well. On most modern maps, the river below the junction of the Pelly and the Lewes is known as the Yukon; this was the great river to the Pacific that Simpson had hypothesized, and although Campbell was still nearly fourteen hundred miles from its mouth when he abandoned his advance and returned to Frances Lake, he missed a chance at a monumental discovery. Writing years later, he regretfully noted that he "was perfectly heedless of what was passing."[106] So too was Governor Simpson, who, on Campbell's return, simply instructed him to erect a new trading post (Fort Selkirk) at the junction of the Pelly and Lewes and to begin draining the fur resources from this rich country. The company, having found what it had been seeking for twenty years, abandoned further search and turned its attention once again to the Northwest and the misunderstood and overestimated Colville.

Since Campbell had explored the connections between the Liard and the great western river, Bell again was instructed to locate a crossing of the divide between the lower Mackenzie and the western stream that was believed to be the Colville but that was, in fact, the Yukon. In 1842 Bell headed west from the company's post on the lower Peel River and crossed the Richardson Mountains, the northernmost section of the Mackenzie Mountains and, thus, the northernmost range of the Rocky Mountains.[107] In four or five days Bell journeyed from the Pelly River across the low Richardson Range to a small stream that, a native guide informed him, flowed into a larger river coming up from the south. Following the small stream, today called the Bell River, Bell and his party reached a larger stream after three days; believing this stream to be simply a branch of the river he had followed from the Richardson divide, rather than the "great river" the natives had reported, Bell determined to travel down the larger stream until he reached the "great river." In fact, the stream he had reached was the Porcupine River, the Yukon's largest northeastern tributary. Like Campbell, Bell had reached a major stream of the Yukon system. Also like Campbell, Bell aborted any further exploration and returned to the Peel River post. His correspondence indicates that he turned back because he was unable to secure an Indian guide to lead him farther downstream;[108] he may also have known that he was near the 141st meridian of longitude, the legal dividing line between British and Russian territory in the Northwest, and may not have wanted to advance into a Russian-controlled region. But if this journey ended somewhat inconclusively, Bell was now able to place the Colville River in his imaginary geography: it was the stream reported by natives as coming up from the south, and it flowed through a rich fur country that, although difficult to reach, was exploitable by the company.

Three years later, in the summer of 1845, Bell made another trip westward into the region he believed to be the drainage basin of the upper Colville. Following the same overland route that he had used to cross the Richardson Range in 1842, Bell and a party of four (two voyageurs and two native guides and interpreters) first reached the Bell River, where they built canoes, and three days later arrived at the Porcupine, which they followed downstream, encountering no obstacles. On 16 June 1845 Bell and his men reached the mouth of the Porcupine River, which here fell into a much larger stream; this larger stream, they learned from natives, was called "the Youcon," meaning "white water" or "swift-flowing river."[109] The British had reached the fourth-longest river of North America, the great western river they had been hearing about since Kutchin Indians had told Mackenzie of it in 1789 and the real-world version of the hypothetical great river that Governor Simpson hoped would open as profitable an area for trade as had the Mackenzie River. After exploring the junction of the Porcupine and the Yukon for a week and after learning that natives in the area traded with whites along the seacoast, Bell returned to the Mackenzie district, where he reported on the Yukon country: "According to their [the natives'] accounts, the country is rich in Beaver, Martens, Bears, and Moose deer, and the River abounds with Salmon, the latter part of the Summer being the season they are most plentifull, when they dry enough for winter consumption. The Salmon ascends the River a great distance but disappear in the fall."[110]

From this account, the Hudson's Bay Company men should have learned something they still did not comprehend. The Yukon was a stream of Pacific rather than Arctic drainage and therefore could not be, as Campbell and Bell and Simpson still believed, the Colville. As far as the company men knew, there was no trade east of Point Barrow; thus, reports of natives trading with whites along the seacoast must have meant that the river led to the Pacific. More important, the reports of salmon in the Yukon's waters should have confirmed that the stream was of Pacific rather than Arctic drainage—since the early 1800s, the defining trait of a Pacific slope stream had been the presence of salmon. However, more important to Bell and Campbell, at least, was the fact that the Pelly River, discovered by Campbell to the south, and the Yukon River, discovered by Bell to the north, were the same stream. Since that stream, flowing from the region explored by Campbell to the region explored by Bell, took a northerly course, they assumed that this course would continue and that the river would therefore empty into the Arctic rather than the Pacific. The Yukon's course is a geographical conundrum, much as that of the Niger in Africa; with some of its headwaters in the south located almost within sight of the Pacific, the river's feeder streams flow first toward the northeast, then turn toward the north, then head westward and eventually southwestward to enter the Pacific Ocean. There was no way, without traveling the river from its junction with the Porcupine to its mouth, that the company men could have understood this mighty looping course. Believing the river to be the Colville simply made more sense, since this belief fit the known geographical facts and was consistent with acceptable geographical logic. For the British, however, this belief may have been a critical mistake that ultimately cost them the possession of Alaska.

The drainage basin of the Yukon River dominates Alaska. The point of discovery by the HBC men was the very heart of the basin and, more important, an area virtually devoid of the influence of other imperial powers—specifically Russia. The Anglo-Russian Convention of 1825 had established the 141st meridian as the dividing line between British America and Russian America, and Bell's advance to the Yukon clearly put him well into Russian territory west of that meridian. But the Porcupine-Yukon confluence was a great distance from any center of Russian fur trade. In spite of an apparent desire to expand trade into the interior, the Russian-American Company had done relatively little in that regard. In 1833 the Russian-American Company had built Fort Saint Michael on the shores of Norton Sound just east of the mouth of the Yukon. From this point, presumably, a drive to the interior could be made, and yet the farthest Russian advance up the Yukon before the 1840s was a 450-mile journey made in 1836 by Vasily Malakhov to the junction of the Yukon and Koyukuk Rivers.[111] Malakhov noted that a profitable trading post could be erected here, and in 1842–43 the Russian-American Company built its major interior post at Nulato. From 1843 on, the only major Russian exploration of the interior was an expedition commanded by Lavrentiy Alekseyevich Zagoskin in the spring of 1843. Zagoskin penetrated only about 150 miles beyond Nulato, however; thus the farthest Russian advance into the interior was about 600 miles from the mouth of the river and still some 1,300 miles from its source. The Yukon Valley above Nulato was left to the British, although the Russians probably did not expect much British activity in the area.[112]

In a sense, the Russians were correct. The Hudson's Bay Company had no plans to further penetrate the Yukon country beyond the advances of Bell and Campbell. Fort Selkirk, at the junction of the Pelly and Lewes Rivers, and Fort Yukon, at the junction of the Porcupine and Yukon Rivers, were built in the mid-1840s to take advantage of the rich fur trade of the region. Governor Simpson specifically warned Campbell (and anyone else) not to follow the Yukon to the sea "as it would bring us into competition with our Russian neighbours, with whom we are desirous of maintaining a good understanding."[113] Simpson's stated desire to be neighborly did not, however, apply to the company's commercial interests. From Fort Selkirk and Fort Yukon, the upper and central portions of the river basin were to be systematically stripped of as many furs as could be obtained from trading with the natives or from trapping. This "scorched earth" policy was similar to that undertaken by the company ten to twenty years before in the Snake River country, and apparently the motivation was much the same: strip the country of furs, and no one else would want it. In both cases the operations were commercial successes, since large quantities of furs were brought into HBC posts; in both cases the operations were imperial and political failures, since the Americans quickly took over Oregon Country after the 1830s and the Russians maintained legal territorial control of North America west of the 141st meridian until selling Russian America to the United States in 1867.

During the remainder of the 1840s, Hudson's Bay Company activity was confined to commerce; moving into the Yukon country in two pincers, from the southeast via the Liard and from the northeast via the Peel, the company began to drain the fur resource of the Yukon Valley. The last major exploration of the fur trade in the farther Northwest was almost an afterthought. In 1851 Campbell, desiring to prove that his and Bell's conjectures regarding the Yukon nearly a decade earlier were correct, set out from Fort Selkirk to travel downstream to Fort Yukon, thus establishing that the Pelly and the Porcupine were both tributaries of the Yukon. This concluding venture of company exploration was, ironically, "an easy, rather matter-of-fact affair."[114] Campbell's trip down the Yukon met no obstacles, and in late June 1851 Fort Yukon came into view. Campbell had linked the company's two thrusts into the interior, a fact that would become even more apparent when he returned to the Mackenzie district via the Richardson Mountain portage and the Peel River. More important, Campbell had demonstrated that his and Bell's geographical conjectures were correct; henceforth the Yukon was known as the single great river of the northwestern interior.[115] No longer would the Colville appear on maps as a great stream draining a vast interior region. Although much of that region remained to be explored by scientists and surveyors in the later years of the nineteenth century, Campbell's 1851 journey was the capstone of fur trade exploration in the Northwest.

## The End of Fur Trade Exploration

Campbell's 1851 journey, the final high-water mark of fur trade exploration by the British in North America, also signaled the peak of British fur trade influence in western North America. Campbell and many other key Hudson's Bay Company personnel left North America for England and Scotland in the early 1850s, and the company abandoned nearly all its trading establishments west of the continental divide, pulling back almost entirely from the Yukon Valley and the interior. Only Fort Yukon remained as a reminder of the commercial and imperial ambitions of the Company of Adventurers, and eventually it too was gone, taken over by the Americans in 1868. The expansion of the Hudson's Bay Company west of the Mackenzie Mountains had not been a success commercially, but it had been a tremendous success geographically, filling in the gaps in the understanding of the five regions of Canada and the Northwest.

The final labors of fur trade explorers would begin to bear fruit as early as 1854, with the publication of the Arrowsmith map of British America. Once again, Campbell was a key player. After returning to Great Britain in 1853, Campbell met with the cartographers of the London firm of Aaron and John Arrowsmith, the premier limners of North American geography since the 1780s. The Arrowsmith company had ready access to data from the archives of the Hudson's Bay Company, but obtaining information from one of the company's most experienced field explorers was even better. Campbell's knowledge allowed the Arrowsmith cartographers to fill in the only major blank region remaining on their maps of North America: "The area west of the Mackenzie River had been filled with little but conjecture, and even the irrepressible, though apocryphal, concept of Cook's River found life there. Arrowsmith's 1854 map of British America, based on the company's explorations, changed that. The great rivers of the Northwest were all accurately laid out: the Peel, the Liard, the Stikine, the Porcupine, the Yukon headwaters, the Pelly, and the Lewes."[116]

The 1854 Arrowsmith map represented the Canadian fur trade's final contributions to geographical knowledge and thus brought the period of exploration to its intellectual end. The symbolic end came three years later, in 1857, with the retirement of Sir George Simpson from his post as governor of the Hudson's Bay Company and with the death of David Thompson, of the North West Company. The era of the fur trade was over, and henceforth the Canadian interior would be explored by scientists. But that initial search for the fur resource—and, more important, for the routes by which that resource could be taken to the entrepôts of the St. Lawrence—contributed the most to the ultimate understanding of the northern and western regions of North America.

# 17 / The Invention of the American West: Fur Trade Exploration, 1821–1839

JOHN L. ALLEN

In 1821 the city-village of St. Louis had probably the most strategic location in North America. A former colonial outpost of both France and Spain, St. Louis had become an American possession with the purchase of the Louisiana Territory in 1803 and continued to serve, as it had since its founding, as the gateway to both the Northwest, containing the drainage basins of the Missouri and the Columbia Rivers, and the Southwest, the area south of the Missouri's drainage basin. In the Northwest, the region east of the Rocky Mountains was indisputably American territory by virtue of the Purchase. West of the continental divide, both British and American interests laid claim to "Oregon Country." In the Southwest, that part lying east of the Rocky Mountains was also within the Territory of Louisiana and was therefore American territory. But Mexico claimed much of the Southwest, particularly south of the Mississippi's western tributaries and west of the Rockies, as part of what had been the "Interior Provinces" of New Spain before Mexican independence. St. Louis, therefore, occupied a geographical location of enormous political and economic significance.

A key aspect of the geostrategic position of St. Louis was its traditional role as the heart of the fur trade of western North America below the forty-ninth parallel.[1] Here, in the waterfront taverns and warehouses nestled under the bluffs of the Mississippi's western shore, fur trade families such as the Chouteaus conducted the business that brought the wealth of "brown gold" to this gateway to the Northwest and the Southwest. Since the mid-1700s, these families had dominated the fur traffic of the Missouri River between St. Louis and the Indian nations of the Missouri's upper reaches—the Sioux and Mandan and Arikara and Hidatsa Indians.[2] The scions of these St. Louis families had rarely engaged in exploration themselves; but they had sent their employees into the region of the Missouri's Great Bend (in central North Dakota) or the areas around the mouths of the Kansas and Platte Rivers. On the upper Missouri these traders had contested with the Canadian traders of the Northwest Company and the Hudson's Bay Company for furs brought into rude, temporary trading posts by Indian hunters. In the valleys of the Platte and Kansas, they had encountered Spanish troops attempting to protect the northern borders of New Spain.

When St. Louis became an American outpost in 1803, its strategic relevance increased. It was from St. Louis that the government-sponsored explorations of Meriwether Lewis and William Clark, Zebulon Pike, and Stephen Long departed for their investigations of the West. These Jeffersonian explorations, grounded in the ideals of the Enlightenment, had been devoted as much to the acquisition of knowledge as to the extension of American political and economic control over the western interior. But even as the official expeditions of the government were taking place, other American explorers engaged in the fur trade of the Rocky Mountain region were beginning to operate out of St. Louis. The older French merchant houses were joined by new companies, beginning with the Missouri Fur Company and culminating in the corporate giants, the American Fur Company and the Rocky Mountain Fur Company, which dominated the Rocky Mountain fur trade until the 1840s.

By 1821 these new economic entities, and the trapper-trader-explorer cadres they sponsored, were no longer Jeffersonian but were now Jacksonian in their operational behavior. That is, they probed the West less for knowledge and more for economic gain; their exploration was entrepreneurial rather than intellectual. But because they operated in geographical regions claimed by several nations—the United States, Great Britain, and Mexico—these St. Louis fur traders and trappers were more than just men seeking a living. They were also "diplomats in buckskin,"[3] engaged in the tricky business of international intrigue as well as in the more common business of obtaining furs; as such, they were ultimately responsible for the eventual success of the United States in gaining economic and political domination over both the Northwest and the Southwest. They were also behind one of the largest and fastest expansions of geographical knowledge resulting from exploration since the first two or three decades following Columbus's discovery of the New World. More than any other group of explorers in the American West, these trappers and traders "invented" the West by presenting the American public with an accessible set of geographical images of mountains and valleys and deserts and lush green prairies.

Traditionally, geographers and historians have viewed the members of the St. Louis fur trade—particularly that breed known as the "mountain men"—as explorers who knew a great deal about the lands they traversed but who seldom communicated this knowledge to those responsible for the institutionalizing of geographical lore in the form of maps, atlases, or geographies.[4] In this view, formal American geographical knowledge was transmitted ex post facto: former "mountain men" served as guides for Oregon and California and Great Salt Lake valley wagon trains; they served as guides and scouts for the U.S. Army in both its military and its exploratory capacities. In these ways alone, according to the customary interpretation, fur trader geographical lore began to appear on the maps and in the journals of the emigrants and army officers and, from there, in published forms available to the American public. This view could not be farther from the truth. Even before 1821, but particularly thereafter, geographical information from the fur trade became a part of the geographical information accessible to the American public relatively quickly through newspapers, personal correspondence, and word of mouth from the waterfront taverns in St. Louis and other frontier cities. To understand this process, we need to comprehend something about the state of American geographical knowledge of the farther West before and after the major period of fur trade exploration between 1821 and 1839.

Before the epic expedition of Lewis and Clark in 1804–6, the prevailing views of the geography of the western interior of the trans-Mississippi West were based on the concept of the West as a uniform garden of great agricultural wealth and on the notion of continental symmetry—that is, the idea that the western half of the continent of North America was a mirror image of the eastern half. In this symmetrical view, the western mountains (only vaguely beginning to be recognized as the Rocky Mountain system) were analogues of the Appalachians, separating the waters that flowed to the Pacific from those that flowed to the Gulf of Mexico just as the Appalachians separated the waters flowing to the Atlantic from those flowing to the Gulf of Mexico via the Mississippi system. Nicholas King's map,[5] drawn in 1803 to provide Lewis with the most current geographical information on western North America, showed five cardinal elements of this conceptual geography of the West. First, the Rocky Mountains formed the core of continental symmetry west of the Mississippi and, as such, acted as a continental divide that parted the Atlantic from the Pacific streams. Second, although the mountains served as a divide between Atlantic and Pacific streams, that divide was not necessarily a long, linear one but may have been a pyramidal height of land or core drainage region where, between the forty-fifth and fiftieth parallels of latitude, all major rivers of the West had their sources. Third, the Rockies were configured as a narrow, single-ridged structure, extending from north to south and not extensive in either height or breadth. Fourth, the sources of the navigable waters of the Columbia and the Missouri lay on opposite sides of this narrow, single ridge and were connected by a short portage. And fifth, the Rockies may have had a southern terminus around 45° north, where a large southern branch of the Columbia had its source. The single most important belief of this conceptual geography was that "a direct & practicable water communication across this continent for the purposes of commerce" could be found by following the Missouri River to its source in the western mountains.[6] From this region, which also served as a source area for virtually all other western rivers, a way could be found to reach the major rivers (especially the Columbia) that flowed west to the Pacific. Between 1804 and 1821, these assumptions were tested by both formal (government-sponsored) and informal (fur-trade based) exploration.

The major government-sponsored expeditions—of Lewis and Clark (1804–6), of Pike (1807–8), and of Long (1819–20)—did little to erode the assumption of a common-source area for western rivers, although they added much to the store of geographical information about the Rocky Mountains. Lewis and Clark, for example, unable to locate this source area in their crossing of the continental divide between the headwaters of the Missouri and those of the Columbia in western Montana, simply moved it farther south in their final maps and reports and postulated a region of some four hundred square miles wherein rose the headwaters of the Missouri, the Yellowstone, the Platte, the Arkansas, the Rio Grande, the Colorado, and the mythical Pacific slope streams of the San Buenaventura (a pure invention but based on some Spanish reports of the late 1700s) and the Multnomah (an overlengthened and oversized version of the Willamette, which enters the Columbia from the south at the present site of Portland, Oregon). Both Pike and Long, exploring the area of the Colorado Rockies, the source region of the Platte, Arkansas, Rio Grande, and Colorado, also continued to speculate about a common-source area somewhere south of Lewis and Clark's crossing of the divide. Pike, for example, described a "grand reservoir of snows and fountains"—the source of the major western rivers.[7]

This "remarkable exercise in fictional geography" was bolstered by the explorations of the early fur trade explorers.[8] From 1806 to 1808 John Colter explored the upper regions of the Yellowstone Basin (the region of the

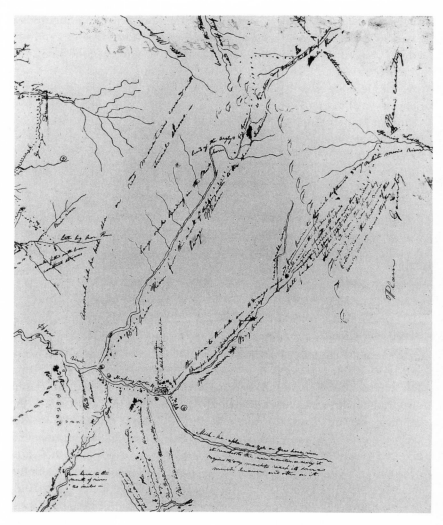

17.1 *Detail from a manuscript map of the Bighorn Basin in northwestern Wyoming (George Drouillard, c. 1810). This first fur trade map of the farther West shows the travels of both Drouillard and John Colter. A legend on the map indicates the belief in the proximity of the source region of the Bighorn (Shoshone) to a "Spanish" river. Courtesy of the Missouri Historical Society.*

Shoshone and the Bighorn-Wind Rivers) and, along with George Drouillard exploring in the same area in 1808–10, confirmed the proximity of the Missouri's headwaters to those of the "Spanish rivers," meaning the Colorado and Rio Grande. Andrew Henry—who, like Colter and Drouillard, worked for Manuel Lisa's St. Louis–based Missouri Fur Company—crossed the divide between the upper Yellowstone and the Snake River and also confirmed the existence of a common-source region for the major western streams. Still another of Lisa's men, Ezekial Williams, traveled south from the Bighorn-Yellowstone confluence to (if his story can be believed) the Arkansas River; he too corroborated the belief in the proximity of the headwaters of major western streams and described, in the area between the Yellowstone and the Arkansas, a "fountain head of the great rivers."[9] Finally, between 1811 and 1813, Wilson Price Hunt and Robert Stuart of John Jacob Astor's Pacific Fur Company (also operating out of St. Louis) covered the extensive country between the Missouri-Platte drainage and the Pacific coast. Neither Hunt, on his westbound journey to the Pacific via the Bighorn-Wind, Snake, and Columbia, nor Stuart, on his eastbound trek via the Columbia, Snake, Green, and Platte, provided any geographical information that eroded the fixed concept of the common-source region. (Stuart did, however, discover South Pass—although the rediscovery of this continental divide crossing by Jedediah Smith over a decade later would be more important for its subsequent use as an avenue of travel.)

These informal explorations by Colter, Drouillard, Henry, Williams, Hunt, and Stuart became a part of conventional geographical lore. Much of their information—including the common-source region—was shown on the large map of western North America that Clark prepared between 1809 and 1811 for publication (1814) with the account of his and Lewis's transcontinental trek.[10] Early fur trade information also figured prominently on John Melish's large "Map of the United States with the Contiguous British and Spanish Possessions" in 1816.[11] Melish showed the Buenaventura flowing from a large lake in the common-source region, which also served as the "principal source" of the Colorado, Multnomah, Rio Grande, Arkansas, Platte, Bighorn, and Snake. No less a geographical authority than Thomas Jefferson wrote Melish, commending him on the "luminous view" the map provided, presumably including Melish's representation of the core drainage region with its implications for Jefferson's continuing dream of transcontinental water travel.[12]

In 1821, at the end of the initial period of governmental and fur trade exploration during the Jeffersonian period, the cardinal elements of western

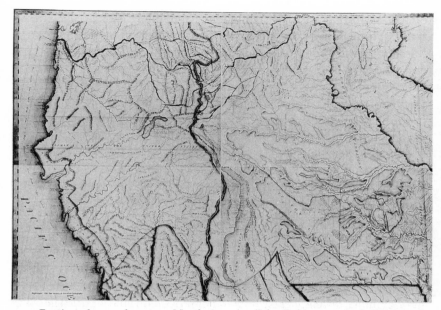

*17.2 Portion of map of western North America (John Robinson, 1819). Robinson's map illustrates the entry of information from the Lewis and Clark and Pike expeditions into American geographical lore. Reproduced from the original by the Institute of Historical Cartography, San Francisco, California.*

geography had changed somewhat. For example, the Rocky Mountains were recognized as more of a barrier than they had been before Lewis and Clark. But the geographical images that resulted from the early period of exploration still held out the hope of a transcontinental water crossing through a common-source region in which lay the headwaters of virtually all of the West's major rivers. The explorations of the American fur trade in the Rocky Mountains between 1821 and 1839, expeditions using as operational bases both St. Louis and the Santa Fe–Taos settlements of New Mexico, would dramatically change that conceptual geography.

## The Early Period of American Fur Trade Exploration: The Taos Trappers

In 1813 Astoria, John Jacob Astor's fur post at the mouth of the Columbia, was sold to the British North West Company. For a time, American influ-

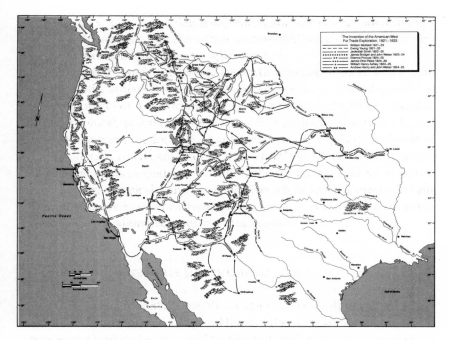

*Map 17.1 The Invention of the American West: Fur Trade Exploration, 1821–1833.*

ence in the Pacific Northwest ended. Continuing fur trade exploration in the regions west of the Rockies would be carried out by members of the North West Company and, after the merger of 1821, the Hudson's Bay Company, with the most important explorations occurring between 1822 and 1829. Their activities (detailed in chapter 16) were extremely important and, through the maps of the British cartographic firm of Arrowsmith, were rather rapidly transmitted to the public, in both Europe and America. While the brigades of the North West Company and the Hudson's Bay Company were exploring the "Snake River Country" of the intermountain West between the Rockies and the Cascades, however, American trading and trapping, out of St. Louis, was taking place east of the Rockies, on the Missouri River, even though a leading figure in the early fur trade, Manuel Lisa, had withdrawn from the field. During this period, the fur trade was confined primarily to the lower Missouri; further penetration of the country beyond the Missouri's Great Bend (in central North Dakota) was effectively limited by the combined might of the Sioux and Arikara Indian nations, who closed the Missouri to American travel (at least partially through the encouragement of British fur traders, who were fearful of American competition in the northern plains) and by the continued hostility of the Blackfeet, who controlled the known passes across the Rocky Mountains at the head of the Missouri. In addition, the St. Louis trade was temporarily weakened by the withdrawal of Lisa, by increasing competition, and by inadequate capitalization.[13] Far to the south, however, in the settlements of Santa Fe and Taos—Spanish colonial settlements until Mexican independence in 1821—other significant fur trade explorations began as early as 1813.

Dozens—perhaps even hundreds—of American trappers had moved into the Mexican settlements of Santa Fe and Taos and the mountains surrounding these settlements in search of furs. After 1816 these "Taos trappers," like all other American trappers, adopted a new fur trade strategy, one developed by Donald McKenzie of the North West Company. Rather than seeking Indian tribes with whom they could trade for furs, they themselves trapped the beaver—in the rich valleys of the Sangre de Cristo, San Juan, and other ranges of the southern Rockies—and then returned to Santa Fe, where they sold the furs to merchants who had crossed the Santa Fe Trail from St. Louis. From 1813 to 1821, the probings of the Taos trappers northward into the New Mexico and Colorado Rockies were tentative. We do not even know precisely who the primary fur trade explorers were or exactly where they went. That they were active in expanding northward and westward is evidenced by the fact that the Mexican governor of Santa Fe in 1824 issued an edict prohibiting American trapping in the northern provinces of New Mexico. Unfortunately, little, if any, of the geographical knowledge gathered by these early adventurers became a part of American geographical lore. After 1821, however, the Taos trappers provided geographical information that was crucial to the American understanding of the entire West up to 1850.

The most important contributions were made by William Wolfskill, Ewing Young, Kit Carson, Etienne Provost, James Ohio Pattie, and Tom "Peg Leg" Smith. In 1821–23 William Wolfskill and a few others trapped beaver streams as far east as El Paso and as far west and north as the Chama and San Juan country of northwestern New Mexico and possibly even into the Colorado Rockies.[14] In the process, they began to clear up the confusion surrounding the headwater regions of the Rio Grande and the Arkansas and concluded that these rivers had sources far south of those of the Yellowstone and Missouri, although this conclusion was not immediately apparent in American maps of the Southwest in this period.[15] A year later, in 1824, as many as five separate parties of Taos trappers, including one led by Ewing Young and another led by Kit Carson, traveled north and west through the Colorado Rockies to the Green River. They may have trapped in the Great Basin streams that flowed from the Wasatch and Uinta Mountains into the Great Salt Lake; if so, they were probably the first Americans to enter that area and the first white men since the Spanish explorations of Fathers Silvestre Vilez de Escalante and Francisco Atanasio Domínguez in the 1770s. One documented visitor to this area was Etienne Provost, who led an American party into the Great Basin in 1824 and possibly discovered the Great Salt Lake.[16] However, none of these trapping parties recognized the Great Basin for what it is—a region of interior drainage from which no rivers flow outward to an ocean. The failure to recognize the peculiar nature of the drainage system of the Great Basin was the primary reason American geographers imagined that such rivers as the Multnomah and the San Buenaventura flowed westward from the Rockies to the Pacific. According to accepted geographical thought, any stretch of country the size of the Great Basin had to be drained by major streams.

One major exploration during this period added to the confusion over the common-source area. The adventures of James Ohio Pattie, who claimed to have made a remarkable trek in 1826, were published and edited in 1831 by Reverend Timothy Flint of Cincinnati.[17] According to the narrative, while trapping on the Gila River, Pattie and his fellow trappers were attacked by Indians near present-day Phoenix, Arizona. Pattie and two others escaped and joined forces with another trapper brigade led by Ewing Young. Then began, if Pattie's story can be believed, one of the most incredible journeys of the fur trade period. According to Pattie, the trapper party journeyed down the Gila River to the Colorado and then turned north up the Colorado, where they were the first white men to see the Grand Canyon since Escalante in 1776. They followed the Colorado northward to its source in the Grand River of the western Colorado Rockies and then crossed the eastern ranges of the Rockies into the source region of the Platte River. Following the Platte northward, they reached the Bighorn and the Yellowstone, which they ascended to its source. They then "crossed the ridges of the Rocky Mountains to Clarke's fork of the Columbia" and ascended the Clark's Fork (Pattie probably meant the Snake River) "to its head which is in Lang's [Long's] Peak, near the head waters of the Platte. We thence struck our course for the head waters of the Arkansas."[18] Crossing the mountains to the east, Pattie's group followed an Indian trail southward down the eastern flank of the Rockies to Taos and Santa Fe. This incredible journey—which would have covered the area from southern Arizona to Wyoming to Idaho and back to Colorado and New Mexico—supposedly took three and a half months. A modern understanding of geography suggests that such a feat would have been impossible. But no modern understanding of western regions existed at the time of Pattie's travels, and his *Personal Narratives* led many to believe in the proximity of the rivers of the Southwest (the Colorado and Rio Grande) with those of the Northwest (the Bighorn, Yellowstone, and Columbia). Pattie claimed: "All these streams upon which we have been trapping, rise from sources which interlock with each other, and the same range of peaks at very short distances from each other. These form the heads of the Red river of the east, and the Colorado of the west, Rio del Norte [Rio Grande], Arkansas, Platte, Yellowstone, Missouri, and Columbia."[19] William Clark himself could not have described his hypothetical common-source region any better. Most of these travels undoubtedly took place either in Pattie's imagination or in Flint's; but the popularity of *The Personal Narratives of James O. Pattie* suggests that, apocryphal or not, the geography described by Pattie became a part of American lore.

Besides the drive northward into the Colorado Rockies and the Great Basin, American trappers also moved west. With Mexican traders out of Santa Fe, Albuquerque, and Taos, Americans followed the Gila River toward the Colorado in an attempt to rediscover an ancient Spanish route that led to California. The best known of these journeys was made in 1827, by Pattie. In his book, Pattie described traveling from Santa Fe to the Gila River and down to the Colorado. He crossed the Colorado into the desert country to the west and struggled through the desert to the Mexican mission at San Diego. His accounts give one of the first pictures of the desert region of the Southwest: "The plain over which we passed should be named the devil's plain . . . that it was more hotter as hell and that none but teyvils could live upon it. . . . During our passage across it we saw not a single bird, nor the track of any quadruped, or in fact any thing that had life, not even a sprig, week or grass blade, except a single shrubby tree, under which we found a little shade."[20] Pattie also presented a glowing picture of California life before the American conquest of the region in the 1840s: "Here they have rich vineyards, and raise a great variety of the fruits of almost all climates."[21] If Pattie's topographical view of the West was faulty, he at least had begun to erode the older notions of the West as a region of uniform fertility and abundance.

After Pattie's California trip, several other parties of Santa Fe and Taos trappers trekked across the barren desert country between the southern Rockies and the California coast. In 1829–30, for example, at least three large parties—one under the command of Ewing Young and guided by Kit Carson, one led by Thomas "Peg Leg" Smith, and one led by William Wolf-skill—followed various versions of the Old Spanish Trail from the New Mexico settlements to California.[22] At least some of the geographical knowledge gained by these travelers began to appear on maps. Much more did not, and although the core of the Southwest—the New Mexico settlements and the southern Rockies—was somewhat well known by the end of the 1820s, most of the remainder was not. The daring Taos trappers who opened up much of the Southwest to fur trade exploitation drew no maps and wrote no geographies. They did not even talk much about their exploits in the taverns and countinghouses of St. Louis. The 1814 publication of the journals of the Lewis and Clark expedition still provided most Americans with their view of the West, and the common-source area for western streams (including the Buenaventura and Multnomah) was still as much a part of this view as it had been immediately after Lewis and Clark. Most Americans continued to think of the West as a region of immense agricultural wealth and potential. Certainly the Taos trappers knew that the deserts of the Southwest would not support an American agricultural civilization, but little of their information became public knowledge.

## William Ashley's "Enterprising Young Men"

The watershed year of 1822, which saw the opening of the important fur trade discoveries in both the Southwest and the Northwest, also marked the beginning of the St. Louis–based fur trade explorers' expeditions into the central and northern Rocky Mountain area. These "free trappers"—the elite of the mountain men—were so named because they were their own bosses. They did not work as wage slaves for one company but contracted to trap the beaver of the Rockies during the winter months and sell their winter's bounty to the highest bidder at the rendezvous, an annual gathering in the mountains. At these summer events, usually held in the valleys west of the Wyoming Rockies, the trappers exchanged their furs for cash, supplies, and the whiskey called "Taos Lightning," a mixture of grain alcohol, red pepper, gunpowder, and worse.

These free trappers have been characterized as "expectant capitalists," a characterization that would fit many other Americans of the early nineteenth century as well.[23] Although just as single-minded in their view of beaver-as-profit as were other trappers, the free trappers' goals differed from those of the members of either the Taos trade or the Snake River brigade of the Hudson's Bay Company. The Taos trappers and the Hudson's Bay men were mostly *explorers* who roamed new country looking for specific objectives—streams and rivers filled with beaver. The free trappers of the St. Louis trade, on the other hand, were primarily *discoverers* who searched the terrain for whatever they might find. The Taos trappers and the Hudson's Bay men reported to their superiors on the unsuitability of the lands for anything other than trapping. The free trappers not only described the West in terms of the rich resource in beaver pelts but also defined the ways to get into the West, to move across the Rockies, to reach the Pacific—and more important, they outlined what could be done with the land once it was settled by people other than trappers. Unlike their counterparts among the Spanish and Mexicans in the Southwest or the British and Canadians in the Northwest, these free trappers sought and found mountain, plains, desert routes that could be used not only by the fur trade brigades but also by the Missouri farmers enticed by the word "Oregon" or the New York shopkeepers bound for the goldfields of California. Between 1822 and 1839 these free trappers reconnoitered virtually the entire West.

The American free trappers relied less on Native American geographical information than did their Canadian and British counterparts to the north. After 1822 the Indians and the American trappers were not partners in the fur trade enterprise but were competitors for the same resource base. Whereas in Canada the fur trade, from its inception, had nearly always depended on the ability of Native Americans to supply white traders with furs in exchange for items of European or colonial manufacture, the American fur trade bypassed the native populations economically. As competitors, whites and Indians in the Rocky Mountain region rarely exchanged geographical information; and because of the reluctance (or inability) of American trappers to keep logs or journals of their travels, little is known about those exchanges that did occur.

Yet there was some interaction between American trappers and natives. A great deal of the technology and knowledge that allowed Americans to survive in the western wilderness was borrowed from Native Americans. Indians (particularly such tribes as the Shoshone and Nez Percé) also supplied a source of horses for trappers whose beasts were well-worn from riding through rugged country and transporting heavy loads of furs from winter campsites to summer rendezvous. However, the Native American tribes of the Rocky Mountain region generally viewed the white trappers as intruders (with some exceptions, such as the Crow—or Absaroka—nation, with whom white trappers often wintered). Hostilities often erupted. Unfortunately, the character of the interaction between Indian and trapper meant that the brilliant culture of the high plains and Rocky Mountain Indians was irrevocably changed and, ultimately, nearly destroyed by the forces of American economic expansion into and utilization of the West, forces that the fur trappers set in motion by their explorations from 1822 to 1839.

While the Hudson's Bay Company was beginning its southward penetration into the Snake River country in 1822 and the Taos trappers were working the beaver streams of the southern Rockies, the free trappers' exploring ventures were beginning to take shape in St. Louis. In 1808, the year of Lisa's return from his first successful year of fur trading on the upper Missouri, a young Virginian named William Henry Ashley moved to St. Louis.[24] During the War of 1812, Ashley developed a business in mining saltpeter (for use in gunpowder) in Potosi, Missouri. Here he met Andrew Henry, one of Lisa's men who had traveled beyond the Rockies in 1810. Since the War of 1812 and the beginning of Indian hostilities in the Missouri Valley, the St. Louis fur trade had been diverted toward Santa Fe and the Southwest, away from the Missouri River. Thus Henry's experience with Lisa in the Northwest was of little value in St. Louis, and he had abandoned the fur trade and gone into lead mining. Ashley, however, became fascinated with Henry's tales of the wealth to be made in the beaver trade; in 1821 the two men formed a partnership to reopen the St. Louis fur trade on the Missouri River. They decided to operate their new fur company along the lines of Donald McKenzie's organization of the Snake River Brigade of the Hudson's Bay Company. Instead of building trading posts and attempting to induce Indians in to trade furs for St. Louis baubles, they would send trappers to hunt the beaver. The trapping season would continue throughout the fall of the year, when the beaver pelts were at their richest. The trappers would then winter either with Indian tribes or at a fort. After a short spring trapping season, they would come together during the summer at some predetermined site to sell their furs to Ashley and Henry.

The first step for the new Ashley-Henry fur company was to gather a trapping brigade. On 13 February 1822 the partners placed the following advertisement in a St. Louis newspaper: "*Enterprising Young Men* . . . to ascend the Missouri to its source, there to be employed for one, two, or three years."[25] The "enterprising young men" who responded to this advertisement included James Bridger, James Clyman, Thomas "Broken Hand" Fitzpatrick, Hugh Glass, Edward Rose, Jedediah Smith, William Sublette, and John Weber. With Henry and Ashley, these men would play a decisive role in bringing the entire West under American control and in expanding the geographical knowledge of the area from the Rocky Mountains to the Pacific Ocean.[26] Unlike James Pattie, Ashley's "enterprising young men" did not write narratives, nor did they draw maps that received wide publication. But they did talk and correspond—to editors of St. Louis newspapers and to friends and relatives back home in Virginia, Kentucky, or Tennessee. Much of the geographical information came, therefore, not through the formal or scientific channels of the published atlas or geography text but through periodical literature, much of it designed for popular consumption.

The Ashley-Henry venture did not begin as successfully as the partners might have wished. An article from the *St. Louis Enquirer* before their departure indicated that their intent was to "direct their course to the three forks of the Missouri, a region it is said, which contains a wealth in Furs, not surpassed by the mines of Peru. . . . They will be gone for three years, during which time it is contemplated to visit the heads of the different rivers under the mountains, and perhaps to go as far on the other side as the mouth of the Columbia."[27] This was an ambitious plan indeed, one that was quickly thwarted by the realities of western travel and Indian hostility. In April 1822 Henry led a party up the Missouri River bound for the beaver country near the mouth of the Yellowstone, having abandoned his original notion of traveling as far as the Missouri's Three Forks. His trip was uneventful, but a second boat sent up the Missouri in May overturned, and most of the expedition's supplies were lost. Back in St. Louis, Ashley outfitted still another boat and headed upstream to join Henry in September near the Arikara villages in what is now northern South Dakota. Henry continued up the Missouri to its junction with the Yellowstone, where he began building Henry's Fort (later called Fort Union). This important outpost was to serve as the base of operations for the Ashley-Henry fur trappers in the Yellowstone-Bighorn country.

Little successful trapping was carried out during the winter of 1822–23, and in early 1823 Ashley and Henry returned to St. Louis for more supplies. In the early spring of 1823 their second flotilla of boats carrying supplies headed up the Missouri, bound for Henry's Fort at the mouth of the Yellowstone. When the boats arrived at the Arikara villages, a battle between the Indians and the Ashley-Henry men broke out. After fourteen of the trappers were killed, Ashley and Henry retreated to their boats and set off down the Missouri for Fort Kiowa, the temporary post they had established at the junction of the Niobrara and the Missouri. Even a campaign against the Arikaras by a detachment of the U.S. Army led by Colonel Henry Leavenworth failed to open the Missouri River for American travel. By this time it was fall, and Ashley and Henry, growing desperate, decided to abandon the Missouri River route in favor of an overland route. The partners planned to send out two overland expeditions from Fort Kiowa: Henry would lead one expedition across South Dakota and north along the present-day border between the Dakotas and Montana toward Henry's Fort; the second party would strike out across South Dakota and Wyoming for the Wind River Range. This decision to abandon the traditional route pioneered by Lewis and Clark was momentous. It not only officially initiated the central Rocky Mountain fur trade but also began the development of the route that would be used by hundreds of thousands of migrants bound for California, Oregon, and the Great Salt Lake in the years to come.[28]

When Henry reached his fort on the Yellowstone, he discovered that most of his horses had been stolen and the Indians were not bringing in furs. He moved his base of operations from Henry's Fort south to the junction of the Powder River and the Yellowstone. From here John Weber and a party of trappers were sent west across the Big Horn mountains and into the Bighorn Basin, following a route pioneered by George Drouillard under Lisa's command more than a decade earlier. From the Bighorn Basin, Weber and his men traveled south to the Wind River valley, the winter home of the Crow nation. They discovered no new territory but did confirm the findings of Drouillard and Colter, including the belief that the Wind River (the upper Bighorn) of the Missouri system headed close to the waters of the "Spanish River"—which could have been either the Rio Grande or the Colorado.

The other overland party sent westward from Fort Kiowa in the fall of 1823 was more important—not because of what it accomplished immediately but because of the young man picked to lead it, Jedediah Strong Smith.[29] Smith was a New Yorker, born into a pioneering family in the Susquehanna Valley of southern New York in 1799. By 1810 his family had moved farther west into Erie County, Pennsylvania; in the Pennsylvania woods, Smith learned wilderness skills from his father, and unlike most other young men on the western frontier, he received a good education from a pioneer physician who was a close family friend. This physician gave Smith a copy of the 1814 publication of the Lewis and Clark journals.[30] Perhaps this gift set young Smith's feet on the path of western adventure, or perhaps the relentless westering spirit of Smith's family and the American frontier culture guided him toward a career in the Far West. By 1817 Smith's family had moved still farther west, into Ashland County, Ohio, and in 1821 Jedediah Smith left home for the Illinois country, where he hunted in 1821–22, and then traveled down the Mississippi River to St. Louis. Here he read the advertisement placed in the *St. Louis Gazette and Public Advertiser* by Ashley and Henry. What an opportunity for an enterprising young man this advertisement must have presented! Smith signed on with the Ashley-Henry company and became a member of Henry's Yellowstone party that built Henry's Fort.

When Smith was selected to lead the second overland party to the mountains in the fall of 1823, he was only twenty-three years old. But he was already a seasoned veteran of the West. He had traveled into the Musselshell River country of central Montana in 1822 as a member of Henry's party. In 1823 he had come back down the Missouri to participate in the fight at the Arikara villages. He had proven himself as one of the most capable men in the entire Ashley-Henry command and was the logical choice to lead one of the two overland parties westward. History proved this decision to be wise; between 1823 and 1831, Smith did more to open the West than any other single member of the American fur trade.

Smith's journey westward in the fall of 1823 led him and his men from the Missouri Valley westward across South Dakota to the Badlands and the Black Hills. With the possible exception of the La Verendrye brothers, French traders in the 1730s, Smith and his trappers were probably the first white men to see this outlying range of the Rockies. From the Black Hills, they traveled across the Thunder Basin region of northeastern Wyoming into the Powder River basin. They continued west toward and across the Big Horn Mountains into the Bighorn Basin, which Smith described as "beautiful, fit for cultivation, and filled with game."[31] They crossed the Bighorn Basin southward, following the Bighorn River through its canyon in the Owlcreek Mountains (where the river's name changes to the Wind River). Following the Wind River upstream, they came to the Wind River valley, where they found Weber's party camped with the Crow Indians. This was the first time the free trappers wintered with the Crows after the fall beaver hunt. It would not be the last.[32]

In early 1824, as the Indians of the northern plains became even more angry with the renewal of white activities in the Yellowstone region, full-scale war broke out between the white trappers and the Blackfeet and Arikara Indians throughout the area. Because of continued Indian hostilities, Ashley and Henry decided to move their base of trapping operations yet again—to the Wind River valley, where the combined Weber and Smith parties had camped during the winter of 1823–24.

From this camp, in early 1824, Smith launched one of the first of his momentous journeys of exploration. He and his men traveled up the Wind River valley and attempted to cross the continental divide by Union Pass, used by Andrew Henry in 1810. They were turned back by heavy snows, and after retreating to the Crow encampment, they journeyed back down the Wind River and southwest along the eastern flank of the Wind River Mountains, "which is here the main Rockey mountains and the main dividing ridge between the Atlantic and Pacific."[33] Near the southern end of the Wind River Range, they came upon the waters of the Sweetwater River (a branch of the North Platte), which they followed westward to its source. According to one member of the party, they traveled "westward through a barren land where their only water was secured from melting snow."[34] Soon after leaving the Sweetwater and crossing the "barren land," Smith and his men came to the Big Sandy River and, shortly after that, the Green or "Seedskadee" River, which Smith recognized as "a Spanish river." By this he meant either the upper waters of the Rio Grande or those of the Colorado. The Green is, of course, the upper Colorado; Smith's party had crossed the South Pass from east to west. Others of Smith's party believed they were on the waters of the "Rio Grande del Norte" and therefore still east of the continental divide.[35] But Smith had his geography correct. Without knowing it, he had almost closed an arc of exploration begun on the other end by Etienne Provost, who, working north out of Taos, was in the same general area at the same time.

Smith had rediscovered the easy continental divide crossing discovered by Robert Stuart more than ten years before. Unlike Stuart's crossing, however, Smith's discovery was crucial to later events. Although nothing in the journals of this exploration indicate that Smith recognized what he had done, from this time on the South Pass was the main route to and from the central Rocky Mountains and the core of the American fur trade region.[36] This was demonstrated in the spring of 1824 when Smith and his men, after a successful spring trapping season, met a party led by Thomas Fitzpatrick and John Clyman, bringing furs south from the Wind River valley. Smith and Fitzpatrick combined their furs, and Fitzpatrick and Clyman carried them down the Sweetwater to the Platte. Not knowing whether they were on "the Platt or the Arkansas," Fitzpatrick and Clyman simply decided to head downriver in an easterly direction, "knowing the civilization could be reached Eastward."[37] The river into which the Sweetwater flowed was, of course, the Platte, and the eastbound party traveled down that river to Fort Atkinson near its junction with the Missouri and then down that river to St. Louis. The eastern portion of the Oregon Trail—from South Platte to St. Louis—had been utilized for the first time for commercial purposes, a fact was not lost on St. Louis newspapers, which reported in 1824 the discovery "of a passage by which loaded waggons can at this time reach the navigable waters of the Columbia River. This route lies South of the one explored by Lewis and Clarke."[38]

After dispatching Fitzpatrick and Clyman to carry the catch of beaver back to St. Louis, Smith had recrossed South Pass to the stream he was now calling the Seedskadee (which means "prairie chicken" in the Shoshone language) or Green River. Here he was joined by Weber, who had followed Smith southward from the Crow camp on the Wind River, also crossing South Pass to get to the valley of the Green River. When the Weber party and the Smith party joined near present-day Big Piney, on the Green River of west-central Wyoming, they created the first fur trade rendezvous, an annual gathering that served as the economic center of the free trapping economy. From this point, the force of "enterprising young men" was again split into two groups. Smith, leading one party, would trap northward along the Green River. The other party, under the command of Weber, would trap the Green River downstream toward the south.[39]

Smith's party, in 1824–25, continued the westward extension of the fur trade along what in a few years would be the Oregon Trail. They trapped up the Green River and then crossed from the upper Green to the Snake River near the site of later Fort Hall in southern Idaho. Then they proceeded overland northward to the Salmon River of eastern Idaho. Here they linked up with a brigade of Hudson's Bay Company trappers under the command of Alexander Ross. They traveled north with the Hudson's Bay men to their post on the Clark's Fork of the Columbia. On this trek, they journeyed through the Bitterroot Valley of western Montana, thereby interlocking the American fur trade of St. Louis with the British fur trade in the Northwest, giving notice that the Hudson's Bay men would now have competition in the inland empire between the Rockies and the Cascades. In making his trip north through the Bitterroot Valley, Smith also linked his discovery of South Pass with the Rocky Mountain crossing of Lewis and Clark nineteen years before. Later that year, Smith traveled back south, in the company of Peter Skene Ogden of the Hudson's Bay Company, to rejoin Weber's party, which had been trapping on the Green River. This reunion took place in the lovely Cache Valley, northeast of the Great Salt Lake. Smith's southward trip had been uneventful, but he noted that he had crossed the "waters of the grand lake or Buenaventura."[40] The great mythical river and, therefore, Clark's common-source region were both still part of Smith's geographical picture of the farther West.

While Smith had been traveling in the Snake River country, the party led by Weber had made significant discoveries of its own. The initial route of the party that was left to trap on "the Spanish River" is uncertain, but apparently most of them traveled down the Green River for a distance, believing themselves to be on the Rio Grande. They then turned westward, across Ham's Fork of the Green River, and crossed the divide between the Green River and the Bear River of the Great Salt Lake drainage. Following the waters of the Bear River, which they believed to be the Multnomah, they crossed into the Cache Valley, where they were joined by Smith in the winter of 1824–25. At some time during the Weber party's travels in this region—either in the late fall of 1824 or the early spring of 1825—another momentous discovery was made.

One of Weber's men, Jim Bridger, followed the Bear River south to its mouth in the Great Salt Lake. Bridger may not have been the first to see the lake. Contemporary sources indicate that Provost, working out of Santa Fe, may have discovered this lake as early as 1820,[41] whereas another claimant to original discovery, Samuel Adams Ruddock, describes a visit to "Lake Timpanogos" (the early name attached to the Great Salt Lake on Spanish maps) in 1821.[42] The Provost claim may be valid; the Ruddock claim is almost certainly not, since Ruddock asserted that Lake Timpanogos was "the principal source of the Multnomah of Lewis and Clark," which he followed to the Columbia through "a rich and delightful valley . . . similar to the lands in Kentucky, Tennessee, and Ohio, producing the same species of wood and timber, and the climate is uncommonly mild." Writing a less apt description of the country between the Great Salt Lake and the Columbia would be difficult to do; Ruddock's journey must be added to others in the western apocrypha. But whether Provost or some other member of the fur trade reached the Great Salt Lake before Bridger in the winter of 1824–25 is irrelevant, since Bridger was the first to document the discovery. As reported in the journals of one of his companions, Bridger at first thought that he had reached the Pacific: "He went to its [Salt Lake's] margin and tasted the water, and on his return reported his discovery. The fact of the water being salt induced the belief that it was an arm of the Pacific Ocean."[43] This belief was rather quickly abandoned, although Bridger and other trappers continued to assume that the lake had an outlet in a river that flowed to the Pacific. A search for this outlet was, however, fruitless. At the same time that Bridger was at the Great Salt Lake, another party of trappers was south of the lake, on the waters of the Weber River, which they believed to be the Buenaventura.

Ashley and Henry's free trappers were learning a great deal about the geography of the central Rocky Mountain region. But in spite of their explorations of 1824–25, their picture of that area was still extremely inaccurate. It is not surprising that the trappers under the command of Smith and Weber were confused about where the continental divide was and about whether the rivers encountered west of South Pass were part of the drainage of the Colorado, Snake, Rio Grande, Multnomah, or Buenaventura. First, there were no accurate maps of the region, and the best map— Clark's map of 1814—showed a common-source region for all western streams in the general location of the South Pass, at approximately 43° north latitude. Second, the geography of the area itself is confusing. South Pass, the true continental divide that separates the drainage basin of the Missouri River from that of the Colorado, is almost unnoticeable. Modern travelers passing through the region today depend entirely on a Bureau of Land Management sign to alert them they have crossed the continental divide. Beyond the valley of the upper Colorado or the Green River, divides that are nearly as imperceptible separate the waters of the Colorado system from both the upper streams of the Snake River basin and the waters that flow to the Great Salt Lake and the Great Basin.

Even today, it is very difficult, from ground level and without good maps, to figure out the drainage systems in this area, where, within a few hundred square miles, rivers rise and flow to the Gulf of Mexico, the Gulf of California, the Columbia River, and the interior Great Basin. For these men in the 1800s, even with all their accumulated wilderness experience, it was equally difficult to determine the correct geographical relationships of the mountains and rivers of the Wyoming Rockies. The state of geographical knowledge at the time was so poor that even if these men had had maps with them, those maps would have been of no help. The Great Basin and its interior drainage system, in which no rivers flow out to an ocean, was not something that had even been dreamed of in 1824–25. Virtually all American maps of the period showed rivers—either the Multnomah or the

Buenaventura or both—draining the vast stretch of country south of the Snake and west of the Rockies.[44]

Geographical confusion aside, the Smith-Weber-Bridger explorations changed the character of the American fur trade, moving it away from the upper Missouri drainage for the first time and into the transmontane West. This locational shift was, of course, partly due to the discovery of South Pass, which facilitated the crossing of the divide into Pacific or interior drainage streams by a route a great deal easier than the northern passes discovered by Lewis and Clark—and well away from the Blackfeet, who continued to block American advances into the headwaters region of the Missouri River. The traditional Missouri River route was also becoming more difficult because of continuing hostility from the Sioux and Arikara Indians, making the newly utilized route of the Platte and South Pass very attractive indeed—a route over which horses rather than boats could serve as the major conveyance of trade and one that quickly became viewed as passable for wagon travel. The avoidance of the Platte as a route to the Rockies had been the result of the innavigability of that stream; the use of horse and wagon travel eliminated that deficiency, and river travel was seen as both unnecessary and inefficient. And the possibility—still a real one in 1825—that the South Pass led to waters that, in the form of the Buenaventura, flowed directly to the Pacific made the central route to the Rockies even more preferable to the northern route of Lewis and Clark.

In an attempt to clear up the geographical confusion surrounding the country west of South Pass (and particularly the question of the direction and course of the Seedskadee), William Ashley himself made a journey in 1825. He hoped to discover the great river or rivers that would lead to the Pacific. Ashley had been back in St. Louis tending to the business side of his and Henry's fur enterprise during the Smith-Weber-Bridger explorations in 1823–24. Late in 1824 he left St. Louis for Council Bluffs, across the Missouri from the mouth of the Platte, and then crossed the Missouri to the Platte Valley, which he followed westward, bound for the Rocky Mountains. With him were twenty-five men, fifty packhorses, and the first wagons to be used in the central Rocky Mountain fur trade.[45] Ashley and his party traveled up the Platte River to the forks of the Platte and then followed the South Platte to the west. Near present-day Fort Collins, Colorado, he took an Indian road up the Cache La Poudre River across the ridge of the Front Range between that tributary of the South Platte and the Laramie plains in southeastern Wyoming; Ashley reported that this crossing was "so gradual as to cause but little fatigue in travelling over them.

The valleys and south sides of the hills were but partially covered with snow, and the latter presented already in a light degree the verdure of spring, while the former were filled with numerous herds of buffaloe, deer, and antelope."[46] He traveled north through the Laramie plains, "delighted with variegated scenery," and across the Great Divide basin of central Wyoming. Unknowingly, he was pioneering the route across Wyoming along which Jim Bridger would guide Captain Howard Stansbury of the U.S. Army in 1850 and that would later be used by the Union Pacific Railroad, the Lincoln Highway (U.S. 30), and Interstate 80.

Beyond the Great Divide basin, Ashley and his men came to Smith's Seedskadee (Green River) in April 1825. From this point, Ashley could see the Wind River Mountains far to the north and noted that they divided "the waters of the Yellow Stone and Bighorn from some of the headwaters of the Columbia . . . [and] separated the southern sources of Lewis's fork of the Columbia [the Snake River] from what I suppose to be the headwaters of the Rio Colorado of the West [the Green River]."[47] At this point, Ashley was clearly viewing his position on the Green River as one that was well within the core drainage regions postulated by Clark and an entire generation of geographers and cartographers. But he still needed to determine whether or not the Seedskadee was the Colorado or the Buenaventura. He divided his command into four parties: one party, commanded by himself, would explore down the Green River (the Seedskadee), which he still hoped would prove to be the Buenaventura and thus provide a water route to the Pacific; a second party, led by James Clyman, would explore up the Green River in an attempt to locate its source; a third party, under the command of Zacharias Ham, would trap in the mountains to the west, near the Bear River; and the fourth party, under Thomas Fitzpatrick, would trap the Green River tributaries entering the river from the Uinta Mountains to the south. All four parties were to meet back at the Green River for a rendezvous in the summer of 1825. This was a well-conceived plan both to open new country and to exploit a new fur resource area.

Ashley left the Green River camp in April 1825 and began floating down the Green River in a "bullboat" made of buffalo hide stretched over supple pieces of wood. He and his men floated through the spectacular Flaming Gorge Canyon and Lodore Canyon through the Uinta Mountains, as far south as the extremely rough canyonland just north of Desolation Canyon in eastern Utah. Throughout this stretch of the Green, Ashley noted that the mountains "approach . . . to the water's edge on either side of the river and rise almost perpendicular to an immense height . . . the river is bounded by lofty mountains heaped together in the greatest disorder, exhibiting a surface as barren as can be imagined."[48] Near Desolation Canyon, Ashley and his men met two trappers from Provost's party out of Taos; the two informed the Ashley men that the river they were on was not the Buenaventura but was the upper portion of the Colorado. This information was corroborated by that obtained from some natives (probably Utes) who indicated that the river did not lead directly to the Pacific but was "the Rio Colorado of the West, [which] continued its course as far as they had any knowledge of it, southwest through a mountainous country."[49] Disappointed that he had not discovered a new route to the Pacific, but with a new and more accurate understanding of the geography of the central Rockies, Ashley turned back north. Leaving the Green River, he followed the Uinta River toward the west and the divide between the Colorado drainage basin and the Great Basin. He followed the small streams that flowed down the western side of this divide toward the Great Salt Lake, which Ashley guessed was the same "Lake Timpanogos" that had appeared on the Spanish maps of the 1770s. He also learned from the Indians in the region that the Great Salt Lake "had a large river flowing out of it on the west end."[50] The Indians did not know whether this river reached the sea, but Ashley concluded that he was finally hearing solid information about the fabled Rio San Buenaventura.

When Ashley returned to the Green River camp to rejoin the other parties in the fall of 1825, he learned that none of them had discovered anything of significance about a large river that was supposed to flow west from this region to the Pacific. Some of his men had talked with Hudson's Bay Company personnel in the Bear River region, however, and had learned that the Great Salt Lake had an outlet to the western ocean and that the outlet was "not the Multnomah, a southern branch of the Columbia, which I first supposed it to be."[51] Smith, returning to meet Ashley after his wanderings with the Hudson's Bay Company brigades in the Snake River country, confirmed that he had actually been on the waters of the "Grand lake or Buenaventura" but could tell nothing of the river or rivers flowing westward from it.[52] It seemed clear to Ashley that a river ran westward out of the Great Salt Lake and that this river would form a logical highway across the arid region west of South Pass all the way to the shores of the Pacific.

It was too late in the season for Ashley to pursue the search for the Buenaventura in 1825, however, and he returned to St. Louis to obtain more trade goods with which to purchase the free trappers' furs. Smith accompanied him on this return trip, the first time Smith had left the mountains in four years. In St. Louis, Smith was promoted to a full partner in the enterprise, buying out Andrew Henry. Ashley determined to settle down to perform the duties of senior partner, running the fur company from St. Louis and staying out of the mountains. He even married a St. Louis society belle and began to enjoy the life of the grand fur trade families of the old French city. But the lure of the mountains and the Buenaventura was too strong. The next summer Ashley was back in the Green River region, having taken the now familiar route up the Platte River and across South Pass. This year, he hoped, he would locate the Buenaventura and the route to the Pacific Ocean from the central Rocky Mountain region.

At the Green River valley, Ashley crossed the divide between the Colorado and Great Basin drainages west of the Green River (the Wasatch Mountains) and descended a river (probably the Weber River of eastern Utah) that he believed to be the upper Buenaventura. Reaching the Great Salt Lake, he and Smith sent some of their men, led by David Jackson, in bullboats to make a circuit of the lake to locate beaver-bearing streams flowing into the lake and, most important, "to locate the river which was supposed to flow out of the western side of the lake to the sea."[53] After a twenty-four-day trip around the lake, the party returned with the news that "they did not exactly ascertain its outlet but passed a place where they supposed it must have been." Again it was too late in the season for Ashley to pursue his dream any further. He returned to St. Louis, this time for good. He retired from the fur business and went into politics, becoming a respected U.S. representative from Missouri. But he did not give up his dream of the Buenaventura. Selling his share of the fur business to Jedediah Smith, David Jackson, and William Sublette, he left Smith, in particular, a legacy: the dream of a water route from the South Pass–Green River–Great Salt Lake region to the Pacific. During a series of epic explorations between 1826 and 1830, Smith would pursue that dream.

The results of the Ashley-Smith explorations were not, perhaps, terribly helpful in increasing the accuracy of geographical information. Ashley's continued belief in either the Multnomah or the Buenaventura seemed to reinforce Clark's old notion of the common-source region of western rivers. Neither Ashley nor Smith probably still believed that the Arkansas and the Rio Grande had their headwaters anywhere near those of the Colorado, Yellowstone, and Snake. But the mythical Multnomah and Buenaventura had entered the imaginary geography of the American West and would not be dispelled until after another decade of exploration. And Ashley and his men had contributed relatively little solid information on western land quality. They had, however, recognized that the country west of South Pass was considerably more arid than the Great Plains east of the Rockies. Speaking of the valley of the Green River, Ashley wrote: "The proportion of arable land (which is almost entirely confined to the valleys of the mountains) is so inconsiderable that the whole country (so far as my observations extended) may be considered of no value for the purpose of agriculture."[54] If there was a Great American Desert, it lay west of the Rockies rather than east as Zebulon Pike and Stephen Long had suggested.

Although the consequences of the Ashley-Smith explorations from 1822 to 1826 may have been inconclusive for geographers and mapmakers, they were significant for politicians and others interested in the westward expansion of the United States. After Ashley's last return from the West, the following item appeared in the *Missouri Herald and St. Louis Advertiser*:

The recent expedition of General Ashley to the country west of the Rocky Mountains has been productive of information of subjects of no small interest to the people of the Union. It has been proved, that overland expeditions in large bodies may be made to that remote region without the necessity of transporting provisions for man or beast. Gen. Ashley left St. Louis in March last and returned in September. . . . The whole route lay through a level and open country, better for carriages than any turnpike road in the United States. Wagons and carriages could go with ease as far as General Ashley went, crossing the Rocky Mountains at the sources of the north fork of the Platte, and descending the valley of the Buenaventura towards the Pacific Ocean.[55]

This was the final legacy of the Ashley-Smith explorations. Fur trade exploration had been converted into public policy for encouraging the settlement of the West by migrants in "wagons and carriages." Ashley and Smith had revealed the way West as far as South Pass and the Great Salt Lake. Perhaps the Buenaventura and a highway to the Pacific lay just beyond.

## Jedediah Smith Explores the West, 1826–1830

In his travels from 1826 to 1830, Jedediah Smith saw more of the American West than any man before him. He was the first to discover the overland route to California, the first to traverse the Great Basin and, perhaps, to recognize it as a region of interior drainage, and the first to travel overland from California to the Columbia River.[56] The contributions his explorations made to geographical knowledge, although not immediately formalized in textbooks and atlases, were greater than those of any other explorer of the West in the first half of the nineteenth century except for those of Meriwether Lewis, William Clark, and John C. Frémont. Several other explorations followed Smith's, completing the cycle of fur trade exploration, but none of those matched his in importance or drama.

Smith left the rendezvous site in the Cache Valley of northern Utah in August 1826 on his epic trip to California. He did not begin this journey intending to go to California but wanted simply to take a small party of men and open new fur country south and west of the Great Salt Lake.[57] Once begun, however, his exploration took on a momentum that carried Smith and his men all the way to the Pacific Ocean. Part of this drive was derived from Smith's desire to locate the Rio San Buenaventura, which Ashley had convinced him would lead Americans to the Pacific. The other part of the driving force was probably Smith's own curiosity: "In taking charge of our S western Expedition, I followed the bent of my strong inclination to visit this unexplored country and unfold those hidden resources of wealth and bring to light those wonders which I readily imagined in a country so extensive might contain . . . I wanted to be the first to view a country on which the eyes of a white man had never gazed and to follow the course of rivers that run through a new land."[58] No explorer before or since has explained the traveler's motivation any better.

On the first leg of his California journey, Smith traveled from the Cache Valley into the valley of the Great Salt Lake and then south to Utah Lake, a freshwater lake that drains north into the Great Salt Lake. From Utah Lake the Smith party traveled southeast along the eastern rim of the Great Basin through country "quite rough and mountainous," continuing to search for the headwaters of the Buenaventura. Hearing of a "great river" to the west, Smith left the divide rim and headed west into the Great Basin; when he reached the Sevier River of southern Utah he was surprised to note that "instead of a River an immense sand plain was before me. . . . The only exception to this interminable waste of sand was a few detached rocky hills that rose from the surrounding plain and the stunted sedge that was thinly scattered over its surface."[59] He followed the Sevier River upstream through "Sandy plains and Rocky hills" until reaching the Great Basin rim again and crossed the divide between the Sevier and the Virgin River near present St. George, Utah.[60] The group traveled southeast down the rough and broken country surrounding the Virgin River, skirting its great gorge, and reached the Colorado. Smith's party had found no good beaver streams throughout this long trek—only barren land covered with alkali flats, mesquite, and sagebrush. When the men reached the Colorado River, they were well below its Grand Canyon and a long way from the Green River of western Wyoming. Yet Smith, with an unerring instinct for geography, recognized the Colorado River as the same stream that "in the Mountains we call seetes-kee-der," or his "Seedskadee" (Green River), which headed in the Wind River Range of Wyoming and joined the Colorado in present-day southern Utah.

Smith and his men traveled through desert country along the Colorado to the villages of the friendly Mojave Indians, near present Needles, California; the Mojave told him "that it was about ten days travel to the spanish settlements in California."[61] By this time, his horses and men were exhausted, and the party had begun to run short of supplies. Knowing somehow that he was closer to the California mission settlements than to his home base in the Cache Valley, Smith struck out westward across the Mojave Desert for the California missions "where I supposed I might procure such supplies as would enable me to move north. In that direction I expected to find beaver and in all probability some considerable river heading up in the vicinity of the Great Salt Lake."[62] After crossing country even more barren than that near the Colorado, Smith and his men reached the San Bernadino Mountains of southern California near present Victorville in November 1826. They crossed over the mountains to Mission San Gabriel, just east of where Los Angeles now sprawls across the Los Angeles basin. The environment of Mission San Gabriel presented a welcome difference to the barrenness of the desert to the east: "The scene was changed and whether it was its own real Beauty or the contrast with what we had seen, it certainly seemed to us enchantment."[63] Smith and his men would not be the last travelers to experience such emotions after crossing the San Bernadino Range into the Los Angeles basin.

Smith was now in Mexican territory, and he sent a letter to the governor in San Diego, announcing his presence and requesting permission to travel north through California in search of furs. He also intended to look for the Buenaventura River, although he did not so inform the governor. Smith and his men crossed over Cajon Pass to the coast and traveled south to San Diego, where, Smith hoped, he would receive permission to explore northward; the Mexican officials retained the American party, however, and Smith remained in southern California for two months before finally getting permission to leave.[64] But, the Mexican governor told them, they were not to explore northward through California; instead they were to cross back over the mountains in the direction from which they had come. Smith and his men dutifully retraced their route over the San Bernadino Mountains to the east; but once on the eastern side of the mountains, safely out of range of Mexican authorities and fearful of recrossing the Mojave Desert, Smith decided to turn north. He and his men skirted the western edge of the Mojave Desert and crossed westward over the Tehachapi Range into the valley of the San Joaquin River. This valley is the southern end of the Great Valley, which stretches almost the north-south extent of California between the Sierras on the east and the California coastal ranges on the south. Smith and his men, the first Americans to enter the Great Valley, recognized it as a land of pastoral abundance—"the most desirable part of the world I ever was in"—and here they found the first beaver streams since leaving the Great Salt Lake.

Smith and his men trapped their way northward along the San Joaquin into the rich beaver country of the rivers that flow west from the Sierras into the Great Valley and, finally, San Francisco Bay. By late April 1827, having trapped and explored on the Stanislaus, Mokelumne, and Cosumnes Rivers (all tributaries of the American River), Smith and his men had accumulated fifteen hundred pounds of beaver pelts and decided to leave California. They headed east across the Sierras, whose "summits could hardly ever be seen as they rose far into the region of perpetual snow and were generally enveloped in clouds,"[65] and after being delayed by late spring snows, they camped on the Stanislaus River. Smith, recognizing the difficulty of attempting a mountain crossing with his full party (and their winter's catch of beaver), left most of his men in the camp on the Stanislaus in May 1827 under the command of his clerk, Harrison Rogers. With two men, Smith crossed the Sierra Nevada south of Lake Tahoe on the present California-Nevada border, back into the Great Basin region of interior drainage. The men followed the Walker River downstream to the east until its waters disappeared in Walker Lake. From here they struck out due east across the barren deserts of central Nevada: "The general appearance of the country . . . is extremely Barren. High rocky hills afford the only relief to the desolate waste for at the foot of these are found water and some vegetation while the intervals between are sand barren Plains."[66] The first American explorer into the central Great Basin country, Smith cogently observed, "The mountains are to this Plain like the island of the Ocean."[67]

The desert crossing was extremely difficult, with little water and scanty provisions, and Smith despaired of ever making it back to his "home in the mountains." Finally, near the present border between Nevada and Utah, the men angled northeast until "the Salt Lake a joyful sight was spread before us."[68]

Smith and his men had done what no one had done before them. They had crossed over the highest mountains and the largest desert in the United States. They had discovered the rich beaver country of the central portions of California's Great Valley and had recognized that valley as a pastoral paradise that could accommodate thousands of American farmers. They had not, however, discovered the Buenaventura River. Although he might have felt a sense of failure at not discovering the desired river route across the Great Basin, when he reached the Great Salt Lake, Smith was on familiar ground. He and his men headed north for the rendezvous site in the Cache Valley. When they got there, Indians told them that the rendezvous had been moved north, to Bear Lake, a day's ride away. Smith and his men rode into the rendezvous camp on 4 July 1827. Smith reported: "My arrival caused considerable bustle in camp, for myself and party had been given up as lost. A small Cannon brought up from St. Louis was loaded and fired for a salute."[69] One of the greatest fur trade explorations was over.

Smith did not remain long at the rendezvous site at Bear Lake. He had left a dozen men and fifteen hundred pounds of beaver on the Stanislaus River of California and was determined to return for them. Less than two weeks later, on 13 July 1827, Smith and eighteen men struck out for California. Not wanting to brave again the fearful desert crossing of his eastbound trip, Smith traveled to the Mojave villages on the lower Colorado by basically the same route that he had followed the year before. This time the Mojave Indians were not so friendly, however, and they attacked the American party; only Smith and less than half his men escaped. They fled west into the desert and, after a grueling crossing, once again traversed the San Bernadino Mountains via Cajon Pass into the Mexican missions.

The Mexicans, like the Mojave Indians, were considerably less hospitable than they had been a year earlier. Smith was threatened with arrest and was taken to San Francisco by sea to deal with Mexican officials there. After two months of delicate negotiations, he was allowed to rejoin his men (who had been brought north overland). At San Francisco, Smith was also joined by Harrison Rogers and the men who had been left the year before at the camp on the Stanislaus. Finally, on 30 December 1827, Smith and all his men were able to depart San Francisco and return to the wilderness, in Smith's words "to the woods, the river, the prairie, the Camp, and the Game."[70]

Smith knew that the route he had taken across the Great Basin to the Great Salt Lake earlier that year had been too far south to prove conclusively that the Buenaventura did not exist. Therefore, he followed the Sacramento River north into the Sierras far enough to convince himself that its source was on the western side of the mountains and that it did not flow through the range from the Great Basin. From the headwaters of the Sacramento, he and his men steered toward the coast and began working their way north. Perhaps they hoped to find another great river that, coming from the east, would prove to be the Buenaventura. In July 1828 Smith's party reached the Umpqua River on the central Oregon coast, where they learned that the Willamette, or Multnomah, was not far to the north. Smith knew of the Hudson's Bay Company fort (Fort Vancouver) where the Willamette joined the Columbia; close to "civilization," he made one of his very few mistakes as a field commander and left his camp unguarded overnight. His party was attacked by the Umpqua Indians, and only Smith and two men who had been hunting game away from camp survived.

The survivors fled north for Fort Vancouver, where they were met with splendid hospitality by Dr. John McLoughlin, the Hudson's Bay Company factor. McLoughlin even sent a party of friendly Indians and Hudson's Bay men south to the site of the battle. Most of Smith's furs were recovered and were purchased by McLoughlin at a fair price. More important, Smith's journals and record books were also recovered. Smith and his two companions remained at Fort Vancouver. Smith kept his eyes and ears open and assessed the strength of the Hudson's Bay Company in the Pacific Northwest. He would report on this to the U.S. secretary of war after his return to the United States in 1830, noting that the country was firmly held by the British but that a "determined force" of Americans could easily take the country from them.[71] He also commented on the enormous potential of Oregon Country for an American agricultural settlement. Before this return, however, Smith still had some exploring to do.

He left Fort Vancouver in March 1829 and traveled with a Hudson's Bay brigade to Fort Colville, a Hudson's Bay Company post on the Columbia River in north-central Washington. From Fort Colville he traveled eastward to the Rockies, where he met his partner, David Jackson, near Flathead Lake in western Montana. Smith and Jackson journeyed south through the Bitterroot Valley and crossed over to Henry's Fork of the Snake in July

1829. Here they met William Sublette, the third member of the partnership that had bought out Ashley. The three partners then proceeded south to Pierre's Hole, east of the Tetons, and the summer rendezvous of 1829.

After the rendezvous, Smith and Sublette traveled across Teton Pass into Jackson's Hole and then west across the mountains south of Yellowstone into the Bighorn Basin. They probably came close to the route followed by John Colter from the Absaroka Mountains into the Bighorn Basin more than twenty years earlier. The partners trapped their way south through the Bighorn Basin and crossed the Owl Creek Mountains into the Wind River valley, where Smith and Weber had wintered their first year in the Rockies. But the beaver were almost gone from this region because of overhunting, and Smith moved north to the Powder River, where they spent the winter of 1829–30.[72] In the spring of 1830, Smith led a trapping party into the Blackfeet country of Montana's Judith River basin. But the Blackfeet were hostile, and the trappers did not linger long, turning southward for the summer rendezvous on the Popo Agie, a tributary of the Wind River.

Smith was exhibiting uncharacteristic homesickness for family and friends, and after the rendezvous, he sold his interest in the fur company to Jackson and Sublette and left the mountains forever. He returned to St. Louis, where he purchased a farm and became active in a merchant company involved in the Santa Fe trade. In the spring of 1831, on a trip to Santa Fe with a caravan of St. Louis traders, Smith was killed on the Cimarron River near the present-day Three Corners area, where Colorado, Kansas, and Oklahoma abut. The fur trade's greatest explorer and one of the greatest explorers of the American West was dead at the age of thirty-two.[73]

Like many other explorers of the fur trade, Smith died before the geographical knowledge he had gathered could be made public. Some historians have concluded that Smith's explorations, as extensive as they were, had little consequence for American views of the Far West. This is simply not true. Although some of Smith's journals were not published until the twentieth century and others were lost altogether, he did influence American knowledge. He wrote several letters to Clark, then U.S. superintendent of Indian affairs in St. Louis, who, since his epic travels with Lewis, had continued to gather intelligence on the West and pass it along to officials in Washington as well as to newspapers. Several of Smith's letters to Clark describing his route to California were widely published in newspapers in different parts of the United States.[74] Obviously, the information provided to Clark by Smith became part of the U.S. government's fund of knowledge on the West. One outstanding example of Smith's practical contribution came in a letter that he wrote in October 1830 to John Eaton, the U.S. secretary of war.[75] Smith detailed many of his explorations, describing, in particular, the rich country controlled by the Hudson's Bay Company in the Pacific Northwest and noting how valuable the area would be for American farmers. He also detailed the route to follow from St. Louis to Oregon Country, the route that would later become the Oregon Trail. A Pulitzer Prize–winning historian of the American West has called this letter of Smith's "one of the most important contributions to a practical knowledge of the West ever made."[76]

Smith's geographical knowledge also appeared on maps after 1830.[77] Although no map drawn by Smith has survived, several maps of the mid-1830s were clearly constructed from various manuscript maps drawn by Smith and presented to government officials and others. An examination of the geographical knowledge contained on these maps reveals Smith's contributions to an improved American image of the West. European maps—such as those by the Brue firm of Paris and the Arrowsmith firm of London—carried Ashley-Smith data as early as 1833. Several Brue and Arrowsmith maps published in 1833 and 1834, for example, showed place-names that could have come only from Smith and Ashley, along with lines indicating Smith's route to California in 1826 and his return to the Great Salt Lake in 1827.

Even more important were two American maps published in 1836. The first of these was published by Albert Gallatin. A man with a long history of public service and "one of the great savants of his time," Gallatin had also played a major role in gathering the geographical data that Nicholas King had used to complete his map in 1803.[78] Gallatin's 1836 map, entitled "Map of the Indian Tribes of North America . . . ," was designed to accompany his "Synopsis of the Indian Tribes," published under the auspices of the American Antiquarian Society,[79] and was thus symbolic of the mainstream of American literary opinion. Like other period maps, most of Gallatin's map was drawn from the traditional formal sources of Lewis and Clark and Pike for the area east of the Rocky Mountains. Gallatin did, however, show "Lorimier's Peak," or Laramie Peak, and Laramie River (unnamed) near the North Platte, information that could have come only from the fur trade, just then becoming active on the North Platte drainage. And in the Snake-Yellowstone core drainage area, Gallatin showed the trappers' "3 Peaks" of the Tetons, although his view of the complex drainage systems of the area was still more primitive than that of the fur trappers.

*17.3 "Map of the Indian Tribes of North America" (Albert Gallatin, 1836). Gallatin's map is one of the very few from the period before John C. Frémont's explorations to show information derived from the travels of Jedediah Smith. Collection of John L. Allen.*

Most of the region west of the continental divide was left blank. Significantly, however, Gallatin did show two rivers originating in the mountains east of the Great Salt Lake and flowing south to join and become the Colorado. These were clearly the Green and Grand Rivers and represented one of the first instances of the inclusion of Smith's geography in American mapping. The Green River heads in the Wind River Range of west-central Wyoming; on Gallatin's map, near the area of present-day Grand Junction, Colorado, the Green is joined by the river now called the Colorado but known to the trappers as the Grand, with its head in the Colorado Rockies—nearly four hundred miles south of the headwaters of the Green River. Smith's geographical image, and by extension Gallatin's, now recognized (and presented for the first time on a map) the two source areas of western rivers in the Rocky Mountains: the northern source region of Wyoming, which gives rise to the Snake, Yellowstone, Bighorn, and Green; and the southern source region of Colorado, from which flow the Grand, Rio Grande, Platte, and Arkansas. Between the two source areas lie the South Pass, the continental divide basin, and the divide itself. None of this geography (other than the accurate distinction between the Green and the Grand branches of the Colorado River) appeared on Gallatin's map, but it was suggested, leading to the assumption that Gallatin probably had this complex geography reasonably well figured out. Certainly Smith (and hundreds of other mountain men) did.

Gallatin's map also showed a line connecting the Colorado and the Pacific coast—but this line was not an apocryphal stream. Rather, it was labeled "J.S. Smith's route 1826." Farther north on the map, east of the Sacramento River (which carries the appellation "Buenaventura") was another dotted line with the caption "J.S. Smith's route 1827." Between these two representations of Smith's trek across the Great Basin appeared the words "Great Sandy Desert," along with rivers that represented the modern Sevier, Beaver, Virgin, and Mojave. We do not know how Gallatin came by information from Smith's travels, but in the final analysis this is unimportant. His map represented the beginning of a new geography, one that did not contain numerous apocryphal features but showed only the observations of responsible explorers such as Smith. The Gallatin map is just as important for what it did not show as for what it did.

The second important American map of 1836 and one that also evidenced American cartographers' growing familiarity with lore from the American fur trade was Henry Tanner's large map of North America published in his *New Universal Atlas*.[80] In most respects, Tanner's map was very similar to Gallatin's, providing further proof that both cartographers had relied on a common body of knowledge, probably obtained from Smith. The differences between the two maps, however, are intriguing. Tanner, for example, did a much less credible job than Gallatin in showing the Green River, placing the source of that stream farther south than Gallatin's approximately correct location. Nor did Tanner show the Laramie Peak and Laramie River geography on the North Platte, although he showed, as Gallatin did not, both Long's Peak and James (Pikes) Peak near the South Platte. South of Pikes Peak, in the area that Gallatin had labeled as part of the Rocky Mountains, Tanner used the term "Mts. of Anahuac"—a trappers' nomenclature that would become increasingly common for the southern Rockies during the next few years. For the region drained by the

Snake River, Tanner's view was much more precise than Gallatin's, including showing the southern branch of the Snake (the Snake proper) heading in "Snow L." or Jackson Lake, the first time this feature had appeared on any published map. Tanner also presented considerably more detail—and generally accurate detail—on the tributary streams of the Snake. For the areas south of the Snake Basin, the region of the Great Basin, Tanner's map was very similar to that of Gallatin, although Tanner used the term "Sandy Plains" rather than Gallatin's "Great Sandy Desert." Tanner also showed a small "Utau L." south of the Great Salt Lake, an important clarification of those two bodies of water, which were combined into one lake on most period maps. And finally, Tanner correctly located, as did Gallatin, the Bear River and its associated (and unnamed) lake to the north of the Great Salt Lake. Viewed together, the Tanner and Gallatin maps were remarkable cartographic achievements and were indicative of the growing importance and volume of fur trade lore.

Knowledge provided by Smith clearly allowed these and other American mapmakers to draw the drainage of the Bighorn and Yellowstone Rivers correctly and to show the first accurate representations of the Platte River route to South Pass and of the valley of the Green River west of the continental divide. The first glimmerings of the Great Basin as a region of interior drainage appeared on maps derived from Smith's geographical data, as did the first accurate views of the Sierra Nevada, the Great Valley of California, and the California coastal ranges. Finally, after Smith, fewer maps showed a mythical Rio San Buenaventura flowing west from the Rockies to the Pacific, and almost no maps contained Clark's fictitious Multnomah. The American West had no greater explorer than the young man who, born in New York and raised and educated in Pennsylvania and Ohio, achieved fame as a captain of the fur brigades of the plains and mountains of the Far West.

## The Later Fur Trade Explorations, 1830–1838

Even before Smith's death in 1831, geographical information from other members of the fur trade began to appear in various places. For example, Joshua Pilcher, the head of the new Rocky Mountain Fur Company, which was formed to compete with the Smith-Jackson-Sublette partnership, also wrote a letter to a government official. Pilcher had spent the years 1827–30 in the Rockies and, like Smith, had visited the Pacific Northwest. His re-

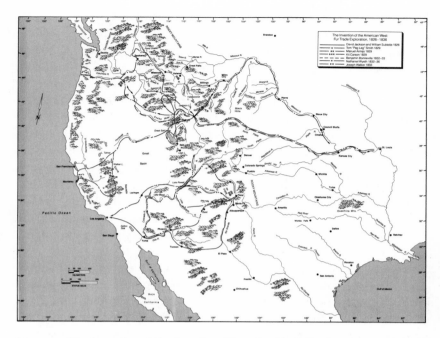

*Map 17.2 The Invention of the American West: Fur Trade Exploration 1826–1836.*

ports on the agricultural potential of Oregon Country were even more enthusiastic than Smith's. Like Smith, he also described the South Pass route
to Oregon Country from the east: "I have crossed . . . often, and always
without delay or difficulty. It is in fact one of the best passes and presents
the best overland route from the valley of the Mississippi to the mouth of
the Columbia."[81] Yet some of his contemporaries may have disagreed with
Pilcher's assessment of South Pass as "the best overland route." An 1827
letter to a national newspaper described another route across the divide,
one that was even more accessible than South Pass: "It would trend directly eastward from . . . Green River and ascending the valley of the Bitter
Creek, thence crossing the north fork of the Platte near the medicine Bow
mountain, and the laramie River in Laramie plains. It would cross the Sher-
man Hill country, of the southern part of the Black Hills [the Laramie Range
of Wyoming, not the Black Hills of South Dakota], and probably descend
the Lodge Pole Creek to its junction with the South Platte."[82] This was precisely the route later followed by the first transcontinental railroad across
southern Wyoming and suggests that as early as 1827—only three years af-

ter Smith's rediscovery of South Pass—members of the fur trade had learned enough of Rocky Mountain geography to begin suggesting alternate routes to South Pass.

This same letter (purportedly written by Bridger, although he was illiterate) indicates that other elements of Rocky Mountain geography were becoming well-known to the fur trade in the closing years of the 1820s. In addition to its description of an alternate route across the divide, the 1827 letter detailed, reasonably accurately, a trapper's visit to the area that became Yellowstone National Park. The unknown trapper crossed a "large rugged mountain" between the Bear River and the Snake River in Jackson's Hole, at the eastern foot of the Teton Range. Following the Snake northward to its head, the trapper came to "the top of the great chain of rocky Mountain which separates the waters of the Atlantic from those of the Pacific"—presumably in the southwestern part of Yellowstone where the Snake River originates in Heart Lake and the Lewis River. The letter described many of the features that later made Yellowstone famous: "a large fresh water lake . . . which is about one hundred by forty miles in diameter, and as clear as crystal" (Yellowstone Lake); and "a number of hot and boiling springs, some of water and others of the most beautiful fine clay, resembling a mush pot, and throwing particles to the immense height of from twenty to thirty feet" (the geysers, mud springs, and "paint pots" of the thermal region west of Yellowstone Lake). Such a description could have come only from someone who had visited this region.

Smith's expeditions were the high-water mark of fur trade exploration of the West. By the time of Smith's death in 1831, the geographical contributions made by the American fur trappers were significant: they had learned the mountains and plains and deserts from the northern Missouri River to southern New Mexico and from St. Louis to the Pacific; they had opened the northern, central, and southern Rockies for economic exploitation; and they had even penetrated into the Great Basin, Oregon Country, and California. There were few, if any, important landmarks of the entire West that were not well-known to the trappers. But during the 1830s, exploration by Rocky Mountain fur trappers began to decline, paralleling the decline of the fur trade itself as increasing competition, more trappers, and fewer beaver began to affect the first economic utilization of the Rocky Mountains by whites.

The work of the fur trappers, however, was not quite done. Although the trappers knew their way around the West like men moving around their own backyard, much of their geographical lore remained to be added to general American information.[83] This addition took place during the 1830s, though not as a result of the trappers themselves. People other than trappers began to move into and across the mountains, using geographical data from the fur trade to draw their maps and chart their courses. The 1830s may have been a decade of decline for the fur trade, but it was a period of expansion for other activities: the first migrant wagon roads across the mountains to Oregon; the first missionaries and settlers in the Rockies and beyond; the first romantic adventurers, writers, and artists. All these western travelers relied on the fur trappers' understanding of western geography. And through these travelers' use of that understanding, the geographical knowledge of the fur trade became part of American geographical lore.

The two best examples of western travelers who used fur trapper lore to further their objectives were Benjamin Bonneville and Nathaniel Wyeth. Bonneville, a West Point graduate, took leave from the U.S. Army in 1831 to engage in the fur trade, though he may actually have been functioning under secret orders from the army to gather knowledge that would allow the United States to gain control over Oregon Country.[84] William H. Goetzmann simply noted that Bonneville "was an instrument of American policy, and a further example of the federal government's interest in the development of the western frontier."[85] One of America's foremost men of letters, Washington Irving (already known as a western writer through his chronicling of the Astorian experience),[86] wrote an enormously popular book about Bonneville's travels in the Rockies and beyond, a book that did much to incorporate fur trapper knowledge as part of American images of the West.[87] Wyeth was a Boston ice merchant whose motives, like Bonneville's, were more than they might have seemed. As a merchant, Wyeth hoped to make money from the fur trade of the farther West. But as a New Englander who had long been interested in the West, he also hoped to aid the American cause in Oregon Country and to extend New England culture to the Pacific Northwest. No major literary figure wrote about Wyeth's travels, but he himself published an account of his adventures in the West. Like Irving's work on Bonneville, this account contributed significantly to American images.[88]

Captain Bonneville set out for the mountains in May 1832 with wagons filled with trade goods and supplies.[89] He used the now-familiar fur trade route up the North Platte and across South Pass. One of his first activities was to build a fort on the Green River near present-day Pinedale, Wyoming, the site of several fur trapper rendezvous. Trappers referred to this fort as "Bonneville's Folly" or "Fort Nonsense," believing it to be too far north on the Green to take advantage of the winter beaver hunt. But Bonneville's military training—and the fact that he may not have been operating completely independently of the army—showed in the strategic location of this fort, well situated to guard South Pass, Jackson's Hole, the Bear River, and the Great Salt Lake.[90] In the summer of 1832 Bonneville divided his command into two parties. One party went to trap on the Bear River while Bonneville, with the remaining men, traveled northwest to Pierre's Hole and camped for the winter on the Salmon River. Clearly Bonneville intended to introduce a permanent American presence in territory that had formerly been controlled exclusively by the Hudson's Bay Company.

In the summer of 1833 Bonneville made his greatest contributions to both exploration and American westward expansion. He decided to take one party himself and retrace the Astorians' route to the junction of the Columbia and Snake Rivers and then travel back to a winter camp on the Bear River. Why he chose to explore country that was already well-known and traveled is unclear, unless he simply wanted to "show the flag" in territory disputed between Great Britain and the United States and viewed by Americans, therefore, as "up for grabs." Bonneville dispatched the other party—consisting of nearly sixty experienced fur trappers and commanded by the fur trapper veteran Joseph Walker—toward the west with an objective that was more apparent than that of Bonneville's travels to the north. Although Irving's account of Bonneville's "adventures" suggest that Walker was instructed to trap only in the Great Salt Lake region, the best source for Walker's exploration—the journal of one of his party, Zenas Leonard—indicates that Leonard signed on with Walker specifically because he "was anxious to go to the coast of the Pacific."[91] Clearly Walker was instructed to locate a route from the Great Salt Lake to the Pacific.

Walker's expedition of 1833–34 was second only to Smith's travels from 1826 to 1830 in opening new territory and developing new geographical knowledge.[92] His route took him from the rendezvous site to the Great Salt Lake and then southwest across a desert "so dry and sandy that there is scarcely any vegetation to be found—not even a spear of grass, except around the springs, too, is so salt that it is impossible to drink it. . . . Every thing here seems to declare that, here man shall not dwell."[93] In eastern Nevada, Walker struck the Humboldt River, that curious stream discovered a few years earlier by Peter Skene Ogden of the Hudson's Bay Company. Believing that he had discovered the Buenaventura, Walker followed the Humboldt downstream until it disappeared into the Sinks area at the eastern base of the Sierra Nevada range. Walker's chronicler, Leonard, noted that the rivers that flowed east from the Sierras, like those that flowed into the Great Basin west from the Rockies, entered lakes with no outlets. The Walker party crossed the Sierras and into California, where he and his party were astounded by the exotic landscapes of the redwoods. They traveled all the way to the Pacific at Monterey Bay—"the feeling of being within hearing of the end of the Far West inspired the heart of every member of our company with a patriotic feeling for his country's honor"[94]— and even experienced an earthquake. From Monterey, where they wintered in 1833–34, Walker and his men crossed back over the coastal ranges to the Great Valley and then southward to cross the southern end of the Sierras by way of Walker's Pass (an important emigrant route in later years), but not before Leonard had penned some of the most lyrical descriptions of the idyllic California landscapes in the years before American occupation.

Once back in the Great Basin, they followed the eastern edge of the Sierras northward until they reached the Sinks of the Humboldt and then followed that river eastward to its source. From here they veered north to the Snake River and then up the Snake a short distance to a point near Bear Lake. Here they left the Snake and struck out overland for the Bear River, where they rejoined Bonneville. On this epic journey, Walker and his men had laid out the Humboldt River trail that would be used by thousands of gold-seekers on their way to California, and they had returned with a view of California that would prove enticing to Americans even before the discovery of gold in northern California. They had also returned with a picture of the Great Basin country rivaled only by Smith's. The difference was that Smith's geography of the Great Basin was never completely published; Walker's was published in Leonard's *Narrative*:

This desert which had presented such an insurmountable barrier to our route, is bounded on the east by the Rocky mountains, on the west by the Calafornia mountain, on the North by the Columbia river, and on the south by the Red, or Colorado river. These two mighty rivers rise in the Rocky mountains adjacent to each other . . . there are numerous small rivers rising in either mountain, winding their way far toward the centre of the plain, where they are emptied into lakes or reservoirs, and the water sinks in the sand. Farther to the north where the sand is not so deep and loose, the streams rising in the spurs of the Rocky and those descending from the Calafornia mountains, flow on until their waters at length mingle together in the same lakes . . . in no place is there a water course through the mountains.[95]

Although this description lacks the geographical precision that marked the first formal mapping of the Great Basin by John C. Frémont in 1843–44, it reveals that the fur trade had, ten years before Frémont, clearly defined the basic concept of a Great Basin of interior drainage.

Washington Irving's *The Rocky Mountains* (1837) was particularly important in presenting the results of the Bonneville enterprise to the American public.[96] This book was widely read and was certainly among the most important literary sources for images of the Rockies and the West before Frémont.[97] The two maps from Irving's work were derived from information provided by the travels of Bonneville and Walker. The first of these was a map of a relatively small area, although it carried the elegant and grandiose title "A Map of the Sources of the COLORADO & BIG SALT LAKE, PLATTE, YELLOW-STONE, MUSCLE-SHELL, MISSOURI; & SALMON & SNAKE RIVERS, branches of the COLUMBIA RIVER." Though convoluted, that title is an apt description of a map that was the first detailed and accurate representation of the northernmost of what fur trappers had, by the mid-1830s, learned were the *two* core drainage regions of the Rockies. Lying symbolically in the exact center of the map, near the northern end of the Wind River Range, appeared that complex interlocking drainage system that gives rise to the Yellowstone, Wind, Green, and Snake. Surrounding that core drainage region are the peripheral areas, also shown in considerable and accurate detail: the Bighorn Basin with its mountain ring surrounding it; the southern end of the Wind River Range and the (unnamed) South Pass between the Sweetwater branch of the Platte and the Big Sandy fork of the Green; the Uintah Range and the Bear River draining into the Great Salt Lake, or "Lake Bonneville"; the course of the Snake across the "Great Lava Plain" with "The 3 Butes" to the north; the course of the Lemhi and Salmon Rivers across the divide from the westernmost stretch of the upper Missouri system (there was no Multnomah); and the Yellowstone River flowing from its lake a short distance north of Jackson's Hole and the headwaters of the Snake. Only the members of the fur trade had the kind of geographical awareness that could allow this precise a picture of this complex a river and mountain system.

The second of the two maps accompanying Irving's *The Rocky Mountains* illustrated the geography of the country between the northern core drainage region and the Pacific, north of the thirty-eighth parallel. On the far

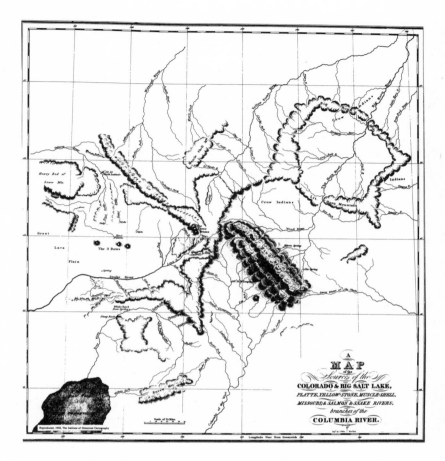

*17.4 "A Map of the Sources of the Colorado & Big Salt Lake . . ." (Benjamin Bonneville, 1837). Published in Washington Irving,* The Rocky Mountains, *this map illustrates the height of fur trade knowledge of the "core region" of the mountain West. Reproduced from the original by the Institute of Historical Cartography, San Francisco, California.*

eastern edge of the map, where the first map left off, was the "Lake Bonneville" version of the Great Salt Lake with its associated Utah Lake, although that lake was shown east rather than south of the Salt Lake. The Snake River and its major tributaries were shown with remarkable accuracy, as were the Willamette entering the Columbia from the south and the Umpqua and the Clamet flowing from the Cascades to the Pacific. The course of the Humboldt ("Mary or Ogden's River") flowing southwest from the area just west of the Great Salt Lake to its terminus east of the Sierras was depicted with considerable clarity, and in the Humboldt's terminal region appeared the large freshwater lakes of the Sierras' eastern front. To the west, the Sacramento and San Joaquin Rivers were shown properly penned up by the Sierras to their east. There was not a hint of any major stream such as the Multnomah, Buenaventura, or Timpanogos draining the area east of the Sierras and west of the Rockies. Indeed, this map showed only one geographical feature that was not closely approximated by reality. Linking the westernmost outliers of the Rockies with the Sierras and lying north of the Great Salt Lake and the Humboldt was a great linear range of mountains bearing the legend "Perpetual Snows." This was the imaginary Snowy Range, a fixture in most geographical images of the time and a forgivable error until Frémont's travels defined the nature of the basin and range country of the intermountain West. Like its companion map, this map was nearly totally dependent on fur trader lore. In the face of the evidence of these maps, it is simply wrong to say, as many have, that the geographical lore of the fur trade did not enter formal American geographical knowledge until Frémont or later.

Nathaniel J. Wyeth, a Boston ice merchant, undertook the second of the major exploratory ventures after Smith. Wyeth had avidly read the Lewis and Clark journals and hoped to resurrect Astor's dream of an American empire in the Pacific Northwest and a trading terminus at the mouth of the Columbia. He was also attracted to the idea of an American farming migration to the Northwest and became an avid member of the Oregon Emigration Society, founded by a fellow New Englander, Hall Jackson Kelley.[98] As one of the country's foremost proponents of Oregon settlement, Kelley had extolled the virtues of Oregon Country: "No portion of the globe presents a more fruitful soil, or a milder climate, or equal facilities for carrying into effect the great purposes of a free and enlightened nation."[99] By 1832, while still accepting Kelley's belief in the "beneficence" of Oregon Country, Wyeth had become convinced that Kelley's scheme to colonize the Pacific Northwest with New England farmers was not going to come to fruition and was now determined to set up his own company and "open" Oregon Country for the United States. After learning what he could of the West from the savants of Boston, Wyeth and sixty New Englanders departed for St. Louis. Here he met with William Sublette of the firm of Sublette & Campbell (the residue of the old Smith-Jackson-Sublette partnership) and was astounded to learn that Sublette and his associates knew a great deal

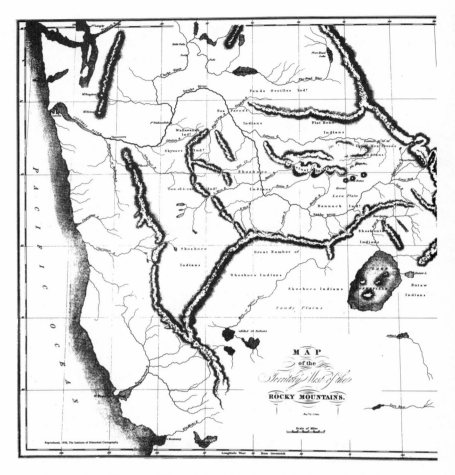

17.5 *"Map of the Territory West of the Rocky Mountains" (Benjamin Bonneville, 1837). Like its companion map, published in Washington Irving,* Scenes and Adventures in the Rocky Mountains, *this map represents the best available information on the Pacific slope at the end of major fur trade explorations. Reproduced from the original by the Institute of Historical Cartography, San Francisco, California.*

more about the West than did the learned men of the New England academies. Wyeth left St. Louis in the spring of 1832, at about the same time that Bonneville departed; crossing the plains with Sublette and a party of fur traders bound for the summer rendezvous, Wyeth and his New Englanders crossed South Pass and traveled northwest to Pierre's Hole. Here a pitched battle broke out between the trappers and the Blackfeet Indians. Wyeth was lucky to escape with his life, exhibiting bravery during the battle and winning the grudging admiration of the mountain men. Unfortunately, he was less fortunate with his own men, many of whom (including his brother and his nephew, who wrote a highly critical account of Wyeth's venture) deserted.[100]

Undaunted, in August 1832 Wyeth headed west from Pierre's Hole, cutting across the plain north of the Snake River. In October he crossed the Blue Mountains to the junction of the Snake and Columbia and traveled down the Columbia to Fort Vancouver. Here he was supposed to meet a ship that he had sent from Boston the year before. Instead he learned that his ship had been wrecked and that, economically, his western venture was a failure. He spent the winter of 1832–33 with the Hudson's Bay Company men at Fort Vancouver, as another of the many travelers succored by Dr. McLoughlin, the factor at Vancouver. The following summer Wyeth journeyed to the Hudson's Bay Company's Flathead Post in western Montana, from which he traveled south to the Tetons, where he met with Bonneville. The two men planned a trip to California (the trip that Walker would take later that summer), but Wyeth backed out of the project and headed home for New England, hoping to recoup his fortune and try again the following year.

In the summer of 1834 Wyeth again left New England for the West. During the winter he had planned an elaborate scheme to control the transportation trade of the farther West. He would again send a ship to the mouth of the Columbia to trade in furs and pick up a load of salmon. Wyeth, meanwhile, would go to the summer rendezvous with trade goods, exchange them for beaver, and head northwest for the Columbia and his waiting vessel, which would carry the wealth in fur back to New England. Two additional features of his plan illustrate the changing character of western travel. Accompanying Wyeth west would be two scientists, botanist Thomas Nuttall and ornithologist John Townsend, and two missionaries, Jason Lee and his nephew Daniel. One western historian has noted that the primary importance of Wyeth's second expedition "was that it opened up the Oregon Trail and the Northwest to the two chief forces of contemporary civilization, science and organized Protestant Christianity."[101]

In terms of the routes followed, Wyeth's second western expedition was almost a duplicate of his first; it also replicated the economic failure of his earlier venture. When Wyeth reached the rendezvous, he discovered that the agreements he had made to purchase furs from trappers had been broken. And when he reached the mouth of the Columbia he learned that, for the second year in a row, the ship that was supposed to meet him there had met with disaster. He attempted to trade in the lower Columbia Valley but could not compete with the powerful Hudson's Bay Company. By the spring of 1836 Wyeth's venture had failed commercially, and in the fall of 1836 he left the West.

Wyeth's attempt at western commerce was an economic failure, but by other measures, his second expedition was a great success. On his way north to the Columbia in 1835, he built Fort Hall near the junction of the Snake and Portneuf Rivers in present-day Idaho. This fort was the first permanent American establishment west of the mountains, giving the United States a foothold that it would never relinquish and providing a strong arguing point in the debate with Great Britain over eventual control of the Pacific Northwest. It also, in later years, served as a critical point on the Oregon Trail. And on Wyeth's return trip in 1836 he mapped the Willamette Valley and proved conclusively that Lewis and Clark's Multnomah was a river of the imagination. A companion of Wyeth's noted: "This week I have returned from an excursion up the river Multnomah or Wallameth. It is far from the stream laid down on your maps, for its most distant source is not probably more than 200 miles in a direct course from its mouth."[102] Wyeth had also laid out the route of the Oregon Trail and, through newspaper articles and letters, made it known to New Englanders, a prime source of the Oregon migrations of the 1840s. And when he left the Columbia in 1836, he left behind the two New England missionaries, Jason and Daniel Lee, who formed the nucleus of the first permanent American settlement in Oregon Country and who would soon be joined in the Northwest by fellow New Englander missionary Marcus Whitman, generally credited with establishing the first permanent American settlement west of the Rockies. Wyeth, drawing on the fur trappers' rich store of geographical lore, had made the Platte River–South Pass–Snake River–Blue Mountains–Columbia River trail known to Americans living in the East. After him, the way to Oregon lay open to American settlement.

Shortly after the New England merchant opened the way to Oregon, another visionary was opening the way to California. Fur trade information was also responsible for the development of the second major overland route to the Pacific in the 1840s. In 1841, guided by Thomas Fitzpatrick, an Illinois schoolteacher named John Bidwell and a wealthy Missouri farmer named John Bartleson drove their wagons westward across the plains, following the fur trade route through the Platte Valley, to South

Pass and beyond to the Bear River. Here they veered south to Joseph Walker's Humboldt River crossing, which they following to the Sinks and thence across the Sierras via Sonora Pass, also discovered by Walker, and down to the Stanislaus River, where Smith's men had wintered, to the Sacramento Valley.[103] The Lees and Whitmans in Oregon and the Bidwell-Bartleson party in California were the forerunners of a huge folk migration between 1842 and the Civil War. Neither these forerunners nor those who followed could have made the transcontinental crossing without the geographical information provided by the fur trade.

## Literary and Artistic Explorers of the West in the 1830s

The Lees and Whitmans and Bidwells and Bartlesons and others who made up the vanguard of the American folk migration to the Pacific based their dreams of western settlement on more than just fur trade information. They also followed a dream that had been made manifest by the literary and artistic explorers who had, as chroniclers of the fur trade in the 1830s, created a romantic western vision that, when added to the more practical and explicit fur trade lore on how to get across the mountains and deserts, shaped powerful images in the American mind. The most important of the literary inventors of the West was Irving, particularly through his chronicling of the Bonneville expeditions and the Astorian venture. But Irving was not alone as a writer of western romance. Sir William Drummond Stewart, a Scottish baronet, wrote several popular (if fairly dreadful) romantic novels about his experiences traveling with the fur trade brigades between 1832 and 1844.[104] Another European aristocrat, Prince Alexander Maximilian of Wied, also traveled west with fur trappers in the 1830s and wrote accounts of his travels, although these were not readily available in the United States.[105] Even the dour missionary Samuel Parker, on an 1838 trip to Oregon with a fur trapper brigade, wrote romantic descriptions of the lands through which he passed and expressed his ultimate objective in his western travel by asking rhetorically, "When will this immensely extended and fertile country be brought under cultivation and filled with an industrious population?"[106] Stewart and Maximilian were accompanied on their travels by two of the three major western artists of that era: Alfred Jacob Miller and Karl Bodmer. These artists, along with George Catlin (who combined his visual art with romantic narratives of western life), presented visionary scenes of the fur trade at its peak, romantic views of western landscapes, and—perhaps most important—fascinating glimpses of the life of the Native Americans of the Far West before their deterioration and virtual disappearance after the onslaught of white American civilization.[107]

During their brief dominance of the western landscape, the members of the fur trade of the Far West were captured on paper by the pens of their literary chroniclers and on canvas by the brushes of the artists. Eventually, these literary and artistic images of the fur trade became just as much a part of the invention of the West as were the travels of the trappers themselves. Listen, for example, to the words of Irving as he describes Bonneville's view of the West from the top of the continental divide:

> Bonneville stood, in fact, upon that dividing ridge which Indians regard as the crest of the world; and on each side of which, the landscape may be said to decline to the two cardinal oceans of the globe. Whichever way he turned his eye, it was confounded by the vastness and variety of objects. Beneath him, the Rocky Mountains seemed to open all their secret recesses; deep, solemn valleys; treasured lakes; dreary passes; rugged defiles, and foaming torrents; while beyond their savage precincts, the eye was lost in an almost immeasurable landscape; stretch on every side into dim and hazy distance, like the expanse of a summer's sea. Whichever way he looked, he beheld vast plains glimmering with reflected sunshine; mighty streams wandering on their shining course toward either ocean, and snowy mountains, chain beyond chain, and peak beyond peak, till they melted like clouds into the horizon.[108]

To this romantic vision, Irving added a bit of hyperbole—an integral part of American images of the West since the fur trade. The ridge on which Bonneville stood when he gained this romantic glimpse was probably, Irving claimed, the highest in North America: "It is certain that the Rocky Mountains are of an altitude vastly superior to what was formerly supposed . . . twenty-five thousand feet above the level of the sea; an elevation only inferior to that of the Himalayas."[109]

Similar romantic and hyperbolic (if less well crafted) passages are to be found in the works of Stewart, who first traveled west with Robert Campbell of the St. Louis trade on a caravan of trade goods bound for the summer rendezvous in 1832. Here he met Bonneville; a year later he traveled to Oregon with Wyeth. In 1837 he traveled west again, this time with the young Baltimore artist Alfred Jacob Miller in tow, and in 1842 he made his final western excursion, accompanied by a young New Orleans journalist, Matthew Field, who wrote his own romantic narratives of the fur trade and the West, describing, for example, the eroded limestone bluffs on the North Platte as "domes, towers, pinnacles and minarettes . . . [of] Oriental magnificence."[110] Stewart found much to enchant him in the western landscape, as witnessed by this lyrical description of the sinks of the Popo Agie River (a tributary to the Wind River): "Several green heights scattered with pines . . . the deep, red jaws of the gorges beneath. Occasional groves of birch and aspen, contrast their tender green with the deeper shades of the cedar and the pine; and the startled antelope bounds from your path, where no eye can follow his rapid course, plunging into the bottom of a deep glen, where the mosaic bed of a torrent is scarcely covered with the water of the placid spring."[111] Stewart displayed an equally romantic view of the Native Americans of the Rockies: "True nobility may be found in the mind of the wild warrior race of these Western mountains, fit to shine in comparison with the long lines of pedigree, which so often transmit to their [European] descendants corrupt blood as well as degenerate habits."[112]

Much more important than Stewart's novels was his patronage of Miller, whose watercolors and oils provide the clearest contemporary views of trapper and Indian life in the 1830s. Miller's West was a region of romantic pastoralism, comfortable and comforting, filled with beauty and offering hope and promise. The Miller landscapes were also often subsumed by the human actors, the trappers and Indians. Miller presented both the trappers and the Native Americans as "nature's noblemen"; more than many other Americans of his time, Miller was encumbered by the mythical baggage of the Enlightenment ideal of the noble savages (among whom he included the white trappers). His Indian women depicted the idyllic side of western life while Indian men and white trappers were often shown mounted in heroic poses reminiscent of Renaissance equestrian monuments. Miller's art clearly indicated that the basest elements of white society that polluted the nobility of the Indian were derived not from those whites on the farthest frontier (the trappers) but from farmers and merchants of "civilization." As portrayed by Miller, the life of the white trapper was little different from that of the Indian, a romantic vision of a life pitted against natural forces, living for the moment in a state of pure innocence.[113]

Although Prince Maximilian's writings were in the form of travel narratives rather than novels, his descriptions of the West were no less romantic than those of his fellow aristocrat. Among the many European scholars who traveled to the American West in the 1800s on scientific excursions or "adventures," Maximilian hoped to collect "data concerning the remnants of its aboriginal population, and the primitive state of its fields and for-

17.6 Trappers Saluting the Rocky Mountains (Alfred Jacob Miller, 1837). This oil painting, a romantic view of both the fur trappers and the landscape they encountered, is representative of Miller's work and of much mid-nineteenth-century western art. Courtesy of the Buffalo Bill Historical Center, Cody, Wyoming. Gift of The Coe Foundation.

est."[114] He and his scientific and artistic entourage, including the artist Karl Bodmer, arrived in St. Louis in 1833, intending to travel west with a fur trade caravan. He was dissuaded from this plan by Clark and others in St. Louis who informed him that such travel would obstruct his scientific purposes; the trading caravans tended to avoid Indians rather than seek them out, and there would be little time to collect botanical samples. Instead, Maximilian should travel up the Missouri River on the American Fur Company's steamboat the *Yellow Stone*.

The German aristocrat concurred with this plan; accordingly, he and his party departed St. Louis in the spring of 1833. They traveled upriver to Fort Pierre in the Sioux country, where they transferred to a newer steamboat, the *Assiniboine*, which they took upstream to Fort McKenzie near the junction of the Marias River and the Missouri in north-central Montana. Here Maximilian spent nearly two months. After his desire to travel west to the Rockies was thwarted by the Assiniboine and Blackfeet troubles on the frontier, he traveled downstream to winter at Fort Clark at the Mandan villages. The following spring, Maximilian returned to St. Louis and then to Europe, where he prepared his journals for publication. Maximilian's travel account was not easily obtained in the United States, either in its German edition or in its English version, published in London in 1839. Regardless, his journals contained little new information on an area that had been well-known to Americans since Lewis and Clark. His landscape descriptions were unabashedly romantic. Like others of his time, he equated the breaks of the Missouri River with ruins of a lost age, giving to the American West an antiquity similar to that of Europe: "Here, on both sides of the river, the most strange forms are seen, and you may fancy that you see colonnades, small round pillars with large globes or a flat slab at the top, little towers, pulpits, organs with their pipes, old ruins, fortresses, castles, churches, with pointed towers, &c.&c, almost every mountain bearing on its summit some similar structure."[115]

Yet Maximilian's ethnological data on the Missouri River tribes were invaluable—especially since many of these natives were decimated (and some, such as the Mandans, nearly exterminated) by the smallpox epidemic that broke out on the northern plains five years after Maximilian's visit. Still, the real significance of Maximilian's journey was the presence of Karl Bodmer. The young Swiss artist was unquestionably the most talented of the artists to portray the American West in the first half of the nineteenth century. His magnificent renderings of the landscapes of the Missouri River, along with his ethnologically and artistically accurate de-

17.7 First Chain of the Rocky Mountains above Fort McKenzie (*Karl Bodmer, 1834*). *Bodmer's oil painting of a scene in what is now west-central Montana shows the highly realistic style that was his trademark. Joslyn Art Museum, Omaha, Nebraska. Gift of the Enron Foundation.*

pictions of the northern plains tribes, were critical for the American view of the West at the end of the fur trapper era. Whereas Miller's paintings fell into the category of romantic pastoralism, Bodmer's were scientifically exotic. His landscapes were absolutely faithful to reality, even if often focused on the fantastic and fabulous; indeed, his work on such areas as the Missouri Breaks country often displays a draftsman-like quality. In his portrayals of Indians and Indian life, Bodmer evinced a fascination with the strange and the wonderful, painting darkly mysterious scenes of Indian burial grounds and ceremonial objects while retaining the same degree of almost photographic precision shown in his landscapes. Bodmer's art, as romantic in its own way as Miller's, formed the basis for many contemporary lithographs appearing in American periodicals, providing the American people "a matchless picture of the American frontier—a collective portrait that was equaled by no other eyewitness artist before the coming of photography."[116]

Arguably of greater importance than either Miller or Bodmer, however, was the American artist George Catlin, whose artistic portrayals of western

Indians and landscapes most clearly represented the West for more than a generation of Americans. Like Maximilian's descriptions, Catlin's writings portrayed the upper Missouri country as relict features of a Golden Age, "one continued appearance . . . of some ancient and boundless city in ruins—ramparts, terraces, domes, towers, citadels and castles may be seen, —cupolas, and magnificent porticoes . . . shedding a glory over the solitude of this wild and pictured country."[117] But it was his artistic portrayals of Indian life that earned Catlin his fame; derivatives of his work appeared in many contemporary journals and periodicals, provided the stylistic bases for illustrations in the western "romances" coming into vogue in the 1830s, and became the primary western iconographic images of the period through imitation in numerous Currier (later Currier and Ives) prints.

Trained for the law in Connecticut and only informally trained in art in Philadelphia, Catlin was not as skilled an artist as either Miller or Bodmer. Although he toured the southern plains and the Southwest extensively after 1833, perhaps his major western work was done in 1832–33 when he traveled up the Missouri River for two thousand miles on the maiden voyage of the American Fur Company's steamboat the *Yellow Stone*. On his way upriver, Catlin painted landscapes, often surreal in quality, of the Missouri Valley, with green, enameled hills and prairies, "a brilliantly colored Eden, peopled with noble warriors who harkened back to the days of ancient Greece, or the pastoral visions of the *Aeneid*."[118] Even more than Miller, Catlin portrayed the western Indians as a romantic and pastoral people, far removed from the "poor, degraded, and humble specimens" that could be seen in areas adjacent to white civilization.[119] Catlin influenced American images of the West primarily through his depiction of the exotic and, to him, Elysian life of the western Indians. Without his work—and that of Miller, Bodmer, Irving, Stewart, Maximilian, and others—the American view of the West at the end of the fur trade era would have been, if reasonably accurate geographically, colorless and sterile.

## The End of the Fur Trade Era, 1839

The last major rendezvous of the fur trappers was held in the summer of 1838; the rendezvous of 1839 was a shadow of what had gone before. The American fur trade's brief dominance of exploration and utilization of the Rocky Mountains and farther West was virtually over by the end of the 1830s. But the fur trappers continued to be an important feature of the American

*17.8* Mandan Village (*George Catlin, 1832*). *Though less skilled as an artist than some of his counterparts, such as Miller and Bodmer, Catlin produced work that was both enormously popular and ethnographically important in portraying a lifestyle soon to pass from the western scene. Courtesy of the Buffalo Bill Historical Center, Cody, Wyoming. Gift of Paul Mellon.*

expansion west. Their future role was typified by Thomas Fitzpatrick's service as guide to the Bidwell-Bartleson party. Other former trappers would guide emigrants across the Great Plains and the Rockies and the Great Basin. Some, like Jim Bridger, would establish posts and forts along the emigrant trails to replenish supplies and refresh livestock. Others, like Kit Carson, would serve as western guides for the wave of government explorers who began to consolidate fur trade lore in the 1840s. In these new capacities, the former members of the fur trade would aid the American westward expansion. They would also contribute to a growing scientific awareness of the West as their geographical information, obtained through years of wading the icy beaver streams and crossing the passes of the mountains, entered the mainstream of American lore.

Two maps, produced in 1839 at the very end of the free-trapping system, demonstrate the degree to which fur trade information had entered established geographical science in the United States. Unlike the maps in Irving's book on Bonneville's adventures, neither of these maps was produced for public consumption. But both were widely circulated among government circles and could be considered as "official maps" and, therefore, as part of the body of formal geographical knowledge on the Rockies at the end of the fur trade's heyday.

The first of these maps was produced by Captain Washington Hood of the U.S. Army Corps of Topographical Engineers. Hood had obtained fur trade data from "frequent conversations with two highly intelligent trappers, William A. Walker, of Virginia, and Mr. Coates, of Missouri, who belonged originally to Captain Bonneville's party, but subsequently continued to roam the mountains as free trappers for six consecutive years; as also that derived from others who were connected with [fur trade] surveys and expeditions as far to the westward as Santa Fe and Taos."[120] Utilizing this information, Hood drew the map "exhibiting the practicable passes of the Rocky Mountains" that his superior, Chief of the Topographical Engineers Colonel J. J. Abert, called "far more correct than [any] other extant."[121] This map existed only in manuscript form, but given its origins in the army's Topographical Bureau, it must have been known to a fairly wide segment of the establishment in Washington. On this map, which extends only from the forty-ninth parallel to the Great Salt Lake and from the Powder River to the Salmon, Hood laid down the routes considered "most practicable" for crossing the Rockies with wheeled vehicles—essentially, the routes used by the fur trappers. This map thus represents a validation not only of the presence of mountain man lore in formal geography but also of the continuing American faith in the belief that the Rockies posed no impenetrable barrier to transcontinental travel.

The second map of 1839 that demonstrated the connection between informal fur trade and formal "official" geographical images of the West was produced by David Burr, "Geographer to the House of Representatives."[122] Burr's map was apparently produced from a manuscript map of Smith's; thus, the West drawn by Burr in 1839 was the West of Jedediah Smith, the most widely traveled of the American fur trappers. Smith's routes back and forth across the vast expanse between the Rockies and the Pacific and from the Columbia to Mexico are clearly marked on Burr's map. Most significant, the Burr map showed the two core drainage regions that, by the end of the 1830s, had become the trappers' image of the Rockies—the northern one in which the Snake, Missouri, Yellowstone, and Green rivers head and the southern one from which rise the source streams of the Platte, Rio Grande, Arkansas, and Colorado or Grand—along with a clear

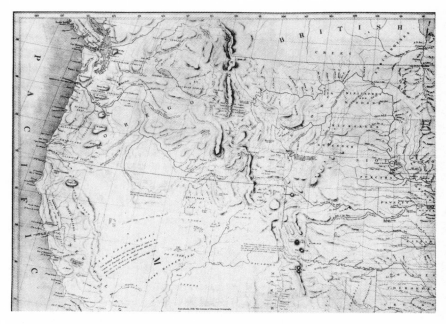

17.9 Portion of map of western North America (David Burr, 1839). Burr's map was apparently copied from a manuscript map by Jedediah Smith and may represent the best depiction of Smith's (and the fur trade's) conception of the Rocky Mountain region. Courtesy of the Library of Congress.

definition of a true continental divide. The correct courses of western rivers were depicted on Burr's map, as were the accurate configurations of the various Rocky Mountain ranges that defined the drainage basins of those rivers. Numerous small legends on the map gave descriptive information on the complex geography of the Rocky Mountain system, information that could have come only from Smith or some equally well informed mountain man of the American fur trade.

The mountain men had put to rest Clark's conceptualization of a single core drainage area for western rivers; these maps are direct evidence of that fact. Even more direct evidence comes from the journal of the last of the mountain men. Referring to James Ohio Pattie's popular published account, which did so much to support the old concept of a common-source area, Osborne Russell wrote: "He [Pattie] says that Lewis' river [the Snake] and the Arkansas head near each other in Long's Peak [of the Colorado Rockies]. I never was at Long's Peak or the head of the Arkansas river but am fully confident these cannot be within 300 mls. of the source of Lewis' river."[123]

Consider what the fur trappers had done in the few years between William Ashley's newspaper advertisement in 1822 and Joseph Walker's journey to California in 1833–34. They had erased the mythical Buenaventura and Multnomah Rivers from the maps and replaced Clark's distorted view of a common-source region with a more rational interpretation of the river and mountain system of the West, one that included the two core regions of northwestern Wyoming and central Colorado—more than four hundred miles apart. They had learned that the centuries-old dream of a water passage across the continent needed to be discarded in favor of a land route. They had pioneered this land route by discovering the Platte River road, South Pass, the Humboldt and Snake plain and other desert crossings, and the passes across the Blue Mountains, the Cascades, and the Sierras. In short, they had created the Oregon and California Trails. They had also learned that the early-nineteenth-century notion of the uniform, garden-like quality of the western lands was inaccurate. Much of the West was desert country, particularly the lands west of the Rockies. But the West contained much prime agricultural land for the needs of an expanding American farm population, especially in Oregon Country and in the Great Valley of California. Based on this information, a wave of migration would soon carry America to the shores of the Pacific and make of the United States a continental nation. The Northwest and the Southwest were added to Louisiana Territory as part of the United States in the 1840s. Without the fur trade of the Far West, without men like William Ashley and Jedediah Smith and hundreds of their companions, both famous and unknown, this could not have happened. In a very real sense—in both literal and symbolic ways—the mountain men and others associated with the American fur trade invented the American West for future generations. In the process, the American fur trappers—romantic characters of a romantic age—created a romantic tradition that still exists. The romance of the fur trade frontier and of the western settlement frontier that immediately followed is still America's creation myth. The words of George Catlin are just as true now as they were when he wrote them in 1840: "The Far West;—the country whose fascinations spread a charm over the mind almost dangerous to civilized pursuits. Few people even know the true definition of the term 'West'; and where is its location?—Phantom-like it flies before us as we travel, and on our way is continually gilded, before us, as we approach the setting sun."[124]

# 18 / Nature's Gullivers and Crusoes: The Scientific Exploration of British North America, 1800–1870

SUZANNE ZELLER

During the 1800s the British territories in North America were more closely scrutinized than ever before. They piqued curiosity during the Napoleonic Wars because they contained natural resources that the British economy required to continue its war effort. Only through rational, "statistical" surveys, borrowed from the German tradition of statecraft in the late 1700s, could the nature and extent of these resources be made known as quickly and efficiently as possible. This practical need to take stock in British North America found reinforcement after the peace of 1815, when an overabundance of British military officers turned their skills to peacetime activities. As a result, geographical investigation was transformed from aesthetic description to the systematic collection and classification of information. Science thus did more than generate abstract data; it offered a means of assessing the habitability of the earth and of making better use of its resources to predict and control the quality of life.

Scientific explorations in British North America after 1800 were conducted along two lines, both etched deeply in the British imagination by travel literature of the time. First, as in Jonathan Swift's *Gulliver's Travels* (1726), explorers sojourned overseas for imperial purposes that were of little direct concern to the colonies. Like Gulliver, they arrived in new lands eager to "see the country and make what discoveries [they] could," and they reported their observations in terms relative to the familiar standards of home. Like Gulliver, these explorers returned home with corrections to current maps and with other useful contributions that were "honourably received."[1] Among the first "Gullivers" were military officers who found themselves underemployed and their positions threatened after the

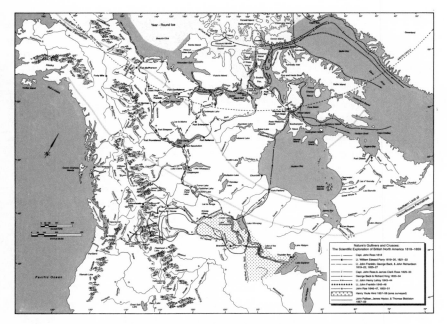

*Map 18.1 The Scientific Exploration of British North America, 1818–1859.*

end of the Napoleonic Wars. In British North America after 1815, the Royal Navy undertook Arctic explorations and hydrographic surveys, and the Ordnance Department surveyed military canals and roads. The military men thus provided the personnel and expertise for major scientific expeditions.[2]

Second, as in Daniel Defoe's *Robinson Crusoe* (1719), British North Americans also used science to explore these new lands, not as visitors but as inhabitants. Like Crusoe, these explorers hoped primarily to replicate the comforts of British life in their own new environment. Their tools included borrowed European ideas reapplied to their North American situation. Later pioneer settlers in British North America could easily appreciate Crusoe's growing conviction that "every man may be in time master" of the skills required to ensure the kind of life he aspired to in his new land; Crusoe himself had landed on his island having "never handled a tool" before in his life. He recorded his progress in a journal, as the environment both modified his tools and raised his expectations. He remarked about one of his inventions, "I had never seen any such thing in England." One of Crusoe's first priorities after building shelter was to undertake "a more particular survey" of his environs by "peering in every corner, and under every rock." With each useful discovery, he realized that more remained to be found, motivating him "to see the whole island." The surveying convinced Crusoe "that this was all my own, that I was king and lord of all this country indefeasibly, and had a right of possession." A parallel process of identification and ownership shaped the thinking of the Crusoes in British North America between 1800 and 1870. [3]

At the end of the War of 1812, many former British military officers were granted land to settle in the colonies. Joined by members of the growing professional and commercial classes in the towns, these highly educated Crusoes were not stranded intellectually. The most obvious example, the author and botanist Catherine Parr Traill (1802–99) immigrated as the wife of a pensioned officer. Traill consciously borrowed from the Crusoe model to fashion her popular writings, including *The Backwoods of Canada* (1836) and *Canadian Crusoes* (1852). She also communicated her botanical findings to the University of Edinburgh, while other immigrants sent their specimens to British scientific institutions such as the Linnean Society and the Geological Society of London, which encouraged submissions from abroad. Moreover, these Crusoes founded similar associations in the colonies and, like the imaginary Crusoe, undertook scientific inventories that they recorded in their own published journals. [4]

The course of scientific exploration in British North America during the nineteenth century was determined largely by the common heritage of the Old World and the New, a heritage that included the strong amateur naturalist tradition in British culture, meshed with the popular tenets of natural theology. [5] Just as crucial was the intellectual impact of the Scottish Enlightenment, with its strong utilitarian bent. [6]

Scientific information, both natural and physical, took various forms, ranging from specimen collections to magnetic and meteorological readings. Yet the approach used was always inventorial, an attempt to take stock of nature in British North America whether for practical or theoretical reasons, usually for both. Indeed, practice and theory were often understood as two ends of the same spectrum of activity. For the Gullivers, scientific knowledge meant the theoretical ability to expand imperial power; for the Crusoes, it meant the practical ability to locate valuable minerals and plants, to combat insect pests and epidemic diseases, even to forecast the weather. For these reasons, scientific exploration changed not only public perceptions of British North America's material potential, both in Great Britain and in the colonies, but also the course of scientific development itself. Scientific successes propelled science to refine its methods to ensure ever greater successes; an important characteristic of the "Victorian rate of progress" was the widespread expectation of its acceleration over time.

## Roots of the Geographical Tradition in Science, 1800–1815

Two eighteenth-century scientific challenges stimulated scientific explorations in British North America during the early 1800s. First, the Linnaean system revolutionized the study of natural history in the 1730s by providing a convenient, universal method of classifying and naming specimens. Although Carolus Linnaeus (1707–78) worked out his system most fully in botany, it nevertheless inspired disciples all over the world to collect, describe, and name animal and mineral specimens as well. Because it rested on only one randomly chosen criterion, plants' reproductive parts, Linnaeus's taxonomic system was admittedly artificial. Still, part of its implicit challenge was to collect specimens as widely as possible in order to arrive at criteria that were more comprehensive, and therefore more "natural," than mere numbers of pistils and stamens. Second, the influential Comte de Buffon (1707–88) in France used a broader geographical approach. He recognized more similarities between Eurasian and North American plants and animals than between those of North and South America. He speculated that European animals had once migrated over a northern land bridge between Asia and North America and that the differences now apparent between them reflected a certain "degeneration" of North American forms. In Buffon's Eurocentric view, these physical changes resulted from climatic influences and seemed to hold out ominous implications for the future of European colonists in North America. His multivolume *Histoire naturelle* (1749) popularized such negative impressions about the New World for a century after its publication. Linnaeus's universal method and Buffon's provocative assumption threw down the gauntlet for more intensive scientific investigations of vast territories like British North America.[7]

In addition, the voyages of Captain James Cook around the world during the 1770s offered a successful model of the potent combination of geography and science. Cook was accompanied by Joseph Banks (1743–1820), a devoted Linnaean who had visited the shores of Newfoundland and Labrador aboard a fishery protection vessel in 1766. Banks returned to England with the most comprehensively documented botanical and zoological specimens ever collected from North America. After accompanying Cook's circumnavigation in 1771, Banks became both scientific adviser to the Royal Botanic Gardens at Kew, which he built into the main imperial clearing-house for plants, and president of the Royal Society of London, a powerful position from which he directed further scientific explorations sponsored by the British government. Cook's second circumnavigation in 1772 included Reinhold Forster and his son Georg, whose broad conceptualizations in turn inspired the influential Prussian scientific traveler Alexander von Humboldt (1769–1859). It was only by overland travel, Humboldt would argue in his widely read and admired *Personal Narrative of Travels to the Equinoctial Regions of America* (1807), "that we can discover the direction of chains of mountains, and their geological constitution, the climate of each zone, and its influence on the forms and habits of organized beings." Humboldt's name became synonymous in both Europe and America with a "cosmical" approach to nature, requiring as systematic a study as possible of the complex interrelations of natural phenomena over the entire earth, with evidence gathered by standardized means.[8]

British scientific exploration gained some of this uniformity of purpose and approach through the influence of Robert Jameson (1774–1854), professor of natural history at the University of Edinburgh. As a youth, Jameson had imbibed from his reading of both *Robinson Crusoe* and Cook's travels a love of nature and an enthusiasm for its exploration. He studied with the famous Saxon geologist Abraham Gottlob Werner (1750–1817) at the Freiberg School of Mines and encouraged his own students to apply Werner's mineralogical techniques to fieldwork, activities that heralded the emergence of geology as an earth science. Wernerians classified rocks on the basis of their location in the ordered strata of the earth's crust, a useful concept for finding minerals and for identifying those lying in situ. They generally worked from "Neptunist" assumptions that the earth's crust had been formed by receding waters. In contrast, their rivals—the followers of James Hutton (1726–97) of Edinburgh—held to "Vulcanist" premises that fire in the earth's core was responsible for these formations. Jameson founded the Wernerian Natural History Society of Edinburgh in 1808 to publish a broad range of evidence on the origins of geological formations, and he cofounded the *Edinburgh Philosophical Journal* in 1819.[9] He convinced "a large share of the best naturalists of the day" of the importance of collecting scientific information and specimens; many of them duly sent back treasures from the far corners of the globe, enabling Jameson to amass an enormous zoological and geological collection second in size only to the British Museum. With this collection, he helped establish the Royal Scottish Museum in 1854.[10]

Among the first to investigate British North America scientifically after 1800 were fur traders. Explorers for both the Hudson's Bay Company and the North West Company penetrated the interior of the continent to map its river routes and assess its fur-bearing potential. David Thompson (1770–1857) included a scientific perspective in his more general task of exploration and mapping. His reports noted both astronomical and temperature readings, which he later submitted to the Smithsonian Institution, as well as his interest in native peoples. Trained by the surveyors Philip Turnor and Peter Fidler, Thompson fitted his observations of the terrain into the surveying tradition prevalent in geology between 1750 and 1820. He described the country he explored less impressionistically than had those before him, noting the inclination of formations to the horizon rather than isolated individual strata. Moreover, Thompson reported evidence of the role of water—and ice in the winter—as an agent of geological change, attempting to comprehend the formations in terms of nearby rivers and lakes.[11]

Several European naturalists reported on areas of British North America outside of the northern territories monopolized by fur-trading companies. In 1803 the French botanist François André Michaux published his *Flora boreali-Americana*, the result of an attempt by his father, André Michaux, to trace the northern tree line as far as Lake Temiskaming in 1792. Michaux's work remained unsurpassed as a source of botanical information until Frederick Pursh's publication in 1814 of a comprehensive Linnaean compilation of North American plants: the *Flora Americae Septentrionalis*. Pursh (1774–1829) had originally come to the United States in 1799 to collect ornamental plants. Little is known about him except that he left in disgrace after falsely claiming important botanical collections, among them some from the Lewis and Clark expedition, as his own. Pursh moved on to Lower Canada, now the province of Quebec, where he marveled at the range of new species and varieties he discovered even in the more densely populated areas around Montreal. There Pursh met John Goldie (1793–1886), a Glaswegian gardener who had come to botanize around the lower Great Lakes in 1819. Fate repeatedly thwarted both collectors' attempts to send specimens safely home to their respective botanical gardens: Goldie's collections were lost at sea three times, and Pursh's contributions to a flora of Canada burned in a Montreal fire shortly before he died there in poverty.

Goldie eventually settled at Ayr in Upper Canada, now the province of Ontario.[12]

The private interests represented by Michaux, Pursh, and Goldie were supported by government-initiated scientific explorations of the British North American colonies during the Napoleonic Wars. In Nova Scotia, Governor Sir John Wentworth, former surveyor general of the King's Woods for the colony, commissioned Titus Smith Jr. (1768–1850) to survey the colony in 1801. Smith, a native of Massachusetts, lived in Dutch Village near Halifax and was known as a botanical gardener skilled in acclimatizing British seeds to North American conditions. Wentworth's practical goal in the survey was to assess Nova Scotia's timber supplies and its potential for growing hemp, valuable to the Royal Navy for rope, and he asked Smith to consider transportation and other economic factors. Smith spent several months deep in the woods, producing much more than a pragmatic economic analysis. He appended to his journals detailed lists and drawings of plants and a map of the province that remained unsurpassed in detail and accuracy for at least a generation.

Thirty years later, convinced that Nova Scotians could contribute uniquely to natural history because so much of the colony, though settled, remained in its natural state, Smith offered remarkable ecological insights into plant succession and the delicate balance of nature. Smith recognized the impact not only of human action on fauna and flora but also of animal migrations on the living patterns of the colony's native peoples. Geology too contributed to Smith's unitary view of nature. Satisfied with neither Wernerian nor Huttonian assumptions, he developed an integrated interpretation of Nova Scotia's geological structures as a low portion of an older mountain range and suggested that some "internal motion" in the earth's core, whether mechanical or chemical, generated a continuous cycle of composition and decomposition in rocks and soils. He believed that this process implied "a necessary connexion" among the mineral, vegetable, and animal kingdoms. But his search for such designs in nature led Smith to postulate that the very advance of "civilization" unwittingly created iron ore deposits by triggering a chemical chain reaction that decomposed iron oxides in the soil when forests were burned for clearing.[13]

A good portion of the other evidence that reached European scientific societies from colonial outposts during the early years of the 1800s came from missionaries to native peoples. Among the earliest were Moravian missionaries, who had lived in Labrador since the late eighteenth century and who regularly sent plant and mineral specimens, including the Labra-

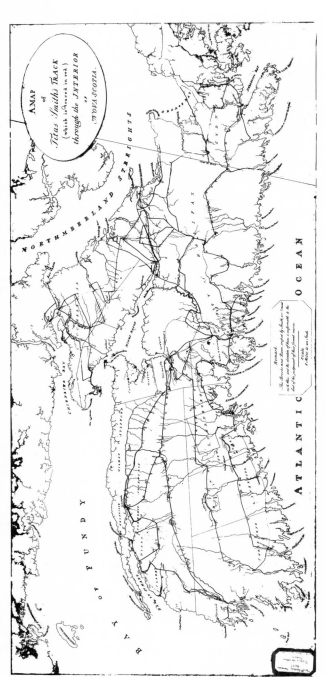

18.1 "A Map of Titus Smith's Track through the Interior of Nova Scotia" (Titus Smith, c. 1805). Smith's map was a pioneering venture in public cartography in eastern Canada. Courtesy of the Public Archives of Nova Scotia.

dorite they discovered, to Britain, the United States, and Europe. In 1814 the Geological Society of London published a note by the Reverend Henry Steinhauer, who collated and synthesized a series of earlier descriptions of the coast of this barren land. Steinhauer promised "interesting results" to geologists who studied Labrador, precisely because its surface remained free of the plant and soil covers that "so often baffle[d] research" in Britain. He recognized Labrador's offshore islands as structurally contiguous with the mainland, and he correctly identified this continuity as key to their interpretation. However, Steinhauer's recommended overview of these "Primitive" formations, the same type that Thompson had described in the Northwest, would have to await the analysis of their prototype, the Canadian Shield, by the Geological Survey of Canada some decades later.[14]

## Science in Polar Exploration, 1815–1819

The hope of finding a Northwest Passage to the Orient had been a recurrent theme in British imperial history for centuries. At the end of the Napoleonic Wars, with the availability of trained military personnel, imperial rivalries now sought expression in nonmilitary forms of engagement, in the peaceful expansion of intellectual as well as territorial frontiers. And nature itself seemed to beckon northward, with a rare breakup of polar ice masses.

British policy regarding Arctic exploration was initiated by Sir John Barrow (1764–1848), secretary of the admiralty, and Sir Joseph Banks, still president of the Royal Society. In his youth, Barrow had voyaged on a Greenland whaler, and he had been interested in nautical and natural sciences ever since. In an influential essay published anonymously in the *Quarterly Review* in October 1817, Barrow insisted that Arctic voyagers would discover "metal more attractive" by allowing themselves to be drawn beyond the familiar waters of Hudson Bay. Reiterating a conviction he had published in 1816, Barrow calculated that a mere "three months out and home" would be sufficient to discover a Northwest Passage. He forged his optimism on Arctic whalers' reports that unusual quantities of polar ice had broken free during the past year or so and had been seen floating into the Atlantic. Barrow perceived a rare window of opportunity to gain not only a competitive edge of geographical knowledge for Britain over its political rivals but also important scientific information that would benefit all of the civilized world.[15]

The diminution of the polar ice cap seemed to carry theoretical as well as practical implications. First, the receding ice masses apparently influenced the earth's magnetism strongly enough to affect navigation. The aurora borealis often made navigators' compass needles "vibrate violently" and even "fly round the whole circumferance." In contrast, Barrow noted a "remarkable coincidence": the westward variation of the compass needle in Baffin Bay, normally the greatest in the world, virtually stopped during the breakup of the ice. This important anomaly implied a link between the appearance of the northern lights and the inability of the polar ice cap to conduct atmospheric electricity safely to the ground. It seemed reasonable to probe the more general relationship of atmospheric electricity and terrestrial magnetism.[16]

Second, Barrow was concerned about the possible climatic effects of the southward movement of the ice. Older Icelanders recalled that normal-sized vegetables had once grown where the visiting British botanist W. J. Hooker (1788–1865) had found cabbages in August 1809 "so diminutive that a half-crown piece would have covered the whole plant." Moreover, the icebergs clearly determined Iceland's daily local weather patterns: crashing offshore, they brought stormy skies; clinging to the coasts, they brought dense fogs and penetrating cold that destroyed vegetation and cattle. Similar effects, Barrow pointed out, had been recorded in Switzerland when glaciers encroached on alpine valleys, and along the Atlantic seaboard in 1816 when corn failed to ripen from Pennsylvania to Massachusetts because icebergs moved as far south as the fortieth parallel. Barrow adduced that France and even England had once supported indigenous wine industries far more extensively than his contemporaries realized. More dramatic effects, he feared, might well be in store for Britain if the process continued.[17]

Barrow also identified more abstract scientific problems that might be resolved with valuable information culled in high latitudes. In addition to determining the degree and magnetic impact of static electricity in the atmosphere, scientists might even locate a north magnetic pole. Moreover, the depth, saltiness, and specific gravity of Arctic seawater, as well as the velocity of Arctic ocean currents, needed further study. Finally, pendulum research data that could be compared with similar measurements at other stations on the globe would help determine mathematically the precise shape of the earth.[18]

Like Barrow, Joseph Banks cultivated contacts with captains of whaling ships in order to benefit from their Arctic experience. In particular he consulted William Scoresby Jr. (1789–1857), whom he had met years earlier through Scoresby's father. The younger Scoresby already had connections with the scientific world through his studies at the University of Edinburgh, where his experience and aptitude had deeply impressed Jameson, who in turn had the ear of Lord Melville in the admiralty. Jameson drew Scoresby into the Wernerian Society and persuaded him to send natural history specimens from his voyages back to Edinburgh. Aboard his whaling ship, Scoresby also recorded valuable meteorological and astronomical readings, and he established that bottom temperatures in Arctic waters exceeded surface temperatures. The Wernerian Society published his important analyses of the varieties of both polar ice and Arctic currents in its *Memoirs* in 1815.[19]

In 1817 Banks approached Scoresby about the receding polar ice cap. Scoresby agreed that science stood only to gain from Arctic voyages, but he pointed out that government support was needed to conduct the specialized and time-consuming investigations. On Banks's advice the Royal Society, whose council included Barrow, urged the admiralty to outfit an Arctic expedition that, while tracing a navigable route from Atlantic to Pacific along the northern coast of America, would also gather specific scientific information. The combined efforts of Barrow, Scoresby, Jameson, and Banks, through their respective and interrelated institutional connections, meshed well with the admiralty's view of its own best interests. In December 1817 the government announced plans to send two pairs of ships to seek a Northwest Passage, one pair to sail in high latitudes via Davis Strait and the other to seek an open polar sea by way of Spitzbergen.[20]

Although Scoresby was eminently qualified to command such a mission, Royal Navy regulations prohibited nonnaval commanders on its expeditions. Perhaps more to the point, Barrow felt defensive about the utter failure of the Royal Navy's last four Arctic ventures, and he was determined to redeem its reputation.[21] In command of the mission were Captain John Ross and Lieutenant William Edward Parry, through Davis Strait, and Captain David Buchan and Lieutenant John Franklin, by way of Spitzbergen. Scientific interests played a primary role in outfitting this expedition, unlike earlier Arctic explorations. On the recommendation of the Royal Society, Captain Edward Sabine (1788–1883) of the Royal Artillery joined Ross as astronomer and naturalist, and Alexander Fisher, a Cambridge mathematician and naturalist, traveled with Buchan as assistant surgeon.

The Ross mission was mandated to pay "every possible attention" to the "advancement of science" by obtaining "correct information on every interesting subject in high northern latitudes which are rarely visited by scientific men." Sabine enthusiastically accepted the assignment, which he hoped would open doors in his intended career straddling the scientific and military spheres. Since one of Sabine's immediate objectives was to determine the length of vibration of the seconds pendulum in high latitudes, the ships carried pendulum clocks fitted with transit instruments. The four ships also carried instruments to measure terrestrial magnetism (dipping needles, azimuth compasses, repeating circles, dip-micrometers and dip-sectors to correct for variations caused by temperature and air pressure, and astronomical instruments for measuring distances), as well as chronometers, a hydrometer, thermometers and barometers, and apparatus for measuring atmospheric electrical charges and component gases and for collecting, preserving, and sketching natural history specimens. Ross devised an armored contraption to bring up samples from the ocean depths. He furthermore instructed that all scientific information and collections from the voyage be submitted to him for distribution and analysis. In general, specimens went ultimately to the relevant London societies, as well as to the British Museum and to Jameson at the University of Edinburgh, after Ross and Fisher described them in published narratives.[22]

The expedition returned home in November 1818, no closer to the discovery of a Northwest Passage. Barrow turned against Ross personally. Ross had followed the Greenland coast of Davis Strait and passed through Melville Bay to examine Smith, Jones, and Lancaster Sounds. After rejecting the first two as unlikely openings to a Northwest Passage, he entered Lancaster Sound but turned back when he believed he saw mountains enclosing it, a decision his officers later refused to support. The expedition returned to England by way of Baffin Island, bypassing Cumberland Sound as well as Frobisher Bay. Sabine escaped Barrow's wrath partly by refusing to hand over his notes and collections to Ross and by publicly disputing Ross's version of the events surrounding the captain's fateful decision.[23] Sabine also insisted that his overriding goal had always been to approach the north magnetic pole as closely as possible. In support of this pristine public image, he dutifully produced extensive tables of astronomical, chronometrical, and painstaking magnetic readings and calculations made in cooperation with Ross's nephew James Clark Ross during the voyage. Sabine also brought back botanical and zoological specimens, among them Sabine's gull *(Xema sabini)*, and received credit for the first sighting of this species. He garnered nothing but praise for his scientific endeavors, the results of which he published separately, including an account of the striking similarities between native peoples living on either side of Bering Strait, evidence that seemed to support Buffon's theory of a prehistoric land bridge between Asia and North America.[24]

Barrow planned a second, even longer, expedition with much the same crew, but with Parry replacing Ross in command. From May 1819 until November 1820 Parry followed Ross's route to Lancaster Sound, the shores of which he traced to Prince Regent Inlet and then to Melville Island, where the expedition wintered. Parry explored parts of the island before setting out to the west again, only to be turned back by ice at Banks Island. The expedition discovered Barrow Strait and returned home by way of Lancaster Sound and Baffin Bay. Sabine accompanied Parry, this time harvesting the "scientifically richest" results of the Arctic expeditions. He pursued research on the length of vibration of the seconds pendulum in various latitudes, earning the Royal Society's Copley Medal in 1821 for contributions to the establishment of the elliptical shape of the earth. He also investigated his other Arctic preoccupation, terrestrial magnetism. In 1817 Christopher Hansteen had argued that the earth had two magnetic poles in each hemisphere and that magnetic fluctuations were related to atmospheric conditions and therefore to meteorology. Sabine built his professional reputation on an attempt to define these relationships more precisely by means of regular and often uninterrupted observations of the tides, the weather, and magnetic dip, force, and variation. In 1825 he published evidence that magnetic force was not greatest where the needle dipped 90 degrees. There was, then, a certain ambivalence in the concept of the earth as a magnet and hence in the meaning of a "north magnetic pole." This discovery, Sabine wrote later, enhanced interest in magnetic researches because now even the broad outlines of the science had to be recast. These researches inevitably turned scientific attention to the north of British North America, where two distinct magnetic poles were now supposed to lie.[25]

Sabine followed the "cosmical" approach of Humboldt, whose outlook deeply influenced the development of the organized British imperial investigations not only of terrestrial magnetism in physical sciences but also of the geographical distribution of species in natural sciences. Humboldt pioneered attempts to typify plant forms in relation to climatic regions, and he formed a matrix for botanical work on species in Britain. Indeed, Sabine brought back Arctic plant specimens to add to Hooker's Icelandic collections. Sabine's colleague Francis Bauer also conducted experiments on red snow samples noticed near Baffin Bay during the first voyage, identifying a fungus as the cause; Arctic zoological specimens attracted considerable interest and increased the thirst for specimens.[26]

Meanwhile, Scoresby continued his Arctic whaling voyages, and in 1820 he published a remarkable work that is still recognized as fundamental to the development of Arctic science. His *Account of the Arctic Regions* collated the geographical, scientific, and practical experiences of a way of life and presented them in the form of an authoritative and captivating classic of whaling literature. His analyses of the natural phenomena of the ocean and its inhabitants ranged from whales to the minutest plankton, which he observed microscopically and recognized as whale food. Scoresby's studies embraced even ocean currents, seawater, and iceforms and included extensive observations of terrestrial magnetism.[27]

## Scientific Explorations Inland, 1820–1829

After Ross's voyage in 1818, scientific explorers' focus shifted from sea to land in the quest for information. Humboldt's geographical approach to science bore fruit in the study of the distribution over the earth of physical and natural phenomena, whether magnetic readings, northern lights, useful minerals, plant and animal species, or even native peoples. In particular, Scandinavian and German disciples of Linnaeus outlined botanical "regions" of the earth in the hope of explaining broad patterns of vegetation in historical terms. The presence of Scandinavian types of plants in the Scottish Highlands raised questions about their distribution among other northern floras, including those in British North America. Such questions could be answered only if collectors traveled abroad to cull specimens, a fact well understood by Hooker, who now began to send others on excursions like the Icelandic journey that had launched his own career.[28]

Unlike the Ross expedition of 1818, Parry's Arctic mission of 1819 was complemented by an overland party instead of a second pair of ships. Lieutenant John Franklin's crew embarked on a remarkable trek from York Factory to Cumberland House, then by way of the Athabasca River and Lake, Slave River, and Great Slave Lake to the Coppermine River and down to its mouth on the Arctic Sea. From there they traveled along the Arctic shore east toward Hudson Bay. The scientist of the expedition was Dr. John Richardson (1787–1865), Franklin's surgeon and naturalist. Richardson had studied medicine at the University of Edinburgh, where he had joined Jameson's expanding network of scientific contacts. Jameson's contribution to Richardson's scientific outlook was reflected most clearly in the Wernerian cast of the geological or "geognostical" observations appended to Franklin's published *Narrative of a Journey to the Shores of the Polar Sea* (1823). As a good Wernerian, Richardson recognized the predominance of "Primitive" formations, which only years later would be understood as metamorphic in origin; he, like Jameson, preferred Neptunian interpretations whenever possible and saw volcanic causes as incidental to the aqueous. Richardson sought out resemblances to European formations described by Werner and Jameson; Jameson, in turn, praised Richardson's descriptions as a "luminous sketch" of Arctic geology.[29]

Richardson's specialty, however, was zoology. His boreal collections were shipped by the Hudson's Bay Company to the British Museum and assigned to the ornithological collector Joseph Sabine, brother of Edward Sabine. Sabine's zoological appendix to Franklin's *Narrative* credited Richardson's painstaking comparisons of his specimens with known species. Richardson also contributed icthyological and botanical lists, the latter compiled with the help of specialists such as Hooker, now regius professor of botany at Glasgow, and Robert Brown (1773–1858), a Scottish taxonomist and curator for the Linnean Society of London. Even without the specimens of the summer of 1821, which exhaustion and near-starvation in the Barren Grounds finally compelled Richardson to abandon, his contribution supplanted earlier fur traders' more impressionistic accounts and placed the natural history of British North America on a new empirical footing. As a result, Parry entrusted his own zoological collections to Richardson.[30]

Richardson was curious about the habitability of northwestern North America. His impression that the ground in the continental interior was not permanently frozen gained significance, in his view, in the light of the Swedish botanist Coran Wahlenberg's *Flora Lapponica* (1812), one of the reference works he selected for the journey. Wahlenberg (1780–1851), much like Humboldt, insisted that vegetation in a given region depended both on actual soil and air temperatures and on their seasonal distributions, rather than on mere annual temperature means; a cold winter did not necessarily preclude agriculture. Space limitations, Richardson claimed, kept him from elaborating in the *Narrative* on either of his pet subjects, the geographical distribution and northern limits of plant species and the effects of climate on the vegetation of the Hudson Bay region. Nevertheless, this continuing interest informed his subsequent scientific explorations, as well as public perceptions of the potential of the Hudson's Bay Company territory for permanent settlement.[31]

Both Parry and Franklin received Arctic assignments again in 1824 and 1825, respectively. In the meantime, Parry had spent two winters in the Arctic from 1821 to 1823, searching for a passage northward from Repulse Bay, and had returned after two unsuccessful attempts to pass through Fury and Hecla Strait, which seemed to him a more promising route than that through Lancaster Sound. On his next voyage, in 1824, Parry again approached Lancaster Sound and wintered at Port Bowen in Prince Regent Inlet. His astronomer, Henry Foster, had been trained by Edward Sabine to record hourly magnetic readings. These data offered standards for simultaneous readings elsewhere on the globe because of their proximity to the north magnetic pole. Parry's failure on this voyage, aborted after the loss of one of the ships, to trace a Northwest Passage highlighted the value of these Arctic data as possibly the last for some time to come. Besides the hope of actually pinpointing the pole, students of terrestrial magnetism believed that copious observations would legitimize their science by leading to the causes of magnetic variations, therefore justifying voyages like Parry's as scientific if not geographical successes.[32]

As physical scientists struggled to systematize growing volumes of geomagnetic data, naturalists worked to assimilate new specimens in the latest attempts at a natural system of classification. Hooker translated A. P. de Candolle's *Théorie élémentaire de la botanique* (1813), which established comparative plant morphology, the study of symmetry in plant forms and structures, as a more reliable taxonomic key than the one Linnaeus had chosen. But de Candolle found Arctic species, on which Hooker was now a recognized authority, problematic. Hooker hoped to solve these taxonomic problems by studying boreal species as widely as possible. Unfortunately, he found little that was new or surprising in Parry's plants, but he did report to the Linnean Society on interesting specimens collected by Edward Sabine on other Arctic expeditions. And evidence from the Parry expedition did erode some long-standing assumptions in geology. First, Arctic traprock samples, undeniably igneous or volcanic in origin, challenged Jameson to modify his Wernerian theoretical framework. Second, Arctic coal samples disproved theories that the mineral was exclusive to warmer climates, opening British North America to new economic expectations. Third, fossil evidence suggested that even the Arctic had once supported a "rich and luxuriant vegetation." All of this new evidence reinforced Jameson's belief in the fundamental uniformity of nature as exhibited in the mineral kingdom. He emphasized the similarities of the Arctic with known lands, ignoring the crucial differences that would be required to be included in a fuller scientific analysis. As scientific mentor to so many explorers, he raised optimism about northern lands far more widely than he could ever realize. Even Scoresby, despite his long experience as a whaling captain, relied heavily on thermometer readings, perhaps more than was warranted, to suggest that Arctic summers could be warmer than Scotland's.[33]

Franklin's second expedition, 1825–27, explored the shore of the Arctic Sea from the mouth of the Mackenzie River both westward to Alaska and eastward to the mouth of the Coppermine. Richardson was assigned to the journey specifically to complete the natural history of the region, and he collected specimens along a route from Cumberland House down the Athabasca, Slave, and Mackenzie Rivers to Great Bear Lake and on down to the Mackenzie delta. While wintering at Fort Franklin, Richardson instructed the crew in current geological principles to help them compare formations they encountered with samples sent along by the Geological Society of London. Richardson reported his own "Topographical and Geological Notices" of his travels up to the Arctic coast and back down along the Coppermine and Dease Rivers, first in the Geological Society's *Proceedings* and then more fully in an appendix to Franklin's *Narrative of a Second Expedition to the Shores of the Polar Sea* (1828). Although both versions noted strong similarities between North American and European formations such as the Old Red Sandstone, as well as the presence of carboniferous strata, his paper to the Geological Society was unusually sanguine in its description of coal found near the mouth of the Mackenzie River, coal deemed "excellent fuel for a steam-vessel." In general, however, his judgment remained conservative. Fearing the dangers of inaccuracy resulting from his admittedly cursory and desultory observations, Richardson dared not even attempt a geological map of the lands he traversed.[34]

Other scientific appendices to the *Narrative* reaffirmed the magnetic effects of the aurora borealis, effects Foster and Parry had recently denied, and charted the progress of spring, the velocity of sound, and the increase of solar radiation in high latitudes. Richardson's main scientific achievement, the natural history collection, was assisted by Thomas Drummond (?–1835), a Scottish botanical collector recommended by Hooker because he specialized in mosses. Since Richardson knew no Canadian botanists, he and Drummond had consulted the American expert John Torrey at West

Point before venturing north. While Richardson collected around Great Bear Lake and northward, Drummond traveled along the Saskatchewan River and across the Rocky Mountains. He returned with 1,500 species of plants, including the most complete set of North American mosses to that date, 150 species of birds, 50 of quadrupeds, and 25 of insects. These specimens and those from the voyage of Captain F. W. Beechey, sent around Cape Horn to Kotzebue Sound and north to Icy Cape to attempt a rendezvous with Franklin's party in 1827, proved so numerous that the British government commissioned elaborate separate publications. Richardson was immediately struck by the degree of similarity between British and British North American mosses, and he hoped to be able to establish the northern limits of many plants indigenous to America.[35]

While Richardson befriended fur traders who agreed to send him specimens from northern territories, the Franklin expedition also encountered fellow Gullivers exploring British North America at the same time. Two in particular—David Douglas (1798–1834), a Scottish gardener sent by the Royal Horticultural Society of London to collect plants, and Dr. John Scouler (1804–71), who accompanied a Hudson's Bay Company brigade as a surgeon—were recommended by Hooker to botanize along the Columbia River. Douglas had collected fruit trees and ornamental plants in southwestern Upper Canada (later Ontario), which he reported as a fertile Eden, in 1823. On a second journey in 1825 via Hudson Bay, he met both Franklin and Scouler before discovering the splendid Douglas fir west of the Rockies. Scouler hoped his proficiency in natural history would earn him additional remuneration for his collections and his report, to supplement the meager wage paid by the Hudson's Bay Company. The northern plants accumulated by Sabine, Richardson, Douglas, Scouler, and others inspired Hooker, in his widely reprinted essay "On the Botany of America," to point out plant distribution patterns that linked high North American latitudes botanically to high Scottish altitudes. Hooker hoped to encourage colonial collectors to discern larger patterns, and he declared his intent to publish a flora of all British North America if no one else would undertake it. Richardson favored this project, but it worried John Torrey, who was also working on a North American flora and was uneasy about increased competition in his field.[36]

Richardson recognized that other scientific research in British North America supplemented his own limited efforts in the Northwest and the Arctic. Among these other investigations was the geological work of another former student of Jameson's at Edinburgh, Dr. John Jeremiah Bigsby

(1792–1881). An assistant staff surgeon in the British Army's medical corps, Bigsby explored the geological structure of Upper Canada, where he collected specimens as far north as Lake Nipissing in 1819. In 1820 he became medical officer to the International Boundary Commission, and for three years he geologized along the Great Lakes, a perfect place to confirm his Neptunist preconceptions about the origins of these rocky shores. Much like Richardson, Bigsby noted successions of strata, their related fossils, and their inclination or uplift. He published detailed geological descriptions of the Montreal and Quebec areas, along with the first detailed geological accounts and maps of the upper Great Lakes.[37]

Bigsby's localized studies in turn complemented the larger-scale hydrographic surveys of the Great Lakes conducted by Lieutenant Henry Wolsey Bayfield (1795–1885) for the Royal Navy. In 1825 Bayfield was surveying Lake Superior when he, like Douglas, met the Franklin expedition just setting out. A keen student of geology, Bayfield perceived the lakes in terms of the rocky structures framing them. He realized that whereas Richardson would gain a wider geological overview by traveling inland, his own assignment allowed him to schematize the stratigraphy of relatively smaller areas in greater detail. His first major geological contribution, on the structure of Lake Superior, was published in Quebec in 1829. Like Bigsby and Richardson, Bayfield classified the formations of the lake in Wernerian terminology, as "Primitive" or "Transition," but he also studied its waters for evidence of sedimentary processes at work. Although he disagreed with Bigsby about the local derivation of beach deposits, suggesting instead that some "convulsion" had carried the shell limestones to Lake Superior from as far away as Hudson Bay, Bayfield's explanation nevertheless predated glacial theory and defaulted to water as the agency of transport.[38]

At the same time, public interest in scientific exploration inspired various immigrants to British North America to promote scientific inventory. David Chisholme (1796–1842), editor of the *Canadian Review*, published Bigsby's essay "On the Utility and Design of the Science of Geology," the first such scholarly study in Canada, in 1824. Chisholme reviewed Bigsby's efforts in 1826, incorrectly presuming that Bigsby's regional studies formed the basis for a more comprehensive geological work on British North America. Chisholme felt sure that valuable minerals awaited discovery in the direction of Lake Huron, and he argued for government support of further geological exploration. If permanent settlement was going to advance to more remote regions, he argued, it was time for inhabitants of both the colonies and Great Britain to turn from romantic landscape aesthetics to a rational investigation of economic resources. Receding forests and rising towns, he insisted, signaled the physical and psychological freedom to address cultural questions beyond those of basic survival.[39]

In an age when intellectual life rested largely on conversation, the growth of colonial towns permitted the organization in British North America of natural history societies modeled on those in London, Edinburgh, Boston, and New York. Interest in the natural history of Nova Scotia and New Brunswick was forged in these eastern colonies by the Reverend William Cochran (1757–1833) of Windsor and Thomas McCulloch (1776–1843) of Nova Scotia, who collected and catalogued native plants. The Pictou Literary and Scientific Society was organized some years later. The lieutenant governor of Nova Scotia, Lord Dalhousie, and his wife, an ardent botanical collector, cultivated a circle of amateur naturalists from among local naval officers and members of the professional and commercial classes. When Dalhousie became governor-in-chief of British North America in 1820, he moved to Quebec City and patronized the Literary and Historical Society of Quebec, founded in 1824. The society's first published transactions reflected both its roots in the amateur naturalist tradition and its interest in Canada's potential for settlement. Montreal's professional, commercial, and largely English-speaking middle classes organized a Natural History Society in 1827 to promote a scientific inventory of the country, including the interior of the continent, with an eye to assessing its commercial and agricultural potential. The society prepared questionnaires for distribution even to the farthest outposts of the Hudson's Bay Company, whose commercial center in North America was in Montreal.[40]

This spirit of collective scientific inventory reached smaller British North American towns and even the backwoods. In addition, British financial matters between 1823 and 1826 favored the formation of joint-stock companies to invest in colonization and mining schemes abroad. One such scheme, the Canada Land Company, contracted to settle over one million acres east of Lake Huron. The company appointed Dr. William "Tiger" Dunlop (1792–1848), an Edinburgh alumnus, as its "Warden of the Woods and Forests" in the Huron Tract. His reports reflect a Wernerian geological outlook puzzled by the overwhelming masses of granite in the region. He wanted to conduct a mineralogical survey of the tract, which he believed promised lucrative results. But his priorities differed from those of the company; in 1830 he moved to York (Toronto), where he helped organize the Literary and Philosophical Society of Upper Canada to promote scientific exploration of British North America "as far as the Pacific and Polar

Seas." The society, somewhat premature in a small town dominated by a narrow elite, barely held together while Dunlop used its auspices to begin lobbying the government for a geological survey of Upper Canada.[41]

One colonial geological survey did result from another such financial scheme in England—the General Mining Association, which gained the rights to Nova Scotia's mineral resources in 1826. Before the association's mining engineers took over, two Boston naturalists, C. T. Jackson (1805–80) and Francis Alger (1807–63), surveyed the colony's geological structures and mineral resources. They saw evidence of a "catastrophic torrent" that had transported rocks from northeast to southwest. They became convinced that both a rejection of Wernerian assumptions in favor of Huttonian theories and a systematic survey of the entire region were warranted. Jackson applied the model of their joint report to his later surveys of Main, New Hampshire, and Rhode Island, and Alger's family established the first smelting furnace in British North America at Halifax in 1829.[42]

Dunlop's counterpart in another colony was William Epps Cormack of Saint John's, Newfoundland. Cormack (1796–1868), a former student of Jameson's who saw himself as a latter-day Crusoe, investigated the natural resources and native peoples of the island's interior in 1822. Cormack submitted his reports, reflecting Wernerian views, to Jameson's journal for publication and his geological specimens to Jameson for examination. Like Dunlop, he founded a short-lived scientific organization, the "Beothick" Institution, where he reported on a second investigation in 1828.[43]

## Scientific Exploration Institutionalized, 1830–1839

After 1829 the impulse to organize scientific exploration in British North America became increasingly formalized and institutionalized. The publication of several important reports marked a watershed in the study of natural as well as physical sciences. In natural history, Richardson's *Fauna Boreali-Americana* appeared in four volumes: 1 (1829) on quadrupeds; 2 (1831), with William Swainson, on birds; 3 (1836) on fishes; and 4 (1837), with William Kirby, on insects. This monumental work embraced collections from explorations by Douglas, Parry, Beechey, and the Hudson's Bay Company and emphasized the search for laws regulating the distribution of animal species. Plants were treated in Hooker's *Flora Boreali-Americana* (2 volumes, 1833–40), which set a new standard for botanical study in British North America. By acknowledging individual contributions from Lake

Huron to the Atlantic seaboard, Hooker apprised his international reader-ship of a remarkable number of plant collectors in British North America. His Glasgow herbarium served as a depot for isolated colonial enthusiasts who would, he feared, otherwise "lose heart in the want of sympathy."[44]

Richardson's decision to entrust the ornithological, entomological, and botanical sections of his report to specialists made sense in a rapidly ex-panding field of knowledge, and Hooker certainly represented a choice above reproach. But Richardson's reliance on Swainson (1789–1855) and Kirby (1759–1850) seems more puzzling, since both were known as "philo-sophical" naturalists who advocated a peculiar idealist "circular" classifica-tion system. Swainson followed the quinary system of taxonomy, which was based on the assumption that a single discernible plan organized the entire natural world. The goal of quinarian taxonomists was to "discover" the details of this plan. They derived clues from their ability to assign plants and animals to groups and subgroups based on apparent structural relationships defined as "affinities," or close similarities, and "analogies," or more distant parallels. Quinarians depicted these groups in sets of cir-cles arranged to reflect these relationships, and as their name implies, they identified the ideal number of members in each category as five.[45]

Although Swainson's transcendental approach to classification never won over most British naturalists, it did influence many. As one leading zo-ologist explained in a commissioned report to the British Association for the Advancement of Science in 1834, "It is difficult to believe that there is not some truth at the bottom of this theory, however erroneous it may be in its details." Quinarianism filled a critical gap in the history of taxonomy dur-ing the late 1820s and 1830s. Linnaeus's "artificial" system could no longer absorb the many new varieties and species collected, and no obvious "nat-ural" system emerged to supplant it. In any case, Richardson needed Swain-son. He was concerned about sales prospects for his *Fauna*, since he had not found anyone willing to classify the birds brought back by Drummond. He met Swainson, who expressed interest, through Hooker and sent him drafts of the bird volume, which Swainson then reworked. Richardson always saw himself as mainly a specimen collector who merely aspired to higher levels of expertise such as description and classification. He deferred easily to specialists, admiring Swainson's attempt at a natural system as "impor-tant and interesting." Jameson, in contrast, noted the "curious body of in-formation" Swainson superimposed on the ornithological material, yet he too recommended the completed volume "very zealously."[46]

In 1835 the British Association commissioned Richardson and Hooker to assess the state of North American zoology and botany, respectively, and to identify scientific questions that could most easily be addressed in America. Richardson's report emphasized the geographical range of groups and species, the relation to climate, and North America's accessibility as a zoological region for migration studies. He noted that the number of breeding birds increased northward even to the edge of the tree line, where as many species bred as did in the neighborhood of Philadelphia, albeit only once a year. Richardson, Hooker, and others also wrote up the natural history collections assembled on Beechey's voyage (1826–28) and on George Back's Arctic land expedition (1833–35). Back and his crew traveled from Fort Alexander on Lake Winnipeg to Fort Resolution, then on to Great Slave Lake, from whence they traced the Great Fish (Back) River northwestward to the Arctic Ocean and returned to winter at Fort Reliance on Great Slave Lake. Back's naturalist, Dr. Richard King (1810–76), developed an interest in ethnology while he also recorded the temperatures of soils, plants, and animals.[47]

The general shift to such land explorations elicited some cooperation between the Hudson's Bay Company and scientific travelers who increasingly passed through its territories. Yet even though company officers guided Franklin and often facilitated scientific collecting, Richardson grew frustrated with their general failure to respond to his requests for more specimens. Very few of them took up the study of nature as a vocation. One exception was George Barnston (1800–1883), an Edinburgh native who met David Douglas at Fort Vancouver and was inspired not only by Douglas's dedication in the field but also by the prospect of participating in the global search for specimens. Barnston spent a lifetime collecting and classifying rocks, insects, and plants during his career as a fur trader. He admired the broad geographical perspective of Humboldt's *Personal Narrative*, and from his earliest entomological observations, he deduced that the Far North might not be quite as inhospitable to human settlement as European opinion suggested.[48]

The natural history societies in Canada shared Barnston's view. William Sheppard, a prominent lumberman and a member of the Literary and Historical Society of Quebec, articulated an important role for both his own society and its sister institutions as clearinghouses for useful knowledge about the Canadas; he accordingly contributed practical information about Canadian trees and grasses to his society's *Transactions*. Sheppard's wife, Harriet, used the example of Canadian songbirds to challenge Buffon's theory of degeneration in the New World. From a scientific perspective, British North America constituted a living laboratory, a unique opportunity to observe the untouched work of nature in progress. The societies in both Quebec and Montreal organized public lectures on the social importance of natural history, and the Natural History Society of Montreal advertised annual prize medals for essays that contributed to the scientific knowledge of the country, hoping to raise the quality of submissions from the public.[49]

While students of natural history groped for a satisfactory taxonomic system, three sources fueled geological exploration in British North America. First, military officers assigned to survey roads, canals, and waterways generated a continuous flow of geological information. Richard Henry Bonnycastle (1791–1847) and Frederick Henry Baddeley (1794–1879), of the Royal Engineers stationed in Quebec, included geological observations in their regular reports, and both men participated in the Literary and Historical Society of Quebec. Although Wernerian influences figured strongly in their early works, Bonnycastle, Baddeley, and Bayfield, of the Royal Navy, all kept abreast of important new geological developments and offered evidence to support a new conceptual synthesis that redressed the balance between fire and water in the creation and shaping of landforms. This second, theoretical boon to geology was represented by Charles Lyell's *Principles of Geology* (3 volumes, 1830–33). Lyell eliminated important anomalies in the Wernerian framework by recognizing the validity of Hutton's theory that unstratified formations, which Lyell called "metamorphic," had solidified from magmas heated in the earth's core. Evidence that had accumulated since the eighteenth century enabled Lyell to transform Hutton's Vulcanism into an elaborate "uniformitarian" theory that postulated geological change over far longer periods of time than previously imagined, through forces that continued to operate and that, in turn, influenced the geographical distribution of plant and animal species. Lyell's historical approach raised the value of geological exploration in British North America and altered the view of the continent itself, which was no longer seen as a primitive, barbaric version of Europe but as a unique repository of cosmological information.[50]

The third source of fuel for geological exploration was the field's transformation from a gentlemanly to an entrepreneurial pursuit. The question of the geographical distribution of useful minerals, especially coal and iron ore, took on practical territorial and economic dimensions for the British Empire, enhancing public interest in government geological surveys to determine the mining and agricultural potential of British North America. Indeed, individual American states had been organizing geological surveys since the 1820s, and in 1835 the British government recognized the importance of the exploratory work begun by the Geological Society of London by launching its own Geological Survey under the Ordnance Department.[51]

Calls for government geological surveys of the Canadas came from several directions. Although the Literary and Philosophical Society of Upper Canada in 1832 petitioned unsuccessfully for an investigation of the entire province, in 1835 Lieutenant Governor Sir John Colborne commissioned a military survey north of the Canada Company's Huron Tract. Baddeley, who joined the expedition specifically to report on the region's geology, was so impressed that he thereafter campaigned for detailed surveys of what he called "the richest mineral country . . . perhaps on this continent." Dunlop's brother Robert (1789–1841), an alumnus of Glasgow and Edinburgh and the elected representative for Huron County, also lobbied for a provincial geological survey. In 1836 he chaired a select committee, composed of a political cross-section of members of the Legislative Assembly, which stressed the importance of such a survey, particularly since valuable coal deposits seemed evident in the colony. In Lower Canada, members of professional and business classes in Quebec and Montreal echoed this call for wider and more specialized geological explorations. The Natural History Society of Montreal petitioned the legislature of Lower Canada in May 1837, hoping to coordinate such a survey with one in Upper Canada. Hopes were put on ice, however, by the outbreak of rebellion in both colonies in 1837.[52]

The government of New Brunswick, free from such immediate threats, in 1838 appointed Abraham Gesner as the first British colonial geologist. Gesner (1797–1864), a Nova Scotian with a London medical education, had followed up Jackson and Alger's revised essay on Nova Scotian geology (1833) with his own, more popular version in 1836. The lieutenant governor of New Brunswick, Sir John Harvey, responded favorably to Gesner's petition for an investigation of that colony for three reasons: first, he was interested in encouraging New Brunswick's economic development; second, the Colonial Office expected its governors to give the "utmost consideration" to the British Museum's request for colonial mineralogical specimens; and third, he shrewdly suspected that coal lay at the root of a festering boundary dispute with Maine. Recently, Gesner had confidentially told Harvey that he believed New Brunswick possessed enough coal to supply "all the continent for a thousand years." With James Robb (1815–61), an Edinburgh-educated lecturer in natural history at King's College, Fredericton, Gesner spent five years analyzing the colony's geological structures and specimens. The two men submitted public reports annually to maintain Harvey's enthusiasm and to ensure the renewal of Gesner's yearly mandate by a frugal and rather skeptical assembly. These reports focused largely on coal deposits and the relation of fossil plants to coal seams, but Gesner also outlined five separate geological districts in the province. Gesner's findings reached even the meeting of the British Association for the Advancement of Science in 1840 through a report by Baddeley; geological surveys of British North America were imperative, agreed the illustrious audience, because valuable coalfields might unwittingly be exchanged for fields of granite in future boundary settlements with the United States. Even so, Gesner's funds were cut off when Harvey left the province.[53]

The optimism generated by Gesner's appointment and his discovery of coal in New Brunswick may well have encouraged the Legislative Assembly in Newfoundland to approve a mineralogical reconnaissance of the island by John Beete Jukes (1811–69) in 1839. Jukes surveyed the coastal regions first and within the year reported negative findings of coal or other desirable minerals. The resulting withdrawal of government support, except for a small continuance for mapping purposes, taught future geological surveyors a crucial lesson about the importance of positive results. Jukes's final report denied both the feasibility of the coal deposits he had seen and, worse still, the possibility of locating any others on the island. Funds for the publication of his final report were secured only through a personal appeal to the new lieutenant governor of Newfoundland, who happened to be Sir John Harvey, in 1841.[54]

The geological inventories exemplified in New Brunswick and Newfoundland and advocated in the Canadas during the 1830s no longer reflected the amateur naturalist tradition in British culture. Supporters and practitioners of geological surveys used strongly utilitarian reasoning; their arguments were linked to notions of overcoming a state of relative economic backwardness. Economic progress meant the growth of industrialism on the British model, invariably the motivation for a scientific search for useful minerals such as coal or iron ore. The use of geology to facilitate and rationalize such an inventory of Canadian resources transformed the science from a systematic method of classification to an ideology forged in the image of British industrial civilization.[55]

While British North America's geological structures and mineral resources justified further geological explorations during the 1830s, its northerly location also attracted scientific attention to its geomagnetic and climatic properties. Just as pendulum experiments allowed mathematicians to calculate the shape of the earth, terrestrial magnetism and meteorology held similar challenges through a new scientific style. This style was strongly inductive, emphasizing large-scale cooperation in the collection of accurate and measurable data to be reduced by mathematical analysis. The new era in magnetic and meteorological observation had dawned with the "cosmical" outlook suggested by Humboldt, the foremost authority on terrestrial magnetism by the 1830s. Humboldt encouraged Edward Sabine to distribute standardized instruments to assemble observations on as grand a scale as possible. They hoped thus to derive a mathematically expressed universal law of terrestrial magnetism based on the Newtonian model of gravitation. For Humboldt and Sabine, the whole earth and its atmosphere became a scientific laboratory for "Humboldtian" studies of magnetic intensity, variation, and dip, as well as lines of force and direction. Networks of magnetic observatories extended across Europe and Russia, and by 1838 Sabine had persuaded both the Royal Society and the British Association to organize a similar chain across the British Empire. The British government agreed to fund the project under the Ordnance Department, with Royal Artillery officers acting as observers under Sabine's supervision.[56]

British North America served as an important quarry of information for both terrestrial magnetism and meteorology. Canada was due south of the magnetic pole of verticity, where the needle dipped 90 degrees, its location pinpointed by Ross in 1831. Waiting now to be discovered somewhere in the adjoining Hudson's Bay Company territories was the pole of intensity, where the magnetic force was greatest. Both Quebec and Montreal were designated as imperial meteorological stations in 1837, and in 1839 Montreal joined a growing list of imperial magnetic observatories. This unsolicited new calling eventually generated interest not only among devotees of physical science but among the Canadian public as well.[57]

However, such public interest was hardly evident when Lieutenant Charles Riddell arrived in Canada in 1839 to begin observations. After consulting Alexander Dallas Bache at Girard College, Philadelphia, and Joseph Henry at Princeton University, Riddell arrived at Quebec only to be informed by Bayfield that he would have to proceed to Toronto to avoid underlying magnetic rock formations that distorted readings taken at Montreal. Riddell leased land from King's College, Toronto, for an observatory to record not only magnetic but also meteorological and auroral observations. But he was dismayed to find no one, not even at nearby Fort York, the least bit interested in assisting him in his tedious tasks. Military engineers, surveyors, and physicians had long been trained to record such observations, and meteorological tables had laced the pages of scientific journals for some time. But the standardized instruments and instructions issued to Riddell—and to anyone who might be induced to help—were new. They had been formulated by Richardson, who was still studying the extent, depth, and seasonal duration of frozen ground in the northern latitudes of British North America. (He contributed these studies to the Royal Geographical Society, founded in London in 1830 to serve as an advisory center for exploration.)[58]

Another locus for meteorological observers was the Natural History Society of Montreal, which anticipated valuable information about the Canadian climate. The scientific search for such patterns in nature constituted another variant of the larger question of geographical distribution and drew on long-held assumptions about the relationship between climate and settlement. Popular mythologies held that Canada's harsh climate would improve with clearing and cultivation and that temperatures were more moderate farther west on the continent. The popular notion that climate would improve with settlement had received the stamp of authority in Edward Gibbon's influential *History of the Decline and Fall of the Roman Empire* (1776). Gibbon had described Canada as "an exact picture of ancient Germany," a frigid forest despite its latitudinal parallels with France and England. Roman accounts that the frozen Rhine and Danube Rivers facilitated barbarian invasions and that reindeer inhabited the ancient forests of Germany and Poland suggested that Europe had once been much colder. It seemed to follow that the European climate had been ameliorated by clearing woods and by draining swamps, permitting the sun's rays to warm the earth. Gibbon fixed this impression of the potential warming of the Canadian climate in the minds of most educated people in the English-speaking world for several generations, predisposing early settlers to attack the forest with unusual vigor. Few people accepted the counterargument of William Kelly, a naval surgeon with Bayfield's hydrographic survey who reminded the Literary and Historical Society of Quebec that Canada's climate had remained fairly constant over the previous two centuries. Like the hope that Canada was as rich in coal deposits as Nova Scotia, the myth of climatic progress died hard, remaining a preoccupation of naturalists in British North America for years to come.[59]

By the end of the 1830s, science had been institutionalized in the exploration of British North America and was perceived as instrumental both in testing older assumptions and in formulating new questions about the nature of these territories. The publication of state-of-the-art floras and faunas, two colonies' temporary forays into geological surveys, the serious attempts in two other colonies to underwrite such surveys, and the establishment of the Toronto magnetic and meteorological observatory exemplified this process of transplanting scientific structures from the Old World to investigate the environment of the New.

## Scientific Exploration Domesticated, 1840–1849

Once institutionalized, the impulse for scientific exploration in British North America showed signs of increasing domestication during the 1840s through both the expanding role of the Toronto observatory and the establishment of the Geological Survey of Canada. An auxiliary function of the Toronto observatory was to serve as a base station for a northern magnetic survey in British North America. This survey of the area of maximum magnetic intensity was conducted by Riddell's successor from the observatory at Saint Helena, Lieutenant John Henry Lefroy (1817–90), who also believed that dedication to his tedious duties would finally set terrestrial magnetism on firm theoretical ground. After consulting with the Hudson's Bay Company, Lefroy and one assistant, with ten boxes of delicate instruments in tow, left Lachine with the first brigade of the season in May 1843. From Norway House, his northern base, Lefroy's travels northeast to York Factory showed magnetic intensity decreasing. This discovery helped locate the major axis of a set of concentric "isodynamic ovals," ellipses used by Sabine to map levels of magnetic intensity. In the United States, Dr. John Locke of Cincinnati contributed measurements from the eastern seaboard to the Mississippi River and determined the corresponding minor axis, allowing the pinpointing of the north magnetic pole of intensity where the two imaginary lines intersected. Lefroy and his assistant proceeded westward to Cumberland House and then wintered at Fort Chipewyan on Lake Athabasca, where they took observations hourly and, during magnetic disturbances, every two minutes, day and night. From there they trekked northward to Fort Simpson near the Arctic Circle and then returned to Montreal via Fort Edmonton and Penetanguishene. In venturing considerably farther north than his orders stated, Lefroy identified three principal lines of magnetic intensity above the fiftieth parallel of latitude, roughly along the Saskatchewan, Peace, and Mackenzie Rivers, and established that North America's isodynamic ovals tilted northwestward, rather than following the meridian as had been assumed.[60]

Lefroy exceeded Sabine's expectations in terrestrial magnetism, but he disappointed Richardson's in natural history. For although he demonstrated far more than merely the northward decrease in magnetic intensity, his rigorous routine left virtually no time to collect flora and fauna. Lefroy recognized the northern part of the continent as a scientific terra incognita, and his journey only whetted his appetite for further, more detailed explorations. After returning to Toronto, he echoed Richardson's call for regular standardized measurements of local soil and air temperatures to permit a more accurate understanding of climate in the Northwest. One means, they agreed, was to enlist officers of the Hudson's Bay Company to include such observations in their regular routines, as a few were already doing.[61]

Accurate temperature readings in the Northwest tested a popular variant of the eighteenth-century myth of climatic progress. During Cook's voyage, Georg Forster had noted that whereas climates on the western and eastern coasts of both Europe and North America contrasted dramatically, the two western coasts shared a relative mildness. He inspired Humboldt to investigate scientifically the popular adage that climate improved "by westing." The idea that the Northwest might be amenable to agriculture found support in Lefroy's 1844 report that soil as far north as the Mackenzie River thawed to a depth of two feet in open places yet to only one foot in the woods. Surprised at Cumberland House to find a field of wheat growing, Lefroy was all the more astonished at Fort Simpson to see a thirteen-acre barley and potato farm. His findings seemed to confirm Richardson's contention that isotherms, lines of equal temperature, tilted northwestward in British North America in the same way as did isomagnetic lines.[62]

A second source of scientific interest in the climate of the Northwest was as Humboldtian as these isotherms. During the 1840s, American physical scientists borrowed the model of Humboldt's magnetic observatories to investigate continental storm patterns. The publication of James Pollard's *The Philosophy of Storms* (1841) inevitably identified the British North American Northwest as a source of winter weather systems. Edward Sabine, ever the opportunist where his observatories were concerned, grasped the significance of Toronto's location to this American meteorological network and used it as added justification for the continuance of the observatory.[63]

Lefroy's duties never again included Arctic travel, but as director of the Toronto observatory, he was ideally situated when Franklin's new search for a Northwest Passage in 1845 renewed enthusiasm about the scientific harvest that could be reaped from this latest venture. Sabine rejoiced at the "extremely valuable" opportunity to compare Lefroy's earlier magnetic readings with Franklin's. When search parties set out in 1848 to track the missing Franklin party, Sabine laid out even more elaborate plans to coordinate with Lefroy at Toronto simultaneous magnetic and meteorological observations by Richardson at Great Bear Lake, Ross at Melville Island, Edward Bird at Barrow's Straits, and Russian observers at Sitka. Richardson and Lefroy coedited the British North American results of these observations while Sabine completed the official report on Lefroy's magnetic survey and prepared similar readings from Nova Scotia and New Brunswick for publication.[64]

Arctic exploration, with its scientific offshoots, had continued coastal surveys begun years earlier. In 1837 the Hudson's Bay Company sent Thomas Simpson and Peter Warren Dease to map the remaining Arctic coastline and, incidentally, to collect magnetic readings and natural history specimens. Dease had accompanied the second Franklin expedition a decade earlier, and he visited Richardson to prepare for this new mission. Yet by then both Richardson and Hooker were feeling stymied by fur trade and naval resistance to "nonservice" naturalists on official expeditions; both investigators required a more specialized selection process to gather specimens.

On the one hand, new zoological subdisciplines opened British North American territories to increased scrutiny. Richardson hoped to update his *Fauna Boreali-Americana* by concentrating on fishes as "the earliest created" vertebrates and as the basis of comparative anatomy, and he much preferred specific rather than random samples of North American fauna. Other zoologists, such as Richard King, surgeon-naturalist to the George Back expedition in 1835, branched off into ethnology and began publishing studies of native peoples for the Ethnological Society of London, which King helped found in 1843. As a result of growing British imperial interest in questions of human capacities for acclimatization, the British Association for the Advancement of Science recognized ethnology as a discipline separate from zoology in 1847. It was becoming increasingly difficult to master scientific knowledge of any one of the three kingdoms of nature.[65]

On the other hand, Hooker, director of Kew Gardens in London since 1841, now possessed the richest collection of North American plants in Europe. Hooker contributed a botanical appendix to Thomas Simpson's *Narrative* (1843), and although he appreciated the contribution of Dease's plant collection to the study of geographical distribution, all the species were nevertheless already noted in his *Flora Borealis-Americana*. Much the same was true for the expedition of John Rae, a medical graduate of the University of Edinburgh and an officer of the Hudson's Bay Company. Only a cactus caught Hooker's interest. Hooker attempted to fill certain gaps in his collections at Kew in 1843 by assigning Joseph Burke, an estate gardener for the president of the Zoological Society of London, the Earl of Derby, to collect trees, especially conifers, and other alpine plants, along Hudson's Bay Company routes to California. Burke's only hope for originality in such well-trodden territory lay well beyond the traditional encampments used by his diligent predecessor Thomas Drummond. Despite hardship and repeated bad luck, he managed to bag the rare golden chinquapin *(Castanopsis chrysophylla)*, but little else pleased his botanical patron.[66]

By the mid-1840s, naturalists felt no closer to discovering general laws that governed the geographical distribution of species. Arctic specialists in particular had difficulty distinguishing new species from familiar ones in climatic extremes and still required cumbersomely detailed descriptions of individual specimens. In 1846 Edward Forbes (1815–54), a former student of Jameson's and a professor of botany at King's College, London, attempted to break this logjam by analyzing British plants and animals in terms derived from uniformitarian geology. Forbes identified characteristic floras and faunas, each correlated to a geographical region from which it had apparently migrated during a particular geological age.[67]

The new hybrid science of paleobotany had already proved its practical value in the recent discovery of the in situ origins of coal by William Edmond Logan, a Canadian of Scottish descent. This discovery helped, in turn, to justify both funding for a geological survey of Canada and Logan's appointment as survey director. Logan (1798–1875) had strong family links to the Montreal business community, had studied natural history at the University of Edinburgh, and had managed his uncle's copper works in Swansea, South Wales, since 1831. There he gained a professional knowledge of coal seams that he recorded on topographical maps and cross-sections so accurately that the Geological Survey of Great Britain adopted his work. Seeking to facilitate the practical search for fuel to smelt the copper, Logan formulated a theory explaining the origins of local coal seams. A great admirer of Lyell's work, Logan offered his evidence to the Geological Society of London in 1840, postulating a direct relationship between the coal seams and the rootlike formations, or *Stigmaria ficoides*, invariably present in the underclay below them. Logan concluded that the plants actually formed coal in the same place where they had lived and died. After his uncle's death that same year, he left the firm to test his theory on the massive Carboniferous formations of Pennsylvania and Nova Scotia. Not only Logan but Lyell himself confirmed the correlation in both places, at-

18.2 *Sir William Logan, first director of the Geological Survey of Canada. Courtesy of the National Archives of Canada, neg. no.* PA74101.

tracting the attention and earning the approbation of eminent geologists who had worked unsuccessfully on the problem of the origins of coal for many years.[68]

Logan's timing could not have been better calculated, first because Lyell happened to be in North America on a geological tour and second because the Legislative Assembly of the newly united province of Canada voted funds for a geological survey just as Logan arrived to visit his brother in Montreal. Logan met Lyell first on a side trip to New York and again at the Pictou coalfield in Nova Scotia. Through Lyell, Logan also met John William Dawson, a Nova Scotian geologist who had recently completed studies in geology at the University of Edinburgh. Lyell encouraged the two British North Americans to cooperate in exploring the extensive geological field before them, convinced as he was that it would yield important scientific discoveries. His uniformitarian geology inspired them not only with new insights into the structures of their native continent but, more important, with a means of integrating these into general geological theory.[69]

Logan and Dawson adapted their general interpretations of British North American geology to Lyell's model; they hoped he would include their discoveries in future editions of his *Principles*. The fact that Lyell spent so much of his time in Nova Scotia corroborating Logan's coal theory in turn intensified the interest of local geologists. Dawson helped develop paleobotany through his analyses of the geological distribution of fossil plants to deduce the climate in which they grew. Richard Brown of the General Mining Association contributed a more localized series of studies of the coal formations and fossils of Cape Breton. Even Abraham Gesner changed his views on the relative position of the Carboniferous strata in order to accommodate the evidence accumulated by Lyell.[70]

Logan's international reputation as a both a geologist and a "practical coal miner of education" only partly explains the founding of the Geological Survey of Canada and his own appointment to direct Canada's first permanent scientific institution. After the rebellions of 1837, the British government deliberately set out to encourage economic development by uniting the two Canadas into one province and providing loans for the improvement of transportation systems. The relative stability signaled by the Act of Union of 1841 freed up time and energy to use science as an investigative tool in assessing Canada's natural resources, especially possible sources of coal and iron ore, and to foster the growth of industrial and agricultural economies based on British and American models. Commercial and professional classes in both Montreal and Toronto strongly supported new opportunities to expand the capital base of the province and had advocated a geological survey for some time.

The question of who was to become provincial geologist was determined largely by the powerful Montreal business community, which promoted Logan as one of its own. Logan received the appointment in the spring of 1842 largely because he convinced politicians and businessmen, as well as geologists, that he could best achieve their various goals. Arguments for a geological survey repeated the necessity of locating in Canada those resources that had made Britain great, namely coal and iron ore. Symbolic in the Victorian view of progress, power, and even civilization itself, these two minerals seemed more desirable than gold. Yet although the proposed survey promised to serve the needs of an incipient industrial community, its inventory component promised also to fulfill more abstract scientific goals by illuminating the geological questions of the day. Logan's consummate skill was his ability to balance these various desiderata as a single spectrum of his geological activities and to encourage the widely held assumption that coal would surely be found in Canada by someone who understood so much about its origins.

Like Sabine and Lefroy, who lobbied the imperial government for continued support of the Toronto observatory, and unlike Jukes in Newfoundland or Gesner in New Brunswick, Logan designed his geological survey to conform to the aims and outlooks of those who determined its (and his) fate, namely the Canadian government and the business communities in the province. At the same time, his strategy extended the vision of many Canadians beyond the political horizons of the province. Logan was well aware that a single grant for one year was insufficient even for a cursory geological glance over such a large territory; and as a good uniformitarian, he firmly believed that the territory under his purview would eventually be extended even further, as part of the natural course of scientific investigation. A good geologist, in Logan's view, followed the boundaries of geological rather than political formations. In his preliminary report of 1842, he established the principle that for the time being, his survey would remain confined to the bounds of settlement, but his first official report of progress in 1843 saw the unique contingencies of Canadian landforms already straining the geographical horizons of this narrow vision.[71]

Logan's first tactic was to search for coal. He masked his own skepticism about the chances of finding it in Canada first with scientific caution and then with new promises of untold mineral wealth. He divided the province into three geological districts—a western, an eastern, and a northern division—and used the enormous limestone formation of the western division from Georgian Bay south to Lake Erie, barren of both mineral fuels and metallic ores, as a base from which to search further. From experience, he knew that metalliferous rocks lay below limestone, and carboniferous above. Yet this axiom also told Logan that the entire province was therefore situated below the strata that contained the coal deposits in the nearby United States. Admitting this likelihood in his first report, he quickly turned his attention eastward to the Gaspé, where he still held out hope for coal because of the proximity of the large deposits in Nova Scotia and New Brunswick. Yet Logan soon confronted the same negative verdict in the violently contorted strata of this eastern division. By 1845 he was forced to admit the irony of his position: that the very predictability afforded by his scientific method could easily breed public disillusionment with the sweeping certainty that no coal would ever be found in the province.[72]

If Logan hoped to continue his geological survey, he had to report something positive. He accordingly devoted the rest of his first report to the shores of the upper Great Lakes in the northern division. From hearsay and from questionable analogies to the example of Michigan, he suggested that rich veins of iron and copper ores might be found on the Canadian side of the lakes. The result was a rush among legislators and businessmen for mining licenses; in addition, when the survey came up for renewal in 1845, Logan wrote his own ticket in a government bill that guaranteed funding for five more years in exchange for annual published reports, a geological map, and more information about copper on the upper Great Lakes. This last condition greatly interested businessmen who hoped that Logan would eventually locate coal to smelt the copper. Nor was this initial enthusiasm dampened during Logan's term to 1849. The governor, Lord Cathcart, was himself a geologist trained by Jameson at Edinburgh; even during this period of economic retrenchment, the government renewed the survey for yet another five years.[73]

## Scientific Exploration Expanded, 1850–1859

Whereas scientific exploration in British North America had been institutionalized and domesticated in various forms by the 1840s, after midcentury such efforts became increasingly expansionist in character. British North American Crusoes not only supplanted but even began to emulate the Gullivers who passed through their lands; they expanded their investigations beyond their own political boundaries and reported discoveries in their newly founded scientific journals. The Royal Canadian Institute, founded at Toronto in 1849 and granted a royal charter in 1851, began publishing the *Canadian Journal of Industry, Science, and Art* soon thereafter, and the Natural History Society of Montreal established the *Canadian Naturalist and Geologist* in 1856. Moreover, these explorations took on a North American orientation, turning away from Britain and toward the United States for their points of reference.

The physical sciences reflected both of these trends. Edward Sabine and Henry Lefroy succeeded in naturalizing the Toronto Magnetic and Meteorological Observatory to create, in effect, Canada's second permanent scientific institution in 1853. Lefroy recognized the intimate connection between the fate of his own observatory at Toronto and Sabine's plans at Woolwich, and the two collaborated in their common cause to justify continued funding for the Toronto station. Their arguments were strengthened when Toronto's magnetic observations for 1840–42 were published as the first volume of a projected imperial series in 1845. While Sabine hoped to gain additional observatories in Newfoundland, Nova Scotia, and Prince Edward Island, Lefroy hoped to persuade either the trustees of King's College at Toronto or the Canadian government to take over the observatory when British funding expired.

Lefroy took advantage of spectacular auroral displays in 1847–48 to analyze the greatest magnetic disturbances ever recorded. In 1848 he added to his network of formal contacts by arranging for nightly weather registers to be kept by Royal Artillery officers at military posts all over British North America. A more general circular, inviting public communication with the Toronto observatory about the aurora, soon established him as the foremost auroral authority on the continent. Lefroy hoped, among other things, to link magnetic and meteorological phenomena to epidemic diseases, such as cholera and influenza, that recurred during those same years, apparently triggered by atmospheric conditions.[74]

Lefroy's expertise, dedication, and growing international reputation impressed American physical scientists such as Joseph Henry of the Smithsonian Institution and Francois Guyot of Harvard University. After visiting the observatory in 1848, they agreed to lobby the British and Canadian governments to continue its funding, since the observatory was crucial to their own proposed North American chain of meteorological stations. Lefroy convinced Egerton Ryerson, chief superintendent of public schools in Canada West (later Ontario), that a series of grammar-school meteorological stations, standardized and directed by the Toronto observatory, would serve multiple scientific and social purposes. Through the Royal Canadian Institute at Toronto, he advocated an even larger series of unbroken meteorological observations across British North America in order to settle, once and for all, the question of climatic progress. In an eleventh-hour reprieve after his own transfer back to England in 1853, Lefroy finally persuaded the Canadian government, impressed with his achievements and reluctant to permit the demise of the observatory when British funding ceased that year, to adopt the institution and to delegate responsibility for the observations to the newly created University of Toronto.[75]

Sabine's and Lefroy's appeals to American influence typified a more general erosion of Canadian dependence on the British scientific metropolis. When Logan's cumulative geological map of the province of Canada required precise longitudinal calculations to fix as many geographical points as possible, it included, in typical uniformitarian fashion, the geologically contiguous territories of New York, New Brunswick, and even Nova Scotia. Logan's appeal to astronomical observatories at Quebec City and Fredericton, New Brunswick, as well as to the Toronto magnetic observatory, raised the issue of whether these calculations should properly be based on standards set at Greenwich or at Boston. G. B. Airy, the British astronomer royal, for practical reasons chose Boston, insisting that "whether right or wrong, it is far more important that continuous districts (British and U.S.) of North America should agree in their basis of Longitude, than that the British Provinces should agree with Greenwich."[76]

Interest in contiguous territories came naturally to uniformitarian geologists, but it was reinforced by British attitudes. In 1851 Logan chose the meeting of the Geological Society of London to announce the survey's important discovery of fossil footprints at Beauharnois near Montreal, the earliest known remains of reptilian forms. Yet during the same visit he was "mortified" to unearth, in the basement of the British Geological Survey's offices, two unopened crates of fossils that he had sent ten years earlier to the survey's director general and his own mentor, Sir Henry Thomas De la Beche, to identify. In the interim Logan had had to travel repeatedly to consult the collections of James Hall of the New York State Geological Survey at Albany, and a cordial friendship developed between the two men. When the fate of Logan's survey rested with a government select committee in 1854, Hall testified to Logan's success in showing Canada "rich in all those mineral products (with the possible exception of coal) which lie at the foundation of modern progress and civilization." Logan, for his part, was pleased to return the favor when the New York survey came under scrutiny in 1855. Meanwhile, Dawson also suffered bitter disappointment when, after the deaths of both Robert Jameson and Edward Forbes in 1854, Dawson's application for the chair of natural history at Edinburgh was rejected, ostensibly because he was a colonial. In 1856 Logan and Dawson invited the American Association for the Advancement of Science to meet in Montreal the following year. Logan there announced his division of the Precambrian formations of the Canadian Shield into Laurentian and Huronian series, which became worldwide prototypes. His analysis enabled Hall, at the same meeting, to introduce the major theoretical concept of the geosyncline, a great downward flexure that helped explain the formation of mountain chains. Just as important was the local public enthusiasm generated by this meeting (which most British scientists did not attend because of the summer heat and travel involved) as "a virtual annexation of American to British American minds, in their action in the wide field of physical and natural science."[77]

While the Geological Survey of Canada was turning away from the British, it was also gaining international recognition. Logan's initial reconnaissance for minerals earned his mineral exhibit rave notices at London's Great Exhibition of 1851, in which he highlighted Canada's rich bog-iron ores, requiring only wood charcoal to produce first-rate iron products, and the presence of coal "upon all sides" of the province as facilitating other industrial enterprises such as copper smelting. His brilliant reprise at the Paris Exposition in 1855 won Logan a knighthood, the Wollaston Medal of the Geological Society, and induction into the French Legion of Honour.[78]

Sir William secured his scientific survey on a solid bedrock of theoretical achievement. He recognized in his northern division of the province his greatest geological challenge, the "Primitive" or "Primary" formations of the Canadian Shield. British geologists had sorted the oldest known fossiliferous rocks, the Upper Primary or Paleozoic formations below the Carboniferous, according to their fossils into Devonian, Silurian, and Cambrian systems, and Canada's vast expanse of unexplored Paleozoic formations offered enough work for anyone's lifetime. Yet there remained in the Shield still older unstratified "Precambrian" formations, barren of fossil guides and often so contorted and chemically altered that their proper order seemed indecipherable. At a time when scientists were just beginning to grasp the chemical and mechanical processes that had forged these metamorphic rocks, British North America's vast and ancient structures offered splendid opportunities to advance Precambrian geology. Logan was certainly up to the challenge.[79]

The enormous territory under Logan's scrutiny called for additional and more specialized staff. Until 1847 his only full-time assistant was Alexander Murray, hired in Britain for his social connections and given a crash course in geology in 1842, who dedicated himself fully to his task even after suffering a serious stroke in 1856. In 1847 the appointment of Thomas Sterry Hunt (1826–92), trained at Yale University, brought to the survey one of the foremost chemical geologists on the continent, and in 1856 Elkanah Billings (1820–76), editor of the *Canadian Naturalist and Geologist*, was hired as the survey's paleontologist to organize its endless supply of fossils. Although the survey also acquired part-time field naturalists, Logan never allotted priority to botanical or zoological studies. Still, paleobotanical advice came readily from Dawson, after 1855 principal of McGill College in Montreal. Dawson's first major publication, *Acadian Geology* (1855), established the eastern colonies of British North America as important sources of knowledge about Devonian and Carboniferous geology. Like Logan's map, Dawson's work followed in Lyell's uniformitarian tradition by defining its purview according to geological rather than political units.[80]

With Dawson's move to Montreal, a growing number of dedicated geologists had no government survey to serve either in Nova Scotia or in New Brunswick. Among them, George F. Matthew (1837–1923) and Frederick Hartt (1840–78) organized the Steinhammer Club in 1857 around Gesner's collections in Saint John, to encourage more detailed explorations of complex local geology. James Robb at the University of New Brunswick, meanwhile, strove to balance Gesner's hyperbolic assessment of the colony's coal supply. Robb argued for a government geological survey and a new map based on developments since Gesner's earlier survey. Dawson and Richard Brown continued to contribute frequent studies of Nova Scotia to the Geological Society of London, and Charles T. Jackson of Boston maintained his geological interest in both colonies.[81]

Meanwhile, much farther west, imperial and colonial concerns combined to intensify public and scientific interest in the habitability of the vast territories northwest of the province of Canada. American manifest destiny, a festering resentment against the Hudson's Bay Company monopoly, Canadian perceptions of agricultural land and mineral fuel scarcities, and British fears of diminishing coal supplies at home all heightened public anxieties that science promised to assuage. Geology, for one, turned to the Hudson's Bay Company territory with greater intensity during the 1850s.

Bigsby, still in England, brooked criticism from the Geological Society of London for publishing several isolated studies of "erratics" in 1851–52, in which he ignored Louis Agassiz's recent glacial or "drift" theories, which demanded a larger geographical perspective. In contrast, John Richardson in 1851 adopted strong uniformitarian tones in a paper that submitted the entire geographical structure of British North America to a sweeping continental analysis. In 1855 the Geological Society published a more speculative collation of previous geological assessments of the Hudson's Bay Company lands, along with a colored map. The author, Alexander Kennedy Isbister (1822–83), had been born at Cumberland House and educated at the Universities of Aberdeen and Edinburgh. A critic of the company's monopoly, he hypothesized that a vast unsurveyed coalfield ran up the base of the Rocky Mountains, perhaps even into the Arctic Sea, and implied that the company had suppressed this information in order to keep out settlers. More important, Isbister's supposed coalfield reappeared in 1857 on an official map of "Canada, Indian Territories, and Hudson's Bay" issued by the Crown Lands Department of the province of Canada, an office dominated by expansionists committed to annexing the territory.[82]

That same year the British House of Commons and the Canadian Legislative Assembly each appointed select committees on the Hudson's Bay Company territories. Although ideology colored both inquiries, the British committee called scientific explorers such as Richardson and Lefroy as key witnesses to the climatic, agricultural, and mineral potential of these lands. Perhaps not surprisingly, however, their testimony proved contradictory and inconclusive. After his last Arctic journey, Richardson had attempted to analyze the northern fauna and flora along Forbesian lines, by geographical and geological regions, and to discern the temperature limits of cereal and potato growth. Much like Hooker at Kew and the Botanical Society of Edinburgh, he was concerned with the question of food supplies on the northern fringes of civilization. Ever the model of cautious inference, he declared the country largely unfit for agriculture or settlement, especially north of the fifty-seventh parallel, where tree trunks froze to the heart. Yet Richardson told the committee that he nevertheless thought the climate might be improved by draining swamps and marshes. Regarding minerals, he was even more optimistic and supported a systematic geological survey in the company's territories. Richardson attributed the failure of copper mining north of Lake Superior to Canadian mismanagement rather than to the quality of the ores or to insurmountable logistical problems.[83]

Lefroy, in contrast, now flatly denied that Gibbon's ideas about climatic

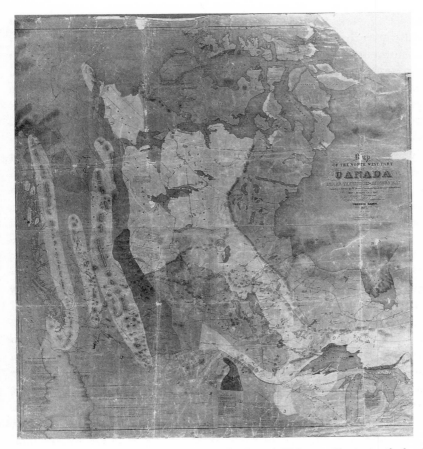

18.3 *"Map of the North West Part of Canada" (1857). This map illustrates the level of scientific knowledge of the Canadian Northwest on the eve of Confederation. Courtesy of the Archives of Ontario.*

progress through settlement and cultivation could apply to British North America. Nor did the presence of trees, he argued, imply agricultural fitness in the Far North; Lefroy attributed the limited success he had witnessed at Fort Simpson to the proximity of the Pacific Ocean. He shocked Canadian expansionists who recalled his earlier enthusiasm in 1844; they discounted Lefroy's apparent change of heart as a party line held by explorers who depended on the fur trade for the routes they traveled. Years later Lefroy himself judged that behind the supposed threat of summer frosts lay the company's misapprehensions about the potential impact of agriculture on the future of its fur trade monopoly.[84]

In the true Baconian spirit of Victorian science, both governments in 1857 sent exploring expeditions to the Northwest for more information. Neither the British party led by John Palliser (1817–87) nor the Canadian group headed by George Gladman (1800–1863) embraced its duties quite free of preconceived expectations. The recent use of Humboldt's isarithms in cartography as propaganda had generated a new wave of public optimism about the climate of the Northwest. Whereas only a decade earlier the Northwest had been marked terra incognita on Humboldt's isothermal maps, the 1857 map of the Canadian Crown Lands Department incorporated lines of equal temperature and the northern limits of common flora and fauna. The ideological applications of these lines were elaborated in an influential work published that same year by Lorin Blodget, a meteorologist for the Smithsonian Institution. Blodget's *Climatology of the United States and of the Temperate Latitudes of the North American Continent* synthesized meteorological data that had been accumulated over the years by Richardson, Riddell, and Lefroy. His continental interpretation of climatic patterns used summer isotherms that slanted northwestward from Toronto and supported expansionists' insistence that the Northwest could be as amenable to settlement and agriculture as Canada was. Isotherms seemed to invite settlement, whether Canadian or American, into the Northwest by finally eliminating the need for a theory of climatic progress. Scientific evidence now caused even the uncommitted to accept expansionist arguments more readily and indeed lent credibility to the still-popular notion that climate improved by westing.[85]

The Palliser and Gladman expeditions constituted both the last of the older geographical explorations with secondary scientific aims and the first of a new hybrid form of exploration in which science clearly penetrated the central geographical questions. Palliser had first proposed his journey to the Royal Geographical Society as a personal project to explore the southern prairies and the Rocky Mountain passes of British North America. The society's appeal to the Colonial Office for financial support propelled his proposal into the political sphere, as a means of answering recent American transcontinental railway surveys and slaking the society's thirst for scientific and geographical information from the western lands north of the forty-ninth parallel. The Colonial Office was anxious to learn whether these lands were accessible from Canada by a route entirely through British territory. As a result of these mixed motives, public financial support

for Palliser's expedition was supplemented by the assignment of four scientific specialists, each with his own instructions: Hooker chose M. E.
Bourgeau of France as botanist; Roderick Murchison of the British Geological Survey and the Royal Geographical Society named Dr. James Hector of
Edinburgh as geologist; Edward Sabine for the Royal Society instructed
Thomas Blakiston of the Royal Artillery as "magnetician"; and John William Sullivan served as astronomer and secretary.

From May 1857 until the return to England in June 1860, Palliser and his
party traveled along several routes in the southern prairies, mainly between the northern and the southern branches of the Saskatchewan River.
The group split and attempted several passes through the Rocky Mountains, until Palliser was satisfied that an all-British route had been traced via
Fort Langley on the Fraser River to Lake Osoyoos. Palliser's lengthy reports, the first careful observations of the prairies to be published, became
an important source of information for future planners of railways and settlement. His reports concluded that any route from Canada to the Red River
settlement, let alone to the Pacific Ocean, would prove superfluous because travel through the United States was so much easier. Only the discovery of extensive mineral deposits, he suggested, might alter this reality.[86]

The scientific verdicts of the Palliser expedition were therefore important. Bourgeau, the botanist, collected sixty thousand specimens of fewer
than five hundred different plant species, some insects, and temperature
readings of soils and tree trunks. His indefatigable efforts revealed that
most of these species had spread over wide expanses of land regardless of
the changing terrain. Hector, the geologist, aided Bourgeau in collecting,
noted the occurrence of timber trees in the Northwest, and reported on botanical distribution throughout the central part of British North America as
an inducement to Canadian agricultural expansion. Hector formulated the
classic distinction of three levels of prairie, the stepwise elevation from the
Red River westward to the Rocky Mountains. Among these relief features,
he sketched the bounds of the arid section that came to be known as "Palliser's Triangle" in present-day Alberta and Saskatchewan. The geologist
had been sent, however, mainly to investigate potential fuel supplies for
the British Empire. Structuring his geological observations on groundwork
laid by Richardson, Isbister, and others, Hector contributed a reliable geological map of the Rocky Mountains in sectional detail that modified Isbister's sweeping claims of a vast coalfield at their base. Yet he did predict the
existence of sufficient coal supplies in British territory to encourage the
consideration of a railway through the prairies to the Pacific.[87]

Blakiston, an outsider who left the expedition in 1858 after a personal dispute, steadfastly eschewed any expansionist ideology. He collected birds as a hobby and contributed incidentally to knowledge of the natural history of the prairie region. In the course of his formal magnetic and meteorological duties, he rejected vague climatic analogies that compared the Northwest to north-central Europe. Instead he sought to explain why the European climate differed so greatly from that of North America, noting the moderating effects of the Gulf Stream in Europe. Blakiston suggested that more informative comparisons might be made of the Pacific Northwest to continental Europe, on the one hand, and of the rest of British North America to Asia, on the other, except that Siberia had no equivalent of Hudson Bay. In the end, he refused to make his meteorological register available to Palliser, although Sabine did duly add the magnetic observations to his volumes of tables.[88]

Science played just as prominent a role when the Canadian government sent its own expedition under George Gladman to assess the agricultural prospects of the area between Canada and the Red River settlement. Sir William Logan nominated Henry Youle Hind as Gladman's geologist because all of his own assistants were busy in the field. Hind (1823–1908), an English immigrant educated at Leipzig and an admirer of Humboldt, was well-known in Toronto as a publicist, the editor of the Royal Canadian Institute's *Canadian Journal of Science, Industry, and Art*, and an outspoken Canadian expansionist. Yet Hind possessed no formal training in the sciences he taught at Toronto's Normal School and Trinity College, affiliated with the recently formed University of Toronto. A peculiar combination of advanced scientific awareness and unproven traditional assumptions supported his optimistic assessment of the lands he traversed, first in 1857 and then in 1858 on a second expedition with Dawson to extend the investigation to the Saskatchewan River. In his published *Narrative* (1860) Hind presumed that the "sterile belt" of the northwestern United States would channel settlement into the Red River and Saskatchewan River valleys, and he was eager to raise Blodget's summer isotherms still higher to confirm this view. Essentially, he skipped the necessary step of collecting information as objectively as possible and relied on a single rapid rise in temperature reported by Lefroy at Fort Simpson in 1844 to conclude that a corresponding "fertile belt," a phrase that seems to have become current through Francis Parkman's immensely popular *The Oregon Trail* (1849), extended from the Lake of the Woods to the Rocky Mountains.[89]

The historical significance of Hind's exploration, and of the positive reception accorded to his *Narrative*, lies in the number and the diversity of the people who, even beyond the expansionist hothouse of Toronto, were prepared to accept his judgment at face value and to take the most positive reading of Palliser's reports. There was a general need at the time for new concepts that were able to grasp the unique geographical realities of the prairie and for a vocabulary that was large enough to contain them. Nor was it yet clear how much emphasis to place on any one science in forming these interpretations. The predominance of meteorology in Palliser's and Hind's day can be understood from a review of Blodget's *Climatology* by G. T. Kingston, Lefroy's successor at the Toronto observatory and a scrupulous outsider to the expansionist movement. Although he ignored the book's final propagandistic chapter, Kingston's whole climatological conception of the North American continent was reoriented by Blodget's approach: the entire region from the Atlantic to the Mississippi Valley now appeared to him as a discrete meteorological unit, vastly different from the area west of the Rockies. For Canadians, unlike Americans, the ideological significance of this expansionist scientific tradition, which ran from Humboldt through Richardson and Lefroy to Blodget and from there through Palliser and especially Hind into the popular perception, was not so much that isotherms transcended the forty-ninth parallel. It was rather that these new meteorological concepts drew the eyes of "civilization" northwestward, beyond the pale.[90]

## Confederation and Conclusion, 1860–1870

The last decade or so before Confederation in 1867 brought both opportunity and instability. During the 1860s, scientific exploration in British North America, like that elsewhere, was characterized by institutional consolidation, increased specialization, and an explosion of expansive activity as a new generation of Crusoes supplanted and emulated the older Gullivers, who had taught them well. The explanation for the growth in complexity of these activities rested not so much with the influence of Charles Darwin as still with Humboldt—with the "spirit of the method" that emphasized geographical distribution and did indeed play itself out in the publication of Darwin's *The Origin of Species by Means of Natural Selection* in 1858–59. Yet the geographical approach in science concerned itself less with origins than with relationships in nature, its ultimate goal being to define laws that patterned natural phenomena, whether floral and faunal ranges, geological and mineral structures, or magnetic and meteorological readings. Most scientific explorers in British North America, whatever the focus of their activities, continued to be guided by the study of geographical distribution. Darwin, after all, anchored the most compelling aspects of his theory in the geographical evidence of the variation and distribution of species, and most British North Americans working within the natural history framework merely resolved to continue collecting evidence on the basis of the uniformitarian assumptions of Lyell in geology and Forbes in natural history.

Both practical motivation and the Edinburgh influence continued to be important in British North America during the 1860s. At least partly in response to recent infestations of potato and wheat crops, botany and entomology increasingly attracted popular interest during the 1860s. John Hutton Balfour (1808–84), professor of medicine and botany and keeper of the Royal Botanical Garden at Edinburgh, encouraged fieldwork on the Edinburgh model in natural history but also advocated botanical investigations of the vast unexplored tracts of the earth. A personal fascination with alpine species focused Balfour's attention on plants of northern regions, where, he taught, even minute lichens and mosses played a role in preparing the soil ultimately for settlement by man. Balfour trained at least two professional botanists who came to teach in British North America, and he equipped them intellectually not only to see in the Canadian Shield much more than an impenetrable armor of Laurentian rock but to spread this vision to their own students and beyond.[91]

The first Balfour-trained botanist was James Barnston (1831–58), a son of George Barnston, the fur trader. James's medical training at Edinburgh nurtured a love of plants, and he returned to Montreal in 1854 determined to organize a Botanical Society of Montreal on the model of its Edinburgh prototype, to assemble a catalogue of Canadian plants, and to teach botany from a chair he helped found at McGill College. Although his untimely death of a mysterious illness in 1858 doomed these incipient botanical institutions, Barnston left behind a growing number of Canadian botanists who realized that their standard reference work, *The Flora of North America* (1838) by John Torrey and Asa Gray of Harvard University, excluded many species found in British North America beyond Montreal and Quebec City. Canada, Barnston had insisted, remained an Eldorado of plants "yet to be made known." His death inspired his father to pursue his studies of plant distribution, especially of the Cruciferae or cress family, in the Hudson's Bay Company territories. Following Balfour, the elder Barnston was struck by the climatic adaptability of these edible plants, which included cabbage, cauliflower, mustard, and turnip. In his view, these plants heralded the northward "diffusion" of civilization over British North America, promising sustenance for human society even in "those dismal regions where ice holds almost eternal empire."[92]

The second student of Balfour was George Lawson (1827–95), professor of chemistry and natural history at Queen's College, Kingston, from 1858. Lawson applied skills honed at Edinburgh to establish the Botanical Society of Canada in 1860. Like Balfour, he intended the society to explore the vegetation found not only locally but also beyond the bounds of settlement, for potato substitutes and chemical dyes as well as botanical species. The society enlisted members from as far away as the Red River and Prince Edward Island, among them Lawson's own students. News of its founding aroused anticipation, even abroad, that the botanical terra incognita between the settled parts of British North America and the Arctic Circle would at last reveal new species as well as the northern limits of those already known.[93]

Botanists and plant collectors also followed Hooker's proposal in 1860 to update British colonial floras. In addition his son, the botanist Joseph Dalton Hooker (1817–1911), published a seminal theoretical article on the "Outlines of the Distribution of Arctic Plants" in the *Transactions* of the Linnean Society in 1862. Although British North American governments were too preoccupied with political and economic problems to commit funds to Hooker's flora, his son's essay offered collectors a refined conceptual framework. Hooker analyzed Arctic floras along Forbesian lines, by geographical region and the geological age of their migration, and defined two regional floras, one western and one eastern, in northern North America. Hooker reoriented botanical attention in a northerly direction, away from a singular concentration on the American border regions, by appealing to both glacial theory and Charles Darwin's theory of "creation by variation" to explain the circumpolar patterns of distribution of these various plant forms. Members of the Botanical Society of Canada, especially Lawson's student Andrew Thomas Drummond and the botanist John Macoun (1831–1920) of Belleville, began characterizing floras they encountered on their own regional terms and expanding their investigations outwardly, whenever possible by joining field expeditions of the Geological Survey of Canada. Lawson expanded his field even further when he moved to Dalhousie University in Halifax in 1863 and began comparing coastal floras with those he had studied inland.[94]

Lawson's expansive or uniformitarian botanical outlook departed from the more traditional localized approach of William Hincks (1794–1871), professor of natural history at the University of Toronto, who adhered to outdated quinarian principles throughout his career. In botany, Hincks was concerned less with exploration, with cataloguing new species not found in Torrey and Gray's *Flora,* than with eliminating from their list those he could not find in Canada. Hincks's greater concern was to compile a Canadian fauna, but there his influence was limited by several factors. With zoology no longer containable as a single unit but subdivided into entomological, ornithological, icthyological, ethnological, and other large subdisciplines, organizing comprehensive collections was difficult. Hincks's impact on the Entomological Society of Canada organized at Toronto in 1863 was further limited by its decentralized structure, with branches in London and Quebec City, and by younger members' wider interests in the dynamic role of wind and water in the geographical distribution of insects. Unlike Hincks, with his more static, traditional approach, these collectors wanted to cover the field, which had remained virtually untouched since small insect collections had been assembled for the British Museum some thirty years before.[95]

While the British and Royal Scottish Museums continued to vie for specimens, especially from fur traders in the Northwest, after 1858 the Smithsonian Institution rivaled these imperial institutions as a repository for zoological items. The Smithsonian sent Robert Kennicott to collect birds and eggs in the Hudson's Bay Company lands during a survey he conducted for the Western Union telegraph company. Through good personal relations with Hudson's Bay Company officers, along with material inducements including firearms and the forbidden luxury of alcohol, ostensibly intended for preserving specimens, the Smithsonian diverted the flow of specimens and artifacts to Washington instead of across the Atlantic, causing traders like George Barnston to consider favoring British and Canadian repositories as a moral and patriotic issue.[96]

For Logan's geological survey, the 1860s brought consolidation and expansion, albeit unofficially. In 1863 Logan published the *Geology of Canada,* the grand synthesis of his previous reports, accompanied by a map three years later. The massive volume marked the end of an era in the history of Canadian scientific exploration and in some ways carried the original mandate of the survey to completion. Canada's geological structures had been outlined and made public with a high degree of scientific expertise, and the term "Laurentian" now applied as the general designation for the most ancient formations of Europe as well as of America. From a practical standpoint, the work uttered the final word on the province of Canada's coal supplies, which constituted little more than "a few carbonized plants." The obvious alternative of turning to the United States for viable sources of the mineral fuel was threatened by the American Civil War at a time when the American abrogation of the Treaty of Reciprocity of 1854 also threatened Nova Scotian coal markets; it appeared increasingly sensible for Canadians and Nova Scotians to turn to one another to solve these apparently complementary problems.[97]

Not only for economic but also for scientific reasons, the Geological Survey of Canada expanded to other colonies well before Confederation. In 1864 Logan assigned Alexander Murray to survey Newfoundland at the invitation of government officials who hoped to develop the island's resources. Logan correctly saw the Laurentian formations of Newfoundland as an extension of the Canadian Shield and was eager to help. Logan included Newfoundland geology in his Canadian entry at the Paris Exposition in 1867. When the island refused to join Confederation that year, the new federal government forbade any further involvement there by the Geological Survey of Canada, now under federal jurisdiction, so Logan sent Murray to continue his survey of Newfoundland on a leave of absence. Similar arrangements to help survey Nova Scotia offended local geologists; yet one of the stipulations of the colony's entry into Confederation was an immediate geological survey of its coal and goldfields by the Geological Survey of Canada. In New Brunswick the government commissioned regional geological reconnaissances by L. W. Bailey in 1863 and H. Y. Hind in 1864, who cultivated links with surveys in contiguous territories, Maine and Canada respectively. Bailey (1839–1925), professor of chemistry and natural history at the University of New Brunswick, was assisted by Matthew and Hartt of Saint John, who strove to fill the geological gaps left by Dawson's *Acadian Geology*. Much like Logan, Bailey was driven by the conviction that "the distribution of mineral ores is as much controlled by principles of order as the distribution of animals or plants, and therefore every observation which tends to increase our knowledge of the position and relation of the rocks which bear them, tends also to their direct development."[98]

When Logan retired from the Geological Survey of Canada in 1869, he left behind the definitive elucidation of Canadian and especially Precambrian geology and an institution prepared to expand. There was little to fault in the broad outlines he had sketched, although his survey had been forced to recant its claims for the Precambrian "fossil" *Eozoon canadense* as the "dawn

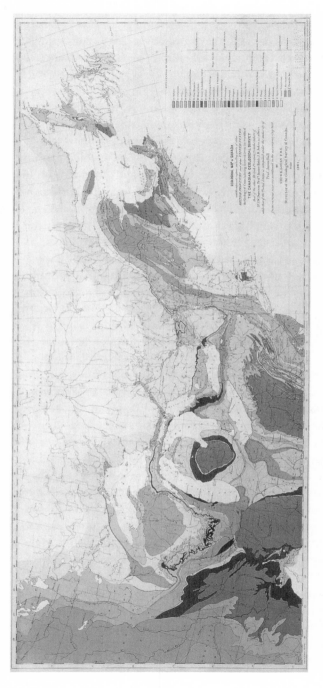

18.4 "Geological Map of Canada and the Adjacent Regions" (Sir William Logan, 1864). Logan's map was one of the earlier geological maps that used color to indicate bedrock and surficial geology. Courtesy of The Geological Survey of Canada (GSC-203212).

animal" of Canada, and some dispute remained over his analy sis of the Quebec Group, which he based erroneously on James Hall's New York system.[99]

The expansive uniformitarian frame of reference in floral, faunal, and mineral explorations had its analogue in terrestrial magnetism and meteorology. In 1853, fourteen years after regular observations had begun at the Toronto observatory, Lefroy admitted that more than twenty-seven quarto volumes of figures had accumulated and needed to be analyzed and reduced and that physical scientists had failed to develop a general theory of the earth's magnetism. This difficulty did not discourage further efforts to organize and coordinate meteorological observations, but it did help to alter their objectives. Attempts within the Royal Canadian Institute to coordinate simultaneous observations of temperature and seasonal variations, the limits of vegetation, the progress of epidemics, and the direction and motion of storms throughout British North America during the 1850s had been widely regarded as premature. Yet by the 1860s, bases for cooperation could be found in other colonies: Frederick Allison of the newly founded Nova Scotia Institute of Natural Science found meaning in local meteorological observations only within the larger context of values at other stations; and J. D. Everett of King's College, Windsor, Nova Scotia, formerly of the Scottish Meteorological Society at Glasgow, established an observatory to carry out meteorological studies even after his return to Scotland in 1864. The astronomical observatories at Fredericton, Quebec, and Kingston served meteorological interests only incidentally, but Montreal benefited from the remarkably complex private magnetic and meteorological observatory built by Dr. Charles Smallwood (1812–74) nearby at Isle Jésus, the operation of which was transferred to McGill College in 1864. Moreover, the Institute of Rupert's Land, founded by fur traders at Fort Garry in 1862 to collect and publish scientific information on the Hudson's Bay Company territories, declared that its membership, scattered from the Pacific Ocean to Lake Superior and north to the Arctic Sea, was willing to undertake regular magnetic and meteorological observations if the society could acquire the necessary instruments.[100]

But more important, the replacement of Lefroy by George Templeman Kingston (1816–86), a former Royal Navy midshipman and principal of the Nautical College at Quebec, marked a distinct shift in the basic aims of the Toronto observatory. Instead of a natural philosopher who undertook long-term climatic studies, the chief meteorologist of Canada now favored practical navigational uses of the science to build a storm-warning system. Recent technological and theoretical developments had forged meteorology into a more exact science. Expanding telegraph networks inaugurated the use of synoptic charts in the study of continental weather systems, and the theory of thermodynamics, which clarified the relationship between heat and motion, helped to explain adiabatic processes that produce precipitation and storms. These developments increased the accuracy of weather forecasting and attracted attention from agricultural, commercial, and insurance interests along the Great Lakes waterways. Kingston bided his time until after Confederation, and in 1872 he organized the Meteorological Service of Canada, centered at the Toronto observatory, to organize the systematic exploration of long-term British North American climatic patterns and also, more immediately, to recruit and train an expanding network of weather observers. Kingston's network communicated telegraphically with American meteorological stations and eventually mounted weather symbols on railway cars. He hoped soon to be able to forecast daily conditions accurately for all whose livelihoods depended on it.[101]

For naturalists and geologists too, Confederation and the annexation of the Northwest that followed in 1870 had a double edge. On the one hand Confederation satisfied expansive impulses inherent in their uniformitarian outlook, but on the other hand, as Torrey and Gray in the United States had discovered decades earlier, transcontinental expansion brought overwhelming numbers of specimens to be analyzed. In Canada, Lawson's goal of a thorough critical examination of Canadian plants resulted in an almost paralyzing mass of materials. Instead of a single published flora, Lawson was forced to contemplate a limited series of monographs on selected aspects of the country's vegetation. Several such studies appeared during the 1870s and 1880s, each highlighting the geographical distribution of one botanical family.[102] But nothing remotely approaching a complete Canadian flora ever emerged from Lawson's pen. This was instead left to A. R. C. Selwyn, Logan's successor in the Geological Survey of Canada, and John Macoun, who became the survey's naturalist in 1877.

Just as Humboldt never completed his multivolume *Cosmos*, Sabine, Richardson, and Hooker never succeeded in modeling laws of geographical distribution in nature on Newton's universal laws of gravitation and motion. The territorial expansion brought by Confederation found the inventory sciences in British North America in various states of readiness to cope with their enlarged fields of investigation: geology, the most highly organized, reveled in the challenge; terrestrial magnetism and meteorology had come to terms with the need to adjust; and the natural sciences, lacking both conceptual focus and government support, were the least prepared. Yet the tradition of scientific inventory in British North America left a far-reaching intellectual legacy. In 1858 Dawson noted: "Physically considered, British America is a noble territory, grand in its natural features, rich in its varied resources. Politically, it is a loosely united aggregate of petty states, separated by barriers of race, local interest, distance, and insufficient means of communication. As naturalists, we hold its natural features as fixing its future destiny, and indicating its present interests, and regard its local subdivisions as arbitrary and artificial."[103] Ten years later, in 1868, he still thought that "Nature" had indeed "already taken hold of the mind of Young Canada" and was "moulding it in its own image."[104]

Scientific modes of exploration, brought to British North America largely by way of the University of Edinburgh, penetrated geographical study between 1800 and 1870 through its Gullivers' and Crusoes' determination to collect useful information on as wide a scale as possible. As the sciences became institutionalized, the Gullivers retreated; and as the sciences became domesticated, the Crusoes behaved more and more like Gullivers. The uniformitarian approach that came to dominate each of the inventorial sciences strongly supported an expansionist ideology and itself became a driving force in Canadian history.

By the 1870s, the preoccupation of scientific explorers with studies of geographical distribution contributed to a unique and complex vision of Canada as a transcontinental nation and of its role as a separate but still connected part of the larger British Empire. In essence, the study of geographical distribution offered romantic nationalists the compelling model of an incipient British North American nation, not as a contradiction in terms but rather as an inevitable historical development, not to be feared as revolutionary or cataclysmic but rather to be welcomed as part of the natural order of things. This new optimism encouraged expansionist believers to reject Buffon's Eurocentric warning that the human animal, like other animals, would deteriorate after migrating to North America. The historical timescale was still too short to judge physical modifications in the animal kingdom, and man required more than two centuries to acclimatize as completely as plants had done in their North American environment. Such assumptions lay at the root of intensified anthropological studies as this new discipline developed in the late nineteenth century. The implicit scientific expectation of a "Victorian rate of progress" in the end created as many problems as it purported to solve, especially for those, such as French Canadians, who did not share its materialist assumptions. For those who did, the righteous sense of harmony with nature was a heady one while it lasted.

# 19 / Nineteenth-Century Exploration of the Arctic

W. GILLIES ROSS

The North American Arctic is usually considered to be the region beyond the northernmost limit of tree growth. The tree line here lacks the nearly latitudinal alignment that it exhibits in Eurasia. Between Labrador and the Aleutian Islands it soars north and swoops south, producing a sinuous pattern with troughs on the coasts of the Labrador and Bering Seas and in Hudson Bay and with crests at Ungava Bay and the northern slope of Alaska. The Arctic region thus includes the two maritime fringes on the Atlantic and Pacific sides, the Arctic mainland extending between northern Labrador and northwestern Alaska, and the islands north of the continental mass, distributed in three tiers aligned from east to west. The maritime Arctic fringes in Labrador and Alaska, which had been explored and partly exploited by Europeans before 1800, are not within the scope of this chapter. The discussion that follows concentrates on the Arctic mainland and islands between Cape Chidley on the east and Point Barrow on the west, from the tree line in the south to the northern tip of Ellesmere Island. This territory, largely unknown in 1800, has a maximum east-west extent of approximately twenty-six hundred miles and a maximum south-north dimension of roughly two thousand miles. Most of this vast domain was thinly inhabited by Eskimo hunters (Inuit), whose ecumene extended as far north as the Parry Channel, the series of waterways running west from Baffin Bay (Lancaster Sound, Barrow Strait, Viscount Melville Sound, M'Clure Strait) and dividing the southern tier of Arctic islands from the two northern tiers. The northern tiers (Queen Elizabeth Islands) did not support a permanent indigenous population in 1800.

Most of the Arctic mainland had been claimed by Great Britain and put under the commercial control of the Hudson's Bay Company. British North America met Russian America in Alaska, and the boundary between them was established along the meridian of 141° west in 1825. Four decades later Alaska was purchased by the United States, and Canada became a self-

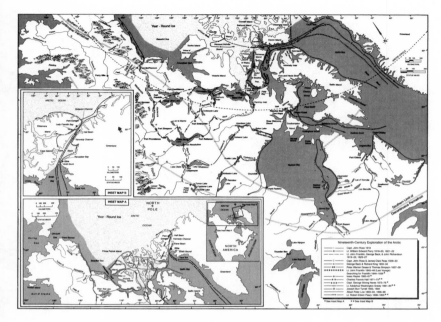

*Map 19.1 Nineteenth-Century Exploration of the Arctic.*

governing dominion. The Arctic islands, however, were not under the sovereign control of any nation before 1880, when Britain, assuming control, transferred them to Canada.

Although a homeland to Eskimo hunters, the Arctic was to Europeans a remote, desolate, and dangerous frontier, "a part of the globe which had no care for human life, which was not built to man's scale, a remnant of the Ice Age which long ago had withered the world."[1] It had no prospects for settlement other than posts and missions; without the incentives of gold and silver, tall trees and fertile fields, or water power and coal, it held little attraction for Europeans except where it provided access to the fur resources of subarctic forests or where its offshore waters yielded bountiful supplies of sea mammal oil, baleen, and ivory.

But exploration is driven by curiosity as well as hunger for land and resources. Thus much of the Arctic mainland and islands became known to Europeans during the 1800s as men slaked their thirst for scientific knowledge and persisted in their quest for a sea route to the Indies—not because they still dreamed that a practical shipping route existed within the icy northern seas but because the question of what lay beyond the known

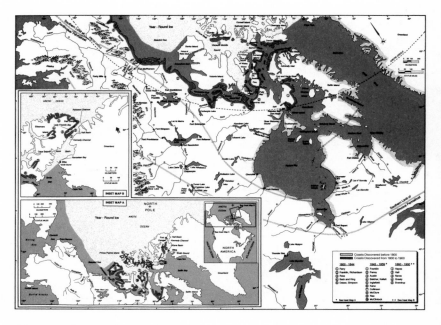

*Map 19.2 Coasts Discovered to 1900.*

world had to be answered. Unrolling the map of the North American Arctic was a slow process, however. The vastness of the region and its severe environment constrained human activities. Before the modern era of air photography, exploration was a linear procedure in which rough observations were made by men traveling along coasts or river valleys. Their speed was limited to a few miles per hour, their observation range restricted to what they could see from hilltop or masthead. Furthermore, Arctic conditions demanded specialized travel and survival methods, which few explorers had learned before going north.

Every climatic zone in North America confronted European explorers with a different set of environmental conditions, some favorable or familiar and some not. The Arctic was arguably the least familiar and least favorable of all. In general, the Arctic is characterized by mean monthly temperatures under 50°F (10°C); long, severe winters; short, cool summers; persistent ice cover on fresh- and saltwater bodies; prolonged winter darkness and summer daylight; ground underlain by continuous permafrost; and a comparatively small number of plant and animal species. Because the North American Arctic was so imperfectly known in 1800, Europeans

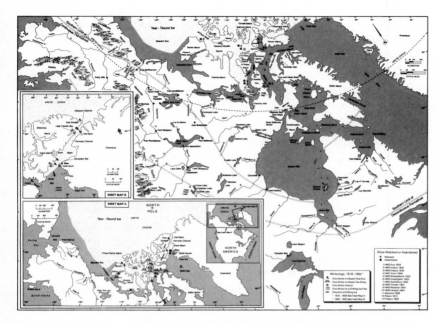

*Map 19.3 Winterings, 1818–1900, and Ships Wrecked or Abandoned.*

lacked reliable quantitative information about these environmental charac-teristics and how they varied from one region to another.

Among these regions, the ancient, glacier-scoured Canadian Shield provides the structural backbone of the Canadian North. Its mountainous eastern rim, running from Labrador to Ellesmere Island, presents to ships approaching from the Atlantic a formidable rampart pierced at sea level in only three places: Hudson Strait, Lancaster Sound, and Jones Sound. This fiord-cut seaward flank of the Shield contains mountain or ice-cap sum-mits of more than five thousand feet in elevation in Labrador and more than eight thousand feet on Baffin Island. Saucer-like, the Shield slopes down to sea level around Hudson Bay and rises again on the opposite side, crossing the Barren Grounds to its less-elevated western margin. Neighbor to the Shield on the west is a region of flat-bedded plains and plateaus. Sedimentary rocks with horizontal aspect create a relatively uniform land-scape sloping gradually northward, carrying the drainage of the Macken-zie River system to the Beaufort Sea, underlying the low, poorly drained coastal plains between Coppermine Gulf and the northwestern corner of Alaska, and forming most of Banks, Victoria, Prince of Wales, and King

William Islands. Most of the Queen Elizabeth Islands are in the Innuitian region of folded rocks. Elevations vary considerably but increase generally northeastward to more than nine thousand feet on the ice caps of Elles-mere Island. The coastal lowlands of Hudson Bay and Foxe Basin compose a fourth physiographic region, one of comparatively slight importance to Arctic explorers. The southwestern parts of Baffin and Southhampton Is-lands were outside the main thrusts of exploration, and the largest low-land, south of Hudson Bay, is subarctic rather than Arctic. The mountain-ous barrier of the Western Cordillera forms a five-hundred-mile-wide belt running along the Pacific coast and curving through Alaska to the Bering Sea and Strait. Within this zone the east-west Brooks Range helped to iso-late the coastal plain of northern Alaska from southern influence.

The pattern of continental drainage was extremely relevant to explorers who traveled overland from Hudson Bay or Montreal to reach the Arctic coast. In fur trade canoes and occasionally boats, they ascended the rivers of the Hudson Bay drainage basin, portaged over the height of land into the Arctic basin, and descended the Mackenzie River System. From Great Slave and Great Bear Lakes they could cross an eastern divide into the headwaters of the Back or Coppermine Rivers, alternative routes to the coast.

The season during which canoes or boats could be used was short. West of Hudson Bay most lakes were frozen from 1 November to 1 July. The rivers, which froze a few weeks later and broke up almost a month earlier, were open for more than five months of the year but were not always navi-gable.[2] In winter the snow-covered ice surfaces of lakes and rivers were perfect highways for sled and snowshoe travel, except during periods of freeze-up and breakup.

Away from the natural routes offered by waterways, summer travel over Arctic tundra was inhibited by the waterlogged ground lying over permafrost (permanently frozen subsoil) and by the spongy mat of sedges, mosses, and lichens common to coastal plains and lowlands. Horses were not considered appropriate for Arctic use, and no suitable vehicle existed for a snowless tundra surface, so summer travel was necessarily by foot, which was both difficult and slow. In winter, the frozen ground surface, mantled with snow for eight or more months during the year, provided ex-cellent conditions for walking (with snowshoes if necessary) and sledding (with either dog or human traction). In the treeless landscape, however, winds could denude exposed areas of their sparse snow cover, confining sled travelers to the low depressions and stream valleys in which snow tended to accumulate. In addition, the physical character of the snow, which changed in response to temperature and humidity, affected sled performance. Extremely cold, dry snow increased the friction of runners, whereas warm, moist snow failed to support their weight.

Arctic summers are tolerably cool, but winters are dangerously cold. Low temperatures, which adversely affected most human activities and often threatened survival, demanded protective measures and equipment. In the month of January, average daily minimum temperatures are below −31°F (−35°C) throughout the central part of the Canadian Arctic.

Locations along the Arctic Circle (66°30' north) experience one twenty-four-hour day and one twenty-four-hour night during the year, and the number of each increases as one goes farther north. At 75° north, the approximate latitude of many explorers in the 1800s, more than three months of continuous darkness and twilight occur after early November, and a corresponding period of continuous daylight occurs after early May. Prolonged darkness depressed men's spirits and made traveling, surveying, hunting, and other outdoor activities difficult, if not impossible. The return of the sun was eagerly awaited by crews wintering at high latitudes, with the period of unceasing sunlight facilitating work.

For maritime expeditions, the extent and the duration of sea ice were of paramount importance. Ships could enter the Arctic in summer only, and their operations were necessarily confined to the region of seasonal, rather than year-round, ice cover. The progressive retreat of the extensive winter ice cover, beginning on the Atlantic and Pacific margins (Labrador Sea, Davis Strait, Bering Sea), enabled ships to reach the eastern coast of Baffin Island or the northwestern coast of Alaska by the start of July and to penetrate Hudson Bay, Lancaster Sound, or the Beaufort Sea by early August. They might navigate passages among the Arctic islands during August and September, if ice conditions were favorable, but soon after, new sea ice would force ships to either sail for home or take up winter quarters in some sheltered harbor. Maritime expeditions were thus severely limited geographically and temporally. The navigation season, scarcely four months long on the seaward flanks, diminished to zero among the Queen Elizabeth Islands. In addition, ice conditions were highly variable from one year to the next.

In 1818 most of this environment was unknown to Europeans. Early in that year, the London mapmaker Aaron Arrowsmith published the first edition of his "Map of Countries Round the North Pole," a circumpolar projection covering the world north of 50° north.[3] Like a tall building disappearing into thick fog, the map is clearest and most detailed in its lower, or southernmost, portions and grows progressively less distinct to the north. No northern limit is shown for the North American continent. Most of the territory north of 70° north is unencumbered space extending to Siberia. In 1818 geographers and mapmakers could not know that much of this blank area is in fact the land-free Arctic Ocean, nearly circular in shape and roughly two thousand miles in diameter. Not knowing the facts, they were obliged to leave embarrassingly large gaps or to resort to conjecture and invention. Intimate experiential knowledge of some parts of the blank regions did exist, but only in the minds of native northern hunters, well beyond the reach of European information systems. Even if there had been access to this knowledge, weaving the separate threads into a complete fabric of geographical relationships would have been difficult because preindustrial native inhabitants perceived, used, and described land, sea, and ice in unfamiliar ways and their occupancy of the Arctic regions was not spatially continuous.

On the Arrowsmith map, North America covers almost a third of the circumpolar zone latitudinally, from about 55° west (eastern Labrador) to 170° west (western Alaska). The Atlantic and Pacific coasts are confidently depicted, their fiords and islands carefully outlined, with a generous sprinkling of place-names representing past voyages, surveys, acts of settlement, and instances of resource utilization. Between these continental margins, the most prominent geographical feature is Hudson Bay, an arm of the sea that, with its narrow connecting corridor of Hudson Strait, extends almost one thousand miles into the Arctic heartland. Here too the geographical detail and nomenclature reflect a reasonably high level of European discovery and activity. Since the initial probes by Henry Hudson and others two centuries earlier, Europeans had explored intensively in search of a Northwest Passage, and the Hudson's Bay Company had established a regular supply route through Hudson Strait to fur trade posts in the bottom of the bay. West of the bay are the main features of the drainage pattern, known through the fur trade, which depended entirely on water transportation, and through exploration carried out by the Hudson's Bay Company and the North West Company. Some interior regions are blank: east of Hudson Bay, the Quebec-Labrador Peninsula appears untracked, and to the far west, the northern part of the Western Cordillera extending into Alaska is unadorned space.

Although the modern eye can easily detect errors in the southern re-

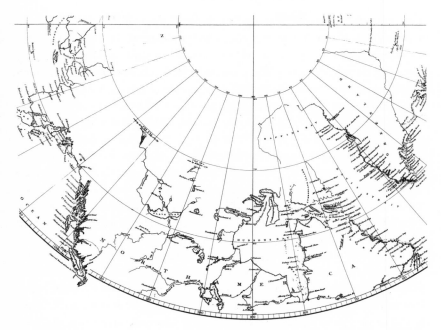

*19.1 "Map of Countries Round the North Pole" (Aaron Arrowsmith, 1818). This map indicates the state of geographical knowledge at the beginning of major Arctic exploration in the nineteenth century. Coolie Verner Collection, Map v331, Special Collections, University of British Columbia Library.*

gions depicted on the Arrowsmith map, the principal geographical features here are readily identifiable. North of 60° north, however, the map becomes less and less reliable. Geographical misconceptions, distortions, and omissions occur, especially in the eastern Arctic, where the complex pattern of land and sea obstructs accurate representation. Ungava Bay is incomplete, the southeastern part of Baffin Island ("Cumberland Island") is unrecognizable, Southampton Island is misshapen, and Foxe Basin is only partly shown. Farther north, coasts are depicted tentatively by thin, discontinuous lines, which leave a good deal to the imagination of the viewer. The most northerly coast, surrounding Baffin Bay, is not securely fastened to either "Cumberland Island" or Greenland, reflecting nineteenth-century doubts about the reliability of the information secured by Robert Bylot and William Baffin two centuries before. Beyond this hesitant outline of Baffin Bay, no land appears on the map.

In the western Arctic, the Alaskan coast bordering Bering Sea, Bering Strait, and the Chukchi Sea is tolerably well shown. The main indentations of Bristol Bay, Norton Sound, and Kotzebue Sound are readily identifiable, and a scattering of place-names reflects Russian and English explorations and the activities of Russian fur traders during the 1700s. The known coast ends, however, at Icy Cape near the northwestern corner of the continent, the most northerly point sighted by James Cook on his third voyage, in 1778.

The most striking aspect of the 1818 map is the absence of a northern limit to the continent. In the vast, empty area between Baffin Bay and Icy Cape, Alaska, only two tantalizing fragments of geographical experience appear. At approximately 69° north and at longitudes of roughly 110° and 135° west are two river mouths. For the first the map inscription reads: "The sea seen by Mr. Hearne 1771." For the second it reads "The sea seen by Mr. Mackenzie July 12th 1789." Separate overland journeys by employees of rival fur-trading companies had reached what seemed to be a northern sea at the mouths of the Coppermine and Mackenzie Rivers. These discoveries provided proponents of the Northwest Passage with some evidence that the North American continent did not extend far north into the "hyperborean sea" to form a barrier against maritime travel between Baffin Bay and the Bering Strait but terminated in an east-west-trending coast at about 70° north, a latitude that had already been attained on both coasts. Despite the fact that innumerable configurations of coastline might connect the scattered known points between Icy Cape and Baffin Bay, and that the geography of the Baffin Bay region itself was not confidently known, opinion favored the notion of a straight-line coast near 70° north. This simple concept accorded well with the historic desire to find a sea route to the Indies round the top of the continent.

The uncertain geography of the eastern Arctic complicated this conjectural picture, however. John Barrow, second secretary of the admiralty, whose determination to find a Northwest Passage colored so much British exploration in the first half of the century, pointed out that no one knew whether the coast of northeastern North America "rounds off to the eastward in a continuous line into Old Greenland, forming what is named Baffin's Bay on the charts, or whether it does not turn in a contrary direction to the westward, and fall in with the general trending of the northern coast of America; which, from three nearly equidistant points, seen by Cook, Mackenzie and Hearne, may be considered to run within a degree either way of the 70th parallel of latitude."[4] Evidently Barrow had already decided in favor of the latter configuration. His frontispiece map showed a dotted coastline connecting Icy Cape, the mouths of the Mackenzie and Coppermine Rivers, and Hudson Bay. And whereas Arrowsmith showed a large, enclosed Baffin Bay, Barrow omitted the discoveries of Baffin altogether and showed a broad Davis Strait leading directly and conveniently to the supposed east-west continental coast. Arrowsmith's map showed observed geographical relationships; Barrow's showed what he hoped would be observed by forthcoming admiralty expeditions.

Arrowsmith's "Map of Countries Round the North Pole" revealed major geographical problems. Eurasia's northern coast was laid down, but North America's was not. Where was the Arctic mainland coast? Did islands exist farther north, and if so, how were they distributed? Was it feasible for sailing ships to travel between the Atlantic and the Pacific Oceans along the continental coast, or among the islands if they existed? From a British point of view, the key to the puzzle was Baffin Bay. Was it the gateway to the elusive passage or merely an immense cul-de-sac?

This simple geographical curiosity was fundamentally important to the British government's decision to renew the Northwest Passage search in 1818. Discussing outstanding global geographical questions still to be resolved, the *Literary Chronicle* asked, "Does the American continent extend into the Arctic region, or, does the sea make an immense island of this new world?"[5] The query was simple enough, but no confident answer could yet be given. The goal now seemed to be more valuable because of the difficulties already experienced in attempting to achieve it. Surely, after so much effort to find a Northwest Passage, the presence or absence of this elusive sea path deserved to be finally determined, lest the work of former expeditions be wasted.

To this desire to finish the job was added a nationalistic dimension. The discovery of a Northwest Passage, as Barrow emphasized, was "an object peculiarly British."[6] The country could not remain indifferent while other countries fitted the last pieces into the puzzle. That other nations might have the gall to contemplate exploration in a region long dominated by British enterprise was made clear in 1815 when Lieutenant Otto Kotzebue of the Russian Navy arrived in England to prepare for an attempt at the Northwest Passage from the western end. He purchased English charts, navigational instruments, a lifeboat, and various foods preserved by Bryan Donkin's newly invented canning method.[7] During his three-year circumnavigation, Kotzebue failed to find the Northwest Passage, but he did chart part of the Alaskan coast overlooked by Cook. His activities worried the

British government. Russia owned Alaska, was well-placed to control the western end of the Northwest Passage, and had ambitions southward along the western coast of North America.[8]

Another factor encouraging the British to renew Arctic exploration was the termination of the Napoleonic wars in 1815, which eliminated the need for a large navy. In the five years after 1812, Royal Navy strength declined from 131,000 to 23,000 men and from 98 to 13 lines of battleships. Officers, including those retained on half-pay, were one-third as numerous as sailors.[9] Exploration and survey were regarded as appropriate employment for a peace-time navy and as suitable outlets for the skills of trained officers. The crude and incomplete map of the Arctic region cried out for refinement and elaboration, and interest in terrestrial magnetism, oceanography, and other branches of science was growing.[10] No one doubted that Royal Navy officers were capable of making the necessary observations.

By themselves, these factors—geographical curiosity, desire to finish the job, reluctance to see other nations discover the passage, intention of keeping naval officers usefully employed, growing interest in science— might not have led immediately to a renewal of British Arctic exploration. But in addition, reports of increasingly favorable ice conditions in northern seas finally convinced influential people that the time was propitious for a major discovery thrust. Unusual quantities of polar ice were reported drifting south into the western sector of the Atlantic Ocean between 1815 and 1818. The phenomenon was especially apparent during the summer of 1817. According to the *Newcastle Chronicle*, the ship *Keddington* sighted four large "islands of ice" in early July.[11] Normally the press would ignore such an event; icebergs were often sighted off Newfoundland by vessels sailing to and from the Gulf of St. Lawrence. But the *Keddington* was on a voyage between Barbados and England and had encountered icebergs roughly five hundred miles southeast of Newfoundland, near the latitude of present-day Boston, far enough outside usual limits to warrant attention. A few months earlier Lieutenant William Edward Parry, soon to become famous for his Arctic voyages, had also noticed icebergs at unusually low latitudes while he was traveling between North America and England.[12] Later in the year the eminent scientist Sir Joseph Banks told him that the increased export of Arctic ice to temperate regions might have been responsible for the declining air temperatures in Britain over the last decade.[13]

At the same time, navigators of the northern seas were encountering abnormally open ice conditions between Greenland and Spitsbergen. In the summer of 1817 the whaling captain William Scoresby Jr. sighted the coast of Greenland, which, because of its fringing barrier of southward-drifting pack ice and icebergs, had been "rarely before seen by any English navigator." A Bremen whaling captain claimed to have sailed along the eastern coast of Greenland to 81°30' north without seeing ice, and some vessels were said to have reached 84° north. Experienced whalemen agreed that "the sea was more open and free from compact ice than in any former voyage they ever made." Scoresby wrote that two thousand square leagues (over seventeen thousand square miles) of the Greenland Sea had become free of ice during the last two years.[14]

These circumstances convinced many people, practical seafarers and armchair travelers alike, that some major convulsions of nature were creating atypical climatic and oceanographic conditions in the North Atlantic sector. Indeed, nature had experienced a convulsion. In 1815 a violent eruption of Mount Tamboro in Sunda Strait, Dutch East Indies, had ejected a large quantity of ash into the stratosphere, where it spread to regions as remote as Greenland and Antarctica, whose massive ice sheets still today contain layers of particulate fallout from that explosive event. The airborne dust appears to have increased the reflection of incoming solar radiation back into space, thereby lowering air temperatures and contributing to crop failures in parts of Europe from 1816 to 1819 and causing the notorious "year without a summer" (1816) in the eastern United States. Changes in atmospheric circulation retarded pack-ice dispersal in southern Hudson Bay, James Bay, and eastern Hudson Bay but augmented ice transport southward from the eastern Arctic in the Labrador Current.[15] Thus a volcanic eruption in the tropics may have influenced the course of exploration in the Arctic.

The increased openness of Arctic seas provided new possibilities for exploratory ventures. Grasping the significance of the improved ice situation, Scoresby suggested to Sir Joseph Banks in early October 1817 that the government might be persuaded to dispatch an expedition of one or more whaleships under his command. Banks supported the idea, which was strongly promoted at the admiralty by John Barrow. Much to Scoresby's annoyance, however, Barrow took full credit for the suggestion without acknowledging Scoresby; he rejected the idea of a whaling master as commander and transformed the proposal into an admiralty expedition with a naval commander and crew. This set the character of British Arctic exploration for many years to come.

# The Northwest Passage: Maritime Approaches, 1818–1833

## Ross (1818)

In the spring of 1818 the British government sent out two polar expeditions, one toward the North Pole and one in search of the Northwest Passage. The latter expedition, under Commander John Ross, consisted of HMS *Isabella* and *Alexander*, both converted whalers. Ross was ordered to enter Davis Strait, "stand well to the northward" along the western coast of Greenland, then turn westward, sail round the North American continent, and enter the Pacific through Bering Strait. The ships were to return to England by the same route if feasible.[16]

The ships arrived off Disko Island, on the western coast of Greenland, in mid-June. Pressing northward as quickly as pack ice permitted, they reached Melville Bay by the end of July. On their way up the Greenland coast they frequently encountered whaleships, whose masters readily offered assistance and advice. At the end of July the discovery vessels worked westward through the ice past Cape York, with the men tracking, warping, and towing the ships through narrow leads, in the manner of the whalers. They were now at the extremity of reliable European knowledge. Behind was a coast familiar to native Greenlanders, their colonial administrators, and transient European whalemen. Ahead was territory possibly, but not certainly, coasted by Bylot and Baffin two centuries before and not subsequently visited by Europeans. As they traveled on, Ross was delighted to find that Baffin's observations were surprisingly accurate.

On the last day of August the two ships stood into the mouth of a large indentation that conformed to Sir James Lancaster's Sound, seen and named, but not entered, by Bylot's ship. Lancaster Sound is the gateway to half a dozen navigable routeways to the Beaufort Sea and Bering Strait. Ross stood on the threshold of a major discovery, but he turned back without taking the step across into the wonderland beyond. In one of the most curious incidents in Arctic exploration, he claimed to have seen a continuous range of mountains extending across the sound. He turned the ships around and headed down the coast of Baffin Island toward Davis Strait and England. On the map in his published narrative, Ross showed Lancaster Sound as a shallow indentation terminating in the "Croker Mountains."[17] But no such mountains exist. Was his error simply "an embarassing trompe de l'oeil" or "an unfortunate fancy, a sad mistake"? Was his vision impaired by snow blindness, deceived by "an effect of cloud," or distorted by "the tremendous refraction of the Arctic"? Perhaps he was too "cautious," as compared with the "resourceful" Parry, or perhaps weak and even cowardly, inventing—as his soon-to-be enemy Sir John Barrow expressed it so contemptuously—"a pitiable excuse for running away home." Could it be that "important discoveries were neither suited to his taste nor within his competence"?[18]

An intentional deception by Ross is highly unlikely. His previous naval service, which included military action and more than a dozen battle wounds, and his subsequent achievements in exploration after 1818, which included five winters in the Arctic, were hardly the actions of a cowardly or unduly cautious man. He was a competent and ambitious officer, and circumstances show that he could not have intentionally invented a sighting; indeed, others had seen the mountains too.[19] The mythical Croker Mountains were probably the result of imperfect and deceptive conditions of visibility at the time. Mirages, the illusory visual effects caused by refraction in the lower atmosphere and frequently associated with temperature inversions in the Arctic regions, are acknowledged to have had "a significant effect on the history of polar exploration."[20]

Ross's letters from the Shetland Islands, where the *Isabella* and *Alexander* stopped on their homeward voyage, stated that there were no prospects of a Northwest Passage. When the vessels reached Hull in mid-November, the local newspaper reported that Ross had "completely succeeded in exploring every part of Baffin's Bay" and had proved "that no passage exists between the Atlantic and Pacific Oceans through Davis' Straits and Baffin's Bay, the whole being found to be surrounded by high land."[21] The *Liverpool Mercury* wrote that Ross "could not discover the smallest opening sufficient to admit the entrance of a ship."[22] But doubts soon surfaced about these discouraging conclusions when Ross's observations about Lancaster Sound and the Croker Mountains were questioned by some of his own officers. As a result, a new admiralty expedition was ordered, this one placed under the leadership of Lieutenant William Edward Parry, who had been second-in-command under Ross.

Despite the embarrassing matter of the Croker Mountains, Ross's expedition could claim some noteworthy achievements. Ross returned with both ships and crews intact, having confirmed the reliability of Baffin's observations concerning the shape and dimensions of Baffin Bay. He and his officers had initiated the scientific investigation of the Arctic regions by gathering data on magnetism, geology, oceanography, meteorology, astronomy, and natural history. He had designed and used a "deep sea clamm" by which bottom samples incorporating organic life were dredged up from a world-record depth of one thousand fathoms—an achievement still regarded as one of the landmarks in the history of oceanographic research.[23] The public was stirred by the discovery that north of 76° north on the coast of Greenland the expedition had found "a newly discovered nation" that had "never tasted the fruits of the earth," apparently living in complete isolation.[24] Yet in the end, instead of constituting the ultimate voyage to crown centuries of effort in search of a sea route to the Pacific, the Ross expedition had simply duplicated Bylot and Baffin's voyage two hundred years earlier. Intended to be the final step in the search, it had proved to be only a new beginning.

### Parry (1819–1820)

Parry's expedition, comprising HMS *Hecla* and *Griper*, departed in May and arrived at the mouth of Lancaster Sound in late July, a month earlier than the ships under Ross in 1818. With "almost breathless anxiety" the crews watched headland after headland fade away astern as the ships sailed through the mythical Croker Mountains and continued west.[25] About 200 miles in from Baffin Bay, Parry turned south into Prince Regent Inlet, correctly guessing that it might connect with Hudson Bay, but after about 150 miles a barrier of ice brought the ships to a halt. They returned to Lancaster Sound and continued westward. Earlier, Parry had worried that a northward extension of the continental landmass might bar his progress, but as he advanced westward without meeting any obstacles, this dismal prospect seemed less and less likely. Ice in the southern part of Viscount Melville Sound forced the ships to hug the northern coast. Passing a succession of large islands (Cornwallis, Bathurst, Byam Martin), they forged westward until heavy polar ice off the southern coast of Melville Island prevented further progress.

In late September, Parry placed the ships in a secure harbor for the winter. Europeans had wintered in Arctic regions before, sometimes ashore and other times on board their ships, but many of these experiences had led to tragedy. As the thin ice spread stealthily out from the shore to encircle the ships in October 1819, Parry and his men may have recalled that only three men of the sixty-five on Jens Munck's expedition had survived the winter of 1619–20 and that every man on James Knight's expedition had died in 1719–21. Both these disasters had occurred in Hudson Bay, between seven hundred and one thousand miles south of Parry's winter harbor. Due to the measures taken by the admiralty to prepare the ships and crews

*19.2 William Edward Parry's vessels, banked with snow and partly unrigged, at Melville Island in 1819–20. Published in William Edward Parry,* Journal of a Voyage for the Discovery of a North-West Passage . . . *(1821), plate 4. Courtesy of the National Archives of Canada, c 28781.*

for wintering, however, as well as the imaginative activities designed by Parry and his officers to combat boredom and depression, they wintered successfully, establishing a useful precedent for subsequent Arctic maritime expeditions. In the following August the ships worked a little farther west but again encountered impassable ice; Parry observed, "There is something peculiar about the southwest end of Melville Island, extremely unfavourable to navigation."[26] Reluctantly the expedition retraced its path back to Baffin Bay and returned to England.

In sailing parallel to the supposed continental coast but about 400 miles north, Parry had not found the unencumbered ocean for which Barrow and others so fervently hoped but instead saw a "sea studded with numerous islands."[27] North of Parry Channel he had seen the southernmost components of the large archipelago now known as the Queen Elizabeth Islands. South of Parry Channel, however, he had seen nothing between

Cape Walker and "Banks Land" some 250 miles farther west. This gap, united with the large expanse of Viscount Melville Sound, appeared on subsequent maps as "Part of the Polar Sea," the "Polar Sea," or the "North American Sea." Three decades later its eastern sector was shown as the "King William Sea."[28] By suggesting that a large island-free sea connected Parry Channel with the supposed continental coast, between Somerset Island on the east and Banks Land on the west, Parry established a seductive geographical concept, one that would form the basis of the admiralty's last attempt to complete the Northwest Passage a quarter-century later.

In seeing this region south of Parry Channel as an arm of the Arctic Ocean, Parry was not entirely mistaken. The surface currents that enter M'Clure Strait import some polar oceanic components, including floes of thick, resistant, multiyear pack ice from the Arctic Ocean and occasionally fragments of thick, flat, ice islands derived from glacier ice shelves at the northern tip of Ellesmere Island. The tough, old ice then drifts southeastward through M'Clintock Channel to near King William Island, where it can go no farther. This stream of heavy ice (Parry's "something peculiar") prevented Parry's ships from passing beyond Melville Island in both 1819 and 1820.

Like a bold brush, Parry's discoveries slashed across the blank maps of Arctic North America, consigning Ross's Croker Mountains to the realm of fable and adding a string of new islands, headlands, and straits with English place-names, from Baffin Bay to Melville Island. Expedition planners now faced a dilemma, however. Parry had sailed six hundred miles west and back again with surprising ease, yet the ice cover of the interior polar sea had prevented him from sailing south toward the supposed continental coast. Should further attempts be made to penetrate this ice barrier, or should a different direction be taken?

Commenting on the direction that exploration should take, the *Hull Advertiser* declared, "One thing is self-evident: that a new course,—for instance, along the north coast of America—must be adopted—that appearing to offer the only chance of success."[29] Parry, contemplating a second expedition, agreed. He proposed a more southerly approach to the supposed westward-trending continental coast, by way of Cumberland Sound or Hudson Bay, where he expected to benefit from a warmer climate, more luxurious vegetation (including antiscorbutic plants), a supply of wood, more abundant wildlife (for meat), and the presence of native people (to forward messages).[30]

*Parry (1821–1823) and Lyon (1824)*

In late April 1821 Parry departed from England with HMS *Fury* and *Hecla*. On reaching Hudson Bay, he first searched the northern end of Roes Welcome Sound for a passage westward. Sailing around the northern tip of Southampton Island through the narrow obstacle course of Frozen Strait, he quickly confirmed a conclusion, of eighty years earlier, that Repulse Bay did not lead to a Northwest Passage. Returning to Foxe Basin, Parry's ships spent the winter at Winter Island, and in the next summer they advanced northward along the coast of Melville Peninsula. Parry hoped that this coast would curve round to connect with the continent's northern coast, a notion supported in a most exciting way by the testimony of Eskimos, who had described and drawn maps of a strait leading west to a large body of water. In August the ships passed the island of Igloolik and entered the strait (named for the *Fury* and *Hecla*) against strong currents. Stopped by ice, Parry sent out exploratory parties, which found that the strait was full of ice but that it did in fact lead to an apparently boundless frozen sea. Parry had no doubt that they were at another margin of the interior polar sea, and he named the eastern end of the strait Cape North-East, for the northeastern corner of the North American continent. But the northern coast did not trend directly toward Alaska. As Eskimos explained, and showed on maps, it curved southward to a point remarkably close to Repulse Bay, from which it was separated by a narrow neck of land only fifty miles across (Rae Isthmus). This appeared on Parry's map, probably the first time that published British charts incorporated information derived from Eskimo informants.[31]

Parry reluctantly concluded that Fury and Hecla Strait did not provide a feasible approach to the continent's northern coast. The strong east-flowing current was a problem for sailing ships, and more important, the strait had remained icebound for two successive seasons, suggesting a permanent condition. Parry's negative assessment was convincing. No other ship attempted to enter the strait during the nineteenth century.

Although he had again failed to complete the Northwest Passage or discover precisely where one lay, Parry had shown where a passage did not exist. Having eliminated M'Clure Strait in 1819–20, he eliminated Fury and Hecla Strait in 1821–23, adding another area to the charts and reducing the vast expanse of unknown territory north of Hudson Bay. And his delineation of Rae Isthmus and the western coast of Melville Peninsula would influence several later expeditions.

Rae Isthmus looked particularly inviting. Eskimos had declared that it

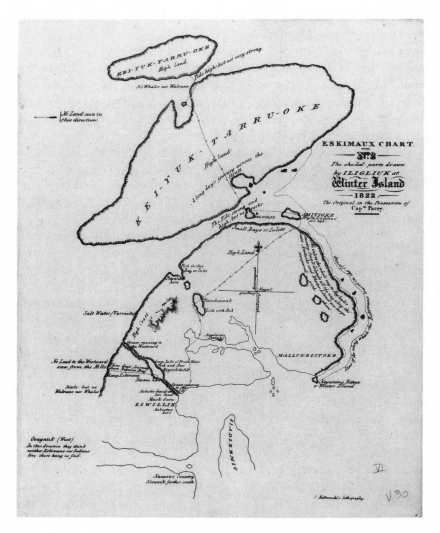

*19.3 Eskimo chart. Maps drawn by Eskimos assisted many explorers to "discover" new lands. This map revealed to Parry that Melville Peninsula ended at a strait (Fury and Hecla) leading westward to a large sea and that the peninsula had a narrow neck (Rae Isthmus) that could be crossed in three days. Published in William Edward Parry,* Journal of a Second Voyage for a North-West Passage . . . *(1824), opposite p. 198. Cartographic and Architectural Archives Division, National Archives of Canada,* NMC 6281.

could be crossed in only three days; on its northern side lay what appeared to be a "portion of the Polar Sea."[32] In the summer of 1824 the admiralty dispatched HMS *Griper*, under the command of Parry's former second-in-command, Captain George Francis Lyon, to winter in Repulse Bay and then send a party across the isthmus to "proceed westerly by land, or by water, as circumstances may admit, until you shall arrive at Point Turn-again" (the easternmost point reached a few years earlier by John Franklin's overland expedition from the Mackenzie River).[33] The novel plan, not without its virtues, failed when the ship encountered unusually difficult ice conditions in Roes Welcome Sound and twice narrowly escaped destruction. Lyon turned homeward without ever reaching Repulse Bay.

The four maritime expeditions that had sailed into the Arctic islands strongly reinforced the notion of a east-west termination to the continent. The task facing the next maritime expedition was to enter Lancaster Sound, cross Parry's interior sea to the continent, and follow the land westward to Point Barrow. But where to attempt the four-hundred-mile traverse to the mainland? Parry, thinking of new possibilities as fast as he eliminated old ones, concluded, "There is no *known* opening which seems to present itself so favourable for this purpose as Prince Regent's Inlet."[34]

### Parry (1824–1825) and Ross (1829–1833)

From Parry's observations of 1819, Prince Regent Inlet appeared to offer a direct route south from Lancaster Sound. But as usual, geographical reality failed to conform to the simple pattern of land and sea envisioned by explorers and cartographers. The inlet appeared to be bounded on the west by continuous land with no sea route to the west. In fact Bellot Strait cuts through this land, making an island of "North Somerset" (Somerset Island) and providing a feasible link in the complex of Northwest Passages. However, neither of the next two expeditions discovered the strait, which escaped detection until 1852.

With his old ships *Fury* and *Hecla*, Parry left England in early May 1824. Unfavorable ice conditions in Baffin Bay used up valuable time, and the ships did not enter Prince Regent Inlet until late September, too late to press southward. They wintered at Port Bowen, but in the following July, when they broke out of the ice and set off down the western coast, gales and wind-driven ice floes forced them inshore, where they took the ground more than once, with the *Fury* sustaining damage. No opportunity could be found to conduct repairs, and in the end Parry and his officers de-

cided to abandon the ship, cache its stores ashore on "Fury Beach," and retreat to England on the *Hecla*.

Ross's expedition on the *Victory* four years later was noteworthy in several respects. For one thing, it was the first British Arctic expedition of the
1800s not to be sent out by the government. The nonexistent Croker Mountains and Barrow's relentless antagonism at the admiralty had damaged
Ross's reputation, and his attempt to get command of another official expedition had failed. Determined to prove himself, he succeeded in obtaining
financial support from Sir Felix Booth, a wealthy distiller.

Ross took one vessel rather than the pair favored by the admiralty. In
1818 he had sailed on ships of 385 and 252 tons; the *Victory* measured only
150 tons. In 1818 he had commanded ninety-five men; now he took a mere
two dozen. In contrast to the admiralty ventures, Ross's expedition was
small, inexpensive, easily managed, maneuverable, and flexible. In addition, the *Victory* was the first vessel to use a steam engine in Arctic exploration and the only one to use retractable paddle wheels for propulsion. Before departure Parry had worried that the technology was untested in
Arctic conditions; it was, he stated, "certainly not the kind of service on
which novelties of that sort ought first to be tried."[35] The words were prophetic. The engine proved to be almost useless and was dismantled and
discarded in the southern part of the Gulf of Boothia.

The expedition was also noteworthy because it stayed out so long. Parry
had wintered once in the Arctic on his first attempt at the Northwest Passage and twice on his second—both bold initiatives at the time—but Ross
and his men spent a record four successive winters in Prince Regent Inlet.
Their long Arctic sojourn was one of necessity rather than choice and included a winter spent in a hut ashore after the ship had been abandoned.

The *Victory* entered Prince Regent Inlet in mid-August 1829 and progressed rapidly toward the south. After stopping at Fury Beach to collect
some of the provisions and equipment left by Parry four years before, the
ship passed the southernmost limit of European exploration (72° north)
and continued as far as Lord Mayor Bay, at the base of Boothia Peninsula,
approximately three hundred miles south of Barrow Strait. Ice prevented
further progress, and since it was by now the end of September, Ross
placed the vessel in winter quarters. In the following April, man-hauling
sled parties began to establish some basic geographical facts about the region, searching unsuccessfully for sea routes to the west (for there was as
yet no sign of the east-west continental coast), crossing the isthmus of
Boothia Peninsula, and traveling over sea ice along the northern coast of

King William Island. Much of the sledding was handled by Ross's nephew James Clark Ross, a keen and capable officer who had served under his uncle in 1818 and had sailed with Parry on three Northwest Passage voyages and one pole-seeking expedition north of Spitsbergen. More receptive to unfamiliar ideas than many other naval officers, he sometimes traveled with Eskimos and experimented with dogsleds and snow houses.

The sea ice did not break up during the summer. A second winter passed. Sled parties set out again in the spring of 1831, and one of them, under James Ross, located and reached the north magnetic pole on the western coast of Boothia Peninsula, an achievement of great scientific interest. The ensuing summer, like its predecessor, brought little reduction of ice cover in the Gulf of Boothia; after shifting the vessel several miles, John Ross and his crew began preparations for their third Arctic winter.

The men now turned their attention to the more immediate problems of survival and escape. Food stocks were diminishing. Two successive summers had passed without a breakup of ice, and Ross could not risk waiting out a third. He therefore decided to abandon the *Victory* in the spring of 1832 and make for Lancaster Sound, with the hope of meeting one of the British whaling ships north of Baffin Island. The trek north was extremely arduous. Unable to haul the two heavy boats (on sleds), the provision sleds, and the camping gear all at once, the men had to backtrack frequently and move everything in stages. After a month, they had walked 329 miles and had advanced a mere 30; almost nine-tenths of the distance still lay ahead.[36] Forced to alter the plan, Ross abandoned the boats and half the provisions, planning to make up the deficiency from Parry's cache of 1825 at Fury Beach. By the first of July all the men were at the depot, where they repaired Parry's old boats and erected a canvas-covered house as a fallback refuge. A month later they started in three boats but were stopped near the mouth of Prince Regent Inlet by extensive pack ice. The weary men retreated to their hut, grandly called Somerset House, for their fourth Arctic winter.

Almost a year later, in mid-August 1833, they departed again in the boats. This time comparatively open ice conditions enabled them to cross Prince Regent Inlet and continue along the northern coast of Baffin Island, sailing when the wind was favorable, rowing during calms, and stopping as seldom as possible for rest and sleep. On the eleventh day they had the remarkable good fortune of being picked up by a Hull whaler off Bylot Island. By an astonishing coincidence, the rescue ship was the *Isabella*, which fifteen years before, under an admiralty commission, had sailed in search of the Northwest Passage under the command of the same John Ross who now appeared out of the Arctic islands with a gang of "repulsive-looking people" who had long ago been given up for dead.[37]

The Ross expedition was right in attaching Boothia Peninsula to the North American continent but wrong in assuming that Somerset Island was a part of Boothia Peninsula. It was right in showing that no strait extended west across Boothia Peninsula but wrong in overlooking Bellot Strait at its northern tip. It was right in delineating much of the northern coast of "King William Land" but wrong in assuming that an isthmus connected it to Boothia Peninsula. The Ross expedition discouraged additional maritime probes into Prince Regent Inlet, pushed westward the area in which a passage might be found between Parry Channel and the continental coast, and reduced the size of Parry's interior polar sea.

## The Northwest Passage: Overland Approach, 1819–1847

While the five maritime expeditions under Ross and Parry were reducing the extent of terrae incognitae west of Baffin Bay and eliminating Foxe Basin and Prince Regent Inlet as feasible gateways to the Northwest Passage, overland expeditions were striking up through subarctic forests to the northern limit of the continent and using boats and canoes to survey the Arctic coast. An overland approach offered several advantages. The final stages of the journey to the Arctic would be undertaken through territory occupied by aboriginal peoples, who could assist as guides, porters, boatmen, and hunters, and by fur traders, who, at their various posts, could supply equipment, food, and practical advice. Relying on local resources in a way that the maritime expeditions could not, the overland parties could be relatively small, mobile, self-sufficient, and inexpensive. Boat and canoe travel would be facilitated by the enormous Arctic watershed west of Hudson Bay, in which the Mackenzie, Coppermine, and Great Fish (Back) Rivers provided convenient highways downstream to the coast. The regular spacing of these river mouths divided the coast between Alaska and Hudson Bay into four nearly equal segments roughly five hundred miles wide, whose investigation could proceed separately.

Each overland expedition from England included several phases. First was the transatlantic journey to Hudson Bay, Montreal, or New York. Next was the trip through the subarctic forest zone to the drainage of the Mackenzie River and down to Great Slave Lake or Great Bear Lake. The third phase was wintering, usually in a cabin erected by the expedition, providing time to prepare equipment and provisions and to transport canoes or boats to appropriate starting places. Fourth was the spring journey from the wintering place to the river and down to the coast. Finally was the summer coastal exploration by boat or canoe, after which the party had to make its way home, repeating in reverse most of the initial phases.

Among the drawbacks to the overland approach was the length of time needed to get a field party from England to its destination. Whereas a maritime voyage to the eastern Arctic could be completed in half a year, an overland expedition required a few years. Most of this time was spent in journeying to and from the Arctic and in wintering, which left little time for active exploration. John Franklin's first overland expedition of 1819–22 was away from England for forty-one months and passed three winters in the northern subarctic, but it spent only five weeks—a mere 3 percent of the time—exploring the Arctic coast. The expedition of George Back and Richard King in 1833–35, which was severely restricted by pack ice, managed little more than two weeks at the coast, only 2 percent of its thirty-one months. Exploration time increased on Franklin's second expedition: approximately 14 percent of the time was occupied by the coastal boat surveys. Distance traveled displayed a similar imbalance. In 1821 Franklin and his party followed the Arctic coast for 555 geographical miles, or 644 statute miles, only 7 percent of the total distance from England and back again.[38]

### Franklin (1819–1822)

Two weeks after Parry departed for Baffin Bay in 1819, the first of the admiralty's overland expeditions left for Hudson Bay under the leadership of Lieutenant John Franklin. The two exploration thrusts were intended to complement each other. While Parry was testing the veracity of Ross's assertion that the "Croker Mountains" blocked Lancaster Sound, Franklin could "amend the very defective geography of the northern part of North America."[39] Specifically, Franklin's task was to trace the continental coast eastward from the mouth of the Coppermine River toward Hudson Bay.

Four naval officers and two seamen formed the nucleus of the expedition. Indians, Eskimos, French-Canadian voyageurs, and a fur trader were recruited in North America. In the spring of 1821 the party of twenty men finally left Fort Enterprise, their winter base north of Great Slave Lake, and began the journey to the coast by way of the Coppermine River. Traveling in birchbark canoes, they reached the river's mouth in mid-July. The Indians turned back, while the Englishmen, voyageurs, and Eskimo interpreters, in two canoes, followed the continental coast eastward as far as the Kent Peninsula. From Turnagain Point, with the summer almost over and food supplies precariously low, the party began its return, heading south into the bottom of Bathurst Inlet, where they abandoned the battered canoes and started overland for Fort Enterprise. But an early winter had driven the caribou herds south, leaving the men without the animal food they had hoped to find on the Barren Grounds. The little band struggled on, fighting desperately to survive. Nearly half the party died, most from starvation but a few by murder. At least one man resorted to cannibalism. The men paid a high price for the charting of a few hundred miles of coastline.

In retrospect, the expedition's deficiencies are obvious. The group was too hastily dispatched, and its members were badly misinformed about the availability of labor and provisions in the fur trade country west of Hudson Bay. Forced to abandon almost two-thirds of their supplies—including ammunition, tobacco, and liquor, highly valued by voyageurs and northern Indians—because they were unable to hire enough boatmen at York Factory, they arrived in the Northwest seriously underequipped, only to find the Hudson's Bay Company and the North West Company involved in a bitter territorial conflict, unaware of the plans of the discovery expedition and unable to give them much help.[40] The naval personnel were not adequately prepared, either by training or by experience, to use the boats and bark canoes of the northern forests, to winter in the subarctic, to set up and strike camp, to sleep in tents, to cook in the open, or to hunt for food. They were novices in the Arctic environment, "sent out to carry out a difficult task with totally inadequate resources."[41] The weight added by scientific instruments and by iron-bladed axes, ice chisels, and other tools for trade with the Eskimos tired the men and slowed the party's progress.[42] The choice of bark canoes for a coastal journey among ice floes was probably unwise. Franklin did not turn for home soon enough, exposing the men to cold weather at the same time that the vagaries of climate deprived them of the caribou meat they so badly needed. Holding themselves aloof from the Canadians, the officers left the tough physical work to the voyageurs and became "a complete dead weight on the party."[43] Franklin's reliance on naval discipline among hired Indians, Eskimos, and French-Canadian boatmen, who neither understood nor sympathized with his objectives, did not earn him their respect.

The attitudes and methods of Franklin and his officers, molded by upbringing, naval training, and social environment, were as inappropriate in the boreal forest and on the tundra as those of the northern Indians would have been in Soho or the central Sahara. But there were few precedents for admiralty planners or the explorers themselves; some mistakes were bound to be made. "The art of survival in the Canadian North is the gift not of nature, but of experience, and . . . it is no reproach to a British naval officer to have starved in those regions."[44] Nonetheless, one suspects that a more tolerant and open-minded attitude toward the Canadians and their methods of travel and subsistence would have helped.

The expedition did suggest changes to be made on subsequent journeys: give the Hudson's Bay Company advance notice; travel to the Northwest faster and arrive earlier in the year; spend fewer winters in the North to obtain one Arctic field season; construct advance bases farther north (near Great Bear rather than Great Slave Lake); use sturdy boats rather than bark canoes for coastal travel; reach the coast by the Mackenzie River rather than the rapids-filled Coppermine; end coastal exploration earlier (20 August became the usual deadline); and use native techniques more often. In addition, the first overland thrust provided a baptism of fire, not only for Franklin but also for his companions Dr. John Richardson and Midshipman George Back. All learned from the experience and participated in later expeditions.

According to Leslie Neatby, Franklin "had put a roof on the map of Canada, and given a definite shape to the North American continent."[45] Undeniably, he had erected a few beams and planks, enough to suggest what form the roof might take, but Franklin's coastal survey had extended across only seven degrees of longitude, less than 10 percent of the longitudinal distance between northwestern Alaska and Hudson Bay. More than 90 percent of the coast remained unexplored.

## Franklin (1825–1827)

The second of the admiralty's Arctic land expeditions set out from England in February 1825. Franklin was again in command, and Richardson and Back were again among his companions. The target was the coastline west of the Coppermine mouth, and the access corridor to be used, on Franklin's suggestion, was the Mackenzie River. After reaching New York by ship, the men used a variety of conveyances to travel to the Northwest— steamboat, coaches, carts, boats, *canôts de maître* (the large freight canoes used by fur traders on the Great Lakes), and finally *canôts du nord* (the smaller, more manageable craft used on the river network beyond the head of Lake Superior). The expedition's three boats, constructed by the admiralty on Franklin's specifications, were shipped through Hudson Bay and taken westward to the Mackenzie Basin to meet the explorers.

While Back and Richardson supervised the construction of a winter residence (Fort Franklin) on Great Bear Lake and the establishment of a depot for the party's journey in the summer of 1825, Franklin set off down the Mackenzie River. His object was to reconnoiter the route he would use to reach the sea in the following summer and to gather information on coastal ice conditions, but he may also have been eager to surpass Mackenzie's achievement of 1789. In mid-August he and his companions stood on one of the outermost islands of the delta, slightly beyond Mackenzie's farthest point north. They then returned upriver to join the others at Fort Franklin.

After wintering, the expedition descended the Mackenzie River and separated into two groups at the delta. One party of a dozen men under Richardson set out to reach the Coppermine River by boat, then return overland to Fort Franklin, while another party of fifteen men under Franklin started for Point Barrow and Icy Cape, hoping to meet HMS *Blossom*, which had been sent round through the Pacific to the western Arctic. If both parties accomplished what they intended, the delineation of the Arctic coast would be complete from northwestern Alaska through approximately fifty-two degrees of longitude to Turnagain Point on Kent Peninsula, Franklin's farthest point east in 1821.

These ambitious objectives were very nearly attained. Richardson and his men, after a tense encounter with Eskimos near the Mackenzie delta, surveyed the coast eastward as far as the Coppermine, abandoned their boats, and walked back to Fort Franklin. They had not only "carried out their mission to the letter"[46] but had sighted new land of unknown extent north of the continent. Their discovery of "Wollaston Land" (the southwestern part of what is now Victoria Island) reduced further the size of the interior polar sea that Parry had depicted south of Parry Channel. Franklin's party narrowly escaped being massacred by a large group of Eskimos in the delta but then advanced westward as fast as the pack ice would permit. The happy prospect of uniting with the *Blossom* and returning comfortably to England by way of the Pacific may have created visions of coral atolls, palm trees, and silver beaches, but time ran out for the rendezvous. On 17 August, a few days from the cautious turn-back deadline established by the admiralty, Franklin realized that the goal, still nearly two hundred miles away, was too distant. At Return Reef, the men reluctantly faced eastward again and began the return to the Mackenzie River. At that moment, HMS *Blossom* was anchored off Icy Cape, and one of its boats was waiting at Point Barrow.

Franklin's second overland expedition had charted the Arctic coast through thirty-five degrees of longitude, covering a latitudinal spread of about 850 miles, a third more than the distance that Parry had sailed westward from Baffin Bay in 1819. This, together with the work accomplished on the first expedition, enabled Franklin to lay down the coast over forty-two degrees of longitude, an east-west latitudinal distance of over 1,000 miles and more than half the distance between northwestern Alaska and Hudson Bay. This was an outstanding achievement.

Two gaps remained. Between his farthest point west at Return Reef and Point Barrow was a short stretch of about 160 miles, which appeared to be a continuation of the relatively uniform westward-trending coast. Between his farthest point east at Turnagain Point and the western coast of Melville Peninsula was a much longer stretch, of immense complexity and importance to the problem of the Northwest Passage.

The admiralty exploration carried out between 1824 and 1828 combined eastern maritime, western maritime, and southern overland approaches. The seaborne assaults from the east by Parry and Lyon attempted to locate and navigate a Northwest Passage. The overland thrust from the south by Franklin endeavored to fix the position of the continent's northern coast. The western maritime expedition under Frederick Beechey waited for Parry and Franklin to emerge at the end of the passage. Communication between the expeditions was envisaged, but the practical problems of contact prevented the three-pronged attack from being effective. The only plausible technique for communicating without actual face-to-face or visual contact was depositing messages in rock cairns in prominent places. That required, however, that both the originator and the receiver of a written message visit the same precise spot during the course of their voyages. Such an event was unlikely in the vast uncharted regions of the Arctic, especially when one expedition could not tell where the other one was. Furthermore, if a message did happen to be retrieved from a cairn, the location of the party that had left it was almost certain to have changed in the intervening months or years. Not surprisingly, the three expeditions of 1824–28 failed to communicate with each other. When HMS *Blossom* returned to Alaska in the summer of 1827 to resume its vigil, there was no way of knowing that Franklin and his men, having come within a few hundred miles of the ship during the previous summer, were now on their way back across the continent to New York to board a steamer for home.

*Back (1833–1837)*

Almost four years after Ross left Scotland on the *Victory* in 1829, concern about his welfare resulted in the dispatch of a search expedition. Supported by public subscription, the government, and the Hudson's Bay Company, the expedition was commanded, on the admiralty's insistence, by Lieutenant George Back. A veteran of both of Franklin's land expeditions, Back not unnaturally proposed an overland approach. The Great Fish River (later renamed for Back), only vaguely known from Indian reports, appeared to be the most direct route toward the region of Prince Regent Inlet, where Ross was thought most likely to be. Back also intended, as secondary objectives, to map unknown coastlines and make some scientific observations.

Back left England by ship in February 1833, accompanied by Richard King as surgeon and naturalist and three other men. They landed in New York, made their way to Montreal, and continued by canoe with voyageurs to the Northwest. Near Great Slave Lake they erected a hut, named Fort Reliance, and spent the winter. Just as they were about to depart in the spring of 1834 they received the news that Ross had arrived safely back in England the previous autumn. Back decided to go on anyway; he could concentrate on tracing the eastern section of the Arctic coast. Leaving Fort Reliance in early June, the small party reached the headwaters of the Great Fish (Back) River and launched its boats.

In contrast to the broad sweep and even flow of the Mackenzie River over the sedimentary lowlands of western Canada, the rivers of the rugged Canadian Shield are tortuous and lively. Back had traversed parts of the Shield and had descended the Coppermine River on Franklin's two overland expeditions, but he knew little about the Great Fish River. It proved to be irregular and tumultuous, a boatman's nightmare. By the time Back's party reached the sea, they had run, portaged around, or lowered down no fewer than eighty-three rapids and falls.[47]

The Back River also differs from the Mackenzie in another respect. Instead of ending in a complex delta with a complex network of distributary channels, the Back River flows neatly into an estuary, which becomes Chantrey Inlet. Instead of emerging directly on the supposed east-west coast along which they could travel westward to Franklin's Turnagain Point, thus closing much of the unexplored gap in the continental coast, the explorers found themselves at the foot of an indentation extending more than seventy miles north. If that was not sufficient cause for disappointment, the inlet was blocked by ice. Working the boats through narrow leads and dragging them over the ice, the men managed to reach the northwestern corner of Chantrey Inlet, but the prospects of further advance were poor. Like Franklin, Back had learned not to stay too late on the Arctic coast, and he was aware that the return trip upriver would be difficult and long. In mid-August, after less than three weeks at the coast, he and his party began their return trip. "No one can regret so much as I do," he wrote later, "that the important and interesting object of ascertaining the existence of a passage along the coast to Turnagain Point was not accomplished." There had been no alternative. He had been contending with an environment in which "the elements war against all intruders and confound the calculations."[48]

Yet the expedition could hardly be considered a failure. It had laid down both coasts of Chantrey Inlet, which, despite the north-south alignment so disappointing to Back, does constitute a segment of the continent's northern coast. The expedition also mapped the Back River and the waterways between it and Great Slave Lake and described the character of the river and the adjacent landscape. These achievements may have seemed of small importance to those who were impatient to see a coastal link with Turnagain Point and the completion of the Northwest Passage, but Back's voyage down and up the Barren Grounds' longest river had a more lasting importance: his maps remained in use until after the Second World War.[49]

Ten months after reaching England, Back was again on his way to the Arctic, this time in command of HMS *Terror* on a combined maritime and overland expedition sent out by the admiralty. The plan, similar to the one employed unsuccessfully by Lyon on HMS *Griper* in 1824, was to sail through Hudson Strait to Repulse Bay, send a party across Rae Isthmus to launch boats on its northern side, and proceed westward along the coast past Chantrey Inlet to Turnagain Point. West of Rae Isthmus the maps were blank as far as the base of Boothia Peninsula, which Ross had explored, but some now suspected that Boothia Peninsula was in fact an island and that a passage could be found south of it. Back's own map from his previous expedition showed (by dotted line) the continental coast extending southeast from the mouth of Chantrey Inlet, supporting this misleading concept.[50] Once again the elements confounded Back's calculations. While attempting to get around the northern side of Southampton Island, as Parry's ships had done in 1821, the *Terror* was caught in the ice and held for the winter, drifting toward Hudson Strait. When released at last in July 1837, the leaking ship had to be sailed back to England. Back had been no more successful than Lyon a dozen years before.

*Dease and Simpson (1837–1839)*

After Back's two successive failures to chart the complex eastern sector of the mainland coast, the initiative was seized by the Hudson's Bay Company. Possessing certain advantages that the admiralty lacked, including "the facilities afforded by their extensive chain of posts, their control over the Indian tribes, the knowledge possessed by their officers of the resources, and their habitude to the hardships of the country," the company decided in 1836 to send out a small party under the joint management of one of its chief traders, Peter Warren Dease, and a younger employee, Thomas Simpson, a cousin of the company's governor.[51] Dease's experience and maturity were intended to complement—and restrain, if necessary—Simpson's driving energy and burning ambition. Their extraordinary objective was to bridge both the western and the eastern gaps in the northern coast, even though these gaps were a thousand miles apart.

Descending the Mackenzie River in two boats, the party of fourteen men reached the sea by 10 July 1837 and started west along the Arctic coast. On the twenty-third, more than three weeks ahead of Franklin's 1826 itinerary, they arrived at Return Reef, his farthest point. With well-founded optimism they pressed rapidly into uncharted territory, but a week later impassable ice stopped the boats approximately fifty miles short of their objective, at a place aptly named "Boat Extreme." Simpson and five men volunteered to walk the rest of the way, carrying a small, collapsible, canvas-covered canoe for crossing streams and leads. On their way they persuaded a band of Eskimos to lend an umiak and provide a rough sketch of the coast to the west, and the men arrived at Point Barrow, the northwestern corner of the continent, on 4 August, having completed the final stage in the European exploration and charting of the western Arctic coastline. The expedition returned to the Mackenzie Valley and wintered at the northeastern extremity of Great Bear Lake in their camp, Fort Confidence.

In early June 1838 they started the eastern part of the survey by crossing the divide east of the Mackenzie drainage basin into the Coppermine system and descending to the sea. This was a far more direct approach than that used in 1821 by Franklin's party, which, by starting farther south at Great Slave Lake, had committed itself to a long and difficult canoe voyage before reaching the coast. Pack ice slowed progress, and it was not until 19 August—the eve of the turn-back deadline—that they approached Turnagain Point, Franklin's farthest point in 1821. Again Simpson, eager to have his name associated with new discoveries, pressed on with some of the men, on foot, to the margin of Queen Maud Gulf, which appeared, tantalizingly, to be an "open sea." The expedition crowned its summer work by sighting a "great northern land" twenty-five miles beyond the continental coast.[52] Lying east of the Wollaston Land discovered by Franklin's eastern division in 1826, this was in fact another part of what is now known as Victoria Island.

The expedition wintered again at Fort Confidence. In June 1839, with "renovated hopes and thankful hearts," Dease, Simpson, and a dozen men set out for the third and last season of coastal exploration. Using the same route, they reached the mouth of the Coppermine in early July and started east through ice-free channels along the shore. They rounded the Kent Peninsula a full month ahead of their 1838 schedule, passed their previous farthest point, and continued along the southern coast of Queen Maud Gulf, experiencing only occasional delays from ice barriers, island groups, shallow water, and head winds.

Excitement must have risen as they pressed on through territory unseen by European eyes, steadily approaching districts explored from the east and south by the expeditions of Ross and Back. On 10 August the party entered a narrow channel, now called Simpson Strait, which separates King William Island from the continental mainland. Since it trended toward the southeast, they wondered if it would lead them into the estuary of the Back River. All doubts were dispelled several days later when they landed on an island halfway up Chantrey Inlet and found a cache of European origin. Gunpowder, caps, fishhooks, rotten chocolate, and decaying pemmican ("literally *alive*") were tangible proof that they had in fact overlapped Back's survey of five years earlier, thus conclusively connecting the mouth of the Back River with Turnagain Point and the rest of the coast to Alaska.[53] They had contributed two long-sought pieces to the incomplete puzzle of the continental shape.

Persevering for a few days more, they passed the easternmost limit of Back's survey and reached the mouth of the Castor and Pollux River (named for their boats) before turning homeward on 20 August. During the long return voyage they crossed over to Victoria Island and traced the course of its southern coast for almost two hundred miles. This was the first European contact with any of the landmasses lying within the polar sea between the continent and the Parry Channel west of King William Island. The men arrived safely back at Fort Confidence in late September, after "by far the longest voyage ever performed in boats in the Polar Sea."[54]

The continental coast was now delineated, albeit in somewhat crude form, from northwestern Alaska almost to Boothia Peninsula. In the east it had been traced from the mouth of Hudson Strait around Hudson Bay, north into Foxe Basin, and down the western side of Melville Peninsula to Rae Isthmus. A separate piece, including all the eastern coast of Boothia Peninsula, had also been charted. Only a few gaps remained, and a child might easily have approximated the true line of the coast by joining up the points. But men's imaginations and ambitions led to unnecessarily fanciful and complex speculations about the geography in the Boothia region.

If Parry and Ross were to be believed, Melville and Boothia were both peninsulas extending north from the continent; the latter (mistakenly thought to include Somerset Island) extended to Barrow Strait (74° north), supposedly the continent's northernmost point; Fury and Hecla Strait was perennially ice-blocked and led only into the Gulf of Boothia and Prince Regent Inlet, with no possibility of a westward passage; therefore the only eastern entrance to a Northwest Passage was through Lancaster Sound and Barrow Strait.

But according to a contrary view, both Melville and Boothia were probably islands; the Hudson Bay coast swung westward after Repulse Bay to connect with the mouth of the Back River; and therefore a Northwest Passage could be effected through Hudson Bay and the Gulf of Boothia. This curious hypothesis, in which the speculative dotted-line evidence on maps by Back and Simpson was accorded higher credibility than the more reliable visual observations of Parry and Ross, was attractive to the Hudson's Bay Company because a coastal Northwest Passage from Hudson Bay to Alaska would be adjacent to the territory over which it held a commercial monopoly.[55] The company decided in 1840 to send an overland expedition under its rising star Thomas Simpson to the disputed Boothia region. Unfortunately the trip was postponed after Simpson's mysterious death.

Dr. Richard King, Back's companion during the descent of the Back River in 1833–35, made repeated, unsuccessful attempts to get support for his own expedition to the Boothia area. One of the most perceptive of all Arctic explorers, but largely ignored by the power-wielding institutions (the admiralty, the Royal Geographical Society, the Hudson's Bay Company), he accepted that Boothia was a peninsula of North America but worried about the relationship between Boothia and King William's Land (King William Island). The map from Ross's second expedition showed the northern coast of King William Island to be connected to Boothia, but only by one of those ambiguous dotted lines.[56] King proposed to travel overland to the region west of Boothia and determine the true relationship of land and sea, but his plan was rejected. In an ironic twist of fate, Franklin was one of its strongest opponents.[57] If King had reached King William's Land and revealed its insularity, Franklin's ships might have avoided catastrophe a decade later by going inside the island rather than into the heavy ice stream northwest of the supposed peninsula.

## Rae (1846–1847)

In 1844 the Hudson's Bay Company revived its plans to complete the exploration and mapping of the northern coast of the continent. Two years later, in mid-June, eleven men left York Factory, Hudson Bay, in two boats under the leadership of John Rae. A native of the Orkney Islands, Rae had obtained a medical degree and entered the service of the Hudson's Bay Company by the age of twenty. During nine years at the fur trade post of Moose Factory, in James Bay, his woodcraft, marksmanship, and ability to cover great distances on foot had attracted the attention of Sir George Simpson, governor of the company's North American territories. Simpson asked Rae to take charge of the Arctic venture: to connect the known coast north of Hudson Bay with the discoveries of Ross, Dease and Simpson, and Back. The mistaken belief that Boothia was an island rather than a peninsula had led to the assumption that one coasting voyage could accomplish the task.[58]

After picking up two interpreters at Churchill, Rae and his men sailed almost seven hundred miles along the western coast of Hudson Bay in open boats only twenty-two feet long and reached Repulse Bay in late July. Learning from Eskimos that just a narrow isthmus lay between Repulse Bay and the sea of Akkoolee (Committee Bay), as indeed Parry had shown from Eskimo information two decades earlier, Rae decided to cross overland instead of sailing the long way round through Foxe Basin and Fury and Hecla Strait. With extraordinary effort the men worked one of the boats through a series of streams, lakes, and marshes and reached the sea on the other side of the isthmus in early August. But closely packed ice lay close to the shore, barring progress westward, so the party retreated to Repulse Bay, built a hut from local stone, and settled down for the winter in Fort Hope. Rae's decision to winter in the Arctic, on slender resources and without "the umbilical cord of an ice-locked vessel," was bold.[59] Only Ross's expedition had lived ashore over a winter, after abandoning the *Victory*, and Ross's men had been able to salvage materials and supplies from Parry's old depot at Fury Beach. Owing largely to Rae's prowess at hunting, the wintering experiment succeeded.

In the following April, Rae set off on foot with a few men, accompanied by two dogsleds carrying provisions and gear; they built snow houses, in

Eskimo fashion, each night. This method of travel was far more successful than boats; in two weeks they were on the coast mapped during Ross's expedition of 1929–33. At Lord Mayor Bay, Rae decided to return, having seen nothing to indicate that Boothia was anything but the peninsula indicated by Ross. Back at Fort Hope by 5 May, he rested, reorganized, and then set out only a week later to explore the western coast of Melville Peninsula. After leaving a support party at the foot of Committee Bay, he continued north over ice and snow on foot with a small group of men, almost reaching the western extremity of Fury and Hecla Strait before turning back. Rae and his men were back at Fort Hope in early June, and in mid-August they sailed for Churchill.

Rae had bridged the gap between the coasts surveyed by Parry in Foxe Basin and Ross in Prince Regent Inlet and had disproved the notion that Melville and Boothia were islands, south of which a convenient sea passage led from Hudson Bay to the central Arctic. Parry, Ross, and various Eskimo informants were vindicated. Rae had also demonstrated what could be accomplished by a small, inexpensive expedition that obtained much of its food by hunting, that used sleds, snowshoes, and snow houses, and that advanced comparatively swiftly over sea ice and snow surfaces during the months of April and May. Like the other company men Dease and Simpson, he had covered impressive distances, but he had concentrated on spring overland excursions rather than summer boat travel, spending a winter on the exposed Arctic tundra several hundred miles north of the shelter of subarctic forests in order to be ready for the spring sledding period. By shunning the customary dependence on subarctic winter bases and by adopting travel methods that enabled him to cover more than twenty miles per day, Rae had added a new dimension to overland and coastal exploration.[60]

## The Franklin Era, 1845–1859

### Franklin (1845–1847)

At the same time that the Hudson's Bay Company decided to renew its exploration of the northern continental coast in 1844 by sending Rae overland, the British government revived its dormant search for the Northwest Passage. Although the Passage had eluded explorers for centuries, experts now thought that a final effort could add the last piece to the puzzle and connect the Atlantic to the Pacific. All that remained, the charts seemed to indicate, was for ships to cross the unexplored polar sea south of Parry Channel and use the handrail of the mainland coast to reach the Pacific. In 1844 John Barrow, nearing the end of his four decades as second secretary of the admiralty, submitted a "Proposal for an Attempt to Complete the Discovery of the North West Passage."[61] The government decided to act.

Captain Sir John Franklin made a strong bid for command of the new expedition. Fifty-nine years old and portly, he had not been in the Arctic in seventeen years. But his reputation had taken some hard knocks during six unpleasant years as governor of the penal colony in Tasmania, and he desperately wanted to repair the damage. With the support of influential friends, he secured the appointment and received his instructions in May 1845. In HMS *Erebus* and *Terror*, he was to sail through Lancaster Sound and Barrow Strait to the vicinity of Cape Walker, or about 98° west, and then "to endeavour to penetrate to the southward and westward in a course as direct towards Bhering's [*sic*] Strait as the position and extent of the ice, or the existence of land, at present unknown, may admit."[62]

Cape Walker lay at the northeastern corner of what has been termed "the unexplored quadrilateral."[63] This area was what remained of the alleged "Polar Sea" or "North American Sea" identified by Parry's first expedition. The size of the area had diminished as portions of landmasses had been discovered within its compass—Banks Land, Wollaston Land, Victoria Land, King William's Land, Boothia, North Somerset, and the land south of Cape Walker itself. None of these regions were completely mapped, however. Most were known only by their exterior coasts facing away from the central sea. How far they extended inward, further reducing the size of the polar sea, and whether other landmasses existed in that region, were questions very relevant to the prospect of a Northwest Passage. Both Barrow, a planner of the Franklin expedition, and John Ross's nephew James Clark Ross, a veteran of all five maritime expeditions and close confidant of both Franklin and his second-in-command during the preparation of the expedition, believed that the unknown region was more or less landless.[64] Parry probably held this view as well.

Finding a link between Parry Channel and the mainland coast seemed straightforward, but the uncertainty of ice distribution and movement concerned experienced navigators. South of Melville Island in 1819–20 Parry had encountered unusually heavy, closely packed ice—formidable, defiant, "as so much land."[65] A decade later Ross had observed similar masses of thick, hard ice floes at King William Island, on the eastern margin of the supposed intervening sea. He believed (correctly as it turned out) that the ice had been transported by currents from Melville Island to King William Island and western Boothia, and he warned that ships sailing southwest from Cape Walker would have to cross the heavy ice stream.[66]

On 19 May 1845 HMS *Erebus* and *Terror*, accompanied by the transport *Baretto Junior*, set off from the Thames with great fanfare. Like Parry's *Hecla* and *Fury*, the *Erebus* and *Terror* had been built originally as bomb vessels, sturdy enough to carry heavy mortars and to withstand powerful recoil during shore bombardment. For the Arctic venture they had been further strengthened, sheathed for work in ice and provided with engines and screw propellers. The total complement was 134 men, of whom 5 were subsequently sent home from Greenland. Many of the officers and seamen were veterans of discovery or whaling voyages in the Arctic regions. They were well clothed and equipped, and their intellectual stimulation had not been neglected: the ships carried more than two thousand books. The men had enough food to last three years. Eighteen live bullocks were taken along to slaughter and freeze in the Arctic; a dozen of these were still alive when the ships reached Greenland. In the opinion of the foremost scholar of the Franklin expedition, this was "the best equipped [party] that the Admiralty had ever sent to the Polar regions."[67]

After taking on board the extra stores carried by the *Baretto Junior* at Disko Island, the *Erebus* and *Terror* continued up the coast of Greenland, often in the company of whaling vessels. In late July they bade farewell to the last of these in northern Baffin Bay and set course for the mouth of Lancaster Sound.

### The Search Begins (1847–1849)

In 1847, Franklin's men had not been heard from since they had left Baffin Bay two years earlier. As concern began to be expressed about the expedition, the admiralty prepared to initiate a search. In fact, for the next dozen years the primary objective of all maritime and overland expeditions would be to find the missing ships and save the men, if they were still alive. During these years, exploration was more intense than in any other period. The many expeditions, although largely unsuccessful in their searches, contributed immensely to European geographical and scientific knowledge.

The absence of records along the route taken by Franklin's ships was a source of real frustration to the admiralty and the search expeditions. Richard Cyriax, who carefully examined the instructions and narratives of a dozen polar expeditions before 1845, concluded that Franklin should not be blamed. Although Parry had left a dozen records ashore during his first voyage, there were no other strong precedents for doing so. Nor had Franklin been instructed to leave records.[68] His instructions included "no mention of rendezvous, nor of depots to fall back upon in case of separation or accident; no expectation held out of relief from home."[69] Nonetheless, John Ross had told Franklin before he left, "I shall volunteer to look for you, if you are not heard of in February, 1847, but pray put a notice in the cairn where you winter, if you do proceed, which of the routes you take."[70] But as Clive Holland has pointed out, "Innovation and personal initiative were never Franklin's outstanding talents as an Arctic explorer."[71] If Franklin had followed Parry's example or Ross's advice, the ensuing search for his missing vessels would have been relatively straightforward. As it was, the search expeditions had little to go on except what was contained in Franklin's instructions.

Before the expedition had departed, Sir Roderick Murchison, president of the Royal Geographical Society, had declared, "The question of a Passage is now almost narrowed to one definite route."[72] This was reflected in Franklin's instructions, which laid down as his first priority a route southward and westward from Cape Walker across the unexplored quadrilateral to the continental coast. Only if this proved almost impenetrable was Franklin to turn to an alternative passage, northward from Barrow Strait into Wellington Channel. Logically, searches should also have given highest priority to the unexplored quadrilateral to which Franklin had been directed, but they did not. Expedition after expedition was sent to Wellington Channel while the area in which a passage seemed most likely to occur, and to which Franklin had been first directed, was neglected. As a result the search was prolonged, the solution of the Franklin mystery was postponed, and much of the region north of Parry Channel (the Queen Elizabeth Islands), which otherwise would have attracted little attention, became well-known.

Why Wellington Channel was suggested as an alternative route deserves explanation, for it leads north instead of west. Conventional maps disguise a fact that is apparent on a polar projection or a globe, namely that a line from Barrow Strait through Wellington Channel, northwest to the Arctic Ocean and on to the Bering Strait, is close to a great circle route, the shortest sea-level distance between two points on the earth's surface. This course, if navigable, would be shorter than one southward through Peel Sound, around King William Island, and west along the mainland coast, the path taken by Roald Amundsen during the first complete Northwest Passage by ship, in 1903–6. This northern route is not navigable, since Wellington Channel leads into a labyrinth of islands and ice-choked straits, beyond which lies the impassable, multiyear ice of the Arctic Ocean, but this could not be known at the time. Instead, in 1819 Parry had observed that the southern parts of Wellington Channel were ice-free; he could not see what lay to the north, and it was commonly believed that an open sea occupied the north polar region. Murchison pointed out, "The only chance of [Wellington Channel] . . . becoming available for the North-West Passage would be that it leads into the open sea, and that the cluster of islands in that direction will be found to cease."[73] Unfortunately, neither of these conditions would prove to be correct.

The myth of the open polar sea exerted an enormous influence on the Franklin search, overriding the reasonable and correct conclusion that his ships had gone south from Barrow Strait. An early search expedition under William Penny found pieces of wood, modified by humans, north of Cornwallis Island. Although they could not be conclusively linked to the Franklin expedition, their presence in a region uninhabited by Eskimos strongly reinforced the belief that the ships had gone up Wellington Channel. Curiously enough, Franklin's vessels *had* passed that way, although that fact would not be known for several years. In the summer of 1845, presumably after failing to find a passage southward from Cape Walker, Franklin had ascended Wellington Channel into Queen's Channel and then, probably after encountering an ice barrier, had returned to Barrow Strait by way of MacDougall Sound, thus circumnavigating Cornwallis Island. After wintering at Beechey Island in 1845–46 he had succeeded at last in sailing south toward King William Island. It is almost as if Franklin had ascended Wellington Channel with the intention of deceiving pursuers, throwing bits of wood overboard to leave a false trail before doubling back to strike for the continental shore. For the searchers, the evidence suggested that Franklin had reached Queen's Channel and continued northward into an ice-free polar sea. They failed to consider the possibility that he had reached Queen's Channel, met impenetrable ice, and then gone south again.

Since no one knew which route Franklin had taken, how far he had penetrated, or whether his ships were still intact or his men still alive, a three-pronged search effort was necessary to cover Franklin's probable route into the Arctic islands, his most likely exit path, and the intervening mainland coast along which he had intended to sail. Since the initial searches adopted the same Atlantic, Pacific, and overland approaches traditionally used by discovery expeditions, they tended to duplicate earlier voyages, thereby adding little to existing geographical knowledge. Soon, however, when no evidence of Franklin was found, the search would expand into unexplored regions.

A party led by Surgeon Sir John Richardson was sent to Hudson Bay in the spring of 1847 to make its way to the Mackenzie River in time for the following summer. In January 1848 HMS *Plover*, under Commander Thomas Edward Laws Moore, sailed for the Bering Strait. In May, HMS *Enterprise* and *Investigator* left for Lancaster Sound, with Captain James Clark Ross, John Ross's nephew, in overall command. In Alaska the *Plover* began a waiting game, which was to last six years, remaining ready to meet and assist Franklin's men if they managed to sail, row, or walk to the western terminus of the Northwest Passage and ready to help any of the search expeditions that might follow the same route. The ship played a relatively stationary and passive—though necessary—role in the Franklin search, with no opportunity to indulge in far-ranging exploration. Investigations of the local region were possible, however; useful hydrographic and ethnographic work was carried out around Point Barrow. One boat expedition went forth from the *Plover*, under Lieutenant William John Samuel Pullen in 1849, to search the northern Alaska coast, which was already reasonably well-known from the work of Franklin in 1826 and Dease and Simpson in 1837. The two boats reached the Mackenzie River without finding any traces of Franklin. Meanwhile, Richardson's party had also reached the Mackenzie River. From here the men journeyed along the coast by boat to the Coppermine River in the summer of 1848, duplicating the voyage Richardson had made twenty-two years earlier while serving under the officer he now sought. But there were no signs that Franklin had been in the area, and the men returned to Great Bear Lake to winter at Fort Confidence.

Of the three thrusts, only the eastern one, under James Clark Ross, came close to the scene of the Franklin disaster and made a significant contribution to geographical knowledge. Ross put the *Enterprise* and *Investigator* into winter quarters at Port Leopold, at the northeastern tip of Somerset Island, in September 1848. No exploration was attempted during the cold, dark winter, but in the following May—when snow surfaces, air temperatures, and duration of sunlight were suitable for excursions with man-hauled sleds—the examination of adjacent coasts got under way. After setting out some advance depots, four sled parties departed from the ships. One of them, comprising two sleds and a dozen men under Ross and another experienced and innovative sled-traveler, Francis Leopold McClintock, set off westward along the unexplored northern coast of Somerset Island toward Cape Walker, Franklin's supposed point of departure for the continental shore. They discovered that instead of continuing to Cape Walker, the coast swung south into a broad inlet (Peel Sound), whose eastern shore they followed for a hundred miles to latitude 72°38′ north. At this point Ross and McClintock were within 200 miles of King William Island, where 105 survivors of Franklin's expedition had abandoned their ships a year earlier to walk south toward civilization. There was, of course, no way of knowing this and no reason to suspect that the *Erebus* and *Terror* had used this convenient southward-trending waterway, for the shore had yielded no evidence whatever and the ice-choked strait did not appear to be navigable. It looked as if the coast would connect with the western coast of Boothia Peninsula, which Ross himself had mapped in 1831 on his voyage to the magnetic pole, but however tempted they must have been to close the gap of approximately 170 miles, it was not feasible to do so. Relying entirely on the food and fuel they were capable of dragging on the sleds, the men had reached their final point of return. They had no choice but to turn back. In doing so, they unknowingly missed the chance to establish the fate of Franklin and his men.

When the various field parties had arrived back at the ships, preparations began for breaking out of the harbor ice, and an emergency depot was established ashore. A house, sleeping bags, blankets, food, tools, stoves, fuel, and a steam launch were left behind, along with a report of progress and plans.[74] The *Enterprise* and *Investigator* had been provisioned for three years and had been out only one, so there was still more time to search. But instead of following up the discovery and mapping of Peel Sound, Ross decided to investigate Wellington Channel. Heading in that direction, the ships were enclosed by drifting pack ice and held fast until September. When they were released in Baffin Bay, Ross gave the signal to return to England.

Although the expedition had failed to find a single clue to Franklin's whereabouts and had returned—some believed prematurely—it had added more than one hundred miles to the charts, secured geological and meteorological data, provided valuable training for a number of officers and men, and improved the techniques of sled travel. Ross's trip "across the boundless regions of ice" was hailed as "a most unparalleled feat in exploration."[75] Ross's sled party had also sighted high mountains on the opposite side of Peel Sound, revealing that the land south of Cape Walker (Prince of Wales Island) extended much farther south then previously known. This finding further reduced the dimensions of the interior sea alleged to extend between Parry Channel and the continent. But from a geographical point of view, the expedition's greatest accomplishment was the discovery of Peel Sound itself, which has composed a link in several Arctic transits during the modern era. Curiously, however, this discovery was not widely appreciated. Owing to its perception as an ice-blocked strait, Peel Sound became an "unpopular direction" in which subsequent expeditions were "shy of attempting anything," as McClintock wrote half a dozen years later.[76] Ironically, the discovery of Peel Sound, through which Franklin's ships had probably sailed, negatively influenced search strategy.

### *Austin, Penny, and Others (1850–1852)*

As Ross struggled to extricate his ships from the ice during the summer of 1849, whalers were keeping a sharp lookout for cairns or other signs of the missing expedition along northern coasts and were seeking information from Eskimos. False or misunderstood reports inflamed the imagination more than once, but they were proved wrong, and hopes for a quick solution of the mystery faded.

In 1850 eleven ships entered Lancaster Sound to intensify the search. Four naval vessels under the command of Captain H. T. Austin, composing "the most complete and well-equipped expedition to have left British shores to that date," and two whaleships under the command of William Penny were sailing under admiralty orders.[77] Two small yachts under the venerable Sir John Ross were supported by the Hudson's Bay Company and private money. Two American ships, commanded by Lieutenant Edwin Jesse de Haven, were privately sponsored but under naval instructions. All of these vessels converged on the mouth of Wellington Channel while one ship, under Commander Charles Codrington Forsyth and sponsored by Lady Franklin, probed southward into Prince Regent Inlet. The Austin and Penny expeditions soon found the place, on Beechey Island, where Franklin's men had passed their first winter (1845–46), but the only written information they could discover was on the headboards of three graves. There was nothing to indicate the direction in which the expedition had proceeded after wintering. De Haven's ships *Advance* and *Rescue* were carried by pack ice halfway up Wellington Channel, back to Lancaster Sound, and down through Baffin Bay to Davis Strait, spending altogether nine months in the ice. Forsyth's *Prince Albert* reached Fury Point but then sailed home to England, accomplishing little. The eight ships under Austin, Penny, and Ross remained to winter within several miles of each other off the southern coast of Cornwallis Island. In late winter, sled parties fanned out in several directions—Penny's men up Wellington Channel,

Ross's men across Cornwallis Island, and Austin's crews westward in Viscount Melville Sound and southwestward beyond Cape Walker. These excursions took the men not only along coasts already laid down on the maps (which they were often able to correct or elaborate) but also along coasts never before observed by Europeans. Although their primary function was to search for evidence of Franklin, they contributed to geographical knowledge while doing so.

Penny's sled and boat parties discovered that Wellington Channel extended north and west into Queen's Channel, which led into Penny Strait, separating Devon Island from Bathurst Island. Penny Strait lay beyond their range, but its existence and the discovery of pieces of wood evidently of European origin convinced Penny that Franklin's ships had passed that way into the alleged open polar sea. Penny and his men thus added a large territory to the maps, pushing the frontier of European knowledge farther north than in any other sector of the Queen Elizabeth Islands except their seaward margin facing Greenland. One geographical misconception resulted from this work, however, when a sled party mistakenly concluded that northern Cornwallis Island was connected to Bathurst Island. Another exploratory party, approaching from the south, was similarly deceived, due to the difficulty of distinguishing between ice and low-lying land when both were hidden beneath a mantle of snow.

Sled parties from Austin's ships traveled along the northern side of Viscount Melville Sound. Parry had mapped the principal headlands in 1819, but Austin's men were able to extend these observations northward. McClintock, already known for his sledding exploits, now performed "the most remarkable of all the journeys" made by Austin's men.[78] Paralleling the track of Parry's ships, he reached Melville Island, passed Winter Harbour, and circled round Dundas Peninsula before starting back. From his farthest point he could see that the island extended much farther; clearly there were still discoveries to be made in that sector. The journey took eighty-one days and covered nearly eight hundred miles, the longest man-hauled sled trip up to that time.

Notwithstanding the traveling exploits of McClintock's party and the extensive discoveries of Penny's crews, it was the third major exploratory thrust that yielded the most significant information on the Northwest Passage. Under the overall direction of Captain Erasmus Ommanney, eight sleds traveled across Barrow Strait to Cape Walker and the "unexplored quadrilateral" beyond. Not a shred of evidence was found at Cape Walker, which had figured prominently in Franklin's instructions, so they continued on to the land beyond (Prince of Wales Island). Splitting up into teams to divide up the work, they managed to survey roughly half the island's perimeter. The island was obviously very large, making additional inroads into the shrinking arm of the polar sea noted by Parry three decades before, and its location south of Cape Walker might have prevented Franklin from adhering to the route laid down in his orders. Could he have sailed southward into Peel Sound? Austin's officers thought not; they shared James Ross's pessimistic view that the strait was perennially blocked by ice, thus strengthening the argument in favor of additional futile searches up Wellington Channel.[79]

Along with Richard King, whose surprisingly accurate predictions were constantly ignored by the admiralty (he "irritated authority for being right"),[80] Lady Jane Franklin repeatedly urged the authorities to direct their efforts to the region specified in her husband's instructions. When they were reluctant to do so, she took action herself, financing a succession of five private search expeditions. After Forsyth's disappointing voyage in the *Prince Albert*, she sent the vessel out again in 1851 under a new commander, William Kennedy. The ship proceeded into Prince Regent Inlet and wintered in Batty Bay. In the spring, while sledding southward along the coast, Kennedy and the French volunteer Joseph-René Bellot discovered the strait that separates Somerset Island from Boothia Peninsula and marks the northernmost extremity of the North American continent. Had Bellot Strait (as it is now called) been known earlier, it might well have played an important role in the quest for a Northwest Passage and the search for Franklin. But in 1852 its discovery had little immediate effect. The strait ended in the southern part of Peel Sound, whose navigability was doubted, and Kennedy now added persuasively to this negative assessment. After a long sled trip, during which he crossed the ice of Peel Sound twice and traveled along its western coast for a considerable distance, he suggested that the sound was not a route to the south after all but was a cul-de-sac terminating in a land bridge that connected Somerset and Prince of Wales islands.[81] Few other Arctic waterways suffered from such bad press as Peel Sound.

*Belcher (1852–1854)*
After the unsuccessful searches of 1850–51, an acrimonious dispute between Austin and Penny led to an official inquiry and damaged the reputations of both men. But the disagreement brought to public attention Penny's strong feeling that Franklin must be sought by way of Wellington

Channel and the alleged open polar sea, using a steam-powered vessel. Whereas the admiralty was unsympathetic to Penny, treating him badly in the inquiry and whenever he applied afterward for further service in the Franklin search, it did not hesitate to adopt some of his ideas.[82] In 1852 it dispatched the largest Franklin search expedition ever, under the overall command of Captain Sir Edward Belcher, to extend the investigation farther north in the Wellington Channel corridor and to search westward along Parry Channel. Four veteran Arctic vessels, all bearing no-nonsense names *(Assistance, Pioneer, Resolute, Intrepid)*, constituted the vanguard of the search. Operating in pairs, they would function as advance bases from which small mobile parties could disperse by boat or sled along adjacent coasts. A depot ship, the *North Star*, would remain at a more accessible place to serve as a warehouse, fallback position, and center for incoming dispatches. In addition three transports *(Breadalbane, Phoenix, Talbot)* would be used later to bring supplies from England and maintain communication with the depot ship. The expedition carried food for four years and, according to the *Illustrated London News*, could stay out for five or six years if it used supplies from the *North Star* and from the depot left on Leopold Island by James Ross.[83]

After a convincing demonstration at Woolwich Dockyard of balloons that could be used to send aerial messages to Franklin and of an electrical device that used exploding charges to blow up ice, the five ships departed from the Thames on 15 April 1852 and arrived at Beechey Island in August. This place, where Franklin and his men had passed their first winter, was well situated for a search base. It was usually accessible from Baffin Bay in August and September, could be visited without serious risk of being cut off by pack ice, and stood at the divergence of routeways to the south, west, and north. The island contained suitable terrain for shore facilities and activities, possessed a supply of fresh water, and enclosed a protected anchorage. Here the flotilla split up, with HMS *North Star* taking up station. The *Assistance* and the steamer *Pioneer*, under the command of Belcher, went north through Wellington Channel and found a secure winter harbor near the northern tip of the Grinnell Peninsula, well beyond Penny's farthest point. The *Resolute* and the steamer *Intrepid*, under the command of Henry Kellett, sailed west along the Parry Channel and froze themselves in at Dealy Island off the southeastern coast of Melville Island.

Both divisions managed to undertake some exploratory trips before the winter forced them into hibernation. In the east, traveling by boat, Belcher's men discovered Cornwall Island about forty miles north of the Grinnell Peninsula. In the west, Kellett's crews laid down a number of caches to extend the range of sled trips in the following spring. During this cache work the Melville Island branch found a message that had been deposited in a stone cairn six months before; it contained the astonishing news that HMS *Investigator*, having entered the Arctic by way of the Bering Strait in 1850, was helplessly icebound in Mercy Bay on the northern coast of Banks Island, less than two hundred miles away. Already entrusted with the sufficiently daunting task of locating Franklin, Kellett now had the additional burden of rescuing Commander Robert McClure and his crew. Frustratingly, he could not attempt a rescue for another half-year, when the sea ice between Banks and Melville Islands would be stable and temperatures and light would be adequate for travel. Kellett's crews settled into their winter routines with the disturbing knowledge that not far away, three-score of their countrymen were facing their third Arctic winter with dwindling food, declining health, no hope of getting free by their own efforts, and not even the consolation of knowing that someone was aware of their plight.

On the afternoon of 6 April 1853, as the dispirited men at Mercy Bay were digging a grave for one of their colleagues, they were amazed to see a stranger approaching over the ice. This turned out to be Lieutenant Bedford Clapperton Trevelyan Pim, from HMS *Resolute*. According to the doctor on the *Investigator*, Pim "made his appearance among us as a deliverer."[84] Because of the urgency of the rescue mission, Pim had set out from Dealy Island on 10 March, a month before the normal sledding season, during very cold weather. With two companions, five dogs, and a sled, he reached Mercy Bay after a month. He started back again the next day with McClure and seven others from the stranded vessel. More sled trips followed; by mid-June the entire crew had been conveyed across the ice of M'Clure Strait to the comparative safety and comfort of the ships at Dealy Island. The empty *Investigator* lay abandoned and lifeless in Mercy Bay, eventually providing a treasure trove for Eskimos.

During the rescue operation, the search for Franklin had gone ahead from the western and eastern bases. Two dozen sleds, each dragged by up to ten men, had left the various vessels on journeys of up to three and a half months. Every sled had a name fit to inspire confidence, such as "Hero," "Fearless," "Dauntless," or "Reliance," and flew its own distinctive flag bearing some motto appropriate to the task: "Hope on, hope ever"; "By faith and courage"; "I watch for your return"; "Mon dieu est ma roche."

The crews were fit, keen, and determined to outdo their shipmates. Pulling the ropes for ten or more hours a day, over a wide variety of surface conditions, in what was probably "the hardest work to which free men have been put in modern times," they advanced painfully slowly—a mile or two an hour—and had good cause to rejoice if they exceeded a dozen miles in a day.[85] Many improvements had been made to sleds, clothing, equipment, food, and logistics since man-hauled sledding had been initiated thirty years before, but it was still brutal and agonizing work. Nine sleds left Dealy Island on 4 April 1853. Of the eighty-eight men on board the two ships, seventy-one participated in the sledding venture. Altogether the western sled parties traveled an extraordinary seven thousand miles and explored approximately eighteen hundred miles of new coastline.[86] There was a similar intensity of spring exploration in the eastern division, and more than once sled parties from east and west met and overlapped, spanning five hundred miles of Arctic territory.

By mid-July disintegrating ice, melting snow, and rising streams ended the sledding season. In less than four months the sled parties sent out by Belcher in the east and Kellett in the west had inscribed a remarkable network of tracks among the Arctic islands. Although they had not uncovered any evidence of Franklin, they must have derived some satisfaction from knowing that, in their plodding but sure way, they had greatly extended the bounds of European experience. The entire second tier of Arctic islands, lying north of the Parry Channel, had been delineated from Devon Island in the east to Prince Patrick Island in the west. Beyond this east-west chain of large islands the explorers had seen no sign of the fabled open polar sea and must have realized that the northern limits of the archipelago had not yet been attained.

In August, Kellett's ships broke out of their harbor ice and headed east carrying the rescued men of the *Investigator*, but they were soon again enmeshed in ice and forced to spend the winter of 1853–54 imprisoned within the pack in Viscount Melville Sound. Meanwhile, Belcher's ships, making their way south, were forced to take up winter quarters on the eastern coast of Wellington Channel. Thus neither the eastern nor the western group reached the base at Beechey Island, where the *North Star* waited. During the winter, becoming fearful that the four ships might not be released in the approaching summer, Belcher gave the order to abandon them all, an extraordinary and unprecedented decision that led to a court-martial on his return. Everyone, *Investigator* survivors included, traveled over the ice to Beechey Island and crowded onto the *North Star* and the transports *Phoenix* and *Talbot* for the voyage home, leaving four of Her Majesty's Ships intact in the ice.

### Inglefield and Kane (1852–1855)

While Belcher's large squadron searched for Franklin in the Wellington and Parry Channels, two small, privately supported expeditions investigated inlets leading off Baffin Bay; if ice had prevented the *Erebus* and *Terror* from entering Lancaster Sound in 1845, Franklin might have looked for a passage north or south. In August 1852 Commander A. E. Inglefield, sent out by Lady Franklin on board the 140-ton screw schooner *Isabel*, probed through Smith Sound to a latitude above 78° north. After turning back, he cruised briefly in Jones Sound and later examined the eastern coast of Baffin Island. Inglefield is credited with having established a new "farthest north" in the Smith Sound sector, sailing 140 miles beyond any point previously attained by Europeans, but British whalers had probably sailed farther north thirty years before.[87]

A year later the American brigantine *Advance*, manned by eighteen men, entered Smith Sound under the command of Doctor Elisha Kent Kane. The vessel had been provided by the industrialist Henry Grinnell, who a few years earlier had sponsored de Haven's expedition, on which Kane had served. Kane thought that the Smith Sound route might prove to be the best path to the supposed ice-free polar sea, in which he could search without impediment for Franklin. His unrealistic hopes were not realized; the ship could get no farther than Rensselaer Bay on the Greenland coast, approximately the same latitude attained by Inglefield. With the *Advance* in winter harbor, boat and sled parties explored the unknown regions to the north and established the outlines of what are now Kane Basin and Kennedy Channel. Most of their travels were along the Greenland coast, which they traced beyond 80° north, but they also observed and named prominent features on the North American side and followed the coast of Ellesmere Island bordering Kane Basin. Kane's expedition thus added to the charts some of the most northerly parts of North America. It also reinforced the notion of an open polar sea, as one sled party reached Kennedy Channel and there looked northward over an apparently interminable body of ice-free water.[88]

### Collinson and McClure (1850–1855)

Although the second tier of Arctic islands, north of Parry Channel, experienced most of the exploration effort from 1850 to 1854, the first, or southern, tier of islands was not entirely neglected. In the vessels *Enterprise* and *Investigator*, Captain Richard Collinson and Commander Robert McClure, approaching by way of the Pacific, revealed the extent of Banks and Victoria Islands. In doing so, they fired a final destructive salvo at Parry's retreating notion that the region between Banks Land and Boothia consisted of a central polar sea.

The plan was for the two ships to work together, but they became separated, partly due to the driving ambition of McClure, the junior officer, whose eyes appear to have been focused on the Northwest Passage rather than on Franklin. McClure was the first to arrive at Point Barrow; ignoring his orders, he pressed impatiently ahead through the Beaufort Sea and past the mouth of the Mackenzie River. Collinson, reaching Point Barrow only a few weeks later, found the coastal passage blocked by ice and had to retreat to winter in the Pacific. Meanwhile McClure had seen the southern part of Banks Island, discovered the narrow Prince of Wales Strait, which divides this island from Victoria Island, and almost sailed to Viscount Melville Sound. From wintering quarters midway up the strait, he was able to reach the sound in late October by sled, thus linking up with Parry's discoveries of three decades before and revealing a potential Northwest Passage. When the ice in this waterway was slow to break up in the following summer, McClure sailed south and worked the vessel around the western side of Banks Island in coastal leads, dangerously exposed to the pressure of the heavy pack ice of the Arctic Ocean. With great difficulty and considerable risk, he rounded the northwestern point of the island and advanced eastward as far as Mercy Bay, where ice closed relentlessly around the vessel. Two years later a very slender thread of circumstance led to the crew's rescue by Lieutenant Pim and the men from HMS *Resolute*.

According to General A. W. Greely: "McClure's voyage was geographically a grand success, but otherwise it must be classed as a failure. Disregarding the spirit of the official instructions he lost his ship, and but for the almost miraculous appearance of Pim would have sacrificed his crew."[89] Fortune treated McClure better than he deserved. For connecting Bering Strait with Parry Channel and thereby discovering a Northwest Passage, he and his crew shared a prize of £10,000. (It could not then be known that Franklin's missing expedition had found an eastern connection between Parry Channel and the continental coast two years before.) If McClure had stayed with the *Enterprise* as instructed, the expedition might have located Franklin, but this probability was generally overlooked. Whereas his superior, Collinson, magnanimously praised his achievements, McClure largely ignored the role of Collinson and that of his rescuers; he insisted that he could have traversed the Passage on his own. "One gets the distinct impression," wrote Pierre Berton, "that McClure was out for McClure."[90]

Collinson, having lost the 1850 season, returned to the Arctic in 1851 and picked up the *Investigator*'s trail. He too failed to reach the top of Prince of Wales Strait, and in attempting to follow McClure round Banks Island, he again found himself too late. McClure had gone north along the coast less than two weeks before, but meanwhile pack ice had closed in upon the land. From this point on, Collinson gave up trying to catch up to his elusive second-in-command and operated independently in regions to the east, a decision that led to more extensive exploration.

After wintering near the base of Prince of Wales Strait, Collinson traced the coast southward to Coronation Gulf and found that "Prince Albert Land," "Wollaston Land," and "Victoria Land" were not separate but were parts of the same landmass (Victoria Island). Passing eastward through relatively well-known territory, he took shelter in Cambridge Bay during the winter of 1852–53. From this spot, sled parties traveled round the southeastern corner of Victoria Island and north past Pelly Point. In the summer of 1853 HMS *Enterprise* started home but had to winter again on the northern coast of Alaska and did not arrive back in England until May 1855, after a record-breaking voyage of five years and four months, including three winters in the Arctic, with only three men dead out of sixty-five. Collinson's voyage has been called "one of the most remarkable and successful on record,"[91] but it was tarnished by Collinson's treatment of his officers, most of whom were under arrest by the time the *Enterprise* sailed out of the Arctic.[92] The geographical significance of Collinson's work was slight because he did not cover new ground. In the region of Prince of Wales Strait and southern Banks Island, he had been forced to follow in McClure's wake. Farther east he had been preceded by Rae, of the Hudson's Bay Company, who had traveled the entire southern coast of Victoria Island by sled and boat during the spring and summer of 1851.

Like Rae two years before, Collinson came within fifty miles of the scene of Franklin's disaster; like Rae, he found and obtained from Eskimos some objects that had almost certainly come from *Erebus* or *Terror*; and like Rae, he was either unable or unwilling to follow up the clues. There was no Eskimo interpreter on board the *Enterprise* to ask the Cambridge Bay Eskimos where, when, and how they had obtained two pieces of metal, one of them stamped with the Queen's broad arrow, to use as blades in their tools. The expedition's interpreter, a Moravian missionary named Johann Miertsching, was on McClure's *Investigator*, icebound on the northern coast of Banks Island without a single Eskimo to talk to. McClure's quest for the Northwest Passage had thus deprived the expedition of an excellent opportunity to discover the circumstances and location of the Franklin disaster.

By using the Bering Sea approach, halfway around the world from admiralty offices in London, Collinson's and McClure's ships had been able to strike directly into the southwestern part of the Arctic islands, a region normally beyond the range of vessels arriving through Lancaster Sound or boat parties reaching the mainland coast by the Mackenzie or Coppermine Rivers. As a result, Banks Island, at the western extremity of the archipelago, was suddenly better mapped than King William Island and the Boothia Peninsula to the east. But the location of Franklin's expedition was still not known. Ship after ship had sailed into the Arctic waterways, each "tracing one warm line through a land so wide and savage," but the mystery persisted.[93]

*Franklin's Expedition Located: Rae and McClintock (1853–1859)*
Following his coastal survey of southern Victoria Island in 1851, John Rae turned in 1853 to the task of mapping the continental coastline on behalf of the Hudson's Bay Company. Uncertainty still existed about the area around King William Land, which was still believed to be a peninsula attached to Boothia, and about the western coast of Boothia Peninsula. Repeating the procedure he had adopted in 1846, Rae traveled by boat along the western coast of Hudson Bay, wintered in Repulse Bay, and in the spring of 1854 crossed the Rae Isthmus with six men, hauling sleds. While following his previous route toward Lord Mayor Bay, he was told by Eskimos at Pelly Bay that a large number of white men had starved to death several years earlier, to the west. Unlike fabulous reports of Franklin before, this account was supported by artifacts that had clearly belonged to Franklin and his companions. Among dozens of items that Rae purchased from Eskimos were a silver plate inscribed with Sir John Franklin's name, one of Franklin's medals, and twenty silver forks and spoons bearing the crests or initials of his officers. Table knives, surgeon's instruments, coins, and fragments of watches, watch chains, and watch cases spoke silently of the tragic fate of the missing men. According to the story, Eskimos had encountered about forty white men on the western coast of King William Island, dragging sleds and a boat southward from crushed or abandoned

vessels and hoping to reach a region in which caribou were plentiful. The men were thin and hungry. The Eskimos supplied a seal, then parted. Later in the year thirty or more corpses were discovered on the mainland south of King William Island near tents, an overturned boat, firearms, other equipment, and a variety of personal belongings. The bodies showed indications of cannibalism.

When Rae heard the news in April, the land was still snow-covered and unsuitable for searching. In addition, he could obtain only a vague idea of the location of the alleged tragedy. Accordingly, he continued on his original mission. On his return to Repulse Bay in late May, Eskimos provided more precise locational information and additional relics, but without a canoe or light boat, Rae could not return westward and cross to King William Island in summer, so he and his men sailed south to Churchill as soon as the sea ice permitted, to report the unwelcome news.

Rae's geographical contribution was to show that "King William Land" was in fact an island, separated from Boothia Peninsula by what is now known as Rae Strait (and James Ross Strait farther north). Some historians have said that if Franklin and his officers had known that the land was actually an island, had been aware of the existence of a waterway leading around the inside of King William Island, they would have been able to avoid being trapped in the heavy pack ice northwest of the island and could have reached the continental coast and continued west to Bering Strait. This supposition raises two questions, however. The first is whether the vessels, from their approach route through Peel Sound and Franklin Strait, could have reached the protected channel inside King William Island without being caught in the heavy pack-ice stream. No one can say precisely what the ice conditions were like in this region during the summer of 1846, but the fact that the ships got within fifteen miles of the northwestern corner of the island before being inextricably beset on 11 September suggests that a course farther eastward, closer to Boothia Peninsula, would probably have been feasible. The second question is whether the deep-draught ships would have been able to navigate through the uncharted, shoal waters of James Ross Strait, Rae Strait, and Queen Maud Gulf. Although the *Erebus* and *Terror* drew nineteen feet, it seems likely that they could have threaded their way carefully through, using the engines, with boats going ahead to sound passageways.[94] The coastal waters between Queen Maud Gulf and Alaska would also have presented a challenge, but Collinson demonstrated the navigability of the route in 1852–53, without the benefit of engines, so this should have been possible for Franklin's ships. However, Arctic sea ice does not move according to a prean-nounced schedule, and it now seems clear that the time was not propitious for a Northwest Passage in the 1840s and 1850s. Oxygen isotope and pollen analyses of cores from ice caps on Devon and Ellesmere Islands have re-vealed that the Franklin expedition and the search expeditions took place at the end of an unusually severe half-century, possibly the worst period in the last seven hundred years. In the region south of Franklin Strait, where *Erebus* and *Terror* were beset, open water probably occurred in only one year out of five.[95]

Rae's news produced various reactions in Great Britain, from resigned acceptance to utter disbelief. Many people, particularly Lady Franklin, urged that further search efforts be undertaken to elaborate on the circum-stances and to look for possible survivors. But months before Rae's discov-eries were made known in England, and while the expeditions of Belcher, Collinson, and McClure were still in the Arctic, the government had al-ready decided to strike the names of Franklin and his officers from the navy list and end the search. Rae's information strengthened their resolve. Fur-ther efforts, if any, would have to be made by nongovernmental organiza-tions or individuals.

Although the full details of the tragedy were not yet known, the area in which it had occurred was at last clear. The target was now King William Island and the estuary of the Back River, the region to which Franklin had first been directed by his official instructions and to which Lady Franklin and Richard King had repeatedly drawn attention, to no avail. The Hud-son's Bay Company dispatched an overland party toward the area in the summer of 1855 under James Anderson. The route, down the Back River, was known; no new territory was explored, and the few relics collected during the short search added little to what Rae had learned.

The final search effort was proposed and sponsored by Lady Franklin, who purchased the steam yacht *Fox*, outfitted the vessel, and selected Com-mander Francis Leopold McClintock to take charge. The *Fox* left Aberdeen in early July 1857 but had the bad luck of being caught up in the pack ice of Baffin Bay, where the party was forced to spend the winter drifting south-ward, a prisoner of the floes. The ship and crew survived, and McClintock, instead of abandoning the original plan, purchased additional provisions from whaling vessels in the following spring and headed north again along the Greenland coast. This time he succeeded in crossing to Lancaster Sound. Peel Sound was found to be blocked by ice, so he turned south into

Prince Regent Inlet and reached the mouth of Bellot Strait, the alternative route of access to the waters west of Somerset Island and Boothia Peninsula. This, however, also proved impassable, and the *Fox* was forced to winter at the eastern end of the strait. From this position McClintock's sled parties set out in the spring of 1859.

Their subsequent discoveries on King William Island and south left no doubt about the validity of Rae's information. McClintock and his officers investigated for themselves instead of relying entirely on the testimony of Eskimos, who, as the prestigious London journal *Athenaeum* had confidently asserted, "like all savages . . . lie without scruple."[96] The relics brought home on the *Fox* were not purchased from natives a few hundred miles away but were collected in situ, where the context of their deposition was clear. The evidence was not limited to the men's material possessions, which Franklin's group could have traded to Eskimos, but included many skeletons, as well as two messages giving the briefest account of events leading up to the disaster.

In contrast to other searching expeditions, McClintock's was narrowly focused. This was less an expedition planned to search for Franklin than a fact-finding mission designed to confirm or refute information already known and to collect evidence that would shed more light on the tragedy. Although aimed specifically at the alleged area of the disaster, however, it could not ignore adjacent coasts because of the possibility that some survivors had pursued a different escape route or that important written records had been deposited elsewhere. In addition, as McClintock and his colleagues well knew, there were still some fundamental geographical questions to be resolved.

Accordingly, McClintock sent sled parties out in various directions. As a result, the insularity of King William Island was confirmed, the continuity of Peel Sound was proved, the mapping of the western coast of Boothia Peninsula was completed, and the southern and western coasts of Prince of Wales Island were charted. The last contribution was particularly significant, since some maps had indicated that Prince of Wales and Victoria Islands might be connected. If so, this would disprove the hypothesis that there was a drift of polar ice from the Arctic Ocean, past Melville Island and southeastward to Boothia Peninsula and King William Island. But now the full extent of Prince of Wales Island was known, and the existence of a broad strait between it and Victoria Island had been revealed. One side of M'Clintock Channel, as it is now named, was charted. Its opposite side, the northeastern coast of Victoria Island, remained unsurveyed—the last major unexplored gap in the southern tier of Arctic islands.

## The Northern Thrust, 1860–1900

With the fate of Franklin and his men ascertained and with several possible sea routes through the Arctic islands discovered, the two most powerful reasons for undertaking exploration in the North American Arctic were removed. A few adventurers later set out in the hopes of finding written records and possibly survivors from the *Erebus* and *Terror*, and at least one person attempted to become the first to navigate a ship all the way through the Northwest Passage, but in general, other motivations stimulated Arctic exploration during the last four decades of the nineteenth century. Since almost all the coasts had been delineated along the continent's northern margin and within the first and second tiers of Arctic islands, attention turned to the unknown region farther north.

After 1860 the primary target of these discovery expeditions was the North Pole, which supplanted the Northwest Passage as the "Arctic grail" coveted by crusading explorer-knights. The apex of the earth's axis of rotation, the point where all meridians converge and where all directions are south, the North Pole is a location undistinguished by any landform or resource. That so much effort should be expended, and so much hardship endured, in a quest for this featureless point, set within a frozen ocean, is vivid testimony to the irrational element in exploration. Although devoid of any practical value, the North Pole exerted a fatal attraction. Attempts to reach the supposed open polar sea by way of Spitsbergen had failed, so attention turned in 1860 to the Smith Sound route, by which Kane's expedition had attained a high latitude seven years before. In this sector a succession of "farthest north" records was established by Pole-seeking parties, but the attainment of the Pole itself, like the first Northwest Passage by ship, did not occur during the 1800s. Nonetheless, the expeditions that struggled toward the top of the world filled in many blank spaces on the Arctic maps.

### Hayes (1860–1861) and Hall (1871–1873)

The three-hundred-mile waterway connecting Baffin Bay with the Arctic Ocean and separating Ellesmere Island from Greenland attracted several polar expeditions in the last four decades of the century. The American

Isaac Hayes, while serving as surgeon with Kane, had become a firm supporter of the theory that the pack ice in northern waters was only a circumpolar ring, a marginal "ice-belt" surrounding a central ice-free sea, and in
1860 he organized his own expedition and sailed through Baffin Bay on the
schooner *United States*. Unfavorable ice conditions forced the ship into
winter quarters much farther south than intended, on the Greenland side
of Smith Sound, a position ill-suited for a poleward thrust. Sled journeys
were made onto the Greenland ice cap and southward along the coast, but
the most important voyage was undertaken toward the north in March
1861. Attempting to cross Smith Sound to the Ellesmere coast, Hayes's
party detoured around rough ice and had to travel eighty miles before
striking the land on the western side of Kane Basin. Backtracking repeatedly to bring up their heavy outfit over rough ice, they traveled more than
five hundred miles to complete the eighty-mile traverse and spent a month
on the crossing.[97] Continuing north along the Ellesmere coast, the party
sledded up Kennedy Channel, passed the highest latitude achieved on the
Greenland side during Kane's expedition, and allegedly reached 81°35'
north, near the mouth of Lady Franklin Bay. From a summit, Hayes saw
that Kennedy Channel, which had been reported entirely open half a
dozen years before, was now full of pack ice. Despite this observation, he
held strongly to his beliefs and later optimistically titled his published narrative *The Open Polar Sea*.[98]

Hayes's claim to have attained a latitude of 81°35' north has been doubted,
but he may indeed have surpassed Kane's farthest point north.[99] He also
contributed to the map of Ellesmere Island's eastern coast. Not all the intri-
cacies of this complex fiord coast could be recorded by the overburdened
sled party during the time available, but Hayes raised one geographical
question of some interest. He drew attention to an indentation (Buchanan
Bay) that was not far north of Smith Sound and that he believed was a strait
leading westward through Ellesmere Island parallel to Jones and Lancaster
Sounds.

A decade later another American, Charles Francis Hall, took up the
quest for the North Pole. Already famous for his two searches for Franklin
relics, he had spent seven and a half years in the Arctic and was recognized
as the leading advocate of Eskimo methods of travel and survival. He appeared to be as likely as any other man to reach the Pole. The U.S. Navy do-
nated a vessel, renamed *Polaris*; Congress apportioned some funds, private subscriptions raised more, and in early July 1871 the expedition sailed
for Baffin Bay. North of Smith Sound, where concentrated pack ice had pre-

vented Hayes from advancing, the *Polaris* made astonishing progress, traveling from Smith Sound through Kane Basin, Kennedy Channel, Hall Basin, and Robeson Channel to 82°11' north in only two and a half days. This was probably farther north than any other vessel had ever gone, and the expedition, poised at the threshold of the Arctic Ocean, was in the best possible position for a sledding assault on the Pole.

Where Hayes's vessel had been confronted by impassable ice, Hall had found navigable water for another three hundred miles. The contrast in summer ice conditions was extraordinary. Less than thirty miles wide for half its length, the waterway between Ellesmere Island and Greenland is filled with sea ice from the Arctic Ocean and glacier ice calved from bordering mountain ranges. A south-flowing current, sometimes opposed by wind and tide, carries the ice toward Baffin Bay. The primeval rhythms of tides, the uncertain pulsations of ice supply, and the variable whims of atmospheric circulation, combined with the constrictions of narrow straits and shallow depths, can result in the formation of persistent ice barriers. "This way to the North Pole," one observer has written, "is less an open door than one that opens and closes rapidly."[100]

Hall's good fortune did not last. After putting his ship into winter quarters on the Greenland coast, he died suddenly after returning from a sled trip in October. The circumstances of his death were suspicious, but an official inquiry held later in Washington concluded that he had died from natural causes. A century later, however, Hall's body, still well preserved in its icy grave, was exhumed; fatally high levels of arsenic in his fingernails and hair pointed to the strong probability that he had been murdered by one of his companions.[101]

Without Hall's zeal and authority, the goals of the expedition were relaxed, although a few sled trips were made in the spring of 1872. When the *Polaris* broke out of winter harbor in August 1872, ice obstructed its passage southward, and for two months the vessel drifted south with the pack, the crew fearing that they would have to spend a second winter in the Arctic. During a gale in October, while half the expedition was on the ice preparing an emergency camp, the ship broke free, and the two groups were separated. Those on the ship managed to move supplies ashore near Etah, and with the cooperation of local Eskimos they survived the winter. In the following June they started south by open boat, headed for Danish settlements on the Greenland coast, and were picked up in Melville Bay by a Scottish whaler. Meanwhile those marooned on the ice floe had experienced one of the most incredible voyages ever, drifting southward with the ice pack for half a year on their exposed and vulnerable raft of frozen water until, on the last day of April 1873, they were rescued off Labrador by a Newfoundland sealing vessel, more than seventeen hundred miles south of the place where they had been separated from the *Polaris*. Of the nineteen whites and Eskimos, five of whom were children, not a life was lost.

## Nares (1875–1876)

Having "slumbered for over twenty years" since the start of the Franklin searches, Great Britain revived its Arctic initiative in 1875 with a large polar expedition under Captain George Strong Nares, former commander of the famous oceanographic research ship *Challenger*.[102] The primary aim was to "attain the highest northern latitude, and, if possible, to reach the North Pole."[103] In addition the men were to explore coasts adjacent to the winter harbors and gather scientific data. A large force was sent out, comprising two ships and 120 men, with an auxiliary transport to carry supplies as far as Disko Island, Greenland. In size the expedition was ominously similar to that of Sir John Franklin's thirty years before. By comparison the Americans Kane, Hayes, and Hall had each used one ship; the combined crews of their three expeditions amounted to only half the number of men serving under Nares.

At the beginning of August 1875 HMS *Alert* and *Discovery* passed through Smith Sound, penetrated Kennedy Channel, and reached Lady Franklin Bay by the end of the month. Their progress in this initial stage was only slightly less spectacular than that of Hall's *Polaris*. Since Nares had been instructed to leave one of the vessels south of 82° north as a fallback precaution, he left the *Discovery* and continued with the *Alert* through Robeson Channel, the last link in the chain of straits and basins between Ellesmere Island and Greenland. The coast, which had been trending northward since Baffin Bay, now began to curve westward to the most northerly point of the North American Arctic. Toward the North Pole, less than five hundred miles away, the vista was discouraging. Closely packed ice, hummocked by the accumulated forces of the vast polar basin, stretched as far as they could see, without the slightest suggestion of an open polar sea. Later, when Albert Hastings Markham published a popular account of his experiences on the expedition, he entitled the work *The Great Frozen Sea*, a pointed rebuke to Hayes for his misleading title *The Open Polar Sea*.[104] Travel over the pressure-ridged pack ice looked difficult if not impossible, but coastal travel along the landfast ice was feasible. Their chances of reaching the Pole, or even a high latitude, rested on whether the Ellesmere coast,

now swinging westward, would later recurve toward the north and provide a handrail to the objective.

At Floeberg Beach, Nares put the *Alert* into winter quarters, having already achieved a farthest north record for ships and men. From each vessel, in its respective harbor, sleds departed on exploratory and depot-
laying journeys during the fall, until darkness and extreme cold forced the
crews into winter hibernation. In April the sledding program was resumed.
From the *Discovery*, sled parties outlined the inner limits of Lady Franklin
Bay and crossed Robeson Channel to explore northernmost Greenland.
From the *Alert*, a large party traveled northwest toward the extremity of
Ellesmere Island. At Cape Joseph Henry, seeing no indication that the
coast turned north, Markham's division, with two sleds and boats, left the
land and headed north over the rough ice while Aldrich, accompanied for
two weeks by a support party, continued westward with one sled to chart
the coastline.

Overburdened and exhausted, Markham and his men struggled northward over the snow-covered ice of the Arctic Ocean to 83°20'26" before
turning back. They were a long way short of the North Pole, but they had
nonetheless traveled to (as a chapter heading in the inevitable book later proclaimed) "the most northern point ever reached by man."[105] As a new farthest north, the ice journey was applauded. In establishing the record,
which would last for six years, Markham had demonstrated a nice awareness of the magic of round figures: on 12 May, with scurvy and fatigue crip-
pling his sled-haulers, he had left seven men and pressed on farther "in order to insure being within four hundred [geographical] miles of the North
Pole."[106] Only when he calculated the remaining distance as 399.5 miles did
he stop. In an arduous, scurvy-ridden ice journey, which took a heavy toll on
everyone's health and claimed the life of one man, Markham and his men
took two months to reach and return from a point less than forty miles off the
coast, and yet they could boast of having only four hundred miles left to go!

Geographically, the ice journey had little significance, other than to
slightly puncture the overblown theory of an ice-free polar sea. Aldrich's
western party contributed more to geographical knowledge. In a journey
lasting almost three months, the small group followed the northern coast
of Ellesmere Island round North America's northernmost headlands to
Yelverton Bay, covering a straight-line distance of about two hundred miles
before returning. No one could say with certainty that no lands existed in
the unexplored region to the west, but this turned out to be the case. Al-

drich's sled trip was one of the last milestones on the path toward knowledge of the full extent of North America. From east to west, from south to north, the continent and most of its Arctic archipelago stood revealed.

All the sledding parties returned with scurvy, having skated on the thin ice of survival by pushing on courageously after the insidious disease had undermined their strength and endurance. Four men had died. Wisely, Nares decided to forgo further efforts and take the vessels home. The *Alert* managed to break out of harbor ice in late July and reach the *Discovery* in Lady Franklin Bay. The two ships left in mid-August and reached England at the end of October. The alarming extent to which scurvy had affected the expedition led to a parliamentary inquiry, in which failure to provide the sledding parties with daily rations of lime juice as an antiscorbutic was identified as the probable cause.

Was the Nares expedition a success or a failure? A Scottish newspaper editorial noted that many would consider it to have failed because it had not attained the North Pole, the only remaining "object of exploration" in the Arctic regions, and some would brand it as "foolhardy" because it had produced nothing of commercial value. Yet, the editorial suggested, the quest for the Pole might lead to great "discoveries and adventures." Regardless, "The whole matter is at least as brave and sensible as war, . . . and the cost to human life is far less."[107]

### Greely (1881–1884)

The year in which Nares departed for Baffin Bay also saw the genesis of a novel approach to the exploration of the polar regions. Lieutenant Karl Weyprecht of the Austrian Navy, an experienced Arctic explorer, outlined to the German Scientific and Medical Association a plan of systematic research, proposing "that scientific investigations, heretofore subordinated to geographical discovery, be now made the primary object."[108] Discovery, he suggested, was of limited value to civilization unless it contributed to an understanding of universal scientific laws. Meaningful scientific work could not be carried out on random, uncoordinated, and hazardous voyages of discovery; it required continuous observations at particular locations, using standardized methods. In a series of annual International Polar Conferences, Weyprecht's concept led to the establishment of fourteen year-round stations in the circumpolar Arctic and subarctic, by eleven nations, to take simultaneous observations in meteorology, magnetism, and other branches of science during an International Polar Year lasting from 1

August 1882 to 1 September 1883. The work was to be coordinated with observations at a number of existing stations in lower latitudes. Three stations were subsequently set up in the North American Arctic, one by Germany in Cumberland Sound, Baffin Island, and two by the United States at Point Barrow, Alaska, and Lady Franklin Bay, Ellesmere Island.[109]

The Lady Franklin Bay expedition of 1881–84, commanded by Lieutenant Adolphus Washington Greely, U.S. Army, used the Smith Sound approach pioneered by Kane, Hayes, Hall, and Nares to establish the most northerly scientific station of the International Polar Year. In several respects this was a curious expedition, one "most oddly out of context."[110] First, it was an army expedition, comprising two dozen soldiers and two Greenland Eskimos. Second, it did not use a vessel for residence, workshop, storage place, and base, as maritime wintering expeditions had done since Parry in 1819. After the men had constructed a building ashore, the chartered steamer *Proteus* left for home. The resultant dependence on people to the south for resupply and evacuation in a region where ice could so easily slam the door in the face of incoming ships made the expedition vulnerable. Third, although designed specifically for the lofty objective of gathering scientific data under an international regime, the expedition indulged in some of the "exploration of the record-breaking kind"[111] that, according to Weyprecht, was the antithesis of valid scientific inquiry. Finally, the number of deaths during the expedition was surpassed in nineteenth-century Arctic exploration only by the Franklin disaster.

After establishing their base, "Fort Conger," on Lady Franklin Bay, where HMS *Discovery* had wintered in 1875–76, the men had initiated the scientific program and undertaken exploratory journeys in various directions. Writing to his wife in June 1882, Greely gloated over Lieutenant James B. Lockwood's achievement in exceeding by a few miles the highest latitude reached by Markham in 1876. Not only had Lockwood set a new world record, but his men had also returned in good health. "Three lives paid for the English discoveries," he wrote. "We beat them and lose none."[112] Sadly, his exuberance was premature. When no supply reached the station in either 1882 or 1883, the situation became perilous. Greely therefore abandoned Fort Conger and took the party 250 miles south by boat to Smith Sound, hoping to find a cache of food left by relief vessels. Instead he found only a message stating that the steamer *Proteus*, one of two ships sent out in the summer of 1883, had been crushed by ice. The expedition wintered at Cape Sabine, slowly starving, until seven emaciated survivors were rescued by the relief ships *Thetis* and *Bear* in late June 1884. Of the eighteen who had died, one had been executed for stealing, one had committed suicide, and the rest had died from starvation, exposure, and frostbite. Another died on the voyage south.

The tragic events of the Greely expedition excited great interest. Much of the comment focused on the most spectacular aspects, including the farthest-north record, disciplinary problems, mismanagement of relief expeditions, starvation, and cannibalism. What the men had accomplished in scientific work and in geographical discovery before the food ran out was largely overlooked. More than any other previous Arctic expedition, Greely's tested the possibilities of year-round exploration: training; keeping the men fit; combating boredom; reconnoitering the land and ice; assessing the condition of food depots left by earlier expeditions; laying out depots for future journeys; hunting musk oxen and other animals for food. From late August to early November at least eighteen trips were made, either walking with packs or using man-hauled or dog-hauled sleds. Four of these excursions were carried out after the sun had set on 16 October. Sled trips were resumed on 19 February, in the coldest month of the year, a week before the sun reappeared, and they continued into June. In summer, exploration was carried out on foot and by boat.

Greely's exploratory parties also utilized a greater diversity of terrain than earlier expeditions. Throughout the searches for the Northwest Passage and Franklin, sled and boat parties had concentrated on delineating coasts, since coasts define waterways. Relatively few expeditions had penetrated into the interior spaces of the Arctic islands. Though appropriate at the time, this practice had nonetheless left vast expanses of land unexplored. Baffin Island alone covers an area twice as large as Great Britain; Ellesmere and Victoria Islands are each twice the size of Ireland. Their interiors were unknown. The inland thrusts made from Fort Conger resulted in the discovery of the extensive ice caps and mountain ranges of Ellesmere Island as well as its largest lake (ironically named for General W. B. Hazen, who was later criticized for inept organization of the relief expedition). Greely's exploration of the area around Lake Hazen has been called "one of the most outstanding feats of polar travel."[113]

## Peary and Sverdrup (1898–1900)

The unquenchable thirst for the North Pole, "the most coveted of trophies," "that Mount Everest of the mind," drove one of the most single-minded explorers of the century, Lieutenant Robert Edwin Peary of the U.S. Navy, to unmatched levels of determination and physical effort.[114] Af-

306 / W. GILLIES ROSS

ter five expeditions to Baffin Bay to explore northern Greenland and collect three large meteorites from Cape York, Peary set off in 1898 to attempt to reach the North Pole by the Smith Sound approach. But the *Windward* was stopped by ice in Kane Basin and forced to winter on the coast of Ellesmere Island, less than 80° north. Peary endeavored to overcome the disadvantage of distance by advancing stores two hundred miles to Greely's Fort Conger by sled in the dead of winter, arriving at Fort Conger in early January 1899 and leaving again for the base in mid-February. In this bold venture he lost most of his toes to frostbite.

Although most of the dog-sled trips undertaken by Peary's expedition were on the well-tracked eastern coast of Ellesmere Island, they did clarify a few geographical misconceptions in the confusing area immediately northwest of Smith Sound. Bache "Island" was found to be a peninsula; Buchanan "Strait" (of Hayes) was proved to be a bay; and "Hayes Sound" was shown to be the end of Buchanan Bay. In addition, Peary traveled inland from this region, ascending more than four thousand feet on glacial ice to a point from which he could see beyond the island's western coast to Axel Heiberg Island. Peary believed he was the first European to sight this large island.

Actually, Axel Heiberg Island had already been discovered by men in Otto Sverdrup's Norwegian expedition a few months earlier. In 1898, as Peary had prepared for his first attack on the North Pole, Sverdrup had entered Smith Sound with a different objective. No stranger to ice navigation, Sverdrup intended to take *Fram* to winter in northern Greenland. From there the men would explore farther by sled, traveling "as far down the east coast as we could attain."[115] Although science was to be taken seriously on the voyage, geographical attainments and political considerations predominated. Sverdrup admitted, "There were still many white spaces on the map which I was glad of an opportunity of colouring with the Norwegian colours."[116]

The expedition spent the first winter on the western shore of Smith Sound near Pim Island, on which most of Greely's men had died and not far from the place where Peary's ship *Windward* was wintering. In the spring two sledding parties traveled west into the interior of Ellesmere Island. One remained two weeks on the inland ice, and the other crossed the island to Bay Fiord on the western coast, resulting in the first sighting of Axel Heiberg Island and Eureka Sound.

Prevented by ice from getting north through Kane Basin in two successive summers and perhaps feeling uncomfortably close to Peary, who "was beginning by this time to feel a strong sense of personal proprietorship" over the Smith Sound routeway toward the Pole, Sverdrup abandoned his original plan in 1899 and took the *Fram* south into Jones Sound.[117] He selected a suitable wintering spot on its northern coast, in Harbour Fiord, from which preliminary exploratory and hunting excursions were conducted before the polar night began. At the close of 1899 he and his fifteen companions (one had died in October) were well situated for extensive journeys of discovery in the untracked region northwest of Jones Sound. In a vast area bounded by the explorations of Parry, Penny, and Belcher on the south, by Kane, Hall, and Peary on the east, and by Nares and Greely on the north, a number of islands still awaited discovery. Sverdrup extensively surveyed this district in the first years of the next century.

Sverdrup's expedition was remarkable for its small size, flexibility, and quiet efficiency. Hunting to keep fit, well-nourished, and free from scurvy and depending on dogsleds for travel over ice and snow, the Norwegians accomplished great deeds in a region where tragedy almost seemed the rule. A millennium before, Norse seafarers had discovered North America, spearheading the European advance; their descendants, including Otto Sverdrup, Roald Amundsen, and Vilhjalmur Stefansson, were now about to complete the map of the continent.[118]

## Behind the Frontier, 1860–1900

While the polar quest carried the discovery of new lands into the ultimate latitudes of Arctic North America, other stimuli drew expeditions to the northern slope of Alaska, the Mackenzie delta area, the Barren Grounds, Hudson Bay and Hudson Strait, and southeastern Baffin Island. These regions, lying far south of the frontier of exploration, were already known in broad outline. Discovery, therefore, was not the main objective. Men sought more-specific goals related to science, commerce, administration, missionary work, and tourism. Yet they often contributed to the incomplete mosaic of geographical information as well. Instead of expanding the outer limits of the world known to Europeans, they filled in some of the missing details behind the frontier of knowledge. This could be termed "secondary exploration" as compared to "primary exploration." Or, using the distinction made by Frank Debenham in 1921, it could be called "exploration" (the "more detailed examination of unfrequented tracts") as distinct from "discovery" (the "search after new fields" and the determination of "main geographical features").[119]

On the Barren Grounds, explorers before 1860 had followed the valleys of the Coppermine and Back Rivers to reach the central coast. Because the voyagers had little cause to depart from the convenient drainage pattern of the Canadian Shield and no reason to descend rivers flowing eastward into Hudson Bay, large expanses of untracked land had remained unknown to Europeans. But between 1865 and 1880, two expeditions traversed the northeastern part of the Barren Grounds. The first was led by Charles Francis Hall; the second was under the command of Lieutenant Frederick Schwatka, on leave from the U.S. Army. In some respects the expeditions were similar. Both were led by Americans, both hoped to recover Franklin records and relics, both obtained passage to and from Hudson Bay on whaleships, and both comprised only a few white men, depending largely on Eskimo companions and native methods of travel. Ebeirbing ("Joe"), the most famous of the Eskimos who assisted Euro-Americans, accompanied both parties.

Hall followed a northerly, mainly coastal route from Repulse Bay through Committee Bay to King William Island in 1869, approximating the path followed by Rae a decade before. Schwatka took a longer course, farther south, starting near Chesterfield Inlet and cutting across the grain of the country to the lower Back River. Of the two journeys, Schwatka's was the more remarkable for duration, distance traveled, and severity of conditions endured. Whereas Hall reached King William Island and returned within three months, Schwatka covered twenty-eight hundred miles over eleven months.[120] On the return trip from the Back River to Hudson Bay, following a more southerly loop than on the outward journey, he and his party sledded across the Barrens between mid-December 1879 and early March 1880, the coldest part of the winter. Although mainly south of the Arctic Circle and therefore not plagued by the midwinter continuous darkness of high latitudes, they were crossing the "cold pole" of the North American Arctic, in which exceptionally low temperatures and high wind chill values occur. For five consecutive months (November to March), the monthly minimum temperature was below $-50°C$ ($-67°F$).[121]

Hall's trip to King William Island was only a part of his extensive travels in the northern Hudson Bay and Foxe Basin regions during an expedition that lasted more than five years. He had close relationships with the Eskimo people and recorded a rich variety of geographical and ethnographical information. Hall's and Schwatka's expeditions, taking place long after Rae and McClintock had discovered Franklin's fate and long after the frontier of primary exploration had shifted north to Smith Sound and Ellesmere

*19.4 Ebeirbing ("Joe"). The most famous of the Eskimos who assisted Euro-Americans, Joe participated in at least six expeditions between 1860 and 1880. Published in J. E. Nourse, ed.,* Narrative of the Second Arctic Expedition Made by Charles F. Hall: His Voyage to Repulse Bay, Sledge Journeys to the Straits of Fury and Hecla and to King William's Land, and Residence among the Eskimos during the Years 1864–'69 *(1879).*

Island, were somewhat anachronistic. Yet they represent the pinnacle of Euro-American success in adopting Eskimo methods of traveling the northern terrain, procuring food, and obtaining shelter.

Science provided the primary motive for many expeditions after 1860. Between 1818 and 1860, most maritime and overland expeditions had done what they could to observe, measure, and collect, but their scientific endeavors had always been secondary to discovering new territory, searching for missing expeditions, or transporting supplies to parties still in the field. Now science became the primary objective of several expeditions. Most were sponsored by government, in Canada by the Department of Marine and Fisheries and the Geological Survey and in the United States by the Coast and Geodetic Survey, the Smithsonian Institution, and the American Museum of Natural History. Much of the scientific research had a strong practical thrust. Since both the United States and Canada became landlords of Arctic territory during the second half of the nineteenth century, the countries desired to determine the geographical extent and resource potential of the northern regions. Surveying and mapping, mineral exploration, and assessment of shipping feasibility were important considerations. Some projects required a continuous recording of data and therefore established year-round stations. Others used small mobile field parties to collect information and specimens regionally or by traverse.

In northern Alaska the general characteristics of the coast were well-known from the work of Northwest Passage and Franklin search expeditions, but the North Slope rising southward to the crest of the Brooks Range had escaped scrutiny.[122] For the International Polar Year, the Point Barrow Expedition, commanded by Lieutenant P. H. Ray of the U.S. Army, established a scientific station in 1881 and operated it until 1883. Although the emphasis was on day-to-day recording of terrestrial and atmospheric properties, Ray undertook sled trips over the wide coastal plain toward the east and south. He mapped part of the Meade River system east of Point Barrow in 1882, and in the next year he traveled south of 70° north and sighted the Meade River Mountains, part of the Brooks Range. The smooth functioning of Ray's expedition contrasted strongly with the disastrous events occurring on the opposite side of the Arctic, on the International Polar Year expedition commanded by Greely. Ray's expedition was better planned; the station was in a more accessible place; the flat coast was better suited to sledding; and the personal relationships were more harmonious.

A few years later the Brooks Range was crossed from the southern side. In December 1885 Lieutenant George M. Stoney, U.S. Navy, starting from the Kobuk River, crossed the drainage divide and reached the headwaters of the north-flowing Colville River, the largest on Alaska's North Slope. A few months later, in another winter trip, he traveled again to the upper Colville but was unable to continue to the coast. In the spring, Stoney's colleague Ensign W. L. Howard ascended the Noatak River, crossed over to the Colville system, descended to the Arctic coast, and continued west to Point Barrow. Farther east, J. H. Turner, of the U.S. Coast and Geodetic Survey, and Frederick Funston, a botanist with the U.S. Department of Agriculture, traveled between the Yukon interior and the Arctic coast in 1890 and 1894 respectively. In 1898 and 1899 Andrew Jackson Stone collected zoological specimens along the coast between Herschel Island (139° west) and Cape Lyon (123° west) on behalf of the American Museum of Natural History.

In the eastern Arctic, scientific activity focused on Cumberland Sound and Hudson Strait and Bay.[123] In 1877–78 the Howgate Preliminary Arctic Expedition, in the *Florence*, wintered at Cumberland Sound. Commanded by the American whaling captain George E. Tyson, a veteran of the extraordinary ice floe drift during Hall's polar quest, the party prepared for the main expedition to northern Ellesmere Island, scheduled for the following year but subsequently canceled, and carried out a broad program of scientific inquiry. A German International Polar Year station operated in the same region in 1882–83 and was succeeded immediately by the German geographer Franz Boas, who, from a Scottish whaling station, undertook extensive travels by dogsled with Eskimo companions and added greatly to the somewhat superficial picture presented on admiralty charts and explorers' maps. Obtaining information from wintering whalemen, the native inhabitants of the region, and his own observations, he described the topography, mapped the seasonal positions of the floe edge, and studied the Eskimo annual hunting cycle, population distribution, and material and intellectual culture. Whereas explorers and scientists usually applied European place-names to the geographical features they mapped, ignoring the Eskimo nomenclature, Boas recorded almost a thousand Eskimo native toponyms then in use and showed their locations on his maps.[124] As a result of whaling activity since 1840, and the work of the three scientific expeditions between 1877 and 1884, Cumberland Sound became one of the best-known parts of the Arctic.

Around Hudson Bay and Hudson Strait, a series of government expeditions after 1876 investigated the region's geology, meteorology, and glaciology. Much of the geological work was carried out by two capable and energetic members of the Geological Survey of Canada, Robert Bell and Albert Peter Low, each of whom made extensive journeys, sometimes traveling overland to James Bay or Hudson Bay by canoe and other times entering Hudson Strait by ship. They examined James Bay, the eastern coast of Hudson Bay, the southern coast of Hudson Strait, and many of the waterways of the immense peninsula of Quebec-Labrador. Low is said to have traveled more than ten thousand miles by boat, canoe, dog-sled, and snowshoe during his northern field excursions.[125] Geologists carried out similar surveys on the western side of Hudson Bay. Joseph Burr Tyrrell completed parallel canoe traverses across the Barren Grounds to the Hudson Bay coast in 1893 and 1894. Near Fort Chimo in Ungava Bay, Lucien McShan Turner recorded weather observations for the U.S. Signal Service and assembled ethnographic and natural history collections for the Smithsonian Institution in Washington. He had already carried out similar work on the Bering Sea coast of Alaska for several years.

Four maritime expeditions were sent out by the Canadian Department of Marine and Fisheries. The first three, on the *Neptune* in 1884 and the *Alert* in 1885 and 1886, were commanded by Lieutenant Andrew Robertson Gordon. Their primary purpose was to set up and supply five temporary stations in Hudson Strait and one in northern Labrador, at which regular observations of ice and weather conditions would be made for two years. The possibility of using the relatively short Hudson Bay sea route to export prairie grain to Europe was under consideration, but first the length and variability of the navigation season had to be determined. In 1897 a fourth expedition went north, on the *Diana*, under William Wakeham, to continue the ice studies. Despite the demands of the glaciological and meteorological work, the ships of the Hudson Bay expeditions were able to undertake other scientific programs, cruise widely, visit settlements, contact native inhabitants and British whalers, and demonstrate Canadian authority.

Missionaries contributed to Arctic exploration after 1860. Endeavoring to reach the most accessible regions of comparatively dense Eskimo settlement, they tended to use either the established subarctic river routes along which missions and fur trade posts were already operating among the northern Indians or the Hudson Bay sea route by which the supply ships of the Hudson's Bay Company sailed annually to Churchill, York Factory, and Moose Factory. Missions and posts provided convenient bases from which the men could make forays into Eskimo territory farther north. The preliminary missionary work among the Eskimos therefore concentrated on the lower Mackenzie River and the southern part of Hudson Bay. In the former the Oblate Father Emile Petitot recorded many geographical and ethno-graphical details during several trips to the Arctic coast in 1864–72. Church of England efforts, beginning in 1871 with Reverend W. C. Bompas, culminated in the establishment of a permanent mission at Herschel Island in 1897 under Reverend I. O. Stringer. In eastern Hudson Bay and James Bay, Reverend James Edmund Peck worked from 1876 to 1884, crossing overland to Fort Chimo on Ungava Bay, a voyage of more than five hundred miles. On the western coast of Hudson Bay, Reverend Joseph Lofthouse traveled more than three hundred miles north from Churchill. Farther north, missionary activities were inhibited by travel and supply difficulties, but transport by whaling vessels enabled the Moravian Mathias Warmow to winter in Cumberland Sound, Baffin Island, in 1857–58, Reverend E. J. Peck to open a permanent mission in the same region in 1894, and A. W. Buckland to spend a winter in Chesterfield Inlet, about four hundred miles north of Churchill, in 1895–96.

Some exploration was motivated by commercial considerations. Fur trade posts of the Hudson's Bay Company existed within the subarctic forest zone from Labrador to Alaska, but the Arctic tundra region, for the most part, lay beyond the range of the company's operations. The possibility of opening trade with the Eskimos led to two exploratory trips, under William Hendry in 1828 and Nicol Finlayson in 1830, up the eastern coast of Hudson Bay and overland to Ungava Bay, culminating in the establishment of the Fort Chimo post. In the late 1840s two reconnaissance trips were undertaken to the Belcher Islands in eastern Hudson Bay by Thomas Wiegand. In the western Arctic, Roderick MacFarland made several journeys to the Anderson River east of the Mackenzie between 1857 and 1861, in preparation for the erection of the Fort Anderson post. Exploratory Arctic journeys by fur traders were thus largely confined to the Mackenzie region, the eastern coast of Hudson Bay, and Ungava Bay. In addition, the Hudson's Bay Company annually sent supply ships from London through Hudson Strait to its posts at the bottom of the bay. Conditions of sea ice, wind, and weather were recorded in logbooks that are still today important sources of glaciological and meteorological data.[126]

In the final decade of the century a new motive stimulated Arctic expeditions. Trophy heads and hides of musk oxen, caribou, and bears—and occasionally, live animals—were the goal of "sport" hunters such as Frank Russell, Caspar Whitney, Henry Toke Munn, and Charles Jesse "Buffalo" Jones. The hunters were attracted to the Barren Grounds, where musk oxen reached the southernmost limit of their range and caribou migrated in herds of immeasurable size. The men usually reached the region by way of Great Slave Lake. The most notable forays into the tundra zone were made by Whitney, who traveled north almost to the Arctic coast, and by Jones, who crossed the Barren Grounds toward Baker Lake in late winter. Although not primarily interested in geographical inquiry, the adventurers wrote popular books in which they described the tundra landscape and its plant and animal life and thus communicated to a wide audience their impressions of the Arctic in a way that fur traders, whalemen, and scientists could not.

Another major commercial motivation for exploration in the North American Arctic was whaling, which also occurred behind the advancing frontier of Euro-American discovery.[127] When British whalemen began to exploit the coast of Baffin Island in about 1820, Baffin and Ross had already circled Baffin Bay, and Parry had shot westward to the verge of the Arctic Ocean. When American whalemen first sailed into Hudson Bay in 1860 and the Beaufort Sea in 1889, they too had been preceded by exploring vessels. Notwithstanding the fact that whalers operated within large regions that were already depicted, albeit roughly, on the charts, they were often the first to enter inlets, straits, and basins contained within the known territory but bypassed by impatient discovery or search expeditions. In revealing the existence, extent, and character of such features, they played a vital but seldom appreciated role in the exploration process.

From northwestern Hudson Bay and Barrow Strait in the east to Amundsen Gulf in the west, a large area remained unaffected by whaling in any direct sense. The commercial exploitation of the Greenland (or bowhead) whale for oil and baleen was confined to three distinct whaling regions, or "whale fisheries," located on the Atlantic and the Pacific flanks and in Hudson Bay. Although these fisheries extended toward the central Arctic, they did not meet. During the Northwest Passage period and the Franklin era, the Davis Strait (Atlantic) whale fishery was the only one in operation. Discovery and search expeditions passed rapidly through the whaling region into the Arctic islands, depriving the whalers of the possibility of being in the vanguard of the exploration thrust. Off the beaten track through Lancaster Sound, however, whalers were occasionally the first to intrude on virgin territory not yet penetrated by Europeans. In 1820 whalers appear to have gone beyond the northern limits of Baffin and Ross. The *Friendship* and *Truelove* apparently reached the latitude of 78°20' north (possibly 78°40' north) in Smith Sound, and the *Lady Jane* sailed far enough north to observe that the sound "widens to the north-west and north-east," in effect reaching what is now called Kane Basin.[128] This was thirty-two years before Inglefield sailed the Franklin search vessel *Isabel* to 78°28' north and claimed to have gone much farther north than any previous ship. Thomas Lee on the whaler *Prince of Wales* was probably the first European to sail into Jones Sound, in 1848, and Captain John Gravill of the *William Ward* was the first to set foot on Ellesmere Island, in the following summer.[129]

Because the main thrust of discovery and search voyages penetrated Lancaster Sound, the eastern coast of Baffin Island was left to the whalers, who normally cruised from Pond Inlet toward Davis Strait during July, August, and September. Unquestionably their most important geographical contribution was the rediscovery and mapping of Cumberland Sound. The largest indentation on the coast (as big as New Jersey), the sound had been discovered by John Davis in 1585 but entirely overlooked during the intervening two and a half centuries. Its rediscovery and exploitation were the result of the foresight and single-minded determination of William Penny, a Scottish whaling captain. Penny had heard Eskimos talk about the large gulf, and in 1839 he took a young man, Eenoolooapik, back to Scotland for the winter. With Penny's help, Eenoo drew a detailed chart of "Tenudiackbeek" (Cumberland Sound). Penny sent it to the admiralty, and in 1840 the Hydrographic Office published the first chart of Cumberland Sound.[130] The map had the unique distinction of being compiled solely on the basis of Eskimo information, before Penny or any other whaleman had entered the sound. Subsequent whaling operations in the region led to improvements in its cartographic representation.

Another locality in which whaling activity led to important discoveries, and revisions of the admiralty charts, was northern Baffin Island. The entrances to Pond, Navy Board, and Admiralty Inlets had been noticed early, but their innermost waters lay beyond the scope of European experience for a surprisingly long time, and their geographical relationship to each other remained a mystery. The admiralty charts simply showed dotted lines extending vaguely into the interior. In 1855 Captain John Gray Sr. sailed through Pond Inlet and discovered that it opened into a large sound, which he named Eclipse Sound after his whaling vessel. His manuscript chart was used to revise the admiralty chart.[131] Gray's interpretation, although a significant improvement, was in two important respects misleading. It showed both Admiralty Inlet and Navy Board Inlet leading into Eclipse Sound (whereas only the latter does so), and it suggested, by dotted lines, that Eclipse Sound crossed Baffin Island to Prince Regent Inlet. Another whaling master, William Adams, was able to correct these errors in 1872. His chart revealed the true relationship of the three inlets and provided new details and place-names.[132] Where some unexplored fiords led south from Eclipse Sound, however, he resorted to the dotted-line treatment.

At a number of places along the coast of Baffin Island, whalemen acquired considerable familiarity with headlands, islands, and inlets that discovery ships, seeking more remote objectives, had quickly passed by. They found protected anchorages in the mouths of a number of fiords and bays between Pond Inlet and Cape Dyer, but because the inner sections of the deep fiords were usually blocked by landfast ice until late in the season and because there was little incentive to explore them, no one could say how far in from the coast they extended. Left to the imagination, some of these fiords assumed the status of trans–Baffin Island routeways and were portrayed as such on certain admiralty charts. But one whaling voyage did survey two fiords. J. B. Walker produced a sketch map covering all of Eglinton Fiord, which extends almost twenty-five miles inland, and all of Scott Inlet, which penetrates forty-five miles into Baffin Island.[133]

The Hudson Bay whale fishery, dominated by American ships from New England ports, began in 1860. Whalemen soon discovered that Southampton and Coats Islands were not connected, as shown on the admiralty charts, but were in fact two islands separated by a wide, navigable strait. Captain Elnathan B. Fisher notified the admiralty of the chart error and submitted a sketch map showing the true relationship of the landmasses.[134] Foxe Basin rarely attracted whaling ships, but in 1879 Captain John O. Spicer sailed the schooner *Era* to its northern reaches and discovered islands not seen by Parry in 1822 and 1823, now called the Spicer Islands, and Era Island.

American whaling operations in the Pacific whale fishery expanded eastward from Point Barrow in the 1870s and reached the MacKenzie delta in 1889. The principal characteristics of the mainland coast and of Banks and Victoria Islands were by this time well-known. The whalemen were too late to make major discoveries or to solve important geographical problems, but they were able to record environmental information relevant to their whaling operations, such as water depths, currents, ice conditions, locations and nature of harbors, and of course distribution and seasonal migration of bowhead whales. A few enterprising captains explored beyond the limits of the whaling grounds. In 1897 the steam whaler *Jeanette* almost duplicated the 1851 voyage of HMS *Investigator*, ascending the western coast of Banks Island into M'Clure Strait and nearly reaching Mercy Bay.[135]

# A Century of Exploration

European exploration of the North American Arctic during the 1800s involved many contacts with the native people. Aside from occasional hostility from western Eskimos, relations were harmonious. Eskimos, and to some extent Indians, were part of the exploration process. They contributed significantly to the Europeans' "discovery" of lands that had been inhabited for thousands of years. Some served as guides, interpreters, boatmen, sled drivers, or hunters on expeditions. Others drew astonishingly accurate maps of large geographical areas.[136] To those Europeans willing to learn, Eskimos taught the techniques of Arctic living and traveling. They were largely responsible for the success of the long journeys made by Hall, Schwatka, Boas, and Peary, for the survival of the group that drifted on an ice floe for more than six months, for Rae's discovery of the fate of the Franklin expedition, and for many achievements often credited solely to the explorers. For the native people, European contact, however scattered in space and time, provided some opportunity to widen their horizons and enrich their material culture, but contact had drawbacks as well. Unfamiliar beliefs and modes of behavior could disrupt traditional societies, and alien diseases could threaten survival.

In addition to face-to-face contact, Europeans and native people had "indirect contact."[137] Shipwrecks and depots provided the inhabitants of some regions with rich stores of useful materials and articles. The Netsilik Eskimos collected items left in the Gulf of Boothia by the Ross expedition of 1829–33, and they later obtained goods abandoned on Franklin's ships near King William Island in 1848. Archaeological work has revealed that a "tremendous quantity of iron, copper, tin, wood and other materials was incorporated into the Inuit material culture system."[138] Metals replaced slate and bone in some of their implements, and the use of wood increased. Formerly dependent on adjacent groups for a limited supply of iron and wood, the Netsiliks found themselves in control of their own sources, changing the geographical pattern of the trading networks in their favor. A similar process occurred in the western Arctic when the Copper Eskimos of Victoria Island discovered supplies unloaded from McClure's ship *Investigator* on the northern coast of Banks Island in 1851–53 and another cache in Prince of Wales Strait. Over about thirty years they appear to have removed "a ton or more of iron, copper and brass, a couple of thousand tin cans, and large but variable amounts of hard and soft woods (including ash, elm, larch, mahogany, maple, oak, pine, and poplar)."[139] Like the Netsiliks, they were able to trade surplus goods to nearby groups, altering the geographical pattern of exchange.

Occasionally explorers took Eskimos home to visit the United States or Great Britain. Some of these Arctic tourists were treated royally, but others were shamefully exhibited as curiosities, and some, like Minik, "the New York Eskimo," were left to shift for themselves in a strange and alien environment.[140]

Eskimos taught the Europeans effective techniques of ice navigation, wintering, snow travel, and cold-weather survival, skills largely unknown to the British naval officers and men who initiated Arctic exploration in the early 1800s. But the explorers learned mainly by trial and error and passed their knowledge on to those who followed. Methods improved as experience accumulated, as participation in Arctic discovery broadened, and as some of the scientific advances of the nineteenth century provided more effective means of traveling and living in the Arctic environment. The inventions of a canning method to preserve food, of marine steam engines and screw propellers, of breech-loading firearms with percussion-cap ignition and rifled barrels, and of waterproofing processes for fabrics all contributed in some way to the performance of Arctic explorers.

In his study of the period 1829–60, Hugh Wallace distinguished between "heavy" and "light" approaches to Arctic exploration.[141] The former, relying mainly on maritime expeditions, was characterized by large ships and crews, elaborate organization, a hierarchical command structure, and the underlying principle of transporting the familiar home environment into the field. The latter, more common on overland expeditions, was characterized by small parties, simple organization, direct command, small loads, rapid movement, and the underlying principle of incorporating native techniques and hunting for food.

The advantages of the heavy maritime approach were that it enabled commodious winter bases to be sailed into the Arctic, loaded with everything needed for the expedition and carrying a large number of men to participate in local exploration. Ships functioned as vehicles, domiciles, storehouses, command centers, bases for sled and boat journeys, scientific stations, hospitals, and social centers. But large, shipboard expeditions were costly, the movement of ships could be severely restricted by sea ice, and if the ship happened to be wrecked, living off the land was not feasible with so many men concentrated at one place. The advantages of the light approach were that it was comparatively inexpensive, flexible, and fast. A small group of men had a far better chance of securing wildlife food, which obviated the necessity of burdening the party with supplies and improved their hopes of getting out of the Arctic if things went wrong. But the light approach, to be effective, demanded very resourceful men, highly skilled in hunting and traveling and accustomed to hard physical work.

Prevailing social mores strongly influenced attitudes toward exploration. According to Stefansson, the outspoken advocate of living off the land in Eskimo fashion, the British thought that the object of exploration was "to explore properly, and not to evade the hazards of the game through the vulgar subterfuge of going native."[142] The means were regarded as more important than the ends; native methods were not quite acceptable. The admiralty and the influential Royal Geographical Society and Royal Society favored the "heavy approach," with its reassuring framework of naval discipline, its value as a naval training exercise, and its obvious advantages for science. On the other hand, the Hudson's Bay Company, with more than a century of experience in northern regions and its core of tough, practical Scotsmen inured to hardship and frugal daily life, inclined toward the "light approach," as did a number of privately sponsored explorers, who either lacked sufficient funds for large ventures or believed strongly in the efficacy of native techniques. Both approaches, and some others not so easy to categorize, played important roles in Arctic exploration and could boast impressive achievements.

Parry's six-hundred-mile traverse from Baffin Bay to Melville Island in 1819 and Collinson's thirteen-hundred-mile thrust from Point Barrow to Victoria Strait in 1851–53 demonstrated that skillfully handled large ships could efficiently thread the waterways of the Arctic islands when ice conditions were favorable. The extensive sled surveys carried out by the two branches of Belcher's expedition of 1852–54 showed what the large crews of wintering ships could achieve in coastal exploration and mapping. Yet large ships, like jumbo-jets today, had a capacity for disaster that far exceeded that of the small mobile parties. Every man in Franklin's expedition of 1845 died, and Belcher felt it necessary to abandon four of his five ships in the Arctic.

Rae, of the Hudson's Bay Company, championed the light method. "Loping relentlessly like a great Arctic fox across the frozen land," he covered prodigious distances.[143] According to his own calculations, he walked (often with snowshoes) 6,555 miles and boated 6,700 miles in Canada.[144] On one Arctic journey he averaged an astounding 28 miles per day for thirty-nine traveling days, hauling a one-hundred-pound sled for much of the distance.[145] Greely called Rae's trip "one of the most remarkable on record."[146] The key to Rae's method, developed during his fur trade years and his first Arctic expeditions, was to sacrifice weight to gain speed and distance. Instead of carrying tents, as the navy man-hauling parties did, Rae and his men built snow houses each night. They hunted for much of their food instead of carrying it with them, thus benefiting from the antiscorbutic properties of fresh meat as well as from reduced weight. Before 1846, overland expeditions had been tied to subarctic winter bases. Rae was the first to winter above the tree line, using local sea mammal oil as lamp fuel.

Because of the shortness of the navigation season in Arctic waters, wintering became a standard feature of most maritime expeditions. Parry established the precedent in 1819–20. His two ships took up winter quarters together. Heated by coal stoves, they were banked with snow on the outside for insulation. Topmasts, yards, and running rigging were removed and stored ashore along with sails and boats, and a plank-and-canvas housing was erected over the upper decks to make an enclosed space for exercise and work in bad weather. To keep men's bodies and minds busy, Parry and his officers organized theatricals, concerts, a weekly newspaper, daily exercise periods, and inspections. On his second expedition Parry introduced a number of improvements to increase comfort below deck. His ships were insulated inside with layers of cork and had more effective duct systems for distributing hot air to sleeping quarters. Air circulation was improved by replacing bunks with hammocks and cots. Exhaust smoke from the galley stove was led around a tank of snow to obtain drinking water. Lemon juice was stored in casks rather than bottles and was laced with spirits to prevent freezing and bursting, and a greater variety of antiscorbutics was taken. The ships themselves (*Fury* and *Hecla*) were of identical dimensions, with fore and main masts of equal size, so that gear was interchangeable and fewer spare parts needed to be carried.

During the remainder of the century approximately sixty ship-winterings occurred. Their locations, plotted by era, reflect the shift from the search for a Northwest Passage to the Franklin search and finally to the quest for the North Pole. Expeditions that spent the winter ashore in the Arctic were less numerous. Except for Rae, who twice established his own winter base above the tree line by traveling there by boat, others had to rely on ships to deliver them to the intended site and collect them later. They were therefore partly dependent on ships without the comfort of having one to live in. Most shore-based expeditions either arranged passage on whalers and the ships of other expeditions or chartered special vessels for the

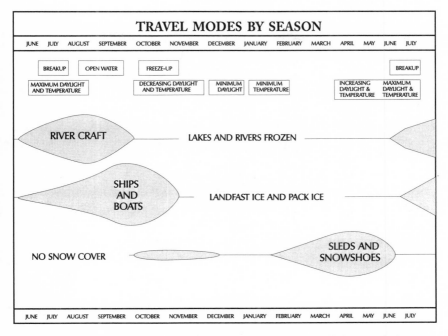

## TRAVEL MODES BY SEASON

| JUNE | JULY | AUGUST | SEPTEMBER | OCTOBER | NOVEMBER | DECEMBER | JANUARY | FEBRUARY | MARCH | APRIL | MAY | JUNE | JULY |

BREAKUP   OPEN WATER   FREEZE-UP   BREAKUP

MAXIMUM DAYLIGHT AND TEMPERATURE   DECREASING DAYLIGHT AND TEMPERATURE   MINIMUM DAYLIGHT   MINIMUM TEMPERATURE   INCREASING DAYLIGHT & TEMPERATURE   MAXIMUM DAYLIGHT & TEMPERATURE

RIVER CRAFT   ———   LAKES AND RIVERS FROZEN   ———

SHIPS AND BOATS   ———   LANDFAST ICE AND PACK ICE   ———

NO SNOW COVER   ———   SLEDS AND SNOWSHOES

| JUNE | JULY | AUGUST | SEPTEMBER | OCTOBER | NOVEMBER | DECEMBER | JANUARY | FEBRUARY | MARCH | APRIL | MAY | JUNE | JULY |

*19.5 Travel Modes by Season. The seasonality of environmental characteristics governed travel methods, confining movement by water to a few months in summer and overland travel to a few months in late winter. Most expeditions, therefore, used a combination of travel methods to extend the duration of their work.*

task. Living in a house ashore eliminated the responsibility of looking after a ship all winter and facilitated scientific programs and missionary work, but the uncertainties of resupply and evacuation were drawbacks, especially at high latitudes, as the unfortunate Greely expedition discovered.

Exploration and searching required mobility. Ships could sail during only three months or less, but other travel modes, sledding in particular, could be used while ships lay icebound. Sledding, however, was also restricted by environmental factors, as its strongest proponent explained: "It can not be commenced until there is sufficient daylight; it cannot be continued after the summer thaw has denuded the land of snow, or rendered the sea-ice unsafe: therefore it can seldom be prosecuted with advantage before the month of April, or later than June."[147] The sledding season, therefore, was approximately as long as the navigation season for ships.

Sleds were of two main types. The first—a flat, toboggan-type that slid over the surface—was most useful on soft, deep snow. The second, on

*19.6 Man-hauled sledding. Much of the exploration of the Franklin era was carried out by small parties traveling on foot from wintering vessels, dragging sleds of camping gear and provisions. The technique persisted into the northern thrust era. Published in Adolphus W. Greely,* Three Years of Arctic Service: An Account of the Lady Franklin Bay Expedition of 1881–84 and the Attainment of the Farthest North *(1886). Courtesy of the Special Collections Division, Babbidge Library, University of Connecticut.*

which the load-bearing floor was elevated above the surface by vertical runners, was most useful on wind-packed snow and on ice. Toboggan sleds were commonly used by the Indians of the northern forests, whereas runner sleds were used by Eskimos on the tundra. For both types, Indians and Eskimos used dog traction. European explorers, however, most often used man-hauling (see figure 19.6).

Beginning with Parry's first two expeditions, naval officers experimented with sleds of various designs and sizes and with both dog and man traction. By 1850 they had committed themselves mainly to man-hauled runner-sleds. These were from eight to thirteen feet in length, about three feet wide, and a foot high. They were led by an officer and dragged by teams of six to ten men. Sleds for long "exploring journeys" averaged about a dozen miles a day, whereas lightly laden sleds on "dispatch journeys" could cover twenty miles. Over time, measures were devised to increase the range of sled travel: depots were set out ahead of the trip along the line of advance and return; auxiliary sleds assisted in the early stages of a trip; and the season was stretched out by leaving earlier (in colder weather) and returning later (over melting snow and ice).

Man-hauling may seem irrational. McClintock, who was responsible for many innovations in sledding technique, was not ignorant of the advantages of dogs; he occasionally used them and admitted that they ate half as much food as men and covered twice the distance.[148] But many of the maritime expeditions operated in uninhabited regions to the west and north of Lancaster Sound; the prospect of purchasing, feeding, and controlling packs of dogs from Greenland or Alaska on board ship was not appealing. In addition, the lack of experience in driving sled dogs appears to have discouraged their use on some expeditions.[149] Regardless of the disadvantages of the man-hauling method, British sledding parties covered almost fifty thousand miles in the Arctic islands.[150]

The men who became most famous for travel by dogsled, including Hall, Schwatka, and Boas, operated within the Eskimo domain, where sledding techniques could be observed, dogs could be purchased, and Eskimos could be hired as drivers, hunters, and guides on voyages. In northwestern Hudson Bay, where the sled voyages of Hall and Schwatka originated, and in Cumberland Sound, where those of Boas began, American and British whalemen had already made good use of Eskimo-operated dog teams in spring whaling operations. Eskimos in these regions were generally centralized near whaling harbors and were accustomed to performing services in return for manufactured goods.

Sledding and other travel in the Arctic climate demanded protective clothing. After 1850 the large maritime expeditions tended to rely on regulation-issue clothing, whereas small, nonmilitary expeditions usually displayed a greater diversity of individual preferences and were more inclined to adopt native garments.[151] In uninhabited regions, traditional Euro-American clothing had to serve, although it was sometimes supplemented by skin parkas, mittens, and boots traded along the coasts of Greenland or Alaska on the incoming voyage. Explorers who wintered within the Eskimo domain, however, were able to observe, assess, and obtain native garments. In addition, sociocultural values influenced clothing choices. According to Barbara Schweger, the British (except for Hudson's Bay Company men) were conservative, maintaining relatively rigid dress codes while generally ignoring the light, comfortable, and thermally superior Eskimo clothing. The Americans were more individualistic, adopting native clothing as a symbol of their enterprise and adaptability on the northern frontier. The Germans, and perhaps the Canadians, were most utilitarian, wearing fur parkas and sealskin boots to accomplish their tasks more efficiently.[152]

Among the shortcomings of European clothing (compared with that of the Eskimos) were its high weight, low insulating value, and close-fitting design, which constricted body movement and thereby promoted fatigue. On wintering ships and at shore bases, mobility was not required; additional layers could be added for warmth. But man-hauling sled trips required movement. A typical sledding outfit was described by McClintock:

> Our system of dressing is thus: soft, warm woolen articles under a cloth which is impenetrable to the wind, and is commonly known as box-cloth; and this again under a suit of closely-textured duck overalls, as snow-repellers.
>
> The feet are wrapped in squares of blanketing, and covered with leather moccasins during extreme cold; or with duck boots, having leather soles, for moderate Arctic cold or for wet.
>
> The entire suit of clothing in wear weighs from 16 lbs. to 21 lbs.[153]

According to Stefansson, a typical Eskimo winter outfit weighed from seven to ten pounds, only half as much.[154]

Another problem was moisture accumulation, not only in clothes but also in tents, ground sheets, ropes, sled sails, knapsacks, sleeping bags, and blankets. On an autumn sled trip during the Nares expedition, the above items together weighed about 107 pounds on departure but 216 pounds on return.[155] The men toiled like plough horses, perspiring freely, then slept in their sodden clothes in the small, clammy tents, releasing moisture into their bedding. They could never get dry. Under the circumstances, wool was probably as good as any other fabric then available.

Just as the Arctic environment affected exploration techniques, explorers influenced the Arctic environment, as outlined in figure 19.7. Given the vastness of the North American Arctic, the comparatively small number of people involved, the mobility of explorers, their reliance on wind and animate energy (rather than fossil fuels) for the propulsion of ships, boats, and sleds, and their tendency to import almost everything they needed rather than utilize the resources of the Arctic, the human impact on the landscape and its biota could not have been great. Nonetheless, because of the treelessness of the tundra, the sparseness of the vegetative cover, and the slow rate of recovery of this cover after disturbance, some tangible signs of nineteenth-century activity are still visible today.

Most obvious are the remains of structures, artifacts, and materials as-

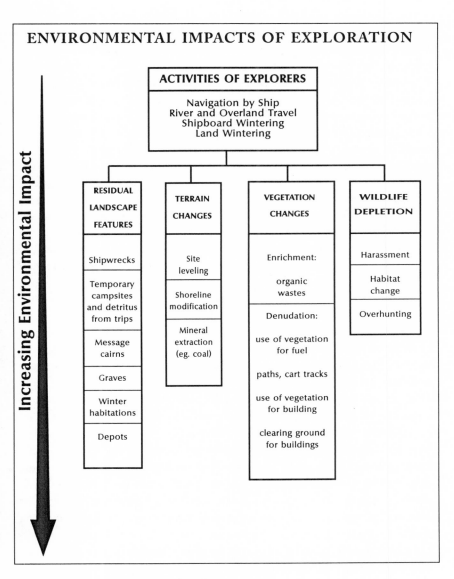

## ENVIRONMENTAL IMPACTS OF EXPLORATION

**ACTIVITIES OF EXPLORERS**

Navigation by Ship
River and Overland Travel
Shipboard Wintering
Land Wintering

**Increasing Environmental Impact**

| RESIDUAL LANDSCAPE FEATURES | TERRAIN CHANGES | VEGETATION CHANGES | WILDLIFE DEPLETION |
|---|---|---|---|
| Shipwrecks | Site leveling | Enrichment: organic wastes | Harassment |
| Temporary campsites and detritus from trips | Shoreline modification | Denudation: | Habitat change |
| Message cairns | Mineral extraction (eg. coal) | use of vegetation for fuel | Overhunting |
| Graves | | paths, cart tracks | |
| Winter habitations | | use of vegetation for building | |
| Depots | | clearing ground for buildings | |

*19.7 Environmental Impacts of Exploration.*

sociated with seasonal habitation sites, depots, and temporary campsites. Wind, water, and ice have contributed to the decay of woods, cloth, and metal in the intervening years, and animal and human scavengers have disturbed the integrity of buildings and dispersed or removed many objects. Yet, these sites still constitute significant elements in the Arctic landscape. Because of their potential use in interpreting and elaborating the history of exploration they are now regarded as a heritage worthy of preservation, but preventing further damage by unscrupulous souvenir-hunters, who use small aircraft and all-terrain vehicles, is difficult.[156]

Less obvious are the remains of abandoned or wrecked ships. Sea ice, tides, and currents are effective scourers of Arctic coasts, and consequently the vessels, intact or dismembered, have probably been transported to unknown submarine localities, forming interesting man-made features on the sea bottom. One sunken wreck, HMS *Breadalbane*, has been found and examined, and attention has now turned to remote-sensing methods of searching for Franklin's ships, the *Erebus* and *Terror*.[157] In those cases where stores were salvaged from stricken ships and deposited ashore, visible relics exist today.

Landscape modification by explorers may have included some local changes to ground contours, stream gradients, and coastline characteristics, resulting from the extraction of coal for heating and the construction of buildings, water supply ponds, and boat ramps. More important, probably, was the impact on vegetation near winter bases. Well-trodden paths persist in the tundra, since trampling denudes the insulating vegetative cover above the permafrost and contributes to a growth of its active (summer melt) layer. The effect of vehicle passage can be severe. The tracks of a narrow-wheeled cart hauled by Parry's men on Melville Island in 1820 were clearly visible to McClintock thirty years later[158] and were almost certainly the faint lines seen by a geologist in the 1950s, a century and a third after the cart had been used.[159] Clearing vegetation to make way for huts, collecting Arctic heather and other shrubs for fuel, and cutting sod to insulate walls undoubtedly altered the character of the ground cover near encampments. The disposal of solid and liquid wastes may have resulted in nutrient enrichment of marine and terrestrial ecosystems, on a local scale. Although the effects of prehistoric Thule Eskimo habitation on soils and vegetation in Hudson Bay have been investigated, the botanical impacts of European explorers have not yet been studied.[160]

Maritime expeditions carried all the food they required with them but supplemented shipboard provisions with the meat of musk oxen, caribou, and a variety of birds. Even the large and well-equipped polar expedition of 1875–76 exploited a dozen species of wildlife.[161] As the concept of living off the land gained adherents, and as evidence mounted that fresh meat prevented scurvy, hunting pressure on the faunal resources increased, particularly on the large, beefy musk ox. Vulnerable in its defensive circle, the musk ox was a common target of expedition hunters from the Barren Grounds to Ellesmere Island. Its numbers may have been significantly reduced, especially in the northernmost regions, where the carrying capacity of tundra pastures was limited and the rate of recovery of animal populations low. The Nares expedition of 1875–76 killed at least sixty-three musk oxen on Ellesmere Island.[162] The expedition's naturalist, Henry Feilden, recognized the danger: "After an invasion such as ours, when every animal obtainable was slaughtered for food, it must take some years to stock the ground."[163] Two decades later the expeditions of Sverdrup and Peary each killed about two hundred musk oxen in the same region.[164] Large catches were also recorded on Melville and King William Islands.

As noted earlier, these "invasions" had various motivations over the years. If one excludes the voyages of whalers, Hudson's Bay Company supply ships, and American revenue vessels, approximately 110 expeditions journeyed to the Arctic region between northwestern Alaska and northern Labrador during the 1800s.[165] Each of these has been assigned to one of seven types, according to what is perceived as its primary purpose, and the expeditions, thus classified, have been graphed by decade (see figure 19.8). Despite obvious problems of categorizing the expeditions, the results indicate some general patterns.

The frequency of expeditions increased during the first half of the century to a peak in 1850–60, fell immediately to a very low level, then rose again to a second peak in 1890–1900. The year 1860 is the boundary between the two similar patterns, each of which occupied four to five decades. The two peak decades, though nearly identical in magnitude, show interesting contrasts in type of exploration. The first consisted almost entirely of Franklin search expeditions, whereas the second included five different types of expeditions.

Franklin's disappearance created the single most important motive for dispatching expeditions to the North American Arctic in the 1800s; nearly a third of all expeditions were organized for this purpose, concentrated around midcentury. Discovery of new lands, waterways, and geographical features constituted the second most important motive, accounting for another quarter of all expeditions; these were relatively evenly distributed

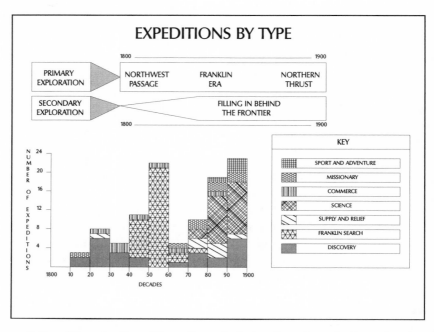

*19.8 Expeditions by Type. The pattern of nineteenth-century Arctic exploration contains two peaks, the first provided by the Franklin search and the second by a diversity of motivations.*

throughout most decades. Voyages for the supply or relief of parties in the field, scientific research, commerce, mission work, or sport hunting make up the remainder; expeditions with these diverse motives increased in number noticeably after 1860.

More than 60 percent of the expeditions originated in Great Britain and approximately 20 percent in the United States. About 60 percent were maritime, comprising more than eighty ship voyages and involving at least sixty individual vessels. Of these seaborne expeditions, 80 percent entered the Arctic by the Atlantic approach, hardly surprising considering their points of origin in Europe and the eastern United States. Of all the expeditions, both maritime and overland, approximately 40 percent passed one or more winters in the Arctic.

The results of all these expeditions are evident in the 1896 edition of Arrowsmith's "Map of the Countries Round the North Pole." Examining this map in conjunction with the 1818 edition shows the extent to which European knowledge of the distribution of Arctic lands and seas improved dur-

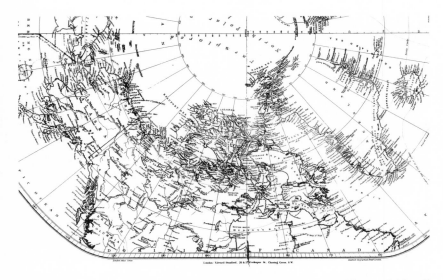

*19.9 "Map of Countries Round the North Pole" (Aaron Arrowsmith, 1896). Detail from* Map of Countries Round the North Pole, *published in* Stanford's London Atlas of Universal Geography *(1896), plate 4. The increase in geographical knowledge of the Arctic during the nineteenth century is illustrated in this Arrowsmith product. Courtesy of the Cartographic and Architectural Archives Division, National Archives of Canada, NMC 8632.*

ing the course of the nineteenth century. Compared with the crude and incomplete 1818 map, the 1896 version was a far more thorough and complete model of the Arctic world. The drainage pattern of northern Canada and Alaska, only partly depicted on the 1818 map, is now reasonably complete. The tree line—the boundary between subarctic forests and Arctic tundra— is now a feature of the map. The continent's northern coast west of Hudson Bay, unknown in 1818 except for the mouths of two rivers, is shown. Baffin Island, of indefinite extent on the earlier map, is now delineated. The first and second tiers of Arctic islands north of the mainland, not even suggested in 1818, are mapped. The coast of Baffin Bay, once a vague, discontinuous outline, is at last firm and full of detail. Beyond Baffin Bay, where nothing but blank space existed before, a series of waterways stretches northward between Greenland and Ellesmere Island for five hundred miles.

The 1896 map represents the culmination of a century of geographical problem-solving. The complex distribution of land and sea had resulted inevitably in a number of questions and misconceptions, some of them controversial and all of them requiring further exploration for their resolution during the nineteenth century: the existence of Ross's Croker Mountains in Lancaster Sound and Parry's polar sea within the Arctic islands; the relationship between Banks, Prince Albert, Wollaston, and Victoria Lands; the insularity of Somerset and King William Islands; the peninsularity of Melville and Boothia Peninsulas; the navigability of Peel Sound; the connection between Pond Inlet and Navy Board Inlet. Woven into the fabric of exploration were the speculative geographical theories based on dubious evidence and the implausible objectives sought more for the glory of the discovery than for any practical benefits: the ice-free Arctic Ocean; the North Pole; the Northwest Passage. They all influenced the direction, intensity, and character of the exploration process.

Not all of North America's Arctic coasts were explored by 1900. Although the frontier of the world known to Europeans had advanced from Labrador, Hudson Bay, and northwestern Alaska to the northernmost tip of Ellesmere Island, there was still unexplored territory in the northwestern sector of the Queen Elizabeth Islands. But at the close of the year 1899, Sverdrup's expedition was wintering in Jones Sound, on the brink of extensive discoveries west of Ellesmere Island, and in another dozen years, Stefansson and the Canadian Arctic Expedition would begin to fill in additional details farther west. Their research would add to the map the most inaccessible part of the Canadian Arctic, finally completing the general outline of North America and its adjacent islands.

But behind the frontier, many smaller geographical details required confirmation, correction, or addition. On the 1896 Arrowsmith map, parts of the western coast of Baffin Island and the northeastern coast of Victoria Island are depicted by dotted lines, their positions doubtful. The northwestern extremity of Baffin Island is incorrectly shown as an island, and many fiords are still of indefinite extent. In Foxe Basin the map fails to show Prince Charles Island and two smaller islands nearby, which together cover more than six thousand square miles; these islands were not discovered until the era of aerial photography following the Second World War.[166]

Although by 1900 the principal geographical features of the North American Arctic had been revealed, the Barren Grounds, the Arctic islands, and the Alaskan North Slope were as vast and wild as ever and, due to the introduction of alien diseases, more thinly populated than in the previous century.[167] Like ocean vessels furrowing the surface of the sea, the

Euro-Americans had come and gone, passing here and there, seldom re-tracing the same line, their tracks fading gradually away like ships' wakes. After probing, searching, and mapping, each expedition had departed, "leaving weathered broken bones, and a long-forgotten lonely cairn of stones."[168]

Before leaving in 1910 for Antarctica, where he and his companions would die using the outdated British Arctic method of man-hauled sled-ding, Robert Falcon Scott wrote a short introduction to a reprint edition of the account of the first overland voyage by Franklin—"a great traveller and a gallant man." Scott referred to the "regions where for ninety years season has succeeded season without change—where few have passed since his day and Nature alone holds sway."[169] The Arctic had not been "conquered" (as so many book titles declare) but merely visited and superficially ob-served. Its geography, known to Eskimo cultures for approximately four thousand years, had at last entered, in crude form, the sphere of knowl-edge of the "civilized" world.

# 20 / The Military Explorers of the American West, 1838–1860

VINCENT PONKO JR.

Exploration and discovery are often integrally intertwined with the spirit of the period in which they occur. For instance, during the mid-1800s, a sense of mission to extend the influence of the United States and its value system was a pervasive factor in the outlook of U.S. government officials, explorers, and the American people. Whether or not it was called "Manifest Destiny," this perception that the United States would and should be a continental nation that was obligated to push its ideals abroad heavily conditioned the objectives and courses of official government exploration from the late 1830s to the beginning of the Civil War.

Previously, the exploration of what is now the western United States—and the extension of American exploring activities to foreign shores in the name of "practical science"—had been largely a mechanism for private citizens of the Republic to expand their utilization of the rich resource base of the North American continent. With the exception of Jeffersonian exploration, in which expeditions like that of Meriwether Lewis and William Clark engaged in government-sponsored investigations, most exploration had been dominated by the commercial interests of the fur trade of the Rocky Mountains and farther West. The explorations of Manuel Lisa's men, of the Astorians, of William Henry Ashley's fur brigades, and of the largely unknown "free trappers" between 1806 and 1842 had not been primarily motivated by national policy (although that policy may ultimately have been shaped by those explorations). By the end of the fur trade era, however, private and commercial interests gave way to national objectives, in particular three desires: to increase the international scientific and philosophical significance of the Republic in the Americas and elsewhere through the application of Humboldtean rather than Enlightenment principles of scientific exploration; to expand American political and economic influence and control not just over the entire continent as far as the Pacific but to island

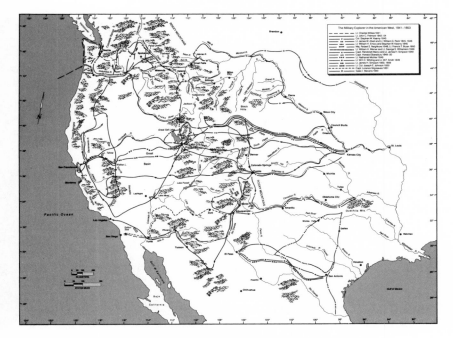

*Map 20.1 The Military Explorer in the American West, 1841–1853.*

groups beyond; and to learn about the resource base of the continental interior not just for the immediate entrepreneurial benefits of the fur trade
but for the longer-range objectives of an expanding agricultural and industrial civilization.

This discussion of military exploration between the end of the fur trade
and the beginning of the Civil War is directed primarily to exploration designed to satisfy the latter two desires. But the beginning of military exploration by the U.S. government during this period was grounded more
firmly in the first desire, that of "showing the flag"—not just of the political
entity of the United States but also of American science—in faraway
places. One aspect of this belief in the worthiness of the transmittal of U.S.
values to other regions was philosophical. Its proponents professed—in a
teleological sense—that all peoples could benefit from the application of
"the American way" to their political and spiritual lives. Although Americans did not, as the British did, refer to their sense of responsibility to
spread the gospel of modern industrial political economy as "the white
man's burden," they felt their obligation no less assiduously than did their

British brethren. A second, more practical aspect of the urge to spread American ways throughout North America and abroad held that those who accepted the supremacy of Western or American economic and political values would be able to engage in economic activity that could make them wealthy. The first full-scale official governmental operation designed with both the philosophical and the practical aspects of exploratory science in the service of the Republic and—by extension—the rest of the world was the U.S. Exploring Expedition or, as it is usually called, "the Wilkes Expedition," named after the U.S. naval officer who served as its commander.[1] Although it began and ended before the first major military explorations of the continental interior, the Wilkes Expedition set the tone for much of the exploration that followed.

## The U.S. Exploring Expedition, 1838–1842

In 1836 Congress appropriated $300,000 for an exploration of the Antarctic region and the area of the Pacific Ocean basin in which the United States had exhibited a commercial interest. The purpose of the expedition was to make hydrographic surveys, chart unknown navigational dangers, and add to scientific knowledge through astronomical observations and the collection of specimens. Captain Thomas ap Catesby was named the commander, with five vessels placed under his command: the frigate USS *Macedonian*, the brigs *Pioneer* and *Consort*, the schooner *Pilot*, and the provision ship *Relief*. After the chosen commander became dissatisfied with his position and requested to be relieved of his command, Lieutenant Charles Wilkes, U.S.N., who had traveled to England to buy instruments for the trip, was named to replace him. The second-in-command was Lieutenant William Hudson, who held two years seniority over Wilkes but who agreed to accept the post on the understanding that the trip was to be purely civil and not military. To clarify this situation, the secretary of the navy, Mahlon Dickson, issued an order stating that the expedition was to be entirely scientific, divested of all military character, and that it would not return to the United States even if the nation became involved in war. The ships originally assigned to the expedition were replaced by the sloop of war USS *Vincennes*, the sloop of war USS *Peacock*, the brig *Porpoise*, two former New York pilot boats, the *Flying Fish* and the *Sea Gull*, and the storeship, the USS *Relief*. After months of preparation that included enticing scientists to accompany the expedition and loading the materials needed for scientific work, the squadron sailed from Norfolk on 19 August 1838.

In the months that followed, Wilkes and his personnel, including the scientists, explored and made notes on the region of Tierra del Fuego and the Strait of Magellan. They then sailed farther south toward what is now called Palmer Peninsula and continued onward to the South Shetlands. In this endeavor, the *Peacock* reached 68°8′ south latitude, 95°44′ west longitude on 25 March 1839, while the *Flying Fish* reported reaching 70° south latitude. During this investigation of the water to the south of South America, the *Sea Gull* became separated from the other ships and was never seen again. The other ships changed their area of operations to the central portions of the Pacific and investigated the Tuamotu Archipelago, the Society Islands, Samoa, the Fijis, New Hebrides, and New Caledonia. By the first week of December 1839, they were in harbor at Sydney, Australia.

On 25 December 1839 Wilkes and his scientists, officers, and crew again sailed their ships southward to try to reach the coastline of Antarctica. The voyage was dangerous, and some ships had to turn back, but on 30 January 1840 Wilkes entered in his journal that the rim of the Antarctic continent had been sighted. Wilkes sailed along this Antarctic coastline until 21 February 1840, even sending some men to land on ice islands in which some rocks were embedded. Both the *Peacock* and the *Porpoise* also thought they had reached the edge of Antarctica, but conditions were so poor that exploration soon gave way to the task of survival. Almost from the beginning of the journey, the job of keeping the *Flying Fish* afloat had occupied the crew and commander's attention, rather than scientific investigation or support for the other vessels in the fleet. Running short of supplies and matériel, Wilkes and his command, on 21 February, had to turn back toward Australia and New Zealand.

After these adventures in the waters off Antarctica, the fleet—except for the *Peacock*, which was being repaired at Sydney and would join the squadron later—met in the Bay of Islands, part of North Island, New Zealand. From here the ships sailed for the Fiji Islands, where survey work, exploration, and scientific endeavors were conducted from May to August. On 11 August the squadron sailed for the Hawaiian or "Sandwich" island group, and by 7 October it had reformed at Honolulu. While the ships were given a general overhaul, the personnel of the expedition found time for rest and relaxation (the first, but not the last, U.S. Navy squadron to utilize Hawaii for that purpose), as well as for the preparation of charts based on the data collected thus far. By mid-November 1840, the work of surveying and exploration was resumed, with individual ships being given different areas to investigate.

On 5 April the *Vincennes* and the *Porpoise* sailed to the northwestern coast of North America. The two ships arrived at the mouth of the Columbia River on 28 April 1841, but because of turbulent conditions across the bar that posed a barrier to the entrance to the river, Wilkes decided to shift exploring activities northward toward the Strait of Juan de Fuca. On 1 May the ships entered the strait. Fog and the danger of running aground on unknown rocks confronted them as they proceeded. The two ships reached Port Discovery—"forty-nine years to the day after Vancouver's arrival"[2]— and, using the chart prepared by George Vancouver, continued into Puget Sound until they reached the southern end of the Hudson Bay's Company port of Fort Nisqually. After being escorted into the harbor by one of the Hudson's Bay Company's sidewheel steamers, the officers and men of the *Vincennes* and *Porpoise* enjoyed the cordiality of the inhabitants of Fort Nisqually and were awed by the majestic surroundings, especially the large trees.

Near Fort Nisqually, Commander Wilkes set up an observatory and dispatched the *Porpoise* to survey Admiralty Inlet, on the eastern end of Puget Sound, while a crew in four boats from the *Vincennes* surveyed Hood's Canal and the coast northward as far as the Fraser River, where they were to meet the *Porpoise*. Although these efforts merely duplicated those of Vancouver two generations earlier, they were the first official U.S. hydrographical surveys of these waters. True to his mission to investigate areas of interest to the United States politically and economically, Wilkes also organized overland expeditions. Lieutenant George Johnson was placed in command of one exploring party, which consisted of Charles Pickering, William Dunlop Brackenridge, T. W. Waldron (the captain's clerk of the *Porpoise*), Sergeant Albert Stearns of the marines, and two crew members. They were to travel east across the Cascade Mountains north of Mount Rainier, eastward to Fort Colville on the Columbia (close to the Columbia's union with Clark's Fork River in the Flathead country), and south to Fort Walla, near the junction of the Columbia and Snake Rivers. They were to return following the Yakima River and cross the mountains again to the coast.

Wilkes commanded another overland trip, taking Joseph Drayton, Purser W. W. Waldron, and a Canadian guide and proceeding to the Methodist mission at Fort Clatsop and thence to the Hudson's Bay Company post at

Fort Vancouver, opposite the entry of the Willamette River into the Columbia where Portland, Oregon, now stands. Headquartered at Fort Vancouver was the governor of all the posts of the Hudson's Bay Company in the West, Dr. John McLoughlin. As the governor had done with other visitors and was to do with many more (including the American migrants who would eventually wrest control of "Oregon Country" from Britain and the Hudson's Bay Company), McLoughlin greeted Wilkes and his party warmly. He furnished Wilkes and Drayton with a commodious bateau, lined with mats for comfort, as well as nine men to act as rowers and miscellaneous equipment to facilitate further travels.

Bolstered by this equipment, Wilkes set out to investigate the Willamette River, noted by previous visitors as an optimum site for the location of an American agricultural colony. Indeed, on his journey Wilkes encountered numerous U.S. settlers who hoped that Wilkes was about to establish the sovereignty of the United States over the region and suppress the rule of the British. Wilkes dissuaded them of this hope and pointed out that until the U.S. government decided to absorb the region into its system, they would be wise not to antagonize the British. Wilkes had closed the loop between official U.S. government exploration and the leading edge of the American migration to the Pacific; as so often happened in American exploration, settlers had preceded explorers. On 17 June Wilkes, having satisfied himself of the size and navigability of the Columbia River and its potential for American access to the interior, started his return to Fort Nisqually and sent orders for the *Peacock* and *Flying Fish* to go to Fort George, the Hudson's Bay Company post at the mouth of the Columbia that had been—until the War of 1812—Astoria, the first American-established settlement on Pacific shores.

In the meantime, the party led by Lieutenant Johnson found its journey into the interior of the Columbian Plateau to be less than pleasant. The arid interior was far different from the lush rain-forest region of the coast; Johnson and his men had to battle mosquitoes and rattlesnakes, purchase provisions from the Indians, swim their horses across the Yakima, and ferry their supplies over the river on "gum elastic bolsters."[3] Finally, they reached the Columbia and followed its banks up to Fort Okanogon, reaching Fort Colville on 15 June. From here they persuaded Indians to ferry them across the Snake River, and moving rapidly—considering they were sailors rather than experienced overland explorers—they arrived at Fort Walla Walla, where they were met by Dr. Marcus Whitman, the American missionary who had pioneered his country's settlement of Oregon Country. During this journey they narrowly avoided a quarrel with some Indians, but otherwise their travels were bothered only by the barren country, dotted with wormwood bushes and tufts of grass, along the Yakima and then the Spipen Rivers. After crossing the mountains again, they reached Fort Nisqually on 15 July, sixty days after their departure. They had traveled through country that was well-known to members of the American fur trade but that had not been visited by U.S. government explorers on an official mission.

While waiting for news of the *Flying Fish* and the *Peacock*, the *Vincennes*, under Henry Eld, was dispatched to survey Gray's Harbor at the mouth of the Chehalis River. The men worked in foul weather in an area of mudflats. To compound their problems, the provisions they had brought with them ran out, and by mid-August they were subsisting on berries, clams, and dead fish washed ashore. With the help of friendly Indians, however, they completed the survey in twenty-four days and traveled back toward Fort George.

Meanwhile, on 17 July, as the *Peacock* crew had prepared to explore and chart the mouth of the Columbia, the ship had attempted to beat the current flowing from the river. Captain Hudson had hoped to gain the aid of the flood tide to cross the bar and enter the river while keeping strict watch for any dangers from shoal water. His preventive measures, however, proved inadequate. The *Peacock* hit the bar and, despite heroic measures, could not be refloated. The ship had to be abandoned. All hands were saved, as were Hudson's journal and the journals of other officers as well as the surveys, the chronometers, a few relics of the crew, and some of the sketches of Alfred T. Agate, the botanical draughtsman. Everything else aboard, including the rest of the hard-earned collection of more than a year of exploration, was lost. As the *Peacock* gradually broke apart, the fragments drifted into deeper water and were lost forever.

In the ship's gig, the officers and crew of the *Peacock* reached Baker's Bay, inside the Columbian estuary. At about the same time, the *Flying Fish* successfully passed through a channel in the bar and anchored in the cove of Baker's Bay. With the help of some members of the American Methodist mission at Point Adams and of James Birnie, the agent of the Hudson's Bay Company at Fort George, the men of the *Peacock* began to establish camp on shore. Even the Indians helped, providing venison and fresh salmon. Near the site of John Jacob Astor's old fort, two miles from the Fort Clatsop of Lewis and Clark, "Peacockville" was established with huts of pine branches and wigwams of old planks. Even Birnie's henhouse was transformed into a living place for the purser of the *Peacock*, William Spieden. The novelty of their new life and the beauty of the primeval forests and sylvan glades, however, could not counteract the idleness that soon confronted the men. Although conditions were favorable and boats were available, only two boats were used in surveying while the *Flying Fish* traced the channel through the bar. Except for some forty men who helped the Hudson's Bay Company harvest its crops, most of the crew of the lost ship remained unproductive for nearly three weeks.

When Wilkes and the *Vincennes* arrived off the mouth of the Columbia, the commander decided not to try to negotiate passage across the bar. After some bargaining with an American merchantman near the Columbia's mouth, he purchased the *Thomas W. Perkins*, which was quickly renamed the *Oregon*, as a replacement for the *Peacock* and started to think of heading for San Francisco. Before departing, however, Wilkes selected several men— Lieutenant George Foster Emmons, midshipman Henry Eld, George M. Colvocoresses, Brackenridge, Agate, botanist William Rich, geologist James Dwight Dana, artist Titian Ramsay Peale, and Sergeant Stearns—for an overland trip to San Francisco, still a very small Mexican mission-presidio. Their objective was simple: to determine if some river other than the Columbia entered the Pacific and made a substantial harbor north of San Francisco Bay (which was, after all, still within Mexican territory). At 2:00 P.M. on 7 September 1841 the party started on its journey. Besides the men of the U.S. Exploring Expedition, the group included various hunters, trappers, coureurs de bois with their squaws, and several families on their way to California, a total of thirty-nine persons. For transport they had eighty horses loaded with stores, powder and ball, and other materials. Altogether it was an impressive caravan.

The trail the party followed south from the Columbia crossed a hilly prairie charred by a recent grass fire, which forced them to ford Tongue Creek and to travel through the Calapuya Hills into the Elk Mountains and the Umpqua area. This part of the trip offered mostly nuisances, except that one day the group was menaced by a grizzly bear. Although several men shot at the bear and a number of rifle balls penetrated its body, the bear did not fall down dead. Emmons was disappointed because he had hoped to preserve the skin. Much like Lewis forty years earlier on the upper Missouri, Emmons recorded his impressions of the animal: "Among all the animals I have ever seen, I do not think that I have witnessed so formidable an enemy."[4] On 18 September the group left the Umpqua territory, continually confronted by lines of grass fires that drove away game and burned forage needed by the horses. In addition, the fires exposed small stones that lamed any unshod horses, forcing the expedition to stop from time to time so that shoes could be nailed on various horses.

Another problem, potentially more serious, was the hostility of the Indians, for whom the Emmons party represented one more incursion into native territory and a potential further disruption of native life. The Indians of the region had already fought a number of conflicts with white invaders and were not disposed to suffer these unwanted intrusions lightly. Pitched battles were avoided, but the Indians hampered the march by placing obstacles on the trail and continually menacing the group. On 22 September the party reached the pass through the Umpquas and discovered that the pack holding Peale's belongings, including his "Oregon Journal," drawing instruments, and sketchbooks, had broken and the material was lost. The travelers stopped for a day to look for Peale's belongings, but they were unsuccessful and started southward again on 24 September. On 25 September the party crossed the Rogue River and continued the journey. By 29 September they had crossed the forty-second parallel (the boundary line between Mexican territory to the south and jointly claimed British and American territory to the north) and caught the first sight of snow-topped Mount Shasta. The explorers found the territory to be full of curiosities and freaks of nature. They encountered huge pine trees and cones, a soda spring with iron-loaded water, another spring with with "Sulphurated hydrogen," a root that—when mashed—could be used as a soap, and antelope.[5]

On 2 October the travelers reached Destruction River in the shadow of Mount Shasta. They followed this waterway to the Sacramento River, through a country rich in plants hitherto unknown to botany and supporting game such as elk, antelopes, deer, and wild cattle, as well as the grizzly bear. Continuing along the banks of the Sacramento, the group reached the Feather River on 18 October, unfortunately at a spot littered with hundreds of skeletons, the remnants of an Indian village that had been wiped out by the "tertian fever" (probably smallpox). In spite of this horrible sight and the weariness of both horses and people, the explorers pushed on to the American River, where they met Captain John A. Sutter, who furnished a boat for the sick. On 23 October the party reached San Francisco Bay, and the naval personnel reported to Wilkes aboard the *Vincennes* at Sausalito, or Whaler's Harbor as it was called. Wilkes commended Emmons on the conduct of the expedition, on which much government policy

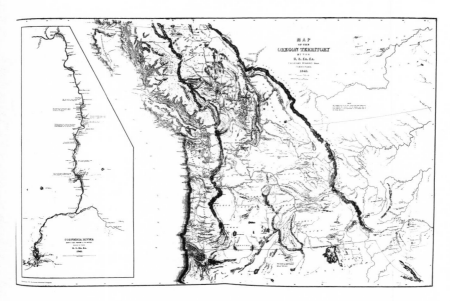

20.1 *Detail from map of the Pacific Northwest coastal region (Charles Wilkes, 1841). This map is typical of the fine cartographic productions of the U.S. Exploring Expedition, led by Wilkes. Courtesy of the Library of Congress.*

and exploration would later be grounded. With the return of Emmons and his party, Wilkes's work was done; on 31 October 1841 the squadron sailed for Hawaii on the first leg of the journey home. After conducting some exploring and scientific work en route, the *Vincennes* arrived in New York on 10 June 1842. The *Oregon* entered the harbor on 29 June and the *Porpoise* on 2 July 1842. The *Flying Fish* had been sold at Singapore for $3,700.

The U.S. Exploring Expedition, or the Wilkes Expedition, signified the official entry of American explorers into the quest for global scientific knowledge. Wilkes had done his job well; his explorations added immeasurably to science, and his investigations of the Pacific Northwest helped to convince the government of the value of Puget Sound, rather than the Columbia River, as America's window to the Pacific. Such convincing would play an important role in the upcoming diplomatic maneuvering over the ownership of Oregon Country. The U.S. Navy would continue to engage in exploration, although not with the same global scope as the U.S. Exploring Expedition. The army would now also enter the field of exploration on a broad scale—both diplomatic and scientific—expanding governmental influence to the continental interior of North America and preparing the way for the increased utilization of the continent's resources by an expansive and expanding population.

## The U.S. Army Corps of Topographical Engineers, 1838–1844

It is not surprising that the factions that favored furthering the mission of the United States, particularly in its trading capacity, would look to the army for help. In the same way that the navy selected special ships, commanders, and crews for its exploring voyages, those interested in overland expansion created special agencies for their purpose. These organizations could operate as official arms of the U.S. government while providing a cloak for the activities of an individual who, while serving his country's interests, sought fame and fortune for himself. Vanity and self-enrichment were present, but they were to prove crucial to the continued expansion of both scientific knowledge and an American population.[6]

One of these created agencies was the U.S. Army Corps of Topographical Engineers, officially founded on 7 July 1838; commanding the Corps for most of its existence was Colonel John J. Abert.[7] The organization became active in the trans-Mississippi West at just about the time the naval squadron under the command of Wilkes was voyaging in the South Pacific and the Arctic and along the northwestern coast of the United States. And the Corps had, as its counterpart to Wilkes, the first major official U.S. government explorer of the continental interior since Stephen Long: Lieutenant John C. Frémont.[8]

Frémont, an advocate of the scientific method of exploration, was hired in 1838 as an assistant to Joseph Nicholas Nicollet, the explorer-cartographer who surveyed the upper hydrographical basin of the Mississippi River. Nicollet's surveys were the first undertaken by the U.S. Army Corps of Topographical Engineers and represented the beginning of the scientific mapping techniques that were to be used by the Corps from Nicollet on. Trained in Europe as a scientist, Nicollet began his surveys from a carefully selected departure point and immersed himself in intricate work involving thousands of astronomical observations and other topographical data for the preparation of maps. He also used the barometer for the measurement of altitude.[9] His expeditions of 1838 and 1839, with the young army officer

Frémont accompanying, were landmarks in scientific exploration and set the pattern for much of Frémont's own work of the 1840s.[10]

On his 1838 expedition, Nicollet covered territory well-known (if not mapped accurately) to the fur trade for over a century. Leaving from Fort Snelling, on the Mississippi, Nicollet and his party traveled across the Coteau du Missouri to the Saint Peter's River and into the Pipestone region, used for thousands of years by native peoples as a quarry for the prized red pipestone. From the quarry he crossed the Big Sioux River but resisted the urge to go into the valley of the James River. When he returned to Fort Snelling, he had covered over one thousand miles of the upper Mississippi Basin in about two months. He had taken numerous astronomical observations, from which he and Frémont would begin compiling a map of the Mississippi's hydrographical basin, the map that was Nicollet's chief contribution to science.

After a winter in St. Louis, Nicollet and Frémont returned to the Coteau du Missouri area west of the main Mississippi Valley and traveled up the James River to the Devil's Lake region, their northernmost point. From here they turned south to the edge of the Coteau and, beyond, to the "vast region of prairies," which they crossed to the Missouri River. They traveled up the Missouri as far as Fort Pierre and then struck out eastward up the Couteau. As they passed the divide between the Missouri and the James River, Nicollet first began thinking of the entire region as not just a land of hills and valleys but as a "basin" within which all the water ultimately flowed to a single outlet—the Gulf of Mexico via the Mississippi River. (This revolutionary geographical conception was to prove critical in Frémont's assessment of the Great Basin between the Rockies and the Sierra Nevada range during his journey of 1843–44.) By the end of 1839, Nicollet and Frémont were back in St. Louis, where they began work on the map that Gouverneur Kemble Warren—an outstanding cartographer in his own right—would refer to as "one of the most important contributions ever made to American geography."[11]

Frémont learned the trade from Nicollet and followed in his footsteps as far as his approach to measurement and mapping was concerned. Frémont had also learned a great deal about the management of an exploratory expedition far from civilization, and although he did not always follow Nicollet's example, his experience with the French scientist proved invaluable during Frémont's first two expeditions. Frémont, however, also had a love of adventure in the West. Enthralled by the way of life in the wilderness, he gained the respect of the "mountain men," who trapped beaver, traded

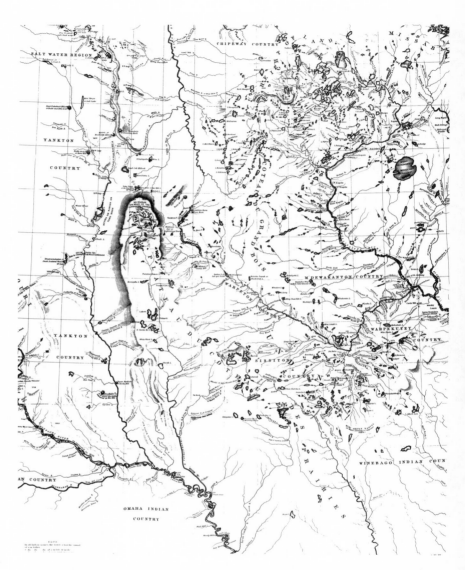

20.2 "Hydrographical Basin of the Upper Mississippi River" (J. N. Nicollet, 1840).
Nicollet's map not only is an excellent example of the cartographer's art in the 1830s
but also is one of the first American-produced maps to correctly illustrate the nature
of hydrographical or drainage basins. Collection of John L. Allen.

with the Indians, and sought adventure or solitude for its own sake. From these precursors of the government explorer and the settler in the West, Frémont learned as much—if not more—about his trade as explorer as he did from his more formal instruction with Nicollet.

Frémont believed in the mission to "civilize" the western regions and bring them under the control of the United States; in this regard, he was supported by a political mentor, Senator Thomas Hart Benton of Missouri, perhaps the country's most influential spokesman for Manifest Destiny. Benton, who also became Frémont's father-in-law after the explorer's marriage to Jessie Benton, cleared the political path for Frémont in many instances. It is often not clear whether Frémont, in his travels, was following the orders of his military superiors or acting according to some grand design of Benton and his coterie.

Frémont's first expedition into the western interior as a commissioned officer and member of the U.S. Army Corps of Topographical Engineers was undertaken and completed in the summer of 1842. Frémont left Washington DC on 2 May 1842 and arrived in St. Louis by 22 May. He was ordered to chart the eastern portion of the trail that had been used by St. Louis merchants to reach the fur-trapping regions of the central Rocky Mountains and that was now being used by American migrants to reach Oregon Country. Before departing St. Louis for the Rocky Mountains, Frémont hired the German draftsman Charles Preuss as mapmaker, the great fur trapper Kit Carson as a guide, and various other personnel, including other mountain men, who, it seemed, were often eager to rally to Frémont's service. Beyond his official purpose of charting the eastern half of what was becoming known as "the Oregon Trail," Frémont intended to make a well-publicized journey to the South Pass area of the Rocky Mountains, to support the belief that such a "popular" venture (meaning one that would receive considerable space in newspapers) would advance the cause of winning Oregon Country for the United States, an objective Benton and his colleagues favored.

On 10 June 1842 Frémont's party left Chouteau Station on the Missouri River west of St. Louis and headed north toward the Platte River and the Rocky Mountains. He followed the Platte to its division into north and south forks (at present North Platte, Nebraska), and then, deviating from the immigrant trail that followed the North Platte, he headed up the South Platte to the Front Range of the Colorado Rockies. From near present Fort Collins, Colorado, he traveled northward along the Front Range (which becomes the Laramie Range in Wyoming) to Fort Laramie, Wyoming.

From here he followed the now well-marked immigrant or Oregon Trail up the North Platte and its tributary, the Sweetwater River, to the famed South Pass across the continental divide. As he traveled, Frémont made calculations to trace his path, including a calculation on the Little Sandy River some eight miles from the South Pass around the southern end of the Wind River range of the Rocky Mountains in west-central Wyoming. This pass, used extensively as a gateway to the Northwest, had been well-known to western travelers since its rediscovery by Jedediah Smith in 1824. According to figures derived from a U.S. Geological Survey cited by the historian Hiram Martin Chittenden in 1901, Frémont was only three miles off in his estimate of the distance from his location on the Little Sandy River to Kansas City.[12] Frémont was not impressed with the famous South Pass (the ascent and the descent were so gradual, he noted, that one could scarcely tell when one had crossed the continental divide), but in his reports and later writings, he did praise the grandeur of the Wind River Mountains. Unfortunately, no altitude readings by barometer could be made, presumably because the barometer had been broken.

After an ascent to the top of a mountain that Frémont believed to be the highest peak (and that he modestly named after himself) in the Wind River Range, Frémont began his trip home. On the way he lost his natural science collections in a boating accident on the Sweetwater River, but on 2 March 1843 his report, after passing through the Topographical Bureau, was placed before the Senate. The report consisted of a narrative by Frémont, a catalog by John Torrey of what plant specimens had survived, a table of astronomical data that included sixty-eight observations for longitude and latitude, six hundred meteorological readings, a brief geological description by James Dwight Dana of Yale College, and a map of the area from Fort Laramie to the Wind River Mountains—the first accurate map of the eastern portion of the Oregon Trail.

As a scientific and mapmaking expedition, Frémont's first trip was not a huge success, having covered terrain long familiar to the fur trader. What it lacked in this area, however, was more than compensated by the symbolism of the journey. The U.S. government had surveyed the first leg of the immigrant trail to Oregon, thus sanctioning that migration. Moreover, Frémont made up for the lack of scientific achievements by arguing for continued exploration and activity in the trans-Mississippi West. As William Goetzmann has noted, Frémont stimulated both the government official and the common person to seek a westward destiny.[13]

On his way to the Wind River Range, Frémont had encountered at least

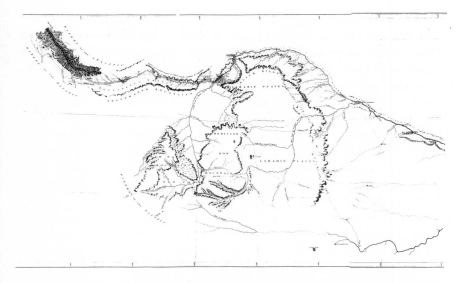

20.3 *"Map to Illustrate an Exploration of the Country, lying between the Missouri River and the Rocky Mountains" (John C. Frémont and Charles Preuss, 1842). Produced by the cartographer Preuss from field sketches by Frémont, this map was the first to accurately portray that portion of the Oregon Trail that lay between Saint Louis and South Pass. Collection of John L. Allen.*

one emigrant caravan bound for the Oregon territory. This movement began to swell immediately after his return in 1842, and another Frémont-led expedition was soon desirable. For his second journey, the orders given to Frémont by Colonel Abert directed the explorer "to connect the reconnaissance of 1842 with the surveys of Wilkes on the coast of the Pacific ocean, so as to give a connected survey of the interior of our continent."[14] It seems clear, however, that Senator Benton's desire to exhibit a U.S. presence in the Northwest for political purposes played a large role in sending Frémont there. Also at issue was the discovery of a river that, many had long suspected, drained the country between the Rockies and the Pacific south of the Columbia-Snake drainage system. This "Rio San Buenaventura," although completely mythical and derived from old Spanish geographical lore of the 1700s, was a focus of Benton's desire for easy transcontinental connections with California as well as Oregon Country.

On this expedition, Frémont again attracted veteran mountain men, such as Thomas Fitzpatrick and Alexis Godey. William Gilpin, a visionary and politician and advocate of western expansion who became the first territorial governor of Colorado, also joined the party as far as the Colorado Rockies. Supported by such adherents and with his preparations completed, Frémont began his journey along the Oregon Trail. After a few days Frémont and his group turned south to explore the line of the Kansas River and reached Big Timbers on 16 June 1843. Here Frémont divided his party into two sections, one group with twelve wagons to travel northward along the emigrant route on the Platte River and the other, with Frémont and fifteen men, to move rapidly straight ahead to the Colorado Rockies, surveying as they proceeded. The two groups were to meet at Saint Vrain's Fort, near the junction of the south fork of the Platte and the Cache la Poudre River east of Longs Peak in north-central Colorado.

The two groups celebrated the Fourth of July at Saint Vrain's Fort. From here, Frémont and his followers went south to Pueblo, Colorado, at that time a crude fur traders' settlement, where they met up with Carson, who had traveled north from Taos, New Mexico, to join the group. Frémont's party was now complete, and he led his force up the Cache la Poudre River, a tributary of the South Platte. No one in the group, not even Carson, knew this region well and could offer advice as to the best route to follow to discover a new pass across the continental divide. Frémont sent the wagons, with most of the group, northward to the emigrant route along the Sweetwater River while he and thirteen men continued up the Cache la Poudre in search of a pass. Unfortunately, the explorers could not find the pass, since the Front Range in this area is not the continental divide but only a divide between the drainages of the North Platte and South Platte. After picking their way over the broken and rocky country of the Laramie Range to the Laramie plains on its western side, they abandoned their search for a pass and turned north to the Sweetwater River, joining the remainder of the party and crossing the divide via the South Pass, known to Frémont from his travels in the previous year. On the way to South Pass, Frémont found coal deposits and fossil specimens that seemed to resemble ones appearing in the stratigraphic sections of Europe. Because of his previous experience and scientific training with Nicollet, Frémont was able to identify them and realize their value.

The explorers traveled through the South Pass and across the Green River (the upper Colorado) and reached the Bear River, a part of the Great Salt Lake drainage. After traveling down the valley of the Bear River and across miles of marshy bottom land, they could see, from a small butte, the Great Salt Lake on 6 September. Frémont was elated. After making camp on the banks of the Weber River, the next morning Frémont and four other explorers dragged their now inflated rubber boat to the shore of the lake and began a reconnaissance of the lake and its islands. Frémont thought that he and his small party were the first to cruise the waters of the lake and visit the islands; he did not know that in 1826, Jim Bridger and a party of trappers had paddled around most of the lake in improvised bull boats.

Frémont and his men spent only a few days near the lake collecting plants and rock specimens. Astronomical observations were also made to fix its location on future maps. From the Great Salt Lake, the party traveled to Fort Hall, close to the Portneuf River (tributary of the Snake River) and north of present-day Pocatello, Idaho, and then up the Snake River past the Hudson's Bay Company post at Fort Boise and onto the Columbia Plateau. Their route took them to Walla Walla and the mission founded by Whitman. From Walla Walla, they followed the Columbia to the Dalles, a series of great falls near where the Columbia enters its gorge through the Cascades. Here Frémont made camp, and leaving his men to rest, he went alone to Fort Vancouver.

Once he reached Fort Vancouver, Frémont had fulfilled his official orders, but his unofficial mission, of locating the fabled Rio San Buenaventura, remained. Instead of returning by the same general route he had followed to reach the Northwest, Frémont and twenty-five men went southward along the course of the Des Chutes River and then eastward into northwestern Nevada to the Truckee and Carson Rivers. On 19 January 1844, concluding that the fabled Rio San Buenaventura was a geographical will-o'-the-wisp, they turned westward to cross the Sierra Nevada toward California (probably via either Walker's Pass or Carson's Pass). Immediately, they ran into deep snow, and the crossing was accomplished only with great difficulty. By 20 February they reached a summit of 9,338 feet; although the rest of the way was downhill, the descent was exhausting and perilous. They finally reached the Sacramento Valley the first week of March and found refuge with Captain John Sutter at Sutter's Fort.

By 24 March the explorers, fit to travel again, started southward through the San Joaquin Valley (the southern portion of the Great Valley of California). Near the site of present-day Bakersfield, they turned southeast and used the Tehachapi Pass to cross the southern end of the Sierra Nevada. On 18 April, near Cajon Pass, they hit the Old Spanish Trail and started across the desert toward the Colorado River. In spite of Indian skirmishes, in which Carson and Godey took the leading role, they soon reached the Las Vegas camping ground, where they were joined by the mountain man Joseph Walker, who guided them to Utah Lake. At this point, just south of the Great Salt Lake, Frémont and his party had virtually completed a large circle of exploration around the Great Basin—a vast region of interior drainage, known previously only to members of the fur trade and never officially recognized on any maps of the region. From Utah Lake, they traveled due east along the Duchesne Fork and the White River across northern Utah into Colorado. They continued eastward until, on 13 June from the top of a mountain in the Colorado Rockies, they saw the valley of the Platte spread before them. Instead of continuing eastward, Frémont turned southward to explore more of central Colorado (the Middle and South Park areas) and reached Pueblo on 29 June. Two days later Frémont and his followers were at Bent's Fort on the Arkansas River near the foothills of the Rockies. Here Carson and Walker remained behind while Frémont and the rest continued to St. Louis. Along the way, Frémont had to avoid a war with Arapaho and Pawnee Indians. Moreover, on 10 July the Kansas River overflowed, and most of the expedition's belongings were lost, including the plant specimens. At around midnight on 6 August 1844 Frémont jumped ashore in St. Louis from a small steamboat he had boarded at Kansas Landing. Thus ended the most spectacular official exploration of western America since that of Lewis and Clark.

What significance did Frémont's journey have for the exploration of the trans-Mississippi West? In terms of discovery and exploration, his investigation determined that the Great Basin region was an area of interior drainage; although this conclusion had probably been reached earlier by members of the fur trade (particularly Jedediah Smith), this was perhaps Frémont's most important contribution to formal geographical knowledge, since this fact helped to dispel the notion of a water route from the central West to the Pacific. He also proved that the northern source region of the Missouri, the Columbia, and the Green Rivers, along with their tributaries, was located in a region different from the source region of the Platte, Rio Grande, and Arkansas in the Colorado Rockies 350 miles to the south. The great rivers of the West did not, as geographical theorists since the seventeenth century had believed, stem from one source region but were geographically divided in their inception and thus flowed in different directions. A new idea of a continental divide was now a factor in the understanding of the river system in the trans-Mississippi West. The only feasible water route across the western part of the United States was still the Platte, Green, and Snake interchange, using as a connection the South

*20.4 Detail from "Map of an Exploring Expedition to the Rocky Mountains in the Year 1842 and to Oregon & North California in the Years 1843–44" (John C. Fré-mont and Charles Preuss, 1845; see p. 538 for the complete map). One of the most important maps of the nineteenth century, this Frémont-Preuss map was the first American map to clearly show the presence of a "great basin" lying between the Rocky Mountains and the Sierra Nevada range. Collection of John L. Allen.*

Pass. In essence, the South Pass was the central point of a land route be-tween the drainages of the Atlantic and the Pacific.

In his assertions about the waters of the trans-Mississippi West, Fré-mont erred, however, in maintaining that the freshwater Utah Lake was part of the Great Salt Lake. On the other hand, his mapmaking was author-itative, since his maps were based not on imaginative meandering but on the astronomical data he collected. As the premier historian of the U.S. Army Corps of Topographical Engineers has pointed out, the real achieve-ment of Frémont's group was to bring the element of trustworthiness in-herent in the scientific method to the making of maps.[15] Although Fré-mont's work was not free from error, he and his cartographer, Charles

Preuss, produced perhaps the most important maps of their time, ones that remained significant until after the Civil War. Constructed by Preuss from computations made by Frémont (and Joseph C. Hubbard of the Coast Survey), the Frémont maps represented the country actually crossed by Frémont or depicted from readings made by reliable sources such as the Wilkes survey. Few other maps at that time were drawn from the actual visual and scientific observations of the mapmaker. Based on thousands of carefully recorded longitude and latitude measurements, these landmark maps, and particularly the great Frémont-Preuss map of the entire West (1845), constituted the first of a series of scientific mappings of the West. They were to be given wide distribution in 1846 when another map using Frémont's field notes and journal was published by the government. Also drawn by Preuss, this later map was titled "Topographical Map of the Road from Missouri to Oregon Commencing at the Mouth of the Kansas in the Missouri River and Ending at the Mouth of the WallahWallah in the Columbia." This seven-section, extremely detailed production clearly outlined the Oregon Trail for prospective emigrants. Printed over the face of the map were excerpts from Frémont's report, describing strategic places along the trail and providing other useful information for the traveler.[16]

In his journey to California and back, Frémont attempted also to advance the cause of science by collecting specimens and fossils. His achievement was less impressive in this respect than in his map construction, but the spirit of contemporary science can be felt on practically every page of his final report. Besides bringing back specimens and fossils, he filled twenty-two pages with meteorological data, important for the calculation of land available for cultivation and providing footnote information for any conclusions that might be made about the "Great American Desert." Frémont paid attention also to the habits, distribution, and physical appearance of a number of Indian tribes. He was not versed in advanced ethnological linguistic techniques, however, and unlike later scientific expeditions, he did not record vocabularies of Indian languages. But he did provide descriptions of the Pawnee, Sioux, Delaware, Kansas, Arapaho, Cheyenne, Snake, Ute, Paiute, Nez Percé, Chinook, Klamath, Diguero, and Mojave Indians (when many of these tribes were almost unknown), with an indication of their attitudes toward white settlement.

Frémont excelled simply in providing a guide and beacon to people who wanted to move westward. In geographical discovery and scientific achievement, he fell short of his contemporary Wilkes, but Frémont's *Report*, his maps, and his other works were used by numerous people in his lifetime. Frémont received acclaim for his activities, whereas Wilkes returned from his epic voyage without fanfare and was plunged almost immediately into controversy over his claims and the way he had conducted his command.[17] The world's preeminent scientist, Alexander von Humboldt, for example, heaped lavish praise on Frémont and gave the explorer special mention in his *Aspects of Nature* published in 1849. As Goetzmann pointed out, "Though Frémont's expeditions were politically conceived and orientated toward practical objectives, as a Topographical Engineer his scientific work added a cubit to the national stature."[18] In this endeavor, he embodied the set of Romantic values characteristic of his age.

## The Corps of Topographical Engineers before and during the Mexican War, 1845–1848

International events soon gave the U.S. Army Corps of Topographical Engineers many opportunities to redeem Frémont's apparent lack of geographical discovery and scientific achievements. For one thing, the war between the United States and Mexico produced a demand for survey work on the area under dispute. Maps in existence at the outbreak of the war included one map in Henry Tanner's *American Atlas* of 1839, which was classified as of doubtful accuracy, a map drawn by Josiah Gregg for his 1844 *Commerce of the Prairies* (a history of the early Santa Fe Trail trade), and some unpublished maps drawn by Lieutenant William H. Emory from various authorities. The War Department did not have a comprehensive original map of the southwestern region being contested by the United States and Mexico during the Mexican War.[19]

To try to rectify this situation, the government launched three trans-Mississippi ventures in the spring of 1845. They were all related to two diplomatic crises: one with Mexico over the independence of Texas and its annexation by the United States, and one with Great Britain over the location of the boundary between British and American territory in the Northwest. As these ventures proceeded, their primary focus turned to the gathering of geographical and scientific information about the western United States. These data were valuable for both settlers and American military leaders; like Wilkes's explorations and Frémont's first two expeditions, these 1845 efforts of the Corps of Topographical Engineers would serve both the official needs of the U.S. government and the demands of an American population clamoring for more land in the West.

The first of the expeditions was headed by Colonel Stephen W. Kearny, who led a contingent of dragoons on a reconnaissance along the Oregon Trail to the South Pass and southward to Bent's Fort. His purpose was to impress the Indians with U.S. military power, keep open the Oregon Trail, and survey the country within the context of its resources. The expedition also functioned as a test of the cavalry as a military force on the plains. Lieutenant W. B. Franklin of the Corps was assigned as topographer and mapmaker. In spite of the somewhat swift nature of Kearny's trip, Franklin was able to compile a carefully drawn map that contained new data but that partially duplicated Frémont's map. Franklin gave credit to Frémont as the source of his information for the country between the Platte and the Arkansas. On his map, however, he suggested that the Grand River (the upper Colorado in the Colorado Rockies) flowed westward from the region of Longs Peak into the Green River to form the Colorado River proper. Although perhaps a guess (albeit an accurate one), this possibility advanced the understanding of the Colorado River system. The only other scientific contribution of Kearny's expedition was a page, in Franklin's report, devoted to geological conclusions, and these were of little significance.[20]

The next expedition was entrusted to Frémont, who was ordered to travel from Bent's Fort through the Rocky Mountains of Colorado. As in his previous expeditions, the true purpose of this journey was known only to Senator Benton and Frémont; possibly, Benton and Frémont, having failed to locate a central river route via the San Buenaventura, were looking for a route suitable for railroad construction across the Rockies to California. On his third expedition into the West, Frémont certainly had no qualms in departing from the orders given to him by Colonel Abert. These instructions called for Frémont to limit his activities to within a reasonable distance of Bent's Fort and to detach Lieutenant James W. Abert, Colonel Abert's son, and a suitable party to explore the southern Rocky Mountains and the regions south of the Arkansas under such instructions as Frémont's experience indicated should be issued. The mission of Abert's journey, the third 1845 expedition, was to explore the country of the Comanche Indians along the Canadian River and the Texas border country. Frémont, meanwhile, was to finish his work in the Colorado Rockies before the adjournment of the next session of Congress so that the information he acquired might be available if military operations in the area became necessary. There was no hint in Colonel Abert's instructions that Frémont was to make a transcontinental expedition to California.

In mid-June 1845 Frémont began to prepare for his trip. On 20 June 1845, with his party assembled, a rapid march was made for Bent's Fort. On the first day into their journey, Frémont read the provisions of martial law, under which the expedition was to be conducted. On 2 August the group reached Bent's Fort, where, a few days later, Frémont presented Lieutenant Abert with his orders instructing the young officer to make a reconnaissance southward and eastward along the Canadian River in the region in which the Kiowa and Comanche Indian tribes lived and roamed. Abert and a companion topographer, Lieutenant William G. Peck, received guidance from Frémont on the correct use of scientific instruments. Abert and Peck, however, were equipped with only a sextant and a chronometer, Frémont having retained the rest of the instruments for use on his forthcoming expedition. Neither Abert's nor Frémont's party seemed to have used barometers.[21]

On 12 August 1845 Abert started his party along the Arkansas River to the Purgatory River (Rio des las Animas) and then westward and over the Raton Pass to the headwaters of the Canadian River. Along the way the group noted existing geological and mineral resources, with the silver mines of New Mexico receiving special attention. He and his men commented on the region through which they were passing and collected specimens of flora and fauna. By 2 September the expedition entered Comanche territory on the northern edge of the Llano Estacado ("Staked Plain") of Texas. Indians were seen and felt constantly, but although Abert's party contacted them and observed their habits, especially those of the Kiowa, no conflicts ensued. During the first week of September, the group turned southward toward the head of the False Washita River. They followed this small stream for a week and then headed again for the Canadian River and proceeded rapidly downstream, leaving hostile Indian country behind them. By 21 October the party reached Fort Gibson in the Arkansas territory, and the expedition officially ended.

Borrowing from earlier maps of Franklin, Frémont, and Gregg, Abert used his own data to construct a carefully drawn map of the route over which he had passed. His depiction was the first truly trustworthy representation of the Canadian River region, although the area had first been crossed more than twenty years before by Stephen Long's party. To supplement his map, Abert produced a written report containing information about Indians, water holes, timber resources, and other information of value both for prospective settlers and for military purposes.[22]

Meanwhile, Frémont, after waiting for Carson to join the group and conducting some final outfitting, was ready to depart on his expedition.

He and his company of about sixty well-armed men left Bent's Fort and proceeded westward along the Arkansas River. Joining Carson and Frémont were Godey, Walker, and other prominent mountain men. Preuss, who had served so well as Frémont's cartographer on the two earlier expeditions, had remained in Washington DC; his place as topographer was taken by Edward Kern, an artist from Philadelphia. Regardless of his official orders to explore the Colorado Rockies, Frémont and his men were headed straight for California. There does not seem to be any question that Frémont's intent—orders or no—had ever been any different. By this time Frémont must have felt secure enough in his role as "Benton's man" in the military to directly disregard the orders of his commanding officer.

The course to the west took Frémont and his command around the Royal Gorge of the Arkansas, through Tennessee Pass across the continental divide, across the Grand (upper Colorado) River near the headwaters of the White River, and along the White River westward across the plateau country of western Colorado and eastern Utah. In time they crossed the Green River and hit the Duchesne River as it flowed through the badlands bordering the Wasatch Plateau. They then found the Timpanogos River and followed it down from the Wasatch Mountains into the Great Basin near Utah Lake. On 10 October they headed for the southern shore of the Great Salt Lake, which they reached three days later. Frémont remained near the Great Salt Lake long enough to make a detailed survey of its southern shores (which he had not seen on his previous expedition), collect plants and animal specimens, and refresh the expedition's horses for a trip across the desert toward the Sierra Nevada.

When they finally left the Salt Lake Valley, Frémont's men traveled to Pilot Peak, west of the Great Salt Lake, where water was found. From here they shifted northward to Whitten's Springs in the Humboldt River Mountains. This route later came to be called the Hastings Cutoff of the California Trail. It gained notoriety because of its use by the Donner Party, victims of trying to cross the wintry Sierra Nevada in 1846. At this point, Frémont divided his followers into two groups. One party, guided by Walker, took the Humboldt River route to Walker Lake at the eastern base of the Sierra Nevada (as a participant in the Rocky Mountain fur trade, Walker had pioneered this route over a decade earlier). Frémont, with ten men, traveled directly across the desert to the same rendezvous, and the two groups came together again on 24 November 1845.

From Walker Lake, Frémont and fifteen men aimed for a crossing of the Sierra Nevada by using the Donner Pass, while the rest of the company, again guided by Walker, headed for Walker Pass. A reunion was planned at the Tulare Lakes. Both groups crossed the mountains successfully. Frémont and his men passed directly through the area that would provide the gold for the rush of 1849, but they did not look for or discover this precious metal on their journey. When they reached the Tulare Lake fork of the Kern River, the rest of the company was not there. Frémont decided therefore to leave his party to winter at Sutter's Fort and wait for the arrival of the larger party. Meanwhile he visited the U.S. vice-consul at Yerba Buena (later, San Francisco), William Alexander Leidesdorff, who in turn escorted him to Pueblo de San Jose. When the second group reached the Tulare Lake region and learned that Frémont was at Pueblo de San Jose, the men headed for that settlement.[23]

The two groups reunited at Pueblo de San Jose, where Leidesdorff had taken Frémont. From the standpoint of the Mexican authorities, a combined party of men under the command of a U.S. Army officer threatened the operations of the Mexican government in California. They thus tried to either disperse or capture Frémont's force, but the U.S. company escaped and headed for the Klamath area in the Oregon territory by way of Lassen's Meadows. At the upper Klamath Lake, two men who had traveled from Sutter's Fort on the Sacramento River informed Frémont that Lieutenant Archibald H. Gillespie of the U.S. Marine Corps was looking for him. Frémont went back the way he had come to meet Gillespie, who then gave Frémont letters from President James Polk, Secretary of State James Buchanan, Secretary of the Navy Hubert Bancroft, and Senator Benton.

After receiving these letters, Frémont gave every indication that he supported the winning of California for the United States by the action of U.S. citizens then in California. He did not at first play an active role in this endeavor, however, because news had not been received of an actual declaration of war between Mexico and the United States. But by June 1846 Frémont decided to make his position known, and so he took charge of the contingent of U.S. citizens already in revolt plus a group who had been waiting for action with him. From this point on, the U.S. push to acquire California was out in the open, and the Californians forcefully resisted. In the subsequent fighting Frémont's forces were at first victorious, and Frémont convinced the rebels who wanted to form a republic that joining the United States was a better plan. To satisfy this movement, the California Battalion was formed on 5 July 1846. Three days earlier, Commodore John Sloat had arrived in Monterey, aboard the uss *Savannah*, with news of the Mexican War and had raised the U.S. flag over the customshouse.

From this point on, events happened very quickly. Commodore Sloat sailed away from Monterey, and Commodore Robert F. Stockton, on board the USS *Congress*, became the ranking naval officer and the highest-ranking military officer on the coast. Stockton quickly gave an official aura to Frémont and the California Battalion by making Frémont a major in charge of the battalion, which was to operate as a member of the horse marines. Frémont, a commissioned officer in the U.S. Army, now had official status resting on the orders of a U.S. naval officer.

Meanwhile, Kearny, now brigadier general, had moved into southern California at a place called Warner's Ranch near Agua Caliente with 110 Dragoons, and in October, Frémont learned that Kearny had appointed him a lieutenant colonel in the army's Regiment of Mounted Riflemen. The confusion surrounding Frémont's dual position as topographical engineer and as field commander of a military force and surrounding the division in command between Stockton and Kearny did not surface, although both Stockton and Kearny issued orders as if they were in overall command. After the battle for California ended, Stockton appointed Frémont governor and commander-in-chief of the territory of California. This move was opposed by Kearny, who apparently gave Frémont a direct order not to change his status as commander of the California Battalion. But in a letter dated 17 January 1847 Frémont wrote that he felt it necessary to disobey Kearny's order. In military terms, Frémont had put himself in a distinctly disadvantageous position by apparently disobeying a direct order from a superior.

In time, Stockton sailed away from California, and his place was taken by Commodore William Brandford Shubrick, who favored Kearny's position in the dispute. Shubrick let Frémont know that he believed Kearny had the authority to control the government of California. In February, Kearny received a letter from the general-in-chief of the army authorizing him to assume the position of governor of California. Holding this authority, Kearny forced Frémont to turn over papers and archives pertaining to the government and to obey any orders Kearny might issue. Frémont was beaten. When Kearny left Monterey on 31 May 1848, Frémont and the members of the Corps who had followed Frémont to California brought up the rear of Kearny's forces and camped separately. Kearny, hoping to disgrace Frémont, refused Frémont's requests and acted harshly toward the younger officer. After arriving at Fort Leavenworth, Kearny placed Frémont under arrest and ordered him to travel to Washington DC and report to the adjutant general of the army for a court-martial.

The verdict of the ensuing court-martial held in Washington DC was curious. The court found Frémont guilty of disobeying a superior officer and sentenced him to be dismissed from the service. Six of the twelve members of the court recommended leniency from President Polk, and in "Remarks by the Court" the full court respectfully commended "Lieutenant Colonel Frémont to the lenient consideration of the President of the United States." Subsequently Polk issued a proclamation on 16 February 1848, within two weeks of the end of the trial, remitting the sentence. In the eyes of Frémont and his supporters (particularly Benton), these moves smacked of political chicanery and double-dealing. His honor had been tarnished; he was—in his opinion—not guilty of anything, and on this note he left the official service of the government.[24]

Because of the intervening military action in California and the subsequent court-martial, Frémont's important narrative of his trip from Bent's Fort to California was not given concentrated consideration by him, and there was scant public demand for its appearance. Congress tabled a measure calling for the immediate publication of his story in the form of a report. Frémont's views did appear, however, as early as 1848, when the Thirtieth Congress provided for the publication of twenty thousand copies of a work by Frémont called *Geographical Memoir upon Upper California* as a companion to a map drawn by Preuss. This publication was not in the form of a journal but rather was a broad description of the natural features of the land from New Mexico to California. No information was provided about the gold regions. Preuss's map was somewhat larger in scope than his earlier productions and filled in previous blank spaces from information acquired since 1845 and 1846. Attempting to present the "whole picture," it suffered in accuracy. For western travelers, however, it was very significant. In addition, an analysis of Frémont's collection of plants appeared as "Plantae Frémontianae" in the *Smithsonian Contributions to Knowledge* (1854).[25]

Frémont's exploration and mapping of the route directly across the Great Basin via the Humboldt was not the only significant contribution of the U.S. Army Corps of Topographical Engineers during the Mexican War. Also important was Kearny's expedition to California. When hostilities with Mexico began in 1846, Kearny had been ordered to go from New Mexico to California. The reliability of existing maps, particularly those for the Southwest, was questioned, and to help Kearny find his way to California and to compile an accurate map of the region traversed, the Corps detailed First Lieutenant William Hemsley Emory as Kearny's topographer, an ap-

20.5 "Map of Oregon and Upper California" (Charles Preuss, 1848). Attributed to Preuss but drawn from field notes of Frémont and others, this is the first accurate map of the Pacific coastal region of the United States. Collection of John L. Allen.

pointment that proved to be an extremely wise choice. Emory's close circle contained prominent astronomers, mathematicians, and geologists; he regularly attended meetings of the American Association for the Advancement of Science and supported scientists in their efforts to make their presence known in Washington DC. Previous topographical duties for Emory included work on the Northeast Boundary Survey of 1843–44 and the completion of a map of Texas in 1844.[26]

After receiving orders to accompany Kearny on the military expedition from New Mexico to California, Emory was given only twenty-four hours to assemble his equipment and to prepare himself and his assistants— Lieutenant James W. Abert (already a veteran of western exploration), Lieutenant William G. Peck, and First Lieutenant William H. Warner. In that time, he was able to gather two large box chronometers, two Gambey eight-and-one-half-inch sextants, a Bunten siphon barometer, and various maps and books.[27] By 2 August, Emory was ready to join Kearny's detachment in New Mexico, and he began the important part of his journal at Bent's Fort on the Arkansas River. On the way south, Emory compared what he saw with what had been written about Mexico and Central America by William H. Prescott and John Lloyd Stephens. In a pioneering statement on land-forming processes, he concluded that the area had once been a level plateau into which valleys had been cut by a "denuding process," but he hesitated to attribute this solely to water erosion. In scientific terms, he confirmed the existence of bituminous coal deposits, and later he investigated the deserted Santa Rita del Cobre copper mine, which had last been worked by Sylvester Pattie and his son James Ohio in 1827.

After the occupation of Santa Fe by Kearny's detachment on 18 August, Emory and his group selected and surveyed the site of Fort Marcy as well as constructed a map of the route followed by Kearny's forces to Santa Fe. As part of this work, Emory concluded that the route from Fort Leavenworth to Santa Fe presented few obstacles for a railroad and speculated that if the rest of the way to the Pacific proved just as good, this could serve as a major transportation route to southern California. Emory also observed the life and customs of the Mexicans and Indians. He was not impressed with the area as farming country or as a source of precious metals, but he noted that the region could be fruitful for wine production, since the soil and weather seemed well suited for grape growing.

After conquering Santa Fe, Kearny set out for California on 25 September. Emory's unit accompanied him. On the march west, Kearny divided his forces into his own detachment and a Mormon Battalion commanded by Captain Philip St. George Cooke. The Mormon Battalion was to accompany a supply wagon train south of the New Mexico mountains and along the Gila River, a more southerly route than Kearny would take, in order to avoid what seemed to be mountainous terrain confronting Kearny's column. Emory, who accompanied Kearny's forces, had the assistance of Warner, Norman Bestor, a civilian statistician, and John Mix Stanley, an artist. Both Abert and Peck had become ill and had been left behind with orders to make a careful map and survey of all of New Mexico.

Much of Emory's interest on the march westward centered on four features of southwestern geography: the ruined pueblos (particularly that of Casa Grande, or Casa Montezuma as it was called by the natives); the Indians that met the U.S. force (especially the Pimas and Maricopas); the geological formations; and the marking of their trail by astronomical observation. Emory, for example, determined by observation the precise location of the junction of the Gila and the Colorado Rivers. As far as the land between New Mexico and the Colorado River was concerned, Emory saw little hope for agricultural settlement except where irrigation was possible, and he advised against slavery in the region—both prescient opinions. Regarding the ruined pueblos, Emory was the first explorer to examine Casa Grande since Padres Pedro Font and Francisco Garces in 1776. At first, he likened some of them to the Aztec cultures of Mexico, but he later came to believe that they were ruins of the modern era whose inhabitants had regressed from a period of earlier brilliance perhaps some four centuries in the past—again, the accuracy of his observations was outstanding. He believed, however, that seven ruined towns on the Rio del San Jose were Coronado's original "Seven Cities of Cíbola," whereas modern research tends to give the Zuñi pueblos as the place of Coronado's conquest.

From the Colorado River, which Kearny forded on 25 November, to Warner's ranch in the Agua Caliente Valley of California, near the hot springs of the same name, the route crossed the desert and over the coastal range of mountains. Because of the weariness of his troops and the arid nature of the region, which provided little in the way of either water or food for the animals on which they rode or on which supplies were carried, the journey was difficult. But by 2 December the journey to the Agua Caliente Valley was completed. Emory fixed the latitude and longitude of their stopping place at Warner's ranch by instrumental observation.

After the battles resulting in the conquest of California, Kearny reached San Diego on 12 December, and the reconnaissance to California was finished. With Kearny, Emory and his group had traveled the entire trans-

Mississippi Southwest by a route relatively unknown, perhaps traveled previously by only a few fur trappers or Indians. This was not the route used by the Spaniards of previous years to get to California; the Old Spanish Trail followed a higher route through Nevada and over the Cajon Pass. Regarding the path he had taken, Emory believed that a railroad might prove feasible along the thirty-second parallel following the Gila River and that emigrants might find this a worthwhile route westward.[28]

The route to California pioneered by the Kearny-Emory expedition had certain geographical disadvantages. The country was rough along the Gila River, the river itself had to be crossed, desert country was difficult to traverse, and the mountainous country just before San Diego offered a further barrier. Few of these difficulties had been encountered by Captain Cooke and his Mormon wagon train because of his more southerly circuitous route; from Cooke's vantage point, this route seemed even more desirable than Kearny's for a railroad and emigrant trail. The fact that Cooke's wagons had succeeded in their passage seemed to confirm this opinion. Because of the routes taken by Kearny and Cooke, Emory advised the secretary of state that in any negotiations for a peace treaty after the war, the United States should seek to establish the boundary with Mexico at 32° north latitude at the least.[29]

Meanwhile, back in New Mexico, Lieutenants Abert and Peck, recovering from their illnesses, had collected specimens, sketched Indians, compiled tribal vocabularies, and studied natural science and ethnology. When their health was restored, they began surveying New Mexico and constructing a map of the region. On 29 September they started southward, visiting the gold-mining region south of Santa Fe along Galisteo Creek, where most of the mines were owned by U.S. citizens. They also investigated the pueblos, some in ruins, west of Albuquerque. Traveling up the Puerco River, they came to the San Jose River and encountered the first of these pueblos, only one of which (the Acoma Pueblo) seemed to fit the stories about the Seven Cities of Cíbola. Acoma was situated high on a limestone mesa and could be reached only by a narrow stairway cut from the face of the cliff. The inhabitants seemed generous and friendly, engrossed in the task of earning their living from farming.

In addition to reporting on Indian life, Abert and Peck gathered data on the population and political organization of the province of New Mexico. An official census report from the records of Santa Fe for 1844 was included in their journal, which gave the population of New Mexico as 100,064. At the conclusion of their work, Abert and Peck traveled east separately, with

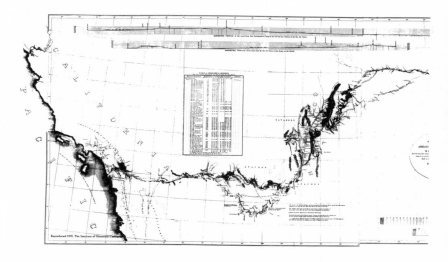

*20.6 Portion of map of the American Southwest (William Emory, 1847). Emory's map was based, in part, on field sketches drawn during the campaigns of the Mexican War in the Southwest. Although a number of small inaccuracies exist in drainage systems, in general the map is a vast improvement over earlier cartography. Courtesy of the Library of Congress.*

Abert being ordered to visit Washington DC to give a firsthand report on conditions in the Southwest.[30]

During their involvement with the Corps of Topographical Engineers during the Mexican War, Emory and his group made an enormous contribution to geographical knowledge. Emory's map of his travels, for example, was the first accurate map of the whole southwestern area. Based on 2,000 astronomical observations with an altitude profile of 357 separate barometric observations, it completed the early outline of trans-Mississippi geography. Errors in the maps of Humboldt's *Atlas*, in Frémont's 1845 maps, and in the commercial maps of Tanner and Samuel Mitchell were all corrected by Emory's work; he and his associates changed the conception of southwestern geography, and their work was widely used during the California gold rush.[31] In addition, the information they gained about the geology, the minerals, the flora, and the fauna of the region was also worthwhile. Special reports on these subjects were issued in conjunction with the final report. As late as 1856, specimens of cacti brought back by Emory, Abert, and Peck were still being discussed by the American Academy of Arts and Sciences.[32] Of special interest also was the impetus that their pioneering investigations of the pueblos had given to the study of Indian archaeological remains. Emory contributed much to the study of pueblo tribes and their past, as well as to the history and life of other Indian groups. Although Emory and his associates never determined the origins of the ruined pueblos, their work provided a foundation for continued research on the subject.[33]

## Transcontinental Expeditions by Frémont and the Corps of Topographical Engineers in 1849

When the war with Mexico was over, the rush to the West began in earnest. News of the discovery of gold in the new state of California in 1848 reached the East late in that year, and from early 1849 onward, gold-seekers tried to get to California as quickly as possible while many other settlers, on more prosaic agricultural migrations, began the trek westward to make a new home for themselves.

The first of the expeditions of the post–Mexican War period was not an official government expedition. Its commander was the erstwhile Frémont, whose service to his country did not end with his extensive California trip of 1845. In 1848 Thomas Hart Benton, senator from Missouri and Frémont's father-in-law, persuaded some businessmen from St. Louis to finance an expedition to the West to be made during the winter, thus proving that a winter crossing of the Rockies was possible. The route of the expedition was to run along the thirty-eighth parallel, a possible central railroad route from St. Louis to San Francisco. Frémont, having just experienced the disgrace of his court-martial, was quick to accept Benton's assignment and eager to reestablish himself as an achiever in the eyes of the nation. He wanted to show that a court-martial should never have happened to a man of his caliber and accomplishments.

During the first week of October 1848 Frémont assembled a party determined to prove that Benton's central path could be used even in the cold and snow of a Rocky Mountain winter. To accomplish this feat, he gathered some thirty-five men, including Godey, Preuss, Edward Kern with his brothers Richard H. and Benjamin, Tom Martin, the botanist Frederick Creutzfeldt, the English adventurer Captain Andrew Cathcart of Prince Albert's Eleventh Hussars, and Theodore McNabb, Godey's fourteen-year-old nephew. On 4 October 1848 the party started upriver from St. Louis by steamboat to a place beyond Westport called Boon Creek. Some two weeks later, on 20 October 1848, the expedition began its journey across the Rocky Mountains by heading for Bent's Fort, which they reached by 15 November 1848. The weather was very unpleasant, and the inhabitants of the area predicted bad winter conditions with much snow in the high mountains. In spite of the dire weather forecasts, Frémont was determined to push on. He took his group to Pueblo, Colorado, where Old Bill Williams, one of the most widely traveled of the former fur trappers, joined the expedition as guide.

The party rode out of Pueblo on 22 November, stopping for a few days at a place twenty-five miles away called Hardscrabble. From here the plan was to cross the Wet Mountains, travel along the eastern side of the Sangre de Cristo Mountains, cross them through Robidoux Pass into the area of the Great Sand Dunes, follow the Rio Grande's headwaters up the San Luis Valley, and travel over the San Juan Mountains and the continental divide at either an unmarked pass (which Williams swore existed) or the better-known Cochetopa Pass. Once they were over the mountains, the trail to California would not be hard to follow. At least that was the plan. But by 17 December 1848 the passage across the San Juan Mountains had not been completed, and the members of the party recognized that they could not continue to go forward. They were 12,327 feet high on Pool Table Mountain; a storm was raging, their food was about gone, they were weakened by cold, and at the height they had reached, they were suffering from a lack of oxygen. To avoid starvation, they killed their mules for food, and to keep warm, they slept together in snow holes. In his private diary, Preuss described their plight under the date of 15 December 1848:

> As far as Hardscrabble, everything went well. We now had the first chain of the Rocky Mountains before our noses, and the great and probably only difficulty of our journey was to find a pass in this season. We were therefore very happy when Frémont decided to engage the services of a guide, Old Bill Williams, who just happened to be here.
>
> The general opinion was that no one knew the country as well as he. . . .
>
> The very second day we made our way through a difficult narrow pass, and we had to contend with a lot of snow. Soon afterwards, Bill's vacillations showed that he was not very much at home, at least in these parts. Trips lasting all day cost us lots of provisions. . . . In

crossing the second chain, Bill definitely missed the promised *Good* pass. . . .

On the summit the wide valley of the Rio Grande opened before our eyes. From here we started through the valley, which we could not cross in one day. . . . Bill kept insisting that we need only cross the mountain range (The San Juan Mountains) in order to reach a snow-free tableland. [italics in original]

On the next day, Sunday, 16 December, Preuss wrote: "Today we (reached) the white summit we had considered the divide of the two watersheds . . . we attempted to cross the summit. Extremely sharp wind and violent snowfall drove us back." Two days later, on 18 December, he wrote that the party had reached the shelter of a small fir grove, but he added:

The cold on the summit was almost unbearable because of the wind and the incessant snowfall. For the animals it was fatal.

Since everything ahead of us, as well as behind us, was white, we decided to return. All but a few of the beasts were dead, and these few were useless. Only Polly was used until her end to drag baggage . . . across the mountain. In slaughtering a few of the animals, we saw that they were not all so very thin and that cold, more than hunger, was responsible for their deaths.

At this juncture, Frémont selected Tom Breckenridge, Henry King, Creutzfeldt, and Williams to try to find a settlement and ask for help. He hoped they would not have to go back to Taos, 160 miles away. The rest of the group moved down the canyon of Embargo Creek to the headwaters of the Rio Grande.

On 9 January 1849 one of the group with Frémont, Raphael Prone, died. No word had been received from a rescue party. In dire circumstances by 11 January 1849, Frémont divided the expedition into groups; the first, under his leadership, consisted of five persons who departed from the others in the hope of finding a settlement. The remainder, led by Lorenzo Vincenthaler, who was not a mountain man or experienced leader, were to remain where they were camped until help arrived. With the Frémont exploring party thus divided into three groups under three leaders, its coherence and will to succeed began to disintegrate. Frémont did find a small settlement near present Questa, New Mexico, on the Red River, and he located the first group, all of them alive except King, whose body bore evidence that parts of it had been eaten. Frémont and his group reached Taos, and a rescue party, under Godey, was sent back into the mountains to find the Vincenthaler group, which by this time had disintegrated into small groups or

single individuals fending for themselves. By 11 February 1849 the last survivors had been brought to Taos. Out of the entire group of twenty-nine
men, however, only ten lived to tell the tale.

Frémont was criticized for his leadership of the expedition, especially by
the Kern brothers. Godey defended Frémont. Frémont himself blamed
Williams for his errors in guidance, but he did not dwell long on the topic
or in Taos. Soon after the survivors of the expedition were relatively fit
again, Frémont announced that he was going to California by the southern
route to operate his Las Mariposas ranch, which he had purchased when
he was in California previously. He invited those who wanted to go to California to accompany him. Cathcart, the Kerns, and Williams refused his
offer. Once in California, Frémont began a career as a rancher and politician.[34] Although he became the Republican Party's first candidate for president in 1856 and served as a general in the Civil War, Frémont's career had
already reached its high point—when he had returned from his great reconnaissance of 1843–44. The disastrous expedition of 1848 was something
from which he would never recover, either personally or professionally.

Following Frémont's disaster in the snows of the southern Colorado
Rockies, other expeditions sought mountain routes that would serve as al-
ternatives to South Pass, which, because of its more northerly location,
was less accessible to migrants from the southern states. The government
appropriated $50,000 for surveys by the Corps of Topographical Engineers
in Nebraska, Texas, New Mexico, and California. One of the first attempts
was centered on Fort Smith, Arkansas. Under pressure from Senator Solon
Borland of Arkansas, the secretary of war ordered a survey to be made for
an emigrant road from Fort Smith across Texas to Santa Fe. On 2 April 1849
Captain Randolph Marcy was ordered to make such a survey; Lieutenant
James H. Simpson was ordered to assist him as topographer.

On his march across Oklahoma and Texas, Simpson verified Abert's
drawings of 1845 and made observations of his own. Although the route
seemed suitable for wagons, Simpson did not think a railroad could be
built because of the absence of population centers, the lack of water, and
the vast distances. He estimated that a railroad could not be built across the
southern plains for another twenty years. When the Marcy-Simpson party
reached New Mexico, it went through Cerro Tucumcari on 16 June and
through the Pecos River town of Anton Chico on Saint John's Day, 24 June;
at 4:00 P.M. on 28 June the men rode into Santa Fe, having covered 819.5
miles in the eighty-six days since leaving Fort Smith. Simpson remained at
Santa Fe, but on 14 August 1849 Marcy began a return trip to Arkansas. He

proceeded southward across the Jornada del Muerto, a barren eighty miles of intense heat that could be bested only at night. By 29 August Marcy and his group reached the village of Dona Ana, in western Texas.

After a short stop at Dona Ana, Marcy departed in the direction of the Organ Mountains and the San Augustine Pass. Traveling through the pass on 2 September, Marcy turned toward the southeast and after two days of travel arrived at the base of the Waco (Hueco) Mountains. Little trouble was encountered in getting through this range, and after subsequent travel through a hard, smooth, and grass-covered valley the group reached the Guadalupe Mountains, 147 miles from Dona Ana by Marcy's measurements. The expedition found and used a narrow gorge flanked by sandstone bluffs to get through this barrier. Passing through the Guadalupe Mountains, the party encountered Delaware Creek, which it followed for 40 miles before arriving on the western bank of the Pecos River. Five days were spent finding a workable ford, one where the wagons and supplies could be floated across the river with the help of a guideline to land them on the opposite shore at a selected site. Several weeks later, after traveling northeast, the company reached the Red River and started across the Llano Estacado of north-central Texas. By 2 October 1849 the men reached the end of the Llano Estacado at what is now Big Spring, Texas, about 600 miles from Santa Fe.

After resting for a few days, the party started marching again. On 7 October, Marcy fell ill with dysentery, and while he was ill one of his men, Lieutenant M. P. Harrison, rode ahead to survey the trail. Harrison was murdered, presumably by Indians; he was scalped, shot through the head, and stripped of his clothing and equipment. His murderers were never found. By 10 October, Marcy had recovered enough to start the journey again, and on 12 October the group reached the Brazos River in present Stonewall County, Texas. In the next few days they survived a torrential downpour and high winds as well as the unwanted attentions of Comanche and Kickapoo Indians. On 22 October they reached the Clear Fork of the Brazos, which Marcy followed to its meeting with the Brazos, where he recommended that a fort be erected. Two years later Fort Belknap was constructed on the site.

From the Brazos, Marcy marched with his men to the Trinity River, and using the road along the ridge that divided the Trinity from the Red River, they reached the Cross Timbers (a region of scrub timber that was a major landmark on the Santa Fe Trail) on 30 October; the group camped near present Gainesville, Texas. Penetrating the Cross Timbers, the group reached the Preston Road connecting Austin with Denison and turned north to Preston (now under the waters of Lake Texoma), about forty miles from Fort Washita. On 7 November the group reached Fort Washita, eighty-five days out of Santa Fe, and from here headed for their home base of Fort Towson, eighty miles due east. Lieutenant Delos B. Sackett and his Dragoons continued to Fort Smith. Marcy had arrived back after an absence of eight months and a journey of nearly two thousand miles across some of the most inhospitable terrain in North America.

A few months later, Marcy's journal was published. Noteworthy for prospective migrants was Marcy's claim of the suitability of his route eastward from Dona Ana as an emigrant road. This route possessed, according to the young officer, the suitable resources for wagon travel; moreover, it shortened the distance between the Mississippi and the Pacific by three hundred miles. Another important feature of the report was Marcy's view that his route constituted a good path for a railroad from Fort Smith to Dona Ana. Sectional politics interfered in the building of the railroad, but by 1850 thousands of emigrants were using his route to travel west. In 1858 the overland Express, established by John Butterfield and running from St. Louis to San Francisco, overlapped Marcy's 1849 route by more than one-third of the 1,795 miles covered by Butterfield's Concord coaches, which touched at Preston, present-day Gainesville, Fort Belknap on the Brazos, Horsehead Crossing on the Pecos (a few miles below where Marcy had crossed), and El Paso. In 1883 the Texas and Pacific Railroad generally followed the Express route across Texas to El Paso, where it joined the Southern Pacific, which for the most part followed Cooke's old California wagon road. After thirty-three years, Marcy's idea of a southern transcontinental railroad across the route he had traversed became a reality.[35]

Perhaps more far-reaching in its implications than the Marcy-Simpson expedition was one commanded by Captain Howard Stansbury, assisted by Lieutenant John W. Gunnison. Within the context of Senator Benton's argument that a railroad should be built from St. Louis to San Francisco, Stansbury was ordered to travel to Fort Hall near the junction of the Snake and Portneuf Rivers via the "emigrant road," or the Oregon-California-Mormon Trail, and begin a detailed study for a military post west of the continental divide to help emigrants prepare for the desert crossing to California. In addition, Stansbury was instructed to survey the entire Great Salt Lake, to map the lake and locate supply routes from Mormon settlements to the emigrant trail, to make a study of both the Mormons and the

Indians of the Salt Lake region, to note all the potential resources of the area, and to return to St. Louis through Santa Fe.

On his way to Fort Hall, Stansbury found the Oregon-California Trail crowded with emigrants and littered with their debris. On 19 June 1849 he reached the new Fort Kearney and on 11 August arrived at Fort Bridger in the southwestern corner of present-day Wyoming on the trail to the regions of the Northwest and just to the east of the Great Salt Lake. Here he enlisted the services of the former mountain man Jim Bridger as a guide. With Bridger's assistance, Stansbury searched for a direct route across the Wasatch Range to the northern side of the Great Salt Lake. Their efforts took them through the Wasatch Mountains to the Mormon Trail about three miles from a place called Brown's settlement, the site of future Ogden. Stansbury thought that a good road for rail travel could be found between Fort Bridger and the Great Salt Lake, but he thought it had to run farther to the north, through Cache Valley and Blacksmith's Fork. From the Mormon settlements in Salt Lake Valley, Stansbury journeyed to Fort Hall, where, after a short survey, he concluded that a wagon road from Fort Hall to the Mormon settlements was practical. He decided, however, that Cache Valley, formerly a site of the American Fur Company's yearly rendezvous, was not suitable for a military post because of the severity of its winter climate.

On 19 October, Stansbury started to explore the western side of the Great Salt Lake. This was a difficult task, made more so by the desert character of the terrain. As he investigated the area, Stansbury concluded that the region had been a vast inland sea and that the mountains hovering over the flat areas must have been huge islands. Years later this conclusion was verified, and the area of the ancient lake, filled with meltwaters from the cordilleran glaciers, was named Lake Bonneville. As part of the survey of the western shore of the Great Salt Lake, Stansbury and his group reached Pilot Peak, the point from which Frémont had begun his successful crossing of the desert in 1845. From here they crossed another seventy miles of desert eastward to the Jordan River and Salt Lake City on the eastern shore. By fully exploring the western margins of the Salt Lake Basin, Stansbury had performed a feat of exploration not previously accomplished (to the best of our knowledge) by mountain men or any others.

While Stansbury was concluding his survey of the Great Salt Lake, Gunnison was making astronomical observations and measuring distances near the freshwater Utah Lake, south of the Great Salt Lake. He con-

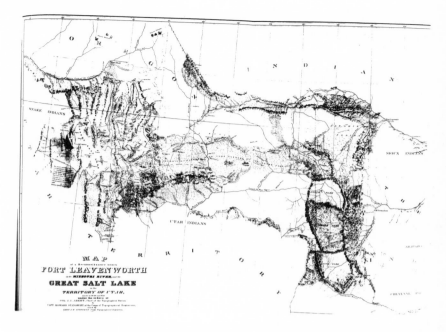

20.7 The central area of Howard Stansbury's reconnaisance for a transcontinental railway route (from a map by Stansbury, 1851). The route shown on Stansbury's map—through the Wyoming or Great Divide Basin—eventually became the route of the Union Pacific Railroad. Courtesy of the Library of Congress.

structed a network of triangles that could be developed to make an accurate map of the valley. Utah Lake was also surveyed, and fourteen triangulation stations were erected in preparation for mapping in the spring. During the winter, field operations were suspended; officers and men now studied the Mormon way of life and constructed boats to be used the following spring in making an extensive survey of the Great Salt Lake. This survey, which lasted until 27 June, formed the basis for the Stansbury-Gunnison map covering five thousand square miles in the Salt Lake region. They had also put down a six-mile-long astronomical baseline and surveyed both the Great Salt Lake and Utah Lake, the Jordan River (connecting the lakes), and all the islands in the Great Salt Lake. The result of their surveys was the first accurate and detailed geographical account of the Wasatch Oasis, a region destined to become the center of the Mormon culture region and the major metropolitan area of the Great Basin.

On his return Stansbury did not take the Santa Fe route eastward but followed the Jordan River eastward to the Weber River. Reaching the Weber River just above a place called Camas Prairie, he used the river as a guide to Echo Creek in the Wasatch Range and over to the Bear River–Muddy River divide to Fort Bridger. From here, Bridger led Stansbury eastward across the Green River valley to a route along Bitter Creek in the Great Divide Basin of south-central Wyoming. After passing through a desert of sage and the traditional Indian war grounds of the Red Desert, Stansbury crossed Bridger's Pass over the northern end of the Medicine Bow Mountains, through the Laramie Basin, and over the Laramie Range via Cheyenne Pass to the upper reaches of the Chugwater River, a small tributary of the Laramie River, in turn tributary to the Platte. In the valley of the Chugwater, Stansbury fell from his horse and was injured so severely that his expedition had to end—but not before Stansbury could report that a usable route through the Rocky Mountains had been found well to the south of the South Pass route, with a more-direct course that saved many days' travel between Fort Laramie and the Mormon settlements. Stansbury's achievement was significant for transportation in the West: the Overland Stage, the Pony Express, the Union Pacific Railroad, the Lincoln Highway (U.S. 30), and Interstate 80 have all used part of the path he blazed on his return. His subsequent map filled in many gaps still present in the picture of the national landscape, and his accompanying written report was second only to the voluminous accounts of Frémont in its ambitious scope. The report was issued first as a Senate executive document in 1851 and was subsequently published in commercial editions between 1852 and 1855, including printings in both London and Stuttgart.[36]

## The Corps of Topographical Engineers and Regional Exploration

In the expeditions of Marcy and Stansbury, the explorations of the U.S. Army Corps of Topographical Engineers reached their pinnacle—at least in terms of exploration conceived and executed on a grand, continental scale. But much work remained to the Corps in filling in, with key geographical details, the existing gaps on the maps of the West. During the period between Stansbury's return and the Civil War, when the Corps was abandoned, the Corps explorations were regionally oriented, directed to investigating the potential of the western interior, which by 1850 had become, through the fulfillment of Manifest Destiny, official U.S. territory.

In Texas, for example, the Corps of Topographical Engineers entered into a sort of military-state-commercial partnership for exploring the region to reveal its economic potential and to erect defenses against Indians. When Texas came into the Union as a state, its citizens were not loathe to seek federal aid to further their own interests. Its representatives in Congress, especially Sam Houston and Thomas Rush, were particularly active in this regard, and the Texas area was one of the first to benefit from federal government exploration in the service of regional economic development. A central objective of exploration in Texas was to find the best-possible routes connecting the urban centers with each other, with the coast, and with northern Mexico for the purpose of furthering trade. Late in the 1840s, San Antonio raised $800 for a road survey to divert the Chihuahua trade from New Mexico to Texas. Thirty-five Texas Rangers, commanded by John Coffee Hays and Captain Samuel Highsmith, left San Antonio on 27 August 1848 to try to find a road to Chihuahua in Mexico, but they accomplished little and merely wandered around the Texas badlands for several months. Another group—led by Major Robert S. Neighbors of the Texas Rangers and John S. Ford, federal Indian agent for Texas—followed the upper Colorado River of Texas to Brady's Creek, found the Concho River and followed it to its sources, crossed the Pecos River at Horsehead Creek, and made it to El Paso. Their return trip took them through the Guadalupe Mountains back to the Pecos and Horsehead Creek. When they reached Brady's Creek, they followed a curve southward to Fredricksburg and into San Antonio. This venture added another route westward.

Meanwhile, General William J. Worth, commanding the Eighth Military District, detailed Brevet Lieutenant Colonel Joseph E. Johnson as the representative of the Corps of Topographical Engineers to make a survey. With four lieutenants under his command, Johnson generally followed the plan for the Texas survey developed by Colonel Abert, who had four desires: to survey Texas in conjunction with the building of a railroad from the eastern border to El Paso; to examine the rivers that ran into the Gulf; to explore the Red River from Natchitoches to Old Fort Washita; and to construct to the Rio Grande a military road that would connect defensive outposts against the Indians in Comanche territory. Houston had been pressing for a bill to authorize the Galveston and Pacific Railroad to build a line westward, and Abert's outlook was partially based on this fact. Robert J. Walker, General James Gadsden, Thomas Rusk, and Volney Howard also played roles in trying to get a railroad built through the Mesilla Valley, an area not included in the Treaty of Guadalupe Hidalgo, which was written as a conclu-

sion to the Mexican War. Their efforts led ultimately not only to the transportation route surveys but also to the Gadsden Purchase, the last remaining area to be added to the United States before the purchase of Alaska and
the annexation of Hawaii.[37]

The first Corps survey under Johnson's supervision was authorized on 9
February 1849, under the command of Lieutenant W. H. C. Whiting, assisted by Lieutenant W. F. Smith. They were to resurvey the Hays-High-
smith route to Presido del Norte and proceed to El Paso. If the outgoing
trail was not satisfactory, they were to pioneer a return trail along the Pecos
and San Saba Rivers to San Antonio. Guided by R. A. Howard, a Texan
Scout, and departing from Fredricksburg, the expedition rode west to the
San Saba River. Here the men ascended the high tablelands; for three days
and four nights, they were without water, until they reached Live Oak
Creek, a tributary of the Pecos. Crossing the Pecos, they traveled through
the Davis Mountains to Presidio del Norte and along the Rio Grande to El
Paso. On their return they followed the Rio Grande to a point above Presidio del Norte and took a cross-country route to the Pecos River. Following the left bank of the Pecos, they traveled over broken, eroded canyon
country to San Pedro and on to Moras Creek. From this junction, the way
to San Antonio was familiar. In his report, Smith noted that the section between the Pecos and San Pedro was the only difficult area. The estimated
distance of their travels was 645 miles. Nine strategic points along the route
were indicated by an approximate latitude determination, a start toward
the construction of a map of the area.

Under the orders of a new commanding officer of the Eighth Military
District, Brigadier General W. S. Harvey, Johnson organized two additional
survey parties. Lieutenant Francis T. Bryan, the leader of one, was ordered
to retrace the Ford-Neighbors passage, while Johnson himself led a second
group to test the Whiting route. Smith and R. A. Howard acted as guides
for Johnson, who attached his party to a battalion of the Third Infantry led
by Major Jefferson Van Horn on its way to El Paso. The expedition started
from San Antonio in a western direction and then changed to a northwestern direction toward Las Moras Creek, the San Pedro, and the Pecos.
The men departed from the Whiting-Smith road by taking another route
between the San Pedro and the Pecos. They also avoided the mountains in
their approach to the Rio Grande and arrived in El Paso on 3 September,
confirming the existence of a practicable road. While preparing for the return journey, Smith surveyed the Sacramento Mountains, west of El Paso,
from 27 September through 3 October 1849. On 11 October, Johnson and his

group started their trip back to San Antonio. They encountered some rough weather but reached San Antonio safely. Johnson thus had a chance to investigate the Whiting route for himself, to analyze the need for defense posts, and to gain an opinion of the suitability of the terrain for a railroad.[38]

While Johnson was testing Whiting's route, Bryan, starting from San Antonio, investigated the more northward course used by Major Robert S. Neighbors and John S. Ford; he found it easy for wagon travel but devoid of water between the head of the Concho River and the Pecos. He suggested that the road could be shortened in three spots: between Fredricksburg and the San Saba, between the San Saba and Brady's Creek, and between the Pecos and the Guadalupe Mountains. He also thought that artesian wells would have to be dug at suitable distances to provide water and to shorten the waterless distances between population centers and rivers.[39] Interestingly, the Texas and Pacific Railroad followed Bryan's route, whereas the Southern Pacific took the lower road.

In the winter, summer, and fall of 1849, another topographical engineer, Lieutenant Nathaniel Michler, explored regions along the Texas coast and investigated routes from the Gulf to San Antonio, particularly from the vicinity of the Arkansas Pass and Corpus Christi. He also developed plans for an army post. His most important work, however, was his road survey conducted in the fall of 1849 from Fort Washita in present Oklahoma to the Pecos River, partially following Marcy's return route from Dona Ana, New Mexico. Later, as part of his duty with the Mexican Boundary Survey, he collaborated with Lieutenant M. L. Smith in tracing a road from Ringgold barracks on the lower Rio Grande to provide a communications link with the settled regions of the state.[40]

The most ambitious of the Texas explorations of the Corps of Topographical Engineers, however, was led by Captain Randolph Marcy, veteran of the long march to Santa Fe in 1849. On 6 March 1852 Marcy received a special order authorizing him to take the needed men from Company D, Fifth Infantry, and to "proceed without unnecessary delay upon an examination of the country between the mouth of Cache Creek to the source of Red River." In Washington DC at the time, Marcy immediately departed for the Southwest. After traveling between Fort Smith, Fort Washita, and Fort Arbuckle while preparing for the expedition, Marcy left for Fort Belknap on 22 April 1852, accompanied by Captain George B. McClellan, his second-in-command, Dr. G. G. Shumard, surgeon and botanist, J. R. Suydam, whose official status is unclear, five Indian scouts, and J. H. Strain, a civilian merchant at Fort Washita. The supply train for the expedition left directly for Cache Creek by the road that Marcy had made during a brief re-connaissance in western Indian Territory in January 1851.

At Fort Belknap, Marcy's escort from Company D, Fifth Infantry, under the command of Lieutenant J. Updergraff, joined him on 30 April 1852. The expedition now consisted of about seventy men, who on 2 May 1852 took up their line of march. In spite of heavy rains and swollen streams, Cache Creek was reached on 13 May 1852. The stream was too high to cross, and while waiting for it to fall, Marcy examined the surrounding territory. Several pieces of ore containing copper were found, along with particles that seemed to be gold dust. Later examination of the ore by Edward Hitch-cock, a prominent pioneer geologist and president of Amherst College, found it poor in quality. Hitchcock named the find "Marcylite" in honor of the explorer, but the ore never found a commercial outlet. On 16 May the expedition crossed Cache Creek and by the seventeenth was on its way again. Animal, plant, and geological specimens were collected, and four daily recordings of weather temperature, barometer reading, and wind velocity and direction were kept by McClellan. Shumard kept a geological journal and collected geological as well as plant specimens. Marcy assimilated zoological information and compiled a small dictionary of 168 common terms used by both the Comanche and the Wichita Indians. This attention to scientific matters accorded with Marcy's instructions. In a letter dated 6 March 1852, from Adjutant General Anson Jones, Marcy had been instructed to "collect and report everything that may be useful or interesting in relation to [the region's] resources, soil, climate, natural history, and geography." He was charged also to determine whether the region could support a considerable Indian population, to discover whether the plains tribes could be induced to settle there and devote themselves to farming, to impress on the Indians the military power of the United States, and to hold out the prospect of punishment if Indian attacks on Texans continued.

By 23 May 1852, somewhere between the present sites of Tipton and Snyder, Oklahoma, the expedition camped for six days close to the foot of the Wichita Mountains. At this point, McClellan took a longitude reading with his pocket lever watch and figured their position to be forty-five seconds east of the one hundredth meridian, by various treaties the western boundary of Texas; Marcy noted in his journal that McClellan was the first surveyor to fix the line. On a nearby cottonwood tree, McClellan blazed on four sides the same inscription saying that the tree marked the beginning of the boundary between the Texas Panhandle and Indian Territory. This action caused confusion in later years because subsequent surveys showed that McClellan had placed the line fifty miles too far east. The boundary was accepted by the Texas Boundary Commission, however, and Texas lost a considerable amount of land to Oklahoma. Marcy's expedition also resulted in the land between the North and the South Forks of the Red River being awarded by the U.S. Supreme Court to Oklahoma rather than Texas.

After their six-day stay near the Wichita Mountains, Marcy and his command continued to advance along the north branch of the Red River from Cache Creek. By mid-June, near the present location of Lefors, Texas, the source of the North Fork seemed at hand. After descending to the bottom of a canyon, leaving the wagons on top, the men came to a floodplain on which the river divided into smaller units. In a grove of cottonwoods, Marcy decided, resided the source of the North Fork of the Red, and he buried a bottle containing a memorandum of their visit under the roots of a tree. He then blazed the tree on both the north and the south sides and penciled in the words "Exploring Expedition, June 16, 1852."

The environment in which the expedition found itself was not as desolate as the men might have expected. A large deposit of gypsum underlay the soil, which was good in many places; grass was abundant, trees grew on the fringe of the river, and the water was drinkable. Large amounts of sulphate of lime were encountered but no hostile Indians. Except for the lack of fresh vegetables and fruits, the party did not suffer from too little food, given the abundance of game—antelope, deer, elk, and buffalo. When the group finished its exploration of the headwaters of the North Fork of the Red River, Marcy and a small party rode north to confirm the existence of the Canadian River, about twenty-five miles north of the Red River, verifying Marcy's 1849 thesis regarding the geographical position and proximity of the Canadian and the Red Rivers.

Returning to camp after this reconnaissance, Marcy was ready to move out on 19 June 1852, and on the following day the entire command moved south to pass the Salt Fork of the Red River. On 26 June 1852 the expedition reached the South Fork of the Red River, and a week later, Marcy and part of his command reached the headwaters of the South Fork. To reach these headwaters, Marcy and his command had traveled through rugged country divided by deep gorges and ridges, across vast stretches of territory inhabited by prairie dogs. Terrain made rough by both the erosive forces of wind and water and the tunneling urges of prairie dogs made wagon travel difficult; Marcy had to leave the wagons and most of his men behind while he and a smaller group of thirteen pushed on to their destination of the source of the Red River. Part of the way, they traveled along the bottom of a huge canyon through which the stream traveled. This was the Palo Duro Canyon, with sandstone bluffs on each side to a height of eight hundred feet or more, separated sometimes by a distance of ten or twelve miles. After penetrating the canyon for a while, the party took a left fork known as Tule Canyon; as they proceeded, the walls came closer together and the floor gradually rose to the level of the surface of the surrounding plains of the Llano Estacado. At the apex of the sandstone cliffs was a spring of cool water. Marcy and his men were the first white men in recorded history to reach this spot—the ultimate source of one of the continent's great rivers. For Marcy, this was a high point in his career.

From the end of Tule Canyon, Marcy and his group traveled back to the main camp along the edge of the Palo Duro Canyon. On 4 July 1852 the groups were united and started for home. The return trip was not easy because of the rough terrain and bitter water. With a lack of vegetables, scurvy hit some of the men. By 12 July 1852 the North Fork was reached and crossed, and that night the command camped near the base of the principal peak of the Wichita Mountains. In his journal Marcy stated that a military post should be established in the region of the Wichita Mountains; in 1869 Fort Sill, Indian Territory (Oklahoma), was established near present-day Lawton, Oklahoma.[41] Marcy's expedition had been a success—in terms of both geographical exploration and scientific knowledge. It certainly typified the "infilling" function of the Corps during the decade immediately preceding the Civil War.

In the Ninth Army District of New Mexico, issues similar to those in Texas occupied the army and the Corps of Topographical Engineers: improvements in transportation; and surveys designed to aid economic development. Unlike Texas, which had solved much of its "Indian problem" by successfully eradicating many of the southern Plains tribes, New Mexico still needed to establish defenses against the Indians or, alternatively, to launch an offensive so that defense would not be necessary. Much of the army's effort in New Mexico was directed toward these aims; a lasting result was additional and detailed studies of old and ruined Indian pueblos.

The topographical engineer on these excursions against the Indians was Lieutenant James Harvey Simpson. On one expedition, he spent some time at the populated pueblo of Jemez, west of Santa Fe on the Rio Grande. Here Simpson examined the way of life of the pueblo inhabitants and was regaled with history as well as myth. The brothers Richard H. and Edward Kern, along with T. A. P. Champlin, assisted him in observation and recording. At the Jemez pueblo, the Kerns made drawings and watercolors, including sketches of the mysterious religious drawings that covered the walls of the *estufa*, the circular meeting room common to all tribes.

After Jemez, the party to which Simpson was attached marched through mesa country and arrived at the Chaco River near 36° north latitude. The men faced canyon country, and as they headed westward into the canyons they began to find evidence of ruined and unknown pueblo civilizations everywhere. The first ruin they examined as they approached Chaco Canyon was called the Pueblo Fintado, and an Indian chief traveling with them declared this ruin to have been the temporary home of Moctezuma when the Aztecs were on their way into Mexico. In all, Simpson and his group discovered ten ruined townsites, constituting one of the most important archaeological discoveries of the time. As he investigated these sites, Simpson noted that they were made out of stone rather than adobe. This and other evidence led him to conclude that they were of Aztec origin, unlike the Casa Grande Pueblo on the Gila River and other pueblos in the Rio del San Jose area investigated by Emory. During the group's stay in the region, Richard Kern made diagrams and sketches on which he indicated dimensions, placed the pueblos in their proper landscape position, and showed their 1849 state of preservation. Generally, his reconstructions embodied Simpson's idea that the pueblos presented a solid wall to the outside on three sides, with an inner courtyard. Simpson also believed that the unit was tiered, with a series of step-back terraces of houses.

From the Chaco ruins, the group traveled westward to the foothills of the Chuska Mountains. After a short fight with some Navajo Indians at this spot, the command marched through the mountains into Canyon de Chelly. The men were the first U.S. citizens to visit this Navajo region, and Simpson again had a chance to study Indian life and ruined pueblos. They also collected numerous specimens of potsherds, some of which Richard Kern later reproduced for Simpson's reports. Both of the Kerns sketched scenes of what they viewed. On the return trip, the expedition marched through Canyon Bonito, the future site of Fort Defiance in Navajo territory on the present boundary of New Mexico and Arizona. More ruins were inspected, and a pueblo room was described carefully by Surgeon John F. Hammond; the description was included in Simpson's report. Besides working on the archaeology of the region, Simpson also carried out his topographical duties and surveyed the Bonito Canyon as a possible wagon roadway to the Rio Grande settlements. The group then made its way across a treeless plain, which spouted cornfields, and approached the village of Zuñi. The men of Alexander W. Doniphan's expedition into Mexico had been there before, but their report was not reliable, perhaps because this force had not included a topographical engineer. The best previous report on the Zuñi pueblos was one written by Josiah Gregg, but this had been based on hearsay. Thus, Simpson again found a gold mine for the study of Indian life and lore. Nearby was Inscription Rock, carved with names and dates in Spanish and Latin—some of them dating back to 1606. This high mesa had been a Spanish landmark, and the Simpson group spent several days making accurate copies of the inscriptions. Simpson even climbed the mesa by way of a spring and a cleft in the side of the rock to examine ruins on the top.

After leaving Inscription Rock, the party passed through the pueblo towns of the Puerco Valley and San Jose River region; Lieutenant Abert had mistaken these for the Seven Cities of Cíbola in his 1846 survey. Here Simpson recommended that a military post be built to guard against Navajo raids. He also advocated that an expedition be sent westward from the Zuñi region in search of an old wagon road to California that was supposed to have been used by the Spanish colonists. Such a road would be nearly on a direct line from Fort Smith through Santa Fe, Cajon Pass, and into Los Angeles. Had it been located (if it even existed), it would have been the most direct and best route for emigrant travel to southern California so far available.

Simpson's fame as a topographical engineer, however, rests not on his search for apocryphal colonial roads but on his advancement of knowledge about the region's Indian life, both ancient and modern. His pueblo investigations, his description of the Indian languages, and his comparative vocabulary analysis, which argued for six different linguistic groups among the southwestern tribes, were impressive. He and his followers were the first U.S. explorers to make an eyewitness survey of the region west of the Rio Grande past the Puerco; they were also the first to penetrate the northern canyonlands. His report on the pueblos he visited must be referenced in any work on the ethnography of the Southwest.

Simpson's recommendation for a survey west of the Zuñi villages was not ignored, and in September 1851 Captain Lorenzo Sitgreaves led a party westward from Zuñi for this purpose. With Sitgreaves was Lieutenant John G. Parke as assistant, S. W. Woodhouse as naturalist, Richard H. Kern as artist, and Antoine Leroux, a former fur trapper, as guide. By 5 November, after crossing the Little Colorado River, the San Francisco Mountains, and other physical barriers that bisected their line of march, Sitgreaves and his party reached the Colorado at a point where the river wandered through a broad valley, something it did not do through much of its course. By marching south along the Colorado through Mojave country and Yuma territory, they reached Fort Yuma on 30 November 1851. From Fort Yuma they proceeded overland to San Diego. Sitgreaves did not write an arresting report, and his scientific work was disappointing. Woodhouse produced a catalog of scientific specimens, but only a few new species were included. Sitgreaves's map was generally accurate as far as the Colorado River, but from the river to San Diego it was based mainly on hearsay and was not carefully laid out by astronomical observation. Perhaps the most noteworthy results of the expedition were the drawings of Richard Kern and the fact that the Santa Fe Railroad elected to follow Sitgreaves's route westward.[42]

An important basic map of the area from Pikes Peak to Cooke's wagon road in Sonora was drawn by Lieutenant John G. Parke. This map was actually completed in 1851 by Richard Kern, under Parke's supervision, before they both left on Sitgreaves's trip westward from the Zuñi villages. Parke's map, which replaced the earlier one drawn by Lieutenant Abert, was based on various sources. Sent to the War Department, it was printed and widely distributed. As new information was received from other expeditions, this was added to Parke's base production; the map thus served as a continuing source of information on the work of the Corps of Topographical Engineers in New Mexico.

In the Tenth Military District of California (including much of what is now Nevada and Arizona), much the same work as was done in Texas and New Mexico was performed by the Corps of Topographical Engineers. The chief topographical engineer for the Tenth District was Captain William H. Warner; he was assisted by Lieutenants George S. Williamson and George Horatio Derby. For a time Warner performed only routine tasks such as mapping the principal battle sites of the Mexican War in California, surveying military roads, and mapping the area around San Francisco and the connection from Monterey to San Luis Obispo. In June 1849, however, he received orders to investigate the terrain from the upper Sacramento River across the Sierra Nevada to the Humboldt River. The object was to find a railroad route across the mountains and to make connections with Stansbury, at that time on his way westward. A railroad route was never discovered because Warner did not believe the terrain was suited for such a form of transportation; but he did find that the way seemed suitable for wagons, and he met many people with wagons following the trail into California.

Warner also found a pass almost at the northern border of California (the forty-second parallel), at Goose Lake, but before he could compile his report detailing this discovery he was killed by Indians. Williamson later completed the report from Warner's notes, and the Warner Range and Warner Pass today stand as a monument to Warner.

In other parts of California, Derby accompanied Brigadier General Bennet Riley as aid and chief topographer on a rapid survey of the San Joaquin and Sacramento Valleys in June and July of 1849. The purpose of the trip was to locate suitable spots in the interior for military posts that would protect miners from Indian attacks as well as keep the peace among the many gold-seekers pouring into California. Riley also verified one pass through the coastal mountains, Pacheco Pass, on a line between the present city of Los Banos and the coast (along present state route 152) as a suitable military supply route from the coast to the interior. One of the most important results of the Derby-Riley excursion was a map that Derby made of the gold regions and that was printed and distributed widely among both civilians and military personnel.

Evidencing the continuing government interest in the gold region of California, on 5 September 1849 Derby received orders to accompany Major Charles P. Kingsbury of the Second Infantry to establish a military reservation at Bear Creek, a tributary to the Feather River. He was also instructed to make a general survey of the country through which they passed and to increase the scope of his work past Deer Creek as far as 39°28' or at "the mouth of the Butte River" where it formed the Sacramento River. Leaving Sacramento on 22 September 1849 at 2:00 P.M., the Kingsbury-Derby group reached the American River at 5:00 P.M.. The men crossed the American River and followed the road north through Nicholas Rancho to a destination near Johnson's Rancho on Bear Creek, where they made camp. This position was, they determined, an excellent site from which to oversee the Truckee emigrant route, which started from a point northwest and came over the mountains; they also were situated in a spot suitable to control the Lassen route coming from the Pit River country to the north. Derby's position placed him in the heart of the gold region, and soldiers during their free time could pan for gold. Derby concluded that the area was excellent for a military reservation, and he completed an extensive survey for its establishment, after which he and his party traveled northward, surveying part of the Lassen trail until they reached Butte Creek. At this point they reversed their travels and headed south toward Sacramento. In his surveying and mapping work, Derby had a number of unfortunate accidents—

including the loss of critical equipment. Nevertheless, his report included a detailed although somewhat inexpert sketch of the region's topography, along with commentary on the region's Indian population. These data later found their way into Philip T. Tyson's *Report on the Geology and Topography of California*, published as a Senate document in 1850. This publication, with an initial printing of five thousand copies, was probably read avidly by gold-seekers.

During April 1850 Derby explored the region south of Tulare Valley. He was supposed to locate a site for a fort between San Miguel and San Luis Obispo, but he was pessimistic in this regard and concluded that the most suitable site was east of the Tulare Lakes on the River Francis. He was also instructed to examine the passes between San Miguel near the coast north of San Luis Obispo and the Tulare Lakes for a military post and to locate a route from the coast to supply such a post. Derby did explore the possible wagon travel routes from the coast, and he recommended the building of a fort at Estrella, so named because it was at a place where four interior valleys met in a star-shaped configuration. He also investigated the interior of an area not far from Walker's Pass but found the region unpleasant because of the mosquitoes and some hostile Indians. In his report, Derby characterized the area as "not more than a desert." He submitted a table of geographical positions and estimated the Indian population at four thousand. His report may be characterized as supplying practical information about road surveying and the location of forts in any area not yet settled by a white population.

Perhaps the most important aspect of Derby's work as a topographical engineer was his attempt to find a supply route from an appropriate depot to Fort Yuma at the meeting of the Colorado and Gila Rivers. The only previous exploration in this area that had utility for geographers and policymakers at midcentury had been attempted in 1826 by Lieutenant R. W. H. Hardy of the Royal Navy. Hardy's book, *Travels in the Interior of Mexico in 1825, 1826, 1827, and 1828*, contained a map drawn by him (along with one drawn by Humboldt in 1806) showing the Gila as meeting the Colorado only a short distance above the mouth of the Colorado at the Gulf of Mexico.[43] Corps topographers' suspicion was that neither the Hardy nor the Humboldt map accurately depicted the lower Colorado, and Derby was charged with correcting the earlier cartography of the region.

Derby and one assistant started their journey from San Francisco on 1 November 1850 aboard the steamer *Invincible*, commanded by Captain A. H. Wilcox and containing a considerable amount of rations for the Fort

Yuma garrison. On 28 November the *Invincible* rounded the tip of Baja California; stopping at Guayamas on the western coast of Mexico for provisions, the party then headed northward for the head of the Gulf. On Christmas Day the ship reached Montague Island at the mouth of the Colorado. The group was in territory previously reached by Hardy in 1826, possibly by mountain man James Ohio Pattie in 1827, and before them, only by the Spanish explorers Hernando de Alarcón and Francisco de Ulloa centuries before. Sounding and surveying operations started immediately, and the vessel went slowly upriver past Pelican Island to the head of navigation at Howard's Point. Between 2 and 11 January the ship's party attempted to make contact with Fort Yuma. On 13 January, while still at the point reached on 11 January, the men met Major Peter Heintzleman, commander of the fort, coming downstream from Fort Yuma, another eighty miles upriver. By 1 February 1850 Derby had finished his work of surveying the lower Colorado, and the *Invincible* started back to its California port. One of the most important aspects of Derby's work was that he proved that the mouth of the Gila was 104 miles upstream from the mouth of the Colorado, hardly the short distance shown on existing maps. He also produced a survey of the river, with soundings, to the place near Point Howard, where the meeting with Major Heintzleman had occurred. Wind and weather information accompanied his report. He concluded that the Colorado could be navigated by a steamboat with a beam of eighteen to twenty feet drawing two and a half or three feet of water at any time of the year.[44]

Derby's later work for the Corps of Topographical Engineers involved projects other than exploration,[45] illustrating the gradually changing role of the Corps in the 1850s from explanation to engineering in the service of developing the transportation and water-control systems of the nation.[46] But Derby's report on the lower Colorado was significant in that it induced Jefferson Davis, the secretary of war, to plan for additional exploration of the Colorado by the Corps. Undoubtedly, Derby's pioneering exploratory efforts in the lower Colorado led, through official circles, to the later upriver journey to the canyons of the Colorado by Lieutenant Joseph Christmas Ives. One of the last and most productive of the U.S. Army Corps of Topographical Engineers explorers, Ives provided the American public with its first look at the extraordinary canyonlands country of the middle Colorado basin.

In October 1857 Ives gathered a remarkable exploring party that included a number of prominent scientists and artists: John Strong Newberry as geologist, surgeon, and naturalist; F. W. von Egloffstein as topographer; P. H. Taylor and C. K. Booker as astronomical and meteorological assistants; and Heinrich Baldwin Mollhausen as official artist.[47] Egloffstein and Mollhausen would produce the visual images of the canyonlands that captured the fancy of the American scholarly community. As engineer and master mechanic, A. J. Carroll handled the shallow-draft steamboat, the USS *Explorer*; this craft had been constructed in Philadelphia, tested on the Delaware River, and shipped to San Diego in sections. The sections were then taken to the mouth of the Colorado on the schooner *Monterey*. After a difficult voyage, the *Monterey* entered the Colorado on 29 November and tied up opposite the northern tip of Montague's Island, where mudflats intervened between a suitable water depth and the shore. Here the parts of the steamer *Explorer* were unloaded, and the boat was assembled from wooden walking platforms erected on the mudflats.

The *Explorer* was not the first steamboat on the Colorado; the Colorado Steam Navigation Company had been conducting a commercial service since about 1852, supplying both Fort Yuma and a civilian settlement across the river. The president of the company, Alonso Johnson, offered Ives the services of one of his pilots, Captain D. C. Robinson, but Ives refused the offer. Paradoxically, Johnson—on a larger steamer, the *General Jessup*—tried to beat Ives in reaching the head of navigation on the Colorado. Johnson got only as far as El Dorado Canyon, which he termed the head of navigation. The remarkable report that Ives wrote after the trip of the USS *Explorer* was factual as well as "literary" (in the nineteenth-century sense) and showed that Ives and his group far exceeded what Johnson had accomplished.[48]

Ives, his party, and the USS *Explorer* left Fort Yuma on 11 January 1858, traveling up the Colorado. At first, their difficulty in navigating through the many sandbars obstructing the river's course brought laughter from onlookers on the shore, but soon they entered country both wild and exotic. The scenery was dazzling, and as the river began to run through gorges, Newberry delighted in being able to study exposed rock strata. At the end of Colorado Valley, they encountered Monument Mountain and near it reached a camp of the friendly Cheniehuevis Indians. Shortly thereafter, they encountered Mojave Canyon and later Mojave Valley, both of which Ives described with great admiration. Some days later they reached Black Canyon, the first of the great canyons of the Colorado, now lost to view by the development of Lake Mead, which was created by the building of Hoover Dam at the head of the canyon. Black Canyon, Ives decided, was the head of navigation—at least for a steamboat—and after reconnoitering Black Canyon in a skiff with Robinson, he sent the *Explorer* back to Fort Yuma with half of the group while the other half continued upstream on foot. This group included Ives, Newberry, Egloffstein, Mollhausen, Lieutenant John Tipton, who had brought supplies by land, and twenty soldiers.[49]

On 23 March 1858 the detachment moved eastward from the river, generally parallel to a wagon road through the Black Mountains and the Cerbat Range; this route had recently been traced by Edward Fitzgerald Beale. Ives's journey seemed to confirm Lieutenant Amiel Weeks Whipple's 1853 guess that a good railroad route could be found west of Cactus Pass in the Aquarius Mountains. Ives also praised the Cerbat Range as providing a good railroad pass from east to west. Before long, on their continuing overland journey upriver, the men encountered the Hualpais Indians, and near Dramond Creek, they approached the lower end of the Grand Canyon of the Colorado. As they continued marching northward, they reached the floor of the Grand Canyon itself, probably the first white men to do so. "Only Cardenas in 1541, Espejo in 1583, Garces in 1776, and perhaps James Ohio Pattie and his fellow trappers in 1823 had ever approached the canyon before, and they had not reached its depths."[50] In his report, Ives reached heights of lyricism in his description of the solemnity and overwhelming immensity of the gorge, while Newberry and the others were caught in the awe-inspiring feeling produced even today in those who travel the floor of the Grand Canyon. For two days after entering the Grand Canyon, the men followed an Indian trail alongside the river; finally they groped and crawled their way to the top, emerging on the Colorado Plateau on the southern rim. Although they tried again to descend to the floor of the canyon, they could not find a suitable trail, and the Hualpais and Yampais Indians of the region were of little help to them. Finally they abandoned their efforts to regain the floor of the Grand Canyon; their barometric readings indicated that the vertical distance from rim to river was slightly over one mile.

Newberry was the first geologist to see the Grand Canyon and its subsidiary canyons. He was able to make a stratigraphic determination that went far back in history, connecting, in its depiction of how the land was built up, with the findings of Henry Engelmann in the central regions east of the Wasatch Mountains as well as with the later geological work of F. V. Hayden and F. B. Meek. Newberry also was fortunate in being able to study the Colorado Plateau, with its hundreds of miles of mesas piled one on top of the other as well as its igneous or volcanic intrusions. Newberry's explanation of this topography was based on the power of water erosion, a pioneering thesis that would later form the basis of the development of fluvial geomorphology as a science. Extending his theories of the canyon's formation and using his examinations of the strata exposed in the canyon walls, he disproved (at least to his own satisfaction) the prevailing geological theory that the North American continent formed a nucleus around Lake Superior and had once been an open sea. If no other observations than Newberry's geology had come out of the Ives expedition, the trip would still have been a success.

On 25 April 1858 the group had reached the northern edge of Bill Williams Mountain (named after the mountain man who had led Frémont to disaster ten years earlier). After traveling around the massive extrusion of San Francisco Mountain, Ives and his party reached the Little Colorado River on 2 May. From here Tipton, with the supply train, struck out eastward along Whipple's trail to Fort Defiance, the army outpost in the country of the Navajos. Ives, meanwhile, decided to explore the Mogui (Hopi) pueblos, which were thought not to have been visited since the era of the Spanish explorers. Taking Newberry and Egloffstein with him, Ives crossed the Little Colorado in Buchanan boats—much like the Missouri River bull boats of the Mandan Indians but made out of canvas instead of buffalo hide stretched over a wooden frame. In front of them was an army of scorpions, spiders, rattlesnakes, and centipedes—along with oppressive heat. Marvelous sights constituted compensation, however, especially for the scientists. On 11 May the group reached the seven Moqui pueblos after crossing the Painted Desert. The pueblos were admirable in their construction and the people orderly and secure. Trying to travel northward again, the three men were defeated by the desert heat and lack of water and finally turned southward toward Fort Defiance, which they reached on 23 May. Tipton, with Newberry continuing his geological labors, marched overland to Fort Leavenworth while Ives returned to Fort Yuma to sell the USS *Explorer* for $1,000. After selling the boat, he went to San Francisco and boarded a ship for Washington DC.

Ives and his group had completed a remarkable journey and had greatly advanced scientific knowledge. Newberry's report contributed to the construction of an increasingly accurate geological picture of the trans-Mississippi West. Egloffstein developed a new procedure in mapmaking so that the party's labors and travels were better illustrated. This depiction, using hachures, can be compared to a sand-table model; reflecting the ruggedness of the country by exposing depth and height, it is a process in use among cartographers even today. Egloffstein's map, moreover, was the first to show the canyon and plateau country. And Mollhausen's sketches—

quickly turned into lithographs for newspaper and magazine publication—provided the country with its first look at some of the most incredible terrain on the planet. Mollhausen also later became famous in his homeland as the "German Fenimore Cooper" for the stories he wrote about the western United States; his travels with Ives thus played a key part in the formation of European as well as American images of the West. However the results of exploration may be measured, Ives's Colorado River expedition was a success. It was also virtually the last of the major exploring ·endeavors of the U.S. Army Corps of Topographical Engineers—other than those conducted as part of such efforts as the Mexican Boundary Survey and the Pacific Railroad Surveys.

## The Mexican Boundary Survey

The Treaty of Guadalupe Hidalgo signed by Mexico and the United States at the end of the Mexican War did not precisely demarcate the boundary between the two countries. This was left to the work of a joint Mexican-American commission, which began its work in 1849; members of the Corps of Topographical Engineers were active in this venture.[51] The first American commissioner was John F. Weller, the official surveyor was Andrew B. Gray of Texas, and various topographical engineers, including Emory and Whipple, were assigned to the commission to do the actual tasks of surveying and measuring. Partly because of the inferior instruments of the Mexican contingent, the personnel of the U.S. unit took the lead in making the astronomical observations needed to lay out and make the azimuth, the straight-line compass bearing along the earth's curvature, which would constitute the boundary between the Pacific and the confluence of the Gila and Colorado Rivers. Each observation, however, was to be verified by a Mexican engineer. As this work proceeded, Gray surveyed the port of San Diego, and Emory organized the boundary survey expedition.

The boundary commission encountered numerous difficulties. The region between San Diego and the junction of the Colorado and Gila Rivers was barren and inhospitable in terms of the resources—especially water—needed for human and animal activity. Moreover, the California gold rush was in full swing, and desertion of personnel to the goldfields proved a problem, as did the high supply prices caused by the gold boom, which depleted the funds of the commission at a more rapid rate than expected. Disputes arose among the military members of the party over the discharge of various duties and responsibilities, and the military personnel also quarreled with the civilian surveyor, Gray; the commission was plagued by immigrants asking for assistance and bothered by hostile Indians and outlaw gangs. Even scientific problems impeded the commission; what, for example, was the accepted length of a marine league? (This latter problem was solved by arbitrarily setting the length at 5,564.6 meters. One suspects the commanders of the various parties wished their other problems could have been solved as easily.)

On 20 June 1849 Weller was replaced as boundary commissioner by John Charles Frémont, who, as he nearly always did, had an agenda somewhat different from the one assigned to him. Instead of assuming the duties of boundary commissioner, he decided to attempt to gain an appointment as a senator from California. In the meantime, jurisdiction over the boundary commission was transferred from the Department of State to the Department of the Interior, and Thomas Ewing of Ohio, as secretary of the interior, ordered Weller to turn over all of his books and property to Emory. Emory did not become boundary commissioner, however, having been insulted by the appointment of Frémont, against whom he had testified at Frémont's court-martial. The intercession of Colonel Abert persuaded Emory to remain with the commission and not to resign either from it or from the army.

In spite of the difficulties, the surveying parties completed the boundary line from the Pacific to the junction of the Gila and the Colorado. The members from the U.S. and Mexican contingents agreed to meet next at El Paso, on the first Monday in November 1850. On 4 May 1850 President Zachary Taylor appointed a new boundary commissioner to replace the errant Frémont: John Russel Bartlett of Providence, Rhode Island, who had lived in New York since 1836, earning his living running a bookstore on the ground floor of the Astor Hotel. Despite the fact that his store specialized in foreign and scientific books and was a meeting place for people and scholars interested in anthropological studies in the United States, Bartlett was obviously not trained for the post of commissioner. Sometimes a seemingly unqualified person rises to the occasion, but this did not prove to be the case here, and Bartlett never functioned as an effective administrator. He did, however, make several excellent appointments to complete the work of the survey. Bartlett selected a group of topographical engineers, civilian surveyors, field scientists sponsored by learned societies, fifty mechanics, and a naval contingent commanded by Lieutenant Isaac G. Strain, U.S.N. The chief topographical engineer was Brevet Lieutenant Colonel

John McClellan. Less wise was Bartlett's inclusion of a number of friends and relatives—most of whom had neither surveying nor exploring experience—in the survey party.

On 3 August 1850 this group, with Bartlett himself in overall command, left New York bound for the Gulf Coast of Texas. After reaching the Texas shore at Indianola, the expedition traveled inland to San Antonio, and from there Bartlett went with a small party to El Paso to meet the Mexican commissioners at the appointed time. The main party, which was expected to follow Bartlett, was rift by disputes over provisions, campsites, and command authority; finally, McClellan—apparently upset at being asked to serve under a civilian—was recalled and placed in charge of the Tennessee River surveys.

When Bartlett and the Mexican commissioners met in November, the most pressing problem involved the definition of the southern boundary of New Mexico. After some discussion, Bartlett and the Mexican commissioners agreed that the boundary should run along a line that extended three degrees west of the Rio Grande and north to the Gila, with the initial point on the Rio Grande at 32°22′ north latitude, or some thirty (rather than eight) miles north of El Paso. This interpretation gave much of the Mesilla Valley to Mexico; Gray, still the official surveyor for the U.S. party, thought this was too liberal an interpretation of the treaty, which stated only that the boundary would be north of "the town called El Paso." Disposal of this territory to Mexico jeopardized the right-of-way for a southern transcontinental railroad and was therefore an issue in railroad as well as sectional politics.

Although Bartlett ordered surveying to begin based on his agreement with the Mexican commissioners, Gray stopped all work on locating the boundary line pending a further conference with the Mexicans. The topographical engineers with the U.S. party, holding generally the same position as Gray, followed his directive. News of this controversy eventually reached Washington, and on 3 October 1851 the secretary of the interior ordered Gray to sign the agreement negotiated by Bartlett and to proceed with the work of surveying. Even before Gray got the chance to refuse, however, he was replaced by Emory, who was given the title of surveyor and chief astronomer.

By this time turmoil was rampant among the commission. The military members disputed Bartlett's authority to issue orders of a scientific nature, orders that they had to obey. Questions of whether the military controlled supplies and could withhold provisions from the civilians also arose. Dur-

ing this situation, Bartlett took trips into Mexico, presumably to seek supplies and encourage trade. He also engaged in negotiations with Apache
war chiefs to try to keep them from interfering with the boundary survey,
and he even traveled to San Diego and "explored" California as far north as
San Francisco. The purpose of this last trip, covering ground well-known
and mapped, was never apparent; it was probably more of a sight-seeing
trip for the commissioner and some of his closest associates.

Gray's removal and the recall of the chief of the topographical engineers, Colonel J. D. Graham, released some tension. Whipple even tried to
survey the Gila River as a means of getting the boundary survey work to
proceed, but his efforts were hampered by the lack of direction and control
from his superiors. When Emory arrived in the fall of 1851, however, he
started to bring order out of chaos, and the work of the Mexican Boundary
Survey began to take shape based on the initial agreement reached between Bartlett and the Mexican commissioners in November 1850. But
Congress—and particularly members from the southern states, including
Texas—were not satisfied with this arrangement. After considerable discussion and acrimony, Congress disbanded the boundary commission on
22 December 1852. Both Bartlett and Emory left the Southwest and arrived
in Washington DC by 1 February 1853.

By May 1853 the fight over the boundary commission had lessened to
the point where a new boundary commission could be appointed to survey
the Rio Grande below the disputed point north of El Paso. That month General Robert Blair Campbell took charge of surveying the river from Laredo
to the Gulf, with Emory again receiving the appointment of chief astronomer and surveyor. This time the work proceeded speedily and smoothly.
With the help of the Coast and Geodetic Survey, the party sounded the
mouth of the Rio Grande, and the line was established with the required
three leagues out to sea. By September 1853 the river survey was virtually
completed. Lastly, the matter of the initial point as set by Bartlett and the
Mexican commission was solved ultimately by the Gadsen Purchase, concluded by treaty in December 1853; under the terms of this treaty, the United
States purchased the disputed territory, including the Mesilla Valley region, from Mexico. The boundaries of the territory acquired by the United
States in this agreement were surveyed under the supervision of Emory,
who on 16 August 1854 once again accepted a post of chief astronomer—
but with the important title of "commissioner" added to his appointment.

Emory quickly laid plans to survey the boundary line as defined by the
purchase. He formed a party, which was divided into two groups, with

himself heading the first group of about a dozen men; with the help of Lieutenant Charles N. Turnbull, this group worked its way west from the Rio Grande. The other party of about six members, commanded by Lieutenant Nathaniel Michler and assisted by the artist-surveyor-collector Arthur Schott, proceeded from San Diego eastward to the Colorado River and onward to the 111th meridian. By the end of November, Emory was at El Paso conferring with the Mexican commissioner sent to work with him. The men got along well, and the surveying process went smoothly. When Michler did not arrive at the expected meeting place of the two parties at the junction of the 111th meridian and the parallel of 31°20' north latitude at the expected time, Emory became angry; Michler was later able to explain his delay, however, and Emory's anger faded. The western half of the survey was finally completed on 14 October 1855. By January 1857 all the necessary documents were signed by both parties, and the field records of the Mexican Boundary Survey were officially closed.

Both before and after the boundary survey ended, important scientific results emerged. From the survey records, the Thirty-fourth Congress authorized the publication of the *Report of the Mexican Boundary Survey* on 15 August 1856. This document was printed in three large quarto volumes; ten thousand copies of the narrative portion, or the first volume, were funded for publication, along with three thousand copies of the botanical or zoological portion. The last volumes of the scientific section were not finished until 1859, and many of these data had been already discussed in papers read before scientific societies. Some of the more important features of this work were the maps produced by Emory. One map was spiced by comments that enhanced its value; this map was based on thousands of astronomical observations that produced 208 separate points of latitude and longitude from the Gulf of Mexico to the Pacific. In addition, a barometric profile revealed variations in altitude along the line. Terrestrial magnetism was not neglected, and eight points of declination, dip, and horizontal intensity of the magnetic field were indicated.

The Emory map was more than just a map of the Mexican boundary region; rather, it was a master map of the whole trans-Mississippi West, drawn to a scale of 1:6,000,000, just half the size of Lieutenant G. K. Warren's map—drawn at about the same time and intended as a supplement to the Pacific Railroad Surveys. In constructing his map, Emory exchanged information with Captain A. A. Humphreys, who supervised production of the Warren map, but Emory's cartography omitted or left blank several important areas included in Warren's map and thus cannot be considered equal to or better than Warren's great map. Emory's map, for example, left most of Oregon Country blank and failed to include a crucial railroad pass through the Chiricahua Mountains above the thirty-second parallel. Emory's map was superior to earlier ones drawn by Preuss and Frémont, however. Other maps that Emory produced were available for study as part of the record but were not published.

Yet the most prominent scientific feature of the report was not its cartography but its section on geology. Emory pointed out that the thirty-second parallel area constituted a great continental depression and—anticipating John Wesley Powell's later work on the "Arid Lands" of the United States—he asserted that the area could not sustain an agricultural population but was suitable only for a mining, pastoral, or wine-making population. From the data that Emory's report placed at their disposal, other "professional" geologists attempted to deduce causal themes and to reconstruct a geological history of the area. From their work emerged a general picture of areas of aqueous or sedimentary deposits pierced by igneous intrusions that resulted in the uplifting of stratified deposits to form areas higher than the surrounding terrain. The influence of inundation periods was also explored, with the conclusion being drawn that there had been several periods during which vast inland seas had existed in the deserts on both sides of the Colorado and Gila Rivers. The scientists also looked at the data from the viewpoint of paleontology and attempted to gauge the comparative ages of the various mountain ranges. As a general foundation, the theory of uniformitarianism (gradual and nearly imperceptible change in the earth's surface) was accepted over catastrophism (abrupt and dramatic change in the earth's surface); this was a conclusion being reached elsewhere in North America by geological science and was a turning point in the emergence of a rational and workable view of earth history.

The botanical sections of the Emory report were the responsibility of John Torrey of Harvard, one of the century's great exploratory botanists and taxonomists. He classified 2,648 species of plants brought back by the field collectors. This work was reviewed by Asa Gray, also of Harvard, in the *American Journal of Science*; Gray said that it was to be considered "the most important publication of [its] kind that has ever appeared." The zoological specimens were divided into sections on mammals, birds, and reptiles. The classification was done mainly by Spencer F. Baird and Charles F. Girard; their work was not equal to that of Torrey, although it was more than acceptable for the standards of science in the mid–nineteenth century.

Perhaps the most important by-products of the work of the boundary survey were not scientific reports as such. In Emory's report were numerous illustrations that gave U.S. citizens a new view of the boundary region. Depictions of Indian groups and individuals were included, as well as views of the inhabited areas and the environment around them. Outline sketches portraying the entire length of the boundary line were also made so that even if the stone markers were destroyed, some idea of their locations would remain. These pictures presented an excellent idea of the topography and characteristic vegetation. In creating these illustrations, Arthur Schott was active in portraying (in color) the Yuma, Co-Co-Pas, Digueno, Lipan, Papago, and other tribes of the region. He also depicted San Antonio, Brownsville, the Rio Pedro, and a giant cactus, or *Cereus giganticus*. Two other persons who also contributed their talents to the pictorial record of the expedition were A. DeVaudricourt, a somewhat eccentric Frenchman from Louisiana, and John Weyess, an Austrian emigrant.

Finally, the work of the boundary commission was brought before the public by its last commissioner, Bartlett, who followed the literary bent of his earlier occupation as bookstore owner and wrote a book entitled *Personal Narrative of Explorations and Incidents in Texas, New Mexico, California, Sonora, and Chihuahua* (1854). Patterned after John Lloyd Stephens's book titled *Incidents of Travel in Central America, Chiapas, and Yucatán* (1841), Bartlett's work contained a detailed (and somewhat self-aggrandizing) account of his travels in northern Mexico, California, and the southwestern United States. In spite of its inaccuracies, *Personal Narrative*, like the publications by Frémont and Gregg, has a place in the literature of travel and exploration; for some, the panoramic view of life in the vast region it covers makes it a classic of its type.[52]

The publication of Bartlett's *Personal Narrative* provided a fitting conclusion to the work of the boundary commission, steeped in politics and less effective than other governmental exploring and surveying activities before the Civil War. Nevertheless, the Mexican Boundary Survey essentially completed the outline of the continental United States, and now the work of making the country solid and settled began. Exploration did not stop, but the efforts of the government and the military turned away from finding trails through the wilderness or establishing national boundaries and toward improving what was known and using the available knowledge to aid in the settlement of the trans-Mississippi West. Chief among the last of these efforts was the work undertaken by military explorers and others in attempting to locate the best routes for a transcontinental railroad.

## The Pacific Railroad Surveys

The resolution of the question of what route to follow in building a transcontinental railroad became of paramount importance to U.S. political leaders in the 1850s. With an American population firmly established on Pacific shores, with Oregon Country, California, Texas, and the Southwest added to U.S. territory, and with growing regional friction between North and South, a transcontinental railroad tying Atlantic and Pacific together was necessary.

To help solve the issue of the most appropriate route, the Thirty-second Congress authorized the survey of all principal potential railroad routes from the Mississippi to the Pacific. Previously, this sort of effort had been almost a routine adjunct to the work of the Corps of Topographical Engineers. Under the new legislation, however, railroad exploration work was placed under the control of the secretary of war, Jefferson Davis. He was instructed to submit a report to Congress in ten months, by the first Monday in January 1854. A separate Bureau of Explorations and Surveys was set up to facilitate the work.[53]

The surveys themselves were to be careful reconnaissances rather than mile-by-mile examinations of grades and curves and were to cover four possible routes: the region between the forty-seventh and forty-ninth parallels of latitude; the thirty-eighth parallel; the thirty-fifth parallel; and the thirty-second parallel. A curious omission was any direct survey along the forty-first parallel—the route ultimately used by the Union and Central Pacific Railroads, the first transcontinental rail link, completed in 1869. Some of this route had been explored earlier by Stansbury in 1849–50 and by the Warner-Williamson expedition of 1849. Other parts of the route would be covered by Lieutenant E. G. Beckwith as a supplement to his work on the thirty-eighth parallel route. Nevertheless, the neglect of the forty-first parallel as a route that directly connected San Francisco and that could have been used as a compromise route is puzzling. In his survey reports Davis later claimed that enough information was already known about this route; another, separate expedition was not justified. Perhaps this was true, but sectional politics obviously played some role in the exclusion of the forty-first parallel route.

The northern survey, covering the region between the forty-seventh and forty-ninth parallels, was under the command of Isaac I. Stevens, a former topographical officer who at that time was governor of Washington Territory and a friend and protégé of Senator Stephen Douglas. The route that Stevens explored led from the Great Lakes westward to the Great Bend of the Missouri and from there to Puget Sound, following trails well-known since the days of Lewis and Clark in the early 1800s. This exploration was the most complex of all the Pacific Railroad Surveys in that it was charged with the widest expanse of territory. The Stevens survey was initially divided into two main parties: one led by Stevens to survey a route across the continental divide from the upper Missouri; and one led by Captain George B. McClellan to travel eastward from the Pacific across the Cascades to locate passes through that last mountain barrier. These two major parties periodically split into smaller groups for regional surveys, and eventually, the entire route was surveyed. But little new information was gained, since the party was covering territory long known to both government explorers and members of the Rocky Mountain fur trade. In terms of exploratory achievement, the northern survey missed discovering perhaps the most important feature along its route—the Snoqualmie Pass across the Cascades—and presented no good information on a route across that range. Snow was on the ground when the expedition reached the region, and Captain McClellan, exhibiting the cautious nature that would cause him problems as a Union general in the Civil War, refused to test the snow depth. Nevertheless, Stevens submitted a glowing report of his accomplishments, a report so lavish in its praise of the northern route that it produced skepticism in Washington DC (particularly among the southerners surrounding Davis). A civilian engineer, Frederick West Lander, was dispatched to survey another route from Puget Sound to the South Pass. Lander's route branched off from the main emigrant trail, and his reports, which were also favorable, were included in the final edition of the Pacific Railroad reports.

The thirty-eighth parallel survey followed the path taken by Frémont in 1848, but it departed from Frémont in using the Cochetopa Pass. The first person to travel over a feasible railroad route along this parallel was Edward Fitzgerald Beale on his way to California in the early summer of 1853 to take up his post as superintendent of Indian affairs for California and Nevada. Beale crossed the Rockies by Cochetopa Pass and followed well-known trails across the Great Basin to California. He was partially funded with a $250,000 appropriation secured by Benton; he was also accompanied by Gwin Harris Heap, a journalist and relative who wrote a report lavish in its praise of Beale's route, calling it the shortest and most perfect road to California.

Beale's unofficial journey notwithstanding, the real work of the thirty-

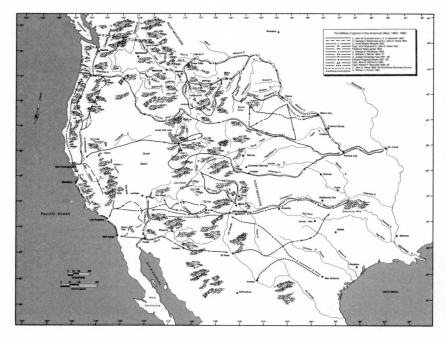

*Map 20.2 The Military Explorer in the American West, 1853–1860.*

eighth parallel survey was undertaken by Captain John William Gunnison, an explorer with previous experience in this region. Senator Benton believed Frémont should have been given the command of the expedition, but his protégé lost out to the army establishment, which always favored regular army officers (usually meaning "officers trained at West Point") over such mavericks as Frémont. Gunnison began his survey from Fort Leavenworth on 23 June 1853 with a party that included a number of veterans of western exploration, including the artist and topographer Richard H. Kern and the German botanist Frederick Crenzefeldt. In his expedition, Gunnison surveyed Cochetopa Pass and crossed the San Juan Mountains to the west by a pass that seemed to be a good wagon road to the valley of the Grand (upper Colorado) River. Near present Grand Junction, Colorado, the party crossed the Green River and made its way through the Wasatch Mountains to the Sevier River valley. Here the men were attacked by Paiute Indians on 26 October 1853; Gunnison, Kern, Crenzefeldt, and John S. Potter, a Mormon guide, were killed, along with four other members of the expedition. With the death of Gunnison, Lieutenant E. G. Beckwith of the Third Artillery became commanding officer of the survey company. After wintering in Salt Lake City, Beckwith reexplored the routes traveled by Stansbury in 1849–50 over the Wasatch Mountains and concluded that Weber River and the Timpanogos Canyon were practical railroad routes.

After receiving clearance from the secretary of war in February 1854 to broaden and continue the survey, Beckwith traveled north to the forty-first parallel and crossed the Great Basin by way of Pilot Peak and the Humboldt River to the base of the Sierra Nevada near Mud Lake. A search located two passes—Madeline Pass and Nobles Pass, the latter already a wagon route that started at Honey Lake—over the mountains into the valley of the Sacramento River. These routes linked Warner's California travels with Stansbury's explorations eastward from the Great Salt Lake area and his discovery of a pass near Lodgepole Creek in the Laramie Range of eastern Wyoming, the northern extension of the Front Range of the Rockies. Through his work, Beckwith anticipated the route of the first cross-country railroad. He did not submit any cost estimate for this portion of his explorations, however, and his contribution to the work of deciding on a transcontinental railroad route did not receive the notice it deserved.

In the meantime, with the support of Senator Benton and private financing, Frémont tried again to blaze a route through the Rockies along the thirty-eighth parallel during the winter of 1853–54. This was his fifth and final western exploration. On this last-ditch attempt to recapture his faded glory as the "Pathfinder," Frémont added a new element to his exploratory work in the form of a daguerreotype camera and its operator. The cameraman was thirty-eight-year-old Solomon Nuñes Carvalho, a descendant of a Sephardic Jewish family and a native of Baltimore. During his travels with Frémont, Carvalho kept a journal, from which much of the information about Frémont's fifth exploration of the West is derived. Frémont hired Egloffstein as topographer and named Oliver Fuller as assistant to Egloffstein. In St. Louis, Frémont found Alexis Godey and persuaded him to join the expedition. A man named W. H. Palmer was allowed to join the group as a "passenger."

By 15 September the party was ready to leave St. Louis, and on 20 September it departed from Westport and struck out across the plains for the Colorado Rockies, where a winter crossing of the mountains would again be attempted. After leaving Westport, Frémont became ill and had to return to St. Louis for medical help. He did not rejoin the expedition until days later. From this point on, the group moved steadily along a westward track, stopping for a while at Bent's Fort beside the Arkansas River; by 3

December the Huerfano River valley had been conquered. From here the party crossed the Wet Mountains and passed through the Sangre de Cristo Mountains via Sand Hill Pass and down into the San Luis Valley. On 14 December 1853 Cochetopa Pass was reached, and the men began their journey through it. Once they got beyond the Cochetopa Pass, the going was very difficult because of the weather and the nature of the ground over which they had to travel—canyons, steep mountains, and deep ravines.

As their food supply began to give out, horses and mules were killed for subsistence, and the Ute Indians harassed the party; Frémont must have begun to fear a repeat of the tragedy of 1848. Fuller, the assistant topographer, died on 7 February 1854, and a pall descended over the expedition. But by this time the group had been almost fifty days in the wild, and there was no turning back. The men continued to struggle through what today is Canyonlands National Park and Bryce Canyon National Park. At a time when their spirits were running very low, they reached the Mormon community of Parowan, whose inhabitants helped Frémont and his men regain their strength. Frémont felt proud that he and his group had crossed some of the roughest country in the West during one of the coldest winters of the region. On 21 February, Frémont and his party, without Carvalho and Egloffstein, who wanted additional rest and went to Salt Lake City for this purpose, left for California. They passed through the new Mormon community of Cedar City, in southwestern Utah, and crossed the line into Nevada near the present town of Pioche, reaching the Sierra Nevada a little south of present-day Bishop, California. Unable to get through Walker Pass because of a snowstorm, Frémont found a passage to a fork of the Kern River and followed the river into the San Joaquin Valley. From here, the trip to San Francisco was relatively easy; on his arrival in San Francisco, Frémont was cheered for his accomplishment. The price of railroad construction would not be low, but Frémont's trip showed that a winter route along the path he had taken was feasible.

Meanwhile, somewhat to the south of Frémont's track, the expedition headed by Lieutenant Whipple explored a route along the thirty-fifth parallel. This route, investigated by Sitgreaves in 1851, promised to satisfy the citizens of Arkansas and other central states. Vigorously supported by Representative J. S. Phelps of Springfield, Missouri, the thirty-fifth parallel route was a direct path that would start in Cairo, Illinois, and would run through an area with a satisfactory climate. Whipple's command began its journey from Fort Smith, Arkansas, in July 1853. The party included Dr. Jules Marcon, a Swiss geologist, and Heinrich Baldwin Mollhausen, the

German artist and naturalist and veteran of the Ives expedition into the Grand Canyon. Whipple's travels took him and his group along the Canadian River trail carved out by Josiah Gregg in 1839 and surveyed by Abert, Marcy, and Simpson ten years later. West of Albuquerque they headed for the Zuñi region, and from there they received the guiding help of Antoine Leroux, who had been with Sitgreaves in 1851 and with Gunnison as far as the Grand River. Leroux took them past the Zuñi region and into the West somewhat south of the route traveled by Sitgreaves. They followed Bill Williams Fork across Arizona to its junction with the Colorado. Reversing his direction, Whipple traveled up the Colorado to present-day Needles, California, and over the Mojave Desert to San Bernadino. In his report, Whipple claimed that the thirty-fifth parallel route was practical and advantageous for a railroad, although in his first financial calculations, he overestimated construction costs by about 100 percent. Later he realized his error when he recalculated the cost for his final estimates. The error, however, stuck in the minds of those who had read Whipple's first report, and the confusion over the building costs along the thirty-fifth parallel did not lead to a favorable hearing for this route.

The final remaining prospective route to be surveyed was that advocated by Davis and his southern coterie—along the thirty-second parallel, already partially explored by Gray before the institution of the Pacific Railroad Surveys. Despite fairly accurate existing information on this southernmost route to the Pacific, however, two parties were sent to investigate this path, one from the West, led by Lieutenant John G. Parke, and the second from the East, commanded by Captain John Pope. During the winter of 1854, Parke explored the route known as "Nugent's Wagon Road" through the Chiracahua Mountains of Arizona, and in the next year he improved the route by locating a more favorable pass. Parke's work occurred after the Gadsen Purchase; if the results of his labors had been known before, the boundaries of the Gadsen Purchase might not have been the same, since the territory it encompassed was not needed for a railroad in the area covered by Parke's investigations.

Later Williamson, accompanied by Parke, looked for a pass through the southern reaches of the Sierra Nevada. Not finding a suitable pass along that portion of the thirty-second parallel, he recommended a route from Fort Yuma through the Cajon or San Gorgonio Pass to Los Angeles, concluding that the western terminus of a railroad should be Los Angeles rather than San Diego; he did point out, however, that a railroad could swing northward into the San Joaquin Valley by using the Tehachapi Pass.

Williamson's efforts were not very favorable to the thirty-second parallel route and seemed to strengthen the arguments for the thirty-fifth parallel. This must not have pleased Davis, and little credence was given to Williamson's opinion. His failure to find a suitable pass through the southern Sierra Nevada was later validated, however, when the Southern Pacific Railroad was forced to dip into Mexico in order to reach San Diego.

With the conclusion of the Parke-Williamson explorations, the official work of the Pacific Railroad Surveys was essentially complete. But in California, other expeditions traveled north and south between the coast range and the Sierra Nevada looking for mountain passes and a satisfactory connection between California and the Northwest. Williamson and Henry L. Abbott, for example, attempted to locate a path from northern California into the Northwest. Even though Indians harassed the people engaged in this work, practical routes both east and west of the Cascade Mountains were found. The route on the western side was approximately along a trail long used by the Hudson's Bay Company and other fur trappers and involved topping a number of ridges between the upper Sacramento River and the Des Chutes River. Although this was country inhabited by hostile Klamath and Pit River Indians, the survey of these routes positioned San Francisco as the leading contender for the western terminus of a transcontinental railroad because branches could run north and south of the city. The little-known efforts to locate north-south railroad routes along the Pacific margin may, therefore, have been more important to the ultimate choice of the western terminus of the first transcontinental railroad than were all the explorations of the Pacific Railroad Surveys combined.

In describing each route, the reports of the Pacific Railroad Surveys varied in quality and in the amount of supporting political argument. All of the Pacific Railroad expeditions were elaborate affairs; scientists, both foreign and domestic, vied for membership in the parties, and much was expected in the way of advancing the cause of science. Scientists saw the surveys as golden opportunities to advance their cause as well as their careers. But the central purposes of the surveys were economic and political, not scientific. And it was in this political and economic context that the reports of the various expeditions were evaluated.

Two steps were used to evaluate the work of the Pacific Railroad Surveys.[54] In the first stage, the Department of War issued a preliminary report in 1855, and in the second stage, a final report, consisting of large quarto volumes, was produced in 1857. As Goetzmann has pointed out, these two reports were quite different in conclusion and intent: in 1855, the thirty-second parallel route was recommended; in 1857, although the thirty-second parallel was still favored, the feasibility of the other routes was addressed. The outcome was confusion; partisanship and regionalism were viewed as the culprits, and Congress failed to decide on a route. The thirty-fifth parallel route would have been an acceptable political compromise, since it was feasible and would have served the South, but Secretary of War Davis ignored this solution. He could not bring himself to accept political expediency over the considerable amount of evidence that had been gathered, particularly by the topographical engineers, in favor of the thirty-second parallel route. The professional reputation of the topographical engineers triumphed over politics, but theirs was a hollow victory.

## Concluding Military Exploration before the Civil War

In the years following the Pacific Railroad Surveys, the search for a transcontinental railroad track continued, but otherwise military and government explorations became somewhat regional in nature and decidedly practical: they now sought new and better ways of transporting emigrants and their supplies to the West. In at least one celebrated instance—the experimentation with the use of camels as beasts of burden and transport in the Southwest—military exploring activities became downright exotic.

In the summer of 1859 Captain James Harvey Simpson conducted an expedition in Utah across the Great Basin from Camp Floyd to Carson City and Genoa at the eastern base of the Sierra Nevada. On the advice of his guide, John Reese, he traveled a route farther south than any path explored previously and learned that this new route was suitable for wagon and stagecoach travel but not for a railroad. The Chopenning Mail Line and the Russell, Majors, and Waddell Overland Stage Company adopted Simpson's route for their services. The geologist Henry Engelmann, who was part of Simpson's party, gained additional geological knowledge. Because of his previous fieldwork, this information enabled Engelmann to complete the first geological transcontinental profile from the Pacific to the Mississippi.[55]

Another regional exploration was that of Captain John M. McComb in 1859 through southern Colorado. McComb went north from Santa Fe on the Old Spanish Trail and crossed the headwaters of the San Juan River. He then marched westward past the southern edge of the Sierra de la Plate, passing and investigating numerous ancient townsites near what is today

Mesa Verde National Park. McComb emerged onto the Colorado Plateau and found his way eventually to the junction of the Green and Grand Rivers (at Grand Junction, Colorado). Newberry, who had accompanied Ives to the Grand Canyon, was with McComb; he gloried in his opportunity for geological work above the Colorado's Grand Canyon, linking his earlier investigations with those of 1859 to form what was perhaps the first integrated view of the complex drainage system of the Colorado River.[56]

Lieutenant G. K. Warren led governmental expeditions in the northern Great Plains from 1855 to 1857. In 1855 Warren (a young officer who resembled Frémont in his demeanor and adventurous spirit) engaged in a huge triangular traverse from Fort Pierre on the Missouri River in South Dakota, south to Fort Kearney on the Platte in Nebraska, west to Fort Laramie in Wyoming, and then back to Fort Pierre. In 1856 Warren traveled up the Missouri and the Yellowstone to the Powder River valley in eastern Montana. And in 1857 he surveyed the Loup Forks–Niobrara River country of Nebraska northwestward to the Black Hills of South Dakota. Even though these explorations covered ground well-known to the fur trade, they were significant in adding to the map of the American West a number of important features, particularly the Black Hills, which Warren, for the first time, located in their proper position. Similar to Warren's explorations was the expedition of Captain William F. Raynolds across the northern plains of Wyoming to the Wind River Mountains in 1859–60. Raynold's ultimate objectives were the location of railroad passes across the Wind River Mountains and an entry into the Yellowstone country. Even though he was guided by Bridger, Raynolds failed to penetrate the Yellowstone territory or to locate adequate passes across the continental divide for railroad travel.[57] His travels through the heart of the region so long traversed by fur trappers typified the later efforts of military explorers, who attempted to formalize existing but informal geographical lore, particularly that of the fur trade.

One of the more unusual aspects of government-sponsored exploration of the West during this final period before the Civil War was the use of camels as a means of transportation. Advocated by Beale and transported from the Middle East by the U.S. Navy, with a native handler, the camels were used in desert regions on an experimental basis. During the period 1859–60, two expeditions in West Texas were designed to locate supply routes for isolated military outposts in the Davis Mountains and the Big Bend area and to find a site near the Rio Grande for a new fort to protect overland migration and stage routes. Both of these expeditions used camels as a means of transportation.

The first of the excursions, in the summer of 1859, was headed by Lieutenant William H. Echols of Alabama, who used twenty-four camels with burdens of about five hundred pounds each. The beasts were difficult to handle at first, and the packs kept falling off, but in his report Echols praised the animals in relation to their purpose. His expedition, in addition to demonstrating the utility of these "ships of the desert" in the American Southwest, resulted in the improvement of the roads between Camps Hudson, Davis, and Stockton and provided a reconnaissance of the Big Bend country. In the following summer Echols again took a camel caravan into the field, departing San Antonio on 24 June 1860 with twenty camels, twenty-five pack mules, and an escort of twenty men of the First Infantry. The region they were to survey was west of the Pecos, and their purpose was again to improve communications and locate a site for a fort on the Rio Grande. At one point during this trek the party went for four days without finding water. Obviously, the camels fared better than the men, but fortunately, water was found just before the party disintegrated; the group reached Presidio del Norte, where, in the midst of greenery, American ranches lined the Rio Grande. Echols scouted the Rio Grande and believed he had found an excellent site for a fort where the Laguna Lengua emptied into the Rio Grande, forming a small valley. This success prompted Echols to return to Camp Stockton, turning Indian trails into military roads as he marched home. Again, the camels had given excellent service.[58]

Camels were also used to help construct a wagon road in the Southwest under the Pacific Wagon Road Program, established in 1857 under the aegis of the secretary of the interior and approved by the federal government as a substitute for the failed Pacific Railroad Program.[59] One proposed wagon route along the thirty-fifth parallel was allowed to remain under supervision of the army, however, and the secretary of war approved work along this route, with Beale, long-time supporter of camels for southwestern transportation, as wagon road superintendent. On 25 June 1857 Beale, with his camels and a polyglot crew, left San Antonio and headed west across the southern plains, reaching Albuquerque on 10 August. At first the camels behaved badly, but after a while they began to prove worthwhile, and their fame spread ahead of them among the Indians. After waiting in Albuquerque for his military escort, Beale moved westward again. Congress had stipulated that this section of the road should start from Fort

Defiance, so Beale made a token ride with twenty men to Fort Defiance and then rode to the Zuñi villages, where the rest of his detachment waited. Departing Zuñi and traveling along the thirty-fifth parallel, the party periodically found and followed the trail surveyed earlier. Avoiding as many natural obstacles as possible, they laid out the road north of Flagstaff and Williams, Arizona, then turned somewhat northwest to use the waters of Gabriel Spring. The expedition reached the Colorado above the present city of Needles, California. Beale and his men had formed a working party that graded roads, constructed bridges, and looked for the best ways for the passage of wagons. They had also formed an exploring expedition, however, for they attempted to ascertain the best and shortest route possible for wagon travel along the thirty-fifth parallel. Crossing the Colorado River ended the official phase of the expedition, and the men and the camels, a huge success, were sent to Fort Tejon, ninety miles north of Los Angeles. Beale owned a ranch in the area, and while the party was in the process of refitting, Beale conducted experiments to see if camels could withstand the cold and snow of the high Sierra Nevada. They could to his satisfaction, but the difficulty of finding trained handlers and camel drivers precluded their ever being utilized significantly in western transportation. Camels were used periodically by the army in the Southwest until the 1880s.

In the Army Appropriations Act of 1858, $50,000 was set aside to improve the road from Fort Smith, Arkansas, through Albuquerque to the Colorado River along the thirty-fifth parallel. Beale was again appointed to head the expedition. This time, with the assistance of Jesse Chisholm, the party followed the Canadian River route. For the use of future travelers, an itinerary was prepared, locating campsites, recording times and distances between the sites, providing water sources and daily temperature data, and noting area game and Indians. In short, the party put together a travel sketch of the country. Of course, as called for by the terms of the assignment, the road was improved as possible, and where necessary, bridges were built. The engineers were operating along the more modern interpretation of their name and function. On Christmas Day 1858 the group feasted with a profitable hunt; the men also consumed a surplus of twenty-five turkeys preserved in the commissary wagon by cold weather. On 26 December the expedition arrived at Hatch's Ranch on the Gallenas River, a tributary of the Pecos. After a month's visit in Santa Fe, Beale started west again on 26 February 1859. On this leg of the journey he determined that travelers could follow the Canadian River route farther than was previously believed. He stated that the Canadian Valley need not be left until the traveler was within fourteen miles of Anton Chico. After much work and perseverance, the detachment reached Santa Fe on 3 March 1859.

West of Albuquerque the group encountered sandhills, the worst part of the trip to California, according to Beale. On the way to the Zuñi villages and Jacobs Wells, the men visited Inscription Rock and worked hard to improve the roadbed, finding fords for stream crossings and estimating the cost of building bridges. This was the general pattern for the remainder of the trip, except for troubles with the Mojave Indians. When Beale reached the Colorado, the road was pronounced excellent for a six-mile team wagon carrying thirty-five hundred pounds. On 2 July 1859 the return trip was begun; by the end of the month, Beale was back in Albuquerque, having covered the distance from the Colorado to the Rio Grande in 108 hours of travel time. From Fort Smith to the Colorado, a road 1,422 miles long had been made fit for wagon travel. In his work as a road builder, Beale did not forget the railroad. He enthusiastically recommended his route along the thirty-fifth parallel, at least part of which was later used by the Atlantic and Pacific and the Santa Fe Railroads.[60]

By 1860 the initial process of outlining the boundaries of the continental United States, discovering its most important and majestic features, and publicizing their existence in a romantic and attractive way was nearly at an end. More important, the process of the advancement of science began to change. Throughout the early period of exploration and discovery, the scientific purpose had emphasized cataloging and classifying. At first, the explorers themselves collected specimens for others to place in the natural order that scientists such as Louis Agassiz thought represented the work of the deity. By the 1850s, however, geologists, botanists, and naturalists started to accompany expeditions to collect and classify specimens and to write about their achievements. The Pacific Railroad Surveys were delayed by applications for membership in the exploring parties, and each expedition was eventually accompanied by a number of savants, some prominent in Europe. There were so many scientists clamoring to go along with each expedition that a special Bureau of Western Explorations and Surveys was used to keep track of them, with a staff to prevent disturbing the organization and work of the expeditions themselves. To help this bureau, the Smithsonian Institution selected the scientists who would go west, furnished them with instruments, and gave advice as needed.

The results of the scientists who accompanied the Pacific Railroad Surveys and other government explorations before the Civil War found their way into scientific discussions or into print between 1855 and 1860 through official reports and papers published or delivered before learned societies. Such disciplines as geology, botany, zoology, meteorology, terrestrial magnetism, paleontology, and others all clearly received stimulation from the exploratory process. Men like F. F. Hayden even conducted subsequent private expeditions to further the work they had started in the 1850s.[61] In addition, the explorations of the 1850s produced magnificent lithographs and other depictions of western scenery. The official reports of the Pacific Railroad Surveys contained 147 lithographs produced by eleven artists: Richard H. Kern, John M. Stanley, F. W. von Egloffstein, Heinrich B. Mollhausen, Lieutenant Joseph Tidball, Albert H. Campbell, Charles Koppel, W. P. Blake, John Young, Gustave Sohon, and Dr. Thomas Cooper. These presentations, often hand-colored by technicians in the Government Printing Office, were of a romantic nature and were intended to depict the grandeur of the western scene in all its glory—even if accuracy occasionally had to be forsaken in the name of art. Some representations of contemporary scenes were also made, including scenes of Indian life.[62]

But the most important scientific achievement of this period of exploration was not the volumes and maps and lithographs of the reports of the Pacific Railroad Surveys but was, arguably, the trans-Mississippi regional map produced by Lieutenant Gouverneur Kemble Warren. The true magnitude of his achievement can be fully recognized only when it is understood that he put together information from distinct and separately functioning expeditions that covered an area of hundreds of thousands of square miles. Warren's master map contained details of landforms, plant distribution, geological data, mineral resources, and even Indian trails. Constructed at a scale of 1:3,000,000, or 47.35 miles to an inch, it measured four feet by three feet ten inches. The projection of meridians and parallels of latitude were made from tables appearing in the annual report for 1854 of Professor A. D. Bache, superintendent of the U.S. Coast Survey, and utilized a new cartographic technique known as the "Polyconic method," which limited distortions in such a way that distances were practically correct for all azimuths or compass bearings. The result was the most accurate map of the trans-Mississippi produced before the extensive surveys following the Civil War. Much of the West remained to be explored, and Americans would continue to be given details on the West until the end of the 1800s, but Warren's great map provided a fitting summary to the work of the military explorers from Frémont to Beale.[63]

Whereas Warren's map marked the zenith of army exploration of the

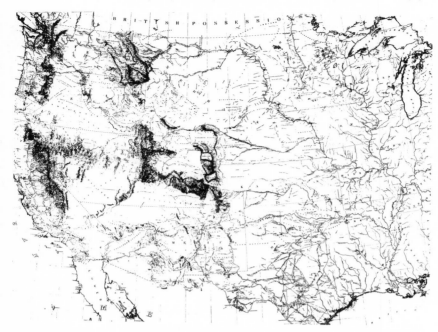

20.8 Map of the trans-Mississippi West (Gouveurneur Kemble Warren, 1857). Warren's map is the culminating cartographic production of the U.S. Army Corps of Topographical Engineers before the onset of the Civil War. It is one of the first maps to show the location and character of the Black Hills of South Dakota as separate from the Laramie Range, a northern extension of the Front Range of the Colorado Rockies. Courtesy of the Library of Congress.

West, the presentation of information about those who inhabited the region before the arrival of the white man marked the nadir. For example, apparently only the expeditions of Whipple and Stevens contributed special information about Indians. Whipple wrote an informative and fairly long essay about the Indians he encountered. Included in this presentation were myths, legends, and descriptions of tribal rituals, to show that Indians had a culture of their own with accompanying expressions in art and ideals. There was nothing definitive about Whipple's essay, but it stood in stark contrast to the more commonly accepted view of the Indian either as a noble savage or as a wild beast of little or no value.[64] Most explorers' reports either ignored native Americans or portrayed them as obstacles to be overcome—in much the same way as grizzly bears, fierce winds, and stinging snows were to be overcome. Although this lack of good ethnological and ethnographical data on Indian life and customs at a time when the Indians were beginning to disappear or, at best, to be altered forever is typical of the times, in hindsight it appears nearly unforgivable.

Thus, though not without faults, the reports of the expeditions of Frémont, of the explorations of the Corps of Topographical Engineers, and of the Pacific Railroad Surveys were a compendium of knowledge based on observations and on the collection of specimens, a collection that helped to make the Smithsonian Institution a world-class museum. The reports reflected a period of science preoccupied with the task of classification, but they also created a door into the world of enthusiasm for future study with a different pattern of questions. The Pacific Railroad Surveys were meant to serve concrete interests, such as the settlement and economic exploitation of the West, but the fact that they included science in the orbit of their work was an ultimate boon to the nation as a whole, as well as a benefit to the scientific community.[65]

For an understanding of western exploration in the 1840s and 1850s, we should remember that the United States was developing an international outlook and that it used its military personnel to advance its interests throughout the world. Money and equipment for forays beyond the Mississippi had to be shared with voyages of exploration in the Atlantic and Pacific Oceans as well as with exploration in other areas of the world. Attempts have been made to examine these land and sea excursions as reflections of the expansionist sentiment of U.S. governmental leaders, but these attempts have not been entirely successful.[66] Government policy in the 1840s and 1850s was often the result of actions by individuals for different purposes. Other people were persuaded to support such endeavors because they were loyal to the cause or because they discerned an advantage for their own situation. Exploration, therefore, was often the outcome of a lobbying effort that succeeded in getting Congress to grant the necessary funds and the president to agree to spend them. The unifying elements were the belief in progress, part of the romantic climate of the time, and the sense of mission that placed the United States in competition on a global scale with older nations and that was manifested in the desire to export Western (particularly American) values throughout the world. For the most part, expansionism and exploration were not ingredients of an independent brew but were reactive to other conditions, such as sentiment or ambition. The military exploration and expansion in the 1840s and 1850s represented the spirit of the age—an age that was ended by the Civil War.

On 3 March 1863 the U.S. Army Corps of Topographical Engineers was disbanded by an act of Congress, and its command function was merged with the Corps of Engineers. Only the memory of its many exploits and successes remained. But the individual heroism displayed by its members remains evident today, in the results of their topographical assignments.

# 21 / The Government Explorer in Canada, 1870–1914

WILLIAM A. WAISER

"It is very commonly supposed, even in Canada, but to a greater extent elsewhere," remarked the speaker, "that all parts of the Dominion are now so well known that exploration, in the true sense of the term, may be considered as a thing of the past."[1] These remarks were made by Dr. George Mercer Dawson before a meeting of the Ottawa Field-Naturalists' Club on 7 March 1890. Widely acclaimed as one of Canada's leading scientists, Dawson had been asked to contribute a paper on "some of the larger unexplored regions of Canada," and he decided to use the occasion to appeal publicly for the continuation of the kind of exploratory surveys that had been performed under government auspices over the past two decades. The comments were typical of Dawson: reasoned, dispassionate, and forthright. Armed with a large map of the Dominion, he identified sixteen "pockets," or areas of mainland Canada (excluding the Arctic Archipelago), that remained "almost or altogether unmapped," and he reported that "the whole topographical fabric of large parts" of existing maps of the country rested on "information of the vaguest kind." Far from believing that Canada's main features had been delineated, Dawson advised his audience that about one million square miles were "for all practical purposes entirely unknown."[2]

Dawson's speech was significant for a number of reasons. In 1870, when Canada acquired Rupert's Land (the area drained by Hudson Bay, including northern Quebec, Ontario, and Manitoba) and the Northwestern Territory (present-day Manitoba, Saskatchewan, Alberta, and the Yukon and Northwest Territories excluding the Arctic islands) and increased seven times in size (from 384,598 square miles to 2,988,909 square miles), the country was scarcely three years old. The following year, after British Columbia joined Confederation, the country covered half a continent and reached the shores of three oceans: the Atlantic, the Pacific, and the Arctic. It was the kind of empire that should have belonged to other, older na-

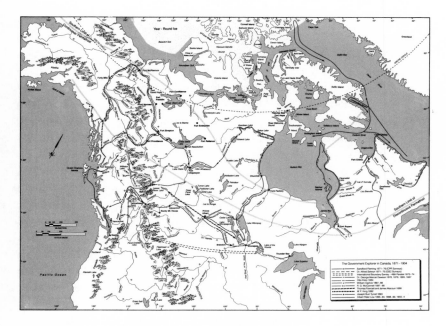

*Map 21.1 The Government Explorer in Canada, 1871–1904.*

tions—not a young dominion that did not have control over its external affairs. Some would argue that Canada should have been concerned about
avoiding possible absorption by the United States.

Canadian expansionists thought otherwise. Believing that Canada faced
a future of stagnation and uncertainty unless it was able to break out from
the constraints of the Canadian Shield and expand westward, they had
successfully transformed the popular image of the Northwest in the 1850s
and 1860s. Once dismissed in Canadian minds as a frozen wilderness, this
area came to be regarded as a potential hinterland that would not only
guarantee political survival but also serve as the means to greatness. This
idyllic vision had such a powerful appeal that westward expansion had
been one of the main themes of the Confederation movement. The Northwest came to be regarded as so fundamental to the future welfare of Canada that its development acquired an element of urgency. Successive federal administrations consequently devoted much energy to opening the
region, naively assuming that any difficulties could be easily overcome.[3]

Dawson was one of dozens of men, attached to various government
agencies, who helped roll back the frontiers of Canada over the subsequent

decades. At the time of the 1870 land transfer, large areas still required general exploration; Canada was largely an unknown country. Two decades later, much had been accomplished: the Canadian-American boundary along the forty-ninth parallel had been marked, large parts of the western interior had been carved into homesteads, the Pacific telegraph and railway were in place, and the vast Canadian Shield had been penetrated by geological and topographical parties. In the process, a substantial amount of scientific information had been gathered. Yet as Dawson advised his audience that day—and he spoke from considerable firsthand experience—to expect that exploration of such a vast region could be achieved within such a short period was far too unrealistic. Much remained to be learned about the country's basic features. Wide-ranging reconnaissance surveys, with their associated mapping and resource assessment, therefore continued under federal sponsorship until the outbreak of World War I.

Dawson justified the need for continued government exploration on practical grounds. "Explorations . . . are absolutely essential to civilized society," he argued. Failure to examine "this great aggregate of territory" would stand "as a certain reproach to our want of enterprise and a justifiable curiosity."[4] This emphasis on positive, constructive information was a hallmark of government-supported exploratory work during the late 1800s. When Canada expanded westward in 1870, the new territory, with its diverse natural life, could have served as an important testing ground, a vast natural-history laboratory, for the celebrated British naturalist Charles Darwin's "theory of natural selection." But Darwin and his ideas were largely ignored in Canada.[5] Instead, scientific exploration was essentially Baconian and concentrated on the careful, methodical observation, listing, and description of resources in an attempt to discover their possible uses. Victorian Canadians put great faith in the problem-solving capabilities of science; scientific knowledge was equated with industry, progress, and power.[6]

This "inventory" science, with its emphasis on statistical information, was precisely the kind of work that Canadian politicians could understand and therefore appreciate. The national development policies of the federal government during this period were based on the widely held assumption that Canada's natural resource wealth was unlimited and that if these resources were made "useful," the country's future as a great nation was ensured.[7] Ottawa thus expected government explorers to provide simple, straightforward, practical information that could be used immediately by private business interests to unlock the resource wealth of the young Dominion. Government officials did not believe in science for its own sake but rather in the use of science to further economic growth and promote national prestige—what one Canadian intellectual historian has described as "an entrepreneurial scientific ideology."[8]

The fact that Dawson delivered his speech on exploration before the Ottawa Field-Naturalists' Club was also no coincidence. Government explorers tended to be all-around investigators, not specialists restricted to a particular field of inquiry. Dawson was thus perfectly at home before his audience. "The explorer or surveyor," he reminded them, "must possess some knowledge of geology and botany, as well as such scientific training as may enable him to make intelligent and accurate observations of any natural features or phenomena with which he may come in contact. He must not consider that his duties consist merely in the perfunctory measuring of lines and delineation of rivers, lakes and mountains."[9] Nor did the government explorer often return from the field empty-handed. Besides making copious notes on numerous varied subjects, he gathered (and preserved) any interesting or unusual specimens that he came across. This collecting activity had an unanticipated effect on institutional development in Ottawa. With field parties returning laden with specimens season after season, the federal government soon found itself in the ironic position of possessing one of the premier museum collections in Canada but having no adequate facility to store these objects safely, let alone display them. Ottawa was eventually forced to open a new national museum building—a testimony to the work of the government explorer.

When Canada officially assumed possession of Rupert's Land and Northwest Territory on 15 July 1870, it did so on the assumption that some, perhaps most, of the land was fertile and that the region would quickly be transformed into the granary of the young Dominion. Yet large-scale agricultural settlement of the western interior at that time was anything but certain. Not only had agricultural activity in the area over the past few decades been extremely restricted in scale, but the results had greatly varied from year to year and from locality to locality. Many environmental factors critical to the growth of cereal grains were still unknown and would be resolved only by the settler after several years (or even decades) of actual experience.

At the time of the land transfer, two images of the region contradicted each other. The land was perceived both as desert and as garden. In the late 1850s, while the future of the Northwest was being debated in London before the select Committee of Inquiry on the Hudson's Bay Company, the British and Canadian government dispatched scientific exploring parties to the western interior to gather more reliable information. The Palliser (1857–59) and Hind (1857–58) expeditions clearly distinguished three prairie levels, or steppes, between northwestern Ontario and the Alberta foothills. They also defined the areas in which agriculture could best be initiated. Neither party was impressed with the grasslands south of present-day Saskatoon, and both concluded that the area formed a triangle of arid and infertile land. Instead, they extolled the merits of the more familiar transitional parkland zone, or "fertile belt," along the Assiniboine and North Saskatchewan Rivers from Winnipeg to Fort Edmonton. This assessment was understandable, for the party members did not know what to make of the peculiar plains environment and innocently assumed that the region's treelessness was a sign of aridity. In describing the sea-like prairies in their reports, both John Palliser and Henry Youle Hind looked to the American trans-Mississippi West and adopted the prevailing notion of a great inland desert, wholly unfit for agriculture, and neatly extended it into British territory to support their pessimistic conclusions about the grasslands' potential. They may not have been so negative about the Canadian plains region had it not been for the perception of a desert south of the forty-ninth parallel.[10] Regardless, the expeditions established basic regional generalizations about the Northwest.

Canadian expansionists had warmly embraced the idea of an exceedingly fertile region in the Northwest. In fact, by the time the region was transferred to Canada, the southern limit of the fertile territory had been extended to the international boundary, even though there had been no further investigation of the Northwest since the Palliser and Hind expeditions. Such sweeping resource generalizations were of limited value. If Canada's great hopes for the new territory were to be realized, a clearer, more detailed knowledge of the land and its resources was urgently required. The Northwest was consequently reexplored over the next few decades under a completely different set of circumstances and objectives. Even though the European fur trade had penetrated much of the region over the past two centuries, the government explorers who now took to the field could in a sense be regarded as "original observers of the land."[11]

## The North America Boundary Commission Survey

One of the first tasks to be undertaken following the land transfer was the surveying of the international boundary line from the Lake of the Woods to the Rocky Mountains. Although the boundary had been formally established by treaty in 1818, the only thing that had been done in the interim was the determination of the so-called northwest angle at the Lake of the Woods in 1826. Curiously, it was the United States that initiated the survey, in the fall of 1870. Anti-British sentiment ran quite high in the United States during these years, and some Americans thought that the country should demand territorial compensation for British actions during the Civil War. In particular, Minnesota, which had been commercially linked with the Red River settlement since the 1850s, was eager to expand northwestward and had gone so far as to pass a resolution along these lines in the state legislature. The administration of U. S. Grant, however, was confident that Canada would soon fall apart—the United States would get the territory in the end—and was apparently more concerned with preventing possible future international incidents because of an ill-defined border.[12]

The British Foreign Office was receptive to the American proposal and first arranged for a preliminary study of the probable costs and the best method of conducting the survey. This assignment was performed by Colonel J. S. Hawkins, of the Royal Engineers, who had served as British commissioner during the 1857–61 Anglo-American survey of the international boundary along the forty-ninth parallel from the Pacific coast to the summit of the Rockies. Drawing on this experience, Hawkins prepared what could best be described as a project blueprint, right down to the need for a portable library. He recommended the same arrangements that were followed during the earlier survey—namely, that the British and the American commissions confer beforehand to work out the details, that British and American astronomical parties be responsible for determining the latitude at alternate observation stations, and that a general survey be made along a narrow belt of land along the boundary. He also suggested that the boundary work proceed from east to west, adding that it would likely require three field seasons. As for the question of whether the marking of the boundary through the broken terrain of the badlands district in present-day southern Saskatchewan and Alberta would be a waste of time and energy, Hawkins argued that this section represented nearly half of the total line to be surveyed (862 miles) and that its exclusion would make a mockery of the exercise. He was, nonetheless, concerned about possible trouble from the Indians and warned, "The working parties should be . . . strong enough to protect themselves."[13]

After further negotiations, including an agreement that Canada would share half the costs of the British commission, the American and the British parties finally took to the field at Pembina, where the Red River intersected the proposed boundary, in the late summer of 1872. The British commissioner was a thirty-seven-year-old British artillery officer, Captain Donald R. Cameron. Unlike most other members of the commission, Cameron had been to the Northwest before, although this was probably an experience that he preferred to forget; three years earlier, as aide-de-camp to Lieutenant Governor–designate William McDougall, he had been turned back by a group of armed métis at the international boundary—probably not far from where they now camped—during the 1869–70 Red River resistance. Cameron had been nominated as commissioner by Canadian Prime Minister John A. Macdonald and was, probably noncoincidentally, the son-in-law of Charles Tupper, a member of Macdonald's cabinet. Cameron's British colleagues were all royal engineers: Commission Secretary A. C. Ward, Chief Astronomer Samuel Anderson, and Assistant Astronomers A. Featherstonhaugh and W. J. Galway. Anderson had worked on the British Columbia boundary survey in the late 1850s. The remaining key positions were occupied by Canadian civilians, many of whom would go on to prominent careers.[14] Subassistant Astronomer W. F. King, for example, became chief astronomer with the Department of the Interior and a British representative on future boundary commissions, and Commissariat Lawrence Herchmer headed the Northwest Mounted Police from 1886 to 1900.

The survey group also included some fifty noncommissioned officers and privates (sappers) of the Royal Engineers. Many performed special tasks, not simply supporting roles. Although the commission's prime objective was the authoritative demarcation of the forty-ninth parallel, the opportunity presented by these kinds of surveys to gather scientific information was fully exploited. Some of the men were consequently assigned to take meteorological and barometric readings and magnetic observations. On Colonel Hawkins's recommendation, two sappers, G. Parsons and J. McCammon, received special instruction in photography before leaving for the field. The camera had been used with encouraging success in the earlier boundary survey and was now seen as an essential tool in recording the commission's activities, the land and its inhabitants, and any interesting phenomena.[15] Hawkins's list of suggested commission personnel also called for men with naturalist proclivities. These duties were largely filled by the young Canadian geologist George Dawson, who had just graduated from the Royal School of Mines in London. He was assisted in this work by Drs. T. J. W. Burgess and T. Millman, commission surgeon and assistant surgeon respectively, who were both avid botanists, and by a trained taxidermist.

The British commission lost little time getting down to work. After determining the position of the forty-ninth parallel at the Red River, it spent the next eight months marking the boundary ninety miles east along the line from its base camp at Pembina, renamed Dufferin in honor of the Canadian governor-general, and south from the Lake of the Woods to the forty-ninth parallel. The location of the boundary line was based on astronomical observations made by the zenith telescope. This instrument, an American invention selected for "its portability, simplicity of observations and computations, and accuracy of results," greatly facilitated the commission's work.[16] The same could not be said of conditions on the ground. The old boundary marker at the northwest angle was eventually found—underwater—after a frustrating three-day search. Given the prevalence of muskeg (subarctic wetlands) in the district, the commission had also decided to conduct its operations in the area during the winter, but it did not bargain on the intense cold (–40°F on average) and the heavy snowfall that regularly brought work to a standstill.

The task of fixing the boundary westward from the Red River began in June 1873. To the unsuspecting observer, all the men, wagons, horses, oxen, equipment, and supplies must have looked like an invasion. The British commission alone, according to Dr. Millman's diary, numbered 257.[17] Many of these men were local teamsters, axmen, and general laborers hired for the season. There were also thirty armed, mounted métis scouts, known as the Forty-Ninth Rangers, who had been recruited in the Red River settlement over the winter. Captain Cameron, the British commissioner, was extremely wary of the interior Indians and feared that his party would be an easy target for a surprise attack. He was also reluctant to accept the American offer to travel under the protection of its military escort. Aware of the poor relations between the U.S. cavalry and the Indians, he did not want the Indians to assume that the two parties were one and the same. Cameron had therefore secured permission from the Foreign Office to employ this special métis corps to serve as an advance party, an intelligence-gathering service, and a liaison between the commission and Indians.[18]

The British commission attacked its work in military-like fashion. To ensure that field operations went as smoothly as possible, Chief Astronomer Anderson, accompanied by the métis scouts, proceeded ahead to find the best travel route, select depot and encampment sites, and prepare a crude

21.1 Men building a boundary mound, 1873. These mounds marked the U.S.-Canadian boundary as laid down by the North America Boundary Commission Survey. Collection of William A. Waiser.

reconnaissance map of the country. He even took preliminary astronomical readings so that the observation stations would be as near the parallel as possible. The remainder of the British commission was largely confined to an eighty- to ninety-mile corridor along the boundary. Three astronomical parties located the boundary at alternate observation stations—spaced at twenty-mile intervals—as well as surveyed the tangent line westward to the next station. This was exacting work; determining the latitude at each observation station usually required seven days.[19] Meanwhile, three surveying parties chained, marked, and mapped a six-mile belt of land west along the boundary. (The area to be surveyed was reduced to three miles once the badlands were reached.) Traveling back and forth between these various parties and the depots was a steady stream of wagons bringing up and distributing supplies.

Just beyond the Missouri Coteau, an escarpment dividing the second and third prairie steppes, the commission ceased its westward advance in early October and quickly retreated back to Dufferin before winter set in. The men could look back on their operations with satisfaction—four hundred miles of boundary (based on observations at twenty-three stations) had been marked without major incident. In fact, the only serious trouble for the commission came from the prairie fires that swept freely across the grasslands, imperiling the parties and their camps at all hours. The other surprise was the densely wooded Turtle Mountain, straddling the border in southwestern Manitoba; a surveying crew was kept busy for the entire summer blazing the boundary through it.

The British commission used the same operational plan for the 1874 field season. Before work could begin, however, a new base camp had to be established. The site selected was a métis wintering settlement at Wood Mountain (in present-day southern Saskatchewan), which Captain Anderson had accidentally found the previous fall. Once the new depot had been stocked with sufficient provisions, especially forage for the animals, and the various parties had been assembled, the marking of the boundary started in June. The first few weeks in the field were extremely exasperating. Although the commission expected the country near the White Mud River to be rough, it did not realize that the men would have to travel several miles north or south of the line to find a suitable route around the wide, deep ravines or the high, conical hills. The broken country eventually gave way to an arid plain that was only a slight improvement. "It was something terrible," Dr. Millman confided to his diary, "when you considered the heat, dust, barrenness—cacti over the whole ground, no water:

21.2 *Badlands south of Wood Mountain, a key reference point during the boundary surveys of the mid-1870s (photography by the Boundary Commission Survey, 1874). Collection of William A. Waiser.*

and the monotony of the scene."[20] The commission came across great herds of buffalo being pursued by Indian and métis hunting parties; within a decade, the animals would be gone.

Near the Milk River and continuing to the Sweet Grass Hills or Three Buttes near the present-day border between Alberta and Montana, the country resumed its rugged character, making simple travel, let alone surveying, difficult. Anxious to complete the work that season, the commission labored on, and by late August it had pushed the boundary up into the foothills to the cairn that had been erected by the 1857–61 Anglo-American survey that had come east from the Pacific. There was little time for reflection, however. Supplies were limited, and the commission had heard rumors that the Indians were planning a surprise attack as the men marched homeward. The different parties hurriedly rendezvoused at Wood Mountain and then retraced their steps back to Dufferin. By the time the main party reached the Red River on 5 October 1874, it had traveled the 862 miles from the Rockies in forty-three days. The next few months were spent preparing and filing final reports, depositing commission records and collections, and disposing of equipment. It was not until May 1876, however, that the work of the boundary commission was formally recognized by the United States and Great Britain.

In retrospect, the North America Boundary Commission Survey was a fine example of international cooperation, particularly considering that relations between the participating countries were strained. It was also a model of organization and coordination of men and equipment over great distances. And it was a feat of scientific precision based on the observation of 167 stars. From the perspective of exploration, the boundary commission provided valuable information about the land and its resources. The region was not a terra incognita, but the commission did provide the first photographic record of the country along the international boundary. It captured on glass plate the diverse landscape of the three prairie steppes or levels, as well as offering glimpses of a rapidly disappearing life-style. Equally important, the commission represented the first major scientific investigation of the so-called Palliser triangle in the post-1870 period.

Although several commission members subsequently expressed opinions on the region's potential, Dawson gave the most complete and penetrating assessment. Dawson's involvement in the boundary survey was largely the doing of his father, Sir William Dawson, principal of McGill University in Montreal. When the elder Dawson had learned that the person originally named as commission naturalist was unavailable, he had

21.3 "Map of the North West Territory Illustrating the British and United States Boundary Line" (R. E. Anderson, 1876). This map, published in the Journal of the Royal Geographical Society in 1876, was the culminating project of the North America Boundary Commission Survey. Collection of William A. Waiser.

written directly to E. A. Meredith, Canadian secretary of state for the provinces, in January 1873, recommending his son's appointment: "He is 23 years old, little in stature, but remarkably agreeable and ready, and an earnest worker, without any bad habits and gentlemanly and refined in his tastes."[21] George, however, had made other plans and was already slated to join the staff of the Geological Survey of Canada and begin fieldwork in British Columbia. In the end his father won out, but the director of the Geological Survey held the other position open for George while he worked with the boundary commission.[22]

Even though he was a somewhat reluctant member of the commission, Dawson vigorously tackled his work. During the 1873 and 1874 field seasons, he wandered widely—sometimes as much as fifty miles from the boundary—investigating any interesting phenomena. He paid particular attention to the geology of the region, especially the lignite exposures and their possible use as fuel for the Pacific railway. He also did his best to work up the natural history of the region, keeping his collecting net, plant press, and can of preserving alcohol close at hand. From his diary, however, it appears that he shot at birds more in the interest of diversifying a monotonous diet than in the hopes of securing specimens. Dawson also had a great interest in anthropology and could not resist the temptation of excavating several Indian graves.[23]

Dawson's findings were published in a lengthy monograph, complete with a colored geological map and several appendices. The report, modestly described by the author as an attempt "to make the 49th parallel a geological base-line with which future investigations may be connected," easily established his reputation as one of Canada's most promising scientists.[24] After first describing the difficulties of trying to unravel the geology of a region in which most rock formations are covered with surface deposits, Dawson correctly suggested that formations originally believed to be of Cretaceous age were more likely Tertiary. Yet in seeking to explain the superficial geology, he scoffed at the idea that the till deposits had been laid down by a great glacier. Rather, he argued that the western interior had once been covered by an inland sea and that the deposits had been made by melting icebergs. Several years passed before he finally changed his mind on this question.

Concerning the potential of the southern grasslands, Dawson stated that the second and third prairie steppes—with their light soils, scanty precipitation, lack of wood, and high incidence of frosts—did not compare favorably with the fertile belt, "which must form the basis of settlement."[25]

At the same time, Dawson was equally determined to correct the false impression that the Palliser and Hind expeditions had generated about the prairie district. Whereas the earlier surveys had projected the Great American Desert into Canadian territory, he observed that a large part of the American plain had since been found not to be typical desert at all: "This country, formally considered almost absolutely desert, is not—with the exception of a limited area—of this character; that a portion of it may be of future importance agriculturally, and that a great area is well suited for pastoral occupation and stock farming."[26] Finally, unlike the earlier explorers, who imposed their values on the grasslands and so naturally concluded that the region was deficient, Dawson urged that the progress of settlement should be "a natural growth taking advantage of the capabilities of the region."[27] His judicious advice could have laid the basis for a sound development of the plains district. Unfortunately, it would be taken to the extreme by subsequent government explorers.

## The Dominion Lands Surveys

While the North America Boundary Commission Survey was marking the southern territorial limit of Canada's new western empire, teams of dominion land surveyors were busy laying out homesteads for the anticipated rush of settlers. Seeing these men as explorers may be difficult: they faced the daunting task of measuring several hundred thousand acres of land and would appear to have had little time to do anything else. At the time of the land transfer, however, Canada had committed itself to a policy of large-scale agricultural colonization of the region on the strengths of the positive aspects of the Palliser and Hind expeditions. No further exploratory work had been undertaken in the interim. The federal government had simply assumed that a good portion of the western interior was fertile. Consequently, the land surveyor was left with the tasks of refining the general concepts of good and bad land and providing the kind of information that would be helpful to prospective settlers.

Ottawa was so anxious that western lands be opened immediately for settlement that actual surveying began several months before the official land transfer. During the summer of 1869, John Stoughton Dennis, soon to be named surveyor general, was sent to the Red River settlement (present-day Winnipeg) to evaluate the situation firsthand and propose a system of land tenure. Rejecting the traditional river-lot system that had been in use

along the Red and Assiniboine Rivers for over half a century, Dennis recommended a grid system based on nine-mile-square townships of sixty-
four equal sections (810 acres); this system was similar to the American one
in use on the western plains except that the sections were deliberately
larger, in an attempt to attract settlers.[28] Dennis and his associates then established the prime or first meridian approximately ten miles west of the
Red River (97°27'28.4" west longitude)—the western limit of settlement at
the time—and were in the process of marking off the major grid lines when
the work was abruptly halted by a group of métis concerned in particular
about the recognition of their landholdings and in general about their fate
as part of Canada.

The ensuing Red River Resistance, during which métis leader Louis Riel
forced the Canadian government to negotiate the region's entry into Confederation, not only delayed the formal land transfer for several months
but also led to a review of the proposed survey system by Ottawa. On
the recommendation of the new lieutenant governor of Manitoba and the
Northwest Territories, Adams Archibald, in March 1871 the size of the
townships was reduced to six miles square (or thirty-six sections) so that
the homestead available to the farmer in either the American or the Canadian West would be identical in size (160 acres); Archibald thought copying
the successful American pattern made sense. This slightly revised system
came into force on 25 April 1871. A few days later, a manual of surveys outlining the system and its astronomical base was issued.[29] Responsibility for
conducting the surveys and gathering related resource information fell to
the new Dominion Lands Branch (of the Secretary of State Department),
which in turn was controlled by the new Department of the Interior as of 1
July 1873.

The first dominion land surveyors who took to the field in the summer
of 1871 faced a formidable challenge. According to an estimate by Surveyor
General Dennis, roughly 1.4 billion acres of land were under direct federal
administration in the Northwest. This number was so enormous because
Ottawa had retained control in 1870 of all public lands and resources for
what it described as "the purposes of the Dominion." Whereas provincial
control of public lands was a recognized right of the four original Canadian
provinces—and later British Columbia (1871) and Prince Edward Island
(1873)—the federal government believed that western settlement and the
construction of a transcontinental railroad through the region could best be
realized if the government exercised exclusive jurisdiction over the land,
including that of the new province of Manitoba. According to a history of

dominion lands policy, federal control of western lands was regarded as "a national necessity"—one that continued well into the twentieth century, even after the new provinces of Saskatchewan and Alberta had been created out of the Northwest Territories in 1905.[30]

Given the size of the area to be surveyed and the urgency attached to the task, the surveying system needed to be applied swiftly yet accurately. Federal control of public lands therefore benefited the Dominion Lands Survey (DLS). Since all of the western interior would be subject to the same grid system, work could proceed at a fairly steady pace, a particularly important consideration because homesteads could be filed only after the land had been surveyed. The system was also precise not simply because it was based on astronomical observation but also because it was uniform throughout the region and therefore less subject to mistake. The natural contours of the land were completely ignored in favor of an artificial, checkerboard ordering. The only major adjustments were "correction lines" that were necessary to take into account the gradual northern convergence of meridians. Once the system was in place and the principles on which it was based were understood, the location of a homestead anywhere in the Northwest would prove a relatively straightforward matter.

As for the actual surveying of the land, the government assumed that settlement would initially be confined to the fertile belt that had been identified by the Palliser and Hind expeditions. The DLS was consequently organized to begin in Manitoba and then proceed northwest along the North Saskatchewan River through central Saskatchewan and Alberta. In their reports, survey officials referred to this area as the "settlement belt," which they fully expected to be fairly uniform in character. They were so confident about the ease with which the work could be performed that surveyors were initially employed under contract at a fixed rate per mile. As surveyors and their support crews took to the field, however, they quickly discovered that very little was actually known about the land and that it was impossible to predict beforehand what physical obstacles might be encountered in a particular district. Each survey was, in a sense, a kind of exploratory activity. Most survey work thus began to be remunerated on a per diem basis; only the subdivision of townships continued to be performed under contract.[31]

In the field, surveyors and their gangs suffered through a host of difficulties, as evidenced by the lively diaries of Otto Julius Klotz. Commissioned as dominion topographical surveyor in November 1877 and later to become assistant astronomer with the Department of the Interior, Klotz faithfully kept a daily journal for fifty-six years. Although his entries at times border on the melodramatic, they provide a vivid picture of the life of a surveyor in the field. In 1879, for example, while laying out township boundary lines near the Pembina River in southwestern Manitoba, Klotz described how he battled forest fires, how the ponies kept wandering off at night, how he suffered from severe bouts of diarrhea because of the brackish water, and how his instrument sometimes came apart in his hands. Klotz's most entertaining entries were reserved for the pesky mosquito:

> The bridgeless river is a small, deep, swift, meandering stream with low muddy banks, the home sweet home of my intimate friend, the mosquito—when writing the word mosquito there is something so enchanting about it that the reality looms up and I am tempted to indulge in some of my "sacred" profanity which I so kindly and so unhesitantly bestowed upon these higher forms of organism. The number we encountered here defied mathematicians to express by finite numbers. . . . Mosquito nets are a delusion and mockery; two will pull the meshes asunder and a third one walk in, without any ceremony of "who comes here."[32]

Despite such irritations, the DLS managed to survey 10.5 million acres in the prairie parkland region between 1871 and 1875. Nevertheless, as the transcontinental railway was pushed across the western interior in the early 1880s, the need to push ahead with the work greatly intensified. From the beginning the government had assumed that the railway—like the survey—would follow the fertile belt. In the spring of 1881, however, the main line of the railway was relocated across the southern grasslands, several hundred miles south of the townships that had been subdivided in the 1870s. The DLS had no choice but to redirect its efforts to the open prairies and try to ensure that there was enough homestead land available for the scores of settlers who would follow in the wake of the railway. Surveyors and their support staff took to the field. In 1883 alone, 119 men surveyed 11,300 miles of township lines and subdivided 1,221 townships. This work translated into some 27 million acres readied for occupation and, as the official department history of the survey boasted, "probably stand[s] unrivalled in the history of land subdivision in any country."[33] The pace did not slacken. By the end of 1887, the total number of subdivided acres topped 70 million.

Given the nature of their work and the speed and economy with which it was to be accomplished, dominion land surveyors would seem to have had little time for much else. One of their official duties, however, was to record the terrain and vegetation and to assess the capabilities of the land. Surveyors were in the ideal position to perform this work, since they saw the country firsthand and became more familiar with its physical and natural features each field season.[34] They also had the chance to observe the soil and subsoil whenever they dug holes for the marker posts. Yet surveyors were not given any specific criteria for judging the soil, which thus became a purely subjective exercise. Surveyors working on opposite sides of a township line often came up with significantly different soil classifications. Moreover, the assessment of the land and its resources remained subordinate to surveying duties, and surveyors often quickly judged a region on the basis of its vegetation.[35] This procedure, also an accepted practice among government explorers at the time, failed to allow for the possibility of varying environmental conditions from year to year. To acquire experience in the western interior and be able to express a competent opinion required detailed study over a number of years, not just a few field seasons.

Surveyors were also involved in general exploratory work. In 1872, the second full season of survey operations, several men were dispatched to different points along the "settlement belt" to examine the country and assess its potential in preparation for the detailed survey. This activity was given official sanction with the creation of the "Special Survey" by federal order-in-council in February 1874. To ensure that the survey was conducted with "all possible precision," advance teams were sent ahead to project the main meridians and baselines into the interior and thereby lay the groundwork for township demarcation and subdivision. As part of this work, these men were also expected "to obtain a knowledge of the character and resources in the way of soil, timber and minerals, as also of the flora and fauna, of the territories covered by the survey."[36] Overnight, then, the survey took on a formal exploration function. While W. F. King, former member of the boundary commission and now astronomical surveyor, spent several consecutive summers in the mid-1870s determining latitude and longitude (including main meridians) at several designated points, other surveyors ran township meridians and baselines across the Northwest. In the process, they mapped the major topographical features, recorded distances, surveyed and marked the main trails, and noted the resources—agricultural or otherwise.

Once the Special Survey had extended the major survey lines up into the Peace River district in present-day northern Alberta, its work became almost exclusively exploratory in character; in fact, it began to investigate territory well north of the region of anticipated settlement. In 1884, for example, Klotz was rescued from the often tedious chore of subdividing townships and did a track survey of the Saskatchewan and Nelson Rivers between Prince Albert and York Factory. Thomas Fawcett made the second of two major exploratory surveys north of the fertile belt in 1888 when he did a micrometer traverse (measurement of angular distances) of the waterways between Lesser Slave Lake in northern Alberta and the Manitoba lakes region. Fawcett was accompanied by a young naturalist, James Macoun, who would eventually become chief of the biological division at the Victoria Memorial Museum. The most dramatic and extensive expedition, however, was that of William Ogilvie. Unlike the other exploratory surveys undertaken by the Special Survey during this period, Ogilvie's included a specific surveying function—the location of the 141st meridian where it intersected the Yukon River (Canadian-American boundary). Ogilvie spent the entire 1887 field season getting to his winter observation site near the small mining settlement of Forty Mile on the Yukon River, all the while making an instrument survey of the route. After ascertaining the location of the boundary (by observing the transits of the moon) and marking it, he then crossed over to the Mackenzie River in the western Northwest Territories in the spring of 1888 and continued his survey south to Fort Chipewyan on Lake Athabasca. This kind of expedition speaks volumes about the caliber of the men who made up the ranks of the DLS and explains why the Special Survey was regarded by some as "the most important surveying work undertaken by the Government since the acquisition of the territory."[37]

The Dominion Lands Branch was also involved in the reappraisal of the region that the Palliser and Hind expeditions had ruled out for settlement. This work was largely undertaken by the plant geographer John Macoun, professor of natural history at Albert College, Belleville, Ontario. Macoun was no stranger to the Northwest; he had favorably assessed the Peace River country in 1872 and 1875 on its ability to support plant species that grew where agriculture was already being practiced in Ontario. He had also told a House of Commons committee in 1876 that the assessment of the Palliser and Hind expeditions was a hasty conclusion and that portions of the region were suited for stock raising and possibly for grain production—even though he had never personally seen the southern grasslands. Now, as the newly appointed explorer for the Canadian government in the Northwest Territories, he was asked in 1879 and 1880 to examine the prairie district south of the Qu'Appelle and South Saskatchewan Rivers, especially those areas that had been condemned. Macoun's findings supported his earlier assertions. Traveling during exceptionally wet summers, he discovered thick swards of luxuriant grasses; he also came across a field of wheat under cultivation in the supposedly sterile soil. Macoun consequently concluded that the shallow and light soils of the second and third prairie steppes would become productive once the ground had been broken and cultivated. He even went so far as to challenge the long-standing assumption that settlement should be initially restricted to the wooded fertile belt, and he extolled the virtues of the treeless plain.[38]

Although Macoun's subsequent statements about western Canada's potential were reckless, he was not alone in his views. As the survey progressed along the North Saskatchewan in the late 1870s, surveyors' field reports indicated that the area of arable land along the fertile belt was much greater than had previously been estimated. Similarly, as the survey moved into the southern district, surveyors found that "what was deemed relatively a desert or barren land, has turned out to be specially fitted, both by fertility of soil and by the nature of its surface, for agricultural production."[39] This sense of discovery, of revealing the region's true character, achieved its fullest expression in the twentieth-anniversary report of survey operations. Indeed, the report argued that "the acquirement of a mass of reliable information" about the region was just as important as the thorough and accurate measurement of the land. "These surveys and explorations exploded the idea, at the time so prevalent, that large portions of the Territories were barren wastes or deserts, and may be said to have settled the question of the adaptability of the large part of the country as a field for successful farming operations . . . in Manitoba and the North-West Territories, the Dominion possesses a heritage which, for healthy climate, richness of soil and general adaptability for agricultural pursuits, compares favourably with any country on the habitable globe."[40]

These findings perfectly matched Canadian expectations. Canada, which had acquired the Northwest in 1870 in the belief that the region would soon become the future home of countless millions, was anxious that its great hopes for the region be substantiated. In particular, the federal government wanted to attract a private builder for the transcontinental railway, and the prospect of wonderfully fertile lands would greatly facilitate this scheme. As for the popular image of the Northwest, during the 1870s an incredible volume of literature waxed enthusiastic about the capabilities and resources of the western interior while downplaying the extent to which the Great American Desert extended into Canada. As early as 1870, for example, A. J. Russell, inspector of Crown timber agencies in Canada, suggested that the value of the southern Saskatchewan country may have been underrated.[41] That same year, a translator's introduction to a book that warned about the incidence of frosts in the fertile belt apologized for its pessimistic outlook.[42]

Given this perception of the Northwest as a possible agricultural garden, the men of the Dominion Lands Branch can be excused for their excesses. As one author has commented about the reevaluation of the southern prairie district, it is "difficult . . . to be objective about the potential use of a marginal area, especially when there are changing resource demands. Each observer tends to have blinders which channel and limit his particular perception of an area."[43] But sweeping generalizations were no substitute for reality. Like the investigators before them, land surveyors, including special explorers such as Macoun, discovered a limited kind of truth. Their findings, though not necessarily wrong, represented only the ideal aspects of the Northwest and were thus misleading and potentially harmful in the long run. The surveyors' statements about the great potential of the western interior suggested that the standard one-hundred-acre homestead allotment was appropriate, even in grassland areas, and that the settler would require little assistance at the pioneering stage. But once settlement of the region got under way, the farmer, especially along the main line of the Canadian Pacific Railway, was confronted with disillusioning agricultural problems and began asking the same questions that Dominion Lands Branch surveyors and explorers had originally sought to answer. The farmer gradually learned that each locality had its unique set of problems and qualities—the potential of desert or garden—and that the successful cultivation of the land depended on experience and the increasing application of science and technology.

A more lasting legacy of the DLS—in comparison with its resource-assessment work—was its activities in the area of phototopography or photogrammetry. By the mid-1880s, the survey had reached the Rockies and faced the perplexing task of how to continue its topographical survey in the mountains. Up to then, the survey had been able to measure so much land each year largely because of the nature of the terrain in the western interior. The surveying of the forty-mile-wide railway belt in British Columbia now promised to be both costly and dangerous. As a prelude to the survey's work in the mountains, Ogilvie made an instrumental traverse along the railway main line in 1885 and thereby established a baseline for future detailed mapping at selected points. When surveying began in the following field season, however, the surveyors quickly realized that conventional methods would not work, particularly when so much climbing was involved. By coincidence, however, the new surveyor general, Edouard Deville, had issued cameras to a number of surveyors in 1886 to take photographs to illustrate their reports, as well as to test the usefulness of photographs in topographical work. Deville now decided that the experiment should be continued in the mountains. In 1887, surveyors J. J. McArthur and W. S. Drewry were supplied with camera equipment and directed to take a series of panoramic views from a number of predetermined (by triangulation) stations. The photographs would then be used to plot the maps back in the office. The results proved satisfactory, and the men repeated the process in the following field season. Thanks to their experience and better camera equipment, they covered seven hundred miles.[44]

Over the next decade, phototopography was increasingly improved and refined and came to be an indispensable surveying aid. In 1892 King, the Canadian commissioner for the International Boundary Survey of the Alaska–British Columbia boundary, elected to use phototopography for the Canadian share of the work. Over the next two field seasons, the Canadian team plotted over five thousand square miles, much to the amazement of their American counterparts. Surveyor A. O. Wheeler also used the camera extensively in his 1901–2 survey of the Selkirk Range in southeastern British Columbia. During the 1902 field season, he took photographs from 120 separate stations reached by a total of sixty-four ascents.[45] The photographs taken during these and other expeditions were secured with practical purposes in mind and hence had little aesthetic value; only rarely were they displayed in public. The technique, however, was a great improvement over conventional surveying methods in that it enabled field parties to cover long distances in a relatively short period of time and at considerably less cost. Phototopography represented a quantum leap in the exploration and mapping of Canada, especially in mountainous regions. In the words of one of the surveyors, "By this widening circle of alpine landmarks one's knowledge of the country is enhanced and takes form."[46]

## The Canadian Pacific Railway Survey

Surveying and measuring western lands constituted only one step—albeit an important one—in the integration of the region with Canada. Until the new territory was linked with the young Dominion, it would remain isolated no matter how much information was gathered about the region and its resources. Providing dependable communication and transportation within and through the region was just as important as knowing what was there. Consequently, much government exploration work was undertaken in the western interior in the 1870s to find the best-possible route for a transcontinental railway and, to a lesser extent, for an electric telegraph. Victorian Canadians looked on steam and electricity as great civilizing agents that would effectively reduce the vast distances of the Northwest, as well as facilitate the establishment of the best features of British civilization in the western interior. Indeed, the new technology and its potential applications helped support the vision of a sea-to-sea nation during the confederation debates and instilled a confidence that the intervening wilderness could be tamed.[47]

The man who was largely responsible for determining the most suitable route for the telegraph and railway was the Scottish-born civil engineer Sandford Fleming. Probably best remembered today as the inventor of standard time, Fleming was appointed chief engineer of the Canadian Pacific Railway (CPR) project by the Macdonald administration in 1871. He was handed the difficult job of fulfilling the Canadian pledge to build a transcontinental railway—the so-called national dream—to British Columbia within ten years. Well-qualified for the task, Fleming not only had distinguished himself during the 1860s as chief engineer of the Intercolonial Railway—a position he retained along with his new assignment—but also had been a strong advocate of western expansion and the construction of a railroad to the Pacific. Less fortunately, he was exceedingly meticulous and tended to avoid making final decisions in favor of doing more fieldwork. He regarded the location of the rail line as a momentous task, one not to be rushed, whatever the urgency.

Fleming firmly believed that a rail line could not be simply pushed across the western interior to the coast but that the development of communication and transportation in the region had to proceed in a prescribed order: first a telegraph line, then a wagon road, and finally a railway. The road would be extremely crude, upgraded and ultimately replaced by the railroad only as settlement progressed. Meanwhile, the telegraph line—seen by Fleming as "the spinal cord of a national nervous system"—had to be erected immediately along the proposed railway route.[48] It was considered essential to western settlement, and thereby to the coming of the railway, in that it would not only guarantee a Canadian presence in the region but also reduce the isolation of the pioneer farmer.

Like the transcontinental railway, the idea of a Pacific telegraph pre-dated the transfer of Rupert's Land and the Northwest Territory to Canada. In the early 1860s, Canadian expansionists had proposed a number of ambitious schemes that portrayed Canada as serving a vital telegraphic link in Anglo-Asian commerce.[49] It was the London-based Hudson's Bay Company, however, that tried to turn the vision into reality. During the summer of 1864, while telegraph supplies were being shipped to Fort Victoria (Vancouver Island), Fort Garry (Winnipeg), and York Factory (on Hudson Bay), famed Arctic explorer and company servant Dr. John Rae made a reconnaissance survey of the northern prairie district and subsequently endorsed a route that linked the fur trade posts of the region between Fort Garry and the Yellowhead Pass (west of present-day Jasper, Alberta). But before construction could begin, the viability of the proposed line was thrown into doubt with the completion of a telegraph between San Francisco and British Columbia in April 1865. The project was dropped, and the telegraph material, still in its shipping containers, was eventually sold to Canada as part of the land-transfer agreement. The equipment would probably have sat unused for several more years had it not been for the 1869–70 Red River Resistance. Frustrated by the poor communications with Red River, Ottawa struck a deal with the Northwestern Telegraph Company to use the Hudson's Bay Company telegraph material to build a government-subsidized telegraph between Fort Garry and existing lines in Minnesota.[50] This line was in operation by November 1871 and was later used by the North America Boundary Commission Survey to determine the location of the forty-ninth parallel along the Red River in the fall of 1873.

While the Red River telegraph line was under construction, Fleming had a number of exploratory teams in the field conducting general reconnaissance surveys for the railway route to the Pacific. Like the Dominion Lands Survey work, railway work in the prairie region was influenced by the conclusions of the Palliser and Hind expeditions and was largely confined in the first field season to the fertile belt—Fleming's tentative choice of a route for the railway. "The whole shape of the developing prairie economy of the 1870's," one historian has noted, "was . . . determined by the assumption that there existed in Canada an extension of the Great American Desert."[51] When the 1871 surveys reported that many of the river valleys along the proposed route through the fertile belt would present significant engineering difficulties, Fleming redirected the line northward through the Manitoba interlake district. Curiously, though, except for a brief, personal inspection of the North Saskatchewan country in 1872, the chief engineer did not arrange for any detailed examination of the revised route but ordered further exploratory work in the mountains and the Shield country north of Lake Superior. He believed that the main features of the prairie region were already known, that construction of the telegraph and the railway across the open country would be relatively easy compared with construction in other sections, and that detailed surveying of the prairie route could be carried out quickly and efficiently when the time arose.[52] Thus when contract tenders were issued by the government of Alexander Mackenzie in June 1874 for four sections of a telegraph line from Lake Superior to the Pacific via the Yellowhead Pass, the exact route across western Canada had yet to be defined.[53]

Over the next two years, surveying of the telegraph line was carried out at a feverish pace. According to the tender documents, the federal government was anxious "to provide a pioneer line throughout the whole extent of the country [Northwest], to assist in the building of the railway and settlement of the country."[54] Ottawa therefore wasted little time in awarding contracts for the various telegraph sections during the winter of 1874–75. According to each agreement, the successful tenderer was to clear the right-of-way, string a one-wire line, and erect stations within at least fifty-mile intervals—all within two years. The subsequent maintenance and operation of the line was also the responsibility of the tendering party. Interestingly, the route of the railway was still under consideration, and the telegraph route was being fixed at the very time that construction of the railway line was getting under way. The process made a mockery of Fleming's "spinal cord" analogy.

During the summer and fall of 1874, an exploratory survey was conducted from Selkirk on the Red River across the Lake Manitoba narrows and then north of the Duck Mountains to Livingstone on the Swan River (in west-central Manitoba). Once the general line was established, the surveying parties were instructed to remain in the field over the winter and perform a more detailed location survey along the same 270-mile route so that the erection of the telegraph along this section could begin in the spring.[55] The determination of the line westward from Livingstone to the Yellowhead Pass was executed under even tighter time constraints. The government surveying crews and the contractor construction crews arrived in the field at roughly the same time in the spring of 1875. Under the circumstances, preliminary and location surveys had to be conducted almost simultaneously. Surveyor Henry Macleod quickly reconnoitred a general line west from Livingstone, sending back directions to the main location parties that followed in his wake. By such means, the surveyors managed to locate the telegraph line throughout the length of the region by the spring of 1876, even though this meant another winter of extreme hardship in the field.[56] Ironically, the only delay to construction was caused when a band of Cree Indians temporarily halted the cutting of poles and laying of wire along the North Saskatchewan River until the government promised to enter into a treaty.

At the end of 1876, Fleming reported that eight hundred miles of telegraph line had been established between Winnipeg and Edmonton along much the same route that the railway was expected to follow. It had been five years since Fleming had taken up his duties, and he could finally point to some concrete results. The completed line, however, fell far short of its assigned role in the civil engineer's grand scheme of things. Because of the speed with which the line was to be fixed, its routing was based less on settlement potential and more on the ease of grades and the availability of construction materials. The information learned about the capabilities of the land, moreover, was sketchy at best and limited to sweeping generalizations and unrealistic expectations. The surveyors were confident, for example, that the muskeg in the Manitoba interlake district could be easily drained for farming purposes.[57] The line was also incomplete and premature. When the federal government called for tenders, it assured the contractors that the telegraph and the railway would follow the same general route, if not the same precise line. However, the route the railroad would follow through the Rockies was uncertain. The builder for the Edmonton–Cache Creek section of the telegraph was consequently ordered to stop construction less than five months after the contract was awarded; only the Kamloops–Cache Creek section in central British Columbia was erected.

The "pioneer" telegraph lived up to its name. Fleming had redirected the line northward to avoid bridging wide river valleys. What he did not seem to realize was that he was trading one set of engineering problems for even more troublesome ones. Several miles of the new telegraph line were located through wet, unstable ground. The difficulties of building these sections were probably not fully appreciated because much of the locational survey work was performed during the winter, when the muskeg was frozen. During the summer, these areas proved a construction nightmare. Poles were continually falling over and damaging the wire, thereby throwing sections of the line out of commission for days, if not weeks. One can only wonder how Fleming's field crews could believe that areas that proved impassable for horses could support a telegraph line, let alone a railway bed.[58]

Once in place, the telegraph line—which was supposed to be an aid to settlement and railway construction—was totally unreliable. Service varied from day to day and could be depended on with any certainty only during the winter. Disillusionment with the line was probably best captured by the Dominion Lands Surveys Special Survey. In 1876 a frustrated King wasted a good part of the summer trying to establish the longitude of Battleford (in west-central Saskatchewan) through the interchange of telegraphic signals with Winnipeg.[59] The following year, he tried to do the same thing at Edmonton but was unsuccessful again. In the words of the official survey history, "This [attempt] . . . , in common with all other attempts to make any use of this worse than useless telegraph line, proved a complete failure."[60]

Over the next few years, work continued along the line in the "woodland" section between Red River and Thunder Bay, so that by the end of the decade, over twelve hundred miles of telegraph line were in place at a cost of more than $1 million. The problems with the line continued, however, and it could be maintained only at considerable expense. In fact, an official government assessment of the telegraph in 1879 concluded that the Lake Winnipeg section had been a serious mistake. A solution to Ottawa's predicament was soon forthcoming when a private syndicate took over the railway project and decided not only to reroute the main line across the southern prairies but also to build its own telegraph along the right-of-way. These changes effectively undermined the rationale for the original telegraph line and led directly to the government abandonment of the section between Winnipeg and Humboldt (central Saskatchewan). Of the remaining line, the Winnipeg–Thunder Bay section was turned over to the syndicate, and the Humboldt-Edmonton section was relocated or rebuilt. It was not until January 1887 that a reliable transcontinental telegraph service was in operation.

Exploration was not to blame for the telegraph fiasco. Government surveyors had been called on to fix a route that had been selected on the basis of limited exploration and evaluation. In addition, their fieldwork had to be completed as quickly as possible so that construction of the telegraph line would not be delayed. This emphasis on the line's rapid completion is perplexing when one compares the construction of the telegraph with that of the railroad. Whereas exploration played a minor, if not negligible, role in the location of the telegraph line, it dominated Fleming's work on the railway. Unable to decide on a route through the mountains, he continued to send out parties year after year to make detailed reconnaissance surveys. Quite likely, the sorry experience of the telegraph line made Fleming more cautious than ever about selecting a route for the railway.

When Fleming assumed his duties as engineer-in-chief of the CPR, he was instructed by the federal government to find the shortest and most practicable route for the railway to the Pacific. To Canadian expansionists, Fleming's job seemed to be a relatively simple matter of plotting a line and then noting and overcoming any engineering problems. Fleming, however, did not see the task in such straightforward terms. Although he believed that the railway would likely proceed along the fertile belt (North Saskatchewan country) and then through the Yellowhead Pass, he was equally determined that all possible routes be thoroughly explored and evaluated. He consequently considered his field of inquiry to be the vast region from the Ottawa Valley (in east-central Ontario) west to the Pacific Ocean and from the international boundary north to the tree line, an area encompassed by fifty-four degrees of longitude and ten degrees of latitude. The area was sparsely inhabited, relatively trackless, and above all, little known. As Fleming would later observe, "We were seeking to gain facts, we had a wilderness to operate upon, and for a time we were working in the dark."[61]

The CPR Survey's first field season was ambitious. Although Fleming would continually complain about the difficulty of finding good men, no less than twenty-one field parties (eight hundred men) were dispatched in the summer of 1871. Fleming saw it as his duty to try to acquire "as much information as possible with the least possible delay."[62] The organization of the parties reflected the areas where Fleming anticipated the greatest trouble in running the rail line. Only one expedition was sent to examine the prairie district (Red River to Rocky Mountains) and the approaches to the two most probable passes, the Yellowhead and the Howse or Kicking Horse (west of present-day Calgary). The remaining parties concentrated their efforts in either the woodland (Ottawa River to Red River) or mountain (Rocky Mountains to Pacific Coast) districts; by coincidence, the British Columbia teams left Victoria for the interior on 20 June 1871, the same day that the province officially entered Confederation. In the field, survey operations were governed by a general set of instructions so that the information secured from the various districts could be easily integrated and analyzed by Fleming.

And detailed information it was. Although the surveys that first summer were considered preliminary, more than two-thirds of the field parties performed instrumental surveys—ironically in areas in which the measurement of the land by chain, transit, and level was exceedingly difficult. All parties, moreover, were required to report on the natural resources of each district. Given the crucial role that the railway would play in settlement and economic development, Fleming recognized that the shortest route was not necessarily the most practicable for generating traffic. "It is most important that as thorough an examination of the country be made before the construction of the road is attempted," he lectured the minister of public works, "an opposite course may result in blunders that could never be entirely remedied at any cost."[63]

In April 1872, one year to the month that he had been appointed, Fleming tabled his first report on the CPR exploratory survey. After briefly reviewing the general organization and duties of the field parties, he announced that the Yellowhead Pass was better suited for a railway than the Howse Pass and that any further examination of southern passes would henceforth be abandoned. He also reported that although a direct route from the Yellowhead to the coast had not been found, a line existed along the Thompson and Fraser Rivers to Burrard Inlet (Vancouver). Fleming refused to endorse this route, however, because of the engineering difficulties it presented, and he recommended that a search be undertaken for a better, less costly interior route. The other trouble spot that the survey had encountered was north of Lake Superior, especially in the Lake Nipigon district. Here the country was so rough and impenetrable in places that the work had to be continued over the winter because the survey line constantly had to be cleared so that the men could see any distance with the equipment. Fleming commented, "The way must be felt little by little."[64]

Over the next two years, the CPR Survey continued its extensive field activities, especially in the mountains and the Shield country. And like the first season of operations, the majority of the surveys involved the exact measurement of heights and distances. "The difficulties met in a field of operations so extensive," Fleming wrote, "called for special examination. Nothing . . . was left undone to gain full information."[65] In the woodland region, after investigating the possibility of locating the line north of Lake Nipigon, survey teams redoubled their efforts to find a feasible route along the northern shore of Lake Superior. Fleming realized that this section of the railway "must be carefully selected to provide cheap transport and thereby facilitate large scale agricultural settlement of the prairies."[66] In the mountain region, parties searched in vain for a more direct route through the Cariboo and Cascade Ranges in south-central British Columbia to the coast. A number of alternative harbors were also investigated in the hope that one might provide better access to the interior. The importance that Fleming attached to this work was underscored by the fact that the British Columbia surveys were placed under the direct supervision of his assistant, Marcus Smith, who was stationed in Victoria as of the spring of 1872.

In the spring of 1874, Fleming issued his second report on explorations for the railway. Although it opened with the disturbing news that a fire in the CPR engineering offices had destroyed most of the plans, field notes, and survey records, the report noted that the recent field results were extremely encouraging. In assessing the work in the woodland district, Fleming downplayed the presence of muskeg and suggested that a line could be built through the rock and bush "without unusually expensive works of construction."[67] This was the same wilderness that had bedeviled survey teams only a few years earlier! The chief engineer also reported that the recent work in the mountains not only had indicated that the Yellowhead was still the best pass for the railway but also had resulted in seven possible routes through the mountains to the coast.[68] Once again, however, Fleming was reluctant to recommend any of the interior routes, in the hope that a more satisfactory one could be discovered, possibly to the north.

The search for this elusive route through the mountains was carried out over the next three field seasons. In 1874 Charles Horetzky examined whether there was a more favorable line from the coast, between Bute Inlet and the Skeena River, to the north bend of the Fraser River in central British Columbia. The following year, E. W. Jarvis traveled nine hundred miles on snowshoes in the dead of winter from the British Columbia interior through the Smoky River Pass to the Athabasca River in northern Alberta. Other CPR surveyors such as Joseph Hunter, John Trutch, and H. J. Cambie added to the growing number of possible routes through the Cascade Range; eventually, these mountains, lying between the coast and the central plateau, would be pierced by twelve different lines, five of which had been surveyed in detail.[69] Exactly the opposite situation confronted explorers in the defiant Cariboo Range: not a single line could be found through the mountains from the Yellowhead Pass to the interior. "So far as known," Fleming reported, "every depression has been examined, and every indentation explored without success. The few lateral valleys, which at wide intervals exist, immediately terminate in gorges, again to disappear in glacial sources at high latitudes."[70] In keeping with Fleming's penchant for thoroughness, selected portions of known routes were reexamined or resurveyed to see whether difficulties could be avoided or distances shortened in any way. The chief engineer even arranged for a midwinter examination of the coast by C. H. Gamsby in 1876 to ascertain ice conditions in the various harbors.

The findings of this latest fieldwork, including a year-by-year recap of CPR Survey operations since 1871, were published in early 1877. The largest, most comprehensive report that Fleming had produced to date, this monograph described an incredible record of exploring activity under government auspices. Over the past six years and at a cost of more than $3 million and thirty-four lives (most from fires or drowning), CPR Survey crews had logged forty-six thousand miles, one-quarter of which had been painstakingly measured yard by yard. According to the report, a practicable route for the railway had been established from Lake Superior to the Rocky Mountains, and the line had been staked out for construction (location surveys) in several places. The mountain section, however, continued to confound Fleming. Although the most recent surveys had demonstrated that the Yellowhead was better than any other possible pass and could be used to reach any harbor in the coast, the chief engineer could still not decide on the route that should be followed through the mountains. His seven routes in the 1874 report had now grown to eleven.[71]

The most logical solution to Fleming's route dilemma was for the federal government to select a route, instruct that location surveys be undertaken, and find a private builder. The British Columbia portion of the railway could be delayed for only so long. In fact, the construction of the line had taken on an urgency. The original assumption had been that the railway would be built as settlement progressed. Fleming, for example, had suggested in the early 1860s that a line to the Pacific could take as much as twenty-five years to complete. When the expected flood of settlers to western Canada did not occur, however, it was concluded that development of the Northwest depended on the railway being first in place—a situation analogous to the American experience in the 1850s.[72]

Besides Fleming's indecision, other factors complicated the route choice. There were sharp regional divisions over the British Columbia terminus. Vancouver wanted the railway to come down Fraser Valley to Burrard Inlet. Victoria, on the other hand, preferred a more northerly route through the mountains to Bute Inlet and then by bridge to Vancouver Island (Nanaimo). The question was further muddied by the actions of Marcus Smith, engineer-in-chief of the British Columbia section. When Fleming left for England on an extended leave of absence in July 1876, Smith was named his temporary replacement and given responsibility for carrying on the survey program. Smith believed himself to be the equal of Fleming—if not better—and he decided to use his new position to propose an alternative route for the railway. Throughout the 1870s, although there had been extremely favorable reports about the Peace River country, Fleming had never given any serious thought to sending the railway through either the low-lying Peace River Pass or the Pine River Pass. Now, in the spring of 1877, Smith secretly dispatched CPR engineer Joseph Hunter to explore the Pine River Pass in northern British Columbia. He then prepared a report on the 1877 surveys in which he recommended that the railway be sent in a northwesterly direction from the Manitoba interlake district through the mountains via the Pine River Pass and then down to Bute Inlet. This proposed change came as a shock to the Liberal government, especially since the new route had never been investigated—or at least so it thought! And when a furious Prime Minister Mackenzie learned of Smith's behind-the-scene intrigues, the acting chief engineer was removed from his position of authority. Fleming was summoned back to Ottawa in the summer of 1878; after reviewing the recent survey work, he confirmed that the railway would best serve the interests of the country if it was sent through the Yellowhead Pass.[73]

There the matter rested until the Macdonald Conservatives romped back into office in the 1878 fall federal election. Given the recent turmoil over where the line should go, Charles Tupper, the new minister of railways and canals, decided to have the various routes examined one more time. CPR survey parties consequently took to the field in the spring of 1879 for the ninth consecutive summer. In the interim, in an effort to aid prairie settlement, Fleming issued a special report devoted almost exclusively to the physical features of the western interior. The region was divided into individual sections or quadrangles, one degree of longitude in breadth by one degree of latitude in length. Each section entry, in turn, provided all the available data that could be culled from existing reports for that particular area. Apart from the format, this resource summary was interesting in that it served to illustrate the extent to which a careful exploration of the prairie district had been neglected for survey work in the woodland and especially the mountain districts. The section entries and the accompanying map reveal that knowledge of the western interior was generally restricted to major travel routes. There were still large areas where "nothing reliable [was] known."[74]

In October 1879 the Macdonald cabinet reviewed the results of the past summer's surveys and officially endorsed the Yellowhead-Burrard route for the railway. All seemed well. Because of the difficulties that were being experienced by the telegraph line in Manitoba, however, the projected railway line was rerouted along the Assiniboine Valley to Brandon in southwestern Manitoba and then northwestward along the North Saskatchewan. But contract work in the Superior section ran up severe cost overruns, prompting the federal government to appoint a royal commission in June 1880 to investigate the CPR project. During the hearings, Fleming's competence became a key issue. The commissioners wondered how over $4 million of exploratory survey work could have failed to draw attention to the muskeg problem in the woodland district. They also questioned the need for sending out costly instrumental surveys when general exploration in the early years would have sufficed. Fleming steadfastly defended his actions during his appearance before the commission in April 1881, but in the end his handling of the survey was declared "a sacrifice of money, time and efficiency."[75]

This verdict seemed to have been confirmed by the actions of the new Canadian Pacific Railroad Syndicate, which assumed control of the project in 1881. Almost from the beginning of the survey work, Fleming had ruled out a southern pass for the railway. In fact, if the Yellowhead Pass was ever deemed impracticable, Fleming would have moved the line north, not south. Thus the syndicate surprised all Canadians when it announced in the spring of 1881 that it would build directly westward from Winnipeg across the open prairie and through a more southerly mountain pass.[76]

What the syndicate decision effectively meant was that Fleming's preoccupation with finding the best route through British Columbia had been for naught. Much of the CPR exploratory work and the accompanying engineering data had not been necessary and would contribute little to the eventual route selection. Perhaps this explains why, in one of the most famous photographs in Canadian history—the driving of the last spike in November 1885 in the mountains near Craigellachie—Sandford Fleming merely looks on wistfully.

## The Geological Survey of Canada

Although the North America Boundary Commission Survey, the Dominion Lands Survey, and the Canadian Pacific Railway Survey were all expected to gather resource information, this activity remained secondary to their surveying duties. Their primary role was to define the geographical limits of the new territory, divide the land into farm-sized parcels, and find the best-possible route for the Pacific railway and telegraph. The major responsibility for locating, examining, and reporting on the resources of the country fell to the Geological Survey of Canada. The federal agency was well qualified for this role. Created in 1842 by the United Province of Canada to investigate and aid in the development of the mineral resources of the country, the survey displayed broad interests that transcended the bounds of traditional geology. It was the only organization of its kind, government or otherwise, concerned with acquiring exact scientific knowledge of Canada's natural resources. From its beginning, moreover, the survey found that many areas required general exploration and topographical mapping, in addition to detailed geological study. The organization was thus already experienced in the kind of wide-ranging field activities that it would be called on to perform in the Northwest. However, the survey's financial and manpower resources were entirely disproportionate to its field responsibilities.[77] This problem existed before the land transfer and was only exacerbated after 1870. Much of the survey's success depended on the energy and initiative of a few government scientists working in difficult and often hazardous conditions in remote areas.

The dramatic expansion in the Geological Survey of Canada's field of inquiry coincided with the appointment of a new director; in fact, Dr. Alfred Selwyn took over the survey helm the same day that the transfer of western lands to Canada was originally scheduled to take place, 1 December 1869. The British-born geologist wanted to make the survey a respected organization in the world scientific community, but at the same time he realized, from his recent experience as first director of the Victoria (Australia) Geological Survey, that the Canadian survey would initially have to concentrate on description and collection as opposed to specialized fieldwork. Selwyn also recognized that the government agency had been founded in the belief that scientific knowledge was to be used for practical and immediate results. Canadian parliamentarians viewed survey officers as collectors of useful facts—and what better facts to collect than those that could be used to guarantee the success of the Pacific railway and the development of the new territory![78] The survey did not neglect Ontario, Quebec, or the Maritime provinces, but the majority of its field endeavors in the 1870s were indeed concentrated in the Northwest, where it cooperated with the

Canadian Pacific Railway Survey whenever possible to gather information about the land and its resources.[79] There was much to be done. The only serious examination of the geology of the region had been conducted by the Palliser and Hind expeditions, and although the parties had made many interesting finds, numerous outstanding puzzles about the geological history of the region remained.

During his first years as survey director, Selwyn led by example. From 1871 to 1875, he spent four of the five summers in the field, examining areas where the railway might possibly be located. In 1871 he explored the British Columbia interior, along the Fraser and Thompson Rivers, and lost several days' observations when his hungry horse devoured pages from his notebook. In the next two field seasons, he examined the proposed Lake Superior–Red River section of the railway and then the fertile belt. His most noteworthy expedition was made in 1875, when in response to growing interest in the Peace River country, he made a special reconnaissance survey of the Peace River Pass and the surrounding district as a possible route for the Pacific railway. The thoroughness with which Selwyn approached his work was evidenced by the fact that he made special arrangements for the botanist John Macoun to accompany the expedition to gather information on the region's flora, climate, and agricultural potential.[80]

Selwyn's information-gathering exercises were typical of survey fieldwork done during the period. Given the vastness of the new territory and the amount of general reconnaissance work that was required, the survey focused on collecting data, including specimens, on a wide range of topics and indicating areas that merited future in-depth study.[81] The tackling of geological problems had to wait for another day. A few survey officers, though, tried to decipher and explain the geological features of a region during their reconnaissance surveys. Dawson, who had distinguished himself during the North America Boundary Commission Survey, was one such government scientist. Appointed to the survey staff on 1 July 1875, Dawson was given specific responsibility for British Columbia and spent five successive field seasons exploring the province. From 1875 to 1877, he worked with Fleming's Canadian Pacific Railway Survey crews and covered an incredible amount of territory bordering the Fraser and Thompson Rivers. The next two summers took him farther afield: first to the northern end of Vancouver Island and the Queen Charlotte Islands and then from the Skeena River up through the Pine River Pass in northeastern British Columbia. During this series of trips, Dawson not only kept detailed notes on just about everything he observed but also made watercolor sketches, took photographs, and even wrote poetry.[82] He later observed that he had "almost felt as if the western mountains belonged to him."[83]

In keeping with the desire for natural resource information, Dawson paid particular attention to the province's coal deposits and prepared an appendix on British Columbia mineral resources for the 1877 railway report. He also shared many of his colleagues' enthusiasm for the Peace River country and reported the existence of over fifteen million acres of good land in the region. His greatest contribution during these years, however, was his unraveling of the geology of the province. On the basis of his explorations, he discovered that British Columbia rock formations differed from those in eastern Canada. He also concluded that a great glacier had once covered the mountains, but he incorrectly attributed the glacial deposits to an inland sea and not glacial decay.[84]

Dawson's ability to extrapolate on the basis of limited observation and to view the bigger picture was unmatched by his survey colleagues. They generally had neither the training nor the expertise. Their fieldwork, however, was no less important. The federal government was eager to proceed with the exploitation of Canada's natural resources and looked to the survey to provide the kind of practical information that would direct and assist this development. In fact, the role of the survey as the chief investigator of Canada's resource potential had been made official in 1877 when the agency was designated a permanent branch of the Department of the Interior, dependent on annual parliamentary grants. It also received a new title, the Geological and Natural History Survey of Canada, which carried with it new duties: henceforth the survey was also responsible for examining the flora and fauna of the Dominion. Any natural history items collected were to be displayed in the survey museum, which at the time housed only geological and mineralogical specimens.

According to the survey's official biographer, Dr. Robert Bell was "the practitioner *par excellence*" of the reconnaissance survey method.[85] And although, like Dawson, he stood above his fellow officers in terms of field accomplishments (both would eventually serve as director), his wide field experience provides insight into the kind of all-inclusive exploratory work that the government explorer was expected to perform. A member of the survey staff since 1857, Bell had been educated in civil engineering and medicine and consequently received his training in the field under the tutelage of other officers, in particular the survey's first director, Sir William Logan. Bell's natural ability made him an outstanding field man, and he soon personified the survey's unofficial credo during this period: observe everything.[86] He spent four successive field seasons (1869–72) mapping the land at the head of Lake Superior, especially around Lake Nipigon and the southern reaches of the Albany River. He then devoted two field seasons to the western interior, working first south and then north of the heralded fertile belt. Like others before him, Bell found his work on the prairies extremely frustrating, for it was virtually impossible to examine the bedrock because of the depth of the overlying glacial drift. In fact, despite the hardships and inconveniences, he was more at home in the subdued Hudson Bay lowlands, and for the remainder of the decade, he explored several of the major rivers (Moose, Hayes, Churchill, Nelson) in this area, as well as the bleak eastern shore of James and Hudson Bays.

Bell's survey work embraced an incredibly diverse range of topics. Little escaped his purview. He took notes on the geological features, the flora and fauna, the climate and soil, the indigenous population, and the exploitable resources. This wealth of information is remarkable considering that Bell performed much of his fieldwork without maps; he had to do the topographical survey work as he went along—a fact that is often overlooked. Nor did Bell's information-gathering cease when he returned to Ottawa at the close of each field season. One winter, for example, he sent a list of questions about the breeding habits of mammals to Hudson's Bay Company posts in the northern districts. He also had a great interest in ethnology, and his papers contain much oral information on Indian legends that traders gathered at Bell's request. As for his formal reports of his field activities, Bell's data were not simply listed but were presented in a manner that left no doubt that Canada had been blessed with a significant natural heritage. He had a great faith in the country and its destiny, and each field trip strengthened this conviction.

By the end of the 1870s, the Geological Survey of Canada had made a respectable start on its huge task of mapping the geology of half a continent. Given the importance of the Pacific railway project, it had concentrated its energies in the western interior, cooperating with Fleming's survey parties wherever possible to outline the general geographical features of the proposed railway route. It had also begun to probe the subarctic, which for years had been the exclusive domain of natives and a handful of traders. And it had produced some of the first topographical maps of many regions, as well as given an indication of the rich natural history of the country. Dr. Selwyn could look back on his first decade as director with justifiable pride.

The federal government, however, did not agree about the value of these reconnaissance surveys. Throughout the 1870s, parliamentarians of both political parties expected the survey to help realize the early development of Canada's mineral wealth by gathering practical information that could be used by private interests. This concern for utility and efficiency had been the reason behind the transfer of the survey and its museum from Montreal to Ottawa in the spring of 1881. Politicians argued that the survey would never produce satisfactory results until it was placed directly under federal control and supervision. Yet with the survey right under Parliament's nose, its failure to provide positive, technical information was only magnified, and the Macdonald government began considering ways to make the agency more development-oriented. In April 1881, in a move to bolster the survey's activities in western Canada, the annual appropriation was increased by 20 percent. The following year, the government transferred the salaries of the permanent officers to the civil service list, thereby making more of the annual federal grant available for field and laboratory operations. Because of this increased funding, politicians looked forward to exercising greater influence over the survey. The improved financial situation appeared to have the opposite effect, however, when Dr. Selwyn began to hire a number of better-educated and more highly specialized officers. For parliamentarians who wanted a more utilitarian agency, these appointments seemed to widen, not close, the gulf between survey objectives and political expectations. The politicians agreed with the general feeling that the survey was more interested in grappling with geological problems than in developing the country's resource wealth.[87]

This growing concern about the kind of work being performed by the Geological Survey of Canada eventually prompted the House of Commons to appoint a select committee in 1884 to investigate the organization. (Curiously, the U.S. Geological Survey was under investigation at the same time and ostensibly for the same reasons as its Canadian counterpart.) Not unexpectedly, the committee's report was a scathing indictment of the survey. It criticized the agency for producing lengthy, complex reports instead of simple, concise summaries, and it recommended that the gathering of practical information should take precedence over pure scientific investigation. Dr. Selwyn, for his part, regarded the investigation as uninformed interference, particularly the suggestion that field operations should concentrate on revealing Canada's mineral resources; under the terms of the 1877 Survey Act, the department was officially required to investigate Canada's natural life.

Moreover, Dr. Selwyn had already taken steps to secure such practical information when he had launched a systematic areal mapping program in 1881. Described as the greatest scientific accomplishment of the survey during the period, the project not only dominated staff activities but also was the longest-running program in survey history. Its objective was the production of a geological map of Canada on a scale of one inch to four miles. A survey team under the leadership of a geologist would be assigned to a specific, limited area over which it would conduct a series of intersecting transverses and then prepare a map and accompanying report. This fieldwork, when combined with further scientific study in the laboratory, resulted in a clearer understanding of Canada's rock formations and their chronological sequence. And with this information, the survey could then locate exploitable ore bodies and mineral deposits.[88]

The survey's systematic mapping operations were initially confined to known areas, in central and eastern Canada, that were readily accessible and were capable of immediate development. The West was not neglected, however. In response to the rerouting of the Canadian Pacific Railway main line, a series of regional surveys were conducted on the prairies, particularly in present-day southern Alberta and Saskatchewan. These studies, developed by Dawson, were more comprehensive than typical reconnaissance surveys but were still limited in scope because of the relatively large area to be covered and the short field period. The 1884 report on the Bow and Belly Rivers in southern Alberta, for example, described an area of more than twenty-five thousand square miles and was based on work conducted over three field seasons. Still, it was a start—and a good one at that. Although the surveys were primarily concerned with delineating the nature and extent of the coal deposits of the region for the transcontinental railway, Dawson, J. B. Tyrrell, and R. G. McConnell described in considerable detail the general topography and geological features of their respective study areas. They also drew attention to a rich trove of dinosaur fossils during their investigation of the southern badlands district. But a satisfactory explanation for the drift deposits of the plains still eluded them.[89]

The Geological Survey of Canada also continued to send out wide-ranging exploratory surveys during the 1880s. This work could not be avoided, since the geological features and the potential resource value of large sections of the Dominion remained mostly unknown. In central Quebec, a veritable terra incognita, Albert Peter Low made the first of what would be a two-decade survey of the area when he examined the reportedly large Lake Mistassini and then followed the Rupert River west to James Bay in

1884–85. Over the next few years, he explored the eastern shore of James Bay, especially the lower reaches of many of the large rivers of the region. Bell, in the meantime, served as a kind of all-around scientific investigator (including physician) to a Department of Marine and Fisheries expedition to Hudson Bay and Hudson Strait to investigate the navigability of the waters. Since the expedition covered a wide area, Bell was in his element, and he used every opportunity to investigate the human and natural life of the area.

The most spectacular survey expedition during this period was an examination of the fabled Yukon territory in the far Northwest. Since the early 1870s, scores of mostly American placer miners had been scouring the rivers of the region for signs of the gold that they intuitively knew was there but that had yet to be found. Although the famous Klondike gold discovery was not made until 1896, this early foreign activity eventually roused the Canadian government from its lethargy in asserting its presence in the region, and it dispatched a three-pronged expedition to explore and map the region in 1887. Under the leadership of the redoubtable Dawson, the exercise marked the first time that the survey's field operations had extended beyond the Arctic Circle. It also served to demonstrate how survey officers were often the first federal agents to visit frontier regions of Canada.[90] Most astonishing, however, was the vast amount of territory covered. Little did the members of the expedition realize that many of the routes they investigated would be used by the Klondike stampeders a decade later.

While Ogilvie of the Dominion Lands Surveys Special Survey located the 141st meridian (Yukon-Alaska boundary), Dawson and his assistant James McEvoy traveled up the Liard River to Frances Lake, where they made an arduous overland crossing to the Pelly in central Yukon. They then continued down the Pelly River to Fort Selkirk, up the Yukon, through the Chilkoot Pass, and on to the Pacific. Because of the constraints of the expedition, Dawson had to rely on interviews with local miners for much of his information about the region's prospects. He did, nonetheless, find evidence suggesting not only that glaciation had occurred from the south but also that parts of the Yukon had actually escaped the great ice sheet.[91]

The exploits of McConnell, the other expedition leader, were equally thrilling. Entering the north country via the Stikine River in northwestern British Columbia, McConnell traveled down the Liard River to Fort Simpson, where he spent the fall and winter of 1887–88 exploring the district, in

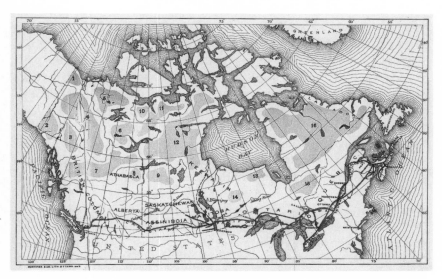

21.4 *"Dominion of Canada—Outline Map Shewing the Larger Unexplored Areas"* *(George Dawson, 1890). Dawson's map, published in the* Ottawa Naturalist *in 1890, ilustrates the vast areas of Canada still unexplored and unmapped. Collection of William A. Waiser.*

particular the western shore of Great Slave Lake. At the time of the spring breakup, he descended the mighty Mackenzie as far as Fort McPherson, where he met Ogilvie, who had finished his work in the Yukon and was continuing his survey southwestward to Lake Athabasca. After exchanging information, McConnell essentially retraced Ogilvie's route; he crossed over to the Porcupine River and then traveled up the Yukon all the way to the Chilkoot Pass and the Pacific. Like Dawson, McConnell also somehow managed to find time to do some work on the geology of the region during his four-thousand-mile journey; he predicted a rich future for the Mackenzie Valley because of the presence of oil-saturated rocks.

Shortly after his return from the Yukon, Dawson delivered his speech to the Ottawa Field-Naturalists' Club on some of the larger, unexplored regions of Canada. Whereas others might have used the occasion to do some chest-pounding about the survey's role in rolling back Canada's frontiers, Dawson confessed that portions of the country were still little more than blank areas on the map. And it was to these unknown areas, or "pockets" as Dawson referred to them, that the survey directed some of its energies over the next decade and a half—under the leadership of Selwyn, then Dawson, and finally Bell. This did not mean that the systematic mapping of Canada's geology no longer had priority. Nor did it mean that the pressure to rein in the survey had lessened since the early 1880s. Many critics still argued that the department was not giving the public its money's worth. But the various survey directors during this period could not in good conscience leave the distant regions unexplored, especially when these areas might provide invaluable scientific information. The great reconnaissance surveys thus continued into the new century. To placate their political masters, the directors emphasized the practical side of the survey's fieldwork at the same time that they tried not to lose sight of the purely scientific aspects. At the beginning of his first annual report as acting survey director, for example, Bell remarked, "Care has been taken to give prominence to any discoveries which may have an economic bearing . . . although scientific discoveries may ultimately prove of greater practical importance."[92]

One of the most sensational field trips during the 1890s was that of Joseph Burr Tyrrell; in fact, he and his party were lucky to return alive. In 1893 the thirty-four-year-old Tyrrell and a small party, including his younger brother, J. W., were sent to examine the Barren Lands west of Hudson Bay. The northern tundra, with its lack of trees and its innumerable water bodies, was a completely foreign landscape and had been visited by only a few white men—the most famous being Samuel Hearne, who had traveled from Churchill to the mouth of the Coppermine River over a century earlier. Tyrrell was now being asked to cross through the heart of the region, from south to north, in one season. The party left Fort Chipewyan on Lake Athabasca in late June 1893 heavily laden with provisions but without Indian guides familiar with the barrens. The men canoed north down Dubawnt River, and by the time they reached Baker Lake in the district of Keewatin in early September, their food supply was nearly exhausted; things would have been much worse had it not been for a chance encounter with a large caribou herd a month earlier. By the time they reached the shores of Hudson Bay on 12 September, they were still several hundred miles from Churchill, and winter was setting in. They had little choice but to push on south along the ice-strewn coast. Only with the greatest exertion and some good luck did they finally reach Churchill on 19 October. The adventure was not over, though. After a few weeks' rest (Tyrrell had lost nearly one-third of his body weight, and his brother had almost died from eating a polar bear's liver), the Tyrrell brothers traveled by dog team and snowshoe the nine hundred miles south to Winnipeg and sent a triumphant telegram to Ottawa.[93]

Tyrrell's ordeal created quite a sensation. Federal politicians were not impressed, however, particularly when they learned that the expedition had cost $7,000. They probably also did not appreciate the important scientific conclusions that Tyrrell drew from his fieldwork. On the basis of his examination of northern Alberta and the Manitoba interlake region in 1887 and 1889 respectively, he had argued that the great drift deposits of the prairie region were glacial in origin. His examination of the striae in the Barren Lands now convinced him that "one of the great gathering grounds for the snow of the Glacial period in North America was a comparatively short distance west of the northern portion of Hudson Bay, and from that centre or gathering ground the ice flowed not only towards the Arctic Ocean and Hudson Bay, but it extended a long distance westward towards the Mackenzie River, and southward towards the great plains."[94]

The other major survey reconnaissance work during this period was performed by Low in present-day Quebec and Labrador; the region could be considered Low's home ground, for he almost single-handedly explored and mapped the little-known territory. In 1893, as part of an overall plan to cross the region from south to north and then east to west, he surveyed from Lake Saint John up through the middle of the region to Fort Chimo, the distant Hudson's Bay Company post on Ungava Bay. Low and his party were then transported by ship south along the northeastern coast of Labrador to Hamilton Inlet, where they spent the winter hauling supplies up the Hamilton (Churchill) River to Grand (Churchill) Falls in preparation for the upcoming field season. In the spring, Low decided to examine the district in detail instead of pushing west across the Labrador Peninsula as originally planned. This change of plans did nothing to lessen the accomplishments of the two-year expedition, for by the time Low emerged from the region on the northern shore of the St. Lawrence River in the fall of 1894, he had traveled fifty-six hundred miles and secured a wealth of information about the land and its resources. He was especially excited about the wide belt of rich iron-bearing rocks that he had discovered southeast of Ungava—the so-called Labrador trough—and about the awesome power potential of Grand Falls.[95]

For the remainder of the decade, Low performed a number of impressive surveys in the region, including the mapping of the entire eastern coast and islands of Hudson and James Bays in 1898–99. Unquestionably, the high point of his exploring career came in 1903–4 when he was appointed commander of the government-sponsored *Neptune* expedition to the eastern Arctic. Since the transfer of the Arctic islands from Great Britain to Canada in 1880, successive federal administrations—both Conservative and Liberal—had made no concerted attempt to assert Canadian sovereignty in the archipelago. Granted, periodic surveys of Hudson Bay and Hudson Strait had been conducted in the 1880s and 1890s (accompanied by survey officers), but these expeditions were largely concerned with the commercial navigability of the coastal waters. The *Neptune* venture was different. Stung by its loss in the Alaska boundary settlement and alarmed by what the activities of foreign whalers and explorers could mean to its tenuous claim in the Arctic, the government of Wilfred Laurier sent the *Neptune* to make formal declarations of Canadian sovereignty at selected points in the region. Low's selection as leader was not surprising, since he was highly regarded and since the expedition carried scientific responsibilities. The choice of Low was also a tacit recognition of the traditional role that officers of the Geological Survey of Canada had played since 1870 as the first representatives of the federal government in many frontier areas.

The *Neptune* left Halifax for the eastern Arctic in August 1903 and paid a quick visit to Cumberland Sound on Baffin Island before taking up winter quarters with an American whaler at Fullerton Harbor on the northwestern shore of Hudson Bay. The following summer, the *Neptune* journeyed north again—this time to Ellesmere Island, Lancaster Sound, and Baffin Island—before returning to Fullerton and from there home to Halifax. During the two-year expedition, Low and his fellow scientists surveyed and mapped coastlines of both the mainland and islands, gathered geological and natural history specimens, made notes on the Inuits they encountered, and took photographs at every occasion. These activities were secondary, however, to the *Neptune*'s sovereignty duties. Foreign whalers were advised that they were in Canadian waters and thereby subject to Canadian jurisdiction and regulations. Northwest Mounted Policemen were deposited at a number of new posts. And the Canadian flag was ceremoniously raised and saluted while a formal document was read aloud on several islands.[96] One can only wonder what the local Inuits thought of all the fuss.

Low gave a full report of these activities, including a candid assessment of the region and its inhabitants, in his popular account of the expedition, *The Cruise of the Neptune, 1903–04*. In fact, these kinds of reconnaissance surveys, whether performed in the great Mackenzie Valley, the rugged

Labrador Peninsula, or the desolate barrens of Keewatin, provided the first real knowledge of many of these regions. Government explorers were the revealers of an unknown Canada. And although federal politicians continually grumbled about sending expeditions to distant areas when districts nearer home remained to be examined, these same politicians had no qualms about taking advantage of the information secured during these explorations. Survey officers made regular appearances before government committees whenever their expertise was sought on a particular area or issue. For example, Bell appeared as an expert witness before the 1888 Senate Select Committee on the Resources of the Great Mackenzie Basin. The brainchild of Senator John Christian Schultz, the committee had been created to gather information on the exploitable resources of Canada's "Great Reserve" north of the Saskatchewan watershed, east of the Rocky Mountains, and west of Hudson Bay. A similar Senate select committee of inquiry was established in 1907 "to give greater publicity to the advantages and resources of northern Canada," and once again, survey employees were asked to describe their experiences, as well as give their impressions of the land's potential in the general areas of agriculture, forestry, fisheries, minerals, climate, settlement, and communication.[97] Thus Tyrrell outlined his travels through Keewatin, and Low commented on the Ungava region, on the area west of Hudson Bay, and on the navigability of Hudson Bay. Their testimony and that of other witnesses was published the following year in book format under the suggestive title *Canada's Fertile Northland: A Glimpse of the Enormous Resources of Part of the Unexplored Regions of Canada*.

Another important consequence of the reconnaissance surveys was the vast array of collected specimens, both natural and physical. According to the 1877 and 1890 Geological Survey Acts, the survey was required to collect, study, and report on Canada's flora and fauna, as well as maintain museums of geology and natural history. Each field season, therefore, survey officers observed the composition and distribution of natural life and gathered any interesting or unusual geological, ethnological, and natural history objects. A few men were particularly active in this regard. Bell usually returned to Ottawa with whatever he could carry; Tyrrell published in 1888 a small catalogue of the mammals of Canada based largely on his work in the western interior. Dawson, for his part, was keenly interested not only in the natural history work of the survey but also in ethnology. During his survey of Vancouver Island in 1885, for example, he spent part of the summer among the Kwakiutl Indians, gathering artifacts, taking photographs, and recording their traditions and linguistics. This and similar work among other Indian groups has stood the test of time and given Dawson a prominent place in the history of Canadian anthropology.[98]

The man who was largely responsible for the survey's flora and fauna collections in the latter part of the nineteenth century was Macoun. In 1881 Macoun was appointed to the Geological Survey of Canada as a political reward for his favorable assessment of the agricultural potential of the western interior in the 1870s. Over the next three decades, first as dominion botanist and then as survey naturalist, he returned from the field each season heavily laden with specimens—including many new to science. This collecting and cataloguing of Canada's natural life was somewhat surprising, given the government's overriding concern with the exploitation and development of Canada's natural resources. Macoun's natural history work, however, was never questioned. For one thing, his broad collecting activity was exactly the kind of science that federal politicians could understand and appreciate. Macoun had no time for Darwin's theory of natural selection, or for that matter, for the growing specialization within the field of biology. He believed that a naturalist should be a kind of jack-of-all-fields whose role was to assemble as complete and accurate an inventory of God's wondrous bounty as possible. Canada's natural life was regarded as simply another resource. Macoun also continually talked about the practical applications of his fieldwork. Whenever he was asked to assess a region's potential on the basis of its natural life, he always returned brimming with optimism. "We have more than half a continent, and if we can raise first-class wheat," he told the House of Commons Committee on Agriculture and Colonization in 1906, "certainly we ought to raise first-class men."[99]

Macoun's wide-ranging collecting efforts, together with the field activity of other survey officers, had an unanticipated effect on institutional development in Ottawa. In the course of exploring Canada's frontiers and retrieving its specimens, the survey soon became the custodian of what was generally acknowledged as a national collection. However, survey headquarters had no room to store or display this material safely. Macoun's herbarium cases, for example, were dispersed up and down the building's corridors. Selwyn and then Dawson consequently pleaded for a new national museum building that would be a fitting repository for these national treasures. Of particular note during this campaign for new facilities were the arguments used to justify the beautiful Victoria Memorial Museum that was eventually built in downtown Ottawa in 1911. Both Selwyn and Dawson wisely realized that they had to do more than emphasize that the survey's magnificent collection needed safeguarding. In keeping with the government's desire for positive, utilitarian information of immediate economic value, they also argued that a new national museum building would be a wonderful advertising medium for the resources of the country. Like the exploratory surveys of the government explorer, then, the institution that showcased this work was also practical in nature. It was not enough to justify the new museum on the grounds of science alone.[100]

## The Dominion of Canada

By the start of World War I, the great explorations that had been performed under government auspices since 1870 began to be replaced with more specialized surveys by more highly qualified personnel. This new phase would not have been possible without the groundwork laid by the government explorers over the past four decades. Indeed, theirs was a remarkable achievement, given the nature of the task and the expectations of the Canadian government. In 1870, in one of the largest real estate transactions in North American history, the young Dominion of Canada had acquired a vast empire of lands to the north and west. The federal government regarded this new territory and its resources as the means to greatness—a way of surviving on the same continent with the United States—and was eager that settlement and development proceed as rapidly as possible. But there was a problem: little was known about the geographical features of the country; many areas were still unmapped. The men who consequently took to the field under government auspices—whether to fix the boundary line, measure the land into units, select the route for the telegraph and railway, or determine the geological formations—were also explorers. In performing their duties, they attempted to gather as much information as possible about the land and its resources, in many instances collecting specimens as well. They were generalists, not specialists restricted to a particular field of inquiry. Like Canada's political leaders, they were also optimistic and were willing to use their field knowledge to help make the country's resource wealth and its potential applications better known. Their work tended to substantiate the expansionist vision for the Northwest. In fact, as western lands were occupied by unprecedented numbers in the early 1900s and as interest turned to the north, anything seemed possible. There was a widespread belief that the limits of the settlement frontier existed only in the imagination—that the twentieth century, in Prime Minister Laurier's words, would be Canada's century. Above all, by mapping the land and gathering information on a wide range of topics, the government explorers filled in many of the blank spaces that had existed in 1870. They gave meaning to the term "Dominion of Canada."

# 22 / Scientific Exploration of the American West, 1865–1900

RICHARD A. BARTLETT

The proper base on which to trace the scientific exploration of the post–Civil War West is not located in the West at all but in Washington DC. There, in surroundings that reminded many visitors of an overgrown southern town, an intellectual awakening occurred during the Gilded Age. In government buildings along the dusty or muddy streets (depending on the weather), new government bureaus employed an increasing number of scientists. By 1900, the Smithsonian Institution administered the National Museum of Natural History, the National Zoological Park, the National Arboretum, the Bureau of American Ethnology, and the Woods Hole Marine Biological Laboratory. The Coast and Geodetic Survey, dating to 1807, was the most active scientific institution in the United States in 1867. The Naval Observatory was located in Washington, and it should not be forgotten that the army and navy conducted scientific work as a part of their duties. The Department of Agriculture, founded in 1862, was rapidly expanding its scientific activities. The predecessors of the U.S. Fish and Wildlife Service began work as early as 1871. Finally, the earth sciences of geology, paleontology, and paleobotany were centered in Washington: Ferdinand Vandeveer Hayden's U.S. Geological and Geographical Survey of the Territories and John Wesley Powell's U.S. Geographical and Geological Survey of the Rocky Mountain Region were administered out of the Interior Department, while Clarence King's U.S. Geological Exploration of the Fortieth Parallel and First Lieutenant George M. Wheeler's U.S. Geographical Surveys West of the One Hundredth Meridian were administered by the War Department. In 1879 these "Great Surveys" were consolidated into the U.S. Geological Survey.

Thus Washington DC, with a population of 131,000 in 1870 (238,000 by 1900), was for a brief time in the late 1800s the nation's center of scientific inquiry; indeed, it was one of the top three or four global centers of science

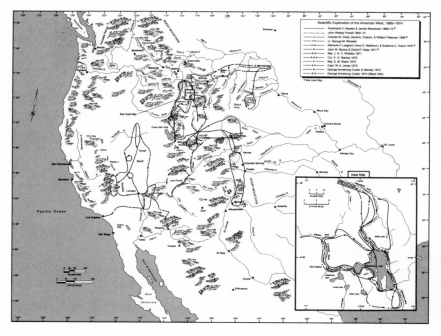

*Map 22.1 Scientific Exploration of the American West, 1868–1874.*

during this period. This fortunate situation—in which scientific investigation was carried on especially but not exclusively by the Smithsonian Institution, the Department of Agriculture, and the Department of Interior—
attracted a coterie of leading scientists to the nation's capital. Aware of their
presence and their common interests, these scientists organized clubs that
helped bring them together with other intellectuals in a social setting. Concentration was at the center of government, which even then constituted
the most lucrative source of funding.[1]

Propitiously, several extremely competent individuals, men seemingly
made for the times, were prominent in Washington DC. Among them was
the brilliant, imaginative scientist-planner-administrator Spencer Fullerton Baird. In 1850 Baird was named assistant to Joseph Henry, secretary of
the Smithsonian Institution. In this position Baird was able to encourage
research and collecting. In 1871 he became commissioner of fish and fisheries; the Woods Hole Marine Biological Laboratory was a result of Baird's
endeavors. In 1878 he succeeded Henry as secretary of the Smithsonian, a
position he held until his death in 1887.

The scope of Baird's activities was incredible. He was a naturalist interested in the world of birds and fishes and everything in between, from insects and plants to large animals. He understood how the office of secretary of the Smithsonian could be used as a catalyst, spawning scientific projects ranging from triangular surveys of the American West to the collection and identification of prehistoric flora and fauna. Baird was the prime mover behind the establishment of the U.S. Museum of Natural History. The ornithologist Robert Ridgeway owed his career to Baird, and the list of those who looked to Baird for advice and aid in obtaining funds reads like a Who's Who of late-nineteenth-century scientists.[2]

Other giants in scientific research and administration also made Washington DC their headquarters. Many of these leaders began their careers with the Great Surveys. Clinton Hart Merriam started his scientific career as a sixteen-year-old member of the Hayden Survey. In his lifetime he was considered the world's leading mammologist; he was also an anthropologist, ornithologist, agronomist, explorer, and administrator. He headed the Biological Survey within the Department of Agriculture from its inception in 1885 until 1910. He was a pioneer in the field of ecology, studying the patterns of geographical distribution of flora and fauna—"life zones," as he called them. He facilitated the change from exploration to interpretation of data and its useful conclusions; he demonstrated, for example, that cotton could grow better in the St. George Valley of Utah than on the gulf plains of Georgia.[3]

Henry Gannett, a topographer with the Hayden Survey, was the greatest American geographer of the time, the "father of Government mapmaking in the United States." He was also an excellent statistician. His greatest contributions were made with the U.S. Geological Survey in the years after 1882. He was also prominent in the creation of the U.S. Board of Geographic Names (now called the U.S. Geographic Board, supervised by the Department of the Interior) in 1890.[4]

Other geologists who served with the Great Surveys and later became administrators of scientific agencies in Washington were Grove Karl Gilbert, William John McGee, Clarence Dutton, and the head of one of the Great Surveys, John Wesley Powell. (For a year Clarence King, who had directed the Fortieth Parallel Survey, served as director of the newly formed U.S. Geological Survey.) Such men had worked well in the field; during their careers with government agencies devoted to science they would also set high scientific research and reporting standards that continue to this day.[5]

Still another branch of scientific endeavor headquartered in Washington DC was the Coast and Geodetic Survey, the first technical bureau of the federal government, having been founded in 1807. In 1871 the survey was charged by Congress to fix the baselines for inland maps. It set out to ascertain the exact longitudes and latitudes of thousands of points across the continent and determine elevations above sea level. It also ran the Canadian-Alaskan and the Canadian–United States boundaries and many state boundaries and was in the vanguard of technical improvements in the fields of cartography, hydrology, and geodesy. During the post–Civil War years its members participated in many international conferences and joint projects.[6]

Within this fertile milieu of scientific research, several people collaborated with the explorers while making their own contributions to the Washington DC scientific renaissance. Among them was zoologist William Temple Hornaday, the principal organizer of the Society of American Taxidermists. He was an authority on the American bison and the first president of the American Bison Society. In 1888 Hornaday was appointed the director of the new Department of Living Animals by Baird's successor at the Smithsonian, Samuel P. Langley. When the U.S. National Zoological Park was created, he was the logical choice as superintendent.[7]

Other scientists included Otis Tufton Mason, the first curator of ethnology at the Smithsonian, who with others founded the Anthropological Society of Washington. Mason's son-in-law was Alexander Graham Bell, who not only invented the telephone but also was interested in aiding the deaf. He too lived and was active in Washington DC.[8] A wealthy, dedicated participant in Washington's scientific activity was Gardener Greene Hubbard, who founded both *Science* magazine and the National Geographic Society and its periodical, the *National Geographic*. Finally, scientists working quietly on farms and in the Washington laboratories of the new Department of Agriculture were frequent attendees at social and official functions that brought the scientists together.

Like the Washington DC scientists, organizations giving them the opportunity to gather proliferated. A loosely organized "Saturday Club"— Baird called it simply "the Washington Scientifics"—existed before the Civil War; in 1871 it was more formally organized as the Philosophical Society. The membership of twenty to thirty convened twice a month at the old Ford's Theater (by then an annex of the surgeon general's office), where participants presented papers, many of such high caliber that they later appeared in scholarly or scientific journals or even in laymen's magazines such as *Harper's New Monthly Magazine*.[9]

Washington had still other clubs of at least a pseudo-scientific quality, such as the Potomac-Side Naturalists' Club and the Metropolitan Club, but all seemed to lack the qualities desired by many members of the scientific community. Finally, in 1878, Powell, Dutton, and Garrick Mallery formed the Cosmos Club. This exclusive organization, which to this day concentrates on a membership of professionals, provided a meeting place where scientists, physicians, top government officials, lawyers, and businessmen could meet and exchange opinions.[10]

By the late 1890s, Washington DC could boast of local societies devoted to most of the sciences: geology, geography, anthropology, zoology, ethnography, botany, biology, paleontology, paleobotany, and entomology. Although Congress and the executive branches of government, such as the Departments of Interior and Army, were always fussy supporters, the fact remained that the most reliable source of funding available was the U.S. government. During this period from 1865 to 1900, leadership that encouraged a favorable environment for scientific research was provided by prominent public men such as Congressmen James A. Garfield (briefly president of the United States) and Senator Henry M. Dawes. They took the scientists under their wings and worked hard to obtain appropriations for scientific projects. It is small wonder, then, that Washington DC became the residence of so many leading savants of the era.

The period from 1865 to 1900 was a watershed era in the history of American science. As the scientists looked to the American West, which was their primary though not exclusive geographical area of interest, they perceived a region becoming well-known but still full of challenging mysteries in all the earth and physical sciences. The West they looked to was changing with great rapidity, so much so that scientific reconnaissance—the wide-ranging survey—would soon give way to more-precise fieldwork and scientific investigation of regions already "explored" in the conventional sense. What picture of the West did the scientists see in this period?

It was certainly not a terra incognita. Meriwether Lewis and William Clark, Zebulon Pike, Stephen H. Long, and John C. Frémont, to name just the outstanding explorers, had trod the American West and reported their discoveries. The Transcontinental Railroad Surveys of 1853–55 had further delineated the American West and tracked viable railroad routes to the Pacific. All of these government-sponsored explorations involved scientific work, especially the collecting, classifying, and storing of specimens. And virtually all of these government-sponsored expeditions resulted in extensive reports that were published by the U.S. Government Printing Office.[11]

Private enterprise also furthered knowledge of the West. Fur trappers had appraised most mountain streams for beaver; in reaching those streams, they had crossed the Great Plains, discovered the major mountain passes, and explored the Great Basin. The California gold rush in 1849, the Pikes Peak frenzy and the opening of the Comstock mines in western Nevada in 1859, and the prospecting carried out by thousands of unnamed miners in 1849 and on meant that, by 1865, white humanity had trod most of the West. Many of these people, such as the mountain man Jim Bridger, knew the terrain as well as a modern traveling salesman knows his territory.

The 1870 census listed approximately 560,000 inhabitants in California, 39,000 in Colorado Territory, but just 9,000 in Wyoming Territory; thirty years later the numbers were 1,485,000 for California, 539,000 for Colorado, and 92,500 for Wyoming (the latter two had achieved statehood). Yet these numbers constituted a mere sprinkling of settlement. When scientists such as Powell, King, and Hayden and survey leaders such as Wheeler scanned a map of the West in 1865, they saw a massive land in which buffalo were still numerous, Indians continued to roam the land at will, and transportation was at best a galloping horse; only the transcontinental telegraph had been completed.

Probably not even the scientists could have contemplated the frenzy of activity that would settle the vast region in the next thirty-five years. With the near-extermination of the buffalo and the segregation of the Indians on reservations, the Great Plains first were dominated by the open-range ranching frontier and then by farmers creeping westward into dry country, learning the hard way about the problems of eking out a living in a near treeless, semiarid region. Technology kept apace, however: the railroads, barbed-wire fencing, a practical windmill, and dryland farming all came to the West. The rancher's open range was closed. Contemporaneously, mining became more sophisticated, with much foreign and eastern capital financing the installation of expensive steam engines, pumps, and hoists; smelters were built to process the ores.

Historians have called the western exploration of the 1840s and 1850s the era of "the Great Reconnaissance," implying that those who followed would carry out more thorough investigations. In this era scientist-explorers studied with a basic premise of God's unity, of His "Great Plan"; they viewed the West as part of a magnificent whole. For scientists, however, the Darwinian revolution ended the concept of God's unified world. Scientific specialties multiplied and became more sophisticated. From the late 1860s on, scientists in the field searched for and discovered evidence and pieced together the geological history of the West. In so doing, they also learned to determine with some accuracy the probability of coal, oil, and precious metals in the western earth.

Settlement of the West occurred even as the compendium of western geographical knowledge was being completed. The basic boundaries of the West were known, but at the beginning of the Great Surveys in 1867, the Grand Canyon of the Colorado had not been explored (except in its lowermost reaches) and the thermal phenomenon of the upper Yellowstone Valley was only a rumor to a handful of former mountain men. Major mountain passes and principal railroad routes were known, but reliable, detailed maps of the American West were lacking. California during the 1860s profited from its own geological survey, directed by Josiah Whitney, but the rest of the vast West awaited geological and other scientific investigation. Stimulated by the scientific environment of Washington, the four Great Surveys, forever associated with the names of their leaders—Hayden, King, Powell, and Wheeler—used the West as their laboratory, enriching American (and global) science beyond measure.

## The Hayden Survey

The first of the men who led the Great Surveys never quite achieved the newer, higher standards being demanded of scientists even as these other scientists became his rivals. Yet, for all his shortcomings, Ferdinand Vandeveer Hayden was a giant among nineteenth-century geologists. The Indians of the northern plains had dubbed him "Man Who Picks Up Stones Running," and indeed, all his active life as a geologist he worked with speed. He conducted reconnaissances, surveys of the geology, of whatever new country in which he might find himself; then he was ready to move on. As the science of geology matured, colleagues and successors faulted him for his haste. Yet more often than not, Hayden's initial interpretations have held. "F. V. Hayden, Geologist in Charge": that is how he was known to his own generation.[12]

Scientists of the post–Civil War generation came by their professions in unusual ways. Science, whatever the specialty, was not quite accepted as a legitimate endeavor. And so the scientifically inclined Hayden, born in

22.1 Dr. Ferdinand Vandeveer Hayden (n.d.). This photo was probably made during Hayden's period of prominence in the geographical surveys, sometime in the mid-to-late 1870s. Courtesy of the U.S. Geological Survey.

Westfield, Massachusetts, in 1829, became a teacher at age sixteen; at eighteen he enrolled at Oberlin College, where he graduated in 1850. He was a quiet, nervous, dreamy young man who, the geologist Charles D. Walcott later wrote, never "would . . . conquer in practical life." Certainly the fundamentalist and abolitionist Oberlin was hardly the place for a lad interested in geology. Hayden appears to have made life tolerable by becoming acquainted with a physician, Dr. John Newberry, who was also an avid geologist; from him, Hayden probably got the idea of becoming a physician. Dr. Newberry also introduced him to James Hall, the leading paleontologist of the time, who resided in Albany, New York. This explains Hayden's matriculation at Albany Medical School. Hall's residence was Hayden's home while he was there; he took his degree in 1854.[13]

Just before this, in the summer of 1853, Hall proposed a season of collecting in the Tertiary and Cretaceous fossil beds of the White River badlands in today's southwestern South Dakota. Accompanied by an older, frail, invertebrate paleontologist named Fielding Bradford Meek, young Hayden made his way up the roiling, muddy Missouri to Fort Pierre. There, across the river from present Pierre, South Dakota, he and Meek assembled their gear. Troubles with the Sioux near the badlands territory changed their plans. They collected fossils in the river basins of the Teton, White, and Cheyenne Rivers, closer to the Missouri and their transportation, the steamboat *Robert Campbell*. All too soon for Hayden, their cart was full and they returned to civilization.[14]

The excitement of the new land, the joy of discovering fossils, the challenge of studying the landforms and the specimens in order to envision and describe what had happened there and how the land had looked millions of years before—all this was too much provocation for Dr. Hayden. He obtained funding from both private and public sources to pursue his first love, geology. In 1854–55 the lone scientist conducted "a single-handed geological and natural history survey of the vast, newly-organized Nebraska Territory."[15] Actually he worked from Fort Benton on the northern Missouri River southward to present northern Nebraska. In 1856 and 1857 he was with Lieutenant Gouverneur K. Warren of the Corps of Topographical Engineers in Dakota; he was with Captain William Franklin Raynolds of the same army branch in 1859 and 1860 in the vast region between the North Platte and the Yellowstone Rivers.[16] Throughout the years from 1853 to 1861, Hayden learned much from his older colleague Meek. The two collaborated in writing several papers widely distributed throughout the scientific community, and they "mapped and described in reconnaissance the geology of much of the northern Great Plains and northeastern Rocky Mountains. They confirmed the existence of Cambrian, Permian, and Jurassic rocks in the western interior . . . [and] . . . they deciphered the structure and geologic history of the Black Hills."[17] As collaborators, he and Meek became the outstanding early stratigraphers of the region from the upper Missouri to the northern Rockies. Hayden was the fast-moving field-worker, whereas Meek was the meticulous laboratory researcher.

During the Civil War, Hayden served in the Union forces as a physician, but as soon as the turmoil was over he once again pursued his first love. In 1866 he was in Dakota's Mauvaises Terres (the badlands), collecting still more fossils. Then in 1867 a propitious situation arose. When Nebraska achieved statehood in that year, some money was still left from its territorial appropriation. Congress allotted the remaining funds to a geological survey of the new state, to be administered by the General Accounting Office. Spencer Baird of the Smithsonian and Senator John Logan of Illinois politicked for Hayden, who received the appointment as Geologist in Charge of the Geological Survey of Nebraska.

Hayden's letter of appointment reveals the concept of scientific field-work at that time. In addition to studying the geology of Nebraska, he was to note "all the beds, veins, and other deposits of ores, coals, clays, marls, peat and such other mineral substances as well as the fossil remains of the various formations." He was also to make barometric observations and collect geological, mineral, and paleontological specimens. In view of Nebraska's essentially agricultural economy, he was to note the soils and subsoils and their adaptation to certain crops. Since the state was nearly treeless, he was to estimate the possibilities of forestation. Finally (probably with a thought to charming Congress) he was asked to submit "graphic illustrations" for inclusion in the General Land Office's annual reports.[18]

Thus was Hayden launched into the work that would occupy him for virtually the rest of his life. With the approximately $5,000—not much money even in 1867 for a season in the field—Hayden built a team well equipped for life on the frontier. In many ways he followed the same organizational procedures for the remainder of his career. Since he was short of funds, he looked to the U.S. Army to supply worn-out horses and mules and surplus army supplies for his use in the field. He obtained scientific instruments and supplies from the Smithsonian Institution. In 1867 he added to his own scientific expertise by bringing along as his professional assistant his friend and frequent collaborator, the paleontologist Meek. And he hired a man Friday who had worked for him since 1856, a young Kentuckian named James Stevenson, who would become the executive officer of the Hayden Survey. (In later years Stevenson and his wife were absorbed in the science of ethnology, spending several seasons with the Zuni and Hopi tribes in the Southwest.)[19]

It must have been an enjoyable season. Hayden and Meek with their little entourage examined all the way to the Front Range of the Rockies in Colorado and into Wyoming. They investigated sections of artesian well borings, paying particular attention to coal veins. In a treeless country, sources of coal were of particular interest to settlers and speculators alike. In his report Hayden commented on the discovery of both lignite veins and iron ore deposits in Colorado, adding the rosy prediction that since the one could smelt the other, such a combination could do for Colorado what iron and coal had done for Pennsylvania.

This awareness of the economic possibilities that he sometimes found in his geological fieldwork and consciously included in his reports became a symbol of Hayden's work. As American science became more mature and sophisticated through the 1870s, Hayden's awareness of the power of mammon—and his catering to it—became a source of irritation to his rivals. Some believed that he was in collusion with certain entrepreneurs, directing the survey toward their regions of interest. His opponents argued that pure science should ignore the wishes of the marketplace. On the other hand, scientists knew that Whitney's California Geological Survey had foundered on the rocks of pure science when the legislators had demanded pragmatic findings from Whitney's state-subsidized organization. In the United States, the debate of pure versus pragmatic science rages to this day.

Nebraskans may have considered Hayden's geological survey of their state a one-year, one-time assignment, but clearly Hayden had other ideas. His sixty-four-page *First Annual Report*, by its very title, indicates the breadth of his plans. It was well received—so much so, and so happy was Hayden with his first year, that he now appeared in Washington and became for several years, until at least 1874, the king of lobbyists among the scientists. The result, in 1868, was that the same $5,000 was there in the Sundry Appropriations Bill, this time for a "general survey of the territories." Hayden had achieved his goal of transferring his field of activities from the state of Nebraska to the territories.[20]

The small expedition comprised a two-horse ambulance, a four-mule covered wagon, and nine men including the paleontologist James Hall, who made their way along the route of the Union Pacific to Fort Sanders (present Laramie, Wyoming). Hayden's tendency to do reconnaissance is apparent in his itinerary. He advanced into the Medicine Bow Mountains (or Snowy Range) west of Laramie and commented on the massive cutting of spruce and pine trees for railroad ties; he suggested that Michigan timber cutters would do well there. Then, accompanied by Generals Francis Preston Blair and Granville M. Dodge, he packed into Colorado's remote North Park. By summer's end he had geologized to Fort Bridger in southwestern Wyoming and had assembled enough fossils to please both Hall and the geologist Louis Agassiz. Then he fulfilled an obligation to a British entrepreneur, William Blackmore, to investigate the Sangre de Cristo Mountains and the parks of southern Colorado. Again, Hayden made highly optimistic reports of the country, predicting profits of 90 percent from sheep raising and of 50 to 60 percent from cattle ranching.[21]

In 1868 he had covered too much territory to do quality geological work except, perhaps, for the collecting of fossils. His "Preliminary Report" was just thirty-five pages long. Yet his lobbying efforts in the late autumn and winter of 1868–69 paid off. In 1869 Congress doubled its appropriation to $10,000. The survey now became known officially as the U.S. Geological and Geographical Survey of the Territories and was transferred administratively from the General Land Office directly to the authority of the secretary of the interior.[22]

This would be Hayden's third year in the field as a U.S. government employee. Both his name and his survey were becoming well-known throughout the United States. Although his survey may appear to have mushroomed already, Hayden clearly envisioned an ever-larger survey with ever-larger assignments. Two impediments, however, continually blocked efficient work, impediments over which neither Hayden nor his rivals had any control. One was the annual lobbying for appropriations. Congress insisted on year-by-year funding. Thus Hayden, Powell, King, and Wheeler were never sure whether the following year their surveys would exist at all or, if they did exist, whether funding would be more or (far more likely) less. Long-range planning was almost impossibile. A second problem was the traditional work lag of Congress. Survey leaders often waited in Washington well into midsummer before the Sundry Appropriations Bill, or the Army Appropriations Bill, was passed. Then, and only then, could they entrain for the West, where summer was already on the wane and the first snows of autumn were likely to fall almost before the survey had entered the field.

If his survey was to expand, additional facets of science had to be added.

In 1869 Hayden hired the twenty-three-year-old artist Henry W. Elliott, who had been Joseph Henry's private secretary at the Smithsonian. In his three seasons with Hayden, Elliott would sketch the shoreline of Yellowstone Lake. His sketches accompanied the 1870 and 1871 reports. Hayden also hired Cyrus Thomas as the survey's entomologist and botanist. After his four years with the survey, this cantankerous scientist, as professor at Southern Illinois Normal and as a member of the U.S. Entomological Commission, vigorously supported the survey. Thomas was the man who wrote convincingly—and utterly erroneously—that rain followed the plow. (He was not alone in believing this: some respected scientists of the time insisted on the validity of the theory, reasoning that breaking the sod resulted in retention of moisture and, somehow, encouraged the coming of rain. Railroads selling land jumped on the bandwagon.) Twenty-five-year-old Percival Frazer Jr. joined the survey as mining engineer and metallurgist; he had trained at the Royal Saxon School of Mines at Freiburg, Germany.

All told, by 1869 Hayden had with him about a dozen men ranging from bright scientists to cooks and packers. His roster included three young "Pilgrims"—1870s terminology for dudes—appointed because of political connections. Eighteen mules and horses—army seconds from Fort D. A. Russell at Cheyenne—two covered wagons, and an ambulance (used for various survey tasks) completed the entourage.

The 1869 field team was still small when compared with personnel of future seasons. This makes it an excellent season in which to analyze Hayden's methodology. His plans were to work south from Fort D. A. Russell all the way into New Mexico, making a geological survey of that vast region. With his geologist's pick and a dirty specimen bag hung over one shoulder, Hayden hopped, skipped, and jumped about the country examining, speculating, and collecting. He dealt with the big questions of geological history, leaving the meticulous work that constituted real proof to those who would come later. Rivals called his work sloppy, but Hayden was surprisingly correct, again and again and again.

Hayden's own reports reveal his methodology and even something of his personality. He was no writer; his reports are dull. Clearly, he worked with a telescope, not a microscope. In his *Third Annual Report* his chapters bear titles like those of a travel itinerary: "From Cheyenne to Denver"; "From Santa Fe to Taos." After about ninety pages, the reader has completed a round-trip. Nor did the geologist in charge sufficiently edit the reports submitted by his fellow scientists. In the 1869 *Annual Report*, Thomas submitted his theory that rain follows the plow. Hayden probably concurred with Thomas's theory, however; in his 1867 report he had implied much the same belief.

Nevertheless the *Third Annual Report* was fairly impressive. In addition to Hayden's report, Frazer's "Mines of Colorado" and Thomas's "Agriculture in Colorado" fleshed out the volume to 146 pages. The generally well received report appealed to the entrepreneurial class. Before a congressional committee, Hayden claimed that eight thousand copies were distributed within three weeks of publication, and he gave himself and the report credit for the decision to construct the Denver and Rio Grande Railroad.

The Hayden Survey continued to expand. More popular than ever, and still with little competition for the funds appropriated for western exploration, Hayden wrested $25,000 out of Congress for his 1870 survey, which, he stipulated, would be conducted primarily in Wyoming. Unfortunately, it was late July when Congress appropriated the money, and cold weather and snow often appear in Wyoming by September. On the way west Hayden, aware of the value of public relations, stopped off in Omaha to meet a young photographer. Here he enlisted twenty-seven-year-old William Henry Jackson as photographer, a move that did his survey inestimable good. Jackson was a dedicated, highly intelligent, and strongly motivated survey member. He possessed a strong tinge of the adventurer's and explorer's psyche, glorying in photographing new and striking discoveries such as the cliff dwellings of southwestern Colorado and the geysers and grand canyon of Yellowstone. He was also healthy, living until age ninety-nine.[23]

The 1870 expedition, in spite of its late start, was productive. Hayden and his men worked west along both sides of the Union Pacific to Fort Bridger. They explored the Wind River Range to the north and the east-west Uinta Mountains to the south, then worked up Henry's Fork of the Green River to Brown's Hole in extreme northwestern Colorado and finally more or less retraced their steps back to Cheyenne. There they entrained for Washington, where offices were set up. During the winter the reports were prepared for publication. Hayden's *Fourth Annual Report* was a substantial book, 511 pages of reports and drawings. It included monographs, often by scientists who were never themselves in the field with Hayden but who were glad for the opportunity to examine, identify, and classify specimens and write reports, even though Hayden paid them nothing for their contributions. Both Meek and the paleontologist Joseph Leidy reported on fossils. In addition, three newcomers to the Hayden reports appeared in the 1870 volume: John S. Newberry, a well-known geologist; Leo Lesquereux, a noted paleobotanist; and the great vertebrate paleontologist Edward Drinker Cope. Along with Leidy and Yale professor Othniel Charles Marsh, Cope was one of the three leading paleontologists of the era.

In his 1870 *Annual Report* Hayden expressed his thanks to such entrepreneurs as Leland Stanford, Edward Harriman, and Ben Crocker of the Central Pacific Railroad, to General Granville M. Dodge of the Union Pacific, and to lesser officials of the Kansas Pacific and Denver Pacific Railroads. "Generosity on the part of such corporations towards men who are devoted to the advancement of knowledge or the good of the world, may be regarded as the index of their tone and character," he wrote. He cultivated the friendship of westerners, noting that his survey was worthwhile for the benefits it would bring to the western people. He spoke of placing "before the world in a proper light the magnificent resources, scientific and practical, of our vast domain in the West."[24] Such pragmatism may not have sat well with the scientists rapidly rising to the fore in Washington, but it sat well with the westerners who studied his reports.

Hayden was riding the crest of the wave. Good public relations, shrewd lobbying, and the cultivation of powerful business interests had created, by 1871, a power base that earned him greatly increased appropriations from Congress. In 1871 he heightened his status by announcing plans to explore northwestern Wyoming, where private explorers had discovered thermal phenomena, a beautiful high-country lake, and a magnificent canyon, Yellowstone. Hayden was aware of the rumored treasures. In 1859–60, as surgeon-naturalist with Raynolds, he had traveled to the headwaters of the Powder River in the Big Horn Mountains southward into the Wind River Range. Raynolds, with Hayden along, had tried to enter the Absaroka Mountains south and east of Yellowstone, but the deep snow prevented penetration. We may assume that Hayden vowed at that time to get to Yellowstone in the future.

The season of 1871 gave him the opportunity. In that year, partly because he advertised his decision to make Yellowstone his area of operations, Congress appropriated $40,000 for the survey. Hayden had better financial backing than ever before, and the geologist intended to use the money well. Moreover, the appropriation came through in late spring, so that Stevenson, Hayden's executive officer, was able to entrain for Ogden, Utah Territory, and begin assembling men and matériel for an early June departure. Most of Hayden's old hands were along, including the best cook in the business, "Potato John" Raymond. A newly appointed mineralogist was Dr. Albert C. Peale, from a distinguished Philadelphia family

*22.2 Map of Yellowstone National Park (1871). An important result of the Hayden Survey, this is the first map of Yellowstone to show the primary features that remain today as tourist attractions. Courtesy of the U.S. Geological Survey.*

involved since early in the century with science, art, and exploration. A German, Anton Schonborn, held a position new for the survey: topographer. This was the first season in which Hayden included triangular topography as one of the survey's duties.

Along as a result of Northern Pacific Railroad subsidization was a Hudson River School landscape painter, Thomas Moran. Tall, angular, thin to the point of scrawny, wearing a cape and a beret, Moran fit well into the corps, in spite of his artist's appearance. He and Jackson, the photographer, got along well.[25] On 11 June the twenty-one men and their seven wagons headed north, bound initially for Fort Ellis (near present Bozeman, Montana) and then southward into the headwater region of the Yellowstone River. The country was new to Hayden, but during the 1860s, miners had made their way north from Ogden to Virginia City and Last Chance Gulch (Helena) and also northwestward to the mines of present Idaho, so the trail was clear. It led through the attractive parks of northern Utah, down the Port Neuf River, past Robber's Roost City, and then up the Snake River valley into Lincoln Valley to the newly established Fort Hall, just north of present Pocatello. As usual at these lonely military outposts, the occupants were glad to have their boredom broken by the surveyors' presence. After a few days at Fort Hall the men advanced to Fort Ellis, just east of Bozeman, where final preparations were made for their trip into the valley of the upper Yellowstone.[26]

Hayden and his men must have experienced the thrill of anticipation. Rumors about the thermal phenomena, a magnificent canyon, and a high-altitude lake had been bandied about for years. Between 1807, when John Colter first entered the area, and the first Hayden expedition into the upper Yellowstone, many white men had seen the region, including fur trappers and gold prospectors. The first well-chronicled expedition into the region took place in September 1869 when three men who were employees of the Boulder (Montana) Ditch Company raised enough money to finance their own exploring trip into the upper Yellowstone. One heavily edited article about their trip was published in the *Western Monthly Magazine*, irritating a few of Montana's prominent citizens who had planned on making such a trip but had failed to bring it about.[27] The following year a substantial party—led by Nathaniel P. Langford, a Montana businessman, General Henry D. Washburn, Montana's surveyor-general, and Lieutenant Gustavus C. Doane, Second Cavalry, U.S. Army, and including several other prominent Montana Territory men—viewed most of Yellowstone's great wonders, including Old Faithful Geyser (which they named). After the Washburn-Langford-Doane Expedition, Yellowstone was no longer unknown. However, scientists of an official expedition sponsored by the U.S. government still needed to give the stories an official stamp of authentication. Hayden found himself in just the right place, with the right kind of survey, at just the right time. Now, in 1871, he was prepared to make the exploration.

On 15 July 1871 the survey set out from Fort Ellis for the upper Yellowstone. Accompanying them was Lieutenant Doane with a small contingent

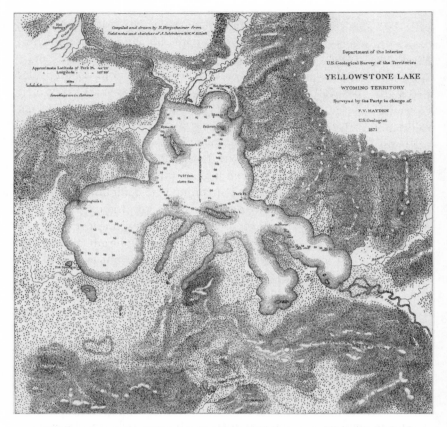

*22.3 "Yellowstone Lake, Wyoming Territory." This map, published in* U.S. Geographical Survey of Montana and Adjacent Territory 1871 *and produced under the supervision of Hayden, was the first precise large-scale map of the lake. Courtesy of the Montana Historical Society.*

of soldiers, more a token of army support than real security. Two other army officers, Colonel John W. Barlow and Captain David P. Heap, traveled along, independently ordered by the army to make a reconnaissance of the region. The group touched at Mammoth Hot Springs (dubbed by Hayden "White Mountain Hot Springs") and worked up to Tower Falls, then over Mount Washburn to the grand canyon of the Yellowstone (where J. Crissman, a Bozeman photographer, watched helplessly as his camera and tripod blew over the precipice, leaving the field for Jackson and Moran). The Hayden men launched a little boat, the *Anna*, on Yellowstone

*22.4 The Hayden Survey camp and sailboat* Anna *at the southwestern arm of Yellowstone Lake (photograph by William H. Jackson, 1871). Courtesy of the U.S. Geological Survey, neg. no. 57-HS-99 in the National Archives.*

Lake and sketched the 175 miles of shoreline, placed its islands at approximately their correct positions, and probed the depths with a lead and line. They then explored the Upper, Middle, and Lower Geyser Basins. Hayden next made his way counterclockwise around Yellowstone Lake, experienced an earthquake while encamped near the southeastern arm, then advanced down the Yellowstone River and crossed the East Fork (now known as the Lamar River) by using a toll bridge run by an English frontiersman named Jack Baronett. Thus Hayden's party worked its way northwestward back to Bozeman. The survey disbanded on 1 October, and many of its members entrained for Washington DC. There specimens would be identified, reports written, and measures taken that resulted, on 1 March 1872, in the creation by Congress of Yellowstone National Park, the nation's first such reservation.

Nothing succeeds like success: in 1872 Hayden received $75,000 for his survey. This season he proposed again to explore scientifically the Yellowstone region and also the area to the south, the Grand Tetons. His survey was by now nationally known. Jackson's photographs were widely disseminated, and his stereopticans of the survey's explorations graced many a marble-topped parlor table.

In 1872 Hayden decided to divide his survey into two divisions, each with about thirty men. Hayden would rendezvous at Fort Ellis and enter Yellowstone as he had the year before. His executive officer, Stevenson, would rendezvous at Ogden, Utah Territory, and advance to Fort Hall, then plunge eastward toward the Tetons, explore Pierre's Hole (now known as the Teton Basin), find a pass and cross it into Jackson's Hole on the east, then head north for a final rendezvous with the Hayden contingent in the Firehole Geyser Basin.

A few scientists who would subsequently gain lasting reputations were added to the survey. One of them was Henry Gannett, the nation's premier geographer and cartographer. Another was William Henry Holmes, who succeeded the artist Henry Elliott, who had resigned. Holmes's magnificent sketches of the land remain one of the artistic achievements of the Hayden Survey. He was a brilliant man, with abilities as geologist, topographer, and anthropologist; later he became director of the National Collection of Fine Arts in Washington. On this expedition, topographical mapping remained a priority, as it had the previous year.

Stevenson's contingent explored the unmapped country. He advanced up Henry's Fork, then over rising, rolling country to Pierre's River and into Pierre's Hole. From camp at the junction of Teton Creek with Pierre's River, the men were drawn to the looming Tetons to the east. The challenge was too much for Stevenson and Langford to resist. With twelve men they started for the highest peak, hoping to reach its summit. Only Langford and Stevenson reached the summit—maybe. Langford always insisted they did, but Stevenson never made the outright claim. By way of Targhee Pass, Stevenson and his men then rode down into the drainage of the Madison River. They followed the Madison upstream and contacted the Hayden contingent at the prearranged point on the Firehole River. After a few days the survey broke into segments once more; Hayden returned to Fort Ellis and entrained east while a few of his scientists remained at work a while longer in Yellowstone. Stevenson's group worked southward through Jackson's Hole, across the mountains to Fort Hall, and south to Ogden, where his corps disbanded.

Hayden's *Sixth Annual Report*, like the previous reports, contained lengthy scientific reports. Lesquereux, Meek, and Cope all submitted

22.5 *The Hayden Survey in Yellowstone National Park during the summer of 1872. Courtesy of the U.S. Geological Survey.*

papers analyzing the fossils turned over to them for examination. Coleoptera (insects including beetles and weevils), Orthoptera (grasshoppers), Odonata (dragonflies), and Mallophaga (bird lice) were all scientifically reported. John Merle Coulter's report identified sixty species of grasses, fifty-three of mosses, and sixty-six of lichens, out of a total listing of twelve hundred species of plants.

Indian troubles may have been Hayden's reason for devoting the next five years to mapping and scientifically examining Colorado, with overlaps into adjoining sections of New Mexico, Utah, and Wyoming. But Yellowstone's challenges to the geologist were so great that he was back in the area with his survey in 1877 and 1878. His reports for those two years (some of which were not published until 1883) are enormous tomes. They contain extensive research into just about every branch of science active at the time. They were not, however, the last word. Arnold Hague, with the U.S. Geological Survey, was assigned to Yellowstone; he worked on the park's geology well into the twentieth century. As the centennial of Yellowstone's discovery approached, a new U.S. Geological Survey investigation began. Using modern methodology, the survey introduced rather startling new concepts, invalidating much of the speculation of Hayden and Hague.[28]

Although Indian troubles in Wyoming and Montana could have prompted Hayden's decision to concentrate on Colorado for the next few years, other circumstances probably entered into his decision as well. Colorado in 1873 was beginning an explosive growth. In 1870 the Union Pacific had completed its line from Denver to Cheyenne, linking Denver to the transcontinental railroad, and just two months later the Kansas Pacific reached Denver from Kansas City. This set off a population boom that lasted for a decade. In Colorado, Hayden realized, were magnificent mountains that held all kinds of treasures, yet its geology, flora, and fauna were hardly known. The hour was late, he felt, and scientific exploration needed to get under way immediately. Maps were an essential component for mining exploration and investment and for railroad expansion. In short, Hayden's pragmatism blended with the needs of dozens of investors and entrepreneurs who looked toward Colorado, with its mighty central Rockies, for potential gain.

The geologist envisioned a beautiful atlas that would be as correct and precise as the methodology of the time allowed. He now had topographers with several seasons' experience in the West; they could form the nucleus of the topographical crews he would be sending into the field. In 1873 he already had at his disposal Gustavus Bechler (an excellent topographer), Gannett, and Holmes. Now he added James Terry Gardner, the highly capable topographer who had worked for King's Fortieth Parallel Survey. Later A. D. Wilson, also previously with King, and Franklin Rhoda and George B. Chittenden joined. In sum, the team constituted the best topographers available, and their work lived up to their promise.

By today's standards, the mapwork of the 1870s was extremely primitive. Yet the basics of modern topographical mapping still use concepts already in use in the 1870s—or even in Jefferson's day. First a baseline was established. For Colorado this was to run approximately down the Front Range of the Rockies (about 104°30'), touching the towns of Greeley, Pueblo, and Trinidad. (Hayden expressed little interest in the high plains of the eastern half of Colorado.) The northern boundary of the Colorado survey would touch King's Fortieth Parallel Survey in southern Wyoming. The southern boundary would be the Mexican border, although this never materialized, since Hayden barely entered New Mexico.

The next step was triangulation. The topographers worked in a half circle with the apex west, touching high points in the distance and linking them to two points elsewhere. Next, they climbed the peaks where triangles touched and extended the triangulation westward in that great half circle. By the end of their third summer in Colorado, Gardner and his men had done primary triangulation of the entire state. Within these huge triangles, secondary triangulation now took place at points six to eight miles apart. When this was completed, all the most outstanding geographical points were represented in fairly close approximation to where they actually stood. They would appear in the right latitude and longitude: Mount Evans would not be where Longs Peak rises, for example, nor would the South Platte be indicated where the Cache la Poudre winds down from the mountains. Altitudes and barometric observations were likewise made, the base points for altitude often being strategic points on railroads.

All of this constituted the scientific part of topography; in the 1870s the artistic aspects were equally important. How does one show on triangulation the peaks, saddles, glacial moraines, cliffs, hills, swales, valleys, canyons, winding rivers, and streams? It was here that the artistic skills of the topographers came in. While one person made the triangulation, another sat on a nearby rock with a sketch pad. The absolute master of this kind of sketching was Holmes, whose work verged on genius. Others, including the young Rhoda, did very acceptable profile sketching also. When the topographers assembled at season's end in the Washington DC offices of the survey, they combined their triangulation with the sketches to produce contour maps of great beauty and, for the time, great accuracy.

For four seasons, 1873–76, the Hayden Survey subordinated all its other work to the compilation of its master *Atlas of Colorado*. By 1873 a routine had been established. In the late spring Stevenson established headquarters at Meier Fisher's ranch outside Denver along Clear Creek. The camp was laid out in military fashion with kitchen and dining facilities as far removed as possible from stables and latrines. Gradually personnel, livestock, and equipment were assembled. Because congressional appropriations usually came in so late in the season, haste inevitably became the hallmark of the headquarters camp. Quickly packers had to become acquainted with their mules and vice versa. Topographers, geologists, paleontologists, and assorted other naturalists had to blend into the camp routine. A few political appointees, often uncooperative spoiled brats, were usually along to do some collecting; and an occasional journalist, such as Ernest Ingersoll, recorded life in the field.[29] The weather was not always sunny, the mules were rarely cooperative, and the haste to complete the season's assignment canceled out anyone's early perception that this was a summer junket.

22.6 (a) "The Quartzite Group—San Juan Mountains" (panorama by William H. Holmes, 1876); (b) "Central Portion of the Elk Mountains" (panorama by William H. Holmes, 1876). These panoramas are among the finest representatives of terrain art ever produced and are nearly photographic in their accurate portrayal of terrain. Courtesy of the National Archives.

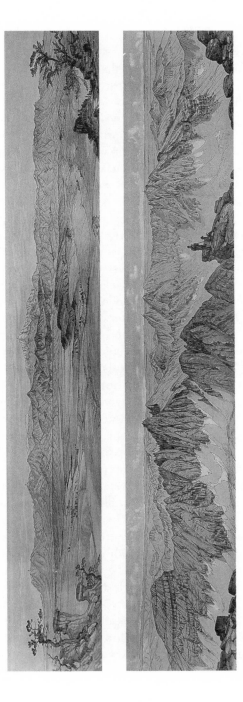

22.7 (a) "The Pike's Peak Group" (panorama by William H. Holmes, 1876); (b) "The La Plata Mountains" (panorama by William H. Holmes, 1876). Courtesy of the National Archives.

In the years 1873–76 Hayden's survey was divided into as few as three and as many as six divisions working as distantly from each other as North Park, on the Wyoming border, to the cliff dwellings along the Mancos River in southwestern Colorado. In 1873, three divisions numbered from eight to twelve men each. Two packers and a cook constituted the usual support team; the rest of the personnel was assigned more professional tasks. Hayden was likely to visit all his divisions during the season; often a primary triangulation team accompanied him. Jackson, the photographer, with his favorite mule, Hypo, was on his own, making his way all over the Colorado Rockies in search of stunning sites. Stevenson was a sort of roving quartermaster, trying to supply all the divisions in the field.

Topographic work in the Rockies was not without its dangers. Besides scientific skill and artistic sketching ability, the topographers had to be men in top physical condition. Day after day, weather permitting, they left their timberline camp as soon as the pink blush of a new day brought enough light to show the way. Early hours were clearest for making observations and sketches; in the high Rockies, afternoons were likely to bring on clouds and rain. Once at the peak, the men often spent six to eight hours taking readings, making and then checking and rechecking triangulation, and sketching; if a geologist was along, he would probably color his sketches to indicate different strata or other geological phenomena.

Some minor scuffles with Indians occurred. In Gannett's party a mule was shot by Indians and three others were lost. Two young men left at camp were surrounded by Indians; luckily one of the young men had been at the nearby agency and recognized some of the Indians, who left them unharmed. A few weeks later Jackson's party was surrounded by Indians, who struck his stock with quirts; his whole party, along with the whooping Indians, rode down the canyon in a wild stampede. Jackson soon met their chief, traded with the Indians, and was allowed to get out safely. In 1878 A. D. Wilson's division was robbed of all its animals and part of its outfit by Indians near Sawtelle's Peak in northeastern Idaho.

The men also had a few scrapes with grizzlies. Archibald Marvine's party in Middle Park lived for two weeks on flour and game brought in by Harry Yount, their hunter. He killed a grizzly by putting a bullet in its front skull, two in its flanks, and one in its heart before it died, too close to its adversary for comfort. Holmes also shot a bear. And Fred Endlich and Rhoda, traversing a razor-edged saddle leading to a high peak, stepped gingerly in the footsteps of a grizzly bear in the snow and thus advanced rapidly toward their goal. Rhoda added that they "were able to put to good use the unerring instinct of the bear in selecting the best route to travel by."[30]

By the close of the 1876 season the Hayden topographers realized that the Great Survey of Colorado was coming to a close. The topographers returned to the Hayden offices in Washington DC—as they had during the past four autumns—to go over their notes, their triangulations, their sketches, and their calculations. They slaved over drafting tables as contour maps emerged slowly from blank sheets of paper. The maps were sent to Julius Bien and Company in New York City, the outstanding U.S. lithography firm that had done considerable work for the government on the Pacific Railway Surveys and on Warren's map of the territories between the Mississippi and the Pacific. In 1877 the Hayden atlas was issued under the title *Geological and Geographical Atlas of Colorado and Portions of Adjacent Territory*. It consisted of ten maps, two cutaways, and two profiles. It was well received. The pragmatic Hayden must have been pleased with its reception by western entrepreneurs such as Colorado railroad builders E. L. Berthoud and William J. Palmer. Even today, geologists find the atlas useful when they are working in remote parts of the state.

Jackson's photographs, including his popular three-dimensional stereoscopic slides, were sold by the thousands throughout the United States. They created in Americans a desire to see the West as tourists and, for many, a desire to settle there. Just as the survey had gained notoriety by bringing the truth about Yellowstone to the American people (and bore much of the responsibility for the creation of the first national park), so too did it gain fame and help advertise Colorado by "discovering" cliff dwellings (though not Mesa Verde) and the Mount of the Holy Cross in Colorado.[31] The transcontinental railroads, rapidly becoming operational during this era, were quick to capitalize on this interest.

In 1879 the surveys of Hayden, Powell, and Wheeler were consolidated into the U.S. Geological Survey. Hayden was allowed to continue work on the preparation of his last reports, and the final, enormous tome appeared in 1883. Today the quarto volumes gather dust in research libraries, but in the 1870s and 1880s they constituted a storehouse of scientific information about the new country in the West. Pragmatically speaking, of the four Great Surveys, Hayden's U.S. Geological and Geographical Survey of the Territories probably had the greatest effect on economic development and settlement in the West.

Hayden and his survey have not, however, fared so well from historians of science, who tend to emphasize the history of geology at the expense of topography and the natural sciences. In geology, Hayden ran into formidable opponents such as Powell and King. They were purists, for the most part, believing in science for science's sake. They emphasized preciseness and meticulousness in geological exploration and caution before publishing theories. Moreover, Gilbert, King, and Powell, a quintessential bureaucrat, were suave, polished, and urbane. They learned how to get what they wanted in Washington. Hayden, who at first had succeeded so well, lost out as these men came to the fore. The Hayden Survey probably deserves more credit than it has been granted, even though much of its work, done in great haste, was indeed unpolished, crude, and below the standards rapidly being established by geologists such as Powell, King, Gilbert, and Dutton.[32]

## The King Survey

The contrasts between the Hayden Survey and the King Survey (the Fortieth Parallel Survey, formally known as the U.S. Geological Exploration of the Fortieth Parallel) exceed the similarities. Both were geological and geographical surveys with representation from other natural sciences. Whereas Hayden concentrated on the Rockies, especially the mountains of Colorado and Wyoming, King focused—in theory, at least—on a one-hundred-mile strip of land in which the Union Pacific Railroad (or its western affiliate, the Central Pacific) ran the main line from Cheyenne, in southeastern Wyoming Territory, to the crest of the Sierra Nevada, where the survey linked up with Whitney's California Geological Survey. Hayden was under Department of the Interior jurisdiction; King was directly under the administrative scrutiny of the U.S. Army chief of engineers, General A. A. Humphreys. Finally, the King Survey displayed a bit of the aristocracy, which was lacking in Hayden's organization.[33]

Clarence King was a product of Yale's distinguished Sheffield Scientific School at a time when that institution numbered on its faculty some of the nation's outstanding scholars: James Dwight Dana, who, with Benjamin Silliman Sr., founded the *American Journal of Science and Arts*; George J. Brush, a leading mineralogist; Chester A. Lyman, an astronomer; and William A. Norton, who taught surveying. Josiah Whitney and William Brewer of the California Geological Survey, with which King and his friend James Terry Gardner would be affiliated in the years 1863–66, were Sheffield men. After his graduation in 1862, King spent the winter of 1862–63 working with the Harvard scientist Alexander Agassiz, son of the famed naturalist and geologist Louis Agassiz.

Gardner was King's closest friend. The two had been students together at Sheffield, and when it became clear that Gardner had better do something about his fragile health in the spring of 1863, the two decided to make a bold move: they would head for California. Their journey west was full of excitement laced with both humor and danger. They worked briefly at a quartz mill at Virginia City, the principal town serving the Comstock Lode, and after saving enough money to continue their journey, they crossed the Sierra Nevada. Then, as fate would have it, on a river steamer bound for San Francisco from Sacramento, they encountered Brewer of the California Geological Survey. This chance meeting determined their futures. For the next four years they were involved with the survey as well as with occasional forays of other employers, such as a geological survey of the Mariposa estate owned by John C. Frémont and a reconnaissance for General Irvin McDowell into the southwestern deserts. Gardner, who at first had not been hired on, eventually became a California Geological Survey topographer, a task he filled so well that he would head up the topographical work for the King Survey and later also for the Hayden Survey.

Late in the summer of 1866, King and Gardner, sitting on the summit of a peak east of Yosemite and gazing as far as they could see into the Great Basin, conceived the idea of the Fortieth Parallel Survey. They were well aware that the transcontinental railroad was rapidly nearing completion— and what did anyone know of the flora and fauna and geological secrets of the vast area along its main line? Such knowledge was necessary, the young men knew, if exploitation of resources was to proceed. Only a scientific survey, they agreed, could define the resource possibilities with any certainty. And since Whitney was in trouble with the California legislature and the future of his survey was uncertain, why not leave his organization, head for Washington DC, obtain federal funds, and undertake the monumental task of resource evaluation along the route of the Union and Central Pacific Railroads?

King arrived in Washington DC in the winter of 1867. He was well prepared, with letters of introduction in hand and letters sent ahead in his behalf. Whitney, Baird, and Dana were among those who wrote, with three letters addressed directly to Secretary of War Edwin Stanton. Despite the presence in Washington of dozens of war veterans searching for employment, King, twenty-five years old and not a veteran, received the appointment. In the *U.S. Statutes at Large* the citation read merely "a geological and topographical exploration of the territory between the Rocky Mountains and the Sierra Nevada mountains, including the routes of the Pacific railroad; Provided, That same can be done out of existing appropriations."[34] The secretary of war handed King his commission as geologist with the following advice: "Now, Mr. King, the sooner you get out of Washington, the better—you are too young a man to be seen about town with this appointment in your pocket—there are four major generals who want your place."[35] After receiving instructions about bookkeeping and other matters that had to be handled the army way, King left Washington. It was already March, and he wanted to be in the field as early into the summer as possible.

His first appointment was his close friend Gardner, an expert topographer. The topographic team included a Swiss named Custer, F. A. Clark, and Allen D. Wilson (always referred to as A. D. Wilson), who would later serve with Hayden and with the U.S. Geological Survey. In geology King also began with friends. He appointed the brothers James Duncan (always known as James D.) and Arnold Hague. These two New Englanders, both slightly older than King, were very well educated. James D. had attended the Lawrence School at Harvard with additional work in mining, geology, and metallurgy in Germany; Arnold had attended the Sheffield Scientific School before also going on to further education in Germany. A third geologist was Samuel Franklin Emmons. He, like the Hagues, had been educated at private schools, first at Harvard and after that at the schools of mines in Europe—in fact, he had met Arnold at the Royal School of Mines at Freiberg.

Choices for collectors and interpreters of flora and fauna worked out well partly through good luck. The botanist's position first went to a young man whose fragile health forced him to resign after nine months. Fortunately, while the young man was still with the survey, a footsore Yankee drifted into the Fortieth Parallel Survey camp in the western Nevada deserts. He had made his way from New England to California, had heard of King's survey, and—against the dangers of dying from thirst, hunger, Indians, or snakebite and of getting lost—had headed into the desert beyond the eastern terminus of the Central Pacific, determined to find King. He looked like a tramp—shabbily dressed, bearded, hungry—but had a Yankee twang, a Yale degree, courses taken at Sheffield, and an interest in flora and fauna. Since he was there, was hungry, and needed a job, King put him to work; within a month King put him on the payroll, and later Sereno

Watson stepped into the job of botanist. So competent was he that he later became curator of the Gray Herbarium at Harvard.

For fauna collections King took a chance on a seventeen-year-old mid-westerner, Robert Ridgeway, recommended to him by Baird. As a lad growing up in Mount Carmel, in southern Illinois, Ridgeway had shown an unusual interest in birds. His parents encouraged the boy, rounding out his rustic education with knowledge of animals as well as birds. It was his mother's suggestion that he write the commissioner of patents in Washington for help in identifying a bird; the letter was sent from the Patent Office to Baird, who replied. A friendship by correspondence began. Baird brought King and Ridgeway together by mail, and thus Ridgeway soon found himself on a railroad car bound for Washington, where he received training from Baird; he then joined King in New York. Later in his career Ridgeway was the curator of birds at the U.S. National Museum of Natural History; he wrote more than five hundred scholarly papers.

King was an innovator. He also understood public relations, hiring Timothy H. O'Sullivan as photographer. O'Sullivan had been with Matthew Brady during the Civil War; his photograph "Harvest of Death," taken the day after Gettysburg, is one of the great photographs of the war. For three years O'Sullivan was with King, and many of his photographs have survived as classics of early photography of the West.[36]

When the advance contingent of King's survey arrived in California, it was enhanced with a troop of twenty soldiers supplied by the Military Division of the Pacific. The survey was also permitted to obtain provisions from the Quartermaster. Ben Crocker, one of the "Big Four" of the Central Pacific, found the members a comfortable campsite in Sacramento and lent them horses and wagons until they received their own. Not until 3 July 1867 did the Fortieth Parallel Survey, more often known as the King Survey, become operational.

The first season was spent in the northern reaches of the Great Basin from the Sierra Nevada and their eastern spur, the Washoe Mountains, eastward theoretically to the Wasatch Mountains of Utah, a distance of about five hundred miles. In reality the surveyors advanced only as far east as the second Humboldt Range: essentially they had covered the north-western quadrant of Nevada. Today's railroad, bus, or automobile traveler knows that every twenty or thirty miles in the Great Basin (which once held two prehistoric inland lakes, Lahontan in the west and Bonneville in the east), the desert is broken by north-south ranges of mountains. Two depressions mark the region, one at the eastern base of the Sierra Nevada (with Death Valley at 282 feet below sea level) and the other far to the northeast, the Great Salt Lake Basin. The Great Basin was then, and remains, an austere, sparsely settled region, much of it true desert occupied by coyotes, rattlesnakes, scorpions, tarantulas, cacti, sagebrush and greasewood, and very little potable water.

King's outfit, including the soldiers, numbered between forty and fifty men. The routine was to establish a base camp, well laid out and with a flagpole flying both the American flag and the flag designed for the Fortieth Parallel Survey. From there the geologists and topographers ranged far and wide in small groups of three or four men plus a cook and a packer. One of the merits of the base camp was that it gave the naturalists Watson and Ridgeway an opportunity to study and prepare their specimens.

The Great Basin was indeed a hostile land, but it was also challenging. Gradually King, the Hagues, and Emmons began piecing together the geological history of this landlocked region in which terraces along the mountainsides indicated the decline of inland seas that had once been more than one thousand feet deep. O'Sullivan took flash pictures of the interior of the Comstock mines. Others built a little boat, the *Nettie*, which they sailed down the Truckee River to Pyramid Lake, in northwestern Nevada.

Ridgeway never forgot the rigors of the Humboldt Sink. The rivers of the Great Basin originally flowed either into low sinks, where they dried up in swampy wastes, or into the Great Salt Lake. The year 1867 had been unusually wet for the region, with the result of more swamp and water and, therefore, more insects. The mosquitoes were so numerous that they snuffed out candles—and they carried malaria. Ridgeway caught the disease, and only the patience of his mule, which allowed him to rest in the animal's shadow at midday in the desert, saved him from probable death. (His companions found him and took him to camp in the ambulance.) The water in the area smelled like rotten eggs, and the decaying vegetation fouled the very air the men breathed. Three-fourths of the expedition came down sick, prompting King by September to move the base camp eastward to more healthful surroundings.

When autumn came, King took his corps into winter quarters, the geologists at Virginia City and the rest at Carson City. His men had conducted a triangular survey from the California boundary at 120° west longitude to about 117°30', consisting of the northwestern quartile of Nevada, "the most difficult and dangerous country to campaign in I know of on the continent," King wrote.[37] Two thousand geological specimens had been collected, three hundred barometrical readings observed, and two thousand meteorological observations made. In the spring of 1868 King split his corps into three divisions, which worked apart from each other for weeks at a time before returning to a prearranged base camp to replenish provisions. Precise geographical boundaries of their work are hard to come by because King was so meticulous in his desire to be correct: he sent his men back over country already surveyed to check and recheck the accuracy of their calculations.

In 1868 the corps worked primarily in northeastern Nevada and northwestern Utah to the Great Salt Lake. They had covered five hundred miles since leaving the crest of the Sierra Nevada, with a width of at least one hundred miles. Crossing some of the higher mountain ranges had to be accomplished in the dark of night when snowdrifts had crusted over sufficiently to carry the weight of mules and men. As geologists, they had exposed as a humbug a supposed coalfield in extreme northeastern Nevada. By mid-October, King pronounced the season's operations at an end. After a month's leave, members reassembled in Washington DC at headquarters established at 294 "H" Street. The task of preparing the reports for publication began.

By 15 May 1869 the corps was once again in the field, this time at Salt Lake City. Again it was split into three groups. King's group was to work the northern end of the Salt Lake valley, Emmons's group the southern end, and the third group—including two topographers and the naturalists Watson and Ridgeway—the Great Salt Lake itself. The last group launched a little boat dubbed the *Eureka* and, at some risk, surveyed the shoreline. King discovered that the lake had risen nine to eleven feet since Captain Howard Stansbury of the Corps of Topographical Engineers had studied it in 1849–50. By summer's end the men were working up the northeastern quartile of Utah Territory (now southwestern Wyoming), a beautiful area. It was essentially a block of land bounded on the south by the east-west Uinta Mountains, the Wasatch Mountains on the west, and, roughly, the Green River on the east; to the north were the plains and mountains of Wyoming, leading to the Snake River valley. When September arrived, some of the personnel entrained for Washington while others, including King, retraced some of their efforts over the past three years, checking and rechecking their readings and computations and making changes where necessary because of new settlements. Finally King and his group departed also—much work remained to be done in Washington.

There, in the winter of 1869–70, they picked up where they had left off

*22.8 The Fortieth Parallel Survey camp near Salt Lake City (photograph by T. H. O'Sullivan, 1871). The pioneer photographer O'Sullivan was one of the more important members of the geological survey of the fortieth parallel because of his precise topographic renderings. Courtesy of the Library of Congress.*

the year before, crystallizing plans for the huge volumes of the Fortieth Parallel Survey reports that would subsequently be printed by the Government Printing Office. By midyear, volume 3, *Mining Industry* by James D. Hague, and volume 5, *Botany*, were ready for submission to General Humphreys for his imprimatur. Plans had initially called for three seasons in the field, followed by the months or years necessary to work up the material and get it published. But King was uncertain of many points involving geology, glaciation, and volcanism and requested further fieldwork. The money was forthcoming, and in 1870 King was once again in the field, accompanied by Arnold Hague and Emmons. Next he concentrated on Lassen Peak and Mount Shasta in northern California while Arnold Hague and A. D. Wilson did similar work at Mount Hood and Mount Rainier. King is due the credit for establishing the existence of living glaciers within the continental United States. At season's end King insisted that their fieldwork had been "an entire success."

There seems to be a pattern to government work: it always expands with a resultant request for more time and money. King, as head of the Fortieth Parallel Survey, was tired of being restricted to that one-hundred-mile strip along the fortieth parallel (although he had already departed widely from it); now he envisioned fieldwork on volcanism from Mount Saint Elias in Alaska southeastward to San Francisco Peak in Arizona. General Humphreys said no. But King's suggestion of carrying the survey from extreme western Wyoming eastward to Cheyenne was approved. Thus in 1871 and 1872 King and his men took to the field once again.

At least the terrain was more pleasant. Range after range of the high Rockies challenged their topographical expertise and geological deductions. The Front Range on the east, the Park Range, the Medicine Bow Range, the Black Hills (or Laramie Range) of Wyoming, and parts of the Uintas to the west all offered challenge; the canyons of the Yampa and Green Rivers invited exploration. The broken, geologically fascinating northwestern corner of Colorado and adjacent areas intrigued them, but snowfall finally forced the party into Fort Bridger on 2 November 1871. Arnold Hague's party, they discovered, had taken refuge from winter at Laramie. King ordered his men to San Francisco, where they went into winter quarters while he recuperated from an illness by taking a six-week vacation in Hawaii.

King would have liked to have boated down the Green River and, one suspects, all the way into the Colorado and down to its mouth in the Gulf of California, but General Humphreys again reined him in. The year 1872 was to be the survey's last in the field. Between 1 May and 15 November, King and his men reexamined the entire range of the specified fortieth parallel country from the 105th to the 120th meridian longitude, always along that one-hundred-mile strip of land embracing the transcontinental railroad. King also worked on glaciation and vulcanism in the Sierra Nevada while Arnold Hague worked in northwestern Colorado; Gardner meanwhile did the topography of the Rabbit Ears Range, the Medicine Bow Range, and the Front Range of Colorado, working down the Cache la Poudre River of northern Colorado to the 105th meridian, the eastern limits of the survey.

Also in 1872, the King Survey gained credence with hard-headed businesspeople by exposing perhaps the greatest hoax ever perpetrated in the American West. During the years of its fieldwork, the Fortieth Parallel Survey covered country that was wide open to exploitation. Thousands of drifting men, many of them veterans of the Civil War, were searching the West for their one big chance, their opportunity to gain wealth. Among them, as always, were some shrewd and unscrupulous men, such as Philip Arnold and John Slack. These two men wanted to parlay perhaps $30,000 paid them for a mining claim into hundreds of thousands or millions of dollars. How did they hope to do this? They planned to salt some diamonds (i.e., place them) in a remote part of the West, stake out a mining claim at the spot, sell the claim, and then disappear!

The two first left for the low countries of Belgium and Holland from Halifax, Nova Scotia; having purchased rough-cut diamonds and a few rubies, they returned, selected a site remote even today in extreme northwestern Colorado, and salted the gems. Then they allowed the rumor to spread in San Francisco that diamonds had been found in the West. Their ruse worked: major financiers of San Francisco and prominent men of New York City purchased the claim after hiring a respected California geologist, Henry Janin, to inspect the site and pronounce it genuine.

King and his men heard the stories about diamonds in the West. In six years of intensive geologizing along the fortieth parallel, they had never found a diamond, nor had they investigated terrain of the kind in which diamonds were said to exist. If diamonds did exist in the West, most especially along the route of the Fortieth Parallel Survey, and King's men had failed to find them, the survey would be humiliated. That alone was sufficient reason to justify an investigation; the thrill of checking out a mystery was certainly present also.

King and his men planned their campaign carefully. They wined and dined known executives of the New York and San Francisco Mining and Commercial Company, the company formed to float stock and exploit the claim, and then innocently asked questions. When King, Emmons, the Hagues, Gardner, and others gathered to compare notes, they found that they had enough evidence to almost pinpoint the location. Quietly they boarded the eastbound train from San Francisco and got off at Fort Bridger, Wyoming Territory. There they rented horses and set out southwest. Soon they had discovered the gulch with the claim notices nailed to nearby trees.

At first they were convinced that diamonds had indeed been discovered. But why were rubies found along with diamonds? Rubies are not found with diamonds. Why were anthills with diamonds identified by a second hole not made by ants? And when they sifted the gravel from the headwaters of the stream, why was the gravel devoid of gems? And why were rough-cut diamonds among those found? Did that not mean that someone had tampered with the gems?

Convinced that they had discovered a massive hoax, King rode through the night to the Union Pacific main line, arriving just in time to flag down the westbound train. When he arrived in San Francisco he called a meeting of the board of directors of the New York and San Francisco Mining and Commercial Company and laid out his evidence. As a result, perhaps thousands of investors were saved from losing their money, there were very red faces among some of San Francisco's best-known financiers, and the "Great Diamond Hoax" became history. What happened to Arnold and Slack? They disappeared, with Arnold later resurfacing in Harlem County, Kentucky, where he used some of his money to open a bank. Probably none of the $600,000 paid out to the two men for their "claim" was ever recovered.

Although General Humphreys reprimanded King for his failure to adequately inform him about the situation, King and his survey benefited greatly from the publicity. As the *San Francisco Bulletin* stated, the hoax exposure emphasized the usefulness "in the ordinary business of society, of scientific education and research."[38] The exposure of the Great Diamond Hoax was a fine way to end six years of fieldwork. Now the survey had to settle down in the New York City headquarters and complete preparations for publication. Still to be written and published were King's own volume, *Systematic Geology*, Arnold Hague's *Descriptive Geology*, an atlas, and several monographs in the natural sciences. King justified his slow progress by explaining that the time had passed "when it is either decent or tolerable to rush into print with undigested field operations."[39] His philosophy about publication was in direct contrast to Hayden's. King and his men pored over their field notes of six seasons, examined and reexamined them, and wrote for publication only when they were sure they were correct. The result was a new standard in American scientific writing.

The seven Fortieth Parallel Survey reports and the atlas were issued over a ten-year period. Volume 3, James D. Hague's beautiful *Mining Industry*, was issued in 1870; not until 1880 did volume 7, Marsh's *Odontornithes: A Monograph on the Extinct Toothed Birds of North America*, make its appearance. Volume 1 in the series, King's *Systematic Geology*, was not issued until 1878. It ran to eight hundred pages, tracing the geological history of what King termed the "Middle Cordilleras"—104°30' west to 120° west, or a distance of eight hundred miles. Much of the geological time chart was found in this vast region. King expressed the hope that his work was a permanent contribution to knowledge and "a stepping-stone . . . built into the great stairway of science."[40] And indeed it was all that, for in *Systematic Geology* King's brilliance as an original thinker shone forth. After years of investigation, he advanced from description to explanation, tracing the West from the Archean or Permian period to the Pleistocene and Recent epochs with their excessive glaciation.

Volume 2, *Descriptive Geology*, an 853-page monograph by Emmons and Arnold Hague, was issued in 1877. Their volume traced the geology of the eight-hundred-mile strip along the fortieth parallel in five major sections, whereas King had outlined the geology historically, tracing 125,000 feet of the earth's crust. Volume 4, *Palaeontology and Ornithology*, also appeared in 1877. Meek wrote Part 1. "He determined the age of the Paleozoic silver-lead ores of the White Pine Mining District in eastern Nevada, the Cretaceous and early Tertiary coals and lignites of the Green River Basin of southwest Wyoming, and other Phanezoic strata in the 40th Parallel Explorations," according to Clifford N. Nelson and Ellis L. Yochelson, authorities on the history of paleontology.[41] James Hall and R. P. Whitfield wrote Part 2, which dealt with certain fossils from the Eureka and White Pine mining districts of Nevada. Ridgeway's three-hundred-page essay on ornithology appears as Part 3 of this volume, a refreshing change after plowing through Meek's, Hall's, and Whitfield's dull tomes.

Volume 5, *Botany*, was written by Watson; the five-hundred-page monograph appeared in 1871. Volume 6, *Microscopic Petrography*, written by Ferdinand Zirkel, a German recruited by King, was distinctly avant-garde. The microscope was just beginning to be used in geology; this volume convinced American scientists of its usefulness and of the validity of the science of petrology.

In 1878 Gardner completed his atlas of the fortieth parallel. One map embraced the entire fortieth parallel country surveyed; five topographic and five geological maps dealt with the region in fifths. Two final atlas sheets carried continuous geological sections from east to west. The King maps did not use the contour system to show elevations but hachures (short parallel lines showing sloping surfaces). Julius Bien did the lithography.

The Fortieth Parallel Survey was worth every cent of the $600,000 it cost the American people. Through its scholarly reports, the survey elevated the standards of American science. It established lofty examples for the other three Great Surveys (standards that they did not always meet), set a fine pattern of format and presentation, and provided a concept of government service and loyalty to science that still stands.

Many of the men of King's Survey went on to distinguished careers in the world of science. King, whose background and cosmopolitan ways ensured his admission to the parlors and offices of the rich and powerful, was the first director of the U.S. Geological Survey, formed in 1879. Although he stepped down after just one year, King's groundwork established the survey as one of the great scientific institutions in the world. He hired twenty geologists and topographers to man the two divisions into which he divided the survey: Mining Geology and General Geology. Strangely, this man who had been so devoted to pure science was quick to use the survey for practical purposes, most especially to aid the mining industry. Yet he encouraged his men to write up their theories on the formation of ore deposits and other significant problems of geology. King also continued to stress "stratigraphic paleontology that determined the relative ages of and correlated fossil-bearing rocks to fix the order and structure of these strata"—a methodology used by the Fortieth Parallel Survey men.[42] His subsequent career, in which he worked as a mining consultant rather than a scientific researcher, was not so satisfactory. He died in Arizona, probably of tuberculosis of the lungs, on 14 December 1901.

## The Powell Survey

The third of the Great Surveys was the Powell Survey, officially known as the U.S. Geographical and Geological Survey of the Rocky Mountain Region. Its director, John Wesley Powell, is imprinted more into the public mind than are Hayden, King, and Wheeler. Actually, Powell's achievements as survey leader and geologist are arguably neither more nor less than those of Hayden and King (Wheeler was not a scientist), but Powell was the quintessential bureaucrat and public relations man. He was responsible for the creation of the U.S. Geological Survey in 1879, and his directorship from 1880 until 1894 did much to establish the permanence of that institution. The Bureau of American Ethnology also exists because of Powell's interests in that science.[43]

Powell, who grew up as a farm boy in Wisconsin, possessed an insatiable taste for knowledge. At age eighteen he convinced a school board of his ability to teach students in a one-room school. To keep ahead of the students, he studied more than they did. He received help and encouragement from educated people with whom he came in contact, and whenever the opportunity presented itself, he enrolled in college. He attended Wheaton College, Illinois College, and Oberlin in Ohio. Interested in geology, he trod whatever countryside surrounded his home at the time. By 1859, when he was twenty-six, he was secretary of the Illinois Natural History Society.

*22.9 Portrait of John Wesley Powell, c. 1897, after his great explorations. The photographer is unknown. Courtesy of the U.S. Geological Survey.*

Then came the Civil War. It was not Powell's nature to stay out of the fray. He enlisted in May 1861 and within a month was a second lieutenant. In November he took leave to marry his cousin, Emma Dean, then returned to Cape Girardeau, Missouri, where he was promoted to captain in charge of Battery F, Second Illinois Light Artillery. On 6 April 1862 his unit was near Pittsburg Landing (Shiloh) in a peach orchard near a sunken road. A little after four o'clock on that afternoon, Powell raised his right arm to signify "Fire." A minié ball struck his right wrist, plowed up his arm to the elbow, and embedded itself in the flesh. On 8 April his right arm was amputated.

Although the ugly stub caused him pain the rest of his life, Powell refused to allow the impediment to dampen his ambitions or change his plans. His interest was in science, at that time especially geology, and the fieldwork would be accomplished in spite of his infirmity. First, however, he continued to serve in the army, ending his career with the rank of major. After the war he accepted the position of geology professor at Illinois Wesleyan University; nearby, at Illinois Normal, he was also appointed curator of the college's natural history museum.

In 1867, the same year that Hayden was named to conduct a geological survey of Nebraska and that King arrived in Washington to gain government funding for his survey of the fortieth parallel, the one-armed army veteran was briefly in the capital, seeking funding for a geological exploration of Colorado. Powell was not as fortunate as the other two, but he did make contacts and got the promise of equipment from the army and of scientific gadgets from the Smithsonian. One suspects that Powell grasped the Washington power structure even better than did Hayden and King— and in later years the major would use that knowledge very successfully. Meanwhile, he had mustered sufficient aid, along with some funding from Illinois sources, to lead a party of eleven to the central Rockies. One of the members was his wife, and two of the others, Frank Bishop and Almon Harris Thompson, would be with him for years to come.

This first exploration was significant in the history of the Powell Survey. Powell met William Byers, publisher of the *Rocky Mountain News*, a valuable public relations contact. And as he explored Middle Park, west-north-west of Denver, and reconnoitered a canyon cut by the Colorado (at that time called the Grand) River, an ambitious project entered Powell's mind. From the thousand and one questions he asked of the miners and mountain men he met, Powell pieced together something of the canyon and mesa country to the west and southwest. Here, he realized, were the chasms along whose walls geological history was written—knowledge awaiting the expert's interpretation. The challenge was enormous and the danger considerable. Powell decided that he was the one to meet that challenge.

Two years elapsed before he could launch his expedition. Meanwhile, in 1868 Powell and Emma and a party of twenty were again in Colorado. With Byers they climbed Longs Peak. Most of the party returned to the East, but Powell and a few others chose a spot near the White River Indian Agency west of Middle Park from which to explore the canyon country of the Bear (today's Yampa) and Grand Rivers. He knew that about 175 miles north of his camp was Green River City, a tiny settlement along the Union Pacific, at the Green River. From here, he had already decided, he would launch boats and float down the Green to the Colorado and on down the Colorado, through the canyons, to some point of debarkation. In March 1869 Powell and his men made their way out of the winter camp by way of the canyons and parks and plateaus leading to Fort Bridger. Now they headed for the railroad at Green River Station and boarded the eastbound train. Powell had to hurry, for he was determined to go down the Green and Colorado that summer.

Again, he raised money from Illinois Normal and Illinois Industrial Universities, obtained supplies from the army and scientific instruments from Henry at the Smithsonian; Powell also used about $2,000 of his own money. In Chicago he pronounced acceptable the three oak boats manufactured to his specifications, double-ribbed and with double stem and stern posts; a fourth boat was made of white pine. The three oak boats were twenty-one feet long; the pine boat was sixteen feet. Bulkheads at each end, called "cabins" by the major, were for supplies, but in 1869 waterproofing was not possible. Within six weeks of his return to Illinois, Powell was ready to leave for Green River Station, where he arrived on 11 May.

In the party were Oramel G. and Seneca Howland, Bill Dunn, Jack Sumner, and Billy Rhodes Hawkins, men whom Powell had met in the West and who had been with him in Middle Park. A young bullwhacker, Andrew Hall (whom they called "Dare-devil Dick"), was another member. An Englishman named Frank Goodman simply appeared at Green River City and asked to join. George Young Bradley was a soldier whom Powell had met; Powell had gotten Bradley out of the peacetime army, and in exchange, Bradley agreed to accompany Powell. Walter Henry Powell, the major's mentally unstable brother, was along on the trip. Finally there was the one-armed, bearded major—happy, enthusiastic, energetic, and willing to take his chances on the river with the boats and the men.

Like most other areas in the American West explored after the Civil War, the region Powell planned to investigate was not unknown. The canyons were known, more or less. Men had traversed parts of them, and Indians knew them. But no one had taken boats all the way down the Green-Colorado to the Grand Canyon, let alone to tidewater. No professional geologist had examined the record of the rocks exposed by the cliffs hundreds of feet high along the river. On the other hand, rumors that towering falls would bring disaster to the Powell expedition were just that—rumors. The major had asked many questions. He was reasonably sure that the canyons were navigable and that dangerous rapids could be traversed by lowering the boats with ropes held by the men along the banks. He knew that space could be found for camps. Of course the expedition would be dangerous, but even in 1869, he knew, the East was eager for any kind of information about the Wild West. After a successful navigation of the Colorado River—followed by excellent published narratives (and the major wrote with a graceful pen), lectures, and contacts with Congress—Powell would be able to mold his future.

The men christened the boats: the sixteen-footer was dubbed the *Emma Dean;* Powell proposed to sit in the middle and take the lead. The three twenty-one-footers (four feet of beam) were dubbed the *Maid of the Canyon, No-Name,* and *Kitty Clyde's Sister.* For nearly two weeks Powell trained his men at Green River City. They packed their bacon, beans, flour, sugar, and coffee in hopes that it would last them until they left the canyons months later. Early in the afternoon of 24 May 1869 the four boats shoved off. The Powell Colorado River expedition was under way.

The journey was one of playfulness, excitement, hard work, miserable living conditions with soaked clothing and poor food, and above all, daring. For when they entered some of the chasms, even though they had trudged ahead along the banks to view the rapids and had charted out in their minds their course, their control over their craft was contested by the waters—and sometimes the waters won. They named the canyons: Flaming Gorge, Canyon of the Rapids, Kingfisher Canyon, Red Canyon, Swallow Canyon, the Canyon of Lodore. The *No-Name* was wrecked. Incredibly difficult portages were made around rapids deemed too difficult to ride the boats through. A fire in camp consumed clothing and cooking utensils.

A month out of Green River City the expedition reached the mouth of the Uinta River, flowing in from the west. Here Goodman departed, leaving nine men to conquer the remaining canyons. Meanwhile a drifter and horse thief named Frank Risdon had spread word in the East that Powell and his men were lost. This drew attention to the expedition and helped Powell attain fame.

Over the next two hundred miles along the Grand, the men passed through what they dubbed the Canyon of Desolation. On 16 July they arrived at the mouth of the Grand. Now, they thought, the river would be more tranquil, but they were wrong. The rapids got worse while the men—tired, wet, and cranky because of the poor food—began to grumble about the major. He was busy taking readings and examining canyon walls: he was being, in short, a scientist. But in carrying on his work, Powell was, the men felt, ignoring their plight. An occasional beaver or mountain sheep, shot by one of the crew, improved their diet.

By 28 August the Howlands and Dunn had had enough. They left the party, climbing out of the canyon. Two and a half days later, the six remaining explorers reached a low, rolling desert, where they met some Indians and finally, at the mouth of the Virgin River, some Mormons fishing. The long ordeal had ended successfully. The three men who had climbed out of the canyon were less fortunate: they had been killed by Indians.

Whatever Powell's career plans had been when he started down the canyons, they were crystallized when he emerged. He was going to make his way as a government scientist and bureaucrat. In Salt Lake City he gave the first of many stirring lectures about his experiences. He returned to Illinois to resign his positions there and then lectured widely throughout the Midwest. Then he went to Washington DC, the fountain of monetary largesse. He sought out congressional leaders such as James Garfield and Abram Hewitt; he had long talks with Spencer Baird of the Smithsonian. He obtained $12,000 from Congress to continue his survey of the "Colorado of the West and its tributaries." Taking a cue from Hayden, King, and Wheeler, he added topography to his assignment. He found a photographer and an artist. And he was able to point out that the canyon and plateau area embraced by his survey had not been preempted by any of the other surveys.

Whereas the 1869 journey down the Green and Colorado Rivers had the aura of an adventure, the major's plans for the second descent were very definitely science-oriented. In 1870 he traveled south of Salt Lake to investigate the terrain drained by the Colorado and its tributaries. He wanted to find two or three points where supplies could be carried to the river edge, cached, and then used as the boatmen arrived at those points. He was intrigued by the Indians, both the prehistoric ones who had built the cliff dwellings he had spotted and the present ones such as the Shivwits. He wanted to find out what had happened to the Howlands and Dunn.

He also observed the land in order to give good advice to the topographers who either would be traveling with him in the boats or would be working on the plateaus while he was descending the river. He had at least three of them with him in 1871; Thompson, his brother-in-law who had been with him in Colorado in 1867, was their leader. Thompson had to learn as he went along, but eventually he became an accomplished surveyor and was later chief geographer for the U.S. Geological Survey.

Much of Powell's personnel in 1871 consisted of relatives, family friends, and Illinois Civil War veterans. Frederick Samuel Dellenbaugh was related to Thompson. The young man possessed artistic abilities and wrote well. In later years he wrote two books about the Colorado River: *The Romance of the Colorado River* and *A Canyon Voyage*. However, E. O. Beaman seems to have been chosen purely for his abilities as photographer. And Andy Hattan, the cook, may have been chosen for his culinary abilities, for he was a good cook.

Powell's plans called for the men to be together some of the time and then to separate into two parties, one of which would be mapping the plateau and canyon country west and north of the river while the other remained with the boats. Their work would extend from May 1871 well into 1872. From 22 May until 26 October 1871, the party was together in the boats from Green River City to Lees Ferry, where the Pariah flows in. Then Powell left the party, putting Thompson in charge. Powell geologized and surveyed the land, on occasion returning to the boats.

From November 1871 until August 1872, Powell, Thompson, Dellenbaugh, Hattan, and two others mapped southern Utah and Arizona north of the Grand Canyon. In the autumn of 1872 they continued downriver in boats from Lees Ferry to the mouth of Kanab Canyon. Not until February 1873 was the preliminary map finished. Placed in a tin tube, it was entrusted to Dellenbaugh to take to Salt Lake City and place on the eastbound train.

The second Powell party, this time in three boats dubbed the *Emma Dean*, the *Nellie Powell*, and the *Cañonita*, had its share of narrow escapes while descending the Green and Colorado Rivers. Something of the mood of the men can be understood by envisioning the major, strapped in a chair in the middle of the *Emma Dean*, reading to his men from Sir Walter Scott's *Lady of the Lake*. Wet clothes were taken off as soon as camp was made and

*22.10 Photograph of Powell's expedition at Green River (photographer unknown, 1871). Courtesy of the U.S. Geological Survey, photo no. 57-PS444 in the National Archives.*

were replaced with dry ones from a rubber bag. Waves of intensely hot air swept up the canyons, enervating the men. Occasionally Indians, or Mormons, were encountered. The crew looked forward to meetings with the supply trains sent by the major. One man wrenched a leg painfully; another was stung by a scorpion that made him ill for days. But work went on: topographer Frank Bishop took astronomical readings with a sextant every forty-five miles along the river and made triangulations from the river to points twenty-five to fifty miles away. He would produce the first scientific map of the Green and Colorado Rivers.

Thompson's work mapping the plateau and canyon country was made difficult because he, unlike topographers on the other surveys, was expected to work through the winter. In addition, his men had been in the field for many months and were tired. Bishop, for example, was in poor physical shape, did not get along well with some of the other members, and was intensely critical of Thompson's topographical skills and Powell's leadership (he did not feel that the major cared enough about the well-being of his men). Thompson was appalled at the amateurishness his map revealed, and yet it proved to be satisfactory and did not, as he was afraid it would, constitute an embarrassment to him for the remainder of his career.

Powell was essentially an empire builder. In 1872 he moved to Washington DC, and from 1874 until 1879 he was far more likely to be in the nation's capital than in the field. Powell—suave, an excellent writer and lecturer, a good hand at a game of whist—was becoming the accepted leader of Washington's scientific community. Meanwhile he administered the survey, sending Thompson back to the scene of mapmaking with whatever topographical assistants Thompson could find. Using fewer men—usually six to eight professionals plus packers and cooks—and considerably less money and ignoring most of the natural sciences, the Powell Survey concentrated on completing the map and on geology.

It was in geology that the survey excelled. The major himself was a competent geologist. His particular ability was in the analyzing and describing of enormous changes in the earth's surface, of uplifts, of wearing away by water and wind, of catastrophic changes. Thus he explained how the Green River flowed through the Uinta Mountains instead of around them because the river ground away even as the mountains rose. He created new terminology and new problems for geologists yet to come. This "new geology," as Powell's colleague Gilbert called it, demanded an understanding of the contours of the land and what caused them to be the way they were. Powell wasted little time with paleontology and paleobotany, although he recognized their significance. His own reports are embodied in the second part of his *Exploration of the Colorado River of the West and Report on the Geology of the Eastern Portion of the Uinta Mountains and a Region of the Country Thereto.*

Powell hired two brilliant geologists. For Grove Karl Gilbert, a theoretician, his meeting with Powell was the turning point of his life. He was sent to study the Henry Mountains, which rise over 10,500 feet in the remote desert of southeastern Utah. This is not a single range of mountains, he discovered, but five separate elevations, each of which had originated as a lava bubble that raised the crust above it, then congealed. His *Report on the Geology of the Henry Mountains* was a landmark in the history of geology, a brilliant analysis by a theoretical geologist who had no peers. Gilbert also became the leading authority on prehistoric Lake Bonneville; his essay on this lake was in the first of the U.S. Geological Survey volumes entitled "Monographs." For many years he was an administrator and chief geologist of the consolidated U.S. Geological Survey, even though he would have preferred an assignment in the field.[44]

The second geologist was Captain Clarence Edward Dutton, who spent fifteen years (1875–90) on special detail to Powell's organization and later to the U.S. Geological Survey. Captain Dutton was specifically interested in the great geological problems posed by the plateau and canyon country of the American Southwest; he was also curious about vulcanism and iso-stasy (the equilibrium of the earth's crust so that pressures tending to ele-vate are squalled by those tending to suppress). Two of his monographs were landmarks of brilliant geological analysis and deduction: *Report on the Geology of the High Plains of Utah* and *Tertiary History of the Grand Canyon District*. Dutton was unusual as a geologist in that he wrote with clarity and grace.

A comparison of the Powell Survey with those of Hayden, King, and Wheeler shows substantial differences. Powell did not expand his survey to include such sciences as botany and zoology; he preferred concentrating on geology and physiography (also known as geomorphology). He did not cater to private interests such as mining investors seeking free geological information. He was not greatly interested in paleontology. He was inter-ested in earth-forming processes, in understanding and describing, in clear laymen's terms, how mountains and canyons (such as in the Plateau Province) were created by natural processes over incredibly long time pe-riods. In many respects, he may properly be considered to be the founder of the modern science of geomorphology.

Powell's interest in many aspects of the scientific exploration of the American West continued unabated. He was so intrigued by the Indians that he began interviewing them and recording their folklore. As a result of this interest, Powell promoted the creation of the Bureau of American Eth-nology, and he later became its first director. In 1875, while in Washington DC, Powell recruited a court stenographer named James C. Pilling. The one-armed major needed an amanuensis to record his notes in the field, to help him assemble the material for his reports, and finally, to record in shorthand the tales the Indians told. Pilling was so engrossed by this last task that in time he established himself as a leading ethnologist; after the creation of the Bureau of American Ethnology, Pilling was one of its lead-ing experts, compiling a bibliography of the languages of North American Indian tribes.

The artist Thomas Moran, who had been with Hayden in 1871 and whose painting of the grand canyon of the Yellowstone helped popularize the park, in 1873 accompanied Powell into southern Utah. Moran's paint-ing *The Chasm of the Colorado* hung for years in the Senate wing of the Cap-itol. Its presence there certainly did no harm to Powell's causes when he testified before congressional committees.

Another of Powell's many interests was the white settlement of the arid West. He had observed the hardships of homesteaders trying to eke out an agricultural living on 160 acres of dry land. He was also aware of the damage done to the land by miners stripping the mountains of timber and of the increase in floods and erosion when timber stands no longer existed to hold the excess rainfall. He was, as usual, several decades ahead of his fellow Americans in noting the wastefulness concomitant with the rush westward. In 1879 he expressed his feelings and suggested corrections in the land system in his *Report on the Arid Regions of the United States*.

In this work, Powell proposed land classification and new land laws that would better fit the region; he also recommended the creation of irrigation districts with fixed land parcels at 80 acres and with water rights attached to landownership. In a democratic manner the landowners of each district would meet to allot water on an equitable basis. Ranchland would be restricted to parcels beginning at 2,560 acres, with no monopoly of water granted to any one owner. In 1888 hydrographic survey work, under the direction of Powell, was begun by the U.S. Geological Survey, which identified and withdrew from public sale dam sites and areas for possible irrigation development. Powell's work aroused resentment among western Congressmen, and although Powell had his defenders, the politicians of the West in 1894 forced Powell out of the director's position of the U.S. Geological Survey.

## The Wheeler Survey

The fourth of the Great Surveys was commonly called the Wheeler Survey, after its head, First Lieutenant George Montague Wheeler; its official designation was the "U.S. Geographical Surveys West of the One Hundredth Meridian." That the U.S. Army would eventually enter the field of exploration and mapping of the American West should come as no surprise. Since the days of Lewis and Clark, both of whom were army men, the American military had been interested in the exploration of the West. In 1813 the army's involvement was further entrenched with the creation of the U.S. Army Corps of Topographical Engineers. Stephen H. Long, John C. Frémont, John W. Gunnison, Howard Stansbury, Gouverneur K. Warren, and W. F. Raynolds are some, but not all, of the army men who led expeditions into the American West before 1861. In 1863 the Corps of Topographical Engineers was abolished, but the army engineers remained, and such outstanding leaders as Brigadier General Andrew A. Humphreys were determined that the army would continue to play a part in the scientific exploration and mapping of the West. The Wheeler Survey was an outgrowth of this plan.

Wheeler was a student at West Point during most of the Civil War, and when he graduated in 1866 the "excitement," as young men would probably have considered it, was over. The army was reduced to a small percentage of its wartime size and was manned for the most part by war veterans, both enlisted men and officers, who for various reasons desired to remain in the service. The prospects for a young man fresh out of West Point, with no combat experience, were not propitious.

But Massachusetts-born Lieutenant Wheeler, graduating sixth in merit in his class of thirty-nine, decided to remain in the army. He began his career as assistant engineer at Point Lobos, near San Francisco, and within a year and a half was appointed engineer on the staff of the commanding general of the Department of California. The next two years found him surveying in the hot desert lands of the Southwest. The results of this work were published, with Daniel Wright Lockwood, as *Preliminary Report upon a Reconnaissance through Southern and Southeast Nevada, Made in 1869.* Though not published until 1875, the report was seen by, among others, General Humphreys. Wheeler was promoted to first lieutenant in March 1867.

His work in the vast wastelands of Nevada had given the twenty-seven-year-old lieutenant an idea. When he submitted his report he suggested that the army extend its operations to embrace a general survey throughout the entire American West. The young army officer was called to Washington DC for consultation. The upshot was the creation of the Wheeler Survey in 1871.[45]

It was not jealousy—at least, not officially—that prompted the army engineers to launch plans for a wide-ranging survey. As Wheeler emphasized, geological maps such as those that Hayden, King, and Powell were producing were not of much use to the army. What the army needed was good topographical maps showing the terrain—its hills and mountains, canyons and valleys, river basins, streams, and lakes, and above all, its human-made phenomena such as roads, towns, railroads, mines, farms, ranches, and factories. Only the army, so he implied, could make maps that were useful for the army.

Wheeler made fourteen field trips into the American West. His operations ranged from south-central Texas to central Washington, although the Wheeler reports, a total of eight volumes and two atlases, concentrate primarily on the Southwest and the central Rockies. Note that the scope of the survey followed the pattern becoming familiar by 1872, when he would have first published under the authority of his survey; the person in charge filed a report, followed by monographs in the natural sciences.[46]

Wheeler took with him competent geologists, including Grove Karl Gilbert, who later joined Powell, and Archibald Marvine, who was later with Hayden. Edward Drinker Cope, the paleontologist, worked under Wheeler's authority in 1874 (Cope worked for Hayden both before and after his employment by Wheeler). Wheeler hired others who collected botanical and zoological specimens, and at one time he enlisted the photographer Timothy H. O'Sullivan, who had been with King. Frederick W. Loring, scion of a prominent Boston family, was on the rolls as "barometric observer and recorder," but he was actually expected to write articles for the eastern press.

Mapping was Wheeler's primary goal. In 1872 he gave his survey its official name, "The U.S. Geographical Surveys West of the One Hundredth Meridian." His long-range plans were to divide the American West into ninety-five rectangles of approximately 150 by 120 miles and map them all. Unlike the topographers of other surveys, Wheeler planned to include not only the physical features but also the habitations of both Indians and whites, railroads and roads, references to vegetation, and precious metal sources. Making a pitch for popular support, Wheeler emphasized the usefulness of his maps to civilians. The lieutenant planned to make these maps rapidly. His survey area for 1871 was central, southern, and southwestern Nevada, eastern California, and southwestern Utah, and at season's end, some 72,250 square miles had been mapped. Because Indians in this barren expanse were still dangerous, he was able to state that his maps, on being published, were of almost immediate use to the army.

His parties—for, like the other survey leaders, he divided up his personnel and gave them assignments to complete—clattered along with full provisions, accompanied by military contingents, making the units much larger forces in the field than those of Hayden, King, and Powell. Wheeler's men used chronometers, six-inch theodolites, gradienters, pivot levels, and mule-drawn odometers. In spite of the fact that his organization was military, Wheeler hired civilian packers and cooks as well as scientists. Usually an army lieutenant commanded each of the parties.

Until 1874, Wheeler's topographers differed from their colleagues in that they followed a meandering system—"meander" here meaning, as a journalist with Wheeler wrote for the *New York Times*, "to make a profile of the course, its windings, ascents and descents, to measure by the odometer and to gather every detail that can possibly be delineated on a map." In 1871 Wheeler's meandering activities were concentrated in southeastern California and Nevada. Wheeler and his men suffered from heat, thirst, and exposure; Wheeler even became descriptive in his otherwise dry reporting: "The route lay for more than 39 miles in light, white, drifting sand, which was traversed between 5 a.m. and 6 p.m., the center of the desert [Death Valley] being reached about meridian. Two of the command succumbed near nightfall, but after they were revived, the march was continued in the moonlight until finally, between three and four in the morning, a 'living stream' was found."

Wheeler not only traversed Death Valley in 1871 but also, in the autumn of that year, conjured up the idea of working his way up the Colorado River two hundred miles from Camp Mojave near the California-Mexican border to Diamond Creek. On 16 September 1871, boatmen, Indians, soldiers, the geologist Gilbert, and the photographer O'Sullivan climbed aboard and began the journey. On 19 October, after terrible hardships, twenty of the original thirty-five reached their destination, nearly all the Indians having deserted. On the way back to the settlements, O'Sullivan lost most of his negatives, and Loring, the journalist, was killed by Indians on the Wickenburg (Arizona) stage. Thus Wheeler's dreams of publicity à la Powell were shattered. Without such publicity, the arduous, dangerous journey had no significance.

In 1873 surveyors for Wheeler and Hayden found themselves working the same area south of Leadville, Colorado. Both groups refused to withdraw, and the duplication of their activities came to the attention of Congress, which forthwith held hearings in front of the Committee on Public Lands. The scientific community, led by Powell, closed ranks in opposition to Wheeler. Although acknowledging that some of his work was meritorious, the scientists found much wrong with the meandering method (Wheeler himself later adopted the triangulation method). The scientists also expressed their frustration in working for authoritarian military men. Finally, they attacked the Wheeler Survey for its brutality toward the Indians.

First Lieutenant Wheeler must share some of the blame for the scientists' attack on the army. Even considering the agonizingly slow promotions that characterized army life from 1865 until 1914, Wheeler's long tenure as a first lieutenant (he was not promoted to captain until 1878) may constitute a tell-tale key to flaws in the man's leadership. Wheeler was accused of not caring about his men as he tried to achieve preset goals. And from 1871 on, his survey was accused of mistreating Native Americans, even of killing and blinding them. His statements of hatred toward the Indians and his attacks on Indian policy imply a narrowness of vision not becoming the leader of an organization dedicated to scientific work. Nevertheless, Wheeler's organization made substantial contributions, not only in the mapping of the American West but in scientific areas also. The survey listed and examined 219 mining districts, surveyed 143 mountain ranges, made profiles of 202 mountain passes, followed 90 rivers and countless streams, determined the heights of 395 peaks above ten thousand feet, explored numerous lakes including the Great Salt Lake, and discovered at least 50 thermal and mineral springs. Natural scientists with Wheeler claimed to have discovered a new species of bird, 8 new reptiles, 32 new fishes, a new mollusk, and 64 new insects. According to Wheeler, he presented the Smithsonian with 61,659 specimens, including rocks and fossils.

## Consolidation and the U.S. Geological Survey

The results of the Congressional Hearing by the Committee on Public Lands in 1873 were negligible. For five more years, all the surveys were allowed to continue their operations. Hayden and Wheeler did not make good appearances before the hearings; Powell, on the other hand, made an excellent showing. Backed by most of the scientific community, Powell over the next years instigated and continued to push for a consolidation of the surveys. When consolidation finally took place in 1879, the army was left in the cold. It was clear that scientists did not want to be under the army system of administration and authority. Victory for the scientists, however, spelled defeat for the American people as well as the army. For perhaps as little as $2 million, Wheeler could have completed his map of the territories and states west of the Mississippi, presenting the nation with a reasonably accurate map of about 1.5 million square miles. Such a map would have been satisfactory for the wants of the people at the time. Instead, at least half a million dollars and ten years of work went for naught.

And so, in 1879, the Great Surveys came to an end, united as the single U.S. Geological Survey. Over the past twelve years Hayden, King, Powell, Wheeler, and the dedicated men working under their direction had mapped enormous areas of the desolate American West—well enough for their work to be useful to the miners, farmers, ranchers, timbermen, railroad builders, and town builders who were rapidly settling the virgin land. It was the Great Surveys that first officially reported the cliff dwellings of the Southwest, the geysers of Yellowstone, and the Grand Canyon of the Colorado. The collection and classification of flora and fauna was enthusiastically pursued by Hayden, King, and Wheeler. Geological problems were first posed by these men and then discussed, sometimes in heated debates still raging today among geologists, paleontologists, and paleobotanists. The hundreds of publications of the Hayden Survey embraced the whole spectrum of science; King's high standards of reporting and publishing raised the stature of American science throughout the world; Powell's interest in geomorphism resulted in great advances in the understanding of the earth's surface; and Wheeler's maps (as well as Hayden's, King's, and Powell's) served a West rapidly being settled.[47] These men laid the foundations.

Building on these foundations was begun by Clarence King, as the first director of the new, highly regarded U.S. Geological Survey. In that crucial first year, King established the pattern of annual reports, bulletins, and monographs; he also sent parties into the field, especially into Colorado and Nevada. King was interested in geological theories, and as his men researched the field for precious minerals—and not-so-precious resources such as coal—he encouraged classification of ores based on their placement and chemical conditions.

King resigned after just one year, and John Wesley Powell succeeded him. A modern cynic would say this had all the markings of a deal, and perhaps it was a surreptitious agreement between the two men, but no proof has ever been found; furthermore, King is known to have wanted to make a fortune, something he could never have done while in government service. Powell greatly expanded the Geological Survey. From 1881 until 1894, when he stepped down under pressure, he obtained congressional permission for the survey to embrace the entire nation, not just the American West; he encouraged topographical mapping, although his standards were somewhat lax; and he assigned such men as Dutton to spend years researching the Grand Canyon of the Colorado and Arnold Hague to devote the rest of his professional life (well into the twentieth century) investigating the geology of Yellowstone Park. Paleontologists and paleobotanists received their due also.

Although the survey was already involved in land classification, publication of Powell's *Lands of the Arid Regions* in 1879 prompted more concentration by the survey on hydrographic work, on the determination of areas of irrigable land and of reservoir and power dam sites, and on the location of forests that balanced and regulated the water flow of rivers. Congress, reacting to western irrigation enthusiasts, in 1888 requested that the Geological Survey identify and withdraw from public sale potentially irrigable lands and possible areas for reservoirs and dams. The survey reacted enthusiastically, partly because Powell was intensely interested in the project. He felt that arid regions necessitated government-controlled, scientifically planned patterns of settlement. The survey set aside too much land, however, forcing some land offices to close. Individualistic westerners endowed with the frontiersmen's belief in the right to settle where they wanted and to do as they wished with the land, even if they ended up starving and bankrupt, protested to Congress. As a result, in 1892 the irrigation survey was abolished, and the survey's budget was cut. In 1894 Powell wisely resigned.

C. D. Walcott, Powell's successor and the director through 1900, restricted survey activities to geology and its auxiliary sciences. For example, the survey was involved in forestry surveys for a few years following the passage of the Forest Management Act of 1897. Meanwhile, scientists such as Arnold Hague and Gilbert continued their geological work throughout the United States.[48]

## Other Scientific Explorers of the American West

Although the federal government's Great Surveys and, later, its U.S. Geological Survey constituted the primary scientific explorations of the American West between 1865 and 1900, other expeditions, both governmental and nongovernmental, did take place. In 1876 Lieutenant Gustavus Doane of the Second Cavalry tried to make a winter journey from Heart Lake, in Yellowstone Park, by boat down the Snake River. He and his men almost died in the useless undertaking, and the scientific results were negligible. Yet it was an exploration of sorts, at the least proving the utter unfeasibility of such a hazardous journey.[49]

A more significant army expedition was led by General George Armstrong Custer. In June and July 1874, from Fort Abraham Lincoln near present Bismarck, North Dakota, Custer led a thousand men south into the Black Hills. Accompanying the expedition was a geologist, Newton H. Winchell, a naturalist, George Bird Grinnell, and a couple of practical miners, Horatio Nelson Ross and William T. McKay. The results of the expedition were momentous as rumors of gold in the Black Hills rapidly spread throughout the West and ultimately throughout the nation.

The official news was not so encouraging. The scientists in their reports were skeptical of the rumors. As a result two more investigators, protected by two companies of cavalry from the Spotted Tail Agency in northern Nebraska, investigated the Black Hills in late August 1874 and subsequently filed a negative report. President U. S. Grant, aware of the mixed rumors, sent out still another expedition in 1875.[50] This group set out in May, protected by six cavalry and two infantry companies. The scientists were in the employ of the Interior Department and were led by Walter P. Jenney of the New York School of Mines; their assignment was to determine if gold was present in the Black Hills. Jenny's report, written with the aid of his assistant, Henry Newton, was conservative but not discouraging. The report was published as a public document.[51]

Interest in natural history, including paleontology and paleobotany in their simpler aspects of collecting fossils, was not and is not restricted to the academician. In the late 1800s, a number of private collectors advanced beyond mere collecting to attacking the intricate problems presented by the fossils they had collected. The paleobotanist Leo Lesquereux, for example, worked independently as well as with Hayden. In 1872, while Lesquereux was out West inspecting the Ellsworth (Kansas) fossil beds, he met an independent collector, Charles H. Sternberg. They immediately became friends and remained so until Lesquereux's death in 1889. Over the years Sternberg sent Lesquereux all his fossilized plants and ferns for classification. The Sternbergs, father and son George, were particularly active near their home along the Smoky Hill River in western Kansas.

Probably all scientists of the time were aware of one of the scientific field's most tempestuous rivalries—between Edward Drinker Cope, a Quaker affiliated with Haverford College and associated some of the time with Hayden and Wheeler, and Othniel Charles Marsh, something of an aristocrat and a professor of vertebrate paleontology at Yale usually associated with Powell and King. Cope and Marsh also carried on independent field research in the American West and hired amateur "bone hunters" to add to their collections.

Marsh's uncle, George Peabody, gave Yale $150,000 to found the Peabody Museum; when Peabody died, Marsh inherited much of his uncle's money. He was, therefore, an independent paleontologist able to finance his own expeditions. His rival Cope, unlike Marsh, did not receive a good formal education. Cope, the frail and religious son of a well-to-do Pennsylvania farmer, was almost entirely self-educated. From an early age he was fascinated by birds and animals, and he possessed the skill of drawing them with preciseness and accuracy. In 1860, when he was twenty years old, he attended lectures by the paleontologist Joseph Leidy at the University of Pennsylvania. Subsequently Cope became a member of the Philadelphia Academy of Natural Sciences. At age twenty-one, with income from a farm he rented out, he traveled to Washington DC, where he absorbed information from Smithsonian scientists including Baird and Henry. Then in 1863 Cope's father sent him to Europe, perhaps to end a love affair, possibly to ensure that he would not be drafted into the Union Army. Cope visited museums and made a point of meeting leading scientists. Returning in 1864, he accepted the position of professor of zoology at Haverford College but resigned after three years.

Marsh first went west along the not-yet-completed Union Pacific in the summer of 1868. He gathered a few bones at the Antelope Springs station in western Nebraska, then went on to the region between Laramie and Rawlins, Wyoming, and Lake Como, passing through a dinosaur graveyard that he ignored. So enthusiastic was Marsh about the potential discoveries to be made in the West that he made plans for a longer and more ambitious expedition the next year. Indian troubles prevented the trip, but in the following year (1870) he, with eleven Yale students paying their own way and with military assistance furnished by General Philip Sheridan, set out for a summer of adventure none would ever forget. First, from Fort McPherson at present Crawford, in northwestern Nebraska, the entourage clattered northward sixty miles to the remote Loup Fork River, where Miocene fossils were found in abundance. Back at the railroad, they got off at Fort D. A. Russell near Cheyenne and advanced southward to the Miocene and Oligocene bluffs of northeastern Colorado. Before the summer ended, they had searched the badlands around Scottsbluff, Nebraska, and the valley of Horse Creek; they entrained for western Wyoming and the Uinta Basin, south of the Uinta Range, and finally collected specimens at the cliffs around Green River and Kemmerer, Wyoming. Then they headed southeast to the Smoky Hill River in western Kansas and eastern Colorado. It was here that Marsh discovered the hollow end of a finger joint of an extinct pterodactyl, "the most remarkable discovery of his life."[52] The study of these reptiles constituted volume 7 of the Fortieth Parallel Survey reports, *Odontornithes: A Monograph on the Extinct Toothed Birds of North America*. In 1871, 1872, and 1873 Marsh again went west with students. He collected at the usual places and added to his itinerary the fossil beds of the Bridger Basin north of the Uinta Mountains and the John Day Basin of eastern Oregon. He was out again in 1874, without students; after that, with a considerable fortune, he hired collectors such as the Sternbergs to do his hunting for him.

Cope was not far behind Marsh. The two men at first got along well, even going on at least one fossil-hunting expedition together. Cope, determined to keep up with the older man, made his first western trip in 1871, as a member of the Hayden Survey. With a small military contingent, he too was in the Smoky Hill badlands in 1871. His collections resulted in his own monograph, published as volume 2 of the Hayden Survey in 1875: *Cretaceous Vertebrata*. In the early 1870s both Cope and Marsh collected in the Uinta and Bridger Basins, in the remote region where Colorado, Wyoming, and Utah meet. Both claimed credit for a number of discoveries. (Credit implies that the discoverer's name is forever attached to the Latin name given to the fossilized creature.)

In 1874 Cope deserted Hayden and joined Wheeler. The paleontologist subsequently angered Wheeler by going over his head to the general commanding the New Mexico region and gaining his permission to remain longer than Wheeler had scheduled at the San Ildefonso beds near Santa Fe. Abundant fossils had been found there. Then the party moved over the Jemez Mountains (also known as Valle Grande Mountains) into extreme northwestern New Mexico and into Colorado's San Jose badlands, which cover the eastern two-thirds of the San Juan Basin just north of the New Mexico border. Later Cope examined mammalian fossils from New Mexico's Puerco formation west of Los Alamos, fossils collected for him by David Baldwin. Cope's discovery and classification of some ninety-three mammalian fauna constitute his greatest contribution to the science.

Cope was again and again in the field, from north-central Texas to the badlands of the Judith River Basin in east-central Montana. Marsh, meanwhile, became more of an administrator, working out of his Yale headquarters with a dozen or more collectors in the field and with other employees helping in his paleontological work at Yale. He was also the more competent public relations man. Because of his inheritance, he did not have to worry about money until late in his career. He was very much the elitist scientist-intellectual, welcomed in the finest salons and cultivating the rich and powerful. Cope was also very much the gentleman, but he had to devote more of his time to earning a living.

Reading of their twenty-five-year feud, one comes to the conclusion that professional jealousy verging on hatred came to dominate many of Cope's and Marsh's actions. They questioned each other's professional skills, accused each other of stealing credit for the discovery and identity of certain vertebrates, and attempted in every way possible to harm each other's reputation among other scientists. Yet in the chronicles of the jealousies and rivalries of scientists, their story is rare only in its length and intensity.

Both men's reputations suffered, but the world of science is probably the better off for the feud. In their hatred they may have worked harder and produced more than they would have as friends. The professional outpourings of both men were prodigious. Cope described more than twice the number of new species than did Marsh, but Marsh knew better what would interest the layman. It was Marsh who collected fossil bones of the thirty-, forty-, and fifty-ton denizens of past geological time and assembled them in museums for all to see. And it was Marsh who traced the evolution of the horse from the primitive *Eohippus* to the modern steed ridden by a Hollywood cowboy. People found his descriptions and sketches of Pterodactyls deliciously horrifying.

The significance of this frenzied paleontological activity in the period 1865–1900 cannot be overestimated. As Henry Fairfield Osborn (a paleontologist of the next generation) has written, the revelations discovered by paleontologists exploring for fossils in the vast Rocky Mountain area clinched the validity of Darwin's theory of evolution. "New and unheard of orders of amphibians, reptiles, and mammals came to the surface of knowledge, revolutionizing thought, demonstrating the evolution theory, and solving some of the most important problems of descent."[53]

The world was fascinated by discoveries of the fossilized bones of inhabitants of past geological eras and by paleontologists' and paleobotanists' structuring of a world that existed millions of years before man appeared. However, we should not forget the work of scientists with less glamorous specialties, scientists who were equally busy in the American West in the period 1865–1900. In ornithology, besides the fine work of Robert Ridgeway, who had begun as a seventeen-year-old with King, Elliot Coues wrote over three hundred articles about birds. As an army assistant surgeon, he traveled widely in the American West. Coues, primarily in the period from 1861 to 1881, published three significant books: *Key to North American Birds*, *Birds of the Northwest*, and *Birds of the Colorado Valley*.[54]

The fields of archaeology and ethnology experienced a surge of activity in the 1880s and 1890s. After about 1878 Powell became engrossed in ethnology and was a prime mover in the creation of the Bureau of American Ethnology. A bureau employee, Frank Hamilton Cushing, lived for four and a half years (1879–84) with the Zunis, becoming fluent in their language and, at their invitation, even joining their secret Priesthood of the

Bow. Because of his work, their myths and folktales have been recorded for history. In 1886 the Hemenway Southwestern Expedition to New Mexico and Arizona, a privately financed enterprise, was initially led by Cushing, who withdrew and was replaced by Adolph Bandelier. This expedition awakened other scientists to the rich heritage of the southwestern Indians and spurred on new research.

In the Far West and Alaska, archaeologists William H. Dall and Max Uhle worked on stratigraphic techniques in building chronologies of past human occupation. Dall's paper "On the Succession in the Shell Heaps in the Aleutian Islands" was published by the Powell Survey (1877). Uhle worked on a shell mound in the San Francisco Bay area, while still another anthropologist, Franz Boas, studied the cultures of the Indians of the Pacific Northwest. A young man who had worked for Marsh, George Bird Grinnell, wrote extensively about the Cheyenne and Blackfeet Indians.

By century's end, the initial scientific exploration of the American West was accomplished. Large areas west of the one hundredth meridian were mapped; geologists were aware, in a general way, of the origins of mountains and plains; watercourses were known, and possible sites for dams, artificial lakes, and irrigation systems had been identified. The flora and fauna had been at least superficially collected, classified, and described. Even the American Indians living in the West had become subjects for studies by anthropologists. In 1865 the vast land west of the one hundredth meridian had not been traversed by a single transcontinental railroad; by 1900 that same expanse of land was spanned by five trunk lines and thousands of miles of feeder lines. Where buffalo had roamed, now cattle grazed or wheat waved in the prairie breeze. And the wonders of the American West had been explored, painted, photographed, and described so that now the traveling public could take the train, and then a stagecoach from the nearest station, to visit Yellowstone, the Grand Canyon of the Colorado, Yosemite, and many another place of beauty. Not for generations to come—and possibly not ever—would humanity have another opportunity to so explore a temperate-zone paradise, which is as good a description as can be given of the American West in 1865–1900.

# 23 / A "Capacity for Wonder": The Meanings of Exploration

WILLIAM H. GOETZMANN

And if by chance you make a landfall on the shores of another sea in a far country inhabited by savages and barbarians, remember you this: the greatest danger and the surest hope lies not with fires and arrows but in the quicksilver hearts of men. (*Advice to Navigators* [1744])
Symmes Chadwick Oliver, *The Shores of Another Sea*

The exploration of North America is at once a stirring story and the exemplification of a process as old as human experience. The story carries with it the basic elements of the Euro-American creation myth that has reverberated down through our history. The twentieth-century American novelist F. Scott Fitzgerald, who was no historian, echoed something of its enduring impact in his best novel, *The Great Gatsby* (1925). Gatsby's friend Nick Carraway, standing near the tip of Long Island in the 1920s, reminds us of the poetry of unintentional discovery: "And as the moon rose higher the inessential houses began to melt away until gradually I became aware of the old island here that flowered once for Dutch sailors' eyes—a fresh, green breast of the new world. Its vanished trees . . . had once pandered in whispers to the last and greatest of all human dreams; for a transitory enchanted moment man must have held his breath in the presence of this continent, compelled into an aesthetic contemplation he neither understood nor desired, face to face for the last time in history with something commensurate to his capacity for wonder."[1]

The chapters in these volumes describe that world event, with its many facets, in modern historical detail incorporating the latest research. In many cases, the point of view has changed, but the currents of mythology run as strong as ever. The "capacity for wonder" is still part of the story.

This chapter is an overview of that story, indeed of the many stories, and of the innate meanings and implications of the process of exploration. In addition, I argue here that in historical times, exploration took place in three "Great Ages of Discovery," each stimulated by a revolution in knowledge that swept over the European or Euro-American world. Whereas every person had the "capacity for wonder," only the peculiar historical convergence of masses of new knowledge, of the advent of new institutions for putting that knowledge to use, of the reconstitution of new epistemologies, of the consequent demand for more and more knowledge, and of the "facts" that constituted geography according to Captain James Cook, made for new, distinctly different "ages of discovery."

These volumes have not told, of course, the whole story of world exploration. They represent a very large case study that, in terms of world exploration, may not even be typical but that is, if not awe-inspiring, revealing. For the most part, they reflect Euro-American ethnocentricity, a European dream acted out with elements of grandeur and horror, though earlier chapters do adopt a Native American point of view and other chapters acknowledge the existence of the Native American perspective. Euro-American ethnocentricity is neither accidental nor arbitrary, however. It was the inevitable product of historical trends, notably the emergence of modern science, which fashioned the distinctive character of European and then Euro-American cultures at a specific time in history that impelled them to explore or search for unknown lands. As one historian has pointed out, "Only exploration's alliance with modern science spared Western 'discovery' from the charge of total ethnocentricity. . . . It made possible an abstraction from the knowledge of various peoples into a more universal framework, a global scholarship of nature. . . . It spoke a universal language and saw from a universal perspective and could, therefore, justify its special form of imperialism."[2]

To a large extent too, the tale of North American exploration is the basis of the American and Canadian myth of progress, whereas virtually the opposite can be said for events or misadventures, particularly, in the Arctic and Mexico. By any measure, however, the exploration and settlement of North America is one of the climactic turning points in world history, which is the reason for this retelling of the story in a more modern and a bit less ethnocentric manner.

For most people, exploration is an adventure compounded of a series of discoveries that prove meaningful to civilization—usually defined as Euro-American civilization. One tends to forget those intrepid Polynesian argonauts who, guided only by the winds, the stars, and the ocean currents, traveled immense distances over the Pacific from New Zealand as far as Hawaii but who did not share their knowledge with the world until Europeans entered the Pacific. Often we forget too that North America was really "discovered" by unknown explorers who traveled in the first of three distinct waves over the icy Pleistocene land bridge between Asia and North America and sometimes as boat people across the North Pacific. When we recall these first people at all from the mists of time, they are loosely dubbed as "ancient man" (now also "ancient woman"). Though they came first, they are considered interlopers on the vast North American continent, as opposed to the third-wave latecomers, whom we now call "Native Americans."[3] But whether Polynesian, Ice Age Asiatic ("ancient man"), or Native American, all seem to have had in common the urge to explore and to migrate.

Certain people, at least, out of such diverse groups felt the urge to explore and, hopefully, to discover not only new lands or new people but also new possibilities for living. With this in mind, one is tempted to say that the urge to explore is intrinsic to the human biological system, with its sensing organs and its capacity to analyze, store, and remember information, as well as its remarkable ability to imagine, to project whole new continents and galaxies of experience. Very probably, imagination and the human "capacity for wonder" are the keys to understanding the urge to explore, which then, for all races and cultures, becomes utilitarian and sometimes rapacious. We should remember, however, that the latter two tendencies are common to all peoples, in one form or another, and are not just confined to the better-documented histories of the Euro-American peoples. Gathering information and crossing over unknown thresholds of geographical experience may well have followed tiny *Zinjanthropus* up out of Africa's Olduvai Gorge and certainly accompanied the Cro-Magnon people across Ice Age Europe. Perhaps one day we will penetrate the biological mystery of this profound urge to explore previously unknown environments—an urge that distinguishes humans from animals, for whom environmental limitations or "niches" generally rule.

## Discovering the Ages of Discovery

Having observed all humans' innate urge to explore, these three volumes focus primarily on the Euro-American drive to explore the mysteries of North America. The reason behind these volumes was twofold. They represent a response to the Columbus Quincentennial and what we Euro-Americans like to think of as the emergence of a "New World." In addition, these volumes may also retrospectively form part of the historical fallout of the 1992 International Space Year, the updated counterpart to the all-important 1957 International Geophysical Year, which produced *Sputnik* and was such a landmark in exploration history. These volumes do not take us into space or even the solar system, however. In that sense, they are provincial and confined to what I have perceived as the Second Great Age of the three Great Ages of Discovery.

The conceptualization of distinct ages of discovery is, to my way of thinking, all-important. It connects geographical exploration not only with history but also with the characteristic mind-sets of people who are concerned with the overall configurations of their culture. Cultures—the traditional values, symbols, and ways of behaving of distinct groups of people—can also be thought of as screens that filter out data that are deemed by a people as useless, meaningless, or even dangerous. Euro-American culture, in contrast to that of Ming Dynasty China, for example, has had a wide-mesh screen permeable to the methods of science and discovery, whereas for a long period, Chinese culture deemed itself self-sufficient at the center of the world. In the Ming Dynasty, Chinese rulers specifically forbade exploration after seven forays across the Indian Ocean to Africa by Admiral Cheng Ho in the first decades of the fifteenth century.[4] This possibly explains why the Chinese, who had the ability for ocean-spanning voyages, did not discover North America.

To connect the act of exploration to culture is to see it as a process tied to mind and values—the *zeitgeist* of a people. In the case of European and, later, Euro-American exploration, ages of discovery in the fifteenth and sixteenth centuries were very closely attuned to the rediscovery of ancient classical knowledge, changing religious values, a search for a mythical land of gold, the rampant growth of mercantile capitalism, and the competition between sovereigns and emergent nation-states for wealth and territorial aggrandizement, what we now call imperialism. Such objectives and values characterize the First Great Age of Discovery, that is, the era of Vasco da Gama, Christopher Columbus, Ferdinand Magellan, and lesser figures of the Renaissance revolution in knowledge.

The Second Great Age of Discovery begins with the emergence of modern science, somewhere in the late seventeenth century, an event certainly marked by the publication of Sir Isaac Newton's *Principia Mathematica* in 1687 and followed by a revolution in epistemology—the skeptical empiri-

23.1 *"Searching the Most Opposite Corners and Quarters of the World." This engraving, probably from the late seventeenth century, symbolizes the ambitions and equipment of the early European seagoing explorers. Courtesy of the National Maritime Museum, Greenwich, England.*

cism of John Locke. The eighteenth and nineteenth centuries have been called "The Greater Enlightenment,"[5] a useful term emphasizing the scientific perception that characterized the eighteenth century but that epistemological perception also carried to its extreme in an exotic world by creating an age of Romanticism, a time when the cascade of information and wondrous specimens from all parts of the globe overwhelmed peoples' imaginations and figuratively exploded the metaphysical Great Chain of Being that had ordered all earthly phenomena in Europeans' minds since the Middle Ages. This new mind-set, which accelerated and diversified European and, later, Euro-American exploration, clearly forms a part of the intellectual history of these cultures. Thus, exploration itself, however it is characterized by action and adventure, is fundamentally a mental process, institutionalized in Euro-America and governed by increasing knowledge, new methodologies, shifting values, and the literal institutionalizing of exploration. Europeans in the eighteenth century were anxious to rid themselves of ancient superstitions in favor of demonstrable knowledge.[6]

Thus, for a time, religious meaning figured in explorers' calculations as being derived from, rather than preceding, scientific knowledge. In the Second Great Age of Discovery, the remarkable Scottish Enlightenment became important as its practitioners revealed the existence of God through nature's design. This climaxed in the Reverend William Paley's *Natural Theology*, published in 1802.

Pantheistic and transcendental beliefs begin to reappear in the wake of that colossus of exploration, Alexander von Humboldt, "the man who would be Faust," who began to explore the western hemisphere in 1806. His mighty expeditions to Mount Chimborazo, and through the green jungle pathways of the Amazon and Orinoco Rivers, reified the subtle metaphysics of Immanuel Kant and Friedrich Schelling in the form of a new discipline—geography. And Humboldtean science, essentially static, lasted at least half a century, until Charles Darwin, a Humboldtean himself, introduced evolution and the chance universe with his *On the Origin of Species* (1859), the faint, but important, beginning of the Third Great Age of Discovery. By that time, however, science, never really neutral and objective, was in full command of exploration. Virtually every expedition included naturalists, and sometimes artists, who pictured new lands and new peoples as exotic or fantastic Romantic specimens. A whole new genre of landscape art appeared. The landscapes, in part derived from cartography (at the time a military, topographical tradition), became then the conventions or preconceptions of landscape developed by Claude Lorrain, Nicolas Poussin, and Salvator Rosa in the seventeenth century, who purported to portray a newer and more realistic view of the earth's creatures and environment. One author, stopping short of the Romantic sublime that emerged in the earthscapes of Frederick Church and Albert Bierstadt, has called the eighteenth- and nineteenth-century landscape a "voyage into substance."[7] Only rarely, however, was this true; both scientists and a whole range of geographical, scientific, and anthropological artists, thanks to what we now know as the "uncertainty principle," were actually linking the observer with the observed, thus making objectivity impossible. Instead, the exploration artists discovered, even engendered, a whole new reality incorporating both environments and peoples, a reality of which North America and its incredibly exotic natives became a part.

Anthropology now included pictures of the "strange" races of the globe, while recorders of mysterious ruins like those of the "lost" civilizations of the Mayans or the Anasazi often overstimulated the minds of the age and brought on an unquenchable thirst for more exploration, which continued the objectives of the Second Great Age of Discovery even while we found ourselves also in the Third Great Age. Later in the nineteenth century, the camera became an instrument of exploration, and soon mass-picture magazines like *National Geographic* brought the exotic lands and peoples into the family living room. Indeed, exotica almost became mundane with the advent of the camera, which people assumed, quite wrongly, produced pictures of "reality," as opposed to art composed according to the dictates of the imagination.

The modern historian J. H. Parry, in *The Discovery of the Sea*, attempted to define two ages of discovery in relatively simple, one-dimensional geographical terms; the first age, or the Magellan Age, discovered, explored, and mapped the world ocean. Later, in *Trade and Dominion*, Parry separated the exploring ages into a more complex division that depended on new technologies, new trading objectives, and a perceived necessity for dominion stemming from nationalistic rivalries.[8] My former student Stephen Pyne, the eminent historian of fire, added that a second age was focused on the exploration of the interiors of the continents.[9] Pyne also agreed, however, that ideas and values had something to do with the aims of exploration, and he pointed out that a third age was geared to space and undersea exploration, which allowed humans to escape the self-reflexivity and solipsism that were the potential products of "no new worlds to conquer." (He was wrong.) A few thousand years ago Alexander the Great was said to have experienced that same kind of crisis, though he did not live in an age as self-referential as ours.[10]

Clearly, a simple ocean-continent (and space) division between the three ages of discovery leaves out such monumental nineteenth-century oceanic expeditions as those of Darwin, Charles Wilkes, the U.S. North Pacific Expeditions, and the celebrated voyage of the *Challenger*. Moreover, sixteenth-century Renaissance explorers, such as Hernán Cortés, Francisco Pizarro, and Francisco Vázquez de Coronado, did spend a great deal of time penetrating the interiors of the North and South American continents in the First Great Age, or the "world ocean" age. The story in these volumes, however, necessarily focuses on continental exploration, since North America is our subject. We also ignore the emergence of the Third Great Age of Discovery, in which we are now living—an age that derives its view of reality, its epistemology, and its values from that Euro-American revolution that occurred in virtually every discipline (including exploration) around 1900: "modernism."[11] Some of the changes have been dramatic: in philosophy, pragmatism and self-reference; in physics, relativity and quantum mechanics involving the "uncertainty principle" (which abolishes the omniscient knower or knowledge as such); in anthropology, the doctrine of cultural relativism; in psychology, the discovery of the subconscious and mythical world archetypes; in literature and philosophy, the stream of consciousness; in art, cubism and abstraction; and in general, through all these disciplines, the "flattening out" or purgation of time as a constant and the abandonment of the dualism between the observer and the observed. The last had always been true, but not sufficiently recognized, in The Greater Enlightenment, though it began to be apparent in the Age of Romanticism. Today, in the Third Great Age of Discovery, we live in an ahistorical, linguistic, and mathematical world of instant self-reference. We have long since subsumed and experienced Marshall McLuhan's "global village," as we live vicariously via satellites and television.

## Native Americans and Exploration

These volumes are designed to recall history and geography and in particular to examine, through modern scholarship, the process of the "discovery" and exploration of North America principally, but not exclusively, by Euro-Americans in the Second Great Age of Discovery. In one of the chapters, G. Malcolm Lewis ventures a brilliant, pioneering reconstruction of Native American exploration of North America, through reconstruction of its impact on Euro-American cartography. Heretofore, only tantalizing clues to preconquest exploration were apparent. Great nineteenth-century historians such as Francis Parkman and Justin Winsor pointed out that the Iroquois knew much about the Ohio, Kentucky, and Virginia country and the Great Lakes, as far west as Michilimackinac. Studies by the eighteenth-century traveler James Adair, and later by Francis Parkman and other historians, also revealed that, via the "warriors' trail" south through Kentucky, northern tribes such as the Shawnees and the Delawares, the Miamis and the Wyandottes, and even the Iroquois had close contact with the major southern tribes. Meriwether Lewis and William Clark were guided up the Missouri by the Hidatsa tribe and through a part of the Rockies by the Shoshone woman Sacagawea, while the mountain men located Wyoming's South Pass, soon the major immigrant route to Oregon and California, through the aid of Wind River valley Crow Indian hunters who drew maps on the ground and used small piles of dirt to represent the Wind River Mountains. In the Southwest, Hopi legend was built around treks by clans of their people far to the north, south, east, and west.[12] In the far North, explorers of the Canadian Arctic relied on the geographical lore of both Inuit and Indian peoples who had incorporated their extensive migratory travels into their worldview. In fact, most tribal legends among both American and Canadian native peoples incorporated knowledge, myth, and lore of extensive travel. One can only speculate that Native American exploration was bound up with trading and warring, but it also demonstrates humanity's universal urge to explore unless that urge is specifically checked by political power, as in the case of Ming China. Thus, the fact that Native Americans were here in North America in great numbers, and that they well knew the continental terrain from the Mackenzie River in far northern Canada to the warriors' trail into Georgia and Florida when the Euro-Americans appeared, makes clear that our principal subject is not discovery but rediscovery, not exploration but reexploration, with the new aims of new ages and with differing consequences—some tragic, some producing much good.

We should also remember that exploration is the process of seeking, though not necessarily of finding, which is discovery. This distinction is important because it indicates that exploration is a human process whereas discovery is an event—a singular episode in human history. Discovery can be an accident, such as when Columbus thought he had found the Indies. Exploration, on the other hand, generally has geographical aims. Sometimes these are very specific, such as the search for the Northwest Passage, or they may be general and flexible, such as the search for various kinds of minerals and promising farmlands. Exploration in North America was particularly distinctive because it was largely focused on a quest for suitable land for immigrant settlers or on a search for other elements of the continental resource base such as furs or minerals or timber, transcontinental transportation routes, and literally thousands of additions to the museums and warehouses of scientific facts. Thus exploration was the vanguard of a particular kind of political and economic, as well as scientific, imperialism. The Euro-American aim, exclusive of Spain's activities in Mexico and Central America, was not to enslave or rule over the native peoples but to brush them aside (not murder them) in the quest for living room on what the northern Europeans arrogantly regarded as a vast empty continent. Moreover, the vision of the vast empty continent included, from the very beginning, immense untapped natural resources, from tall trees for ship

23.2 Pehriska-Ruhpa (Two Ravens), Chief of the Hidatsa Dog Dancers *(Karl Bodmer, 1833). This Bodmer watercolor is one of the finest examples of the artist's ethnographic depictions of Missouri River native peoples. Courtesy of the Joslyn Art Museum, Omaha, Nebraska. Gift of the Enron Art Foundation.*

23.3 Stewart & Antoine Confronted by Crow Indians (*Alfred Jacob Miller, 1837*). *Miller's paintings of the farther West in the 1830s captured the interaction between white trappers and the native peoples of the western interior. Courtesy of the Walters Art Gallery, Baltimore, Maryland.*

masts to Niagara-like free waterpower to immense quantities of gold. The Spaniards had found a Golconda in Mexico and Central America; why would a similar bonanza not be found in North America? Clearly, North America was one immense cornucopia of exploitable or developable resources, though settlement on the Great Plains (a region comparable on other continents only to the pampas of South America, the steppes of Russia, and the savannahs of East Africa) was carried out in spite of some of the first explorers' vision of the plains as "the Great American Desert." Today, this "desert" helps feed the world.

The chapters in these volumes deal with such specifics, with human adjustments in North America, from Alaska's "icy mountains" to Florida's "sunny clime." The thrust of this chapter is to examine the fundamental nature of exploration, to discuss the issues raised by exploration, and for what it is worth, to underscore the good (while at the same time recognizing the evil) that came of the North American exploration into the many and varied wildernesses in what are now the United States, Canada, and Mexico but were once the dwelling places of peoples so mysterious that we have continued to compound Columbus's error by calling them "Indians."

## Exploration as Moral Drama

When we speak of exploration by Euro-Americans, we must speak in terms of a moral drama[13] that had begun to unfold since the days of Columbus and that, a bit later, became explicit in Father Bartolomé de Las Casas and Juan Ginés de Sepúlveda's debates—at Valladolid, Spain, in 1550–51—concerning the human status of the Native Americans or the "Indians," as they were mistakenly called. That sense of moral drama, with its overtones of forcible conquest of regions already settled by complex societies, has now become all too apparent to students of American history. Dr. Samuel Johnson perhaps put the proposition most succinctly when he declared, according to Boswell, "I do not much wish well to discovery [sic] for I am always afraid that they will end in conquest and robbery."[14]

Interestingly enough, Johnson made that statement in the eighteenth century, the first of those two centuries that formed what I have earlier called the Second Great Age of Discovery[15]—the age in which the United States was born and the Canadian Confederation created, both expanding over the North American continent on what they considered to be a divinely inspired mission to disperse enlightened republican and Christian civilization around the globe. In its particular American version, this mission was a "Manifest Destiny," as termed by the Jacksonian editor J. L. O'Sullivan. And it *was* a religious mission in the eyes of Euro-Americans. It spread the gospel of Christianity and the benefits of Republican democracy and of modern science, which, revealing Nature, revealed the thoughts of the Creator.[16] Thus, globe-encircling scientific exploration could, in theory, uncover very nearly the "mind of God." That the indigenous inhabitants of the places discovered, including North America, did not understand these "Divine" blessings from Western civilization was, some thought, a "great pity."

As far as the United States and Canada and North America in general are concerned, historians and cultural critics, from James Fenimore Cooper to contemporary Native American spokesmen such as Vine Deloria Jr., have seen discovery and exploration as pure moral drama. Alfred Crosby, in *The Columbian Exchange*, has seen it not only as human but as biological imperialism; he has wrestled with such questions as who gave syphilis to whom first—the Europeans to the New World peoples or the New World peoples to the Europeans.[17] (The eighteenth-century French explorer Louis Antoine de Bougainville blamed it on the fun-loving Tahitians, who cavorted with his sex-starved sailors in 1769.)[18] Disease has ranked high as a horror in the history of exploration. Some authorities have claimed that as many as ten million Native Americans were killed by European diseases but that, oddly enough, no Europeans were killed by Native American diseases.[19] One commentator has even referred to the Euro-peopling of North America as a "Holocaust" (a term that may soon be tragically debased by overuse).[20] The American novelist William Faulkner saw *both* native and white Americans as guilty. Chief Doom (Issetibbeha) sold land that he could not and did not own to the white man, who also could not own it, any more than he could "own" imported and enslaved black people.[21] A more recent book has chronicled the *many* sins of the conquest—sins that are still with us and that desperately need to be expiated.[22] (Even Euro-American evacuation from the North American continent seems not out of the question as an option to some contemporary American historians and a horde of interested journalists.) One historian has put the case of the onset of the American national creation myth even more bluntly in an article entitled "Frontiersmen, Fur Traders, and Other Varmints."[23]

In the 1830s and 1840s the explorer-artist George Catlin railed against "the juggernaut of civilization" plainly enough in his treatises on the American Indian, and in terms of today's ambiguous "discourse," we cannot be quite sure that James Fenimore Cooper even considered his own archetypal creation, Leatherstocking, a moral equal.[24] Was Natty Bumppo really, for Cooper, a primitive lower-class outcast, absurdly roaming the wilds of nature (the "Devil's Den," it was once called),[25] or was he the harbinger of that evil juggernaut of crude bourgeois civilization that Thomas Jefferson called yeoman? The reason anybody reads Cooper's works today is *because* his Leatherstocking represents the Euro-American dilemma vis-à-vis nature and nurture, the dilemma that lies at the moral center of the history of the American and Canadian civilization that followed the paths of the explorers.[26]

John Gast insouciantly visualized the march of empire in his popular 1872 picture *American Progress*. Is his central female figure the sweet goddess of liberty and civilized progress? Or is she the camp follower of ruthless conquest? The retreating parties of Gast's image, including growling bears and surly Indians, are not exactly happy. Their "defeat" was made possible not only by disease but also by science and technology and a belief in imperialism and capitalism (forms of political and economic ownership), which swept over the globe in the Second Great Age of Discovery—the age in which the American colonies revolted from England, Captain Cook discovered and took possession of South Seas paradises, and Adam Smith published that free-trade, capitalist bible *The Wealth of Nations*.

## The Dynamics of Cultures, Civilization, and Exploration

Both Native American and Euro-American cultures suffered continuing and massive dislocations of structures of thought, philosophical fractures, and psychological turmoil during the Second Great Age of Discovery, even while modern scientific civilization came to "flower" in the United States and Canada by the mid–twentieth century.

If one considers culture a construct of societal beliefs, rules, and accustomed ways of doing things—a social grid that screens out unwanted data (or habits) and only grudgingly admits new data that are deemed useful in a traditional context—then one gets a picture of the impact of the hundreds of exploring expeditions and the millions of bytes of data bombarding existing Euro-American culture. Walter Webb, thinking only of the economic consequences, called the result a "400-year boom."[27] Rather than just a dubious economic boom, both the First and the Second Great Ages of Discovery shattered European, as well as Native American, philosophical structures that had been erected to control cultural information. The result was continuous and relentless change in the perceptions of reality, values, and common utility, originating in the emergence, as noted, of modern science—an activity that sees reality merely as process and not amenable to the erection of final or ultimate philosophical structures of order. This has made North American civilization a scientific civilization. It is the product of the Second Great Age of Discovery—when new lands, new people, new oceans, new continents, new ecologies, new beauties, new wonders, and a whole restructuring of time, as well as space, resulted as this new data penetrated Euro-America, the United States, and Canada and especially as the United States and Canada incorporated more of the new than did any other cultures in all of history before the sudden advance of Japan in the nineteenth and twentieth centuries and now of all of South Asia. The story

23.4 "Harry Yount atop Berthold Pass" (photograph by William H. Jackson, 1875). Jackson was both graphic artist and photographer on a number of scientific expeditions of the post–Civil War era. His photography, in particular, provided Americans with some of their first views of the western United States. Courtesy of the National Archives.

of the exploration of North America is merely a dramatic historic episode, or perhaps an episteme of this process.

If we are being asked today to evaluate this process by hindsight, using today's self-referential values, we should at least be aware of and understand the meaning of the moral, aesthetic, social, scientific, and institutional discourses of the past. Michel Foucault has called this the "Archeology of Knowledge," which we must try to understand much as we try to understand remote tribal totems and taboos as anthropologists before we judge the society or culture that we can only partially recover.[28] We must beware of excessive contemporary self-reference, which is an ultimate form of "ethnocentrism," that is, "egocentrism."[29] Writing history and historical geography is as much an attempt to distance ourselves from our egos and prejudices and present-day journalistic fads as it is an attempt to recover the past. Lately we have been too quick to make North American history and exploration a scapegoat for our favorite contemporary special interests, as well as the ecstasies of fashionable guilt.

## Exploration's Positive Impacts

Having outlined some of the negative legacies of exploration and discovery—or conquest—I should like to focus the rest of my text on some of the ways in which exploration as a cultural process has had a positive impact on North American, Canadian, Mexican, and Euro-American civilization.

1. Explorers mapped and defined the North American continent. We have gone from the maps of Lewis and Clark or those of Alexander Mackenzie and David Thompson to sophisticated satellite maps that explore not only space but also planet earth, taking us into the Third Great Age of Discovery, largely an age of prosthetic or nonhuman explorers and far-flung space probes.[30] Mapping, a form of commodification with reference to exploitable resources, is an obvious aid to capitalistic development and nationalism, but it also now highlights the urgent agenda of ecological survival, as well as having created in the United States and Canada one of the highest standards of living in the world.

2. Explorers located the mountain passes, traversed the rivers, and laid out the trails, wagon routes, and railroads that would lead millions of settlers onto the various frontiers where, more often than not, the poor and the weary and the middle class, who swarmed in from Europe and Asia, could find opportunities for living. There settlers established their "dwellings," in the Heideggerian sense of the word. They found true "homes"— places where one could live with nature and where one could always, in theory, return.[31]

3. Explorers established a network of commerce in the West—the fur trade, mining, mustanging, the Santa Fe trade, agriculture, logging, even wine-making—and then, of course, much more, including the locations for towns and cities that became homes and workplaces, or stages of creativity, for millions of people.

4. Explorers helped to shape a continental geopolitics. In what is now the United States, as men such as Christopher Gist and Daniel Boone crossed over the Alleghenies into the interior, they found the Ohio country and hence a river that connected the settlements that followed. Even more important, the French discovery of the Mississippi, and then the American reexploration of the great Mississippi-Missouri river system, the longest river in the world, revealed a crucial geographical feature that linked the peoples below the forty-ninth parallel in a network of almost explosive economic development. The United States became a "heartland country," with a vast internal market for over a hundred years, and still remains so,

mythologically. This river-connected internal market stands in sharp contrast to the Australian experience and that of our neighbors, Canada and Mexico.

5. Explorers, especially on the Great Plains of both Canada and the United States and in California's Great Valley, eventually enabled the United States and Canada to assume a major role in feeding the world in the twentieth century.

6. Explorers made a major contribution to the establishment of organized science in North America—the result not only of continental but of global exploration. One need only call the roll of U.S. and Canadian governmental scientific expeditions: the three-thousand-mile reconnaissance of Lewis and Clark; Major Stephen Long's expedition over the Great Plains to the Rockies; the many expeditions of the U.S. Army Corps of Topographical Engineers from 1840 to 1860, culminating in the Pacific Railroad Surveys of 1853–54; the Royal Navy surveys and the Ordnance Survey in mapping the Arctic coasts of Canada; the great post–Civil War geological surveys, the work of hundreds of intrepid members of the U.S. Geological Survey and the Geological Survey of Canada; the U.S. Biological Survey and the investigations of the Botanical Society of Canada; the Smithsonian-sponsored expeditions; the Bureau of Explorations and Surveys in the United States and the Dominion Land Surveys in Canada; the Coast and Geodetic Survey; and the many global seaborne ventures of the Royal Navy and the U.S. Navy, especially the U.S. Exploring Expedition of 1838–42, sometimes known as the Wilkes Expedition, which proved Antarctica a continent and mapped the Northwest Coast of America, pointing up the greater value of Puget Sound as a harbor in comparison with the Columbia River[32] and making cities like Seattle possible.

7. Explorers such as John Wesley Powell, F. V. Hayden, N. P. Langford, George M. Dawson, John Palliser, J. B. Tyrrell, and John Muir played an important role in seeing the West as a laboratory for social planning. Water basin culture in the arid lands, national parks, and wilderness preservation, as well as land classification systems, were initially devised by these farseeing statesmen of North America's richly varied landscape.

8. Explorers, through biology, geology, paleontology, and archaeology, helped to rediscover time, three kinds of time: historical time, prehistorical human time, and the earth's four- or five-billion-year history that replaced the biblical count of 4004 years. This had a powerful effect on religion and all other organized thought as well.

9. Explorers, through their scientific work, helped make the continent,

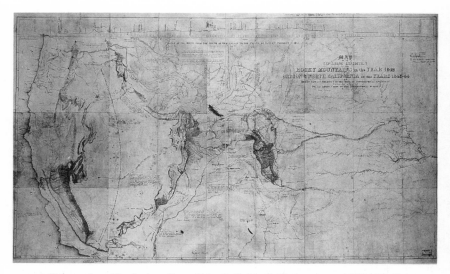

23.5 *"Map of an Exploring Expedition"* (John C. Frémont and Charles Preuss, 1845). This map combined the results of two expeditions, of 1842 and 1843–44. It was the first map to show the Great Basin accurately. Courtesy of the Geography and Map Division, Library of Congress.

especially the Far West, the world's laboratory for structural geology, enhancing the understanding of nature's forces at work on the earth.

10. Explorers such as O. C. Marsh, Joseph Leidy, and Charles Wright contributed the crucial proofs for Darwin's theory of evolution. Marsh and Leidy reconstructed the paleontological proofs for the evolution of the horse, whereas Wright supplied the plant distribution data that enabled Asa Gray, an evolutionist, to vanquish the theories of Louis Agassiz, the Harvard zoologist-creationist.[33]

11. Explorers, as part of the global reconnaissance of the Second Great Age of Discovery, mapped the oceans, the ocean floor, and the Arctic and discovered and mapped two new continents—Australia and Antarctica.

12. Explorers mapped the western coast of North America and proved that no Northwest Passage existed—including the mythical Straits of Anián and Juan de Fuca. John C. Frémont and Charles Wilkes finally demolished the myth of the Rio Buenaventura, which was supposed to flow, according to the explorer manqué Baron Lahontan, from a great interior sea straight to the Pacific Ocean.[34]

13. Explorers, including Parson John Heckewelder, Conrad Weiser,

Lewis Evans, George Catlin, Karl Bodmer, Prince Maximilian of Wied-Neu-Wied, Horatio Hale, Captain John Gregory Bourke, John Wesley Powell, and dozens of anthropologists studied the Native Americans and helped to create not only a science of anthropology but also the world's first institution for the study of primitive peoples, the Bureau of American Ethnology, established by Congress in 1879 with Powell as its first director. The bureau was also one of the first government agencies to employ women as field explorers and archaeologists, for example Matilda Cox Stevenson and Alice Fletcher. The study of Native Americans also advanced through the work of Hale, a philologist with the Wilkes Expedition who studied the cargo cult language of the Northwest Coast Indians. From his pioneering work came the concept of comparative linguistics and early cultural relativism (just a bit before a sailor, Herman Melville, articulated it in his novels of the 1840s and 1850s). Hale then passed on his idea of cultural relativism to Franz Boas, and thus began modern anthropology—an anthropology that already had enough data on American Indian tribes and South Seas natives to locate and call attention to alternative moral universes that began to cast light on, and even to serve as a critique of, Euro-American values.[35] Young men and women under the direction of the great Bronisław Malinowski began to study remote cultures such as the Trobriand Islanders so that they could better understand the Long Islanders.[36] They also studied the pueblo dwellers of the Southwest so that they could get a more serene angle on the cliff dwellers of Manhattan.

14. Explorers served, for Euro-Americans, as the heroic leaders of the redemption of, rather than the conquest of, the continent—something that Americans, in particular, have been naive enough, or perhaps proud enough, to adopt as their national creation myth. The explorers were considered our Odysseus or, as Bernard DeVoto once put it in a typical overstatement, the "Odysseus Jed Smith" and the "Wing-Shod Fitzpatrick."[37] James Fenimore Cooper, whatever his ambiguities, described the vision and emotions of the crude yeoman prairie squatters. They saw Leatherstocking as no less than a nature god coming out of the sun:

The sun had fallen below the crest of the nearest wave of the prairie, leaving the usual rich and glowing train in its track. In the center of this flood of fiery light, a human form appeared, drawn against the gilded background, as distinctly, and seemingly as palpable, as though it would come within the grasp of any extended hand. The figure was *colossal*, the attitude musing and melancholy, and the situation directly in the route of the travellers. But embedded, as it was,

*23.6 Hayden surveyors on Silverton Mountain, Colorado Territory (1875). Expedition member and artist William Holmes is shown sketching a landscape for later conversion to a lithograph. Courtesy of the National Archives.*

23.7 *The Gardiner River, (Mammoth) Hot Springs, Yellowstone (photograph by William H. Jackson, 1873). Jackson's photo was one of the first to show the thermal wonders of the Yellowstone region. Courtesy of the U.S. Geological Survey.*

in its setting of garish light, it was impossible to distinguish its just proportions or true character.

The effect of such a spectacle was instantaneous and powerful. The man in front of the emigrants came to a stand, and remained gazing at the mysterious object with a dull interest, that soon quickened into superstitious awe.[38]

15. Explorers took us deeply into nature—its great "prairie oceans," its "American Zaharas [sic]" and "Death Valleys" and "Barren Lands," its extraordinary mountain ranges (one marked by a great, shining snowy cross), its lakes and rivers and pastoral paradises, where flocks and herds abounded in a land of plenty, redeemed by explorers and settlers as the "instruments of the Almighty." All this helped to establish an identity for the confederated Canadians and to create a character for the American people, whom David Potter once called a "People of Plenty"[39] and who lived in a country that historian Perry Miller patriotically described as "Nature's Nation."[40] Dramatically, American western explorers led us into very special places in the West: Yosemite's immense silent glacial valley, the titanic scientific drama of the Grand Canyon, and the wonders of Yellowstone. These became "sacred spaces"—the world's first wilderness parks,

as full of philosophical, even religious, meaning as tourists, or better, "nature pilgrims," entered into them.

16. Explorers in the Second Great Age of Discovery played a significant role in the creation of an age of artistic, literary, and intellectual Romanticism on both sides of the Atlantic—a part that has not been sufficiently recognized by European scholars.

It is worthwhile to try briefly visualizing this romanticizing process that led beyond North America to England and Europe. The historian J. C. Beaglehole commented on Tahiti's influence on Western civilization: "Wallis [when he discovered Tahiti] had not merely come to a convenient port of call. He had stumbled on a foundation stone of the Romantic Movement. Not as a continent, not as vast distances, was the ocean thought to be known. The unreal was to mingle with the real, the too dramatic with the undramatic; the shining light was to become a haze in which every island was the one island, and the one island a Tahitian dream."[41]

Tahiti's American counterpart perhaps lay deep in the mountain fastnesses of the West. As we have expressed it elsewhere:

In *The Rocky Mountains, Lander's Peak,* the artist Albert Bierstadt became the orchestrator of a mighty, Wagnerian scene, which exaggerated the vertical thrust of the Wind River Range to achieve the monumental grandeur which Americans had come to expect from their continent. It is a synthesis of a myriad of natural facts: from the snow-covered mountain summit and knife-edged peaks—the like of which challenged the bravery of Clarence King as he cavorted in the Sierras—to plunging waterfalls, natural meadows and peaceful Indians who are reminiscent of the Westphalian peasants in Bierstadt's European views. The artist dared, not merely a literal transcription of nature, but an act of creation itself, replete with all of the creatures which, as his friend Louis Agassiz, the Harvard naturalist, would suggest, were the outward manifestations of the mind of the Deity.[42]

The artists and photographers who accompanied exploring expeditions into the American and Canadian West in the nineteenth century often had a very special "capacity for wonder" that matched the Tahitian dream of eighteenth-century mariners in the Pacific. Geographical marvels like the sublime immensity of the Great Plains, which reached to infinity, stunned their imaginations. And as they grew accustomed to the plains, next the "Mountains of the Wind" deep in the West or the wonders of Yellowstone—an unexpected paradise of cerulean paintpots, sky-high geysers, and a grand canyon comparable to that in far-off Arizona—only began to

23.8 The Mirage (Thomas Moran, 1879). Moran's romantic paintings of the American West helped to popularize an idealized image of the region and were instrumental in winning congressional approval of the national park concept. Courtesy of the Stark Museum of Art, Orange, Texas.

reveal the wonders of the American West. In addition the West, with its noble savages and rugged fur trappers, heroic cowboys and stoic cavalrymen, became a domain of the world's imagination, far transcending the proprietary claims of North Americans who happened to live on the same continent or who inhabited that hallowed region. The American continental frontier, with its many explorers—red men, Hispanic gold-seekers, and intrepid white scouts in the vanguard of a relentlessly growing modern civilization—was a vast, wondrous adventure and then an extraordinary exploitation as people (refugees and immigrants from all over the globe) poured into the United States and Canada. Rudyard Kipling drew a distinction between explorers and exploiters, a distinction that we hope is clear in these volumes. In one of his finest poems, *The Explorer*, he wrote:

"There's no sense in going further—it's the edge of cultivation,"
So they said, and I believed it—broke my land and sowed my crop—
Built my barns and strung my fences in the little border station
Tucked away below the foothills where the trails run out and stop:
Till a voice, as bad as Conscience, rang interminable changes
On one everlasting Whisper day and night repeated—so:
"Something hidden. Go and find it. Go and look behind the Ranges—
"Something lost behind the Ranges. Lost and waiting for you. Go!"
So I went, worn out of patience; never told my nearest neighbours— . . . .
. . . . . . . . . . . . . . . . . . . . . . . . . . . .
I remember lighting fires; I remember sitting by 'em;
I remember seeing faces, hearing voices, through the smoke;
I remember they were fancy—for I threw a stone to try 'em.
"Something lost behind the Ranges" was the only word they spoke.
I remember going crazy. I remember that I knew it
When I heard myself hallooing to the funny folk I saw.
'Very full of dreams that desert, but my two legs took me through it . . .
And I used to watch 'em moving with the toes all black and raw.
But at last the country altered—White Man's country past disputing—
Rolling grass and open timber, with a hint of hills behind—
There I found me food and water, and I lay a week recruiting.
Got my strength and lost my nightmares. Then I entered on my find.
. . . . . . . . . . . . . . . . . . . . . . . . . . . .
Well I know who'll take the credit—all the clever chaps that followed—
Came, a dozen men together—never knew my desert-fears;

Tracked me by the camps I'd quitted, used the water-holes I'd hollowed.
They'll go back and do the talking. *They'll* be called the Pioneers!
. . . . . . . . . . . . . . . . . . . . . . . . . . . . . .
Yes, your "Never-never country"—yes, your "edge of cultivation"
And "no sense in going further"—till I crossed the range to see.
God forgive me! No, *I* didn't. It's God's present to our nation.
Anybody might have found it, but—His Whisper came to me![43]

# Notes

## 15. Exploring the American West in the Age of Jefferson

1. Donald Jackson, ed., *The Letters of the Lewis and Clark Expedition with Related Documents, 1783–1854*, 2d ed., 2 vols. (Urbana, 1978), 2:668.

2. *Niles' Weekly Register*, 23 November 1822.

3. William Goetzmann, *Exploration and Empire: The Explorer and the Scientist in the Winning of the American West* (New York, 1966), 4.

4. My use of republicanism draws heavily on Drew R. McCoy, *The Elusive Republic: Political Economy in Jeffersonian America* (New York, 1980), chap. 8.

5. North West Company, petition, 30 June 1812, C042/70/16, No. 2, Public Record Office, London, England.

6. Alexander Ross, *Adventures of the First Settlers on the Oregon or Columbia River, 1810–1813* (1849; reprint, Lincoln, 1986), 40.

7. Thomas Jefferson to John Hollins, Washington, 19 February 1809, in Jefferson Papers, Document Collection, Library of Congress, Washington DC (hereafter cited as JP-DLC).

8. James King to Banks, October 1780, quoted in David Mackay, "A Presiding Genius of Exploration: Banks, Cook, and Empire, 1767–1805," in Robin Fisher and Hugh Johnston, eds., *Captain James Cook and His Times* (Seattle, 1979), 29.

9. Jefferson to John Manners, Monticello, 22 February 1814, in JP-DLC.

10. This approach is best exemplified in the work of John L. Allen. See especially his "Lands of Myth, Waters of Wonder: The Place of Imagination in the History of Geographical Exploration," in David Lowenthal and Martyn J. Bowden, eds., *Geographies of the Mind: Essays in Historical Geography in Honor of John Kirtland Wright* (New York, 1976), 41–61.

11. Pierre Margry, ed., *Decouvertes et etablissements des Francais dans l'ouest et dans le sud de l'Amerique Septentrionale, 1614–1754*, 6 vols. (Paris, 1876–86), 6:534. See also Pierre F. X. Charlevoix, *Journal of a Voyage to North America*, 2 vols. (London, 1761), 2:180. I am grateful to W. J. Eccles for drawing my attention to this important material.

12. John L. Allen, *Passage through the Garden: Lewis and Clark and the Image of the American Northwest* (Urbana, 1975), 23.

13. Jonathan Carver, *Travels through the Interior Parts of North America* (London, 1781), 118. See also John Parker, ed., *The Journals of Jonathan Carver and Related Documents, 1766–1770* (St. Paul, 1976).

14. Carver, *Travels*, 542.

15. J. C. Beaglehole, ed., *The Journals of Captain James Cook: The Voyage of the "Reso-lution" and "Discovery," 1776–1780* (Cambridge, U.K., 1967), pt. 1: cxxvii, 367. See also Glyndwr Williams, "Myth and Reality: James Cook and the Theoretical Geography of North America," in Fisher and Johnston, *Cook and His Times*, 59–80.

16. Pond, "A Map Presented to Congress, New York, March 1, 1785," in Henry R. Wagner, *Peter Pond: Fur Trader and Explorer* (New Haven, n.d.), map 1.

17. James P. Ronda, *Astoria and Empire* (Lincoln, 1990), chap. 1.

18. Allen, *Passage through the Garden*, 56–57; Carl I. Wheat, *Mapping the Trans-Mississippi West, 1540–1861*, 5 vols. (Menlo Park CA, 1958–62), 1:151, 246 (plate 244).

19. Gilbert Imlay, *A Topographical Description of the Western Territory of North America* (London, 1979), 76.

20. Allen, *Passage through the Garden*, 83; Wheat, *Mapping the Trans-Mississippi West* 1:155, 175, 178, 242, 249 (plates 231 and 253).

21. Allen, *Passage through the Garden*, 58; Wheat, *Mapping the Trans-Mississippi West* 1:159, 183, 250 (plate 259).

22. Allen, *Passage through the Garden*, 54.

23. Allen, *Passage through the Garden*, 53–55.

24. W. Kaye Lamb, ed., *The Journals and Letters of Sir Alexander Mackenzie* (Cambridge, U.K., 1970), 417. Jefferson's response is spelled out in Donald Jackson, *Thomas Jefferson and the Stony Mountains: Exploring the West from Monticello* (Urbana, 1981), 121–24.

25. Alexander DeConde, *This Affair of Louisiana* (New York, 1976), chap. 7.

26. Albert Gallatin to Jefferson, Washington, 21 November 1802, in JP-DLC.

27. Jefferson, "Message to Congress," 18 January 1803, in Jackson, *Letters of the Lewis and Clark Expedition* 1:13.

28. Jefferson to C. F. de C. Volney, Washington, 11 February 1806, in JP-DLC.

29. Jefferson to Meriwether Lewis, Washington, 23 February 1801, in JP-DLC. See also Jackson, *Jefferson and the Stony Mountains*, 117–21.

30. The relevant documents for this period are in Jackson, *Letters of the Lewis and Clark Expedition* 1:16–55.

31. James Boswell, *The Life of Samuel Johnson*, 2 vols. (1791; reprint, London, 1904), 2:227.

32. Gallatin to Jefferson, Washington, 13 April 1803, in JP-DLC.

33. Levi Lincoln to Jefferson, Washington, 17 April 1803, in JP-DLC.

34. Jefferson to Lewis, Washington, 20 June 1803, in Jackson, *Letters of the Lewis and Clark Expedition* 1:61.

35. Jefferson to George Washington, Annapolis, 15 March 1784, in JP-DLC. See also Jefferson to G. K. van Hogendorp, Paris, 13 October 1785, in JP-DLC.

36. Jefferson to Lewis, Washington, 20 June 1803, in Jackson, *Letters of the Lewis and Clark Expediton* 1:64. For an extended treatment of expedition-Indian relations, see James P. Ronda, *Lewis and Clark among the Indians* (Lincoln, 1984).

37. Jefferson to Lewis, Washington, 20 June 1803, in Jackson, *Letters of the Lewis and Clark Expedition* 1:62. See also James P. Ronda, "Lewis and Clark and Enlightenment Ethnography," in William F. Wellingham, ed., *Enlightenment Science in the Pacific Northwest* (Portland OR, 1984), 5–17.

38. Reuben Gold Thwaites, ed., *The Original Journals of the Lewis and Clark Expedition*, 8 vols. (New York, 1904–5), 4:89–90.

39. Jefferson to Robert Smith, Monticello, 13 July 1804, in JP-DLC.

40. Annie H. Abel, ed., *Tabeau's Narrative of Loisel's Expedition to the Upper Missouri* (Norman, 1939), 108–9.

41. The analysis in this section is based on Ronda, *Lewis and Clark among the Indians*, chap. 2.

42. William Clark, "Estimate of the Eastern Indians," in Gary E. Moulton, ed., *The Journals of the Lewis and Clark Expedition*, 11 vols. to date (Lincoln, 1983-), 3:418 (hereafter cited as *JLCE*).

43. Allen, *Passage through the Garden*, 268–79; *JLCE* 4:242.

44. Allen, *Passage through the Garden*, 269.

45. Jefferson to Charles Thompson, Paris, 20 September 1787, in JP-DLC.

46. *JLCE* 4:271.

47. Jefferson, "Annual Message to Congress," 2 December 1806, in Jackson, *Letters of the Lewis and Clark Expedition* 1:352.

48. Lewis to Jefferson, Saint Louis, 23 September 1806, in Jackson, *Letters of the Lewis and Clark Expedition* 1:319–24. See also James P. Ronda, "The Writingest Explorers: The Lewis and Clark Expedition in American Historical Literature," *Pennsylvania Magazine of History and Biography* 112 (October 1988): 608–13.

49. *JLCE*, atlas, plate 125.

50. "The Conrad Prospectus," c. 1 April 1807, in Jackson, *Letters of the Lewis and Clark Expedition* 2:395.

51. Jefferson to Alexander von Humboldt, Monticello, 6 December 1813, in JP-DLC.

52. Paul Cutright, *Lewis and Clark: Pioneering Naturalists* (Urbana, 1969), chaps. 22–23 and appendices A and B.

53. Thwaites, *Original Journals* 5:299.

54. Jefferson to William Dunbar, Washington, 13 March 1804, in JP-DLC.

55. Dunbar to Jefferson, Natchez, 13 May 1804, in JP-DLC.

56. Jefferson, "Instructions for Thomas Freeman," Monticello, 14 April 1804, printed in Dan L. Flores, ed., *Jefferson and Southwestern Exploration: The Freeman and Custis Accounts of the Red River Expedition of 1806* (Norman, 1984), 320–25.

57. Dunbar to Jefferson, Natchez, 13 May 1804, in JP-DLC.

58. Flores, *Jefferson and Southwestern Exploration*, 45.

59. Flores, *Jefferson and Southwestern Exploration*, 45; Jackson, *Thomas Jefferson and the Stony Mountains*, 225–26.

60. Flores, *Jefferson and Southwestern Exploration*, 56–62.

61. Nemesio Salcedo to Casa Calvo, Chihuagua, 8 October 1805, in Donald Jackson, ed., *The Journals of Zebulon Montgomery Pike with Letters and Related Documents*, 2 vols. (Norman, 1966), 2:111–12. See also Jackson's perceptive comment at 2:108–9.

62. Flores, *Jefferson and Southwestern Exploration*, 132.

63. Flores, *Jefferson and Southwestern Exploration*, 143.

64. Flores, *Jefferson and Southwestern Exploration*, 204.

65. Flores, *Jefferson and Southwestern Exploration*, 205.

66. Flores, *Jefferson and Southwestern Exploration*, 205.

67. Flores, *Jefferson and Southwestern Exploration*, 317.

68. Jackson, *Thomas Jefferson and the Stony Mountains*, 234–36.

69. Jackson, *Thomas Jefferson and the Stony Mountains*, 242. There is no scholarly biography of Wilkinson. The best popular account is Thomas R. Hay and M. R. Werner, *The Admirable Trumpeter* (Garden City NJ, 1941).

70. Jackson, *Thomas Jefferson and the Stony Mountains*, 244.

71. Henry Dearborn to James Wilkinson, Washington, 26 February 1805, in Jackson, *Journals of Zebulon Montgomery Pike* 2:99.

72. Wilkinson to Dearborn, Saint Louis, 26 November 1805, in Jackson, *Journals of Zebulon Montgomery Pike* 2:250.

73. My understanding of the Wilkinson-Burr relationship is built on the documents and editorial notes in Mary-Jo Kline, ed., *Political Correspondence and Public Papers of Aaron Burr*, 2 vols. (Princeton, 1983), 2:903–1037.

74. Pike to David Bissell, Saint Louis, 15 June 1806, in Jackson, *Journals of Zebulon Montgomery Pike* 2:114.

75. Wilkinson to Pike, Saint Louis, 25 June 1806, in Jackson, *Journals of Zebulon Montgomery Pike* 1:285–86.

76. Jackson, *Journals of Zebulon Montgomery Pike* 1:286.

77. Pike to Wilkinson, LaCharette, 22 July 1806, in Jackson, *Journals of Zebulon Montgomery Pike* 2:124.

78. Jackson, *Journals of Zebulon Montgomery Pike* 1:358.

79. Jackson, *Journals of Zebulon Montgomery Pike* 1:367.

80. Jackson, *Journals of Zebulon Montgomery Pike* 1:368–74.

81. Jackson, *Journals of Zebulon Montgomery Pike* 1:377–78 and Jackson's note at 2:132.

82. Jackson, *Journals of Zebulon Montgomery Pike* 2:122–24 and Jackson's important commentary at 2:126. Interpretations of Pike by earlier historians were based on the wholly inadequate Elliot Coues edition of his works.

83. Jackson, *Thomas Jefferson and the Stony Mountains*, 263.

84. *JLCE* 2:260.

85. Richard E. Oglesby, *Manuel Lisa and the Opening of the Missouri Fur Trade* (Norman, 1963).

86. Lewis to Dearborn, Washington, 15 January 1807, in Jackson, *Letters of the Lewis and Clark Expedition* 1:368. For a broad, popular treatment of Drouillard, see M. O. Skarsten, *George Drouillard, Hunter and Interpreter* (Glendale CA, 1964).

87. Burton Harris, *John Colter: His Years in the Rockies* (New York, 1952), chaps. 4–5. Goetzmann, *Exploration and Empire*, 20–22, 25, offers a somewhat different reconstruction of Colter's 1807 journey.

88. Thwaites, *Original Journals* 5:387.

89. Thwaites, *Original Journals* 5:387.

90. Wilkinson to Dearborn, Saint Louis, 8 September 1805, in Clarence E. Carter, ed., *The Territorial Papers of the United States: The Territory of Louisiana-Missouri, 1803–1806*, vols. 13 and 14 (Washington DC, 1948), 13:199.

91. My analysis of the McClellan expedition is drawn from Harry M. Majors, "John McClellan in the Montana Rockies, 1807: The First Americans after Lewis and Clark," *Northwest Discovery* 2 (November–December 1981): 554–630.

92. Thompson to the North West Company, Kootenay House, 23 September 1807, in *Oregon Historical Quarterly* 38 (December 1937): 394–95.

93. Pinch to Thompson, 29 September 1807, printed in Majors, "McClellan," 608.

94. Majors, "McClellan," 611–12.

95. Manuel Lisa to William Clark, Saint Louis, 1 July 1817, printed in the *Missouri Gazette*, 5 July 1817.

96. Oglesby, *Lisa*, chap. 3. These ideas were not unique to Lisa but had already been articulated by trader-explorers such as Jacques Clamorgan and James Mackay. See A. P. Nasatir, ed., *Before Lewis and Clark: Documents Illustrating the History of the Missouri, 1785–1804*, 2 vols. (Saint Louis, 1952).

97. Thomas James, *Three Years among the Indians and Mexicans* (1846; reprint, Chicago, 1953); Ralph Ehrenberg, ed., "Sketch of Part of the Missouri and Yellowstone Rivers with a Description of the Country," *Prologue* 3 (fall 1971): 73–78.

98. Goetzmann, *Exploration and Empire*, 25. Drouillard's map is in Skarsten, *Drouillard*, end pocket.

99. *Louisiana Gazette*, 11 October 1811.

100. *JLCE*, atlas, plate 126.

101. Allen, *Passage through the Garden*, chap. 14.

102. Everett S. Brown, ed., *William Plumer's Memorandum of Proceedings in the United States Senate, 1803–1807* (New York, 1923), 520.

103. Ronda, *Astoria and Empire*, chap. 2.

104. Astor to De Witt Clinton, New York, 25 January 1808, in vol. 4, pp. 5–6, De Witt Clinton Papers, Butler Rare Book and Manuscript Library, Columbia University, New York.

105. Memorandum for Secretary of the Navy William Jones, Washington, 19 April 1813, in Astor Papers, Beinecke Library, Yale University, New Haven, Connecticut.

106. Ronda, *Astoria and Empire*, chap. 2.

107. James R. Gibson, *Imperial Russia in Frontier America* (New York, 1976), 3–15, 153–61.

108. Ronda, *Astoria and Empire*, chap. 3.

109. For a full discussion of the various Astoria expeditions, see Ronda, *Astoria and Empire*, chaps. 4–6.

110. Hunt to John Wesley Hunt, Saint Louis, 14 October 1806, in John Wesley Hunt Papers, Filson Club, Louisville, Kentucky.

111. Clark to William Eustis, Saint Louis, 12 September 1810, in Carter, *Territorial Papers* 14:414.

112. Thwaites, *Original Journals* 5:319–20.

113. *Louisiana Gazette*, 8 April 1811.

114. Washington Irving, *Astoria; or, Anecdotes of an Enterprise beyond the Rocky Mountains* (1836; reprint, Norman, 1964), 256. Irving here paraphrases from a now-lost Hunt overland journal.

115. John Bradbury, *Travels in the Interior of America* (Liverpool, 1817), 78–79; Ronda, *Astoria and Empire*, chap. 5. A fuller sense of what Henry and his men believed to be the best route over the continental divide can be seen in Henry M. Brackenridge's interview with Henry printed in the *Louisiana Gazette*, 11 October 1811. Henry's "Southern Pass" route is marked, probably too far north, on Clark's 1810 master map.

116. Ronda, *Astoria and Empire*, chap. 6.

117. Ronda, *Astoria and Empire*, chaps. 8–9.

118. Jefferson to John Melish, Monticello, 31 December 1816, in JP-DLC.

119. Irving, *Astoria*, xlvii.

120. Ross, *Adventures*, 34.

121. Ronda, *Astoria and Empire*, chap. 10.

122. John C. Calhoun to A. Smyth, Washington, 29 December 1819, in *American State Papers: Military Affairs*, 7 vols. (Washington DC, 1832–61), 2:33.

123. Roger L. Nichols, ed., *The Missouri Expedition: The Journal of Surgeon John Gale with Related Documents* (Norman, 1969), 82.

124. The Long scientific expedition produced a number of important narratives: Edwin James, *Account of an Expedition from Pittsburgh to the Rocky Mountains*, 2 vols. (Philadelphia, 1823); Harlin M. Fuller and LeRoy R. Hafen, eds., *The Journal of Captain John R. Bell* (Glendale CA, 1973); Asa O. Weese, ed., "The Journal of Titian Ramsay Peale, Pioneer Naturalist," *Missouri Historical Review* 41 (January 1947): 147–63, 266–84. The most reliable scholarly account is Roger L. Nichols and Patrick L. Halley, *Stephen Long and American Frontier Exploration* (Newark DE, 1980). Maxine Benson's forthcoming biography of Edwin James should add much to our understanding of the expedition.

125. Weese, "Journal of Titian Ramsay Peale," 149.

126. *Niles' Weekly Register*, 24 June 1819.

127. James, *Account of an Expedition* 1:460.

128. James, "Diary," quoted in Maxine Benson, ed., *From Pittsburgh to the Rocky Mountains: Major Stephen Long's Expedition, 1819–1820* (Golden CO, 1988), xi.

129. Martyn J. Bowden, "The Great American Desert and the American Frontier, 1800–1882: Popular Images of the Plains and Phases in the Westward Movement," in Tamara K. Hareven, ed., *Anonymous Americans: Explorations in Nineteenth-Century Social History* (Englewood Cliffs NJ, 1971), 48–79.

130. Long, "General description of the country traversed by the Exploring expedition . . . January 20, 1821," appended to James, *Account of an Expedition* 2:361.

131. Long, "General description of the country traversed by the Exploring expedition . . . January 20, 1821," appended to James, *Account of an Expedition* 2:361.

132. Richard Rush to James Monroe, London, 1 October 1818, in James Monroe Papers, Document [Collection], Library of Congress.

133. Ross, *Adventures*, 34.

134. Seymour I. Schwartz and Ralph E. Ehrenberg, *The Mapping of America* (New York, 1980), plate 145 and 238–39; W. W. Ristow, "John Melish and His Map of the United States," *Library of Congress Quarterly Journal* 19 (1962): 159–78.

135. Wheat, *Mapping the Trans-Mississippi West* 2:66, 220 (plate 328).

136. John L. Allen, "Patterns of Promise: Mapping the Plains and Prairies, 1800–1860," in Frederick C. Luebke, Frances W. Kaye, and Gary E. Moulton, eds., *Mapping the North American Plains: Essays in the History of Cartography* (Norman, 1987), 46.

137. Wheat, *Mapping the Trans-Mississippi West* 2:77, 80, 224, 226 (plates 343 and 353).

138. Henry R. Schoolcraft, *Narrative Journal of Travels . . . from Detroit . . . to the Sources of the Mississippi River* (Albany, 1821), xii.

139. Schoolcraft, *Narrative Journal of Travels*, 250.

140. Martha Coleman Bray, *Joseph Nicollet and His Map* (Philadelphia, 1980), 166.

141. Joseph Conrad, *Heart of Darkness* (London, 1952), 50. I am indebted to Richard Van Orman for this citation.

142. Governor-General Francisco Carondelet to Marques de Branceforte, New Orleans, 7 June 1796, in Nasatir, *Before Lewis and Clark* 2:440.

143. Jefferson to John Breckinridge, Monticello, 12 August 1803, in JP-DLC.

144. Jefferson to John Holmes, Monticello, 22 April 1820, in JP-DLC.

145. Charles Francis Adams, ed., *Memoirs of John Quincy Adams*, 12 vols. (Philadelphia, 1874–77), 4:438–39.

# 16. Canadian Fur Trade and Exploration of Western North America

1. Cited in Arthur S. Morton, *A History of the Canadian West to 1870–71*, 2d ed. (Toronto, 1973), 48.

2. Edwin Ernest Rich, *Hudson's Bay Company, 1670–1870*, 3 vols. (New York, 1961); Peter C. Newman, *Company of Adventurers*, 2 vols. (New York, 1985–87); Douglas MacKay, *The Honourable Company* (Freeport NY, 1970).

3. Marjorie Wilkins Campbell, *The North West Company* (Toronto, 1957); Gordon Charles Davidson, *The North West Company* (New York, 1918).

4. Theodore J. Karamanski, *Fur Trade and Exploration: Opening the Far Northwest, 1821–1852* (Norman, 1983), xiii. xvi.

5. Barry Gough, *The Northwest Coast: British Navigation, Trade, and Discoveries to 1812* (Vancouver, 1992), is particularly useful for the early phase of nineteenth-century fur trade exploration in the Pacific region; also see James P. Ronda, *Astoria and Empire* (Lincoln, 1990), chap. 1, and William H. Goetzmann, *Exploration and Empire: The Explorer and the Scientist in the Winning of the American West* (New York, 1966).

6. Goetzmann, *Exploration and Empire*, 92.

7. Eric Ross, *Beyond the River and the Bay* (Toronto, 1970), maps and chap. 1; R. Cole Harris and John Warkentin, *Canada before Confederation* (New York, 1974), 232–84.

8. J. B. Tyrrell, ed., *David Thompson's Narrative of His Exploration in Western America, 1784–1812* (Toronto, 1916).

9. The Hudson's Bay Company archives are the most extensive record of Canadian exploration; much of the archival material exists in published form through the auspices of the Hudson's Bay Record Society. A recent historian of the Hudson's Bay Company has noted, "The Hudson's Bay Company is probably the best-documented institution in the world, next to the Vatican" (Newman, *Company of Adventurers* 1:xii).

10. Tyrrell, *David Thompson's Narrative*, 170.

11. Tyrrell, *David Thompson's Narrative*, 170.

12. Tyrrell, *David Thompson's Narrative*, 179.

13. John L. Allen, *Passage through the Garden: Lewis and Clark and the Image of the American Northwest* (Urbana, 1975), 207–8 and n.4.

14. Tyrrell, *David Thompson's Narrative*, 183, 192.

15. Campbell, *The North West Company*, 111.

16. Cited in Campbell, *The North West Company*, 124.

17. Lawrence J. Burpee, *The Search for the Western Sea*, 2 vols. (Toronto, 1908), 2:536; Tyrrell, *David Thompson's Narrative*, 385, 430.

18. Davidson, *The North West Company*, 96.

19. John Warkentin, *The Western Interior of Canada: A Record of Geographical Discovery, 1612–1917* (Toronto, 1964), 105–8; Elliot Coues, ed., *New Light on the Early History of the Greater Northwest: The Manuscript Journals of Alexander Henry, Fur Trader of the Northwest Company, and of David Thompson, Official Geographer and Explorer of the Same Company, 1799–1814*, 2 vols. (New York, 1897), 1:420, 285, 118–19, 297; Daniel Williams Harmon, *A Journal of Voyages and Travels in the Interior of North America* (Andover CT, 1820).

20. Cited in Campbell, *The North West Company*, 174. Daniel Harmon noted in his journal: "It is a curious fact, in the geography of North America, that so many of the lakes and rivers, on the west side of this lofty range of mountains, discharge their waters through one narrow passage, in this great barrier, and eventually enter the North Sea" (Harmon, *Journal of Voyages and Travels*, 191).

21. Cited in Campbell, *The North West Company*, 175.

22. Tyrrell, *David Thompson's Narrative*, 375.

23. Tyrrell, *David Thompson's Narrative*, part 2, chap. 3.

24. Tyrrell, *David Thompson's Narrative*, part 2, 473.

25. Tyrrell, *David Thompson's Narrative*, part 2, 501.

26. Tyrrell, *David Thompson's Narrative*, part 2, lx.

27. Cited in Davidson, *The North West Company*, 101.

28. Ronda, *Astoria and Empire*, 277–301.

29. Washington Irving, *Astoria; or, Anecdotes of an Enterprise beyond the Rocky Mountains* (New York, 1836).

30. Ross Cox, *Adventures on the Columbia River* (London, 1831), 137–38, 147.

31. Alexander Ross, *Adventures of the First Settlers on the Oregon or Columbia River*, vol. 7 of *Early Western Travels*, ed. Reuben Gold Thwaites (Cleveland, 1904), 78, 89, 92, 114, 134, 145.

32. David Lavender, *Land of Giants* (New York, 1958), 110–18.

33. Hiram M. Chittenden, *The American Fur Trade of the Far West*, 2 vols. (1935; reprint, Lincoln, 1986), 1:32–50.

34. Goetzmann, *Exploration and Empire*, 88–89.

35. Richard I. Ruggles, *A Country So Interesting: The Hudson's Bay Company and Two Centuries of Mapping, 1670–1870* (Montreal, 1991), 68.

36. Morton, *History of the Canadian West*, 511.

37. Ruggles, *A Country So Interesting*, 63; John L. Allen, "To Unite the Discoveries: The American Response to the Early Exploration of Rupert's Land," in Richard C. Davis, ed., *Rupert's Land: A Cultural Tapestry* (Waterloo ON, 1988), discusses the relationship between Fidler's maps and the Aaron Arrowsmith productions.

38. Ruggles, *A Country So Interesting*, 64–65.

39. Ruggles, *A Country So Interesting*, 69.

40. Ruggles, *A Country So Interesting*, 70.

41. Cited in Morton, *History of the Canadian West*, 734–35.

42. Goetzmann, *Exploration and Empire*, 92.

43. E. E. Rich, ed., *Peter Skene Ogden's Snake Country Journals*, 5 vols. (London, 1950–61).

44. Gloria G. Kline, *Exploring the Great Basin* (Norman, 1963), 121.

45. Rich, *Snake Country* 1:40.

46. Rich, *Snake Country* 1:50.

47. Rich, *Snake Country* 1:xxx.

48. Rich, *Snake Country* 1:49.

49. Rich, *Snake Country* 1:xxxiii.

50. Rich, *Snake Country* 1:32.

51. Cited in Frederick Merk, ed., *Fur Trade and Empire: George Simpson's Journal . . .* (Cambridge MA, 1931), 275.

52. K. G. Davies, A. M. Johnson, and Dorothy O. Johansen, eds., *Peter Skene Ogden's Snake Country Journal, 1826–27* (London, 1961), 115.

53. Glyndwr Williams, ed., *Peter Skene Ogden's Snake Country Journals, 1827–29* (London, 1971), 3–94.

54. Williams, *Ogden's Snake Country Journals*, 109.

55. Williams, *Ogden's Snake Country Journals*, 119.

56. Williams, *Ogden's Snake Country Journals*, 137.

57. Williams, *Ogden's Snake Country Journals*, Appendix C, 175–81.

58. Goetzmann, *Exploration and Empire*, 98–99.

59. See John L. Allen, "Division of the Waters: Changing Concepts of the Continental Divide, 1804–44," *Journal of Historical Geography* 4 (1978): 362.

60. John Work, *Fur Brigade to the Bonaventura; John Work's California Expedition, 1832–33* (San Francisco, 1945), 9. Work's later travels in the Flathead Lake and Blackfoot country are chronicled in John Work, *The Journal of John Work . . . with an Account of the Fur Trade in the Northwest*, ed. W. S. Lewis and P. C. Phillips (Cleveland, 1923).

61. Work, *Fur Brigade*, xviii.

62. Goetzmann, *Exploration and Empire*, 102–3.

63. Ruggles, *A Country So Interesting*, 74.

64. Ruggles, *A Country So Interesting*, 75.

65. Ruggles, *A Country So Interesting*, 75.

66. Ruggles, *A Country So Interesting*, 75.

67. Ruggles, *A Country So Interesting*, 76.

68. Cited in Ruggles, *A Country So Interesting*, 76.

69. Ruggles, *A Country So Interesting*, 76–77. The Beads-Spencer map is reproduced as plate 31.

70. E. E. Rich, *The Fur Trade and the Northwest to 1857* (Toronto, 1967), 274.

71. Karamanski, *Fur Trade and Exploration*, 58.

72. Merk, *Fur Trade and Empire*, 203.

73. E. E. Rich, ed., *Black's Rocky Mountain Journal, 1824* (London, 1955): see the introduction by R. M. Patterson.

74. Rich, *Black's Rocky Mountain Journal*, 22.

75. Karamanski, *Fur Trade and Exploration*, 76.

76. Rich, *The Fur Trade and the Northwest*, 275.

77. Ruggles, *A Country So Interesting*, 90.

78. Cited in Rich, *The Fur Trade and the Northwest*, 275.

79. Ruggles, *A Country So Interesting*, 96–105, gives a good account of this latter phase of Hudson's Bay Company activities, particularly in the transition between exploring new routes and developing company surveyors as preparers of cadastral charts for settlement purposes.

80. Ruggles, *A Country So Interesting*, 94–95.

81. Cited in Karamanski, *Fur Trade and Exploration*, 41.

82. Cited in R. M. Patterson, "The Nahanny Lands," *Beaver* (summer 1961): 293, 40.

83. Patterson, "The Nahanny Lands," 47.

84. An excellent early scientific account of the upper Liard may be found in R. G. McConnell, "Report on an Exploration in the Yukon and Mackenzie Basins, N.W.T.," *Geological and Natural History Survey of Canada Reports for the Year 1887* (Montreal, 1891).

85. Karamanski, *Fur Trade and Exploration*, 106.

86. Richard Finne, *The Headless Valley*, (New York, 1967), 111.

87. Gloria Griffen Cline, *Peter Skene Ogden and the Hudson's Bay Company* (Norman, 1974), 113–15.

88. E. H. Oliver, ed., *The Canadian North-West: Its Early Development and Legislative Records*, 5 vols. (Ottawa, 1915), 2:692.

89. Cited in Karamanski, *Fur Trade and Exploration*, 125–27.

90. Karamanski, *Fur Trade and Exploration*, 129.

91. Karamanski, *Fur Trade and Exploration*, 129.

92. John W. Todd Jr., ed., *Two Journals of Robert Campbell (Chief Factor, Hudson's Bay Company), 1808 to 1853* (Seattle, 1958), introduction.

93. Todd, *Two Journals of Robert Campbell*, 42.

94. Todd, *Two Journals of Robert Campbell*, 43.

95. Karamanski, *Fur Trade and Exploration*, 154–56.

96. Todd, *Two Journals of Robert Campbell*, 56.

97. See W. Gillies Ross, "Nineteenth-Century Exploration of the Arctic," chapter 19 of this volume.

98. Ruggles, *A Country So Interesting*, 79–80.

99. Ethel G. Stewart, "Fort McPherson and the Peel River Area" (master's thesis, Queen's University, Kingston ON, 1955), 343.

100. Cited in Karamanski, *Fur Trade and Exploration*, 165.

101. Alexander Kennedy Isbister, "Some Account of Peel River, N. America," *Journal of the Royal Geographical Society* 15 (1845): 335–39.

102. Todd, *Two Journals of Robert Campbell*, 58.

103. Todd, *Two Journals of Robert Campbell*, 59.

104. Cited in Clifford Wilson, *Campbell of the Yukon* (Toronto, 1970), 43.

105. Todd, *Two Journals of Robert Campbell*, 61–64.

106. Todd, *Two Journals of Robert Campbell*, 69.

107. G. P. De T. Glazebrook, ed., *The Hargrave Correspondence* (Toronto, 1938), 380–82.

108. Glazebrook, *The Hargrave Correspondence*, 408.

109. Karamanski, *Fur Trade and Exploration*, 223.

110. Cited in Karamanski, *Fur Trade and Exploration*, 224.

111. Henry N. Michael, ed., *Lietuenant Zagoskin's Travels in Russian America, 1842–1844* (Toronto, 1967), 10.

112. Michael, *Lietuenant Zagoskin's Travels*, 183.

113. Cited in Karamanski, *Fur Trade and Exploration*, 233.

114. Karamanski, *Fur Trade and Exploration*, 266.

115. Todd, *Two Journals of Robert Campbell*, 93–123.

116. Karamanski, *Fur Trade and Exploration*, 279.

## 17. The Invention of the American West

1. William H. Goetzmann, *Exploration and Empire: The Explorer and the Scientist in the Winning of the American West* (New York, 1966), 14.

2. Hiram M. Chittenden, *The American Fur Trade of the Far West*, 2 vols. (1935; reprint, Lincoln, 1986); Paul C. Phillips, *The Fur Trade* (Norman, 1961).

3. Goetzmann, *Exploration and Empire*, 4.

4. Bernard DeVoto, *Across the Wide Missouri* (Boston, 1947), 1–6; Goetzmann, *Exploration and Empire*, 78.

5. John L. Allen, *Passage through the Garden: Lewis and Clark and the Image of the American Northwest* (Urbana, 1975), 97–108.

6. "Jefferson's Instructions to Lewis," in Donald Jackson, ed., *Letters of the Lewis and Clark Expedition with Related Documents, 1783–1854* (Urbana, 1962), 61.

7. Donald Jackson, ed., *The Journals of Zebulon Montgomery Pike with Letters and Related Documents*, 2 vols. (Norman, 1966), 2:26.

8. Goetzmann, *Exploration and Empire*, 25.

9. David H. Coyner, *The Lost Trappers: A Collection of Interesting Scenes and Events in the Rocky Mountains* (Cincinnati, 1847).

10. Paul Allen, *History of the Expedition under the Command of Captains Lewis and Clark . . .* , ed. Nicholas Biddle (Philadelphia, 1814).

11. *Niles' Weekly Register*, 9 November 1816, 2:164; Carl I. Wheat, *Mapping the Trans-Mississippi West, 1540–1861*, 5 vols. (Menlo Park CA, 1958–62), 2:63–64.

12. Wheat, *Mapping the Trans-Mississippi West* 2:64.

13. Harrison C. Dale, *The Ashley-Smith Explorations and the Discovery of a Central Route to the Pacific, 1822–1829* (Glendale CA, 1941), 41–42.

14. Dale Morgan, *Jedediah Smith and the Opening of the West* (New York, 1953), 147–48. The primary and best source on the Taos trappers is David J. Weber, *The Taos Trappers: The Fur Trade in the Far Southwest, 1540–1846* (Norman, 1971).

15. Morgan, *Jedediah Smith*, 148.

16. Goetzmann, *Exploration and Empire*, 67.

17. James O. Pattie, *The Personal Narratives of James O. Pattie of Kentucky*, facsimile ed. (Lincoln, 1984). For an excellent treatment of the Pattie saga, see Richard Bateman, *James Pattie's West: The Dream and the Reality* (Norman, 1986).

18. Pattie, *Personal Narratives*, 92.

19. Pattie, *Personal Narratives*, 93.

20. Pattie, *Personal Narratives*, 150.

21. Pattie, *Personal Narratives*, 152.

22. Goetzmann, *Exploration and Empire*, 75–78.

23. William H. Goetzmann, "The Mountain Man as Jacksonian Man," *American Quarterly* 15 (1963): 402–15. An excellent treatment of the economy and ecology of the fur trade during this period is David J. Wishart, *The Fur Trade of the American West, 1807–1840: A Geographical Synthesis* (Lincoln, 1979).

24. Dale, *Ashley-Smith Explorations;* Dale L. Morgan, *The West of William Ashley* (Denver, 1964).

25. Cited in Goetzmann, *Exploration and Empire*, 105. For an excellent treatment of Ashley, see Richard M. Clokey, *William H. Ashley: Enterprise and Politics in the Trans-Mississippi West* (Norman, 1980).

26. Goetzmann, *Exploration and Empire*, 110–25; Dale, *Ashley-Smith Explorations,* 65–165; Morgan, *Jedediah Smith*, 59–174.

27. *Saint Louis Enquirer*, 13 April 1822, 6–7.

28. Dale, *Ashley-Smith Explorations*, 82–87.

29. LeRoy R. Hafen, ed., *The Mountain Men and the Fur Trade of the Far West*, 10 vols. (Glendale CA, 1965–72), 8:331–48.

30. Morgan, *Jedediah Smith*, 23–26.

31. Goetzmann, *Exploration and Empire*, 115.

32. Charles L. Camp, "Jedediah Smith's First Far-Western Exploration," *Western Historical Quarterly* 4 (1973): 151–70.

33. Charles L. Camp, ed., *James Clyman, Frontiersman* (Portland OR, 1960), 25.

34. Dale, *Ashley-Smith Explorations*, 88.

35. Dale, *Ashley-Smith Explorations*, 97.

36. Goetzmann, *Exploration and Empire*, 117.

37. Camp, *James Clyman*, 27.

38. *Arkansas Gazette* (Little Rock), 16 November 1824, 1. This reference was repeated in a number of newspapers shortly after its original publication. Most important of the papers, perhaps, was the nationally circulated *Niles' Weekly Register*, which reprinted the story on 4 December 1824.

39. Dale, *Ashley-Smith Explorations*, 92–101.

40. Dale, *Ashley-Smith Explorations*, 102.

41. Letter from William Marshall Anderson to the *National Intelligencer* (Washington DC), 16 February 1860.

42. *Report to U.S. Congress, May 15, 1826*, by Mr. Baylies, 19th Cong., 1st sess., 1826, H. Doc. 213.

43. Cited in Goetzmann, *Exploration and Empire*, 118.

44. Dale, *Ashley-Smith Explorations*, 99 n.183. See also: Mathew Carey, *General Atlas* (Philadelphia, 1814); John Melish, *Map of the United States . . .* (Philadelphia, 1816); and William Darby, *Map of the United States* (Philadelphia, 1818).

45. Dale, *Ashley-Smith Explorations*, 115–75.

46. Dale, *Ashley-Smith Explorations*, 127.

47. Dale, *Ashley-Smith Explorations*, 132.

48. Dale, *Ashley-Smith Explorations*, 138–39.

49. Dale, *Ashley-Smith Explorations*, 147.

50. Dale, *Ashley-Smith Explorations*, 150.

51. Dale, *Ashley-Smith Explorations*, 150–51.

52. Dale, *Ashley-Smith Explorations*, 151.

53. Dale, *Ashley-Smith Explorations*, 162.

54. Dale, *Ashley-Smith Explorations*, 134–35.

55. Dale, *Ashley-Smith Explorations*, 192.

56. Goetzmann, *Exploration and Empire*, 130–41; Morgan, *Jedediah Smith*, 193–317; George R. Brooks, *The Southwest Expedition of Jedediah Smith: His Personal Account of the Journey to California, 1826–27* (Glendale CA, 1977); Harvey L. Carter, "Jedediah Smith," in Hafen, *Mountain Men and the Fur Trade* 8:331–48; Maurice S. Sullivan, ed., *The Travels of Jedediah Smith* (Santa Ana CA, 1934).

57. Morgan, *Jedediah Smith*, 335.

58. Brooks, *Southwest Expedition of Jedediah Smith*, 36–37.

59. Brooks, *Southwest Expedition of Jedediah Smith*, 47.

60. Carter, "Jedediah Smith," 338.

61. Brooks, *Southwest Expedition of Jedediah Smith*, 77.

62. Brooks, *Southwest Expedition of Jedediah Smith*, 77–78.

63. Brooks, *Southwest Expedition of Jedediah Smith*, 98.

64. "Harrison Roger's Journal," in Morgan, *Jedediah Smith*, 198–228. See also David J. Weber, ed., *The Californios versus Jedediah Smith, 1826–1827: A New Cache of Documents* (Spokane, 1990).

65. Brooks, *Southwest Expedition of Jedediah Smith*, 149.

66. Brooks, *Southwest Expedition of Jedediah Smith*, 178.

67. Brooks, *Southwest Expedition of Jedediah Smith*, 184.

68. Brooks, *Southwest Expedition of Jedediah Smith*, 193.

69. Sullivan, *Travels of Jedediah Smith*, 26.

70. Goetzmann, *Exploration and Empire*, 137.

71. *Message . . . Relative . . . to the British Establishments on the Columbia and the State of the Fur Trade*, 21st Cong., 2d sess., 1831, S. Doc. 39.

72. Dale Morgan and Carl I. Wheat, *Jedediah Smith and His Maps of the American West* (San Francisco, 1954), 78–79.

73. Goetzmann, *Exploration and Empire*, 130.

74. Cf. *Missouri Republican* (Saint Louis), 11 October 1827, 1, and *Saratoga Springs (N.Y.) Sentinel* 9, no. 28 (1827): 2.

75. Morgan, *Jedediah Smith*, 343–48.

76. Goetzmann, *Exploration and Empire*, 130.

77. Wheat, *Mapping the Trans-Mississippi West*, vol. 3.

78. Wheat, *Mapping the Trans-Mississippi West* 2:151.

79. Albert Gallatin, "Synopsis of the Indian Tribes . . . ," in *Transactions of the American Antiquarian Society* 2 (1836).

80. Wheat, *Mapping the Trans-Mississippi West* 2: map no. 422.

81. Cited in Goetzmann, *Exploration and Empire*, 139–40.

82. *Niles' Weekly Register*, 6 October 1827.

83. DeVoto, *Across the Wide Missouri*, 5.

84. Chittenden, *American Fur Trade* 1:399; Goetzmann, *Exploration and Empire*, 148–50; DeVoto, *Across the Wide Missouri*, 58–60.

85. Goetzmann, *Exploration and Empire*, 150.

86. Washington Irving, *Astoria; or, Anecdotes of an Enterprise beyond the Rocky Mountains* (New York, 1836).

87. Washington Irving, *The Rocky Mountains: or, Scenes, Incidents, and Adventures in the Far West*, 2 vols. (Philadelphia, 1837).

88. F. G. Young, ed., "The Correspondence and Journals of Captain Nathaniel J. Wyeth, 1831–36," *Sources of the History of Oregon* (Eugene, 1899).

89. The account of Bonneville's travels is taken from Irving, *The Rocky Mountains*.

90. Goetzmann, *Exploration and Empire*, 150.

91. Zenas Leonard, *Narrative of the Adventures of Zenas Leonard* (Clearfield PA, 1839), 64–65.

92. The account of the Walker expedition is taken from Leonard, *Narrative*.

93. Leonard, *Narrative*, 35.

94. Leonard, *Narrative*, 47.

95. Leonard, *Narrative*, 69.

96. The most accessible version of Irving's work is the reprint edition, edited by Edgely Todd: *The Adventures of Captain Bonneville* (Norman, 1962).

97. John L. Allen, "Horizons of the Sublime: The Invention of the Romantic West," *Journal of Historical Geography* 18 (1992).

98. DeVoto, *Across the Wide Missouri*, 61–62.

99. Hall Jackson Kelley, *A Geographical Sketch of That Part of North America Called Oregon* (Boston, 1830), 4.

100. John B. Wyeth, *Oregon; or, A Short History of a Long Journey*, vol. 21 of *Early Western Travels*, ed. Reuben Gold Thwaites (Cleveland, 1905); John K. Townsend, *Narrative of a Journey across the Rocky Mountains to the Columbia River*, vol. 21 of *Early Western Travels*, ed. Thwaites.

101. Goetzmann, *Exploration and Empire*, 165.

102. Warren Angus Ferris, *Life in the Rocky Mountains* (Denver, 1940), first published in *Western Literary Messenger*, April–May 1844, citation from 4 May 1844, 4.

103. John Bidwell, *Journey to California* (San Francisco, 1937); George Stewart, *The California Trail* (New York, 1962).

104. Mae Reed Porter and Odessa Davenport, *Scotsman in Buckskins: Sir William Drummond Stewart and the Rocky Mountain Fur Trade* (New York, 1963); Sir William Drummond Stewart, *Altowan: or, Incidents of Life and Adventure in the Rocky Mountains*, 2 vols. (New York, 1846).

105. Alexander Maximilian, Prince of Wied, *Travels in the Interior of North America*, 2 vols., vols. 22–24 of *Early Western Travels*, ed. Thwaites (1906).

106. Samuel Parker, *Journal of an Exploring Tour beyond the Rocky Mountains* (Ithaca NY, 1838), 142.

107. William H. Goetzmann, *The West as Romantic Horizon* (Lincoln, 1981); William H. Goetzmann and William N. Goetzmann, *The West of the Imagination* (New York, 1986), 44–68; David C. Hunt and Marsha Gallagher, *Karl Bodmer's America* (Omaha, 1984); Marvin C. Ross, *The West of Alfred Jacob Miller* (Norman, 1968); Ron Tyler, ed., *Alfred Jacob Miller: Artist on the Oregon Trail* (Fort Worth, 1982).

108. Irving, *The Rocky Mountains* 1:191.

109. Irving, *The Rocky Mountains* 1:191.

110. [Matthew Field], *Prairie and Rocky Mountains Sketches*, ed. Kate L. Gregg and John F. McDermott (Norman, 1957).

111. Stewart, *Altowan* 1:122.

112. Stewart, *Altowan* 1:247.

113. Goetzmann, *Romantic Horizon*, 11–27.

114. Maximilian, *Travels in North America* 1:12.

115. Maximilian, *Travels in North America* 2:78.

116. William Goetzmann, introduction to Hunt and Gallagher, *Karl Bodmer's America*, 3.

117. George Catlin, *Letters and Notes on the Manner, Customs, and Condition of the North American Indians* (London, 1841), 60. See also William H. Truettner, *The Natural Man Observed: A Study of Catlin's Indian Gallery* (Washington DC, 1979).

118. Goetzmann and Goetzmann, *The West of the Imagination*, 19.

119. Catlin, *Letters and Notes*, 172.

120. Gouverneur K. Warren, *Memoir to Accompany the Map of the Territory of the United States from the Mississippi to the Pacific Ocean . . .* , 33d Cong., 2d sess., 1859, S. Doc. 78, 19.

121. J. J. Abert, "Practicable Route for Wheeled Vehicles across the Rocky Mountains" (manuscript, Missouri Historical Society, Saint Louis, 1843).

122. Wheat, *Mapping the Trans-Mississippi West* 2:169, map no. 441.

123. Osborne Russell, *Journal of a Trapper; or, Nine Years in the Rocky Mountains* (Lincoln, 1965), 127–28.

124. Catlin, *Letters and Notes*, 62.

## 18. Nature's Gullivers and Crusoes

1. Passages quoted from the Jonathan Swift, *Gulliver's Travels*, Bantam classic ed. (New York, 1986), 93–95, 116–17, 147, 180–84.

2. Hew Strachan, "The Early Victorian Army and the Nineteenth-Century Revolution in Government," *English Historical Review* 95 (1980): 782–809; Peter Burroughs, "The Ordnance Department and Colonial Defence, 1821–1855," *Journal of Imperial and Commonwealth History* 10 (1982): 125–49.

3. Passages quoted from Daniel Defoe, *Robinson Crusoe*, Penguin classics ed. (Hammondsworth, U.K., 1986), 85–86, 90, 93, 95, 98, 112–14, 121, 134–35.

4. For an early example of soldiers' interest in natural history, see Major General Thomas Davies, "An Account of the Jumping Mouse of Canada," *Linnean Society Transactions* 4 (1798): 155–57. Such accounts were widely reprinted. On Traill, see Michael A. Petermann's entry in *Dictionary of Canadian Biography* (Toronto, 1966–90), 12:996–97.

5. Robert M. Young, "Natural Theology, Victorian Periodicals, and the Fragmentation of a Common Context," *Darwin's Metaphor: Nature's Place in Victorian Culture* (Cambridge, U.K., 1985), 126–63; David N. Livingstone, "The History of Science and the History of Geography: Interactions and Implications," *History of Science* 22 (1984): 271–302; A. B. McKillop, *A Disciplined Intelligence: Critical Inquiry and Canadian Thought in the Victorian Era* (Montreal, 1979), chaps. 2–3; Carl Berger, *Science, God, and Nature in Victorian Canada* (Toronto, 1983), chaps. 1–2; William Lauder Lindsay, "The Place and Power of Natural History in Colonisation," *Edinburgh New Philosophical Journal* 18 (1863): 145; Richard Yeo, "An Idol of the Market-Place: Baconianism in Nineteenth-Century Britain," *History of Science* 23 (1985): 251–98.

6. David Daiches, Peter Jones, and Jean Jones, eds., *A Hotbed of Genius: The Scottish Enlightenment, 1730–1790* (Edinburgh, U.K., 1986); Roy Porter, "The Industrial Revolution and the Rise of the Science of Geology," in M. Teich and R. Young, eds., *Changing Perspectives in the History of Science* (London, 1973), 320–43.

7. R. J. Harvey-Gibson, *Outlines of the History of Botany* (London, 1919), 88; W. B. Turrill, *Joseph Dalton Hooker* (London, 1963), 10; A. G. Morton, *History of Botanical Science* (London, 1981), 432–33; David Goodman, "Button's *Histoire naturelle* as a Work of the Enlightenment," in J. D. North and J. J. Roche, eds., *The Light of Nature* (Dordrecht, 1985), 57–64.

8. A. M. Lysaght, *Joseph Banks in Newfoundland and Labrador, 1766* (London, 1971), 36–37; David Mackay, "A Presiding Genius of Exploration: Banks, Cook, and Empire, 1767–1805," in Robin Fisher and Hugh Johnston, eds., *Captain James Cook and His Times* (Vancouver BC, 1979), 23, 27; H. C. Cameron, *Sir Joseph Banks* (London, 1952), 63; Lucile Brockway, *Science and Colonial Expansion: The Role of the British Royal*

*Botantic Gardens* (London, 1979); Alexander von Humboldt, *Personal Narrative* (1807), ed. and trans. Thomasina Ross, 3 vols. (1814–26; reprint, London, 1907), 1:ix. On "Humboldtian science," see Susan Faye Cannon, *Science in Culture: The Early Victorian Period* (New York, 1978), esp. chap. 2.

9. Roy Porter, *The Making of Geology: Earth Science in Britain, 1600–1815* (Cambridge, U.K., 1977), 152, 171–73 n. 5; Anand D. Chitnis, "The University of Edinburgh's Natural History Museum and the Huttonian-Wernerian Debate," *Annals of Science* 26 (1970): 85–94.

10. Joan M. Eyles, "Jameson, Robert," in *Dictionary of Scientific Biography* (London, 1960–86), 7:69–71; "Biographical Memoir of the Late Professor Jameson," *Edinburgh New Philosophical Journal* 57 (1854): 5; John Challinor, "The Progress of British Geology during the Early Part of the Nineteenth Century," *Annals of Science* 26 (1970), 187–88; Jessie M. Sweet, "Robert Jameson and the Explorers," part 1, *Annals of Science* 31 (1974): 21–47.

11. John Warkentin, *The Western Interior of Canada: A Record of Geographical Discovery* (Toronto, 1964); Lawrence J. Burpee, "David Thompson: A Great Land Geographer," *Canadian Geographical Journal* 30 (May 1945): 238–39; John Warkentin, "David Thompson's Geology: A Document," *Journal of the West* 6 (July 1967): 468–90, esp. 476, 481–82, of the reprinted document.

12. R. B. Thomson, "A Sketch of the Past Fifty Years of Canadian Botany," in Royal Society of Canada, *Fifty Years Retrospect* (n.p., 1932), 173; Joseph Kastner, *A World of Naturalists* (London, 1977), 210, 259; William H. Goetzman, *Exploration and Empire: The Explorer and the Scientist in the Winning of the American West* (New York, 1966), 182; C. U. Hay, "John Goldie, Botanist," *Royal Society of Canada Transactions*, 2d ser., 3, sec. 4 (1897): 125–30.

13. Andrew H. Clark, "Titus Smith, Junior, and the Geography of Nova Scotia in 1801 and 1802," *Annals of the Association of American Geographers* 44 (1954): 291–314; Eville Gorham, "Titus Smith: A Pioneer of Plant Ecology in North America," *Ecology* 36 (1955): 116–23; William Smith, "Some Account of the Life of Titus Smith," *Nova Scotia Institute of Natural Science Proceedings and Transactions* 1 (1866): 152; Titus Smith Jr., "A Lecture on the Mineralogy [and the Geology] of Nova Scotia," *Magazine of Natural History* 9 (1836): 371–72, 575, 577, 582–86, 592–93; Titus Smith Jr. "Conclusions on the Results on the Vegetation of Nova Scotia," *Magazine of Natural History* 8 (1835): 641–42; Titus Smith Jr., "On the Operations of Fungi in Disintegrating Vegetable Substances," *Halifax Monthly Magazine* 1 (1830–31): 339–42; Titus Smith Jr. "A List of the Principal Indigenous Plants of Nova Scotia," *Halifax Monthly Magazine*, 1 (1830–31): 342–45.

14. Henry Steinhauer, "Notice Relative to the Geology of the Coast of Labrador,"

*Geological Society of London Transactions* 2 (1814): 488–94; Augustus C. Thompson, *Moravian Missions* (New York, 1890), 218.

15. [John Barrow], review of *Narrative of a Voyage to Hudsons Bay*, by Lieut. William Chappell, R.N., *Quarterly Review* (October 1817): 199–200; John E. Caswell, "Canadian Arctic Exploration," part 1, *Beaver* 299 (1969): 4–13, part 2, 300 (1969): 38–45, part 3, 300 (1969): 26; Glyndwr Williams, *The British Search for the Northwest Passage in the Eighteenth Century* (London, 1962); L. P. Kirwan, *The White Road: A Survey of Polar Exploration* (London, 1959), esp. chaps. 1–5.

16. [Barrow], review of Chappell, 199–203.

17. [Barrow], review of Chappell, 204–5.

18. [Barrow], review of Chappell, 222–23.

19. Tom and Cordelia Stamp, *William Scoresby: Arctic Scientist* (Whitby ON, [1976]), chap. 7; Kirwan, *White Road*, 75–79; William Scoresby, "On Some Circumstances Connected with the Original Suggestion of the Modern Arctic Expedition," *Edinburgh New Philosophical Journal* 20 (1836): 93–100; Anita McConnell, "The Scientific Life of William Scoresby Jr.," *Annals of Science* 43 (1986): 257–86; Sweet, "Jameson and the Explorers," 22–26.

20. Caswell, "Canadian Arctic Exploration," part 3, 27–28; [Barrow], review of Chappell, 365–66.

21. [Barrow], review of Chappell, 213.

22. Ernest S. Dodge, *The Polar Rosses: John and James Clark Ross and Their Expeditions* (London, 1973), 71, 73; John Ross, *A Description of the Deep Sea Clamms, Hydraphorus, and Marine Artificial Horizon* (London, 1819); John Ross, *A Voyage of Discovery, Made under the Orders of the Admiralty, in His Majesty's Ships Isabella and Alexander, for the Purpose of Exploring Baffin's Bay, and Inquiring into the Probability of a North-west Passage* (London, 1819); Alexander Fisher, *Journal of a Voyage of Discovery to the Arctic Regions, in His Majesty's Ships Hecla and Griper, in the Years 1819 & 1820* (London, 1821); [Edmund Jameson], "Account of the Expedition to Baffin's Bay," *Edinburgh Philosophical Journal* 1 (1819): 154; Sweet, "Jameson and the Explorers," 41–44.

23. Dodge, *Polar Rosses*, chap. 4; Edward Sabine, *Remarks on the Account of the Late Voyage of Discovery to Baffin's Bay* (London, 1819); John Ross, *An Explanation of Captain Sabine's Remarks* (London, 1819).

24. Joseph Sabine, "An Account of a New Species of Gull," *Linnean Society Transactions* 12 (1818): 520–23; Joseph Sabine, "An Account of the Esquimaux," *Quarterly Journal of Science, Literature, and Art* 7 (1819): 72–94; Joseph Sabine, "Observations on the Dip and Variation of the Magnetic Needle, and on the Intensity of the Magnetic Force," *Royal Society of London Philosophical Transactions* 109 (1819): 132–44; Ian R. Stone, "Profile: Edward Sabine, Polar Scientist, 1788–1883," *Polar Record* 22 (1984): 305–9.

25. Joseph Sabine, "An Account of Experiments to Determine the Acceleration of the Pendulum in Different Latitudes," *Royal Society of London Philosophical Transactions* 111 (1821): 176–90. On Hansteen, see *Edinburgh Philosophical Journal* 3 (1820): 124–38 and 4 (1820–21): 114–24; [Christopher Hansteen], "On the Number and Situation of the Magnetic Poles of the Earth," *Edinburgh Philosophical Journal* 12 (1825): 328–34; [Christopher Hansteen], "Observation on the Position and Revolution of the Magnetic Poles of the Earth," *Edinburgh Philosophical Journal* 5 (1826): 65–71; Edward Sabine, "Contributions to Terrestrial Magnetism," *Royal Society of London Philosophical Transactions* 136, part 3 (1846): 237–55.

26. W. J. Hooker, "On the Botany of America," *Edinburgh Journal of Science* 2 (1825): 108–29, also published in *American Journal of Science and Arts* 9 (1825): 263–84.

27. William Scoresby, *An Account of the Arctic Regions with a History and Description of the Northern Whale-Fishery*, 2 vols. (1820; reprint, New York, 1969).

28. Alexander von Humboldt, "New Inquiries into the Laws Which Are Observed in the Distribution of Vegetable Forms," *Edinburgh Philosophical Journal* 7 (1822): 47–55; Malcolm Nicholson, "Alexander von Humboldt, Humboldtian Science, and the Origins of the Study of Vegetation," *History of Science* 25 (1987): 167–94; M. J. Bowen, "Mind and Nature: The Physical Geography of Alexander von Humboldt," *Scottish Geographical Magazine* 86 (1970): 222–23.

29. Robert E. Johnson, *Sir John Richardson: Arctic Explorer, Natural Historian, Naval Surgeon* (New York, 1976); John McIlraith, *Life of Sir John Richardson* (London, 1868); C. Stuart Houston, ed., *Arctic Ordeal: The Journal of John Richardson, Surgeon-naturalist with Franklin, 1820–1822* (Kingston, 1984); John Richardson, "General View of the Geognostical Structure of the Country Extending from Hudson's Bay to the Shores of the Polar Sea," *Edinburgh Philosophical Journal* 9 (1823): 372–76; John Franklin, *Narrative of a Journey to the Shores of the Polar Sea* (1825; reprint, Edmonton AB, 1969), appendix 1.

30. Franklin, *Narrative*, appendices 5, 6, 7; Houston, *Arctic Ordeal*, 197–200; William Edward Parry, *Journal of a Second Voyage for the Discovery of a North-West Passage from the Atlantic to the Pacific in the Years 1821–22–23, in His Majesty's Ships Fury and Hecla . . .* (London, 1824), appendix.

31. Franklin, *Narrative*, appendix 1, 497–99, 534–37; Houston, *Arctic Ordeal*, xxvii; McIlraith, *Richardson*, chap. 14.

32. W. E. Parry, "Analysis of Scientific Books and Memoirs: *Journal of a Second Voyage*," *Edinburgh Journal of Science* 1 (1824): 154–55; [W. E. Parry], "A Concise Statement of the Magnetical and Other Philosophical Experiments and Observations Made during the Recent Northern Expedition under Captains Parry and Hoppner, 1824–5," *Edinburgh Philosophical Journal* 14 (1826): 345–46; [W. E. Parry], "Notice of Captain

Parry's Last Expedition to the Arctic Regions in 1824 and 1825," *Edinburgh Journal of Science* 4 (1826): 147.

33. [Parry], "Notice of Captain Parry's Last Expedition," 150; Suzanne Zeller, *Inventing Canada: Early Victorian Science and the Idea of a Transcontinental Nation* (Toronto, 1987), 186–89; Robert Jameson, "General Observations on the Former and Present Geological Condition of the Countries Discovered by Captains Parry and Ross," *Edinburgh New Philosophical Journal* 2 (1827), 105–6. For the importance of the concept of uniformity, see W. H. Fitton, "Presidential Address," *Geological Society of London Proceedings* 1 (1828–29): 125; cf. Scoresby, *Account of the Arctic Regions* 2:123–26, and Thomas Latta, "Observations on the Arctic Sea and Ice," *Edinburgh New Philosophical Journal* 2 (1827): esp. 92–93.

34. John Franklin, *Narrative of a Second Expedition to the Shores of the Polar Sea* (1829; reprint, Edmonton AB, 1971), 56, appendix 1; John Warkentin, *Geological Lectures by Dr. John Richardson, 1825–26*, National Museums of Canada Syllogeus, no. 22 (Ottawa, 1979); John Richardson, "Intelligence from the Land Arctic Expedition," *Edinburgh New Philosophical Journal* 1 (1826): 161–66; John Richardson, "Overland Arctic Expedition," *Edinburgh New Philosophical Journal* 2 (1827): 161–63; John Richardson, "Account of the Expedition under Captain Franklin," *Edinburgh Journal of Science* 6 (1827): 107–17.

35. Franklin, *Narrative of a Journey*, xxviii and appendices 2–7; John Richardson, "On the Aurora Borealis," *Edinburgh New Philosophical Journal* 5 (1828): 241–43; John Richardson, "Account of the Expedition under Captain Franklin, and of the Vegetation of North America," *Edinburgh Journal of Science* 6 (1827): 110–13; Frederick W. Beechey, *Narrative of a Voyage to the Pacific and Bering's Strait*, 2 vols. (1845; reprint, Bibliotheca Australiana no. 34, Amsterdam, 1969), 1:xvi–xvii; Barry M. Gough, ed., *To the Pacific and Arctic with Beechey* (Cambridge, U.K., 1973), 44–49.

36. Harold R. Fletcher, *The Story of the Royal Horticultural Society* (London, 1969), 9, 16, 27, 100; William Morwood, *Traveller in a Vanished Landscape* (London, 1973), 11, 21; Franklin, *Narrative of a Second Expedition*, 314–15; "Notice Respecting Mr. Scouler's and Mr. Douglas's Recent Voyage to the North-West Coast of America," *Edinburgh Journal of Science* 5 (1826): 378–79; "Account of the Expedition under Captain Franklin," *Edinburgh Journal of Science* 6 (1827): 113–17; A. Grace Gray, "David Douglas," *Beaver* 268/2 (1938): 27–29; J. W. Eastham, "A Note on Archibald Menzies and David Douglas, Botanists," *British Columbia Historical Quarterly* 12 (1948): 247–48.

37. Franklin, *Narrative of a Second Expedition*, appendix 1, liii–liv. The International Boundary Commission also recorded magnetic variation on the Great Lakes: see *Edinburgh Journal of Science* 2 (1825): 366; Jeremiah Bigsby, "Outline of the Mineralogy, Geology, &c. of Malbay, in Lower Canada," *American Journal of Science* 5

(1822): 205–22; [Jeremiah Bigsby], "Notes on the Geography and Geology of Lake Huron," *Geological Society of London Transactions*, ser. 2, part 2 (1824), 175–209; [Jeremiah Bigsby], "Sketch of the Geology of the Island of Montreal," *Lyceum of Natural History of New York Annals* 1 (1825): 198–219; [Jeremiah Bigsby], "Notes on the Geography and Geology of Lake Superior," *Quarterly Journal of Science* 18 (1825): 1–34, 228–67; [Jeremiah Bigsby], "On the Geology of Quebec and Its Vicinity," *Geological Society of London Proceedings* (1827–28), 37–38; Fitton, "Presidential Address," 125; G. B. Morey, "Early Geologic Studies in the Lake Superior Region: The Contributions of H. R. Schoolcraft, J. J. Bigsby, and H. W. Bayfield," *Earth Sciences History* 8 (1989): 38–39.

38. Morey, "Early Geologic Studies," 40; cf. also H. W. Bayfield, "Outlines of the Geology of Lake Superior," *Literary and Historical Society of Quebec Transactions* 1 (1829): 2, 42–43; Neil C. Hultin, "Captain Bayfield, Some Admiralty Clerks, and the Naming of Islands," *Ontario History* 78 (1986): 48–56; Roy F. Fleming, "Charting the Great Lakes," *Canadian Geographical Journal* 12 (1936): 69–77; Don W. Thomson, *Men and Meridians* (Ottawa, 1966), 186–87.

39. J. J. Bigsby, "On the Utility and Design of the Science of Geology," *Canadian Review and Literary and Historical Journal* 2 (1824); "Review of William Bell, *Hints to Emigrants*," *Canadian Review and Literary and Historical Journal* 1 (1825): 287.

40. Thomas Bender, *New York Intellect* (Baltimore, 1987), 39; Thomas C. Haliburton, *History of Nova Scotia*, vol. 2 (1829; reprint, Belleville NS, 1973), 405–13; Allan C. Dunlop, "The Pictou Literary and Scientific Society," *Nova Scotia Historical Quarterly* 3 (June 1973): 99–116; Marjorie Whitelaw, ed., *The Dalhousie Journals*, vol. 1 (n.p., 1978), 7; Richard Jarrell, "The Rise and Decline of Science at Quebec, 1824–1844," *Historie sociale* 9 (1977): 77–91.

41. Zeller, *Inventing Canada*, 19–22.

42. Donald C. Macleod, "Miners, Mining Men, and Mining Reform: Changing the Technology of Nova Scotian Coal Mines and Collieries, 1858–1910" (Ph.D. diss., University of Toronto, 1981), 301–4; see also Fitton, "Presidential Address," 133.

43. W. E. Cormack, "Account of a Journey across the Island of Newfoundland," *Edinburgh Philosophical Journal* 10 (1823–24): 156–62; W. E. Cormack, "Civilization of the Aborigines of Newfoundland," *Edinburgh New Philosophical Journal* 4 (1828): 205–6; "Report of Mr. W. E. Cormack's Journey in Search of the Red Indians in Newfoundland," *Edinburgh New Philosophical Journal* 6 (1828–29): 318–29; see also Patrick O'Flaherty, *The Rock Observed* (Toronto, 1979), 42–48.

44. John Richardson, *Fauna Boreali-Americana*, 4 vols. (London, 1829–37), 1:xi–xix (1829), 2:xvii (1831); W. J. Hooker, *Flora Boreali-Americana*, 2 vols. (London, 1833–40), 1:39 (1833), 2:205 (1834). Edinburgh too continued to function as an important center for immigrants interested in collecting plants; cf. Catharine Parr Traill, *The Back-*

*woods of Canada* (1836; reprint, Toronto, 1980), 91–92; see also Steven Shapin, "Nibbling at the Teats of Science: Edinburgh and the Diffusion of Science in the 1830s," *Metropolis and Province: Science in British Culture, 1780–1850* (Philadelphia, 1983).

45. On quinarianism, see Philip F. Rehbock, *The Philosophical Naturalists* (Madison, 1983), 26–28; Mary P. Winsor, *Starfish, Jellyfish, and the Order of Life* (New Haven, 1976), 82–87; David Knight, "William Swainson: Types, Circles, and Affinities," in North and Roche, *The Light of Nature*, 83–94. The clearest contemporary explication was William Swainson, *A Treatise on the Geography and Classification of Animals* (London, 1835), 196–348.

46. Adrian Desmond, "The Making of Institutional Zoology in London, 1822–1836," *History of Science* 23 (1985): part 1, 153–85, part 2, 22–50; Mario A. Di Gregorio, "In Search of the Natural System: Problems of Zoological Classification in Victorian Britain," *History and Philosophy of the Life Sciences* 4 (1982): 225–54; Richardson, *Fauna* 2:xvii, xi; "New Publications: Fauna Boreali-Americana; or, The Zoology of the Northern Parts of British America, Part Second—The Birds," *Edinburgh New Philosophical Journal* 12 (1831–32): 393, 395.

47. John Richardson et al., *The Zoology of Captain Beechey's Voyage*, 2 vols. (London, 1832, 1841); George Back, *Narrative of the Arctic Land Expedition* (1836; reprint, Edmonton AB, 1970), appendices; Richard King, *Narrative of a Journey to the Shores of the Arctic Ocean*, 2 vols. (London, 1836); Hugh N. Wallace, *The Navy, the Company, and Richard King: British Exploration in the Canadian Arctic, 1829–1860* (Montreal, 1980).

48. Richardson, *Fauna* 1:xix; Suzanne Zeller, "The Spirit of Bacon: Science and Self-Perception in the Hudson's Bay Company, 1830–1870," *Scientia Canadensis* 13 (fall/winter 1989): 79–101; William Fraser Tolmie, *Physician and Fur Trader* (Vancouver, 1963), 11, 387; Jean Murray Cole, *Exile in the Wilderness: The Biography of Chief Factor Archibald McDonald, 1790–1853* (Don Mills ON, 1979), 175, 209–11.

49. William Sheppard, "Notes on Some of the Plants of Lower Canada," *Literary and Historical Society of Quebec Transactions* 3 (1837): 39–40; Harriet Sheppard, "Notes on Some of the Canadian Song Birds," *Literary and Historical Society of Quebec Transactions* 3 (1837): 222; A. Benedict, "On the Vegetation of the Ottawa and Some of Its Tributaries (L. Canada)," *American Journal of Science and the Arts* 18 (1830): 352.

50. "New Army Regulations in Regard to Natural History and Botany," *Edinburgh New Philosophical Journal* 14 (1833): 208; Charles Lyell, "Presidential Address," *Geological Society of London Proceedings* 2 (1837): 381–82; Stephen Jay Gould, *Time's Arrow, Time's Cycle*, Jerusalem-Harvard Lectures (Cambridge MA, 1987); Porter, *Making of Geology*, 129; D. R. Oldroyd, "Historicism and the Rise of Historical Geology," part 1, *History of Science* 17 (1979): 242–46.

51. Robert A. Stafford, "Geological Surveys, Mineral Discoveries, and British Expansion, 1835–71," *Journal of Imperial and Commonwealth History* 12 (May 1984): 5–32;

James A. Secord, "King of Siluria: Roderick Murchison and the Imperial Theme in Nineteenth-Century British Geology," *Victorian Studies* 25 (1982): 413–42; Robert Stafford, *Scientist of Empire: Sir Roderick Murchison, Scientific Exploration, and Victorian Imperialism* (Cambridge, U.K., 1989).

52. Zeller, *Inventing Canada*, 23–28.

53. C. T. Jackson and F. Alger, *Remarks on the Geology and Mineralogy of the Peninsula of Nova Scotia* (Cambridge MA, 1833); Abraham Gesner, *Remarks on the Geology and Mineralogy of Nova Scotia* (Halifax NS, 1836); L. M. Cumming, "Abraham Gesner (1797–1864): Author, Inventor, and Pioneer Canadian Geologist," *Geological Association of Canada Proceedings* 23 (1971): 5–10. For an interesting use of geological theory for political ends, see Alex McEwen, ed., *In Search of the Highlands: Mapping the Canada-Maine Boundary, 1839* (Fredericton NB, 1988), 107. See also Alfred Goldsworthy Bailey, ed., *The Letters of James and Ellen Robb* (Fredericton NB, 1983), xxv.

54. John B. Jukes, "Report on the Geology of Newfoundland [1839]," reprinted in *Edinburgh New Philosophical Journal* 29 (1840): 103–111; J. B. Jukes, *Excursions in and about Newfoundland*, 2 vols. (London, 1842), 1:vii, 2–3; J. B. Jukes, *General Report of the Geological Survey of Newfoundland* (London, 1843), 152.

55. For an elaboration of this argument, see Zeller, *Inventing Canada*, chap. 2.

56. David Philip Miller, "The Revival of the Physical Sciences in Britain, 1815–1840," *Osiris*, 2d ser., 2 (1986): 126, 127–29, 134; John Cawood, "The Magnetic Crusade: Science and Politics in Early Victorian Britain," *Isis* 70 (1979): 493–518.

57. James Clark Ross, "On the Position of the North Magnetic Pole," *Royal Society of London Philosophical Transactions* 124 (1834): 47–51; Sir John Ross, *Narrative of a Second Voyage in Search of a North-West Passage*, 2 vols. (1835; reprint, New York, 1969), 2: appendices.

58. John Richardson, "Notice of a Few Observations Which It is Desirable to Make on the Frozen Soil of British North America," *Edinburgh New Philosophical Journal* 30 (1841): 117–20; Richardson, "Note on the Best Points, in British North America, for Making Observations on the Temperature of the Air," *Royal Geographical Society Journal* 9 (1839): 121–24.

59. Edward Gibbon, *The History of the Decline and Fall of the Roman Empire*, 3 vols. (London, 1791), 1:347–48; Kenneth Kelly, "The Changing Attitude of Farmers to Forest in 19th-Century Ontario," *Ontario Geography* 1 (1974): 64–67; William Kelly, "On the Effect of Clearing and Cultivation on Climate," *Literary and Historical Society of Quebec Transactions* 3 (1837): 309; see also William Kelly, "Abstract of the Meterological Journal," *Literary and Historical Society of Quebec Transactions* 3 (1837): 46–65, and William Kelly, "On the Temperature, Fogs, and Mirages of the River St. Lawrence," *Literary and Historical Society of Quebec Transactions* 3 (1837): 1–45.

60. Zeller, *Inventing Canada*, 125–29; see also Trevor H. Levere, "Magnetic Instru-

ments in the Canadian Arctic Expedition of Franklin, Lefroy, and Nares," *Annals of Science* 43 (1986): 63–67.

61. Zeller, *Inventing Canada*; John H. Lefroy, "Barometric and Thermometric Measurements of Heights in North America," *Royal Geographical Society Journal* 16 (1846): 292; see also Francis Walker, "Descriptions of Some Chalcidite of North America," *Annals and Magazine of Natural History* 14 (1844): 14–18, 331–41, 407–10.

62. John H. Lefroy, *Autobiography*, ed. Lady Lefroy (London, [1896]), 104; Richardson, "Notice of a Few Observations," 110–22; John Richardson, "On the Cultivation of the Cereals in the High Latitudes of North America," *Edinburgh New Philosophical Journal* 30 (1841): 123–24; John Richardson, "Register of the Temperature of the Atmosphere, Kept at Fort Simpson, North America," *Edinburgh New Philosophical Journal* 30 (1841): 124–26; John Richardson, "Observations on Solar Radiation, Made at Fort Franklin," *Edinburgh New Philosophical Journal* 30 (1841): 240–51; John Richardson, "Observations on the Progress of the Seasons as Affecting Animals and Vegetables at Martin's Falls," *Edinburgh New Philosophical Journal* 30 (1841): 252–56.

63. Zeller, *Inventing Canada*, 140.

64. "The Arctic Expedition under the Command of Sir John Franklin," *Annals and Magazine of Natural History* 16 (1845): 163–66; John Lefroy and John Richardson, *Magnetical and Meteorological Observations at Lake Athabasca and Fort Simpson and at Fort Confidence, in Great Bear Lake* (London, 1855); Edward Sabine, "Contributions to Terrestrial Magnetism," *Royal Society of London Philosophical Transactions* 136 (1846): 237.

65. Alexander Simpson, *The Life and Travels of Thomas Simpson* (London, 1845), 176, 178, 183, 185, 190; Thomas Simpson, *Narrative of the Discoveries on the North Coast of America* (London, 1843), appendices; Richard King, "On the Physical Characters of the Esquimaux," *Edinburgh New Philosophical Journal* 36 (1844): 296–310; Richard King, "On the Intellectual Character of the Esquimaux," *Edinburgh New Philosophical Journal* 38 (1845): 306–32; see also Wallace, *The Navy, the Company, and Richard King*, 36; John Scouler, "On the Indian Tribes Inhabiting the North-West Coast of America," *Edinburgh New Philosophical Journal* 41 (1846): 168–92; J. C. Prichard, "On the Relations of Ethnology to Other Branches of Knowledge," *Edinburgh New Philosophical Journal* 41 (1846): 307–35.

66. [Asa Gray], "Notice of European Herbaria, Particularly Those Most Interesting to the North American Botanist," *Annals and Magazine of Natural History* 42 (1841): 180; Simpson, *Narrative*, 409–18; see also Richard Glover, "The Man Who Did Not Go to California," *Canadian Historical Association Historical Papers* (1975), 95–112.

67. Edward Forbes, "On the Connexion between the Existing Flora and Fauna of the British Isles, and the Geological Changes Which Have Affected Their Area," *Geological Survey of England and Wales Memoirs* 1 (1846): 336–432.

68. Charles Lyell, "Remarks on Some Fossil and Recent Shells, Collected by Captain Bayfield, R.N., in Canada," *Geological Society of London Transactions* 6 (1842): 135–41; Charles Lyell, "On the Ridges, Elevated Beaches, Inland Cliffs, and Boulder Formations of the Canadian Lakes and Valley of St. Lawrence," *American Journal of Science and the Arts* 46 (1844): 314–17; William E. Logan, "On the Character of the Beds of Clay Lying Immediately below the Coal Seams of South Wales," *Geological Society of London Proceedings* 3 (1840): 275–77; full text in *Geological Society of London Transactions*, 2d ser., 6 (1842): 491–97; William E. Logan, "On the Coal-Fields of Pennsylvania and Nova Scotia," *Geological Society of London Proceedings* 3, part 1 (1842): 707–12; Zeller, *Inventing Canada*, 42–43.

69. Zeller, *Inventing Canada*, 43–44; Charles Lyell, *Travels in North America*, 2 vols. (New York, 1845); "Mr. Lyell's Expedition to America," *Edinburgh New Philosophical Journal* 31 (1841): 200–201; E. A. Collard, "Lyell and Dawson: A Centenary," *Dalhousie Review* 22 (1842–43): 133–44.

70. Charles Lyell, "On the Upright Fossil-trees Found at Different Levels in the Coat Strata of Cumberland, Nova Scotia," *Geological Society of London Proceedings* 4, part 1 (1843): 176–78; Charles Lyell, "On the Coal Formation of Nova Scotia," *Geological Society of London Proceedings* 4, part 1 (1843): 184–87, and *American Journal of Science and the Arts* 45 (1843): 356–59; J. W. Dawson, "On the Newer Coal Formation of the Eastern Part of Nova Scotia," *Geological Society of London Quarterly Journal* 4, part 3 (1844–45): 504–12; J. W. Dawson, "Notices of Some Fossils Found in the Coal Formation of Nova Scotia," *Geological Society of London Quarterly Journal* 2 (1846): 132–35; Abraham Gesner, "A Geological Map of Nova Scotia, with an Accompanying Memoir," *Geological Society of London Proceedings* 4, part 1 (1843): 186–90. On Dawson's paleobotanical work, see Zeller, *Inventing Canada*, 225–26.

71. Zeller, *Inventing Canada*, 53.

72. Zeller, *Inventing Canada*, chap. 3.

73. Zeller, *Inventing Canada*, chap. 3.

74. Edward Sabine, *Observations Made at the Magnetic and Meteorological Observatory at Toronto in Canada*, vol. 1 [1840–42] (London, 1845); D. Olmsted, "On the Late Periodical Visitation of the Aurora Borealis in North America," *Edinburgh New Philosophical Journal* 51 (1851): 293–98; John Lefroy, "Preliminary Report on the Observations of the Aurora Borealis," *Philosophical Magazine* 36 (1850): 456–66, and *British American Journal*, n.s., 6 (1850): 72–79; John Lefroy, "Second Report," *Philosophical Magazine*, 4th ser., 4 (1852): 59–68, and *American Journal of Science and the Arts*, 2d ser., 14 (1852): 153–60. See also Zeller, *Inventing Canada*, 134–39.

75. Zeller, *Inventing Canada*, 141–43, 155–56; *Edinburgh New Philosophical Journal* 54 (1853): 144–47.

76. Richard A. Jarrell, *The Cold Light of Dawn* (Toronto, 1988), 36–39; J. E. Ken-

nedy, "The Development of Astronomy in Fredericton, New Brunswick, between 1847 and 1876," *Royal Astronomical Society of Canada Journal* 70 (October 1976): 238–46.

77. William E. Logan, "On the Occurrence of a Track and Foot-Prints of an Animal in the Potsdam Sandstone of Lower Canada," *Geological Society of London Quarterly Journal* 7 (1851): 247–52; Charles Lyell, "Presidential Address," *Geological Society of London Quarterly Journal* 7 (1851): lxxv–lxxvi; William Hopkins, "Presidential Address," *Geological Society of London Quarterly Journal* 8 (1852): lxxx; Morris Zaslow, *Reading the Rocks* (Ottawa, 1974), 54–55; William E. Eagan, "Is There a Huronian Group? The Debate over the Canadian Shield, 1880–1905," *Isis* 80 (1989): 232–53; Zeller, *Inventing Canada*, 100.

78. "London: Exhibition of 1851," *Official Description and Illustrative Catalogue*, part 2 (London, [1851]), 957–58.

79. Archibald Geikie, *The Founders of Geology*, reprint ed. (New York, 1962), chap. 13; Archibald Geikie, *Life of Sir Roderick Murchison* (London, 1875), chaps. 9–10; Martin J. S. Rudwick, *The Meaning of Fossils*, rev. ed. (New York, 1976), chap. 4; Martin J. S. Rudwick, *The Great Devonian Controversy* (Chicago, 1985); James A. Secord, *Controversy in Victorian Geology: The Cambrian-Silurian Dispute* (Princeton, 1986).

80. See reports of W. S. M. D'Urban and R. Bell in Geological Survey of Canada, *Report of Progress* (Montreal, 1859), 226–63; "Canadian Natural History," *Canadian Journal*, n.s., 3 (1858): 461–62.

81. Randall F. Miller and Diane N. Buhay, "The Steinhammer Club: Geology and a Foundation for a Natural History Society in New Brunswick," *Geoscience Canada* 15 (1988): 221–26; J. F. W. Johnston, *Report on the Agricultural Capabilities of the Province of New Brunswick*, 2d ed. (Fredericton NB, 1850), 14, 18.

82. J. J. Bigsby, "On the Erratics of Canada," *Geological Society of London Quarterly Journal* 7 (1851): 215–38; J. J. Bigsby, "On the Physical Geography, Geology, and Commercial Resources of Lake Superior," *Edinburgh New Philosophical Journal* 53 (1852): 55–62; J. J. Bigsby, "On the Geology of the Lake of the Woods, South Hudson's Bay," *Geological Society of London Quarterly Journal* 8 (1852): xxxi–xlii; Louis Agassiz, "Global Theory of the Erratics," *Edinburgh New Philosophical Journal* 49 (1850): 97–117; E. Desor, "On the Drift of Lake Superior," *American Journal of Science*, n.s., 13 (1852): 93–109; John Richardson, "On Some Points of the Physical Geography of North America in Connection with Its Geological Structure," *American Journal of Science*, n.s., 7 (1851): 212–15; A. K. Isbister, "On the Geology of the Hudson's Bay Territories," *Geological Society of London Quarterly Journal* 2 (1855): 497–520.

83. Select Committee on the Hudson's Bay Company, House of Commons, Great Britain Parliament, *Report* (London, 1857), questions 2898, 2901, 2935, 3083–113; John Richardson, *Arctic Searching Expedition*, 2 vols. (London, 1851), vol. 2, ap-

pendix 3, "On the Geographical Distribution of Plants North of the 49th Parallel of Latitude."

84. Select Committee, *Report*, questions 213–28, 238–42, 265–302; Zeller, *Inventing Canada*, 173–76.

85. G. S. Dunbar, "Isotherms and Politics: Perception of the Northwest in the 1850s," in A. W. Rasporich and H. C. Classen, eds., *Prairie Perspectives*, vol. 2 (Toronto, 1973), 80–101; John Warkentin, "Steppe, Desert, and Empire," in Rasporich and Classen, *Prairie Perspectives* 2:102–36; D. R. Owram, *Promise of Eden: The Canadian Expansionist Movement and the Idea of the West* (Toronto, 1980), chap. 3; Alexander Morris, *Canada and Her Resources* (Montreal, 1855), 136–43.

86. See Irene M. Spry's succinct account in *Dictionary of Canadian Biography* 11:661–64.

87. James Hector, "Exploration of North America," *Edinburgh New Philosophical Journal*, n.s., 11 (January 1860): 169–72; James Hector, "Notes on the Geology of Captain Palliser's Expedition in British North America," *Edinburgh New Philosophical Journal*, n.s., 12 (1860): 225–28; George Lawson, "Hector on the Areas of Botanical Distribution throughout the Central Part of British North America," *Canadian Naturalist and Geologist* 6 (1861): 395–97; W. O. Kupsch, "Hector's Geological Explorations of the Canadian Prairie West (1857–1859)," *Geological Association of Canada Proceedings* 23 (1971): 31–41.

88. Zeller, *Inventing Canada*, 170, 173, 175; John Palliser, *The Journals, Detailed Reports, and Observations Relative to the Exploration of British North America* (London, 1863), 264.

89. Henry Y. Hind, *Narrative of the Canadian Red River Exploring Expedition*, 2 vols. (1860; reprint, Edmonton AB, 1971), 2:234, 354, 357, 370; W. L. Morton, *Henry Youle Hind* (Toronto, 1980), 26, 78; Zeller, *Inventing Canada*, 150–51, 174; see Irene M. Spry, ed., *The Papers of the Palliser Expedition, 1857–1860*, Publications of the Champlain Society, vol. 44 (Toronto, 1968), 260.

90. "Canadian Expeditions to the North-West Territory," *Canadian Journal* 5 (1860): 550; Alexander Morris, *The Hudsons Bay and Pacific Territories* (Montreal, 1858), 79. See also Warkentin, "Steppe, Desert, and Empire," 102–36; W. A. Waiser, *The Field Naturalist: John Macoun, the Geological Survey, and Natural Science* (Toronto, 1989).

91. Balfour had helped found the Botanical Society of Edinburgh, which was still sending collectors to British North America, and the Botanical Club of Edinburgh, both of which inspired similar Canadian organizations: see John Hayman, ed., *Robert Brown and the Vancouver Island Exploring Expedition* (Vancouver, 1989); J. H. Balfour, *Manual of Botany*, 3d ed. (London, 1855); J. H. Balfour, *Class Book of Botany* (Edinburgh, U.K., 1854); J. H. Balfour, *Phytotheology* (Edinburgh, U.K., 1851); I. B.

Balfour, "A Sketch of the Professors of Botany in Edinburgh, U.K.," in F. W. Oliver, ed., *Makers of British Botany* (Cambridge, U.K., 1913), 296–98.

92. George Barnston, "Remarks of the Geographical Distribution of Plants in the British Possessions of North America," *Canadian Naturalist and Geologist* 3 (1858): 28–32.

93. George Lawson, "Botanical Society of Canada: Abstract of Recent Discoveries in Botany and the Chemistry of Plants," *Botanical Society of Canada Annals* 1 (March 8, 1861): 174–75.

94. Zeller, *Inventing Canada*, 235–37 and chap. 13; William Sheppard, "On the Geographical Distribution of the Coniferae in Canada," *Edinburgh New Philosophical Journal*, n.s., 15 (1861): 206–11; J. D. Hooker, "Outlines of the Distribution of Arctic Plants," *Linnean Society Transactions* 23 (1862): 251–310. After the death of his father in 1865, J. D. Hooker entrusted the whole of North American botany to the care of Asa Gray at Harvard University.

95. William Hincks, "Materials for a Fauna Canadensis," *Canadian Journal* 7 (1862): 446–61; William Hincks, "Review of Catalogue of Birds Known to Inhabit Western Canada," *Canadian Journal* 11 (1867): 244–47.

96. Greg Thomas, "The Smithsonian and the Hudson's Bay Company," *Prairie Forum* 10 (1985): 283–306; Robert Kerr, "For the Royal Scottish Museum," *Beaver* (1953): 32–35.

97. Zeller, *Inventing Canada*, 102, 105.

98. Zeller, *Inventing Canada*, 107–8; Michael Staveley, "Saskatchewan-by-the-Sea: The Topographic Work of Alexander Murray in Newfoundland," *Newfoundland Quarterly* 77 (summer and fall 1981): 31–41.

99. William Logan, "On the Occurrence of Organic Remains in the Laurentian Rocks of Canada," *Geological Society of London Quarterly Journal* 21 (1865): 45–50; for the nationalist implications of *Eozoon canadense*, see Zeller, *Inventing Canada*, 104–5; William E. Eagan, "'I would have sworn my life on your interpretation': James Hall, Sir William Logan, and the Quebec Group," *Earth Sciences History* 6 (1987): 47–60.

100. Zeller, *Inventing Canada*, 163–67.

101. Zeller, *Inventing Canada*, 162–70; Canada, Parliament, House of Commons, *Sessional Papers* (1872), nos. 5, 53.

102. George Lawson, "On the Ranunculaceae of the Dominion of Canada and of Adjacent Parts of British America," *Canadian Naturalist and Geologist* 4 (1869): 407; George Lawson, "Descriptions of the Plant Species of Mysotis," *Canadian Naturalist and Geologist* 4 (1869): 398–407; George Lawson, "North American Laminarlaceae," *Canadian Naturalist and Geologist* 5 (1870): 99–101; George Lawson, "Remarks on the Flora of the Northern Shores of America," *Royal Society of Canada Transactions* 5, sec. 4 (1887): 207–8.

103. *Canadian Naturalist and Geologist* 3 (1858): 392–93.

104. Zeller, *Inventing Canada*, 258–68.

## 19. Nineteenth-Century Exploration of the Arctic

1. John Buchan, quoted in George Malcolm Thomson, *The North-West Passage* (London, 1975), 263.

2. Donald MacKay and Olav H. Loken, "Arctic Hydrology," in Jack Ives and Roger C. Barry, eds., *Arctic and Alpine Environment* (London, 1974), 118, 119.

3. During the year 1818, with a resurgence of interest in the search for the Northwest Passage, at least nine arctic maps were published in London. Arrowsmith's map, which was based on the most reliable information and was frequently revised, effectively mirrors the expanding knowledge of the Arctic regions during the nineteenth century. Its first state (1818) and twenty-eighth state (1896) are used to frame this chapter. The map's evolution has been carefully documented in Francis Herbert, "A Cartobibliography (with Locations of Copies) of the Arrowsmith/Stanford North Pole Map, 1818–1937," *Association of Canadian Map Librarians Bulletin* 62 (1987): 1–16.

4. John Barrow, *A Chronological History of Voyages into the Arctic Regions . . .* (1818; reprint, Devon, U.K., 1971), 375.

5. "Questions Still to Be Solved in Geography," *Literary Chronicle*, 23 October 1819, 361, 362. Cited in Alan Edwin Day, *Search for the Northwest Passage: An Annotated Bibliography* (New York, 1986), 345.

6. Barrow, *Chronological History*, 364.

7. Otto von Kotzebue, *A Voyage of Discovery, into the South Sea and Beering's Straits . . . in the Years 1815–1818 . . . in the Ship Rurick*, 3 vols. (1821; reprint, Bibliotheca Australiana no. 17, Amsterdam, 1969), 1:14–19.

8. Barry M. Gough, "British-Russian Rivalry and the Search for the Northwest Passage in the Early 19th Century," *Polar Record* 23 (1986): 301–17.

9. Christopher Lloyd and Jack L. S. Coulter, *Medicine and the Navy, 1200–1900*, vol. 4, *1815–1900* (Edinburgh, 1963), 91, 92.

10. Trevor H. Levere, "Science and the Canadian Arctic, 1818–76, from Sir John Ross to Sir George Strong Nares," *Arctic* 41 (1988): 127–37. See also Trevor H. Levere, *Science and the Canadian Arctic: A Century of Exploration, 1818–1918* (Cambridge, U.K., 1993).

11. *Newcastle (U.K.) Chronicle*, 5 July 1817, 3, col. 2.

12. A. G. E. Jones, "Sir John Ross and Sir John Barrow," *Notes and Queries*, August 1972, 298.

13. A. M. Lysaght, *Joseph Banks in Newfoundland and Labrador, 1766: His Diary, Manuscripts, and Collections* (London, 1971), 285.

14. "West Greenland," *Liverpool Mercury*, 5 September 1817, 75; "North-west Passage," *Liverpool Mercury*, 12 December 1817, 75; Tom Stamp and Cordelia Stamp, *William Scoresby Arctic Scientist* (Whitby, U.K., 1976), 66.

15. A. J. W. Catchpole and Marcia-Anne Faurer, "Ships' Log-books, Sea Ice, and the Cold Summer of 1816 in Hudson Bay and Its Approaches," *Arctic* 38 (1985): 123.

16. John Ross, *A Voyage of Discovery, Made under the Orders of the Admiralty, in His Majesty's Ships Isabella and Alexander, for the Purpose of Exploring Baffin's Bay, and Inquiring into the Probability of a North-west Passage* (London, 1819), 4, 5.

17. Ross, *Voyage of Discovery*, opposite page 175.

18. Daniel Francis, *Discovery of the North: The Exploration of Canada's Arctic* (Edmonton AB, 1986), 79; Jeanette Mirsky, *To the Arctic: The Story of Northern Exploration from Earliest Times to the Present* (New York, 1948), 100; Ernest S. Dodge, *The Polar Rosses: John and James Clark Ross and Their Expeditions* (London, 1973), 92; G. S. Ritchie, *The Admiralty Chart: British Naval Hydrography in the Nineteenth Century* (London, 1967), 139; Douglas Wilkinson, *Arctic Fever: The Search for the Northwest Passage* (Toronto, 1971), 85; John Barrow, *Voyages of Discovery and Research within the Arctic Regions, from the Year 1818 to the Present Time* (London, 1846), 49; James M. Savelle and Clive Holland, "John Ross and Bellot Strait: Personality versus Discovery," *Polar Record* 23 (1987): 416.

19. A. G. E. Jones, "Rear Admiral Sir William Edward Parry: A Different View," *Musk-Ox* 21 (1978): 5.

20. W. G. Rees, "Polar Mirages," *Polar Record* 24 (1988): 193.

21. *Hull Advertiser*, 14 November 1818, 21 November 1818.

22. "Polar Expedition," *Liverpool Mercury*, 20 November 1818, 166.

23. Harold V. Thurman, *Essentials of Oceanography* (Columbus OH, 1983), 21.

24. "Polar Expedition," *Liverpool Mercury*.

25. William Edward Parry, *Journal of a Voyage for the Discovery of a North-West Passage from the Atlantic to the Pacific . . . in the Years 1819–1820, in His Majesty's Ships Hecla and Griper . . .* (London, 1821), 31.

26. Parry, *Journal of a Voyage*, 297.

27. Parry, *Journal of a Voyage*, 296.

28. Parry, *Journal of a Voyage*, opposite page 296; Alexander Fisher, *Journal of a Voyage of Discovery to the Arctic Regions, in His Majesty's Ships Hecla and Griper, in the Years 1819 & 1820* (London, 1821), frontispiece; *Letters Written during the Late Voyage of Discovery in the Western Arctic Sea, by an Officer of the Expedition* (London, 1821), frontispiece; John Rae, *Narrative of an Expedition to the Shores of the Arctic Sea in 1846 and 1847* (London, 1850), end map.

29. "Discovery Ships," *Hull Advertiser*, 17 November 1820, 3.

30. Parry, *Journal of a Voyage*, 296–99.

31. William Edward Parry, *Journal of a Second Voyage for a North-West Passage from the Atlantic to the Pacific in the Years 1821–22–23, in His Majesty's Ships Fury and Hecla . . .* (London, 1824), end maps.

32. George Francis Lyon, *A Brief Narrative of an Unsuccessful Attempt to Reach Repulse Bay . . .* (1825; reprint, Toronto, 1971), iii.

33. Lyon, *A Brief Narrative*, xiv.

34. Parry, *Journal of a Second Voyage*, 489.

35. Parry, quoted in Dodge, *Polar Rosses*, 119.

36. John Ross, *Narrative of a Second Voyage in Search of a North-west Passage* (London, 1835), 642.

37. Ross, *Narrative*, 720.

38. John Franklin, *Narrative of a Journey to the Shores of the Polar Sea in the Years 1819–20–21–22* (1823; reprint, London, 1910), 342.

39. Franklin, quoted in Paul Nanton, *Arctic Breakthrough: Franklin's Expeditions, 1819–1847* (London, 1970), 2.

40. Clive Holland, "John Franklin and the Fur Trade, 1819–22," in Richard C. Davis, ed., *Rupert's Land: A Cultural Tapestry* (Waterloo ON, 1988), 97–111.

41. C. Stuart Houston, ed., *Arctic Ordeal: The Journal of John Richardson, Surgeon-naturalist with Franklin, 1820–1822* (Kingston ON, 1984), xxiv.

42. In 1983 an expedition unearthed some of the excess equipment jettisoned by Franklin's overburdened party, including eight iron axheads. See John W. Lentz and Todd Buchanan, "Clues to a Tragic Trek on Canada's Hood River," *National Geographic* 169 (1986): 140.

43. Vilhjalmur Stefansson, *Unsolved Mysteries of the Arctic* (New York, 1939), 40.

44. Leslie Neatby, *In Quest of the Northwest Passage* (London, 1958), 81.

45. Neatby, *In Quest of the Northwest Passage*, 80.

46. Robert E. Johnson, *Sir John Richardson: Arctic Explorer, Natural Historian, Naval Surgeon* (London, 1976), 57.

47. George Back, *Narrative of the Arctic Land Expedition to the Mouth of the Great Fish River, and along the Shores of the Arctic Ocean, in the Years 1833, 1834, and 1835* (1836; reprint, Edmonton AB, 1970), 390.

48. Back, *Narrative*, 426.

49. Alan Cooke and Clive Holland, *The Exploration of Northern Canada, 500 to 1920: A Chronology* (Toronto, 1978), 160.

50. Back, *Narrative*, end map.

51. Thomas Simpson, *Narrative of the Discoveries on the North Coast of America* (London, 1843), 2.

52. Simpson, *Narrative*, 296.

53. Simpson, *Narrative*, 370, 371.

54. Simpson, *Narrative*, 388.

55. Back, *Narrative*, end map; Simpson, *Narrative*, end map.

56. Ross, *Narrative*, opposite page 1.

57. Richard King, "On the Unexplored Coast of North America," *London, Edinburgh, and Dublin Philosophical Magazine and Journal of Science*, 3d ser., 20 (1842): 491, 492.

58. Rae, *Narrative*, 1.

59. Pierre Berton, *The Arctic Grail: The Quest for the Northwest Passage and the North Pole, 1818–1909* (Toronto, 1988), 159.

60. Hugh Wallace, *The Navy, the Company, and Richard King: British Exploration in the Canadian Arctic, 1829–1860* (Montreal, 1980), 68.

61. Christopher Lloyd, *Mr. Barrow of the Admiralty: A Life of Sir John Barrow, 1764–1848* (London, 1970), 144.

62. Richard J. Cyriax and J. M. Wordie, "Centenary of the Sailing of Sir John Franklin with the *Erebus* and *Terror*," *Geographical Journal* 106 (1945): 176.

63. Cyriax and Wordie, "Centenary," 176.

64. Richard J. Cyriax, "Sir James Clark Ross and the Franklin Expedition," *Polar Record* 3 (1942): 528, 529.

65. Cyriax and Wordie, "Centenary," 171.

66. Cyriax, "James Clark Ross," 529.

67. Richard J. Cyriax, *Sir John Franklin's Last Arctic Expedition: A Chapter in the History of the Royal Navy* (London, 1939), 55.

68. Richard J. Cyriax, "Sir John Franklin: A Note on the Absence of Records on the Shores Past Which He Sailed during His Last Voyage," *Scottish Geographical Magazine* 75 (1959): 35.

69. John Brown, *The North-West Passage, and the Plans for the Search for Sir John Franklin: A Review* (London, 1858), 37.

70. Berton, *Arctic Grail*, 145.

71. Holland, "Franklin and the Fur Trade," 100.

72. Murchison, quoted in Brown, *North-West Passage*, 30.

73. Murchison, quoted in Brown, *North-West Passage*, 30.

74. James D. Gilpin, "Outline of the Voyage of H.M.S. *Enterprize* and *Investigator* to Barrow Strait in Search of Sir John Franklin," *Nautical Magazine* 19 (1850): 168.

75. "The Arctic Expeditions: Return of Sir James Ross," *Hull Advertiser*, 9 November 1849, 5.

76. Francis Leopold McClintock, "Reminiscences of Arctic Ice-Travel in Search of Sir John Franklin and His Companions," *Journal of the Royal Dublin Society* 1 (1856–

57): 183–250; Francis Leopold McClintock, *The Voyage of the Fox in the Arctic Seas: A Narrative of the Discovery of the Fate of Sir John Franklin and His Companions* (London, 1859).

77. Andrew Taylor, *Geographical Discovery and Exploration in the Queen Elizabeth Islands*, Department of Mines and Technical Surveys, Geographical Branch, Memoir 3 (Ottawa, 1955), 42.

78. Taylor, *Queen Elizabeth Islands*, 38.

79. A. G. Findlay, "On the Probable Course Pursued by Sir John Franklin's Expedition," *Journal of the Royal Geographical Society* 26 (1856): 29.

80. A. G. E. Jones, "Sir James Clark Ross and the Voyage of the *Enterprise* and *Investigator*, 1848–49," *Geographical Journal* 137 (1971): 165.

81. Brown, *North-West Passage*, 261–63.

82. Clive Holland, "The Arctic Committee of 1851: A Background Study," part 2, *Polar Record* 20 (1980): 117.

83. "Sir Edward Belcher's Arctic Searching Squadron," *Illustrated London News*, 17 April 1852, 305, 306.

84. Alexander Armstrong, *A Personal Narrative of the Discovery of the North-West Passage* (London, 1857), 560.

85. C. S. Mackinnon, "The British Man-Hauled Sledging Tradition," in Patricia D. Sutherland, ed., *The Franklin Era in Canadian Arctic History, 1845–1859*, Mercury Series, Archeological Survey of Canada Paper no. 131 (Ottawa, 1985), 133.

86. Francis Leopold McClintock, "On Arctic Sledge Travelling," *Proceedings of the Royal Geographical Society* 19 (1875): 470, 472.

87. Taylor, *Queen Elizabeth Islands*, 45.

88. Elisha Kent Kane, *Arctic Explorations in Search of Sir John Franklin* (London, 1879), 180.

89. A. W. Greely, *Handbook of Arctic Discoveries*, Columbian Knowledge Series, no. 3 (Boston, 1896), 147.

90. Berton, *Arctic Grail*, 212.

91. Greely, *Handbook*, 150.

92. Berton, *Arctic Grail*, 301.

93. Stan Rogers, "The Northwest Passage," *Northwest Passage* (Dundas ON: Fogarty's Cove and Cole Harbour Music, 1980), record album.

94. Berton, *Arctic Grail*, 145.

95. B. T. Alt, R. M. Koerner, D. A. Fisher, and J. C. Bourgeois, "Arctic Climate during the Franklin Era, as Deduced from Ice Cores," in Sutherland, *The Franklin Era*, 69–92.

96. "Sir John Franklin's Expedition," *Aberdeen Journal*, 1 November 1854, 7. The belief that Eskimos lied (a belief shared by Charles Dickens and others) may have

arisen because two Eskimo reports during the Franklin search had proved to be false (or, perhaps, had resulted from misunderstanding). On the other hand, Eskimo information about the configuration of coastlines was so reliable that some explorers, and even the British admiralty, sometimes incorporated it on their charts. Eskimo accounts relating to the Franklin disaster are summarized in David C. Woodman, *Unravelling the Franklin Mystery: Inuit Testimony* (Montreal, 1993). Much effort has been expended to discover why the entire expedition died on or near King William Island in 1847–48. Skeletal material reveals scurvy and suggests that lead poisoning from the solder used in food canning may have contributed to the tragedy. See Owen Beattie and John Geiger, *Frozen in Time: Unlocking the Secrets of the Franklin Expedition* (Saskatoon SK, 1987).

97. George Bryce, *The Siege and Conquest of the North Pole* (London, 1910), 66.

98. Isaac I. Hayes, *The Open Polar Sea: A Narrative of a Voyage of Discovery towards the North Pole, in the Schooner "United States"* (London, 1867).

99. Bryce, *Siege and Conquest*, 68; J. R. Lotz, "Northern Ellesmere Island: A Study in the History of Geographical Discovery," *Canadian Geographer* 6 (1962): 154.

100. Lotz, "Ellesmere Island," 151.

101. Chauncey C. Loomis, *Weird and Tragic Shores: The Story of Charles Francis Hall, Explorer* (London, 1971).

102. George Henry Richards, introduction to George Strong Nares, *Narrative of a Voyage to the Polar Sea during 1875–6 in H.M. Ships "Alert" and "Discovery,"* 2 vols. (London, 1878), 1:xxxi.

103. Nares, *Narrative* 1:xi.

104. Albert Hastings Markham, *The Great Frozen Sea: A Personal Narrative of the Voyage of the "Alert" during the Arctic Expedition of 1875–76* (London, 1894).

105. Markham, *The Great Frozen Sea*, 298.

106. Markham, *The Great Frozen Sea*, 309.

107. "Arctic Exploration," *East Aberdeenshire Observer*, 3 November 1876, 3.

108. Adolphus W. Greely, *Three Years of Arctic Service: An Account of the Lady Franklin Bay Expedition of 1881–84 and the Attainment of the Farthest North*, 2 vols (London, 1886), 1:20.

109. William Barr, *The Expeditions of the First International Polar Year, 1882–83*, AINA Technical Paper no. 29 (Calgary AB, 1985).

110. L. P. Kirwan, *The White Road: A Survey of Polar Exploration* (London, 1959), 187.

111. Kirwan, *White Road*, 187.

112. Greely, quoted in A. L. Todd, *Abandoned: The Story of the Greely Arctic Expedition, 1881–1884* (New York, 1961), 46, 47.

113. Lotz, "Ellesmere Island," 155.

114. Kirwan, *White Road*, 177; Alan Cooke, "A Gift Outright: The Exploration of the Canadian Arctic Islands after 1880," in Morris Zaslow, ed., *A Century of Canada's Arctic Islands, 1880–1980* (Ottawa, 1981), 52.

115. Otto Sverdrup, *New Land: Four Years in the Arctic Regions*, 2 vols. (London, 1904), 1:1.

116. Sverdrup, *New Land* 1:1.

117. Taylor, *Queen Elizabeth Islands*, 69.

118. Cooke, "A Gift Outright," 57.

119. Frank Debenham, quoted in William C. Wonders, "Unrolling the Map of Canada's Arctic," in Zaslow, *A Century of Canada's Arctic Islands*, 10.

120. Heinrich Klutschak, *Overland to Starvation Cove: with the Inuit in Search of Franklin, 1878–1880*, ed. and trans. William Barr (Toronto, 1987), 175.

121. Klutschak, *Overland to Starvation Cove*, 185.

122. This summary of North Slope exploration is based largely on the following sources: Barr, *International Polar Year*; John Edwards Caswell, *Arctic Frontiers: United States Exploration in the Far North* (Norman, 1956); Herman R. Friis, "A Brief Review of Official United States Geographical Exploration of the Arctic Realm and Subarctic Portion of the North Pacific Ocean as It Was Conducted from the Pacific Coast Prior to 1914," in *Proceedings of an Archival Symposium Held at the California Historical Society* (San Francisco, 1971); Greely, *Handbook*; and Ernest de K. Leffingwell, *The Canning River Region, Northern Alaska*, U.S. Geological Survey, Professional Paper no. 109 (Washington DC, 1919).

123. Convenient works describing nineteenth-century activities in the Canadian Arctic south of the region of primary exploration include the following: Cooke and Holland, *Northern Canada*; Edwin Ernest Rich, *The History of the Hudson's Bay Company, 1670–1870*, vol. 2, *1763–1870* (London, 1959); Morris Zaslow, *The Opening of the Canadian North, 1870–1914* (Toronto, 1971); Morris Zaslow, *Reading the Rocks: The Story of the Geological Survey of Canada* (Toronto, 1975). See also the chapters by William A. Waiser and Suzanne Zeller in this volume.

124. Douglas Cole and Ludger Muller-Wille, "Franz Boas' Expedition to Baffin Island, 1883–1884," *Etudes Inuit /Inuit Studies* 8 (1984): 52.

125. Fabien Caron, "Albert Peter Low et l'exploration du Québec-Labrador," *Cahiers de Géographie de Québec* 9 (1965): 182.

126. Catchpole and Faurer, "Ships' Log-books."

127. Secondary works on Euro-American whaling in the North American Arctic include the following: John R. Bockstoce, *Steam Whaling in the Western Arctic* (New Bedford MA, 1977); John R. Bockstoce, *Whales, Ice, and Men: The History of Whaling in the Western Arctic* (Seattle, 1986); Daniel Francis, *Arctic Chase: A History of Whaling in Canada's North* (St. John's NF, 1984); W. Gillies Ross, *Whaling and Eskimos: Hudson Bay,*

*1860–1915*, Publications in Ethnology, no. 10 (Ottawa, 1975); W. Gillies Ross, "Whaling, Inuit, and the Arctic Islands," in Zaslow, *A Century of Canada's Arctic Islands*, 33–50; W. Gillies Ross, *Arctic Whalers, Icy Seas: Narratives of the Davis Strait Whale Fishery* (Toronto, 1985).

128. "Lancaster Sound," *Liverpool Mercury*, 6 September 1820, 119: *Newcastle Chronicle*, 30 September 1820, 3.

129. Lotz, "Ellesmere Island," 151.

130. "Davis Strait, Cumberland Isle: From the Observations of Captain Penny of the Greenland Ship *Neptune* of Aberdeen, and from the Information of Eenoolooapik, an Intelligent Esquimaux," 12 February 1840, Chart 1255, in Great Britain Hydrographic Office.

131. "A Chart of a New Fishing Ground Just Discovered by Captain John Gray Senr of the Ship *Eclipse* of Peterhead, 25 July 1855," in Taunton, Somerset, England, Hydrographic Department.

132. "Chart by Capt. W. Adams of Eclipse Sound, Navy Board, and Admiralty Inlets, 1872," in Taunton, Somerset, England, Hydrographic Department.

133. J. B. Walker, "Sketch Map of Scott's Inlet, and Eglinton Fiord, September 1st, 1877," in Taunton, Somerset, England, Hydrographic Office.

134. Ross, *Whaling and Eskimos*, 41.

135. John Bockstoce, "Contacts between American Whalemen and the Copper Eskimos," *Arctic* 28 (1975): 298–99.

136. John Spink and D. W. Woodie, *Eskimo Maps from the Canadian Eastern Arctic*, "Cartographica" Monograph no. 5 (Toronto, 1972).

137. James M. Savelle, "Effects of Nineteenth-Century European Exploration on the Development of the Netsilik Eskimo Culture," in Sutherland, *The Franklin Era*, 193.

138. Savelle, "Effects of Nineteenth-Century European Exploration," 204.

139. Clifford G. Hickey, "An Examination of Processes of Cultural Change among Nineteenth-Century Copper Inuit," *Etudes Inuit /Inuit Studies* 8 (1984): 24.

140. Kenn Harper, *Give Me My Father's Body: The Life of Minik, the New York Eskimo* (Frobisher Bay NT, 1986).

141. Wallace, *The Navy, the Company, and Richard King*.

142. Stefansson, *Unsolved Mysteries*, 126.

143. Peter C. Newman, *Company of Adventurers*, 2 vols. (New York, 1985–87), 1:294.

144. Robert L. Richards, *Dr. John Rae* (Whitby, U.K., 1985), 186, 187.

145. Richards, *Dr. John Rae*, 183.

146. Greely, *Handbook*, 135.

147. McClintock, "Sledge Travelling," 465.

148. McClintock, "Sledge Travelling," 474.

149. Richard J. Cyriax, "Arctic Sledge Travelling by Officers of the Royal Navy, 1819–49," *Mariner's Mirror* 49 (1963): 137; Mackinnon, "Man-Hauled Sledging," 132.

150. McClintock, "Sledge Travelling," 478.

151. Barbara Schweger, "Documentation and Analysis of the Clothing Worn by Non-native Men in the Canadian Arctic Prior to 1920, with an Emphasis on Footwear" (master's thesis, University of Alberta, 1983), 179.

152. Schweger, "Clothing."

153. McClintock, "Sledge Travelling," 469.

154. Vilhjalmur Stefansson, "Clothes Make the Eskimo," *Natural History* 64 (1955): 39.

155. Nares, *Narrative* 1:172.

156. Caroline Phillips, "The Camps, Cairns, and Caches of the Franklin and Franklin Search Expeditions," in Sutherland, *The Franklin Era*, 149–73.

157. Joseph B. MacInnis, "The Breadalbane Project," in Sutherland, *The Franklin Era*, 174–84; M. J. Muirhead, "The Application of a Sophisticated Canadian Subsea Technology to the Determination of the Location of the *Erebus* and *Terror*," in Sutherland, *The Franklin Era*, 215–19.

158. Mirsky, *To the Arctic*, 103.

159. Dr. Ray Thorsteinsson, personal communication with the author, 1990.

160. Nancy McCartney, "Effects of Thule Eskimos on Soils and Vegetation at Silimiut, N.W.T.," in Allen P. McCartney, ed., *Thule Eskimo Culture: An Anthropological Retrospective*, Mercury Series, Archeological Survey of Canada Paper no. 88 (Ottawa, 1979), 495–527.

161. Nares, *Narrative* 2:352, 353.

162. Elisabeth Hone, *The Present Status of the Muskox in Arctic North America and Greenland*, Special Publication no. 5, American Committee for International Wild Life Protection (Cambridge MA, 1934), 39.

163. Nares, *Narrative* 2:201.

164. Hone, *Present Status*, 39. Nonnative commercial and subsistence utilization of musk oxen is summarized in William Barr, *Back from the Brink: The Road to Muskox Conservation in the Northwest Territories*, Komatik Series no. 3 (Calgary, 1991).

165. This is based on the annotated chronological compilation of expeditions in Cooke and Holland, *Northern Canada*, and on Leffingwell, *Canning River*.

166. J. Keith Fraser, "The Islands in Foxe Basin," *Geographical Bulletin* 4 (1953): 5.

167. The population of Canadian Eskimos is believed to have decreased from approximately 26,000 in the seventeenth century to about 8,000 by 1906 (Robert M. Bone, "The Numbers of Eskimos: An Arctic Enigma," *Polar Record* 16 [1973]: 554).

168. Rogers, "Northwest Passage."

169. R. F. Scott, introduction to Franklin, *Narrative*, vii.

## 20. Military Explorers of the American West, 1838–1860

1. The following account of the U.S. Exploring Expedition of 1838–42, or the Wilkes Expedition, is based on Vincent Ponko Jr., *Ships, Seas, and Scientists: U.S. Naval Exploration and Discovery in the Nineteenth Century* (Annapolis, 1974), 19–32, and William Stanton, *The United States Exploring Expedition of 1838–1842* (Los Angeles, 1975), 247–65. Ponko's account in *Ships, Seas, and Scientists* is based on Philip I. Mitterling, *American Exploration in the Antarctic to 1840* (Urbana, 1959), and David B. Tyler, *The Wilkes Expedition: The First United States Exploring Expedition, 1838–1842*, American Philosophical Society Memoirs, no. 73 (Philadelphia, 1968). Curiously, Stanton does not mention Tyler's full-scale work in his text, footnotes, or bibliography. Wilkes left New York on 19 August 1838 and returned on 10 June 1842, sailing about 85,000 miles and surveying some 280 islands, 800 miles of streams and coastline in Oregon territory, and 1,500 miles of the Antarctic coastal region. The narrative produced by Wilkes, *Narrative of the United States Exploring Expeditions during the Years 1838, 1839, 1840, 1841*, 5 vols., is being republished in part by the University of Illinois Press. Information about specimens collected by this expedition and scientific papers written related to the expedition can be found in Harley Harris Bartlett, *The Reports of the Wilkes Expedition, and the World of the Specialists in Science*, Proceedings of the American Philosophical Society, no. 82 (Philadelphia, 1940), and Daniel C. Haskell, *The United States Exploring Expedition, 1838–1842, and Its Publications, 1844–1874* (1942; reprint, New York, 1968). See also the Accession Files, Office of the Registrar, Smithsonian Institution, Washington DC; catalogs and other material in the Division of the Museum of Natural History of the Smithsonian. The Smithsonian Institution held an exhibit, "Magnificent Voyagers," in the Museum of Natural History from 14 November 1985 to 7 November 1986, which dealt with the Wilkes Expedition. The catalog of this exhibit was published: Herman J. Viola and Carolyn Margolis, eds., *Magnificent Voyagers: The U.S. Exploring Expedition, 1838–1842* (Washington DC, 1985); at the same time, the Smithsonian published Charles Erskine, *Twenty Years before the Mast with the More Thrilling Scenes and Incidents while Circumnavigating the Globe under the Command of the Late Admiral Charles Wilkes, 1838–1842* (Washington DC, 1985).

2. Stanton, *The United States Exploring Expedition*, 254.

3. Stanton, *The United States Exploring Expedition*, 258.

4. Stanton, *The United States Exploring Expedition*, 261.

5. Stanton, *The United States Exploring Expedition*, 263.

6. Ponko, *Ships, Seas, and Scientists*, 1–18.

7. William H. Goetzmann, *Army Exploration in the American West, 1803–1863* (New Haven, 1959), 435. The commander of the U.S. Army Corps of Topographical Engineers for most of its existence was Colonel John J. Abert. For a brief biographical account of his career, see [John Charles Frémont], *Narratives of Exploration and Adventure*, ed. Allan Nevins (New York, 1956), 254 n.5. See also "Legacy of the Topographical Engineer: Textual and Cartographic Records of the Western Exploration, 1819–1860," *Government Publications Review* 7A, no. 2 (1980): 111–16.

8. For two readable accounts of Frémont's life, see Allan Nevins, *Frémont, Pathmaker of the West* (New York, 1939), and Ferol Egan, *Frémont, Explorer for a Restless Nation* (Garden City NY, 1977). Also a good source is John C. Frémont, *Memoirs of My Life* (Chicago, 1877).

9. Herman Friis, "The Documents and Reports of the United States Congress: A Primary Source of Information on Travel in the West, 1783–1861," in John Francis McDermott, ed., *Travelers on the Western Frontier* (Urbana, 1970), 112–67.

10. The major sources for Joseph Nicolas Nicollet and his explorations are Martha Coleman Bray, *Joseph Nicollet and His Map* (Philadelphia, 1980), Martha Coleman Bray, *The Journals of Joseph N. Nicollet: A Scientist on the Mississippi Headwaters with Notes on Indian Life* (Minneapolis, 1970), and Martha Coleman Bray, *Joseph N. Nicollet on the Plains and Prairies* (Minneapolis, 1976).

11. Gouverneur Kemble Warren, *Memoir to Accompany the Map of the Territory of the United States from the Mississippi River to the Pacific Ocean*, 36th Cong., 2d sess., 1855–60, S. Doc. 11, 24.

12. Hiram M. Chittenden, *The American Fur Trade of the Far West*, 2 vols. (1935; reprint, Lincoln, 1986), 2:458–81.

13. The 1842 expedition of Frémont is based on Goetzmann, *Army Exploration*, 77–85. See also Ralph Ehrenberg and Herman Viola, "Exploring the American West Series," introduction to John Charles Frémont, *The Exploring Expedition to the Rocky Mountains* (Washington DC, 1988).

14. The expedition of Frémont in 1843–45 is taken from Frémont, *Memoirs*, and John Charles Frémont, *Report of the Exploring Expedition to the Rocky Mountains in the Year 1842, and to Oregon and North California in the Years 1843–44*, 28th Cong., 2d sess., 1845, S. Doc. 174, serial 461 (commercial edition, New York, 1848). See also [Frémont], *Narratives of Exploration*, 182–426; Nevins, *Frémont*, 127–326; Egan, *Frémont*, 133–261; Goetzmann, *Army Exploration*, 85–108; and William H. Goetzmann, *Exploration and Empire: The Explorer and the Scientist in the Winning of the American West* (New York: 1966), 244–50. Frémont's official reports have been republished a number of times. The best documentary source on Frémont, including reprints of his re-

ports published by the government, is Donald Jackson and Mary Lee Spence, eds., *The Expeditions of John Charles Frémont*, 3 vols. and map portfolio (Urbana, 1970–84).

15. Goetzmann, *Army Exploration*, 103.

16. Goetzmann, *Army Exploration*, 104–6; Goetzmann, *Exploration and Empire*, 313–14.

17. Ponko, *Ships, Seas, and Scientists*, 28–29.

18. Goetzmann, *Army Exploration*, 108; for positive views of Frémont's scientific accomplishments, see Allan Nevins, "A Record Filled with Sunlight," *American Heritage* 7 (August 1956): 12–19, 106–7, and John L. Allen, "Division of the Waters: Changing Concepts of the Continental Divide, 1804–44," *Journal of Historical Geography* 4 (1978): 366–70.

19. Henry Tanner, *American Atlas* (Philadelphia, 1839), pl. 10; Josiah Gregg, *Commerce of the Prairies; or, The Journal of a Santa Fe Trader, during Eight Expeditions across the Great Western Prairies and a Residence of Nearly Nine Years in Northern Mexico*, ed. Max Moorhead (Norman, 1954); Goetzmann, *Army Exploration*, 110. The best source on maps of the trans-Mississippi West is Carl I. Wheat, *Mapping the Trans-Mississippi West, 1540–1861*, 5 vols. (Menlo Park CA, 1958–62). See also Frederick C. Luebke, Frances W. Kaye, and Gary Moulton, eds., *Mapping the North American Plains: Essays in the History of Cartography* (Norman, 1987). In this last work, note especially: Raymond W. Wood, "Mapping the Missouri River through the Great Plains, 1673–1895," 27–40; John L. Allen, "Patterns of Promise: Mapping the Plains and Prairies, 1800–1860," 41–62; and John B. Garver Jr., "Practical Military Geographers and Mappers of the Trans-Missouri West, 1820–1860," 111–26.

20. Stephen W. Kearney, *Report of a Summer Campaign to the Rocky Mountains . . . in 1845*, 29th Cong., 1st sess., 1846, S. Doc. 1; see also Carl I. Wheat, "Mapping the American West, 1540–1847," *Proceedings of the American Antiquarian Society* 64 (1954): 19–94, 107.

21. Goetzmann, *Army Exploration*, 123–24.

22. James W. Abert, *Journal of Lieutenant James W. Abert from Bent's Fort to St. Louis*, 29th Cong., 1st sess., 1846, Exec. Doc. 438.

23. Goetzmann, *Army Exploration*, 116–23; Egan, *Frémont*, 317–463.

24. Egan, *Frémont*, 280–317.

25. John C. Torrey, "Plantae Fremontianae; or, Descriptions of Plants Collected by Colonel J. C. Fremont in California," *Smithsonian Contributions to Knowledge* 6 (Washington DC, 1854): art. 2; Goetzmann, *Army Exploration*, 122–23; Egan, *Frémont*, 462–46. Frémont's *Geographical Memoir upon Upper California* is reprinted in Jackson and Spence, *Expeditions of John C. Frémont* 3:495–570, as is Torrey's "Plantae Fremontianae" (3:570–608).

26. For a biographical sketch on Emory, see the *Dictionary of American Biography*,

20 vols. (New York, 1928–55), 6:153–54, and *Biographical Register of the Officers and Graduates of the United States Military Academy*, 2 vols. (New York, 1891), 1:481.

27. William H. Emory, "Memorandum of Property Received from the Topographical Bureau 'To Be Used West of the Mississippi River'" (1846), in William H. Emory Papers, Yale Collection of Western Americana, Sterling Memorial Library, Yale University, New Haven.

28. William H. Emory, *Notes of a Military Reconnaissance from Fort Leavenworth in Missouri, to San Diego in California Including Parts of the Arkansas, Del Norte [Rio Grande], and Gila Rivers*, 30th Cong., 1st sess., 1848, H. Doc. 41, accompanied by subreports of Philip St. George Cooke, A. R. Johnson, and James V. Abert. The Senate version of this document (S. Doc. 7) also includes Emory's map "Military Reconnaissance of the Arkansas, Rio del Norte, and Gila Rivers" but does not include the subreports by St. George Cooke, Johnson, and Abert. See also Ross Calvin, ed., *Lieutenant Emory Reports: A Reprint of Lieutenant W. H. Emory's Notes of Military Reconnaissance* (Albuquerque, 1951); Norman J. W. Thrower, "William H. Emory and the Mapping of the American Southwest Borderlands," *Terrae Incognitae* 22 (1990): 67–91; William H. Emory, "Extracts from His Journal while with the Army of the West," *Niles' Weekly Register*, 31 October 1846; and Philip St. George Cooke, "Journal of the March of the Mormon Battalion," in Ralph P. Bieber, ed., *Exploring Southwestern Trails, 1846–1854* (Glendale CA, 1938), 26–29, 63–240.

29. "Buchanan to Trist, Washington, D.C., July 19, 1847," in John Basset Moore, ed., *The Works of James Buchanan*, 12 vols. (Philadelphia, 1908), 3:368–69.

30. *Report of the Secretary of War Communicating in Answer to a Resolution of the Senate, a Report and Map of the Examination of New Mexico Made by Lieutenant J. W. Abert of the Topographical Corps, Feb. 10, 1848*, 30th Cong., 1st sess., 1848, S. Doc. 23; see also John Galvin, ed., *Western America, 1846–1847*: The Original Travel Diary of Lieutenant J. W. Abert, Who Mapped New Mexico for the United States Army, with Illustrations in Color from His Sketchbook (San Francisco, 1936), 1–116.

31. William H. Emory, *Report on the United States and Mexican Boundary Survey*, 34th Cong., 1st sess., 1847, H. Doc. 135, 1–17; Goetzmann, *Army Exploration*, 142; Daniel T. Groggin, *Preliminary Inventory of the Records Relating to International Boundaries* (1968), in Record Group (hereafter cited as RG) 76, National Archives, Washington DC.

32. Max Weisel, *A Bibliography of American Natural History: The Pioneer Century, 1769–1865*, 3 vols. (New York, 1967), 3:17.

33. Goetzmann, *Army Exploration*, 143–44; Justin Winsor, *Narrative and Critical History of America*, 8 vols. (Boston, 1889), 1:396.

34. Accounts of Frémont's fourth expedition may be found in William Brandon, *The Men and the Mountain: Frémont's Fourth Expedition* (New York, 1955); Erwin G.

Gudde and Elisabeth K. Gudde, eds., *Exploring with Frémont: The Private Diaries of Charles Preuss, Cartographer for John C. Frémont on His First, Second, and Fourth Expeditions to the Far West* (Norman, 1958), 143–53; Leroy R. Hafen and Ann W. Hafen, eds., *Frémont's Fourth Expedition: A Documentary Account of the Disaster of 1848–1849 with Diaries, Letters, and Reports by Participants in the Tragedy* (Glendale CA, 1960). See also Nevins, *Frémont*, 343–72; Goetzmann, *Exploration and Empire*, 266–70; and Jackson and Spence, *The Expeditions of John Charles Fremont* 3:xix–xxxi, 3–110.

35. Randolph B. Marcy, *Report of a Route from Fort Smith to Santa Fe*, 31st Cong., 1st sess., 1850, S. Doc. 64; James Harvey Simpson, *Report and Map of the Route from Fort Smith, Arkansas, to Santa Fe, New Mexico*, 31st Cong., 1st sess., 1850, S. Doc. 12; Grant Foreman, *Marcy and the Gold-Seekers* (Norman, 1939), 14–15, 118–19, 128; Eugene W. Hollon, *Beyond the Cross Timbers: The Travels of Randolph E. Marcy, 1812–1887* (Norman, 1955), 59–90.

36. Goetzmann, *Army Exploration*, 219–25. The most recent publication of the report of the Stansbury expedition is Brigham D. Madsen, *Exploring the Great Salt Lake: The Stansbury Expedition of 1849–50* (Salt Lake City, 1988). See also Howard Stansbury, *Exploration and Survey of the Valley of the Great Salt Lake of Utah, Including a Reconnaissance of a New Route through the Rocky Mountains*, 32nd Cong., spec. sess., 1851, S. Doc. 3, and John W. Gunnison, *The Mormons or Latter Day Saints in the Valley of the Great Salt Lake: A History of Their Rise and Progress, Peculiar Doctrines, Present Conditions, and Prospects* (Philadelphia, 1852).

37. Goetzmann, *Army Exploration*, 194–95, 206, 208, 226, 273; Goetzmann, *Exploration and Empire*, 232, 263, 290. See also Robert V. Hine, *Bartlett's West: Drawing the Mexican Boundary* (New Haven, 1968).

38. W. F. Smith, *Report . . . of Routes from San Antonio to El Paso*, 31st Cong., 1st sess., 1850, S. Doc. 64. See also Averam B. Bender, "Opening Routes across West Texas, 1848–1850," *Southwestern Historical Quarterly* 37 (1933–34): 119; W. Turrentine Jackson, *Wagon Roads West: A Study of Federal Road Surveys and Construction in the Trans-Mississippi West, 1846–1869* (Lincoln, 1979), 39–42.

39. This recommendation found its way later into an appropriation of $100,000 to experiment with digging artesian wells in the Llano Estacado ("Staked Plain") and Jornada del Muerto regions of Texas and New Mexico. Goetzmann, *Army Exploration*, 365–68.

40. Goetzmann, *Army Exploration*, 233–34; Jackson, *Wagon Roads West*, 36–47. Michler worked with Bryan during part of his work in Texas, and their reports are found in Smith, *Report . . . of Routes from San Antonio to El Paso*; see also Gouverneur Kemble Warren, *Memoir to Accompany the Map of the Territory of the United States from the Mississippi to the Pacific Ocean . . . .*, 33d Cong., 2d sess., 1859, S. Doc. 78.

41. Hollon, *Beyond the Cross Timbers*, 127–61; Goetzmann, *Army Exploration*, 234

n.68; Grant Foreman, ed., *Adventure on the Red River* (Norman, 1937). Marcy's own reports were published as *Exploration of the Red River of Louisiana in the Year 1852*, 32d Cong., 2d sess., 1853, S. Doc. 54.

42. James Harvey Simpson, *Journal of a Military Reconnaissance from Santa Fe, New Mexico, to the Navajo Country Made with the Troops under Command of Brevet Lieutenant-Colonel John M. Washington, Chief of the Ninth Military Department and Governor of New Mexico*, 31st Cong., 1st sess., 1850, S. Doc. 64, 55–168; Frank McNitt, ed., *Navajo Expedition: Journal of a Military Reconnaissance from Santa Fe, New Mexico, to the Navaho Country Made in 1849 by Lieutenant James H. Simpson* (Norman, 1964), 5–162. See also David Weber, *Richard H. Kern: Expeditionary Artist in the Far Southwest, 1848–1853* (Albuquerque, 1985), 72–113, 143–86; William J. Heffernan, *Edward M. Kern: The Travels of an Artist-Explorer* (Bakersfield CA, 1953); Lorenzo Sitgreaves, *Report of an Expedition down the Zuni and Colorado Rivers*, 32d Cong., 2d sess., 1853, S. Doc. 59.

43. Wheat, "Mapping the American West," 131–32; Averam B. Bender, *The March of Empire: Frontier Defense in the Southwest, 1848–1860* (Lawrence, 1952).

44. Francis P. Farquhar, "The Topographical Reports of Lieutenant George H. Derby," part 2, *California Historical Society Quarterly* 11 (1932): 247. The reports of Derby's expedition are R. S. Williamson, *Report of a Reconnaissance of a Route through the Sierra Nevadas by the Upper Sacramento*, 31st Cong., 1st sess., Part II, 1848–50, S. Doc. 47, and George H. Derby, *Topographical Memoir Accompanying Maps of the Sacramento Valley*, 31st Cong., 1st sess., 1850, S. Doc. 47; see also George Rippey Stewart, *John Phoenix, Esq., the Veritable Squibob: A Life of George H. Derby* (New York, 1937), 57–72.

45. In 1851 Derby was assigned the task of diverting the San Diego River into False Bay in an attempt to keep the harbor from filling with silt. See Goetzmann, *Army Exploration*, 160–261, and Stewart, *A Life of George H. Derby*, 135–37.

46. Goetzmann, *Army Exploration*, 431–34.

47. Joseph C. Ives, *Report upon the Colorado River of the West*, 36th Cong., 1st sess., 1861, H. Doc. 90.

48. Arthur Woodward, *Feud on the Colorado* (Los Angeles, 1955), provides details on the competition between Ives and Johnson.

49. Goetzmann, *Army Exploration*, 380.

50. Goetzmann, *Army Exploration*, 387–90.

51. Goetzmann, *Army Exploration*, 153–54; a general treatment of the Mexican Boundary Survey is Edward S. Wallace, *The Great Reconnaissance: Soldiers, Artists, and Scientists on the Frontier, 1848–1861* (Boston, 1955), 3–101.

52. John Russel Bartlett, *Personal Narrative of Explorations and Incidents in Texas, New Mexico, California, Sonora, and Chihuahua, Connected with the United States and Mexican Boundary Commission during the Years 1850, 1851, 1852, and 1853*, 2 vols. (New

York, 1854). A good reprint edition is Odie B. Faulk, ed., *Personal Narrative* . . . , 2 vols. (Chicago, 1965). Asa Gray's quote about the botanical report of John Torrey is in Andrew Rodgers, *John Torrey* (Princeton, 1942), 227. The quotations from Bartlett's book are on pages 201–7.

53. The Pacific Railroad bill finally passed Congress on 2 March 1853; see the *Congressional Globe*, 32d Cong., 2d sess., 1853, 841.

54. Evaluation of the Pacific Railroad Surveys took place in two stages. A preliminary report was issued in 1855 as A. A. Humphreys and G. K. Warren, "An Examination by Direction of the Hon. Jefferson Davis, Secretary of War, of the Reports of Explorations for Railroad Routes from the Mississippi to the Pacific, Made under the Orders of the War Department in 1853–54 . . . ," 33d Cong., 1st sess., 1855, H. Doc. 129. Beginning in 1857, in a series of thirteen large quarto volumes, the final report was issued: *Reports of Explorations and Surveys to Ascertain the Most Practicable and Economical Route for a Railroad from the Mississippi to the Pacific Ocean* (Washington DC, 1857–60). It is difficult to use in reference to the location of specific reports, but help may be found in Adelaide Hasse, *Reports of Explorations Printed in the Documents of the United States Government* (Washington DC, 1899). Useful as an outline is George Leslie Albright, "Official Explorations for Pacific Railroads, 1853–55," *University of California Publications in History* 2 (1921). The primary written report of Frémont's unofficial fifth trip of exploration is Solomon Nuñes Carvalho, *Incidents of Travel and Adventure in the Far West, with Col. Fremont's Last Expedition across the Rocky Mountains: Including Three Months' Residence in Utah, and a Perilous Trip across the Great American Desert to the Pacific* (New York, 1860). Beale's trip across the Southwest was given publicity by Gwin Harris Heap, *Central Route to the Pacific with Belated Material on Railroad Explorations and Indian Affairs by Edward F. Beale, Thomas H. Benton, Kit Carson, and Col. E. A. Hitchcock, and in Other Documents, 1853–54*. First published in 1854, it has been edited by LeRoy R. Hafen and Ann W. Hafen (Glendale CA, 1957).

55. "Report of the Secretary of War Communicating . . . Captain Simpson's Report and Map of Wagon Roads in Utah Territory," 35th Cong., 2d sess., 1859–60, S. Doc. 40. See also Goetzmann, *Army Exploration*, 397–403.

56. John N. Macomb, *Report of the Exploring Expedition from Santa Fe, New Mexico, to the Junction of the Grand and Green Rivers of the Great Colorado of the West in 1859* (Washington DC, 1860); see also Goetzmann, *Army Exploration*, 394–97.

57. Goetzmann, *Exploration and Empire*, 309–10; William F. Raynolds, *Report on the Exploration of the Yellowstone and the Country Drained by That River*, 40th Cong., 2d sess., 1868, S. Doc. 77. See also F. V. Hayden, *Geological Report of the Exploration . . . under the Direction of Captain (Lt. Col. and Brevet Brig. Gen.) W. F. Raynolds, Corps of Engineers, 1859–60* (Washington DC, 1869).

58. A somewhat popular account of the use of camels by the army is Robert Froman, "The Red Ghost," *American Heritage* 12 (April 1961): 35–37, 94–98.

59. For the best account of the government's wagon-road program, see Jackson, *Wagon Roads West*.

60. Bertha S. Dodge, *The Road West: Saga of the 35th Parallel* (Albuquerque, 1980), 92–109, 113–16, 123–32, 166, 174–78, 190–201.

61. Goetzmann, *Exploration and Empire*, 490–529.

62. See Robert Taft, *Artists and Illustrators of the Old West* (New York, 1953); Peter Bacon Hales, *William Henry Jackson and the Transformation of the American Landscape* (Philadelphia, 1988); and Robert V. Hine, "An Artist Draws the Line," *American Heritage* 19 (February 1968): 28–35, 102–3.

63. Goetzmann, *Army Exploration*, 313–16, 440–60; Frank N. Schubert, "Emory and Warren Mapping the Trans-Mississippi West," *A. B. Bookman's Weekly* (October 18, 1982), 2590–98. The best account on Warren is his own *Memoir to Accompany the Map of the Territory of the United States from the Mississippi River to the Pacific Ocean*, 33rd Cong., 2d sess., 1859, S. Doc. 78, vol. 11, serial set no. 801.

64. Goetzmann, *Army Exploration*, 331–32.

65. Goetzmann, *Army Exploration*, 427–31.

66. Cf. Russell Blaine Nye, *Society and Culture in America, 1830–1860* (New York, 1974), and Martin Ridge, "Why They Went West: Economic Opportunity on the Trans-Mississippi Frontier," *American West* 1 (1964): 40–57.

## 21. The Government Explorer in Canada, 1870–1914

1. G. Dawson, "On Some of the Larger Unexplored Regions of Canada," *Ottawa Naturalist* 4 (1890–91): 29.

2. Dawson, "On Some of the Larger Unexplored Regions," 30.

3. D. R. Owram, *Promise of Eden: The Canadian Expansionist Movement and the Idea of the West* (Toronto, 1980), 59–78.

4. Dawson, "On Some of the Larger Unexplored Regions," 31, 39.

5. See A. B. McKillop, *A Disciplined Intelligence: Critical Inquiry and Canadian Thought in the Victorian Era* (Montreal, 1979).

6. C. Berger, *Science, God, and Nature in Victorian Canada* (Toronto, 1983), 6–16.

7. R. C. Brown, "The Doctrine of Usefulness: Natural Resource and National Park Policy in Canada, 1887–1914," in J. G. Nelson, ed., *Canadian Parks in Perspective* (Montreal, 1970), 55.

8. T. Levere, "What Is Canadian about Science in Canadian History?" in R. A. Jarrell and N. R. Ball, eds., *Science, Technology, and Canadian History* (Waterloo ON,

1980), 20; see also V. de Vecchi, "Science and Government in the Nineteenth Century" (Ph.D. diss., University of Toronto, 1978).

9. Dawson, "On Some of the Larger Unexplored Regions," 39–40.

10. John Warkentin, "Steppe, Desert, and Empire," in A. W. Rasporich and H. C. Classen, eds., *Prairie Perspectives*, vol. 2 (Toronto, 1973), 113–21.

11. Owram, *Promise of Eden*, 65.

12. J. G. Snell, "American Neutrality and the Red River Resistance, 1867–70," *Prairie Forum* 4, no. 2 (fall 1979): 183–96.

13. J. S. Hawkins to F. Chapman, March 1871, f. 856, vol. 228, Department of the Interior, RG 45, Government Archives Division, National Archives of Canada (hereafter cited as NAC).

14. Surveyors: A. G. Forrest, A. L. Russell; Subassistant astronomers: W. A. Ashe, G. F. Burpee, G. C. Coster, W. F. King; Surveying officer/commander of scouts: D'Arcy East; Assistant surveyor: G. G. Crompton; Commissariat: L. W. Herchmer; Surgeon: Dr. T. J. W. Burgess; Surgeon's assistant: Dr. T. Millman; Veterinary surgeon: Dr. W. G. Boswell; Naturalist: G. M. Dawson.

15. A. Birrell, "Survey Photography in British Columbia, 1859–1900," *BC Studies* 52 (winter 1981–82): 41–48.

16. A. Featherstonhaugh, *Narrative of the Operations of the British North American Boundary Commission, 1872–76* (Woolwich, U.K., 1876), 30.

17. T. Millman, "Impressions of the West in the Early 'Seventies from the Diary of the Assistant Surgeon of the B.N.A. Boundary Survey," *Women's Canadian Historical Society of Toronto* 26 (1927–28).

18. D. R. Cameron to Secretary of State for Foreign Affairs, 20 December 1872, f. 1824, vol. 229, Department of the Interior, RG 45, Government Archives Division, NAC.

19. For an explanation of how the boundary was astronomically determined, see S. Anderson, "The North American Boundary from the Lake of the Woods to the Rocky Mountains," *Journal of the Royal Geographical Society* 46 (1876): 259–62.

20. Millman, "Impressions of the West," 21 July 1874.

21. J. W. Dawson to E. A. Meredith, 22 January 1873, f. 2002, vol. 229, Department of the Interior, RG 45, Government Archives Division, NAC.

22. D. Cole and B. Lockner, eds., *The Journals of George Mercer Dawson: British Columbia, 1875–1878*, vol. 1, *1875–1876* (Vancouver, 1989), 7–8.

23. A. R. Turner, "Surveying the International Boundary: The Journal of George M. Dawson," *Saskatchewan History* 21, no. 1 (winter 1968).

24. G. M. Dawson, *Report on the Geology and Resources of the Region in the Vicinity of the 49th Parallel, from Lake of the Woods to the Rocky Mountains* (Montreal, 1875), v.

25. Dawson, *Report on the Geology and Resources*, 292.

26. Dawson, *Report on the Geology and Resources*, 299.

27. Dawson, *Report on the Geology and Resources*, 301.

28. D. W. Thomson, *Men and Meridians: The History of Surveying and Mapping in Canada*, vol. 2, *1867–1917* (Ottawa, 1972), 7–19.

29. For an excellent description of the survey system and the activities of the Dominion Lands Branch, see W. F. King and J. S. Dennis, "General Report of Operations from 1869 to 1889, Together with an Exposition of the System of Survey of Dominion Lands, and a Schedule of Dominion Land and Topographical Surveys," Canada, Parliament House of Commons, *Sessional Papers*, no. 13 (1892), part vi.

30. C. Martin, *"Dominion Lands" Policy* (Toronto, 1973), 9.

31. King and Dennis, "General Report of Operations," 6–8.

32. Diary, 29 July 1899, 350–51, O. J. Klotz Papers, MG 30 R1B, Manuscript Division, NAC.

33. King and Dennis, "General Report of Operations," 25.

34. During the 1885 North-West Rebellion, surveyors believed that they could play a deciding role as an intelligence corps because of their familiarity with the region. See W. A. Waiser, "Surveyors at War: A. O. Wheeler's Diary of the North-West Rebellion," *Saskatchewan History* 38, no. 2 (spring 1985): 42–52.

35. T. R. Weir, "Settlement in Southwest Manitoba, 1870–1891," *Historical and Scientific Society of Manitoba Transactions*, 3d ser., no. 17 (1960–61): 54–64; J. L. Tyman, *By Section, Township, and Range: Studies in Prairie Settlement* (Brandon ON, 1972), 17, 19.

36. King and Dennis, "General Report of Operations," 9.

37. King and Dennis, "General Report of Operations," 9.

38. For a discussion of John Macoun's assessment of western Canada's potential, see W. A. Waiser, *The Field Naturalist: John Macoun, the Geological Survey, and Natural History* (Toronto, 1989), 16–54.

39. "Report of the Department of the Interior for 1881," Canada, Parliament, House of Commons, *Sessional Papers* 20, no. 18 (1882), part i, 4–5.

40. King and Dennis, "General Report of Operations," 21, 31.

41. A. J. Russell, *The Red River Country, Hudson's Bay, and the North-West Territories Considered in Relation to Canada* (Montreal, 1870), 43–45.

42. A. A. Taché, *Sketch of the North-West of America* (Montreal, 1870), translator's introduction.

43. Warkentin, "Steppe, Desert, and Empire," 128.

44. Thomson, *Men and Meridians*, 131–39.

45. Thomson, *Men and Meridians*, 139–40.

46. Thomson, *Men and Meridians*, 140.

47. Owram, *Promise of Eden*, 32–42.

48. S. Fleming, *Memorial of the People of Red River to the British and Canadian Governments* (Quebec, 1863), 27.

49. See A. Robb, "Edward Watkin and the Pacific Telegraph, 1861–1865," *Ontario History* 64, no. 4 (December 1973): 189–209.

50. A. Ronaghan, "The Pioneer Telegraph in Western Canada" (master's thesis, University of Saskatchewan, 1976), 12–16; J. S. Macdonald, *The Dominion Telegraph* (Battleford ON, 1930).

51. Owram, *Promise of Eden*, 115.

52. S. Fleming, ed., *Report on Surveys and Preliminary Operations on the Canadian Pacific Railway up to January 1877* (Ottawa, 1877), 36–37.

53. Contract 1 (awarded 17 October 1874): Selkirk to Livingstone, 295 miles; Contract 2 (awarded 30 October 1874): Livingstone to Edmonton, 517 miles; Contract 3 (awarded 10 November 1874): Edmonton to Cache Creek, 557 miles; Contract 4 (awarded 9 February 1875): Fort William to Selkirk, 410 miles.

54. Canada, Parliament, House of Commons, *Journals*, 1877, 25.

55. H. A. F. Macleod, "Progress Report on the Surveys Made in the North-West Territories during the year 1875," in Fleming, *Report on Surveys*, appendix M, 189–203.

56. H. A. F. Macleod, "Progress Report on the Surveys Made in the Western Prairie Region, and on the Eastern Slope of the Rocky Mountains," in Fleming, *Report on Surveys*, appendix Y, 337–52.

57. G. C. Cunningham, "Report on Preliminary Survey between Lake Winnipegosis and Livingstone during the Summer and Autumn of 1874," in Fleming, *Report on Surveys*, appendix L, 185.

58. Cunningham, "Report on Preliminary Survey."

59. The telegraph was an important tool in survey operations and was often used, to pinpoint locations. A location whose longitude is known is made the base station. From this point, as well as at the point whose longitude is wanted, observations of the transits of certain stars are taken and the times of the transits carefully noted by a chronometer. The astronomers then go to the telegraph office at their respective locations and compare the transits by means of the telegraph. The difference in time between the base station and that whose longitude is required is ascertained and verified. The longitude is then determined by performing a series of mathematical calculations.

60. King and Dennis, "General Report of Operations," 18.

61. S. Fleming, *Letter to the Secretary of State, Canada, in Reference to the Report of the Canadian Pacific Railway Royal Commission* (Ottawa, 1887), 5.

62. S. Fleming, ed., *Progress Report on the Canadian Pacific Railway Exploratory Survey* (Ottawa, 1872), 6–7.

63. S. Fleming to Minister of Public Works, 19 April 1872, Sandford Fleming Papers, vol. 64, 210–11, MG 29 B1, Manuscript Division, NAC.

64. S. Fleming, ed., *Report on Surveys and Preliminary Operations on the Canadian Pacific Railway up to January, 1877* (Ottawa, 1877), 57.

65. Fleming, *Report on Surveys*, 16.

66. S. Fleming, ed., *Canadian Pacific Railway Report of Progress on the Exploration and Surveys up to January, 1874* (Ottawa, 1874), 32.

67. Fleming, *Canadian Pacific Railway Report*, 34–35.

68. For a listing of the various routes, see Fleming, *Canadian Pacific Railway Report*, 18–19.

69. Fleming, *Canadian Pacific Railway Report*, 32–33.

70. Fleming, *Canadian Pacific Railway Report*, 31–32.

71. Fleming, *Report on Surveys*, 33–34.

72. Owram, *Promise of Eden*, 122–23.

73. A. Wilson, "Fleming and Tupper: The Fall of the Siamese Twins," in J. S. Moir, ed., *Character and Circumstance* (Toronto, 1970), 108–13. For an assessment of the two routes, see S. Fleming to Minister of Public Works, 2 May 1879, Fleming Papers, vol. 65, 11–21, Manuscript Division, NAC.

74. S. Fleming, ed., *Report in Reference to the Canadian Pacific Railway* (Ottawa, 1879).

75. *Report of the Canadian Pacific Railway Royal Commission*, vol. 3 (Ottawa 1882), 495.

76. This decision to reroute the main line through the southern grasslands was not based, as is widely assumed, on a reassessment of the agricultural potential of the region. Rather, the syndicate was determined to secure all the potential traffic of the Northwest by eliminating possible competition from American-based railways. Since the main line could serve or control only a limited area, the CPR builders decided to crowd the international boundary as closely as possible as would be permitted by the federal government. This attempt to exclude American inroads into western Canada was further necessitated because the railway was to be an all-Canadian route running through the wilderness north of Lake Superior. Western traffic had to be secured to support this nonrevenue-producing region. The syndicate therefore thought primarily in terms of national strategy, not local conditions; it would have built across the prairies even if the area was poorly regarded, relying on branch lines north into the fertile belt. For a detailed discussion of this question, see W. A. Waiser, "A Willing Scapegoat: John Macoun and the Route for the CPR," *Prairie Forum* 10, no. 1 (summer 1985): 66–81.

77. Morris Zaslow, *Reading the Rocks: The Story of the Geological Survey of Canada, 1842–1972* (Toronto, 1975), 34, 107–8.

78. Thomson, *Men and Meridians*, 288.

79. For an outline of survey activities in central and eastern Canada in the 1870s, see Thomson, *Men and Meridians*, 116–20.

80. Waiser, *The Field Naturalist*, 28–31.

81. Zaslow, *Reading the Rocks*, 114, 154.

82. See D. Cole and B. Lockner, eds., *The Journals of George M. Dawson: British Columbia, 1875–1878*, 2 vols. (Vancouver, 1989).

83. Quoted in A. H. Lang, "G. M. Dawson and the Economic Development of Western Canada," *Canadian Public Administration* 14, no. 2 (summer 1971): 239.

84. Cole and Lockner, *Journals of George M. Dawson* 1:13–18.

85. Zaslow, *Reading the Rocks*, 121.

86. Zaslow, *Reading the Rocks*, 108.

87. Zaslow, *Reading the Rocks*, 135; de Vecchi, "Science and Government in the Nineteenth Century," 222–23.

88. Zaslow, *Reading the Rocks*, 177–83.

89. John Warkentin, *The Western Interior of Canada: A Record of Geographical Discovery, 1612–1917* (Toronto, 1964), 263–64.

90. Zaslow, *Reading the Rocks*, 158.

91. Zaslow, *Reading the Rocks*, 159.

92. "Summary Report of the Geological Survey of Canada for 1901," Canada, Parliament, House of Commons, *Sessional Papers* 36, no. 19 (1903): 1.

93. J. W. Tyrrell subsequently wrote a popular account of the expedition: *Across the Sub-Arctic of Canada* (Toronto, 1897).

94. J. B. Tyrrell, "Notes on the Pleistocene of the North-West Territories of Canada, North-West and West of Hudson Bay," *Geological Magazine*, decade 4, vol. 1, no. 363 (September 1894): 397.

95. Zaslow, *Reading the Rocks*.

96. W. G. Ross, "Canadian Sovereignty in the Arctic: The *Neptune* Expedition of 1903–04," *Arctic* 29, no. 2 (1976): 87–104.

97. E. Chambers, *Canada's Fertile Northland: A Glimpse of the Enormous Resources of Part of the Unexplored Regions of the Dominion* (Ottawa, 1908).

98. Cole and Lockner, *Journals of George M. Dawson* 1:18–22.

99. Canada, Parliament, House of Commons, *Journals* 42, appendix 4, "Report of the Select Standing Committee on Agriculture and Colonization," 18. Macoun's son, James, made a negative assessment of the Peace River country in 1904 and nearly lost his position. See W. A. Waiser, "A Bear Garden: James Melville Macoun and the 1904 Peace River Controversy," *Canadian Historical Review* 67, no. 1 (March 1986): 42–61.

100. For a discussion of the national museum question, see Waiser, *The Field Naturalist*, especially chap. 4.

## 22. Scientific Exploration of the American West, 1865–1900

1. Michael James Lacey, "The Mysteries of Earth-Making Dissolve: A Study of Washington's Intellectual Community and the Origins of American Environmentalism in the Late Nineteenth Century" (Ph.D. diss., George Washington University, 1979); J. Kirkpatrick Flack, *Desideratum in Washington: The Intellectual Community in the Capital City, 1870–1900* (Cambridge MA, 1975). See also George Browne Goode, ed., *The Smithsonian Institution, 1846–1896: The History of the First Half* (Washington DC, 1897).

2. Lacey, "Mysteries of Earth-Making Dissolve," 14–28; "Baird, Spencer Fullerton," *Dictionary of American Biography*, 20 vols. (New York, 1928–55). See also William Healey Dall, *Spencer Fullerton Baird: A Biography* (Philadelphia, 1915).

3. Lacey, "Mysteries of Earth-Making Dissolve," 29–43.

4. Lacey, "Mysteries of Earth-Making Dissolve," 51–59, quotation p. 51; "Gannett, Henry," *Dictionary of American Biography*. See also S. N. D. North, "Henry Gannett," *National Geographic Magazine* 26 (December 1914): 609–13.

5. Lacey, "Mysteries of Earth-Making Dissolve"; Thomas G. Manning, *Government in Science: The U.S. Geological Survey, 1867–1894* (Lexington KY, 1967); and A. Hunter Dupree, *Science in the Federal Government: A History of Policies and Activities to 1940* (Cambridge MA, 1957).

6. A. Joseph Wraight and Elliott B. Roberts, *The Coast and Geodetic Survey, 1807–1957* (Washington DC, 1957).

7. "Hornaday, William Temple," *Dictionary of American Biography*.

8. Lacey, "Mysteries of Earth-Making Dissolve," 70–82.

9. Flack, *Desideratum in Washington*, 55–98.

10. Flack, *Desideratum in Washington*, 55–98.

11. William H. Goetzmann, *Exploration and Empire: The Explorer and the Scientist in the Winning of the American West* (New York, 1966). Papers of individual explorers as well as their biographies have in most instances been published.

12. Richard A. Bartlett, *Great Surveys of the American West* (1962; reprint, Norman, 1986), 3–34; Goetzmann, *Exploration and Empire*, 489–529.

13. Bartlett, *Great Surveys*, 4–6, quotation p. 4; Clifford M. Nelson and Fritiof Fryxell, "The Ante-Bellum Collaboration of Meek and Hayden in Stratigraphy," in Cecil J. Schneer, ed., *Two Hundred Years of Geology in America* (Hanover NH, 1979), 187–200.

14. Nelson and Fryxell, "Ante-Bellum Collaboration of Meek and ·Hayden," 188–89.

15. Nelson and Fryxell, "Ante-Bellum Collaboration of Meek and Hayden," 190.

16. Bartlett, *Great Surveys*, 3–7; Nelson and Fryxell, "Ante-Bellum Collaboration of Meek and Hayden," 190, 192.

17. Nelson and Fryxell, "Ante-Bellum Collaboration of Meek and Hayden," 196–97. See also Mike Foster, "The Permian Controversy of 1858: An Affair of the Heart," *Proceedings of the American Philosophical Society* 133 (1989): 370–90.

18. *U.S. Statutes at Large* 14:470.

19. Unless otherwise stated, the essay on the Hayden Survey is based on Bartlett, *Great Surveys*, 3–120.

20. *U.S. Statutes at Large* 15:119.

21. Government publications of the Great Surveys are listed in Laurence F. Schmeckebier, *Catalogue and Index of the Hayden, King, Powell, and Wheeler Surveys* (Washington DC, 1904).

22. *U.S. Statutes at Large* 15:306.

23. William Henry Jackson, *Time Exposure* (1940; paperback reprint, Albuquerque, 1986).

24. F. V. Hayden, "Letter to the Secretary," *Fourth Annual Report* (Washington DC), 6–8. A brief survey of Hayden's activities into the early 1870s is Gilbert F. Stucker, "Hayden in the Badlands," *American West* 4 (February 1967): 40–45, 79–85.

25. Richard A. Bartlett, "From Imagination to Reality: Thomas Moran and the Yellowstone," in Jack Salzman, ed., *Prospects: An Annual of American Cultural Studies* 3 (1977): 111–24.

26. Richard A. Bartlett, *Nature's Yellowstone* (1974; paperback reprint, Tucson, 1989). See also Aubrey L. Haines, *The Yellowstone Story*, 2 vols. (Boulder, 1977), vol. 1.

27. Charles W. Cook, David E. Folsom, and William Peterson, *The Valley of the Upper Yellowstone*, ed. Aubrey L. Haines (Norman, 1965).

28. William R. Keefer, *The Geologic Story of Yellowstone Park*, U.S. Geological Survey Bulletin no. 1437 (Washington DC, 1972).

29. Ernest Ingersoll wrote two travel books largely based on his experiences with the Hayden Survey: *Knocking Around the Rockies* (New York, 1883), and *The Crest of the Continent* (Chicago, 1885).

30. Bartlett, *Great Surveys*, 99.

31. Clarence S. Jackson and Lawrence W. Marshall, *Quest of the Snowy Cross* (Denver, 1952).

32. At the time of this writing (1991), Hayden, unlike King and Powell (but like Wheeler) lacks a full-length, scholarly biography.

33. Unless otherwise stated, the essay on the King Survey is based on Bartlett, *Great Surveys*, 123–215. See also Thurman Wilkins, *Clarence King* (1953; paperback reprint, Albuquerque, 1988); Harry Crosby, "So Deep a Trail" (Ph.D. diss., Stanford University, 1953); Goetzmann, *Exploration and Empire*, 430–66; and Clifford M. Nelson and Mary C. Rabbit, "The Role of Clarence King in the Advancement of Geology in the Public Service, 1867–1881," in A. E. Leviton, P. U. Rodda, E. L. Yochelson, and M. L. Aldrich, eds., "Frontiers of Geological Exploration of Western North America," *Proceedings of the American Association for the Advancement of Science, Pacific Division* (San Francisco, 1982).

34. *U.S. Statutes at Large* 14:457.

35. Quoted in Bartlett, *Great Surveys*, 144.

36. Jarres D. Horan, *Timothy O'Sullivan: America's Forgotten Photographer* (New York, 1956), 151–214.

37. Quoted in Bartlett, *Great Surveys*, 144.

38. Bartlett, *Great Surveys*, 203.

39. Bartlett, *Great Surveys*, 206.

40. Bartlett, *Great Surveys*, 207.

41. Clifford N. Nelson and Ellis L. Yochelson, "Organizing Federal Paleontology in the United States, 1858–1907," *Journal of the Society for the Bibliography of Natural History* 3 (1980): 607–18.

42. Nelson and Yochelson, "Organizing Federal Paleontology," 609–10.

43. Bartlett, *Great Surveys*, 218–329: see also Goetzmann, *Exploration and Empire*, 530–76, and William Culp Darrah, *Powell of the Colorado* (Princeton, 1951). The diaries were reprinted in *Utah Historical Quarterly* 15–17 (1947–49); Wallace Stegner, *Beyond the Hundredth Meridian* (Boston, 1953).

44. Stephen J. Pyne, *Grove Karl Gilbert: A Great Engine of Research* (Austin, 1980).

45. There is no biography of Wheeler or history of his survey. This essay is based on Bartlett, *Great Surveys*, 333–72; see also Goetzmann, *Exploration and Empire*, 467–89, and Peter L. Guth, "George Montague Wheeler, Last Army Explorer of the American West" (master's thesis, West Point, 1975).

46. George M. Wheeler, *Report on the United States Geographical Surveys West of the One Hundredth Meridian*, 7 vols. (Washington DC, 1875–89).

47. Bartlett, *Great Surveys*, Goetzmann, *Exploration and Empire*, Dupree, *Science in the Federal Government*, and Wilkins, *Clarence King*, discuss the consolidation. See also National Academy of Sciences, *A Report on the Surveys of the Territories*, 45th Cong., 2d sess., 1879, H. Doc. 270.

48. See Ellis L. Yochelson, "Charles Doolittle Walcott, 1850–1927," in National Academy of Sciences, *Biographical Memoirs* 39 (1967): 471–540. A paper encapsulat-

ing the history of paleontology in the United States between 1804 and 1904 is Clifford M. Nelson, "Paleontology in the United States Federal Service, 1804–1904," *Earth Sciences History* 1 (1982): 48–57.

49. See Orrin H. Bonney and Lorraine G. Bonney, *Battle Drums and Geysers: Lieutenant Doane* (Chicago, 1970).

50. Leland D. Case, "History Catches Up," in Roderick Peattie, ed., *The Black Hills* (New York, 1952), 75–96; see also Donald Jackson, *Custer's Gold: The United States Cavalry Expedition of 1874* (1966; reprint, Lincoln, 1972), 46–73.

51. Walter P. Jenney, *Report on the Mineral Wealth, Climate and Rainfall, and Natural Resources of the Black Hills of Dakota*, 44th Cong., 1st sess., 1877, S. Exec. Doc. 51.

52. Url Lanham, *The Bone Hunters* (New York, 1973), 79–100, quotation p. 84.

53. Lanham, *Bone Hunters*, 187.

54. See Paul Russell Cutright and Michael J. Brodhead, *Elliott Coues: Naturalist and Frontier Historian* (Urbana, 1981).

## 23. A "Capacity for Wonder"

1. F. Scott Fitzgerald, *The Great Gatsby* (1925), ed. Malcolm Cowley (New York, 1953), 137.

2. Also see Stephen Pyne, "A Third Great Age of Discovery," in Carl Sagan and Stephen Pyne, *The Scientific and Historical Rationales for Solar System Exploration*, Space Policy Institute, Elliott School of International Affairs, George Washington University, SPI 81-1 (Washington DC, 1988), 31–32.

3. Terence Grieder, *Origins of Pre-Columbian Art* (Austin, 1982), chaps. 2, 4, 6.

4. Joseph Needham, *The Shorter Science and Civilization in China: An Abridgement*, 2 vols., ed. Colin A. Ronan (Cambridge, U.K., 1986), 128–59.

5. Pyne, "A Third Great Age of Discovery," 27.

6. Peter Gay, *The Enlightenment, an Interpretation: The Rise of Modern Paganism* (New York, 1968).

7. Barbara Stafford, *Voyage into Substance: Art, Science, Nature, and the Illustrated Travel Account, 1760–1840* (Cambridge, U.K., 1984).

8. J. H. Parry, *Trade and Dominion* (London, 1971), 3–13; Parry, *The Discovery of the Sea* (Berkeley, 1981).

9. Pyne, "A Third Great Age of Discovery," 23.

10. Pyne, "A Third Great Age of Discovery," 35.

11. Pyne elegantly dated the end of the Second Great Age of Discovery with the advent of self-reflexivity in a work published in 1902, Joseph Conrad's *The Heart of Darkness*, where the protagonist, far up the Congo, ultimately finds only himself

and can only utter "the horror, the horror" at such knowledge, and with Robert Falcon Scott's tragically documented 1912 journey into white nothingness at the South Pole that resulted only in self-recognition and death. In *New Lands, New Men,* I have come to an almost identical conclusion for the end of the Second Great Age of Discovery: Robert E. Peary's reaching the North Pole in 1909, after which he became a virtual recluse for the rest of his life.

12. Frank Waters, *The Book of the Hopi* (New York, 1963), 31–124.

13. Pyne, "A Third Great Age of Discovery," 36–46.

14. Quoted in Richard A. Van Orman, *The Explorers: Nineteenth-Century Expeditions in Africa and the American West* (Albuquerque, 1984), 71.

15. See especially William H. Goetzmann, *New Lands, New Men: America and the Second Great Age of Discovery* (New York, 1986), 1–15.

16. See Herbert Hovencamp, *Science and Religion in America, 1800–1860* (Philadelphia, 1978).

17. See Alfred W. Crosby, *The Columbian Exchange: Biological and Cultural Consequences of 1492* (Westport CT, 1972), 122–60. Also see Crosby, *Ecological Imperialism: The Biological Expansion of Europe 900–1900* (Cambridge, U.K., 1986).

18. See Louis Antoine de Bougainville, *A Voyage round the World,* trans. J. R. Forster (London, 1772).

19. See Francis Jennings, *The Invasion of America: Indians, Colonialism, and the Cant of Conquest* (Chapel Hill, 1975).

20. Jennings, *The Invasion of America.*

21. William Faulkner, "The Bear," *Go Down Moses and Other Stories* (New York, 1942).

22. Patricia Nelson Limerick, *The Legacy of Conquest: The Unbroken Past of the American West* (New York, 1987).

23. Wilbur Jacobs, "Frontiersmen, Fur Traders, and Other Varmints," *American Historical Association Newsletter,* 1970–71.

24. See James Fenimore Cooper, The Leatherstocking Tales, especially *The Prairie* (1827) and the *Pioneers* (1826).

25. It was so termed in Michael Wigglesworth, *The Day of Doom* (1662).

26. See Henry Nash Smith, *Virgin Land: The American West as Symbol and Myth* (Cambridge MA, 1950).

27. Walter P. Webb, *The Great Frontier* (Austin, 1951), 21–28, 413 ff.

28. See Michel Foucault, *Archeology of Knowledge and the Discourse on Language,* trans. A. M. Sheridan Smith (New York, 1972). Also see Michel Foucault, *The Order of Things: An Archeology of the Human Sciences (Les Mots Et Les Choses)* (New York, 1973).

29. See Limerick, *The Legacy of Conquest,* 30 n.23.

30. See Pyne, "A Third Great Age of Discovery," 2 n.3. However, expeditions in the Third Great Age of Discovery need not be prosthetic and nonhuman. The current projections for a manned trip to Mars are between eight months and eighteen months, depending on the route. This makes a Mars trip, even a manned expedition, easily comparable in terms of time frames to the voyages of the Second Great Age of Discovery.

31. Martin Heidegger, *Basic Writings* (New York, 1977), 319–40.

32. Goetzmann, *New Lands, New Men*, 265–97.

33. Goetzmann, *New Lands, New Men*, 357–58.

34. William H. Goetzmann, *Exploration and Empire: The Explorer and the Scientist in the Winning of the American West* (New York, 1966), 246–47. See Goetzmann, *New Lands, New Men*, 68, for Baron de Lahontan's map showing the "Morte or Rivier Longue," that is, the Buenaventura.

35. See Lee Clark Mitchell, *Witnesses to a Vanishing America: The Nineteenth Century* (Princeton, 1981), chaps. 7 and 8, 189–251.

36. Professor Norman Holmes Pearson to Professor Bronislaw Malinowski, story related to William Goetzmann, 1954, Yale University; also see Norman Holmes Pearson, "The Nature and Possibilities of American Studies," in Joseph Milton Nance, ed., *Some Reflections upon Modern America* (Austin, 1968), 3.

37. Bernard DeVoto, introduction to *The Life and Adventures of James P. Beckwourth*, ed. T. D. Bonner (New York, 1931), xxvii.

38. James Fenimore Cooper, *The Prairie* (New York, 1950), 8.

39. David Potter, *People of Plenty: Economic Abundance and the American Character* (Chicago, 1954).

40. Perry Miller, *Nature's Nation* (Cambridge MA, 1967).

41. J. C. Beaglehole, ed., *The Journals of Captain James Cook on His Voyages of Discovery*, 4 vols. in 5 (Cambridge, U.K., 1955–74), 1:xciv–xcv.

42. William H. Goetzmann and William N. Goetzmann, *The West of the Imagination* (New York, 1986), 155.

43. Rudyard Kipling, "The Explorer" (1898).

# Selected Bibliography

## North American Exploration, Volume III

The third volume of *North American Exploration* encompasses the nineteenth-century transition from the Humboldtean explorers of the Age of Enlightenment, who sought confirmation of God's grand design in new lands and new peoples, and the post-Darwinian scientific explorers, who were less concerned with fitting all they saw and sensed into a cosmos than they were with compiling data that would verify theory and generate hypotheses. Given the enormous numbers of exploratory expeditions in North America during this period—beginning with Meriwether Lewis and William Clark and concluding with the Great Surveys of the post–Civil War period—the literature is voluminous. The following bibliographic listing, therefore, is partial and somewhat arbitrary, although it should be understood as a reasonably complete coverage of the key explorers and expeditions in the United States and Canada from 1800 to 1900. Because the nineteenth century has generated such a large collection of articles in periodicals and professional journals, I have chosen to avoid those sources in this selection in favor of book-length studies and, of course, the primary sources of the journals and accounts of the explorers themselves. Readers wanting more bibliographic information will find it in the reference notes accompanying each of the chapters in this volume. The items listed in this selected bibliography should be available in both medium-sized public libraries and most college and university libraries. The secondary sources tend to dominate the collections in public libraries. For a good selection of primary materials, the reader will need to visit college and university libraries, along with some specialized larger private and municipal libraries. The secondary sources by scholars and others describe the processes of exploration and provide details on routes and on the explorers themselves. The secondary sources offered here are among the very best of a huge collection, and the stories they tell are rich and rewarding. As always, even more rewarding are the words of the explorers and their contemporaries. For the reader whose interest in nineteenth-century North American exploration is profound, the primary sources should be sought out. Follow Lewis and Clark as they "proceeded on" up the Missouri and across the plains and Rockies to the Pacific and back; enjoy the fullness of their experience as they perceived it (and the uniqueness of their spelling). See the Great Basin unfold in the mind of John Charles Frémont as he solves one of the great geographical riddles of the continent. And experience the quest for scientific knowledge that motivated men such as John Wesley Powell and

F. V. Hayden to endure incredible hardship while their academic counterparts were as comfortable as late Victorian technology allowed. The word-pictures of the participants in the romanticism and exoticism and utilitarianism and Darwinism of the nineteenth century are, like those of earlier players in the drama of North American exploration, the best sources of all. They enable us to feel the chill of the Wind River as its waters penetrate the elkskin moccasins of a fur trapper, to smell the sagebrush of the Great American Desert, to shiver with cold in the ice-bound ships during the final search for the Northwest Passage. They also enable us to experience the thrill of the awakening awareness of the role of landscapes in the understanding that humans attempt to bring to their view of the world.

Abel, Annie H., ed. *Tabeau's Narrative of Loisel's Expedition to the Upper Missouri*. Norman, 1939.

Abert, James W. *Journal of Lieutenant James W. Abert from Bent's Fort to St. Louis*. 29th Cong., 1st sess., 1846, Exec. Doc. 438.

Allen, John L. *Passage through the Garden: Lewis and Clark and the Image of the American Northwest*. Urbana, 1975.

Allen, Paul. *History of the Expedition under the Command of Captains Lewis and Clark.* . . . Ed. Nicholas Biddle. Philadelphia, 1814.

Armstrong, Alexander. *A Personal Narrative of the Discovery of the North-West Passage*. London, 1857.

Back, George. *Narrative of the Arctic Land Expedition to the Mouth of the Great Fish River, and along the Shores of the Arctic Ocean, in the Years 1833, 1834, and 1835*. 1836. Reprint, Edmonton, Alberta, 1970.

Bailey, Alfred Goldsworthy, ed. *The Letters of James and Ellen Robb*. Fredericton, New Brunswick, 1983.

Barrow, John. *A Chronological History of Voyages into the Arctic Regions*. . . . 1818. Reprint, Devon, U.K., 1971.

———. Review of *Narrative of a Voyage to Hudsons Bay*, by Lieut. William Chappell, R.N. *Quarterly Review* (October 1817): 199–200.

———. *Voyages of Discovery and Research within the Arctic Regions, from the Year 1818 to the Present Time*. London, 1846.

Bartlett, John Russel. *Personal Narrative of Explorations and Incidents in Texas, New Mexico, California, Sonora, and Chihuahua, Connected with the United States and Mexican Boundary Commission during the Years 1850, 1851, 1852, and 1853*. 2 vols. New York, 1854.

Bartlett, Richard A. *Great Surveys of the American West*. 1962. Reprint, Norman, 1986.

———. *Nature's Yellowstone*. 1974. Paperback reprint, Tucson, 1989.

Bateman, Richard. *James Pattie's West: The Dream and the Reality*. Norman, 1986.

Beaglehole, J. C., ed. *The Journals of Captain James Cook: The Voyage of the "Resolution" and "Discovery," 1776–1780*. Cambridge, U.K., 1967.

Beattie, Owen, and John Geiger. *Frozen in Time: Unlocking the Secrets of the Franklin Expedition*. Saskatoon, Saskatchewan, 1987.

Beechey, Frederick W. *Narrative of a Voyage to the Pacific and Bering's Strait*. 2 vols. 1845. Reprint, Bibliotheca Australiana no. 34, Amsterdam, 1969.

Bender, Averam B. *The March of Empire: Frontier Defense in the Southwest, 1848–1860*. Lawrence, 1952.

Benson, Maxine, ed. *From Pittsburgh to the Rocky Mountains: Major Stephen Long's Expedition, 1819–1820*. Golden CO, 1988.

Berton, Pierre. *The Arctic Grail: The Quest for the Northwest Passage and the North Pole, 1818–1909*. Toronto, 1988.

Bidwell, John. *Journey to California*. San Francisco, 1937.

Bieber, Ralph P., ed. *Exploring Southwestern Trails, 1846–1854*. Glendale CA, 1938.

Bockstoce, John R. *Steam Whaling in the Western Arctic*. New Bedford MA, 1977.

———. *Whales, Ice, and Men: The History of Whaling in the Western Arctic*. Seattle, 1986.

Bonney, Orrin H., and Lorraine G. Bonney. *Battle Drums and Geysers: Lieutenant Doane*. Chicago, 1970.

Bradbury, John. *Travels in the Interior of America*. Liverpool, 1817.

Brandon, William. *The Men and the Mountain: Frémont's Fourth Expedition*. New York, 1955.

Bray, Martha Coleman. *Joseph N. Nicollet on the Plains and Prairies*. Minneapolis, 1976.

———. *Joseph Nicollet and His Map*. Philadelphia, 1980.

———. *The Journals of Joseph N. Nicollet: A Scientist on the Mississippi Headwaters with Notes on Indian Life*. Minneapolis, 1970.

Brooks, George R. *The Southwest Expedition of Jedediah Smith: His Personal Account of the Journey to California, 1826–27*. Glendale CA, 1977.

Brown, John. *The North-West Passage, and the Plans for the Search for Sir John Franklin: A Review*. London, 1858.

Bryce, George. *The Siege and Conquest of the North Pole*. London, 1910.

Burpee, Lawrence J. *The Search for the Western Sea*. 2 vols. Toronto, 1908.

Calvin, Ross, ed. *Lieutenant Emory Reports: A Reprint of Lieutenant W. H. Emory's Notes of Military Reconnaissance*. Albuquerque, 1951.

Camp, Charles L., ed. *James Clyman, Frontiersman*. Portland OR, 1960.

Campbell, Marjorie Wilkins. *The North West Company*. Toronto, 1957.

Carvalho, Solomon Nuñes. *Incidents of Travel and Adventure in the Far West, with Col. Fremont's Last Expedition across the Rocky Mountains: Including Three Months' Residence in Utah, and a Perilous Trip across the Great American Desert to the Pacific*. New York, 1860.

Carver, Jonathan. *Travels through the Interior Parts of North America*. London, 1781.

Caswell, John Edwards. *Arctic Frontiers: United States Exploration in the Far North*. Norman, 1956.

Catlin, George. *Letters and Notes on the Manner, Customs, and Condition of the North American Indians*. London, 1841.

Charlevoix, Pierre F. X. *Journal of a Voyage to North America*. 2 vols. London, 1761.

Chittenden, Hiram M. *The American Fur Trade of the Far West*. 2 vols. 1935. Reprint, Lincoln, 1986.

Cline, Gloria Griffen. *Peter Skene Ogden and the Hudson's Bay Company*. Norman, 1974.

Clokey, Richard M. *William H. Ashley: Enterprise and Politics in the Trans-Mississippi West*. Norman, 1980.

Cole, D., and B. Lockner, eds. *The Journals of George Mercer Dawson: British Columbia, 1875–1878*. Vol. 1, *1875–1876*. Vancouver, 1989.

Cole, Jean Murray. *Exile in the Wilderness: The Biography of Chief Factor Archibald McDonald, 1790–1853*. Don Mills ON, 1979.

Cooke, Alan, and Clive Holland. *The Exploration of Northern Canada, 500 to 1920: A Chronology*. Toronto, 1978.

Coues, Elliot, ed. *New Light on the Early History of the Greater Northwest: The Manuscript Journals of Alexander Henry, Fur Trader of the Northwest Company, and of David Thompson, Official Geographer and Explorer of the Same Company, 1799–1814*. 2 vols. New York, 1897.

Cox, Ross. *Adventures on the Columbia River*. London, 1831.

Coyner, David H. *The Lost Trappers: A Collection of Interesting Scenes and Events in the Rocky Mountains*. Cincinnati, 1847.

Cutright, Paul. *Lewis and Clark: Pioneering Naturalists*. Urbana, 1969.

Cutright, Paul Russell, and Michael J. Brodhead. *Elliott Coues: Naturalist and Frontier Historian*. Urbana, 1981.

Cyriax, Richard J. *Sir John Franklin's Last Arctic Expedition: A Chapter in the History of the Royal Navy*. London, 1939.

Dale, Harrison C. *The Ashley-Smith Explorations and the Discovery of a Central Route to the Pacific, 1822–1829*. Glendale CA, 1941.

Darrah, William Culp. *Powell of the Colorado*. Princeton, 1951.

Davidson, Gordon Charles. *The North West Company*. New York, 1918.

Davies, K. G., A. M. Johnson, and Dorothy O. Johansen, eds. *Peter Skene Ogden's Snake Country Journal, 1826–27*. London, 1961.

Davis, Richard C., ed. *Rupert's Land: A Cultural Tapestry*. Waterloo ON, 1988.

Dawson, G. M. *Report on the Geology and Resources of the Region in the Vicinity of the 49th Parallel, from Lake of the Woods to the Rocky Mountains*. Montreal, 1875.

Day, Alan Edwin. *Search for the Northwest Passage: An Annotated Bibliography*. New York, 1986.

DeVoto, Bernard. *Across the Wide Missouri*. Boston, 1947.

Dodge, Bertha S. *The Road West: Saga of the 35th Parallel*. Albuquerque, 1980.

Dodge, Ernest S. *The Polar Rosses: John and James Clark Ross and Their Expeditions*. London, 1973.

Egan, Ferol. *Frémont, Explorer for a Restless Nation*. Garden City NY, 1977.

Ehrenberg, Ralph, and Herman Viola. "Exploring the American West Series," introduction to John Charles Frémont, *The Exploring Expedition to the Rocky Mountains*. Washington DC, 1988.

Emory, William H. *Notes of a Military Reconnaissance from Fort Leavenworth in Missouri, to San Diego in California Including Parts of the Arkansas, Del Norte [Rio Grande], and Gila Rivers*. 30th Cong., 1st sess., 1848, H. Doc. 41.

———. *Report on the United States and Mexican Boundary Survey*. 34th Cong., 1st sess., 1847, H. Doc. 135.

Erskine, Charles. *Twenty Years before the Mast with the More Thrilling Scenes and Incidents while Circumnavigating the Globe under the Command of the Late Admiral Charles Wilkes, 1838–1842*. Washington DC, 1985.

Faulk, Odie B., ed. *Personal Narrative. . . .* 2 vols. Chicago, 1965.

Featherstonhaugh, A. *Narrative of the Operations of the British North American Boundary Commission, 1872–76*. Woolwich, U.K., 1876.

Ferris, Warren Angus. *Life in the Rocky Mountains*. Denver, 1940.

[Field, Matthew]. *Prairie and Rocky Mountains Sketches*. Ed. Kate L. Gregg and John F. McDermott. Norman, 1957.

Fisher, Alexander. *Journal of a Voyage of Discovery to the Arctic Regions, in His Majesty's Ships Hecla and Griper, in the Years 1819 & 1820*. London, 1821.

Fleming, S., ed. *Progress Report on the Canadian Pacific Railway Exploratory Survey*. Ottawa, 1872.

———. *Report in Reference to the Canadian Pacific Railway*. Ottawa, 1879.

———. *Report on Surveys and Preliminary Operations on the Canadian Pacific Railway up to January 1877*. Ottawa, 1877.

Flores, Dan L., ed. *Jefferson and Southwestern Exploration: The Freeman and Custis Accounts of the Red River Expedition of 1806*. Norman, 1984.

Foreman, Grant. *Marcy and the Gold-Seekers*. Norman, 1939.

———, ed. *Adventure on the Red River*. Norman, 1937.

Francis, Daniel. *Arctic Chase: A History of Whaling in Canada's North*. St. John's NF, 1984.

———. *Discovery of the North: The Exploration of Canada's Arctic*. Edmonton, Alberta, 1986.

Franklin, John. *Narrative of a Journey to the Shores of the Polar Sea in the Years 1819–20–21–22*. 1823. Reprint, London, 1910.

———. *Narrative of a Second Expedition to the Shores of the Polar Sea*. 1829. Reprint, Edmonton AB, 1971.

Frémont, John C. *Memoirs of My Life*. Chicago, 1877.

———. *Narratives of Exploration and Adventure*. Ed. Allan Nevins. New York, 1956.

———. *Report of the Exploring Expedition to the Rocky Mountains in the Year 1842, and to Oregon and North California in the Years 1843–44*. 28th Cong., 2d sess., 1845, S. Doc. 174, serial 461. Commercial edition, New York, 1848.

Fuller, Harlin M., and LeRoy R. Hafen, eds. *The Journal of Captain John R. Bell*. Glendale CA, 1973.

Galvin, John, ed. *Western America, 1846–1847: The Original Travel Diary of Lieutenant J. W. Abert, Who Mapped New Mexico for the United States Army, with Illustrations in Color from His Sketchbook*. San Francisco, 1936.

Gibson, James R. *Imperial Russia in Frontier America*. New York, 1976.

Goetzmann, William H. *Army Exploration in the American West, 1803–1863*. New Haven, 1959.

———. *Exploration and Empire: The Explorer and the Scientist in the Winning of the American West*. New York, 1966.

———. *The West as Romantic Horizon*. Lincoln, 1981.

Goetzmann, William H., and William N. Goetzmann. *The West of the Imagination*. New York, 1986.

Gough, Barry M. "British-Russian Rivalry and the Search for the Northwest Passage in the Early 19th Century." *Polar Record 23* (1986): 301–17.

———, ed. *To the Pacific and Arctic with Beechey*. Cambridge, U.K., 1973.

Greely, Adolphus W. *Three Years of Arctic Service: An Account of the Lady Franklin Bay Expedition of 1881–84 and the Attainment of the Farthest North*. 2 vols. London, 1886.

Gregg, Josiah. *Commerce of the Prairies; or, The Journal of a Santa Fe Trader, during Eight Expeditions across the Great Western Prairies and a Residence of Nearly Nine Years in Northern Mexico*. Ed. Max Moorhead. Norman, 1954.

Gudde, Erwin G., and Elisabeth K. Gudde, eds. *Exploring with Frémont: The Private Diaries of Charles Preuss, Cartographer for John C. Frémont on His First, Second, and Fourth Expeditions to the Far West*. Norman, 1958.

Gunnison, John W. *The Mormons or Latter Day Saints in the Valley of the Great Salt Lake: A History of Their Rise and Progress, Peculiar Doctrines, Present Conditions, and Prospects*. Philadelphia, 1852.

Hafen, LeRoy R., ed. *The Mountain Men and the Fur Trade of the Far West*. 10 vols. Glendale CA, 1965–72.

Hafen, Leroy R., and Ann W. Hafen, eds. *Frémont's Fourth Expedition: A Documentary Account of the Disaster of 1848–1849 with Diaries, Letters, and Reports by Participants in the Tragedy.* Glendale CA, 1960.

Haines, Aubrey L. *The Yellowstone Story.* 2 vols. Boulder, 1977.

Hales, Peter Bacon. *William Henry Jackson and the Transformation of the American Landscape.* Philadelphia, 1988.

Harmon, Daniel Williams. *A Journal of Voyages and Travels in the Interior of North America.* Andover CT, 1820.

Harris, Burton. *John Colter: His Years in the Rockies.* New York, 1952.

Haskell, Daniel C. *The United States Exploring Expedition, 1838–1842, and Its Publications, 1844–1874.* 1942. Reprint, New York, 1968.

Hayden, F. V. *Geological Report of the Exploration . . . under the Direction of Captain (Lt. Col. and Brevet Brig. Gen.) W. F. Raynolds, Corps of Engineers, 1859–60.* Washington DC, 1869.

Hayes, Isaac I. *The Open Polar Sea: A Narrative of a Voyage of Discovery towards the North Pole, in the Schooner "United States."* London, 1867.

Hayman, John, ed. *Robert Brown and the Vancouver Island Exploring Expedition.* Vancouver, 1989.

Heap, Gwin Harris. *Central Route to the Pacific with Related Material on Railroad Explorations and Indian Affairs by Edward F. Beale, Thomas H. Benton, Kit Carson, and Col. E. A. Hitchcock, and in Other Documents, 1853–54.* 1854. Reprint, ed. LeRoy R. Hafen and Ann W. Hafen, Glendale CA, 1957.

Heffernan, William J. *Edward M. Kern: The Travels of an Artist-Explorer.* Bakersfield CA, 1953.

Hind, Henry Y. *Narrative of the Canadian Red River Exploring Expedition.* 2 vols. 1860. Reprint, Edmonton AB, 1971.

Hine, Robert V. *Bartlett's West: Drawing the Mexican Boundary.* New Haven, 1968.

Hollon, Eugene W. *Beyond the Cross Timbers: The Travels of Randolph E. Marcy, 1812–1887.* Norman, 1955.

Horan, Jarres D. *Timothy O'Sullivan: America's Forgotten Photographer.* New York, 1956.

Houston, C. Stuart, ed. *Arctic Ordeal: The Journal of John Richardson, Surgeon-naturalist with Franklin, 1820–1822.* Kingston, 1984.

Humboldt, Alexander von. *Personal Narrative.* 1807. Ed. and trans. Thomasina Ross. 3 vols. 1814–26. Reprint, London, 1907.

Hunt, David C., and Marsha Gallagher. *Karl Bodmer's America.* Omaha, 1984.

Irving, Washington. *Astoria; or, Anecdotes of an Enterprise beyond the Rocky Mountains.* 1836. Reprint, Norman, 1964.

————. *The Rocky Mountains; or, Scenes, Incidents, and Adventures in the Far West.* 2 vols. Philadelphia, 1837.

Ives, Joseph C. *Report upon the Colorado River of the West.* 36th Cong., 1st sess., 1861, H. Doc. 90.

Jackson, Donald, ed. *The Journals of Zebulon Montgomery Pike with Letters and Related Documents.* 2 vols. Norman, 1966.

————. *The Letters of the Lewis and Clark Expedition with Related Documents, 1783–1854.* 2d ed., 2 vols. Urbana, 1978.

————. *Thomas Jefferson and the Stony Mountains: Exploring the West from Monticello.* Urbana, 1981.

Jackson, Donald, and Mary Lee Spence, eds. *The Expeditions of John Charles Frémont.* 3 vols. and map portfolio. Urbana, 1970–84.

Jackson, W. Turrentine. *Wagon Roads West: A Study of Federal Road Surveys and Construction in the Trans-Mississippi West, 1846–1869.* Lincoln, 1979.

Jackson, William Henry. *Time Exposure.* 1940. Paperback reprint, Albuquerque, 1986.

James, Edwin. *Account of an Expedition from Pittsburgh to the Rocky Mountains.* 2 vols. Philadelphia, 1823.

James, Thomas. *Three Years among the Indians and Mexicans.* 1846. Reprint, Chicago, 1953.

Johnson, Robert E. *Sir John Richardson: Arctic Explorer, Natural Historian, Naval Surgeon.* New York, 1976.

Kane, Elisha Kent. *Arctic Explorations in Search of Sir John Franklin.* London, 1879.

————. *Arctic Explorations in the Years 1853, '54, '55.* 2 vols. Philadelphia, 1856.

Karamanski, Theodore J. *Fur Trade and Exploration: Opening the Far Northwest, 1821–1852.* Norman, 1983.

Kearney, Stephen W. *Report of a Summer Campaign to the Rocky Mountains . . . in 1845.* 29th Cong., 1st sess., 1846, S. Doc. 1.

Kelley, Hall Jackson. *A Geographical Sketch of That Part of North America Called Oregon.* Boston, 1830.

King, Richard. *The Franklin Expedition from First to Last.* London, 1855.

————. *Narrative of a Journey to the Shores of the Arctic Ocean.* 2 vols. London, 1836.

Kirwan, L. P. *The White Road: A Survey of Polar Exploration.* London, 1959.

Kline, Gloria G. *Exploring the Great Basin.* Norman, 1963.

Kotzebue, Otto von. *A Voyage of Discovery, into the South Sea and Beering's Straits . . . in the Years 1815–1818 . . . in the Ship Rurick.* 3 vols. 1821. Reprint, Bibliotheca Australiana no. 17, Amsterdam, 1969.

Lamb, W. Kaye, ed. *The Journals and Letters of Sir Alexander Mackenzie.* Cambridge, U.K., 1970.

Leonard, Zenas. *Narrative of the Adventures of Zenas Leonard.* Clearfield PA, 1839.

Lloyd, Christopher. *Mr. Barrow of the Admiralty: A Life of Sir John Barrow, 1764–1848.* London, 1970.

Luebke, Frederick C., Frances W. Kaye, and Gary E. Moulton, eds. *Mapping the North American Plains: Essays in the History of Cartography.* Norman, 1987.

Lyell, Charles. *Travels in North America.* 2 vols. New York, 1845.

MacKay, Douglas. *The Honourable Company.* Freeport NY, 1970.

Macomb, John N. *Report of the Exploring Expedition from Santa Fe, New Mexico, to the Junction of the Grand and Green Rivers of the Great Colorado of the West in 1859.* Washington DC, 1860.

Madsen, Brigham D. *Exploring the Great Salt Lake: The Stansbury Expedition of 1849–50.* Salt Lake City, 1988.

Manning, Thomas G. *Government in Science: The U.S. Geological Survey, 1867–1894.* Lexington KY, 1967.

Marcy, Randolph. *Exploration of the Red River of Louisiana in the Year 1852.* 32d Cong., 2d sess., 1853, S. Doc. 54.

———. *Report of a Route from Fort Smith to Santa Fe.* 31st Cong., 1st sess., 1850, S. Doc. 64.

Markham, Albert Hastings. *The Great Frozen Sea: A Personal Narrative of the Voyage of the "Alert" during the Arctic Expedition of 1875–76.* London, 1894.

Maximilian, Alexander, Prince of Wied. *Travels in the Interior of North America.* 2 vols. Vols. 22–24 of *Early Western Travels,* ed. Reuben Gold Thwaites. Cleveland, 1906.

McClintock, Francis Leopold. *The Voyage of the Fox in the Arctic Seas: A Narrative of the Discovery of the Fate of Sir John Franklin and His Companions.* London, 1859.

McDermott, John Francis, ed. *Travelers on the Western Frontier.* Urbana, 1970.

McEwen, Alex, ed. *In Search of the Highlands: Mapping the Canada-Maine Boundary, 1839.* Fredericton NB, 1988.

McNitt, Frank, ed. *Navajo Expedition: Journal of a Military Reconnaissance from Santa Fe, New Mexico to the Navaho Country Made in 1849 by Lieutenant James H. Simpson.* Norman, 1964.

Merk, Frederick, ed. *Fur Trade and Empire: George Simpson's Journal. . . . Cambridge.* MA, 1931.

Michael, Henry N., ed. *Lieutenant Zagoskin's Travels in Russian America, 1842–1844.* Toronto, 1967.

Mirsky, Jeanette. *To the Arctic: The Story of Northern Exploration from Earliest Times to the Present.* New York, 1948.

Mitterling, Philip I. *American Exploration in the Antarctic to 1840.* Urbana, 1959.

Morgan, Dale L. *Jedediah Smith and the Opening of the West.* New York, 1953.

———. *The West of William Ashley.* Denver, 1964.

Morgan, Dale, and Carl I. Wheat. *Jedediah Smith and His Maps of the American West.* San Francisco, 1954.

Morton, Arthur S. *A History of the Canadian West to 1870–71.* 2d ed. Toronto, 1973.

Morton, W. L. *Henry Youle Hind.* Toronto, 1980.

Moulton, Gary E., ed. *The Journals of the Lewis and Clark Expedition.* 11 vols. to date. Lincoln, 1983–.

Nanton, Paul. *Arctic Breakthrough: Franklin's Expeditions, 1819–1847.* London, 1970.

Nares, George Strong. *Narrative of a Voyage to the Polar Sea during 1875–6 in H.M. Ships "Alert" and "Discovery."* 2 vols. London, 1878.

Nasatir, A. P., ed. *Before Lewis and Clark: Documents Illustrating the History of the Missouri, 1785–1804.* 2 vols. St. Louis, 1952.

Neatby, Leslie. *In Quest of the Northwest Passage.* London, 1958.

———. *The Search for Franklin.* London, 1970.

Nevins, Allan. *Frémont, Pathmaker of the West.* New York, 1939.

Newman, Peter C. *Company of Adventurers.* 2 vols. New York, 1985–87.

Nichols, Roger L., ed. *The Missouri Expedition: The Journal of Surgeon John Gale with Related Documents.* Norman, 1969.

Nichols, Roger L., and Patrick L. Halley, *Stephen Long and American Frontier Exploration.* Newark DE, 1980.

Oglesby, Richard E. *Manuel Lisa and the Opening of the Missouri Fur Trade.* Norman, 1963.

Owram, D. R. *Promise of Eden: The Canadian Expansionist Movement and the Idea of the West.* Toronto, 1980.

Palliser, John. *The Journals, Detailed Reports, and Observations Relative to the Exploration of British North America.* London, 1863.

Parker, John, ed. *The Journals of Jonathan Carver and Related Documents, 1766–1770.* St. Paul, 1976.

Parker, Samuel. *Journal of an Exploring Tour beyond the Rocky Mountains.* Ithaca NY, 1838.

Parry, William Edward. *Journal of a Second Voyage for the Discovery of a North-West Passage from the Atlantic to the Pacific in the Years 1821–22–23, in His Majesty's Ships Fury and Hecla. . . .* London, 1824.

———. *Journal of a Voyage for the Discovery of a North-West Passage from the Atlantic to the Pacific . . . in the Years 1819–1820, in His Majesty's Ships Hecla and Griper. . . .* London, 1821.

Pattie, James O. *The Personal Narratives of James O. Pattie of Kentucky.* Facsimile ed. Lincoln, 1984.

Pharand, Donat. *The Northwest Passage: Arctic Straits.* Dordrecht, Netherlands, 1984.

Phillips, Paul C. *The Fur Trade.* Norman, 1961.

Ponko, Vincent, Jr. *Ships, Seas, and Scientists: U.S. Naval Exploration and Discovery in the Nineteenth Century*. Annapolis, 1974.

Porter, Mae Reed, and Odessa Davenport. *Scotsman in Buckskins: Sir William Drummond Stewart and the Rocky Mountain Fur Trade*. New York, 1963.

Pyne, Stephen J. *Grove Karl Gilbert: A Great Engine of Research*. Austin, 1980.

Rae, John. *Narrative of an Expedition to the Shores of the Arctic Sea in 1846 and 1847*. London, 1850.

Raynolds, William F. *Report on the Exploration of the Yellowstone and the Country Drained by That River*. 40th Cong., 2d sess., 1868, S. Doc. 77.

Rich, E. E. *The Fur Trade and the Northwest to 1857*. Toronto, 1967.

————. *The History of the Hudson's Bay Company, 1670–1870*. Vol. 2, *1763–1870*. London, 1959.

————, ed. *Black's Rocky Mountain Journal, 1824*. London, 1955.

————. *Peter Skene Ogden's Snake Country Journals*. 5 vols. London, 1950–61.

Richardson, John. *Arctic Searching Expedition*. 2 vols. London, 1851.

Ronda, James P. *Astoria and Empire*. Lincoln, 1990.

————. *Lewis and Clark among the Indians*. Lincoln, 1984.

Ross, Alexander. *Adventures of the First Settlers on the Oregon or Columbia River, 1810–1813*. 1849. Reprint, Lincoln, 1986.

Ross, Eric. *Beyond the River and the Bay*. Toronto, 1970.

Ross, John. *Narrative of a Second Voyage in Search of a North-west Passage*. London, 1835.

————. *A Voyage of Discovery, Made under the Orders of the Admiralty, in His Majesty's Ships Isabella and Alexander, for the Purpose of Exploring Baffin's Bay, and Inquiring into the Probability of a North-west Passage*. London, 1819.

Ross, Marvin C. *The West of Alfred Jacob Miller*. Norman, 1968.

Ross, W. Gillies. *Arctic Whalers, Icy Seas: Narratives of the Davis Strait Whale Fishery*. Toronto, 1985.

————. *Whaling and Eskimos: Hudson Bay, 1860–1915*. Publications in Ethnology, no. 10. Ottawa, 1975.

Ruggles, Richard I. *A Country So Interesting: The Hudson's Bay Company and Two Centuries of Mapping, 1670–1870*. Montreal, 1991.

Russell, Osborne. *Journal of a Trapper; or, Nine Years in the Rocky Mountains*. Lincoln, 1965.

Schoolcraft, Henry R. *Narrative Journal of Travels . . . from Detroit . . . to the Sources of the Mississippi River*. Albany, 1821.

Schwartz, Seymour I., and Ralph E. Ehrenberg. *The Mapping of America*. New York, 1980.

Scoresby, William. *An Account of the Arctic Regions with a History and Description of the Northern Whale-Fishery.* 2 vols. 1820. Reprint, New York, 1969.

Sherwood, Morgan B. *Exploration of Alaska, 1865–1900.* New Haven, 1965.

Simpson, Alexander. *The Life and Travels of Thomas Simpson.* London, 1845.

Simpson, James Harvey. *Journal of a Military Reconnaissance from Santa Fe, New Mexico, to the Navajo Country Made with the Troops under Command of Brevet Lieutenant-Colonel John M. Washington, Chief of the Ninth Military Department and Governor of New Mexico.* 31st Cong., 1st sess., 1850, S. Doc. 64.

————. *Report and Map of the Route from Fort Smith Arkansas, to Santa Fe, New Mexico.* 31st Cong., 1st sess., 1850, S. Doc. 12.

Simpson, Thomas. *Narrative of the Discoveries on the North Coast of America.* London, 1843.

Sitgreaves, Lorenzo. *Report of an Expedition down the Zuni and Colorado Rivers.* 32d Cong., 2d sess., 1853, S. Doc. 59.

Skarsten, M. O. *George Drouillard, Hunter and Interpreter.* Glendale CA, 1964.

Smith, W. F. *Report . . . of Routes from San Antonio to El Paso.* 31st Cong., 1st sess., 1850, S. Doc. 64.

Spry, Irene M., ed. *The Papers of the Palliser Expedition, 1857–1860.* Publications of the Champlain Society, vol. 44. Toronto, 1968.

Stafford, Robert A. *Scientist of Empire: Sir Roderick Murchison, Scientific Exploration, and Victorian Imperialism.* Cambridge, U.K., 1989.

Stansbury, Howard. *Exploration and Survey of the Valley of the Great Salt Lake of Utah, Including a Reconnaissance of a New Route through the Rocky Mountains.* 32nd Cong., spec. sess., 1851, S. Doc. 3.

Stanton, William. *The United States Exploring Expedition of 1838–1842.* Los Angeles, 1975.

Stefansson, Vilhjalmur. *Unsolved Mysteries of the Arctic.* New York, 1939.

Stegner, Wallace. *Beyond the Hundredth Meridian.* Boston, 1953.

Stewart, George. *The California Trail.* New York, 1962.

Stewart, Sir William Drummond. *Altowan: or, Incidents of Life and Adventure in the Rocky Mountains.* 2 vols. New York, 1846.

Sullivan, Maurice S., ed. *The Travels of Jedediah Smith.* Santa Ana CA, 1934.

Sutherland, Patricia D., ed. *The Franklin Era in Canadian Arctic History, 1845–1859.* Mercury Series, Archeological Survey of Canada Paper no. 131. Ottawa, 1985.

Sutherland, Peter C. *Journal of a Voyage in Baffin's Bay and Barrow Straits, in the Years 1850–1851, Performed by H.M. Ships "Lady Franklin" and "Sophia," under the Command of Mr. William Penny. . . . * 2 vols. London, 1852.

Sverdrup, Otto. *New Land: Four Years in the Arctic Regions.* 2 vols. London, 1904.

Taft, Robert. *Artists and Illustrators of the Old West.* New York, 1953.

Thomson, D. W. *Men and Meridians: The History of Surveying and Mapping in Canada.* Vol. 2, *1867–1917.* Ottawa, 1972.

Thomson, George Malcolm. *The North-West Passage.* London, 1975.

Thwaites, Reuben Gold, ed. *The Original Journals of the Lewis and Clark Expedition.* 8 vols. New York, 1904–5.

Todd, A. L. *Abandoned: The Story of the Greely Arctic Expedition, 1881–1884.* New York, 1961.

Todd, Edgely, ed. *The Adventures of Captain Bonneville.* Norman, 1962.

Todd, John W., Jr., ed. *Two Journals of Robert Campbell (Chief Factor, Hudson's Bay Company), 1808 to 1853.* Seattle, 1958.

Tyler, David B. *The Wilkes Expedition: The First United States Exploring Expedition, 1838–1842.* American Philosophical Society Memoirs, no. 73. Philadelphia, 1968.

Tyler, Ron, ed. *Alfred Jacob Miller: Artist on the Oregon Trail.* Fort Worth, 1982.

Tyrrell, J. B., ed. *David Thompson's Narrative of His Exploration in Western America, 1784–1812.* Toronto, 1916.

Tyrrell, J. W. *Across the Sub-Arctic of Canada.* Toronto, 1897.

Viola, Herman J., and Carolyn Margolis, eds. *Magnificent Voyagers: The U.S. Exploring Expedition, 1838–1842.* Washington DC, 1985.

Waiser, W. A. *The Field Naturalist: John Macoun, the Geological Survey, and Natural Science.* Toronto, 1989.

Wallace, Edward S. *The Great Reconnaissance: Soldiers, Artists, and Scientists on the Frontier, 1848–1861.* Boston, 1955.

Wallace, Hugh N. *The Navy, the Company, and Richard King: British Exploration in the Canadian Arctic, 1829–1860.* Montreal, 1980.

Warkentin, John. *The Western Interior of Canada: A Record of Geographical Discovery, 1612–1917.* Toronto, 1964.

Warren, Gouverneur K. *Memoir to Accompany the Map of the Territory of the United States from the Mississippi to the Pacific Ocean. . . .* 33d Cong., 2d sess., 1859, S. Doc. 78.

Weber, David J. *Richard H. Kern: Expeditionary Artist in the Far Southwest, 1848–1853.* Albuquerque, 1985.

———. *The Taos Trappers: The Fur Trade in the Far Southwest, 1540–1846.* Norman, 1971.

———, ed. *The Californios versus Jedediah Smith, 1826–27: A New Cache of Documents.* Spokane, 1990.

Wheat, Carl I. *Mapping the Trans-Mississippi West, 1540–1861.* 5 vols. Menlo Park CA, 1958–62.

Wheeler, George M. *Report on the United States Geographical Surveys West of the One Hundredth Meridian.* 7 vols. Washington DC, 1875–89.

Wilkes, Charles. *Narrative of the United States Exploring Expeditions during the Years 1838, 1839, 1840, 1841.* 5 vols. Philadelphia, 1845.

Wilkins, Thurman. *Clarence King.* 1953. Paperback reprint, Albuquerque, 1988.

Wilkinson, Douglas. *Arctic Fever: The Search for the Northwest Passage.* Toronto, 1971.

Williams, Glyndwr. *The British Search for the Northwest Passage in the Eighteenth Century.* London, 1962.

———, ed. *Peter Skene Ogden's Snake Country Journals, 1827–29.* London, 1971.

Williamson, R. S. *Report of a Reconnaissance of a Route through the Sierra Nevadas by the Upper Sacramento.* 31st Cong., 1st sess., Part II, 1848–50, S. Doc. 47.

Wilson, Clifford. *Campbell of the Yukon.* Toronto, 1970.

Winsor, Justin. *Narrative and Critical History of America.* 8 vols. Boston, 1889.

Wishart, David J. *The Fur Trade of the American West, 1807–1840: A Geographical Synthesis.* Lincoln, 1979.

Work, John. *Fur Brigade to the Bonaventura: John Work's California Expedition, 1832–33.* San Francisco, 1945.

———. *The Journal of John Work . . . with an Account of the Fur Trade in the Northwest.* Ed. W. S. Lewis and P. C. Phillips. Cleveland, 1923.

Wyeth, John B. *Oregon; or, A Short History of a Long Journey.* Vol. 21 of *Early Western Travels,* ed. Reuben Gold Thwaites. Cleveland, 1905.

Zaslow, Morris. *The Opening of the Canadian North, 1870–1914.* Toronto, 1971.

———, ed. *A Century of Canada's Arctic Islands, 1880–1980.* Ottawa, 1981.

Zeller, Suzanne. *Inventing Canada: Early Victorian Science and the Idea of a Transcontinental Nation.* Toronto, 1987.

# Contributors

**John L. Allen** is a professor of geography at the University of Connecticut. He is the author of several books, including *Passage through the Garden: Lewis and Clark and the Images of the American Northwest* and *Jedediah Smith and the Mountain Men of the American West*, and numerous articles in scholarly periodicals, edited volumes, and conference proceedings. Dr. Allen is also the editor of *Annual Editions: Environment*. He has served his academic department as its first head (1976–81) and as acting head (1986–87) and has held many other administrative and committee posts at the University of Connecticut, where he has spent his entire academic career. Dr. Allen has served as a National Councilor of the Society for the History of Discoveries and as a member of the editorial board of *The Journal of Historical Geography*. He is an authority on the role of images in exploration. Dr. Allen holds academic degrees from the University of Wyoming (B.A. and M.A.) and Clark University (Ph.D., 1969) and was an NSF Post-Doctoral Fellow at Clark University in 1970–71.

**Richard A. Bartlett** is a professor emeritus of history at the Florida State University, where he spent most of his professional career. He also held an academic appointment at Texas A&M University and was employed at the National Archives and the Library of Congress. Widely known as one of the foremost historians of the nineteenth-century American West, Dr. Bartlett is the author of the award-winning *Great Surveys of the American West*, *Nature's Yellowstone*, and *Yellowstone: A Wilderness Besieged*. In addition to these and other works, Dr. Bartlett has edited over half a dozen books and written many articles. He is the winner of the Spur Award for the best nonfiction book on the American West in 1962 and the Ray Allen Billington Award for the best article on the West in 1969. In addition to his teaching and research responsibilities, Dr. Bartlett has acted as a consultant on many public history projects and has been a member of the Governing Council of the Western History Association and a member of the editorial board of the *Journal of the West*. Dr. Bartlett received his baccalaureate at the University of Colorado, his master's degree at the University of Chicago, and his doctorate at the University of Colorado (1953).

**William H. Goetzmann** holds the Jack S. Blanton Jr. Chair in History and American Studies at the University of Texas at Austin. One of the nation's most celebrated historians and perhaps the world's leading authority on the nineteenth-century American West, Dr. Goetzmann received the Joseph Pulitzer Award for History for his 1967 book *Exploration and Empire: The Role of the Explorer and the Scientist in* *the Winning of the American West*. Among Dr. Goetzmann's other books are the seminal *Army Exploration in the American West, 1803–63* and *New Lands, New Men: America and the Second Great Age of Discovery*. The author of over fifty scholarly articles, Dr. Goetzmann has received a number of prizes and awards in addition to the Pulitzer, including the Francis Parkman Award of the Society of American Historians, and is the recipient of many research-grant awards. Dr. Goetzmann has served as an adviser and consultant to countless museums, associations, and projects. He has taught at Yale University, the University of Texas, and Cambridge University, where he was a Fulbright Visiting Lecturer. He has also held a number of administrative posts, including the chairman of the Department of History at the University of Texas and director of American Studies at the University of Texas. Dr. Goetzmann received his undergraduate and graduate degrees (Ph.D., 1957) from Yale University.

**Vincent Ponko Jr.** has retired as professor of history and academic dean at Dominican College, New York. He also held administrative positions at California State University, Bakersfield, and the University of Scranton, as well as an academic appointment at Villanova University. An authority on U.S. military and government exploration in the nineteenth century, Dr. Ponko is the author of *Ships, Seas, and Scientists: U.S. Naval Exploration and Discovery in the Nineteenth Century* and over a dozen articles in scholarly publications. He has received several research grants from the American Philosophical Society, is a former National Councilor of the Society for the History of Discoveries, and serves on the National Archives Advisory Council. Dr. Ponko received his baccalaureate degree from Brown University, his master's from DePaul University, and his Ph.D. from Loyola University of Chicago (1959).

**James P. Ronda** is Henry G. Barnard Professor of History at the University of Tulsa. He was formerly at Youngstown State University, Ohio. Internationally recognized for his work on Native American history and the early exploration of the American West, Dr. Ronda is the author of many books, including *Lewis and Clark among the Indians* and *Astoria and Empire: The Clash of Cultures and Nations in the Pacific Northwest*. He also has authored over a dozen articles in scholarly journals and has contributed widely to conference proceedings and collections. Dr. Ronda has received a number of awards for his scholarly endeavors. He received his baccalaureate from Hope College and his graduate degrees from the University of Nebraska–Lincoln (M.A., 1967, Ph.D., 1969).

**W. Gillies Ross** is a professor of geography at Bishop's University in Quebec, where he has taught since 1961. He has also been on appointment to the Scott Polar Research Institute in Cambridge, England. Dr. Ross is an authority on Arctic maritime exploration and the whaling industry in Arctic waters and is the author of

*Whaling and Eskimos: Hudson Bay, 1860–1915* and *Arctic Whalers, Icy Seas: Narratives of the Davis Strait Whale Fishery*. He has also edited a number of books and contributed many articles to the professional and scholarly literature. In addition to his research activities, Dr. Ross has served Bishop's University in a number of administrative and committee posts, including head of the Department of Geography. He has also exhibited his photographs in leading museums, including the Metropolitan Museum of Art, and in 1953 he sailed across the Atlantic Ocean. Dr. Ross was educated at McGill University, where he received his baccalaureate and master's degrees, and at Cambridge University, where he received the Ph.D. in 1971.

**William A. Waiser** is associate professor of history at the University of Saskatchewan and was formerly historian at Parks Canada, Prairie Regional Office. He is recognized for his work on government exploration in Canada and is the author of *The Field Naturalist: John Macoun, the Geological Survey, and Natural Science*, as well as a number of articles in the professional literature. He has served on the editorial board of *Saskatchewan History* and was the editor of the *NeWest Review*. In addition to his academic activities, Dr. Waiser has extensive experience as a practicing and consulting historian for Canadian museums and the Canadian national park system. He received, among other fellowships, the Queen's Fellowship of the Canadian Council in 1975–76. Dr. Waiser was educated at Trent University (B.A., 1975) and the University of Saskatchewan (M.A., 1976, Ph.D., 1983).

**Suzanne Zeller** is associate professor of history at Wilfred Laurier University, Ontario, and has also held academic appointments at both Trent University and the University of Windsor. Her 1987 book, *Inventing Canada: Early Victorian Science and the Idea of a Transcontinental Nation*, as well as a number of articles in the scholarly literature, has enhanced her growing reputation as a scholar of scientific exploration in nineteenth-century Canada. In addition to her academic work, Dr. Zeller has served as a consultant and writer of educational films in the history of Canadian science. She received her baccalaureate and master's degrees from the University of Windsor and her Ph.D. from the University of Toronto (1986).

# Index